THE JOSEPH SMITH PAPERS

Dean C. Jessee
Ronald K. Esplin
Richard Lyman Bushman
GENERAL EDITORS

PREVIOUSLY PUBLISHED

THE JOSEPH SMITH PAPERS

HISTORIES

VOLUME 1:
JOSEPH SMITH HISTORIES, 1832–1844

Karen Lynn Davidson
David J. Whittaker
Mark Ashurst-McGee
Richard L. Jensen
VOLUME EDITORS

THE CHURCH
HISTORIAN'S
PRESS

The Church Historian's Press is an imprint of the Church History Department
of The Church of Jesus Christ of Latter-day Saints, Salt Lake City, Utah,
and a trademark of Intellectual Reserve, Inc.

www.josephsmithpapers.org

The Joseph Smith Papers Project is endorsed by
the National Historical Publications and Records Commission.

Art direction: Richard Erickson.
Cover design: Scott Eggers. Interior design: Richard Erickson and Scott M. Mooy.
Typography: Alison Palmer and Riley M. Lorimer.

Library of Congress Cataloging-in-Publication Data

Smith, Joseph, 1805–1844, author.
Joseph Smith histories, 1832–1844 / Karen Lynn Davidson, David J. Whittaker, Mark R. Ashurst-McGee,
Richard L. Jensen, volume editors.
pages cm — (The Joseph Smith Papers. Histories; volume 1)
Includes bibliographical references and index.
ISBN 978-1-60641-196-4 (hardbound: alk. paper)
1. Church of Jesus Christ of Latter-day Saints—History—19th century. 2. Smith, Joseph, 1805–1844.
I. Davidson, Karen Lynn, editor. II. Whittaker, David J., editor. III. Ashurst-McGee, Mark, editor. IV. Jensen,
Richard L., editor. V. Title. VI. Series: Smith, Joseph, 1805–1844. Joseph Smith papers. Histories; volume 1.

BX8611.S655 2012   289.309'034—dc23   2011048106

Printed in the United States of America on acid-free paper.
10 9 8 7 6 5 4 3 2 1

The Joseph Smith Papers

Contents

JOSEPH SMITH HISTORIES, 1832–1844

REFERENCE MATERIAL

Illustrations and Maps

MAPS

OTHER VISUALS

Timeline of Joseph Smith's Life

1805   1810   1815   1820   1825   1830   1835   1840   1845

1805
Born in Vermont.

1816–1817
Family moved
to New York.

1820
First vision
of Deity.

1823
First vision of angel Moroni.

1827
Married Emma Hale.
Obtained Book of Mormon gold plates.

1829
Bulk of Book of Mormon translated.
Received authority to
baptize and ordain.

1830
Book of Mormon published.
Organized church.
Commenced revision of Bible.

1831
Moved from New York to Ohio.
Revelation locating Mormon
gathering place in Missouri.

1833
Bible revision ended.
Book of Commandments printed.

1834
Led military expedition to Missouri
to assist exiled Latter-day Saints.

1835
Organized Quorum of the Twelve Apostles.
Doctrine and Covenants published.

1836
Temple completed in Ohio.
Visions of Jesus Christ,
Moses, Elias, and Elijah.

1837
Sent missionaries to England.
Dissension and financial
problems in Kirtland.

1838
Moved from Ohio to Missouri.
Surrendered to Missouri militia.
Incarcerated pending trial.

1839
Allowed to escape.
Relocated to Illinois.
Met with U.S. president
Martin Van Buren seeking
redress for Missouri grievances.

1841
Commissioned as lieutenant
general of Nauvoo Legion
of Illinois militia.

1842
Organized Female Relief Society.
Introduced temple
endowment ceremony.
Elected mayor of Nauvoo.

1843
Revelation on plural wives
and eternal marriage recorded.

1844
Nominated as U.S.
presidential candidate.
Murdered by mob.

For a detailed overview of Joseph Smith's life for the period
covered in this volume, see the chronology in the back of the
volume. For the sources of the information presented in this
timeline, see the Joseph Smith Papers website.

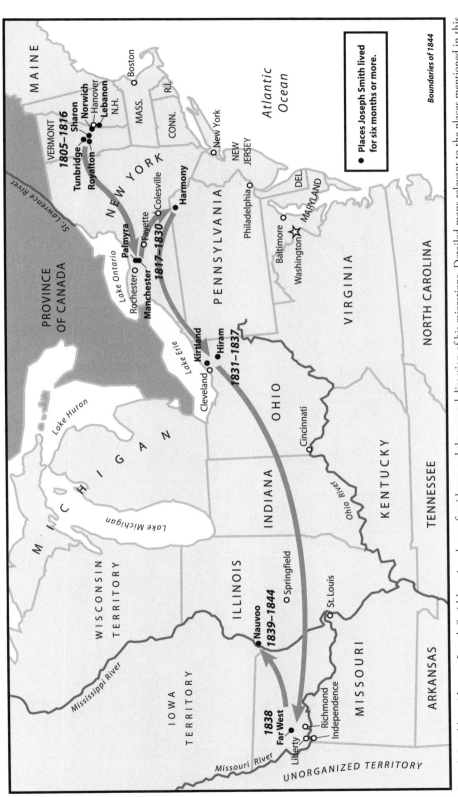

Joseph Smith's residences. Joseph Smith's major places of residence and the general direction of his migrations. Detailed maps relevant to the places mentioned in this volume appear on pages 567–575 herein. (Design by John Hamer.)

Joseph Smith's Historical Enterprise

When historian and publisher Hubert H. Bancroft asked in 1880 how the Latter-day Saints came to have a historian's and recorder's office, considering that "other people, generally, are so careless of recording their proceedings," church historian Franklin D. Richards replied that "at the organization of this Church, the Lord commanded Joseph, the Prophet, to keep a record of his doings, in the great, and important work, that he was commencing to perform. It thus became a duty imperative."[1] The revelation to which Richards referred, dated 6 April 1830, instructed, "There shall be a record kept among you, and in it thou shalt be called a seer, a translator, a prophet, an apostle of Jesus Christ, an elder of the church."[2]

The "duty imperative" that rested on the church founder and his followers resulted in a rich documentary record. Joseph Smith, along with those working under his direction, created and collected minutes of church meetings, priesthood licenses, revelations, journals, correspondence, and other papers. These documents appear in the appropriate series of *The Joseph Smith Papers:* the Journals series, Documents series, Revelations and Translations series, Legal and Business Records series, and Administrative Records series. In addition to such papers, several important narrative histories were undertaken during Smith's lifetime, and the resulting texts constitute the Histories series. The first volume, *Joseph Smith Histories,* comprises histories written, dictated, or signed by Smith or created under his direct supervision. The documents in volume 2 of the series, *Assigned Historical Writings,* have a less direct connection to Joseph Smith. They were begun at his official direction but did not receive his sustained supervision. The balance of the Histories series, published electronically at josephsmithpapers.org, will present the massive multivolume history that Joseph Smith initiated in Missouri in 1838 and that church historians concluded in Salt Lake City in 1856, more than a decade after Smith's death. Although the Histories series will include only writings conceived as narrative histories, these writings were often based on individual documents, including

---

1. Richards, "Bibliography of Utah," 3–4.
2. Revelation, 6 Apr. 1830, in Doctrine and Covenants 46:1, 1835 ed. [D&C 21:1].

letters, petitions, and revelations, and in many cases the source documents were copied directly into the histories.

The turbulent conditions of Joseph Smith's life hindered his attempts to write and oversee the creation of a history. Violent opposition threatened the Saints from without and dissension divided them from within. Lawsuits and financial problems were a constant distraction. Smith's history identifies the factors that complicated his literary efforts, describing "long imprisonments, vexatious and long continued Law Suits[,] The treachery of some of my clerks; the death of others; and the poverty of myself and brethren from continued plunder and driving."[3] Record keeping and history writing did not thrive in these unsettled and sometimes bloody years, and the documents that were produced are fragmentary, recording only a fraction of Smith's activities and teachings. For example, the written record carries only traces of the vigorous oral tradition of preaching, debate, and the sharing of beliefs that existed from the earliest days of the church.[4] And yet, despite the long list of impediments to history writing, Joseph Smith showed sustained interest in documenting the church's rise and progress, and his repeated efforts to do so bore fruit. Their necessarily incomplete nature notwithstanding, the histories that were written document significant aspects of his life and of the early days of the church, including some details recorded nowhere else.

The Earliest Historical Accounts

Even before the April 1830 injunction to keep a church record, Joseph Smith began recording sacred texts, including the extensive Book of Mormon translation. In connection with these revelatory documents, Smith produced and published two short narratives. The first, his earliest known historical text,

---

3. JS History, vol. C-1, 1260. As explained later, scribes continued to employ the first-person pronoun in the sections of history—including the passage quoted here—that were written after Smith's death.

4. Joseph Smith's sermons, in particular, were a vital part of the experience of the early Saints, but Smith left no notes or texts of his preaching, and those who attended his sermons in the early years made no attempt to capture his words. Smith's early histories are all but silent regarding his sermons, but other documents of the time often allude to oral transmission of doctrine and instruction. For example, in a June 1835 letter to his wife, William W. Phelps reported hearing Joseph Smith speak on the subject "This is my beloved son; hear ye him," which likely included an account of his first visionary experience. Phelps reported: "He preached one of the greatest sermons I ever heard—it was about 3½ hours long—and unfolded more mysteries than I can write at this time." Even when official church record keeping improved in the 1840s, only a fraction of Smith's sermons were recorded in detail. By Dean C. Jessee's count, fewer than one-fifth of Smith's known sermons were captured in any text (very few of them adequately), and the majority of those texts date from the last few years of Smith's life. (William W. Phelps, Kirtland, OH, to Sally Phelps, Liberty, MO, 2 June 1835, JS Collection, CHL; Jessee, "Priceless Words and Fallible Memories," 23–25; see also Parley P. Pratt, Kirtland, OH, to John Taylor, Toronto, Upper Canada, 27 Nov. 1836, John Taylor, Collection, CHL.)

is found in the preface to the first edition of the Book of Mormon. Probably written in mid-August 1829, just before the first pages of the Book of Mormon manuscript were delivered to the printer, the preface explained Smith's response to the loss of the earliest pages of the Book of Mormon translation in summer 1828:

> As many false reports have been circulated respecting the following work, and also many unlawful measures taken by evil designing persons to destroy me, and also the work, I would inform you that I translated, by the gift and power of God, and caused to be written, one hundred and sixteen pages, the which I took from the Book of Lehi, which was an account abridged from the plates of Lehi, by the hand of Mormon; which said account, some person or persons have stolen and kept from me, notwithstanding my utmost exertions to recover it again—and being commanded of the Lord that I should not translate the same over again, for Satan had put it into their hearts to tempt the Lord their God, by altering the words, that they did read contrary from that which I translated and caused to be written; and if I should bring forth the same words again, or, in other words, if I should translate the same over again, they would publish that which they had stolen, and Satan would stir up the hearts of this generation, that they might not receive this work: but behold, the Lord said unto me, I will not suffer that Satan shall accomplish his evil design in this thing: therefore thou shalt translate from the plates of Nephi, until ye come to that which ye have translated, which ye have retained; and behold ye shall publish it as the record of Nephi; and thus I will confound those who have altered my words. I will not suffer that they shall destroy my work; yea, I will shew unto them that my wisdom is greater than the cunning of the Devil. Wherefore, to be obedient unto the commandments of God, I have, through his grace and mercy, accomplished that which he hath commanded me respecting this thing. I would also inform you that the plates of which hath been spoken, were found in the township of Manchester, Ontario county, New-York.[5]

The second narrative, dated shortly after the organization of the Church of Christ on 6 April 1830 in Fayette, New York, constituted a historical prologue to a text setting forth the "articles and covenants" of the new institution. It provides the first known references to key events of the beginning of Mormonism:

> The rise of the Church of Christ in these last days, being one Thousand eight Hundred & thirty years since the coming of our Lord & Saveiour Jesus Christ in the flesh; it being regularly organized & established agreeable to the Laws of our Country, by the will & commandments of God in the fourth Month & on the Sixth day of the Month, which is called April: which Commandments were given to Joseph, who was called of God & ordained an Apostle of Jesus Christ, an Elder

---

5. Preface to Book of Mormon, 1830 ed., iii–iv. These events were also recorded in JS History, ca. summer 1832, pp. 15–16 herein; and JS History, vol. A-1, pp. 244–252 herein (Draft 2).

The rise of the Church of Christ in these last days, being one Thousand eight Hundred & thirty years since the coming of our Lord & Saviour Jesus Christ in the flesh it being regularly organized & established agreeable to the Laws of our Country, by the will & commandments of God in the fourth Month & on the sixth day of the Month, which is called April: which commandments were given to Joseph the seer who was called of God & ordained an Apostle of Jesus Christ an Elder of this Church & also to Oliver who was also called of God & ordained an Apostle of Jesus Christ, an Elder of this Church & ordained under his hand & this according to the grace of our Lord & Saviour Jesus Christ to whom be all glory both now & forever AMEN

For after that truly was manifested unto this first Elder that he had received a remission of his sins he was entangled again in the vanities of the world but after truly Repenting God ministered unto him by an holy angel whose countenance was as lightning & whose garments were pure & white above all whiteness & gave unto him Commandment which inspired him from on high & gave unto him power by the means which were before prepared that he should translate a Book which Book contained a record of a fallen People & also the fulness of the Gospel of Jesus Christ to the Gentiles & also to the Jews proving unto them that the holy Scriptures are true & also that God doth inspire men in & call them to his holy work in these last days as well as in days of old that he might be the same God forever amen Which Book was given by inspiration & is called the Book of Mormon & is confirmed to others by the ministering of angels & declared unto the World by them Wherefore having so great witnesses by them shall the world be judged even as many as shall hereafter receive this work either to faith & righteousness or to the hardness of heart in unbelief to their own condemnation for the Lord God hath spoken it for we the Elders of the Church have heard & bear witness to the words of the glorious majesty on high to whom be glory for ever & ever amen

Historical prologue to 10 April 1830 "Articles and Covenants." This summary of the "rise of the Church of Christ in these last days" begins the "Church Articles & Covenants," copied into an early compilation of revelations. It gives the earliest known account of key events of early Mormon history. Handwriting of John Whitmer. Revelation Book 1, p. 53, Church History Library, Salt Lake City. (Photograph by Welden C. Andersen.)

of this Church, & also to Oliver who was also called of God an Apostle of Jesus Christ, an Elder of this Church & ordained under his hand, & this according to the grace of our Lord & saveiour Jesus Christ to whom be all glory both now & forever. Amen.

For after that it truly was manifested unto this first Elder, that he had Received a remission of his sins he was entangeled again in the vanities of the world but after truly Repenting God ministered unto him by an Holy Angel whose countenance was as Lightning & whose garments were pure & white above all whiteness & gave unto him Commandments which inspered [inspired] him from on high & gave unto him power by the means which were before prepared that he should translate a Book which Book contained a record of a fallen People & also the fulness of the Gospel of Jesus Christ to the Gentiles & also to the Jews proveing unto them that the Holy Scriptures are true & also that God doth inspire men & call them to his Holy work in these last days as well as in days of old that he might be the same God forever amen Which Book was given by inspiration & is Called the Book of Mormon & is confirmed to others by the ministering of Angels & declared unto the World by them Wherefore having so great witnesses by them shall the world be Judged even as many as shall hereafter receive this work either to faith & righteousness or to the hardness of heart in unbelief to their own condemnation for the Lord God hath spoken it for we the Elders of the Church have heard & bear witness to the words of the glorious majesty on high to whom be glory for ever & ever amen[.][6]

Development of Extended Historical Narratives

The two short examples above constitute the only extant historical writings from the first years of the Latter-day Saint movement. The 6 April 1830 revelation commanded that a church *record* be kept, and accordingly, the early response to the command was primarily the compilation of revelations, minutes, and other records of church conferences and administrative meetings. At a conference on 9 June 1830, Oliver Cowdery was "appointed to keep the Church record and Conference minutes," thus becoming the church's first official record keeper.[7] His minutes of the 9 June conference, besides noting who was present and who spoke, included a record of the ten ministerial licenses

---

6. Articles and covenants, 10 Apr. 1830, in Revelation Book 1, p. 53, in *JSP*, MRB:77 [D&C 20:1–16].

7. Minute Book 2, 9 June 1830. Cowdery, who had earlier served as scribe for Joseph Smith, was not given a formal title for this new clerical assignment, but he performed duties that came to be associated with the roles of scribe, clerk, and recorder. He signed the 9 June 1830 minutes using the title "Clerk." In early Mormon usage, though the distinctions were not always clear, a "scribe" usually kept records such as revelations, translations, correspondence, and journal entries; a "clerk" kept minutes of conferences, councils, and other meetings; and a "recorder" created or certified official institutional documents. The title of "recorder," with its legal implications, was probably borrowed from the contemporaneous terminology of government record keeping.

that were issued.[8] Cowdery's departure with other church elders in fall 1830 on a proselytizing mission to the West effectively ended his early work to keep general church records.

Before Cowdery left, David Whitmer received a short-term appointment to keep the records until January 1831, and in April 1831 John Whitmer accepted official record-keeping responsibilities.[9] As part of John Whitmer's new assignment, Joseph Smith asked not only that he keep records of church proceedings but also that he "keep the Church history."[10] In response, Whitmer requested divine confirmation, and in March 1831 a revelation assigned him to "write and keep a regular history" and to "keep the church record and history continually."[11] Beginning with Whitmer's appointment, writing a narrative history of the Latter-day Saint movement became a permanent part of the church's record-keeping activities. Whitmer recorded minutes of church meetings, as Oliver Cowdery and David Whitmer had done, and on 12 June 1831 he began work on a history.[12] An additional revelation in November 1831 defined Whitmer's responsibilities more expansively. He was instructed to receive reports from those serving missions "abroad in the earth" and to travel widely among church members, "that he may the more easily obtain knowledge: preaching and expounding, writing, copying, selecting and obtaining all things which shall be for the good of the church, and for the rising generations." All this material was to be used to create "a history of all the important things" relative to the church.[13]

Whitmer retained responsibility for the history as he moved from Ohio to Missouri in late 1831, back to Ohio in 1835, and back again in 1836 to Missouri, where he also served as a member of the Missouri church presidency. During this time he accumulated historical records and drafted narrative material, beginning with the October 1830 departure of Cowdery and colleagues. "The Book of John Whitmer" ultimately included copies of dozens of revelations,

---

8. The minutes for this conference became the first item recorded in Minute Book 2. A regular system for issuing and recording licenses was finally established in March 1836. Early church records may also have included membership lists as new converts joined the church. (Minute Book 1, 3 Mar. 1836; see also Cannon, "Licensing in the Early Church," 96–105.)

9. Minute Book 2, 26 Sept. 1830 and 9 Apr. 1831.

10. Whitmer, History, 24, in *JSP*, H2:36.

11. Revelation, ca. 8 Mar. 1831–B, in Doctrine and Covenants 63:1–2, 1835 ed. [D&C 47:1, 3]; see also Minute Book 2, 9 Apr. 1831.

12. Whitmer's history indicated that Oliver Cowdery had previously written "the commencement of the church history commencing at the time of the finding of the plates, up to June 12, 1831," and that Whitmer began where Cowdery had left off. Besides Whitmer's account, however, there is no contemporaneous evidence that Cowdery wrote a narrative history prior to 1834, when he began publishing a series of historical letters in the *Latter Day Saints' Messenger and Advocate*. (Whitmer, History, 25, in *JSP*, H2:36.)

13. Revelation, 11 Nov. 1831–A, in Doctrine and Covenants 28:1–2, 1835 ed. [D&C 69:3, 7–8].

letters, and other documents, interspersed with historical narrative. Whitmer was excommunicated on 10 March 1838 following disagreements with other church leaders, but he continued to add to his history until after Joseph Smith's death in 1844.

The years after John Whitmer's call in 1831 saw a significant expansion of church record creation. Joseph Smith continued to oversee Whitmer's record keeping, including the copying of manuscripts of revelations into bound volumes, and he gave Whitmer occasional instruction on writing a history. Additionally, Smith in 1832 began a letterbook, a journal, and a formal history. In this history, twenty-six-year-old Smith provided a narrative of his early life, focusing on the foundational events that supported his claims as God's prophet and seer. He recounted his first vision of Deity[14] and the ministering of angels he had received, including a visitation from the angel Moroni, who set him to the task of retrieving and translating the gold plates. Joseph Smith's circa summer 1832 history provides the earliest written account of these events, and it is the only one that includes his own handwriting.

In June 1832, William W. Phelps and other church members in Independence, Jackson County, Missouri, began printing the first Mormon periodical, *The Evening and the Morning Star.* Joseph Smith had high expectations for the newspaper, and he saw in it an opportunity to disseminate information about the church's history. In a postscript to a January 1833 letter to Phelps, Smith instructed him to include in the *Star* items that set forth "the rise progress and faith of the church."[15] That counsel led Phelps to begin a series in the newspaper that summarized the church's continued growth and missionary work. The first installment was Phelps's own summary of early church events, titled "Rise and Progress of the Church of Christ." Later that year, after the Mormon printing office in Independence was destroyed and the Latter-day Saints were expelled from Jackson County, church leaders Parley P. Pratt, Newel Knight, and John Corrill printed an account of the expulsion, titled

---

14. All of Joseph Smith's written accounts of his first vision of Deity are found in *Histories, Volume 1;* see JS History, ca. summer 1832, pp. 11–13 herein; JS History, 1834–1836, pp. 115–116 herein (a later version of JS, Journal, 9–11 Nov. 1835, in *JSP,* J1:87–88); JS History Drafts, ca. 1838–1841, pp. 210–215 herein; JS, "Church History," p. 494 herein; and JS, "Latter Day Saints," p. 508 herein. The appendix to volume 1 includes the first published account of the vision (pp. 522–523 herein), found in Orson Pratt, *A[n] Interesting Account of Several Remarkable Visions,* which was later used by Joseph Smith when composing the "Church History" article. For contemporaneous reports by witnesses who heard Joseph Smith's narration of the vision, see [David Nye White], "The Prairies, Joe Smith, the Temple, the Mormons, &c.," *Pittsburgh Weekly Gazette,* 14 Sept. 1843, [3]; and Neibaur, Journal, 24 May 1844.

15. JS, Kirtland, OH, to William W. Phelps, [Independence, MO], 11 Jan. 1833, in JS Letterbook 1, p. 20.

Portrait of Joseph Smith. Oil on canvas, 30 × 24 inches. The artist, a Latter-day Saint named David Rogers, painted this portrait and a companion portrait of Emma Smith while visiting Nauvoo, Illinois, from New York in September 1842. The paintings hung in Emma's home in Nauvoo for many years. (Courtesy Community of Christ Library-Archives, Independence, MO.)

"'The Mormons' So Called."[16] Because Pratt was not an official church historian and did not write under direct assignment from Joseph Smith or other church leaders, his account is not included in the Histories series of *The Joseph Smith Papers*. Nonetheless, his account is significant as one of the earliest examples of a historical narrative written by a Latter-day Saint.

Within five months of the destruction of the Missouri printing office in July 1833, church leaders established printing operations in Kirtland, Ohio, and again the church newspaper served as a forum for publishing the story of the Latter-day Saint movement. In 1834, Oliver Cowdery, as editor of the *Latter Day Saints' Messenger and Advocate* (the successor to *The Evening and the Morning Star*), wrote a series of eight letters chronicling Joseph Smith's early spiritual experiences and the origins of the Book of Mormon. Although there is no evidence that Joseph Smith assigned Cowdery to write the letters, he offered his assistance to ensure that the "narrative may be correct."[17] The published letters were also copied into Smith's next history, begun by Cowdery in late 1834 and continued by other scribes into early 1836. At its inception, this new project promised to be an impressive and comprehensive institutional history, including a genealogy of the presidency of the church and a day-by-day narrative. But most of the genealogy was left blank, and the daily chronicle ended after just two entries (5 and 6 December 1834). After a handwritten transcription of Cowdery's published historical letters, the final section of the history drew heavily on Smith's 1835–1836 journal, beginning with the entry of 22 September 1835 and continuing until 18 January 1836. At that point, as had been the case for the three previous sections of the 1834–1836 history, the final section was discontinued.

The Missouri Experience

Following the Mormons' expulsion from Jackson County in 1833 and their agreement to leave neighboring Clay County in 1836, the state legislature created Caldwell County, encompassing sparsely settled land in northwest Missouri, for Latter-day Saint settlement. In early 1838, Joseph Smith relocated from Kirtland to Far West, in Caldwell County. After his arrival, the Mormon population in northwest Missouri swelled as church members fled the increasingly hostile

---

16. See "'The Mormons' So Called," *The Evening and the Morning Star,* Extra, Feb. 1834, [1]–[2]. This account was originally printed as a broadsheet, probably in 1833 in Liberty, Missouri. No copies of the original are known to exist. The text was later incorporated into Pratt's 1839 *History of the Late Persecution.* "'The Mormons' So Called" will be available as a supplementary document on the Joseph Smith Papers website, josephsmithpapers.org. (See Crawley, *Descriptive Bibliography,* 1:42–43.)

17. Editorial, *LDS Messenger and Advocate,* Oct. 1834, 1:13 (see also later version, p. 39 herein).

conditions in Kirtland and converts gathered from across the United States and Upper Canada.

Even with pressing church responsibilities, Joseph Smith continued to emphasize the writing of history during his time in Missouri. After church historian John Whitmer's excommunication in March 1838, Smith took three steps in rapid succession to strengthen the church's history-keeping enterprise: he called for the appointment of two new historians, John Corrill and Elias Higbee, "to write and keep the Church history";[18] he sought unsuccessfully to obtain from John Whitmer the historical materials in his custody;[19] and, with Sidney Rigdon, his counselor in the church presidency, he began writing a new narrative.[20]

After being appointed church historian, John Corrill began working on a history, but the booklet he completed and published was an independent project written from his own perspective. His narrative summarizes many of the doctrines that were taught by Joseph Smith, and it provides particularly valuable details of the conflicts between the Mormons and the other Missouri settlers. In the opening chapters, Corrill described his conversion to Mormonism; in the final chapters, he explained the gradual erosion of his confidence in Smith's prophetic leadership. Corrill was excommunicated in 1839, the same year he published at his own expense the work he titled *A Brief History of the Church of Christ of Latter Day Saints, (Commonly Called Mormons;) Including an Account of Their Doctrine and Discipline; with the Reasons of the Author for Leaving the Church.*

Elias Higbee, though assigned as historian at the same time as Corrill, produced no formal narrative history. He did, however, travel to Washington DC in late 1839 with Joseph Smith to present to Congress a petition for redress, which included a survey of the Latter-day Saints' immigration to and forced exodus from Missouri. Higbee may have helped write this petition, and he also signed a second congressional petition a year later.[21]

When John Whitmer declined to turn over the historical records in his possession, Joseph Smith and Sidney Rigdon began their own project, conceived of as "a history of this Church from the earliest perion [period] of its existance up to this date."[22] With assistance from George W. Robinson, "general Church

18. Minute Book 2, 6 Apr. 1838.

19. JS and Sidney Rigdon, Far West, MO, to John Whitmer, 9 Apr. 1838, in *JSP*, J1:249.

20. JS, Journal, 27 and 30 Apr. and 1–4 May 1838, in *JSP*, J1:260, 263–264.

21. JS et al., Memorial to U.S. Senate and House of Representatives, 27 Jan. 1840, in Record Group 46, Records of the U.S. Senate, Committee on the Judiciary, Records, 1816–1982, National Archives, Washington DC; Petition of the Latter-Day Saints, H.R. Doc. 22, 26th Cong., 2nd Sess. (1840).

22. JS, Journal, 27 Apr. 1838, in *JSP*, J1:260.

Clerk & Recorder" and "Scribe for the first Presidency,"[23] they devoted six days in late April and early May 1838 to the task.[24] Work then halted as Smith turned his attention to other responsibilities, including preparations to accommodate the arrival of hundreds of Saints migrating from Canada and Ohio. No manuscript of their 1838 work is extant, but the work was incorporated into the later surviving history manuscripts.

Hopes for a peaceful Latter-day Saint gathering in northwest Missouri were short lived. As in previous Missouri settlements, confrontation ignited in and around Caldwell County over religious, cultural, and ideological differences between the Mormons and their neighbors and over fears of Mormon political and economic domination. As the Latter-day Saints' growing population expanded beyond the boundaries of Caldwell County, significant numbers of Missourians actively opposed the Saints and refused to tolerate their presence. The ensuing "Mormon War" culminated in Missouri governor Lilburn W. Boggs's "extermination order," the imprisonment of Joseph Smith and other church leaders, and the forced migration of Mormons eastward across the Mississippi River to western Illinois.

While incarcerated at Liberty, Missouri, during the winter of 1838–1839, Smith wrote a letter "to the church of Latterday saints at Quincy Illinois and scattered abroad and to Bishop [Edward] Partridge in particular." Later published in the church's Illinois newspaper, *Times and Seasons,* the letter instructed the Saints to write about their persecutions as an aid in seeking redress from the federal government:

> And again we would suggest for your concideration the propriety of all the saints gethering up a knoledge of all the facts and suffering and abuses put upon them by the people of this state and also of all the property and amount of damages which they have sustained both of character and personal Injuries as well as real property and also the names of all persons that have had a hand in their oppressions as far as they can get hold of them and find them out. and perhaps a committe can be appointed to find out these things and to take statements and affidafets and also to gether up the libilous publications that are afloat and all that are in the magazines and in the Insiclopedias and all the libillious histories that are published and that are writing and by whom and present the whole concatination of diabolical rascality and nefarious and murderous impositions that have been practised upon this people that we may not only publish to all the world but

23. Minutes, 6 Apr. 1838, in *JSP,* J1:250; see also Minute Book 1, 17 Sept. 1837.
24. JS, Journal, 27 and 30 Apr. and 1–4 May 1838, in *JSP,* J1:260, 263–264.

present them to the heads of the government in all there dark and hellish hugh [hue] as the last effort which is injoined on us by our heavenly Father[.]²⁵

Included in this series of *The Joseph Smith Papers* is Edward Partridge's response, published as "A History, of the Persecution, of the Church of Jesus Christ, of Latter Day Saints in Missouri" in the church's Illinois periodical. The "History, of the Persecution" series also excerpted from other important works that Smith's mandate had set in motion.²⁶

Joseph Smith's instructions invited all Latter-day Saints to become historians. By calling on each Saint to add a personal chapter to the collective history, Smith's letter effectively democratized Mormon historical writing. Moving beyond the personal, religious history of Smith's own life and the sacred history of the church, the call for Latter-day Saints to put their persecution narratives in writing helped create an enduring self-understanding. As well as providing evidence for redress petitions and attempting to draw public sympathy for their plight, the community effort to create history served to strengthen the church's cohesion and solidify what it meant to be Mormon. History, then, became a means not only to share their story but to forge a shared Latter-day Saint identity.

History Keeping in the Nauvoo Period

In April 1839, Joseph Smith escaped from custody in Missouri and made his way to Quincy, Illinois, near what became the Mormon gathering place at Nauvoo. As the Latter-day Saints built a new community, Joseph Smith directed a twofold effort to produce history, one focused on the Missouri experience and

---

25. JS et al., Liberty, MO, to the church members and Edward Partridge, Quincy, IL, 20 Mar. 1839, in Revelations Collection, CHL [D&C 123:1–6]; see also "Copy of a Letter," *Times and Seasons,* May 1840, 1:99–104; and "An Extract of a Letter," *Times and Seasons,* July 1840, 1:131–134.

26. Once the Saints received Smith's directive, a variety of important historical records began to pour forth. Some church members wrote extensive journal accounts of their Missouri experiences. Others were assigned to gather these accounts from among their fellow Mormons, and still others wrote petitions and pamphlets intended for the American public. Many of these documents may be found compiled in Clark V. Johnson's *Mormon Redress Petitions: Documents of the 1833–1838 Missouri Conflict* (Provo, UT: Religious Studies Center, Brigham Young University, 1992). Among accounts published at the time, John P. Greene's *Facts Relative to the Expulsion of the Mormons or Latter Day Saints, from the State of Missouri, under the "Exterminating Order"* (Cincinnati: R. P. Brooks, 1839) became a significant source of information for later histories. John Taylor wrote an eight-page pamphlet titled *A Short Account of the Murders, Roberies, Burnings, Thefts, and Other Outrages* (Springfield, IL: 1839). In the fall of 1839, Parley P. Pratt published *History of the Late Persecution Inflicted by the State of Missouri upon the Mormons* (Detroit: Dawson and Bates). An eighty-four-page publication titled *An Appeal to the American People* appeared in 1840 (Cincinnati: Shephard & Stearns) without an author's name, but later references indicate Sidney Rigdon was the author. Long excerpts from both Pratt's and Rigdon's work were included in the "History, of the Persecution" series.

the other on the overall story of the church. Within two weeks of Smith's arrival in Quincy, a church conference appointed a committee to compile records of the injustices suffered by the Saints in Missouri, as Smith had suggested in his letter from jail. The committee, consisting of Almon Babbitt, Erastus Snow, and Robert B. Thompson, was assigned to "gather up and obtain all the libelous reports, and publications . . . that they can possibly obtain," as well as to compile records from church members. Thompson was assigned to use these sources to draft a history.[27] Although no formal narrative resulted, the committee collected affidavits, and Thompson and Elias Higbee prepared and signed a petition to the United States Congress in 1840 recounting the Latter-day Saints' losses.[28] Other individuals, responding to Smith's appeal to the general membership of the church, wrote petitions and pamphlets filled with personal narratives and documentary compilations of their suffering. Such accounts were designed to draw public opinion and governmental support to their side. Smith himself composed a "Bill of Damages against the State of Missouri," which narrated from his perspective the persecution of the Mormons in 1838.[29]

Turning from his campaign to publicize and seek redress for Mormon suffering in Missouri, Smith devoted five days of June and three more days in July 1839 to a renewed focus on what his journal called simply "history." He enlisted his scribe James Mulholland to take dictation and called on Newel Knight, an early convert to Mormonism from Colesville, New York, to assist in reconstructing events in upstate New York.[30] Further work was forestalled by other concerns, including a local malaria epidemic and the departure of members of the Quorum of the Twelve for a mission to the British Isles.

Two extant manuscripts resulted from Mulholland's work with Joseph Smith: the 1839 draft and the start of the large history manuscript. The 1839 draft (designated Draft 1 herein), written on twenty-five pages of a makeshift gathering of paper, was likely composed to pick up the story where the now nonextant 1838 history ended; it begins immediately after the baptism of Joseph Smith and Oliver Cowdery in May 1829 and concludes in late September 1830. Mulholland's inscription in the large history manuscript occupies fifty-nine pages (Draft 2 herein) and begins at Joseph Smith's birth in 1805. Beginning with May 1829, where the 1839 draft starts, the large history manuscript appears to be an edited copy of the draft. The draft and Mulholland's portion of the large history manuscript end at the same point, with the September 1830

---

27. Minutes, 4 May 1839, in JS Letterbook 2, p. 140; Snow, Journal, 1838–1841, pp. 52–53.

28. Petition of the Latter-Day Saints, H.R. Doc. 22, 26th Cong., 2nd Sess. (1840).

29. JS, "Bill of Damages against the State of Missouri[:] An Account of the Sufferings and Losses Sustained Therein," Quincy, IL, 4 June 1839, JS Collection, CHL.

30. JS, Journal, 10–14 June and 3–5 July 1839, in *JSP*, J1:340, 345.

conference of the church. The original source for the pre-May 1829 material in
the large history appears to be the nonextant 1838 Smith-Rigdon manuscript.[31]
Thus, Mulholland copied first the Smith-Rigdon manuscript (or Joseph Smith
may have dictated a revised version) and then copied in the 1839 draft, thereby
creating in the large history volume a seamless narrative.

In the same year, Joseph Smith and others began publishing histories of
the events that occurred in Missouri. In July 1839, the first issue of the *Times
and Seasons* included a revised and expanded version of Smith's "Bill of
Damages" under the title "Extract, from the Private Journal of Joseph Smith Jr."
In October of that year, Smith traveled to Washington DC to present the
Saints' petitions to Congress and to President Martin Van Buren. During
Smith's absence, Edward Partridge, to whom Smith had addressed "in particular" his mandate from prison to gather accounts of the Saints' Missouri depre-
dations, published in the December 1839 issue of the *Times and Seasons* the first
installment in a series of articles that gave his account of "the persecutions of
the church of Jesus Christ of Latter day Saints, in the State of Missouri."[32]
After Partridge's death in May 1840, the editors of the newspaper continued
the series by printing excerpts of two previously published accounts: Parley P.
Pratt's *History of the Late Persecution* and Sidney Rigdon's *Appeal to the
American People.* In all, eleven installments of "A History, of the Persecution, of
the Church of Jesus Christ, of Latter Day Saints in Missouri" appeared in the
newspaper from December 1839 to October 1840.

At the church's general conference in Nauvoo on 3 October 1840, Robert B.
Thompson was appointed to replace George W. Robinson as the "general
church clerk," the latter having announced his intention to move across the
river to Iowa.[33] Thompson served in various clerical, editorial, and administrative capacities and succeeded Mulholland—who died suddenly in November
1839—as scribe for Joseph Smith's history. Beginning where Mulholland left
off in the large history volume, Thompson recorded sixteen pages that carried
the narrative through mid-November 1830, describing the conversion of Sidney
Rigdon and many of his followers in Ohio and including an extensive biographical sketch of Rigdon. Thompson died 27 August 1841.[34]

At about the time Thompson was inscribing Smith's history, Smith
assigned Edwin D. Woolley and Howard Coray to draft additional historical

31. The large history manuscript notes the date of composition as 2 May 1838. (JS History, vol. A-1,
p. 238 herein [Draft 2]; compare JS, Journal, 2 May 1838, in *JSP*, J1:264.)
32. "A History, of the Persecution," *Times and Seasons,* Dec. 1839, 1:17, in *JSP*, H2:206.
33. "Minutes of the General Conference," *Times and Seasons,* 12 Oct. 1840, 1:185.
34. "Death of Col. Robert B. Thompson," *Times and Seasons,* 1 Sept. 1841, 2:519–520; Hyrum Smith and
JS, Nauvoo, IL, to Oliver Granger, 30 Aug. 1841, Henry E. Huntington Library, San Marino, CA.

material, using sources Smith provided. Woolley eventually withdrew from the project and was replaced by a "Dr. Miller."[35] Their work evidently resulted in two different kinds of drafts. According to Coray's later reminiscences, the first grew out of instructions "not only to combine, and arrange in chronological order, but to spread out or amplify not a little, in as good historical style as may be."[36] No manuscript matching this description has survived, but their work may have provided the basis for material subsequently copied into the large history by other scribes. Coray did, however, produce an edited version of the narrative inscribed in the large history volume. According to Coray's later account, Joseph Smith was directly involved in this reworking of the history, reading aloud and dictating revisions from the large volume as Coray and Miller wrote.[37] Two drafts of this work have survived.[38] However, there is no indication that either draft was used in subsequent compiling or in publication of the history, as writing proceeded in the large history volume. Though a short-lived effort, Coray's manuscript represents the intention to revise the history, suggesting that Joseph Smith had not yet settled on a final historical product even after he had directed scribes to begin inscribing the history in the large, more permanent volume in 1839.

Work on the large history manuscript continued throughout the church's Illinois period. William W. Phelps, former editor of the Latter-day Saint newspaper in Jackson County, performed clerical duties in Nauvoo for Joseph Smith starting in late 1842. Phelps's inscription in Smith's church history extended from pages 75 to 157 in the large history volume, carrying the narrative to 1 November 1831. As the work continued to take shape, arrangements were made for its publication. In its 15 March 1842 issue, during Phelps's tenure of stewardship for the history and Smith's general editorship of the newspaper, the *Times and Seasons* began serial publication of the work under the title "History of Joseph Smith." Editorial comments made by Joseph Smith elsewhere in the newspaper explained that although the previous issue had featured a brief historical essay, he would "now enter more particularly into that history, and extract from my journal."[39] This repeated the practice, seen earlier with the publication of Smith's bill of damages, of identifying as an extract from Smith's journal a document that was produced for specific purposes quite different from a typical journal.

---

35. Coray, Reminiscences, 2.

36. Coray, Reminiscences, 4.

37. Howard Coray, Statement, 1869, in JS History, [ca. 1841]; see also pp. 200–201 herein.

38. See pp. 191–192 herein. The earlier draft is transcribed as "Draft 3" on pp. 205–463 herein.

39. JS, Notice, *Times and Seasons,* 15 Mar. 1842, 3:726.

The first part of the history benefited from Smith's direct input, and its first-person narrative resembles a journal account. The history goes on to weave together the texts of Smith's revelations and other documents with a narration of events and developments in the early years of the church. The revelation texts were an essential component of the history; Orson Pratt later stated that Joseph Smith intended the revelations to "be published more fully in his History" than in the published compilations of revelations.[40] Only a handful of the revelations Smith dictated after April 1835 were included in the 1844 edition of the Doctrine and Covenants, and when the history was printed, it served as the most accessible repository for the others. Willard Richards, a later member of Smith's clerical staff, began working on the history in early December 1842 and was appointed Joseph Smith's "private se[c]retary & historian" later that month.[41] He inscribed 659 pages of the manuscript over a period of two years. After working closely with Sidney Rigdon, George W. Robinson, and James Mulholland in 1838 and 1839 to compose the history, Joseph Smith delegated most of the later work to others, though he occasionally reviewed the text and made revisions. As Willard Richards and his colleagues and successors continued the narrative with material that was for the most part neither written nor dictated by Smith, they maintained the first-person approach so it would appear as though Smith was the narrator throughout. When the clerks reached the point that Smith's journals could provide information, the journals became a key component of the history. Scribes also used other documents created under Smith's direction or by others associated with him.

At the outset, the "History of Joseph Smith" appeared to be only the most recent of numerous historical narratives published by the Latter-day Saints. However, with its continued publication stretching almost four years in Nauvoo and many years thereafter in England and in Utah, it became the standard, official history of the church. Even after publication began in the *Times and Seasons,* revisions were made in the manuscript instead of in a copy of the printed version. Thus the manuscript volumes, rather than the serialized publication, were used as the definitive source for subsequent publications.[42]

Addressing a Larger Audience

Besides assisting in the compilation of the institutional history in the 1840s, Joseph Smith wrote about the church's beginnings in response to inquirers

---

40. Orson Pratt, "Restoration of the Aaronic and Melchisedek Priesthoods," *LDS Millennial Star,* 25 Apr. 1857, 19:260.

41. Richards, Journal, 1–2 and 21 Dec. 1842; JS, Journal, 21 Dec. 1842, in *JSP,* J2:191.

42. The chart on p. 203 herein provides an overview of the relationships among the various versions of Joseph Smith's multivolume manuscript history.

outside the Mormon community. Efforts by early Mormon leaders to spread information about the church, along with skeptical curiosity from the public concerning Mormonism and repeated published attacks against its founder, made Joseph Smith a well-known figure outside the Latter-day Saint community. By 1842, reporters and authors were seeking out the Mormon prophet for information both personal and historical. Smith welcomed opportunities to explain his own story and that of the church, recognizing that the press, though often negative, could serve as an important means of enlightening the public and correcting misconceptions. One such opportunity came in March 1842 when John Wentworth, editor of the *Chicago Democrat,* requested information on the church in behalf of his friend George Barstow, who intended to use it in a history of New Hampshire. Drawing in part on a pamphlet published by Orson Pratt two years earlier,[43] and probably assisted by scribes, Smith compiled a brief sketch of the church's history and beliefs. The Latter-day Saint movement ultimately fell outside the chronological scope of Barstow's published book, but the letter to Wentworth was printed in the *Times and Seasons* in March 1842 under the title "Church History."

In 1843, in response to another request for information, Joseph Smith and William W. Phelps sent an updated version of "Church History" to editor I. D. Rupp, who published it with the title "Latter Day Saints" in the 1844 publication *He Pasa Ekklesia* [The whole church]: *An Original History of the Religious Denominations at Present Existing in the United States.* After receiving a copy of Rupp's volume in the spring of 1844, Smith sent a letter thanking Rupp for "so valueable a treasure" and praising both the volume and its compiler. Smith agreed to recommend the book in the church newspaper and offered, "I shall be pleased to furnish further information, at a proper time, and render you such service as the work, and vast extension of our church may demand."[44] Within a month of writing this letter, however, Smith was murdered at Carthage, Illinois.

The publication of *An Original History of the Religious Denominations* marked a milestone. Before this time, Joseph Smith and his new church had suffered repeated attacks in books and articles; except for church-owned periodicals, the printed word seemed the church's enemy. With the publication of "Latter Day Saints," Smith's message appeared in a prominent, nationally

---

43. Pratt, *Interesting Account of Several Remarkable Visions,* pp. 517–546 herein.

44. JS, Nauvoo, IL, to Israel Daniel Rupp, Lancaster City, PA, 5 June 1844, copy, JS Collection, CHL. A notice recommending the Rupp volume to Latter-day Saints appeared in the *Nauvoo Neighbor* the same week that Smith died. ("He Pasa Ekklesia," *Nauvoo Neighbor,* 26 June 1844, [2].)

Multivolume manuscript history of Joseph Smith. These manuscript volumes, labeled "A-1" through "F-1," were compiled and written between 1839 and 1856, starting from work done in 1838. The history began under the supervision of Joseph Smith and had reached page 812 in volume B-1 by the time of his death. Between 1842 and 1863, this history was published serially in various church periodicals. Under the editorship of B. H. Roberts, the history was published in six volumes as *History of the Church of Jesus Christ of Latter-day Saints, Period 1* between 1902 and 1912, with Joseph Smith listed as author. JS History, vols. A-1–F-1, Church History Library, Salt Lake City. (Photograph by Welden C. Andersen.)

distributed volume, signaling that the Church of Jesus Christ of Latter-day Saints had become an established presence on the religious landscape.

Completion of Joseph Smith's History

Near the end of his life, Joseph Smith gave high priority to his history, and he was finally able to devote the resources to make it a substantial production. In May 1843, he told William W. Phelps of a message that came to him in a dream: "The history must go ahead before any thing."[45] When noise from a school hindered the work of his scribes, Smith told the schoolmaster to relocate, "as the History must continue, and not be disturbed."[46] In December 1842, Willard Richards was assigned to write for the history, and soon after, he became supervisor of the other scribes and compilers. Under Richards's direction, the enterprise made substantial progress. Addressing the Saints in Nauvoo a month before he was killed, Joseph Smith noted with satisfaction that during the past three years his "acts and proceedings" had been recorded by "efficient Clerks in constant employ," who had accompanied him everywhere and "carefully kept my history, and they have written down what I have done, where I have been & what I have said."[47]

When Smith was killed in June 1844, the manuscript history numbered 812 pages in two bound manuscript volumes, but it recorded events only up to 5 August 1838.[48] The commitment to write the history did not die with the church's founder, however, and by January 1846, when the manuscript was packed up for removal from Nauvoo, it totaled 1,486 pages and continued the narrative to 1 March 1843. The exodus from Nauvoo to the Great Basin interrupted writing for more than eight years. On 1 December 1853, Richards dictated one sentence of the history, but illness prevented further work, and he died 11 March 1854.[49] His successor was George A. Smith, a church apostle, cousin of Joseph Smith, and eyewitness to much of the Latter-day Saints' history. By 1856 the massive history was completed up to Joseph Smith's death. It filled 2,332 pages in six manuscript volumes.

Serial publication of the "History of Joseph Smith" in the Nauvoo *Times and Seasons* continued to 15 February 1846, the newspaper's final issue. In April 1845, church leaders made plans to publish the history in book form in Nauvoo, and a fair copy of the multivolume history was begun, apparently intended to

---

45. JS, Journal, 19 May 1843, JS Collection, CHL.

46. JS History, vol. E-1, 1768; see also JS, Journal, 7 Nov. 1843, JS Collection, CHL.

47. "Sermon of Joseph the Proph[et]," 26 May 1844, p. 2, JS Collection, CHL.

48. See JS History, vol. B-1, 812; see also Jessee, "Writing of Joseph Smith's History," 441, 466.

49. JS History, vol. D-1, 1486.

aid in the typesetting of the book.⁵⁰ These publication plans were not carried out, however, perhaps because of growing opposition to the Mormons in Nauvoo. The duplicate copy of the history was used as the source text in Utah when the *Deseret News* picked up serial publication of the history where the *Times and Seasons* left off; the series ran from 15 November 1851 to 20 January 1858.⁵¹ It was also published in England in the *Latter Day Saints' Millennial Star,* first from June 1842 to May 1845 and continuing from 15 April 1852 to 2 May 1863. Beginning in 1902, the history was edited and published in six volumes under the editorship of Latter-day Saint theologian and historian B. H. Roberts, as *History of the Church of Jesus Christ of Latter-day Saints, Period I. History of Joseph Smith, the Prophet by Himself.* An accompanying seventh volume edited by Roberts covered the history of the church through 8 October 1848. *History of the Church* has served as the most comprehensive single source for the study of the beginnings of Mormonism since its publication. The Histories series of *The Joseph Smith Papers* will make available the manuscript behind B. H. Roberts's widely used publication, and it will identify, in turn, the sources behind the manuscript itself, thereby facilitating more informed use of the history.

---

50. Historian's Office, Journal, 3 Apr. 1845, 1:35.

51. Creation of the second copy of the history was discontinued 6 August 1856, by which time the history had been copied to 18 July 1843 and the copy numbered five volumes, designated volumes A-2 through E-2. Beginning in December 1856, the first copy of the history again became the source for publication in the *Deseret News.* (JS History, vol. E-2, 83.)

History Creation Dates, Narrative Spans, Scribes, and Precursor Documents

This chart lists each history in volumes 1 and 2 of the Histories series, along with the date of creation or publication, the years covered within the history, the scribes in whose handwriting the history appears (not applicable to published histories), and the major documents that were copied into the history or that served as sources. This overview is intended as a convenience in understanding the sequence and often overlapping span of the various histories. Because such a chart necessarily simplifies and summarizes many complex issues, readers will wish to consult the source note and historical introduction that preface each of the histories for additional information.

Document	Created/Published	Narrative Span	Scribes	Precursor Documents
Volume 1: Joseph Smith Histories				
JS History, ca. summer 1832	ca. summer 1832	23 Dec. 1805–5 Apr. 1829	JS, Frederick G. Williams	Possibly earlier draft (nonextant)
JS History, 1834–1836	ca. 5 Dec. 1834–ca. Apr. 1836	ca. 1823–18 Jan. 1836	Warren Parrish, Warren Cowdery, Frederick G. Williams, Oliver Cowdery	Eight letters from Oliver Cowdery to William W. Phelps, in *LDS Messenger and Advocate*, Oct. 1834–Oct. 1835; JS, Journal, 1835–1836
JS History, 1838–ca. 1841 (Draft 1)	ca. June 1839	15 May 1829–26 Sept. 1830	James Mulholland	Possibly JS History, 1838 (nonextant)
JS History, 1838–ca. 1841 (Draft 2)	ca. July 1839–ca. 1841	23 Dec. 1805–26 Sept. 1830	James Mulholland, Robert B. Thompson	JS History, 1838 (nonextant); Draft 1; Doctrine and Covenants, 1835 ed.; Book of Mormon, 1837 ed.
JS History, 1838–ca. 1841 (Draft 3)	ca. 1841	23 Dec. 1805–26 Sept. 1830	Howard Coray	Draft 2
JS, "Extract, from the Private Journal"	July 1839	14 Mar. 1838–Apr. 1839		JS, "Bill of Damages," 4 June 1839
JS, "Church History"	1 Mar. 1842	23 Dec. 1805–ca. 1841		Orson Pratt, *A[n] Interesting Account of Several Remarkable Visions*, 1840
JS, "Latter Day Saints"	1844	23 Dec. 1805–ca. Sept. 1843		JS, "Church History," 1842; William W. Phelps, "Additions to an Article in the Times & Seasons," Sept. 1843
Volume 2: Assigned Historical Writings				
John Whitmer, History	1831–ca. 1847	Oct. 1830–ca. 1847	John Whitmer	Earlier notes or drafts (nonextant); revelations, letters, and other documents as selected by Whitmer
William W. Phelps, "Rise and Progress"	Apr. 1833	6 Apr. 1830–Apr. 1833		
John Corrill, *A Brief History of the Church*	ca. 11 Feb. 1839	fall 1830–ca. Feb. 1839		John Corrill, "Brief History," manuscript, ca. 1838–1839; *Extract from the New Translation of the Bible*, [ca. 1835?]
"A History, of the Persecution"	Dec. 1839–Oct. 1840	winter 1831–winter 1839		Edward Partridge, History, manuscript, ca. 1839; Parley P. Pratt, *History of the Late Persecution*, 1839; [Sidney Rigdon], *Appeal to the American People*, 1840

Relationships among Histories and Precursors

The texts featured in volumes 1 and 2 of the Histories series are found in the center column, arranged chronologically based on the date manuscripts were commenced or printed works were published. Documents found in volume 1 are indicated with "H1," documents in volume 2 with "H2." An asterisk (*) marks works of which Joseph Smith is not credited as an author and which did not result from his direct assignment. Double asterisks (**) indicate nonextant works. An arrow from one document to another indicates that the former was a source for the latter. A dashed arrow indicates a possible source.

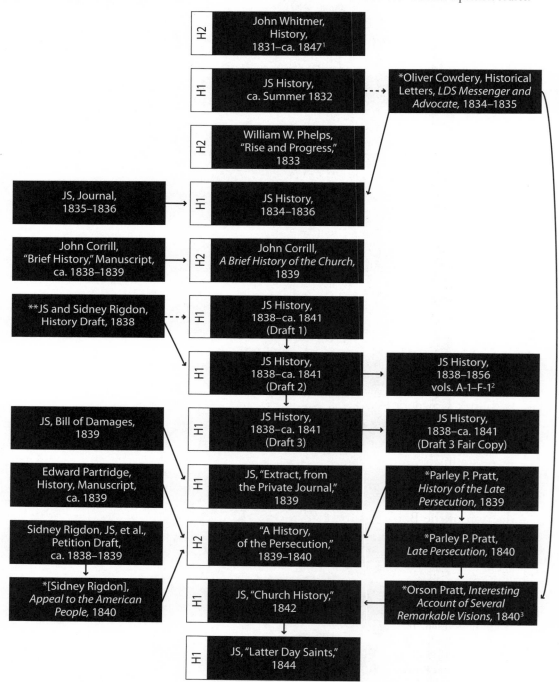

1. Whitmer began writing or keeping notes for a history in 1831. The extant manuscript of his history was begun circa 1838.

2. "Draft 2" constitutes the first sixty-one pages of this history, which will be published at josephsmithpapers.org. See page 203 herein for a detailed chart of the relationships among the different versions of JS's 1838–1856 history.

3. This document is reproduced in the appendix, pages 517–546 herein.

The Histories of Joseph Smith, 1832–1844

The eight histories in the main body of this volume were all part of Joseph Smith's own record-keeping endeavors, though they vary widely in their creation date, purpose, format, length, and scope. These documents all qualify as Joseph Smith histories; that is, Smith wrote or supervised the writing of each, under circumstances that allowed him to be closely involved in their creation. Although he had considerable assistance from scribes and other associates, Smith himself assumed authorial responsibility for the histories herein.[1]

The first of these narratives was probably begun in Hiram, Ohio, in summer 1832, when Joseph Smith hired Frederick G. Williams to serve as his scribe. The circa summer 1832 history is the earliest extant attempt by Smith to write an account of his life, and it is the only narrative history that contains his own handwriting. The document alternates between the handwriting of Smith and of Williams.

Joseph Smith's 1834–1836 history, which includes the handwriting of four of his scribes—Warren Parrish, Warren Cowdery, Frederick G. Williams, and Oliver Cowdery—was written in Kirtland under Smith's supervision. The bulk of the history was copied from two sources: a series of historical letters written by Oliver Cowdery in 1834–1835 and Smith's 1835–1836 journal. Although the history was not written by Joseph Smith, he clearly took ownership of it, referring to the book as "my large journal," in which "my scribe commenced writing . . . a history of my life."[2]

Following the 1834–1836 history are transcripts of three related documents that narrate in detail Joseph Smith's formative visionary experiences, the production of the Book of Mormon, and the first few months of the church he organized. These documents, which together trace the progression of history

---

1. In contrast, the four histories in volume 2 of the Histories series, *Assigned Historical Writings, 1831–1847,* share a less direct link to Joseph Smith than do the histories in volume 1. Although each history in volume 2 was begun in response to an official assignment, none came under Smith's immediate and sustained supervision. These histories are John Whitmer's history, titled "The Book of John Whitmer"; William W. Phelps, "Rise and Progress of the Church of Christ," published in *The Evening and the Morning Star* in April 1833; John Corrill, *A Brief History of the Church of Christ of Latter Day Saints;* and "A History, of the Persecution, of the Church of Jesus Christ, of Latter Day Saints in Missouri," published in the *Times and Seasons* from December 1839 to October 1840.

2. JS, Journal, 29 Oct. 1835, in *JSP,* J1:76.

writing in the late 1830s and early 1840s, are labeled herein as Draft 1, Draft 2, and Draft 3. They are presented in parallel columns to facilitate comparison. The first, an incomplete draft in the hand of scribe James Mulholland, was probably penned in June and July 1839. It was evidently the continuation of a history, no longer extant, that Smith initiated a year earlier in April 1838, with assistance from Sidney Rigdon and scribe George W. Robinson.

In the second column is a later draft of the same material, as it existed in about 1841. Draft 2 was written in the same large volume as Joseph Smith's 1834–1836 history, turned over so the back cover became the front; it now constitutes the first sixty-one pages of the initial volume of Smith's multivolume history. It is transcribed here as it appeared in about 1841, excluding later redactions and additions. Mulholland inscribed the first fifty-nine pages sometime before his death in November 1839. The first seventeen pages of Draft 2 have no surviving source, though they were apparently copied from the nonextant 1838 history. Beginning on manuscript page 18, Draft 2 contains an edited version of Draft 1. The two texts correspond until the end of page 59 of the large volume, where Draft 1 concludes and Mulholland's handwriting in the large history manuscript ends. Draft 2 continues for two more pages, which recount the October 1830 beginnings of the mission to the West undertaken by Oliver Cowdery and others. These pages were inscribed by Robert B. Thompson and are included in the present volume because they correspond to the end of Draft 3, the draft found in the third column of the presentation in this volume.

Draft 3 is a 102-page manuscript written in the hand of Howard Coray. It is a lightly edited version of Draft 2 and was copied from the large history volume. Coray began work on this draft in late 1840 or early 1841, and he later made a fair copy. His project was discontinued, however, and his efforts on this iteration of the history went unused as writing and revising proceeded in the large bound volume.

By the time historians and clerks concluded their work on Joseph Smith's history in 1856, twelve years after his death, it consisted of more than 2,300 pages in six large volumes. That entire work will be found on the Joseph Smith Papers website, josephsmithpapers.org. The first sixty-one pages of the history reproduced in the present volume facilitate comparison with the earlier draft in Mulholland's hand and the later draft in Coray's hand. Of the massive six-volume manuscript, the excerpt reproduced as Draft 2 in the present volume includes the material Smith worked on most closely.

"Extract, from the Private Journal of Joseph Smith Jr." was printed in the church's periodical in Illinois, *Times and Seasons*. The article gives an account of the conflicts between the Mormons and other citizens of northwestern

Missouri. Despite its name, "Extract" was not excerpted from any known journal account; the principal source for the article was Smith's petition for the redress of losses in Missouri. The petition, titled "Bill of Damages against the State of Missouri," is in the hand of scribe Robert B. Thompson.[3]

Joseph Smith was also named as the author of the last two documents in this volume: "Church History," published in the *Times and Seasons;* and its later version, "Latter Day Saints," published as an essay in an 1844 anthology of religions. Although he relied on scribal assistance, and although "Church History," and therefore "Latter Day Saints" also, drew in part from Orson Pratt's earlier work, Smith assumed authorial responsibility for both histories in their final form.

The appendix to the present volume reproduces Orson Pratt's *A[n] Interesting Account of Several Remarkable Visions, and of the Late Discovery of Ancient American Records,* a thirty-one-page pamphlet published in Edinburgh, Scotland, in 1840 as part of the author's proselytizing efforts in Great Britain. Although the pamphlet was not written by Joseph Smith or created by his assignment, it is included as an appendix because of its importance as a source for the historical article "Church History." Gray shading in the appendix indicates wording or content that was incorporated into "Church History." Other texts that served as precursors to the documents in this volume will be available at josephsmithpapers.org.

---

3. JS, "Bill of Damages against the State of Missouri[:] An Account of the Sufferings and Losses Sustained Therein," Quincy, IL, 4 June 1839, JS Collection, CHL.

Editorial Method

The goal of the Joseph Smith Papers Project is to present verbatim transcripts of Joseph Smith's papers in their entirety, making available the most essential sources of Smith's life and work and preserving the content of aging manuscripts from damage or loss. The papers include documents that were created by Joseph Smith, whether written or dictated by him or created by others under his direction, or that were owned by Smith, that is, received by him and kept in his office (as with incoming correspondence). Under these criteria—authorship and ownership—the project intends to publish, either in letterpress volumes or electronic form, every extant Joseph Smith document to which its editors can obtain access. This volume of the Histories series presents an unaltered and unabridged transcript of seven histories written by Smith or under his direction, as well as an excerpt from the history he began in 1838, which eventually comprised six volumes and which will be published in its entirety in electronic form at the Joseph Smith Papers website, josephsmithpapers.org. An appendix included herein provides the transcript of a document used as a source for the Joseph Smith histories titled "Church History" and "Latter Day Saints."

Document Selection

This volume includes transcripts of both handwritten and printed documents. When a history was intended for print, the earliest printed version is presented, rather than subsequent printings or any earlier manuscript version. However, in the case of the history Joseph Smith began in 1838, which was printed serially in church newspapers beginning in 1842, early manuscript versions are presented to aid readers in understanding the development of that history. For one of these documents, presented here as "Draft 3" of the 1838–circa 1841 history, there are two manuscript versions of the original, a rough draft and a fair copy. In this instance, the rough draft was chosen as the featured text because the revisions evident in this draft provide more information about the creation process. Several of the documents in this volume are based at least in part on earlier texts, such as histories that include copies of revelations or printed works typeset from a manuscript (see the chart on page xxxiii herein for a list of the documents in this volume and their antecedent texts). The texts transcribed in this volume have been compared to all known extant source texts (and in the case of Draft 3 of the 1838–circa 1841 history, to the later fair copy), and any significant differences are described in annotation.

Rules of Transcription

Handwritten documents of course present greater transcription challenges than do printed documents. Because of aging and sometimes damaged texts and imprecise penmanship, not all handwriting is legible or can be fully deciphered. Hurried writers often rendered words carelessly, and even the best writers and spellers left out letters on occasion or formed them imperfectly and incompletely. Text transcription and verification is therefore an imperfect art more than a science. Judgments about capitalization, for example, are informed not only by looking at the specific case at hand but by understanding the usual characteristics of each particular writer. The same is true for interpreting original spelling and punctuation. If a letter or other character is ambiguous, deference is given to the author's or scribe's usual spelling and punctuation. Where this is ambiguous, modern spelling and punctuation are favored. Even the best transcribers and verifiers will differ from one another in making such judgments. Interested readers may wish to compare our transcriptions with images of the original documents at the Joseph Smith Papers website to better understand how our transcription rules have been applied to create these transcripts. Viewing the originals also provides other information that cannot be conveyed by typography.

To ensure accuracy in representing the texts, transcripts were verified three times, each time by a different set of eyes. The first two verifications were done using high-resolution scanned images. The first was a visual collation of the manuscript images with the transcripts, while the second was an independent and double-blind image-to-transcript tandem proofreading. The third and final verification of the transcripts was a visual collation with the original document. At this stage, the verifier employed magnification and ultraviolet light as needed to read badly faded text, recover heavily stricken material, untangle characters written over each other, and recover words canceled by messy "wipe erasures" made when the ink was still wet or removed by knife scraping after the ink had dried. The verified transcripts meet or exceed the transcription and verification requirements of the National Archives and Records Administration's National Historical Publications and Records Commission.

The approach to transcription employed in *The Joseph Smith Papers* is conservative by historical documentary editing standards. The transcripts render most words letter by letter as accurately as possible, preserving the exact spelling of the originals. This includes incomplete words, variant spellings of personal names, repeated words, and idiosyncratic grammatical constructions.

The transcripts of handwritten documents also preserve substantive revisions made by the writer. Canceled words are typographically rendered with the strikethrough bar, while inserted words are enclosed within angle brackets. Cancellations and insertions are also transcribed letter by letter when an original word was changed to a new word simply by canceling or inserting letters at the beginning or end of the word—such as "sparingly" or "attend⟨ed⟩". However, for cases in which an original word was changed to a new word by canceling or inserting letters in the middle of the word, to improve readability the original word is presented stricken in its entirety, followed by the revised word in its entirety. For example, when "falling" was revised to "failing" by canceling the first "l" and inserting an "i", the revision is transcribed as "falling ⟨failing⟩" instead of "fal⟨i⟩ling". Insubstantial cancellations and insertions—those used only to correct spelling and punctuation—are silently emended, and only the final spelling and punctuation are reproduced.

The transcription of punctuation differs from the original in a few other respects. Single instances of periods, commas, apostrophes, and dashes are all faithfully rendered without regard to their grammatical correctness, except that periods are not reproduced when they appear immediately before a word, with no space between the period and the word. Also, in some cases of repetitive punctuation, only the final mark or final intention is transcribed while any other characters are silently omitted. Dashes of various lengths are standardized to a consistent pattern. When asterisks are used in the original to signify an ellipsis, they have been standardized to ellipsis points. The short vertical strokes commonly used in early American writing for abbreviation punctuation are transcribed as periods, but abbreviation punctuation is not reproduced when an abbreviation is expanded in square brackets. Flourishes and other decorative inscriptions are not reproduced or noted. Punctuation is never added silently.

Incorrect dates, place names, and other errors of fact are left to stand. The intrusive *sic,* sometimes used to affirm original misspelling, is never employed, although where words or phrases are especially difficult to understand, editorial clarifications or corrections are inserted in brackets. Correct and complete spellings of personal names are supplied in brackets the first time each incorrect or incomplete name appears in a text (unless the correct name cannot be determined). Place names that may be hard to identify are also clarified or corrected within brackets. When two or more words were inscribed or typeset together without any intervening space and the words were not a compound according to standard contemporary usage or the writer's or printer's consistent practice, the words are transcribed as separate words for readability.

Formatting is standardized. Original paragraphing is retained, except that the original datelines in journal-like entries are always run in with the first paragraph of the entries. Standardized editorial datelines and section headings—typographically distinguishable from the text—have also been added where appropriate for convenience of use. All paragraphs are given in a standard format, with indention regularized and with blank lines between paragraphs omitted. Block quotations of letters, minutes, revelations, and other similar items within the texts are set apart with block indentions, even when such items are not set off in the original. Horizontal rules and other separating devices inscribed or printed in the original are not reproduced. Where blank horizontal space was used between sentences to signal breaks in thought, a convention found most frequently in James Mulholland's writing, they are rendered as paragraph breaks. Line ends are neither typographically reproduced nor symbolically represented. Because of the great number of words broken across a line at any point in the word, with or without a hyphen, end-of-line hyphens are not transcribed and there is no effort to note or keep a record of such words and hyphens. This leaves open the possibility that the hyphen of an ambiguously hyphenated compound escaped transcription or that a compound word correctly broken across a line ending without a hyphen is mistakenly transcribed as two words. As many end-of-line hyphens have been editorially introduced in the transcripts, a hyphen appearing at the end of a line may or may not be original to the document.

In transcripts of printed sources, typeface, type size, and spacing have been standardized. Characters set upside down are silently corrected. When the text could not be determined because of broken or worn type or damage to the page, the illegible text is supplied based on another copy of the printed text, if possible. Printers sometimes made changes to the text, such as to correct spelling mistakes or replace damaged type, after printing had already begun, meaning that the first copies to come off the press often differ from later copies in the same print run. No attempt has been made to analyze more than one copy of the printed texts transcribed here, aside from consulting another copy when the one used for transcription is indeterminable or ambiguous.

Redactions and other changes made on a document after the original production of the text are not transcribed. Labeling and other forms of archival marking are similarly passed by in silence.

Transcription Symbols

The effort to render mistakes, canceled material, and later insertions sometimes complicates readability by putting Joseph Smith and his scribes behind the "barbed wire" of symbolic transcription. However, conveying such elements with transcription symbols can aid in understanding the text and the order and ways in which the words were inscribed. Typesetting can never effectively represent all the visual aspects of a document; it cannot fully capture such features as the formation of letters and other characters, spacing between words and between paragraphs, varying lengths of dashes and paragraph indentions, and varying methods of cancellation and the location of insertions. Despite its limitations, a conservative transcription method more faithfully represents the process by which the text was inscribed—especially cancellations and insertions—rather than just the final result.

The following symbols are used to transcribe and expand the text:

/ⁿ	In documents inscribed by more than one person, the slash mark indicates a change in handwriting. A footnote identifies the previous and commencing scribes.
[roman]	Brackets enclose editorial insertions that expand, correct, or clarify the text. This convention may be applied to the abbreviated or incorrect spelling of a personal name, such as Brigham Yo[u]ng, or of a place, such as Westleville [Wesleyville]. Obsolete or ambiguous abbreviations are expanded with br[acket]s. Bracketed editorial insertions also provide reasonable reconstructions of badly miss[p]elled worsd [words]. Missing or illegible words may be supplied within brackets in cases where the supplied word is based on textual or contextual evidence. Bracketed punctuation is added only when necessary to follow complex wording.
[roman?]	A question mark is added to conjectural editorial insertions, such as where an entire word was [accidentally?] omitted and where it is difficult to maintain the sense of a sentence without some editorial insertion.
[*italic*]	Significant descriptions of the textual medium—especially those inhibiting legibility—and of spacing within the text are italicized and enclosed in brackets: [*hole burned in paper*], [*leaf torn*], [*blank*], [*9 lines blank*], [*pages 99–102 blank*].
[*illegible*]	An illegible word is represented by the italicized word [*illegible*] enclosed in brackets.
◊	An illegible character within a partially legible word is rendered with a hollow diamond. Repeated diamonds represent the approximate number of illegible characters (for example: sto◊◊◊◊s).
[p. x]	Bracketed editorial insertions indicate the end of an originally numbered page, regardless of the location of the page number on the original page.
[p. [x]]	Bracketing of the page number itself indicates that the page was not originally numbered and that the number of the page is editorially supplied.

<u>underlined</u>	Underlining is typographically reproduced. <u>Individually</u> <u>underlined</u> <u>words</u> are distinguished from <u>passages underlined with one continuous line</u>.
superscript	Superscription is typographically reproduc^{ed}.
~~canceled~~	A single horizontal strikethrough bar is used to indicate any method of cancellation: strikethrough, cross-out, wipe erasure, knife erasure, overwriting, or other methods. ~~Individually canceled words~~ are distinguished from ~~passages eliminated with a single cancellation~~. Characters individual~~ly~~ canceled at the begin~~ning~~ or end of a word are distinguished from ~~words canceled in their entirety~~.
⟨inserted⟩	Insertions in the text—whether interlinear, intralinear, or marginal—are enclosed in angle brackets. Letter⟨s⟩ and other characters individual⟨ly⟩ insert⟨ed⟩ at the beginning or end of a word are distinguished from ⟨words⟩ inserted in ⟨their⟩ entirety.
bold	Joseph Smith's handwriting is rendered in boldface type. Bracketed editorial insertions made within passages of **Smith's own h[and]w[riting]** are also rendered in boldface type.
[roman]	Stylized brackets represent [brackets] used in the original text.
TEXT	The word TEXT begins textual footnotes describing significant details not comprehended by this scheme of symbolic transcription.
|	A line break artificially imposed in an original document is rendered as a vertical line in textual notes.

Annotation Conventions

The Joseph Smith Papers do not present a unified narrative. Annotations—including historical introductions, editorial notes, and footnotes—supply background and context to help readers better understand and use the documents. The aim of the annotation is to serve scholars and students of early Mormon history and American religious history generally, whose familiarity with these fields may vary widely.

The *Papers* cite original sources where possible and practical. Secondary sources of sound scholarship are cited when they usefully distill several primary sources. Quotations from primary sources preserve original spelling but silently emend cancellations and insertions (unless judged highly significant).

Certain conventions simplify the presentation of the annotation. Joseph Smith is usually referred to by the initials JS. The terms *Saints, Latter-day Saints,* and *Mormons*—all used by mid-1834 in reference to church members—are employed interchangeably here. Most sources are referred to by a shortened citation form, with a complete citation given in the Works Cited. Some documents are referred to by editorial titles rather than by their original titles or the titles given in the catalogs of their current repositories. These editorial titles are in some cases similar to informal names by which the documents have come to be known. The editorial titles are listed in the Works Cited along with the complete citations by which the documents can be found in repositories. The most important sources used in annotating a volume are discussed in the Essay on Sources preceding the Works Cited.

This volume uses a citation style that lists all source citations at the end of the footnote. Because of the complexity of some footnotes and the difficulty readers might have in determining which source citations document particular statements within such footnotes, superscript letters are sometimes used to key specific statements to their corresponding documentation. Though it goes beyond conventional citation style, this detailed approach may best serve researchers using this volume as a reference work.

The annotation extensively cites Joseph Smith's revelations. In the 1830s, Smith and his followers at first used the terms *commandments* and *revelations* interchangeably in referring to these dictations that they viewed as divine communications. Usage patterns in early documents suggest that in the earliest years, Latter-day Saints may have seen subtle differences in the meaning of these terms: *commandment* may have denoted communications that required action or obedience, whereas *revelation* may have referred to communications on doctrinal topics. During the mid-1830s, *revelation*—the term used throughout *The Joseph Smith Papers* to refer to these works—became standard. Many of these revelations were first collected and published in 1833, with numbered chapters and paragraphs (or verses), as the Book of Commandments. An expanded collection, organized into sections and with new versification, was published in 1835 as the second part of the Doctrine and Covenants. In 1844, at the time of his death, Smith was overseeing publication of a revised edition of the Doctrine and Covenants, which was published later that year. Since then, the Doctrine and Covenants has been published in several editions, each including newly canonized revelations or other items.

Source citations in this volume identify revelations by their original date and by a citation of the version most relevant to the particular instance of annotation (usually the 1835 edition of the Doctrine and Covenants). In cases in which two or more revelations bear the same date, a letter of the alphabet is appended to the date so that each revelation has a unique editorial title—for example, May 1829–A or May 1829–B. Revelation citations also include a bracketed "D&C" reference that provides the Doctrine and Covenants section and verse numbers that have been standard in The Church of Jesus Christ of Latter-day Saints since 1876. For example, the last portion of the revelation that provided a basis for the Mormon health code is cited as Revelation, 27 Feb. 1833,

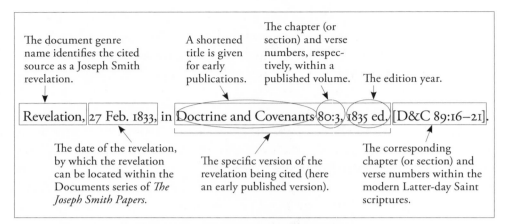

The document genre name identifies the cited source as a Joseph Smith revelation.

A shortened title is given for early publications.

The chapter (or section) and verse numbers, respectively, within a published volume.

The edition year.

Revelation, 27 Feb. 1833, in Doctrine and Covenants 80:3, 1835 ed. [D&C 89:16–21].

The date of the revelation, by which the revelation can be located within the Documents series of *The Joseph Smith Papers.*

The specific version of the revelation being cited (here an early published version).

The corresponding chapter (or section) and verse numbers within the modern Latter-day Saint scriptures.

Citation format for Joseph Smith revelations.

in Doctrine and Covenants 80:3, 1835 ed. [D&C 89:16–21] (see figure). Bracketed D&C references are provided for the benefit of Latter-day Saints, who can easily access the revelations in their familiar canon of scriptural works, and other students of early Mormonism who may wish to access the most widely available editions of these revelations. A table titled Corresponding Section Numbers in Editions of the Doctrine and Covenants is provided following the Works Cited to help readers refer from the cited version of a canonized revelation to other published versions of the same revelation. For more information about revelation citations, see the aforementioned table and the introduction to the Works Cited.

Smith's revelations and revelatory translations published outside of the Doctrine and Covenants, such as the Book of Mormon, are referenced in *The Joseph Smith Papers* to an early published or manuscript version, with references to modern Latter-day Saint publications added in brackets. These books of Latter-day Saint scripture are described in more detail in the introduction to the Works Cited. When the Bible is used in annotation, the King James Version—the version read by Smith and his followers and contemporaries as well as by English-speaking Latter-day Saints today—is referenced.

In addition to the annotation in the main body of a volume, several supplementary resources in the back of each volume aid in understanding the text. As many of the places, people, organizations, and terms mentioned in the histories appear more than once, the reference material serves to remove duplicate footnotes and to otherwise systematically reduce the annotation in the main body. To minimize repetition and interruption, only rarely will annotation within the histories directly refer readers to the reference material in the back.

Many of the people whose names appear in these histories have been identified. In most cases, information about these people appears in the Biographical

Directory rather than in the notes. Some names have silently been left without identification either because resources did not permit research or because no information was found. Complete documentation for reference material in the back and for the timeline and map included earlier in the volume may be found at josephsmithpapers.org, as may other resources, including a complete calendar of Smith's papers and expanded versions of many of the reference resources.

The first two volumes of the Histories series will be indexed cumulatively in the second volume of the series. A printable, searchable index will also be available at the Joseph Smith Papers website.

JOSEPH SMITH HISTORIES
1832–1844

Joseph Smith's earliest narrative history. Sometime in or around summer 1832, Joseph Smith and Frederick G. Williams recorded a history of Smith's early years in this marbled-cover blank book. This document contains the earliest written account of Joseph Smith's first vision of Deity and of his obtaining the gold plates. The volume was later used as a letterbook. JS History, ca. summer 1832, in JS Letterbook 1, JS Collection, Church History Library, Salt Lake City. (Photograph by Welden C. Andersen.)

HISTORY, CIRCA SUMMER 1832

Source Note

JS, "A History of the life of Joseph Smith Jr. an account of his marvilous experience and of all the mighty acts which he doeth in the name of Jesus Ch[r]ist the son of the living God of whom he beareth record and also an account of the rise of the church of Christ in the eve of time according as the Lord brought forth and established by his hand firstly he receiving the testamony from on high seccondly the ministering of Angels thirdly the reception of the holy Priesthood by the ministring of—Aangels to adminster the letter of the Gospel—the Law and commandments as they were given unto him—and the ordinencs, forthly a confirmation and recep-tion of the high Priesthood after the holy order of the son of the living God power and ordinence from on high to preach the Gospel in the administration and demonstration of the spirit the Kees of the Kingdom of God confered upon him and the continuation of the blessings of God to him &c—," [ca. summer 1832]; hand-writing of Frederick G. Williams and JS; six pages; in JS Letterbook 1, JS Collection, CHL.

JS's circa summer 1832 history was inscribed in the front of a medium-size, commercially pro-duced blank book. The book's ledger paper is horizontally ruled with thirty-six (now faint) blue lines and vertically ruled with four red lines. The original book apparently contained nine gatherings of twelve leaves each, but eight leaves have been cut from the final gathering. The text block was sewn all along over recessed cords. The leaves measure 12⅝ × 7¾ inches (32 × 20 cm). The pastedowns and fly-leaves were blank white paper. The volume was constructed with front and back covers of pasteboard and a tight-back case binding with a brown calfskin quarter-leather binding. The bound book measures 12⅞ × 8 × ⅞ inches (33 × 20 × 2 cm). The outside covers are adorned in shell marbled paper, with brown body and veins of blue and red. The front pastedown bears the inscriptions "c=c/i" and "/i=", possibly original merchandising notes. The original front flyleaf, together with any inscriptions it may have borne, is no longer extant.

The history was inscribed by Frederick G. Williams and JS with quill pen, in ink that is now brown, on the first three leaves of ledger paper. The first five pages of the history were numbered by Williams. Later, the book was turned over so the back cover became the front and the last page became the first. One or more texts were inscribed in this side (the back) of the book, as is evident from inscrip-tions visible on the remaining stubs of the eight now-excised leaves. The volume was also repurposed as a letterbook. Beginning on the recto of the fourth leaf in the front of the book (immediately following the history) are ninety-three pages of copied outgoing letters, dated 14 June 1829 through 4 August 1835, in the handwriting of Williams, JS, Orson Hyde, and Oliver Cowdery. The book's pagination also began anew with the copied letters. The first page of letters bore the inscription "1a", which is only par-tially legible on the now-trimmed page but is complete in photocopy and microfilm copies at the Church History Library.[1] The front flyleaf is missing; perhaps it bore a title related to the history and

---

1. The photocopy may have been made from the microfilm. The letterbook was filmed on 12 November 1968. (Microfilming report, entry no. JP 1068, Historical Department, Microfilm Reports, 1949–1975, CHL.)

was removed when the volume was converted to a letterbook. The back flyleaf is also missing. At some point, Williams began an index for the letters. This incomplete index is inscribed on paper that does not match the original ledger paper. It was apparently a loose leaf inserted in the volume—as is Williams's index to the contents of Revelation Book 2[2]—although it is currently bound in the front of the volume as a result of late twentieth-century conservation. This index does not list the history.

A reconstruction of the physical history of the artifact helps explain the current material context of the document. Photocopy and microfilm images of the book, as well as an inspection of the conservation work now present in the volume, indicate that the text block separated from the binding at some point. Also, the initial three leaves containing the history were excised from the volume. The eight inscribed leaves in the back of the volume may have been cut out at the same time.[3] Manuscript evidence suggests that these excisions took place in the mid-twentieth century. A tear on the third leaf, which evidently occurred during its excision, was probably mended at the time. This tear was mended with clear cellophane tape, which was invented in 1930.[4] The three leaves of the history certainly had been removed by 1965, when they were described as "cut out," although they were archived together with the letterbook. The size and paper stock of the three excised leaves match those of the other leaves in the book. Also, the cut and tear marks, as well as the inscriptions in the gutters of the three excised leaves, match those of the remaining leaf stubs, confirming their original location in the book.[5] The three leaves were later restored to the volume, apparently in the 1990s.[6] This restoration was probably part of a larger conservation effort that took place, in which the entire volume was rebound, including binding the formerly loose index of letters. The first gathering, which contains the history, was slightly trimmed in connection with this conservation work. The volume shows marked browning, brittleness, and wear. It is listed in Nauvoo, Illinois, and early Salt Lake City, Utah, inventories made by the Church Historian's Office, as well as in the 1973 register of the JS Collection, indicating continuous institutional custody.[7]

Historical Introduction

JS's circa summer 1832 history is the only narrative of the foundational spiritual events of JS's early life that includes his own handwriting. It begins in an imposing manner, announcing "A History of the life of Joseph Smith Jr. an account of his marvilous experience and of all the mighty acts which he doeth in the name of Jesus Ch[r]ist . . . and also an account of the rise of the church of Christ in the eve of time." Following this introduction, JS started with his own birth and then quickly moved to the events that marked the beginning

---

2. At some point, Williams's index for the Revelation Book 2 was attached with adhesive wafers to the inside front cover of the revelation book. (See *JSP,* MRB:412–413.)

3. These eight leaves have not been located.

4. Cole et al., *Encyclopedia of Modern Everyday Inventions,* 22; Edelman, "Brief History of Tape," 45–46.

5. Cheesman, "Analysis of the Accounts Relating Joseph Smith's Early Visions," 126; Jessee, "Early Accounts of Joseph Smith's First Vision," 277–278.

6. The leaves were still detached when they were photographed for a 1984 publication.[a] They were reattached by 2000, when scanned images that show them as such were made by the Church Archives of The Church of Jesus Christ of Latter-day Saints.[b] The leaves are also reported as being reattached in a 25 February 2001 register of the JS Collection, which states that they were "reattached in the 1990s."[c] (a. Jessee, *Personal Writings of Joseph Smith,* 15–20. b. Turley, *Selected Collections,* vol. 1, disc 20. c. Faulring, "Annotated Catalog of the Joseph Smith Collection.")

7. "Schedule of Church Records. Nauvoo 1846," [1]; "Inventory. Historian's Office. 4th April 1855," [1], Historian's Office, Catalogs and Inventories, 1846–1904, CHL; Johnson, *Register of the Joseph Smith Collection,* 7.

of his career as a prophet: his study of the Bible, his early visions, the reception of the gold plates, the financial and scribal assistance of Martin Harris at the beginning of JS's translation of the plates, and Harris's loss of the early translation manuscript and dismissal as a scribe. Then, following a brief mention of Oliver Cowdery, who in the account had not yet met JS but would soon provide him desperately needed scribal and financial assistance, the document ends abruptly after only six pages. The introductory prospectus to the history refers to four foundational events in JS's life: "the testamony from on high," later explained as his first vision of Deity; "the ministering of Angels," or the angel Moroni's revelation of the gold plates of the Book of Mormon; the "reception of the holy Priesthood"; and "a confirmation and reception of the high Priesthood." JS related the first two events in some detail, providing a firsthand account of his childhood and early religious experiences, but this history includes nothing further about the reception of priesthood authority.

It is not clear why JS ended his earliest history before completing his stated intentions. Some of his other documentary endeavors, including the journal he began the same year, are similarly incomplete, perhaps indicating that other activities simply took precedence.[8] It is possible, however, that JS deliberately ended the history where he did, viewing it as part of a larger historical record that would include the work of others assigned as record keepers. Even though JS wrote his own history in about summer 1832, he continued to affirm John Whitmer's role as church historian, demonstrating that JS's historical venture did not relieve Whitmer of the responsibility to continue the church history.[9] For his part, Whitmer viewed his history as continuing work begun by Oliver Cowdery, whom he replaced as church record keeper.[10] The question of whether JS expected Cowdery's or Whitmer's work to fit together with the account begun in his own history cannot be settled for certain; JS's narrative does, however, cover only earlier history for which JS alone could provide a firsthand account, and it concludes just before Cowdery enters the scene.[11]

---

8. Although JS began his first journal with the explicit intention "to keep a minute acount of all things that come under my obsevation," there were substantial gaps in his journal keeping. (JS, Journal, 27 Nov. 1832, in *JSP*, J1:9.)

9. See JS, Hiram, OH, to William W. Phelps, [Independence, MO], 31 July 1832, JS Collection, CHL; JS, Kirtland, OH, to William W. Phelps, [Independence, MO], 27 Nov. 1832, in JS Letterbook 1, pp. 1–4; Revelation, 11 Nov. 1831–A, in Doctrine and Covenants 28:1, 1835 ed. [D&C 69:3]; and JS and Sidney Rigdon, Far West, MO, to John Whitmer, 9 Apr. 1838, in *JSP*, J1:249.

10. Minute Book 2, 9 June 1830; Revelation, ca. 8 Mar. 1831–B, in Book of Commandments 50 [D&C 47]; Whitmer, History, 25, in *JSP*, H2:36; see also Historical Introduction to Whitmer, History, in *JSP*, H2:8.

11. Although no narrative history by Oliver Cowdery predating JS's first history is known, Cowdery wrote a series of historical letters in 1834–1835 that were published in the *Latter Day Saints' Messenger and Advocate* and were later copied into JS's 1834–1836 history, pp. 39–89 herein. Cowdery may have taken JS's history into account when he began the first letter, as he picked up the story just where JS had left off— when the two first met in Harmony, Pennsylvania, on 5 April 1829. Cowdery went on to describe the receipt of the lower (Aaronic) priesthood. Thus, whether by design or coincidence, Cowdery detailed the third event outlined in the prospectus to JS's history ("the reception of the holy Priesthood by the ministring of—Aangels"). In chapter 7 of his history, Whitmer covered the fourth event (the "confirmation and reception of the high Priesthood"). (Oliver Cowdery, Norton, OH, to William W. Phelps, 7 Sept. 1834, *LDS Messenger and Advocate*, Oct. 1834, 1:13–16 [also in JS History, 1834–1836, pp. 39–44 herein]; JS History, ca. summer 1832, p. 10 herein; Whitmer, History, 27, in *JSP*, H2:40; see also 40n40 herein.)

The circa summer 1832 history came about as part of a new phase in JS's record-keeping practices. During the first four years of Mormon record keeping (1828–1831), JS focused primarily on preserving his revelatory texts. The records surviving from the early period of his prophetic career are almost exclusively sacred texts, including the Book of Mormon manuscripts, his revision of the Bible, and his own contemporary revelations. Scriptural record keeping overshadowed personal and institutional record keeping. This focus changed in 1832, when JS began documenting his personal life in detail for the first time, both in his history and in the journal he began on 27 November 1832. He and his scribes also began compiling a minute book and a letterbook, providing material recording day-to-day events. With this broader record-keeping focus, JS began to document his role as revelator and church leader in addition to preserving the texts of revelations and visions.

In the early 1830s, when this history was written, it appears that JS had not broadcast the details of his first vision of Deity. The history of the church, as it was then generally understood, began with the gold plates. John Whitmer mentioned in his history "the commencement of the church history commencing at the time of the finding of the plates," suggesting that Whitmer was either unaware of JS's earlier vision or did not conceive of it as foundational.[12] Records predating 1832 only hint at JS's earliest manifestation. The historical preamble to the 1830 "articles and covenants," for example, appears to reference JS's vision in speaking of a moment when "it truly was manifested unto this first elder, that he had received a remission of his sins."[13] Initially, JS may have considered this vision to be a personal experience tied to his own religious explorations. He was not accustomed to recording personal events, and he did not initially record the vision as he later did the sacred texts at the center of his attention. Only when JS expanded his focus to include historical records did he write down a detailed account of the theophany he experienced as a youth. The result was a simple, unpolished account of his first "marvilous experience," written largely in his own hand. The account was not published or widely circulated at the time, though in later years he told the story more frequently.

Understanding the production of the circa summer 1832 history is complicated by the possibility that it was copied from an earlier manuscript, a possibility suggested by the known record-keeping practices of JS and Frederick G. Williams, in whose alternating handwriting the history is inscribed. In the same time period, they jointly copied six revelations from 1831 and 1832, some of which JS originally dictated to Williams, into the beginning of a compilation of revelations.[14] They also divided inscription work when they copied JS's 27 November 1832 letter to William W. Phelps, which JS originally dictated, into JS's first letterbook (begun in the same volume that contains the circa summer 1832 history). Thus, the other extant 1832 documents inscribed in both JS's and Williams's handwriting are all copies.[15] In their early record-keeping efforts, JS and his scribes established

---

12. Whitmer, History, 25, in *JSP,* H2:36.

13. Articles and covenants, 10 Apr. 1830, in Book of Commandments 24:6–7 [D&C 20:5–8]. In the circa summer 1832 history, Christ's first message to JS is "thy sins are forgiven thee."

14. See Revelation Book 2, 1–10, 12–15, 18–31, in *JSP,* MRB:415–433, 437–443, 449–475.

15. See Vision, 16 Feb. 1832, in Revelation Book 2, pp. 1–10, in *JSP,* MRB:415–433 [D&C 76]; Revelation, 4 Dec. 1831, in Revelation Book 2, pp. 12–15, in *JSP,* MRB:439–443 [D&C 72]; Revelation,

the practice of copying loose minutes, letters, and revelations into more permanent blank books. In fact, the large blank books used in church record keeping through 1832 were filled entirely or almost entirely with material copied from loose leaves.[16] Thus, the fact that the extant history exists in a record book and not as loose leaves suggests it is a copy.

Textual clues also indicate that the extant 1832 history may not be an original composition. The handwriting of Williams and JS passes back and forth with little or no correspondence to the narrative progress of the history; the two sometimes alternate inscription mid-sentence. In JS's writing, moreover, the disruptions to inscription caused by changing or sharpening a quill and dipping it in ink occur in the middle of a thought and even in the middle of a word, suggesting he was copying rather than composing.[17]

Other textual evidence, however, indicates that the circa summer 1832 history may be the original inscription. In their work on the history, neither JS nor Williams made inscription errors that one might expect to find if it were a copy, errors that both men made in contemporary copying work. For example, when copying a 27 November 1832 letter into his first letterbook, JS inadvertently repeated a phrase from a line above and then struck the phrase after realizing his error.[18] Similarly, in copying a December 1833 letter into the same volume, Williams apparently skipped a line of the original before catching himself and fixing the mistake.[19] Errors like these do not appear in the circa summer 1832 history.

The history also contains several significant contemporaneous revisions in JS's handwriting, which may indicate that JS was composing original narrative. For instance, at the bottom of page 3 he wrote, "about that time my mother and," but then apparently decided he did not want to include this detail and canceled the passage. Such revisions, however, could have been made during copying, not during composition. JS and his scribes made similar revisions as they copied drafts and other antecedent documents into the 1834–1836 history and the multivolume manuscript history initiated in 1838. Likewise, JS and Williams may have been modifying the circa summer 1832 history as they copied it from an earlier text.

Although JS's earliest history bears no date, its approximate creation date can be determined by considering the language of the text, the volume in which it is found, and the larger historical context. Frederick G. Williams first met JS in summer 1831, but there is no

---

7 Mar. 1832, in Revelation Book 2, pp. 18–19, in *JSP*, MRB:449–451 [D&C 80]; Revelation, 22 and 23 Sept. 1832, in Revelation Book 2, pp. 20–31, in *JSP*, MRB:453–475 [D&C 84]; and JS, Kirtland, OH, to William W. Phelps, [Independence, MO], 27 Nov. 1832, in JS Letterbook 1, pp. 1–4. A small section of JS inscription among his Bible revisions may be an exception; it was made in either 1832 or 1833. (Faulring et al., *Joseph Smith's New Translation of the Bible*, 72.)

16. Later JS documents, however, such as his journals for 1835–1836, March–September 1838, and 1841–1842, provide examples of original material inscribed directly into large blank books. Frederick G. Williams evidently also began inscribing topical indexes of scriptural references directly into several blank books beginning 17 July 1833. (See Jensen, "Ignored and Unknown Clues of Early Mormon Record Keeping," 136–139.)

17. On the second page of the manuscript, for example, the quill sharpness changes between the *u* and the *r* of "courses" in the phrase "the stars shining in their courses."

18. JS, Kirtland, OH, to William W. Phelps, [Independence, MO], 27 Nov. 1832, in JS Letterbook 1, p. 4.

19. JS, Kirtland Mills, OH, to Edward Partridge et al., Liberty, MO, 10 Dec. 1833, in JS Letterbook 1, p. 71.

Frederick G. Williams. Approximately half of Joseph Smith's circa summer 1832 history is in the handwriting of Joseph Smith himself; the other half of the six-page document was inscribed by Frederick G. Williams. Williams was officially appointed clerk and scribe to Smith on 20 July 1832 but had done copying work as early as February of that year. (Courtesy Church History Museum, Salt Lake City.)

evidence that he began work as a scribe before 16 February 1832, the date of the first item he copied into JS's second revelation book.[20] Although none of the revelations he transcribed into the book bears a transcription date, the inconsistent copying styles of the various transcripts and the interspersed transcripts of older revelations that appear among the March 1832 revelations suggest that the book had become the active record-keeping repository for the revelations by March 1832.[21] If JS and Williams were copying revelations in March 1832, it is not implausible that they created the history around the same time.

The volume containing the history provides clues to determine the latest date by which the history was written. Sometime after the history was inscribed, the volume was repurposed as a letterbook, beginning with a letter dated 27 November 1832. The uneven copying styles of the letters from January to April 1833 indicate that the letterbook was being used as an active copy book during that period, with letters being transcribed into the volume in chronological order as they were written, prior to mailing them.[22] JS probably followed this same pattern the previous fall, making a contemporaneous copy of the 27 November 1832 letter in the letterbook before sending the original. If indeed the volume that contains the circa summer 1832 history was repurposed as a letterbook at the end of November, the history must have been written before then.

The date range for likely composition of the history can be narrowed even further. Williams took on increasing clerical work in July 1832 during a suspension of Sidney Rigdon's position as JS's principal counselor and scribe.[23] In a later statement, Williams wrote, "I commencd writing for Joseph Smith Jr July 20th 1832 as may be seen by S Rigdon permission dated as above."[24] Following this 20 July appointment, Williams's clerical duties expanded and he recorded revelations, Bible revisions, and letters as JS dictated.[25] JS's earliest history was probably inscribed between the 20 July appointment and 22 September 1832,

---

20. Williams, "Frederick Granger Williams," 245–247; see also Revelation Book 2, pp. 1–10, in *JSP,* MRB:415–433.

21. See Revelation Book 2, pp. 1–20, in *JSP,* MRB:415–453. John Whitmer had earlier inscribed revelations into a blank book, Revelation Book 1, but because Whitmer took this book to Missouri in late November 1831, another book was needed for copying revelations. Revelation Book 2 filled this need, and it was apparently begun in February or March 1832. (See *JSP,* MRB:408–410.)

22. See JS Letterbook 1, pp. 14–36.

23. At a Sunday meeting held in Kirtland on 8 July 1832, JS demanded that Rigdon surrender his priesthood license because Rigdon had declared three days earlier that the "keys of the kingdom" had been taken from the church and that he alone retained them.[a] Three weeks later JS reinstated Rigdon in the church presidency.[b] (a. "History [of] Charles Coulson Rich," 3–4, Historian's Office, Histories of the Twelve, ca. 1858–1880, CHL; Cahoon, Diary, 5–17 July 1832; Lucy Mack Smith, History, 1844–1845, bk. 13, [6]; Dibble, "Philo Dibble's Narrative," 79–80. b. Hyrum Smith, Diary and Account Book, 28 July 1832; JS, Hiram, OH, to William W. Phelps, [Independence, MO], 31 July 1832, JS Collection, CHL.)

24. Frederick G. Williams, Statement, no date, Frederick G. Williams, Papers, CHL. Although the cited permission is not extant, the language of this undated statement indicates that Williams was basing his information not on memory but on contemporaneous documentation.

25. See, for example, Revelation Book 2, pp. 19–31, in *JSP,* MRB:451–475; Faulring et al., *Joseph Smith's New Translation of the Bible,* 59, 70–72; JS, Hiram, OH, to William W. Phelps, [Independence, MO], 31 July 1832, JS Collection, CHL; and JS, Kirtland, OH, to Vienna Jacques, Independence, MO, 4 Sept. 1833, JS Collection, CHL. Williams later wrote that from the time of his employment on 20 July 1832 until January 1836, he "was constantly in said Smiths employ." (Frederick G. Williams, Statement, no date,

the date of a revelation that changed JS's lexicon regarding priesthood. The history refers to the first priesthood JS received as the "holy priesthood," which was then followed by the reception of the "high priesthood," but the September 1832 revelation reserved the adjective "holy" for the higher priesthood.[26] JS's subsequent writings and revelations consistently reserved the word "holy" to describe the greater priesthood only.[27] The terminology of the existing documentary record, therefore, coupled with the date of Williams's appointment as scribe, suggests that the history was most likely composed between 20 July and 22 September 1832.

Regardless of when it was created, the circa summer 1832 history provides the most personal, intimate account of JS's early visions available and preserves details of those visions not recorded elsewhere.

——————— ☙ ———————

/[28]A History of the life of Joseph Smith Jr. an account of his marvilous experience[29] and of all the mighty acts which he doeth in the name of Jesus Ch[r]ist the son of the living God of whom he beareth record and also an account of the rise of the church of Christ in the eve of time according as the Lord brought forth and established by his hand ⟨firstly⟩ he receiving the testamony from on high seccondly the ministering of Angels thirdly the reception of the holy Priesthood by the ministring of—Aangels to adminster the letter of the ~~Law~~ ⟨Gospel—⟩ ⟨—the Law and commandments as they were given unto him—⟩ and ~~in~~[30] ⟨the⟩ ordinencs, forthly a confirmation and reception of the high Priesthood after the holy order of the son of the living God power and ordinence from on high to preach the Gospel in the administration and demonstration of the spirit **the Kees of the Kingdom of God confered upon him[31] and the continuation of the blessings of God to him &c——**

Frederick G. Williams, Papers, CHL; compare Frederick G. Williams, "Account on Farm," no date, Frederick G. Williams, Papers, CHL.)

26. Revelation, 22 and 23 Sept. 1832, in Doctrine and Covenants 4:2–3, 1835 ed. [D&C 84:6, 18–19]. For examples of pre–September 1832 use of "holy" to describe both the higher and lower priesthoods, see Book of Mormon, 1830 ed., 73–74, 258–260 [2 Nephi 5:26, 6:2; Alma 13:1–19]; Elder's license for John Whitmer, 9 June 1830; Teacher's license for Christian Whitmer, 9 June 1830, Western Americana Collection, Beinecke Rare Book and Manuscript Library, Yale University, New Haven, CT; and Priest's license for Joseph Smith Sr., 9 June 1830, JS Collection, CHL.

27. See, for example, Plat of City of Zion, 1833, CHL; JS to Oliver Cowdery, Blessing, 18 Dec. 1833, in Patriarchal Blessings, 1:12; and Instruction on priesthood, ca. Apr. 1835, in Doctrine and Covenants 3:1, 8, 10, 1835 ed. [D&C 107:3, 14, 20].

28. TEXT: Frederick G. Williams handwriting begins.

29. In contemporaneous religious writing, "experience" often denoted personal enlightenment through divine communication. ("Experience," in *Oxford English Dictionary*, 3:430.)

30. TEXT: "it" changed to "in" and then "in" canceled.

31. See Matthew 16:19; Revelation, 30 Oct. 1831, in Doctrine and Covenants 24:1, 1835 ed. [D&C 65:2]; and Revelation, 15 Mar. 1832, in Doctrine and Covenants 79:1, 1835 ed. [D&C 81:2].

I was born in the town of Charon [Sharon] in the ⟨State⟩ of Vermont North America on the twenty third day of December AD 1805 of goodly Parents[32] who spared no pains to instruct⟨ing⟩ me in ⟨the⟩ christian religion[.] at the age of about ten years my Father Joseph Smith Seignior moved to Palmyra Ontario County[33] in the State of New York and being in indigent circumstances were obliged to labour hard for the support of a large Family having nine chilldren[34] and as it required their exertions of all that were able to render any assistance for the support of the Family therefore we were deprived of the bennifit of an education suffice it to say I was mearly instructtid in reading and writing and the ground ⟨rules⟩ of Arithmatic which const[it]uted my whole literary acquirements.[35] At about the age of twelve years my mind become seriously imprest [p. 1] with regard to the all important concerns of for the wellfare of my immortal Soul which led me to searching the scriptures believeing as I was taught, that they contained the word of God thus applying myself to them and my intimate acquaintance with those of differant denominations led me to marvel excedingly for I discovered that ⟨they did not adorn⟩ instead of adorning their profession by a holy walk and Godly conversation[36] agreeable to what I found contained in that sacred depository this was a grief to my Soul thus from the age of twelve years to fifteen I pondered many things in my heart concerning the sittuation of the world of mankind the contentions and divi[si]ons the wicke[d]ness and abominations and the darkness which pervaded the of the minds of mankind my mind become excedingly distressed for I become convicted of my sins and by searching the scriptures I found that mand ⟨mankind⟩ did not come unto the Lord but that they had apostatised from the true and liveing faith and there was no society or denomination that built upon the gospel of Jesus Christ

---

32. Compare Book of Mormon, 1830 ed., 5 [1 Nephi 1:1].

33. Palmyra became part of Wayne County at its creation in April 1823. (An Act to Erect a New County, from Parts of the Counties of Ontario and Seneca, by the Name of Wayne, and for Other Purposes [11 Apr. 1823], *Laws of the State of New-York* [1823], chap. 138, pp. 158–162.)

34. When the Smith family moved to Palmyra there were only eight children (two children had died in infancy). Lucy, the ninth child, was born 18 July 1821, when JS was fifteen.

35. The Smith family embarked on a new effort to clear land and establish a family farm in New York after years of financial misfortune in Vermont and New Hampshire. JS and his siblings did, however, receive some formal schooling in their youth and probably received some rudimentary education at home. (See Palmyra, NY, Attendance record, first school district, Sept.–Nov. 1817, Macedon Historical Society, Macedon, NY; see also Marquardt, *Rise of Mormonism,* 33–34.)

36. See 1 Peter 1:15; 2 Peter 3:11; and Articles and covenants, 10 Apr. 1830, in Book of Commandments 24:48 [D&C 20:69].

as recorded in the new testament³⁷ and I felt to mourn for my own sins and for the sins of the world³⁸ for I learned in the scriptures that God was the same yesterday to day and forever³⁹ that he was no respecter to persons⁴⁰ for he was God for I looked upon the sun the glorious luminary of the earth and also the moon rolling in their magesty through the heavens and also the stars shining in their courses and the earth also upon which I stood and the beast of the field and the fowls of heaven and the fish of the waters and also man walking forth upon the face of the earth in magesty and in the strength of beauty whose power and intiligence in governing the things which are so exceding great and [p. 2] marvilous even in the likeness of him who created him ⟨them⟩ and when I considered upon these things my heart exclaimed well hath the wise man said the ⟨it is a⟩ fool ⟨that⟩ saith in his heart there is no God⁴¹ my heart exclaimed all all these bear testimony and bespeak an omnipotant and omnipreasant power a being who makith Laws and decreeeth and bindeth all things in their bounds⁴² who filleth Eternity who was and is and will be from all Eternity to Eternity and when ⟨I⟩ considered all these things and that ⟨that⟩ being seeketh such to worshep him as worship him in spirit and in truth⁴³ therefore I cried unto the Lord for mercy for there was none else to whom I could go and to obtain mercy and the Lord heard my cry in the wilderness and while in ⟨the⟩ attitude of calling upon the Lord ⟨in the 16th year of my age⟩⁴⁴ a piller of fire light above the brightness of the sun at noon day come down from above and rested upon me and I was filled with the spirit of god and the ⟨Lord⟩ opened the heavens upon me and I

37. Like the Disciples of Christ and other primitivists, JS believed that the mainline churches of his day had strayed from the order and teachings of the New Testament church. (See Hughes and Allen, *Illusions of Innocence,* chap. 6.)

38. See, for example, 1 John 2:2; and Book of Mormon, 1830 ed., 518 [4 Nephi 1:44].

39. See Hebrews 13:8; and Book of Mormon, 1830 ed., 111, 116 [2 Nephi 27:23, 29:9].

40. See Acts 10:34–35; Revelation, 1 Nov. 1831–B, in Book of Commandments 1:6 [D&C 1:35]; and Revelation, 2 Jan. 1831, in Book of Commandments 40:14 [D&C 38:16].

41. See Psalms 14:1, 53:1.

42. The teleological argument for the existence of God, the "argument from design," was standard in the Christian tradition of the philosophy of religion. ("Design Argument," in *Dictionary of the History of Ideas,* 1:670–677; Cosslett, *Science and Religion in the Nineteenth Century,* 25; see also Book of Mormon, 1830 ed., 308 [Alma 30:44]; and Revelation, 27 and 28 Dec. 1832, in Doctrine and Covenants 7:9–12, 1835 ed. [D&C 88:36–47].)

43. See John 4:24; and Book of Mormon, 1830 ed., 321 [Alma 34:38].

44. TEXT: Insertion in the handwriting of Frederick G. Williams. JS later recounted that this vision occurred in early spring 1820, when he was fourteen years old. (JS History, vol. A-1, p. 212 herein [Draft 2]; compare JS, Journal, 9–11 Nov. 1835, in *JSP,* J1:87–88 [see also later version, pp. 115–116 herein]; JS, "Church History," p. 494 herein; and JS, "Latter Day Saints," p. 508 herein.)

saw the Lord[45] and he spake unto me saying Joseph ⟨my son⟩ thy sins are forgiven thee. go thy ⟨way⟩ walk in my statutes and keep my commandments behold I am the Lord of glory I was crucifyed for the world that all those who believe on my name may have Eternal life ⟨behold⟩ the world lieth in sin ~~and~~ at this time and none doeth good no not one they have turned asside from the gospel and keep not ⟨my⟩ commandments they draw near to me with their lips while their hearts are far from me and mine anger is kindling against the inhabitants of the earth to visit them acording to thir ungodliness and to bring to pass that which ⟨hath⟩ been spoken by the mouth of the prophets and Ap[o]stles[46] behold and lo I come quickly as it [is] written of me in the cloud ⟨clothed⟩ in the glory of my Father[47] and my soul was filled with love and for many days I could rejoice with great Joy and the Lord was with me but could find none that would believe the hevnly vision nevertheless I pondered these things in my heart[48] ~~about that time my mother and~~[49] but after many days [p. 3] /[50]I fell into transgressions and sinned in many things which brought a wound upon my soul and there were many things which transpired that cannot be writen and my Fathers family have suffered many persicutions and afflictions and it came to pass when I was seventeen years of age I called again upon the Lord and he shewed unto me a heavenly vision for behold an angel of the

---

45. JS later recounted that he saw two "personages," that one appeared after the other, and that "they did in reality speak unto me, or one of them did." Other accounts identify the two personages as the Father and the Son. (JS History, vol. A-1, p. 214 herein [Draft 2]; JS, Journal, 9–11 Nov. 1835, in *JSP*, J1:87–88 [see also later version, p. 116 herein].)

46. The importance of the biblical prophecies appears as a persistent theme in JS's religious thought. Pomeroy Tucker, who was acquainted with JS during their adolescence, affirmed JS's claim to have studied the Bible and reminisced that the "Prophecies and Revelations were his special forte." Whereas the prophets of the Old Testament promised the restoration of Israel and a Messianic reign, Jesus and John proclaimed a future apocalypse and a millennium of peace. JS's earliest revelations conveyed the message of both an end-time restoration and an imminent apocalypse. (Tucker, *Origin, Rise, and Progress of Mormonism,* 17.)

47. Christ's declaration is saturated with scriptural allusions and phraseology from both the Bible and JS's revelatory texts. See, for example, Leviticus 26:3; Vision, 16 Feb. 1832, in Doctrine and Covenants 91:4, 1835 ed. [D&C 76:41]; Revelation, ca. 7 Mar. 1831, in Book of Commandments 48:9–10 [D&C 45:8]; Revelation, 22 and 23 Sept. 1832, in Doctrine and Covenants 4:7, 1835 ed. [D&C 84:49]; Psalm 14:3; Isaiah 29:13; Deuteronomy 29:27; and Matthew 24:30.

48. Compare Luke 2:19.

49. This canceled fragment may refer to the Presbyterian affiliation of JS's mother and three of his siblings. In 1838, JS recounted that they "were proselyted to the Presbyterian faith" in connection with the revivalism preceding his vision. ("Records of the Session of the Presbyterian Church in Palmyra," 10, 24, and 29 Mar. 1830; JS History, vol. A-1, p. 208 herein [Draft 2].)

50. TEXT: Frederick G. Williams handwriting begins.

Lord[51] came and stood before me and it was by night and he called me by
name and he said the Lord had forgiven me my sins and he revealed unto me
that in the Town of Manchester Ontario County N.Y. there was plates of gold
upon which there was engravings which was engraven by Maroni & his fathers
the servants of the living God in ancient days and deposited by th[e] commandments of God and kept by the power thereof and that I should go and get
them and he revealed unto me many things concerning the inhabitents of of
the earth which since have been revealed in commandments & revelations and
it was on the 22d day of Sept. AD ~~1082~~ 1822[52] and thus he appeared unto me
three times in one night and once on the next day and then I immediately
went to the place and found where the plates was deposited as the angel of the
Lord had commanded me and straightway made three attempts to get them
and then being excedingly frightened I supposed it had been a dreem of Vision
but when I considred I knew that it was not therefore I cried unto the Lord in
the agony of my soul why can I not obtain them[53] behold the angel appeared
unto me again and said unto me you have not kept the commandments of
the Lord which I gave unto you therefore you cannot now obtain them for the
time is not yet fulfilled therefore thou wast left unto temptation that thou
mightest be made accquainted ~~of~~ with the power of the advisary [adversary]
therefore repent and call on the Lord thou shalt be forgiven and in his own due
time thou shalt obtain them [p. 4] for now I had been tempted of the advisary
and saught the Plates to obtain riches and kept not the commandme[n]t that I
should have an eye single to the Glory of God[54] therefore I was chastened and
saught diligently to obtain the plates and obtained them not untill I was
twenty one years of age and in this year I was married to Emma Hale Daughtr
of Isaach [Isaac] Hale who lived in Harmony Susquehan[n]a County
Pensylvania on the 18th January AD, 1827, on the 22d day of Sept of this same

---

51. JS identified this angel as Moroni, the last ancient American prophet to write in the Book of
Mormon. ([JS], Editorial, *Elders' Journal,* July 1838, 42–44; see also Oliver Cowdery, "Letter VI," *LDS
Messenger and Advocate,* Apr. 1835, 1:112 [see also later version, p. 71 herein]; and Revelation, ca. Aug.
1830, in Doctrine and Covenants 50:2, 1835 ed. [D&C 27:5]. For JS's other accounts of this experience, see
JS, Journal, 9–11 Nov. 1835, in *JSP,* J1:88–89 [see also later version, pp. 116–117 herein]; JS History Drafts, 1838–
ca. 1841, pp. 220–233 herein; JS, "Church History," pp. 494–495 herein; and JS, "Latter Day Saints,"
pp. 508–509 herein.)

52. Later accounts clarify that Moroni first appeared late in the night of 21–22 September 1823. (JS
History, vol. A-1, p. 220 herein [Draft 2]; Oliver Cowdery, "Letter IV," *LDS Messenger and Advocate,* Feb.
1835, 1:78–79 [see also later version, p. 57 herein].)

53. In 1835, Oliver Cowdery wrote that JS was "sensibly shocked" each time he attempted to remove the
plates from their repository. (Oliver Cowdery, "Letter VIII," *LDS Messenger and Advocate,* Oct. 1835,
2:197–198 [see also later version, p. 82 herein]; see also Knight, Reminiscences, 1; and Lucy Mack Smith,
History, 1844–1845, bk. 5, [5].)

54. See Matthew 6:22; and Book of Mormon, 1830 ed., 533 [Mormon 8:15].

year I obtained the plat[e]s—and ~~the~~ in December following we mooved to Susquehana by the assistence of a man by the name of Martin Har[r]is who became convinced of th[e] vision and gave me fifty Dollars to bare my expences and because of his faith and this rightheous deed the Lord appeared unto him in a vision and shewed unto him his marvilous work which he was about to do **and ⟨h[e]⟩ imediately came to Suquehannah and said the Lord had shown him that he must go to new York City ⟨with⟩ some of the characters so we proceeded to coppy some of them and he took his Journy to the Eastern Cittys and to the Learned[55] ⟨saying⟩ read this I pray thee and the learned said I cannot but if he would bring the blates [plates] they would read it but the Lord had forbid it and he returned to me and gave them to ⟨me⟩ ⟨to⟩ translate and I said ~~I said~~ cannot for I am not learned but the Lord had prepared ~~spectticke~~ spectacles[56] for to read the Book therefore** /[57]I commenced translating the characters and thus the Propicy [prophecy] of Isiaah was fulfilled which is writen in the 29 chaptr concerning the book[58] and it came to pass that after we had translated 116 pages[59] that he desired to carry them to read to his friends that peradventur he might convince them of the truth therefore I inquired of the Lord and the Lord said unto me that he must not take them and I spake unto him (Martin) the word of the Lord [p. 5] and he said inquire again and I inquired again and also the third time and the Lord said unto me let him go with them only he shall covenant with me that he will not shew them to only but four persons and he covenented withe Lord that he would do according to the word of the Lord[60] therefore he took them and took his journey unto his friends to Palmire [Palmyra] Wayne County & State of

---

55. In early 1828, Harris visited Luther Bradish in Albany, New York, and Charles Anthon and Samuel Mitchill in New York City. An extant document bearing the title "Caractors," which contains several rows of copied characters, appears to be related to the document Harris carried with him. (JS History, vol. A-1, pp. 240–244 herein [Draft 2]; "Caractors," [ca. 1829–1830], CCLA; see also reproduction and discussion of this document in *The Joseph Smith Papers,* Documents series, vol. 1 [forthcoming].)

56. JS recounted that he found these spectacles with the plates. (JS History, vol. A-1, p. 232 herein [Draft 2]; JS, "Church History," p. 495 herein; see also "Urim and Thummim," in Glossary.)

57. TEXT: Frederick G. Williams handwriting begins.

58. See Isaiah 29:11–14.

59. This page count may be a retrospective approximation based on the later manuscript copy of the Book of Mormon used by the printer. The top of page 117 in that copy marks the beginning of the book of Mosiah, which corresponds to the end of the period covered in the pages lost by Harris. (See Skousen, *Printer's Manuscript,* 284.)

60. Martin Harris was permitted to show the translation manuscript to five members of his extended family: his wife, Lucy Harris Harris; his brother Preserved Harris; his father, Nathan Harris; his mother, Rhoda Lapham Harris; and his wife's sister Polly Harris Cobb. (JS History, vol. A-1, p. 244 herein [Draft 2]; Pilkington, Autobiography and statements, 15–16; "Married," *Geneva [NY] Gazette,* 3 June 1812, [3]; Tuckett and Wilson, *Martin Harris Story,* 176–179; see also Lucy Mack Smith, History, 1844–1845, bk. 6, [10]–[12]; bk. 7, [1].)

N York and he brake the covenent which he made before the Lord and the Lord suffered the writings to fall into the hands of wicked men[61] and Martin was Chastened for his transgression and I also was chastened ~~also~~ for my transgression for asking the Lord the third time wherefore the Plates was taken from me by the power of God and I was not able to obtain them for a season and it came to pass afte[r] much humility and affliction of Soul I obtained them again[62] when Lord appeared unto a young man by the name of Oliver Cowd[e]ry and shewed unto him the plates in a vision and also the truth of the work and what the Lord was about to do through me his unworthy Servant[63] therefore he was desiorous to come and write for me ~~and~~ to translate now my wife had writen some for me to translate and also my Brothr Samuel H Smith[64] but we had become reduced in property and my wives father was about to turn me out of doores ~~I~~ & I had not where to go and I cried unto the Lord that he would provide for me to accomplish the work whereunto he had commanded me[65] [4 lines blank] [p. [6]]

61. Sometime after Harris read or showed the manuscript to other acquaintances, it was lost or stolen.[a] Martin Harris and several others believed that his wife, Lucy Harris Harris, stole the manuscript. Conflicting accounts claim she burned it or gave it to others.[b] (a. Preface to Book of Mormon, 1830 ed., iii; JS History, vol. A-1, p. 246 herein [Draft 2]. b. Howe, *Mormonism Unvailed*, 22; Clark, *Gleanings by the Way*, 247–248; Lucy Mack Smith, History, 1844–1845, bk. 7, [5]–[8].)

62. JS later recounted that he again received the plates from the angel "in a few days." (JS History, vol. A-1, p. 252 herein [Draft 2]; compare Lucy Mack Smith, History, 1844–1845, bk. 7, [9]; see also Revelation, July 1828, in Book of Commandments 2:3–5 [D&C 3:6–13].)

63. Cowdery heard about JS and the gold plates while residing in Wayne County, New York, and then boarded with JS's parents. (Morris, "Conversion of Oliver Cowdery," 7–8.)

64. Emma and Samuel Smith wrote down the words of the Book of Mormon as JS spoke them. (Joseph Smith III, "Last Testimony of Sister Emma," *Saints' Herald*, 1 Oct. 1879, 289–290; see also Givens, *By the Hand of Mormon*, 26–37.)

65. JS and Emma Smith were living in a house on the property of her father, Isaac Hale. On 6 April 1829, the day after Oliver Cowdery arrived at his home, JS entered into an agreement with Hale to buy the home and thirteen acres of surrounding land and made a down payment on the purchase. Cowdery most likely supplied money for this payment, and he then began work as the principal scribe for JS's translation of the Book of Mormon. (Isaac Hale to JS, Agreement, Harmony, PA, 6 Apr. 1829, JS Collection, CHL; Oliver Cowdery, Norton, OH, to William W. Phelps, 7 Sept. 1834, *LDS Messenger and Advocate*, Oct. 1834, 1:14 [see also later version, p. 41 herein]; Oliver Cowdery, Far West, MO, to Warren Cowdery, [Kirtland, OH], 21 Jan. 1838, in Cowdery, Letterbook, 81; see also Revelation, Mar. 1829, in Book of Commandments 4:11 [D&C 5:34].)

A History of the life of Joseph Smith Jr. an account of his marvilous experience and of all the mighty acts which he doeth in the name of Jesus Christ the son of the living God of whom he beareth record and also an account of the rise of the church of Christ in the eve of time according as the Lord brought forth and established by his hand firstly he receiving the testamony from on high seccondly the ministering of Angels thirdly the reception of the holy Priesthood by the ministring of Angels to adminster the letter of the Gospel——the Lord and commandments as they were given unto him—and the ordinencs, forthly a confirmation and reception of the high Priesthood after the holy order of the son of the living God power and ordinence from on high to preach the Gospel in the administration and demonstration of the spirit the Kees of the Kingdom of god confered upon him and the continuation of the blessings of God to him &c——

I was born in the town of Charon in the [S]tate of vermont North America on the twenty third day of December AD 1805 of goodly Parents who spared no pains to instructing me in the christian religion at the age of about ten years my Father Joseph Smith Siegnior moved to Palmyra Ontario County in the State of New York and being in indigent circumstances were obliged to labour hard for the support of a large Family having nine Childreen and as it required the exertions of all that were able to render any assistance for the support of the Family therefore we were deprived of the bennifit of an education suffice it to say I was mearly instructed in reading and writing and the ground rules of Arithmatic which constuted my whole litterary acquirements. At about the age of twelve years my mind become seriously imprest

Joseph Smith's circa summer 1832 history, pp. 1–[6] (transcribed on pp. 10–16 herein), in JS Letterbook 1, Church History Library, Salt Lake City. (Photographs by Welden C. Andersen.)

2

with regard to the all important concerns for the well
-fare of my immortal Soul which led me to search
-ing the Scriptures believing as I was taught, that
they contained the word of God thus applying
myself to them and my intimate acquaintance
with those of different denominations led me to
marvel exceedingly for I discovered that they did not
adorning their profession by a holy walk and God
-ly conversation agreeable to what I found contain
-ed in that Sacred depository this was a grief to
my Soul thus from the age of twelve years
to fifteen I pondered many things in my heart
concerning the situation of the world of mankind
the contentions and divions the wickeness and
abominations and the darkness which pervaded
the minds of mankind my mind become
exceedingly distressed for I become convicted of my
sins and by searching the Scriptures I found
that mankind did not come unto the Lord but that
they had apostatised from the true and living
faith and there was no society or denomination
that built upon the gospel of Jesus Christ as
recorded in the new testament and I felt to mourn
for my own sins and for the Sins of the world
for I learned in the Scriptures that God was
the same yesterday to day and forever that he was
no respecter to persons for he was God for I
looked upon the sun the glorious luminary of
the earth and also the moon rolling in their
majesty through the heavens and also the stars
shining in their courses and the earth also upon which
h I stood and the beast of the field and the fowls of
heaven and the fish of the waters and also man walking
forth upon the face of the earth in majesty and in
the strength of beauty whose power and intelligence
in governing the things which are so exceeding great and

marvilous even in the likeness of him who created ~~him~~ them
and when I considered upon these things my heart exclaimed
well hath the wise man said it is a ~~fool~~ fool ~~saith~~ in
his heart there is no God my ~~heart~~ exclaimed all all
these bear testimony and bespeak an omnipotent
and omnipresent power a being who maketh Laws and
decreeth and bindeth all things in their bounds who
filleth Eternity who was and is and will be from all
Eternity to Eternity and when I considered all ~~these things~~
and that that being seeketh such to worship him as worship
him in spirit and in truth therefore I cried unto
the Lord for mercy for there was none else to whom I could go and
to obtain mercy and the Lord heard my cry in the wilderness
and while in the attitude of calling upon the ~~Lord~~ in the 16th year of my age a pillar of
fire light above the brightness of the sun at noon day
come down from above and rested upon me and I was filled
with the spirit of god and the Lord opened the heavens upon me
me and I saw the Lord and he spake unto me saying
Joseph my son thy sins are forgiven thee. go thy way walk in my
statutes and keep my commandments behold I am the
Lord of glory I was crucifyed for the world that all those
who believe on my name may have Eternal life ~~behold~~ the world
lieth in sin ~~and~~ at this time and none doeth good no
not one they have turned asside from the gospel and
keep not my commandments they draw near to me with their
lips while their hearts are far from me and mine anger
is kindling against the inhabitants of the earth to visit
them according to their ungodliness and to bring to pass
that which hath been spoken by the mouth of the prophets
and Apostles behold and lo I come quickly as it was
written of me in the cloud clothed in the glory of my Father
and my soul was filled with love and for many days I
could rejoice with great joy and the Lord was with me
but could find none that would believe the heavenly
vision nevertheless I pondered these things in my heart
~~about that time~~ ~~my mother~~ ~~and~~ but after many days

I fell into transgression and sinned in many things which brought a wound upon my soul and there were many things which transpired that cannot be writen and my Fathers family have suffered many persicutions and afflictions and it came to pass when I was seventeen years of age I called again upon the Lord and he shewed unto me a heavenly vision for behold an angel of the Lord came and stood before me and it was by night and he called me by name and he said the Lord had forgiven me my sins and he revealed unto me that in the Town of Manchester Ontario County N.Y. there was plates of gold upon which there was engravings which was engraven by Maroni & his father the servant of the living God in ancient days and deposited by the commandments of God and kept by the power thereof and that I should go and get them and he revealed unto me many things concerning the inhabitants of the earth which since have been revealed in commandments & revelations and it was on the 22d day of Sept. AD 1822 and thus he appeared unto me three times in one night and once on the next day and then I immediately went to the place and found where the plates was deposited as the angel of the Lord had commanded me and straightway made three attempts to get them and then being exceedingly frightened I supposed it had been a dream vision but when I considered I knew that it was not therefore I cried unto the Lord in the agony of my soul why can I not obtain them behold the angel appeared unto me again and said unto me you have not kept the commandments of the Lord which I gave unto you therefore you cannot now obtain them for the time is not yet fulfilled therefore thou wast left unto temptation that thou mightest become acquainted with the power of the adversary therefore repent and call on the Lord thou shalt be forgiven and in his own due time thou shalt obtain them for now I had been tempted of the adversary and sau[ght] th[e] Plates to obtain riches and kept not the commandm[ent] that I should have an eye single to the glory of God therefore I was chastened and sought diligent[ly] t[o] obtain th[e] Plates and obtained them not untill I was twenty on[e] years of age and in this year I was married to Emma Hale Daughter of Isaac Hale who lived in Harmony Susquehaned county Pensylvania on the 18th January A. 1827, on the 22d day of Sept of this same year I ob- -tained the Plates and th[e] in december following we removed to Susquehana by the assistence of a man by the name of Martin Harris who became convinced of th[e] vision and gave me fifty Dollars to bare my expences and because of his faith and this righteous deed the Lord appeared unto him in a vision and shewed unto him his marvilous work which he was about to do and imediately came to Suquehannah and said the Lord had shown him that he must go to new york city with some of the characters so we proceeded to coppy some of them and he took his journey to the Eastern Cittys and to the Learned saying read this I pray thee and the learned said I cannot but if he wo- =uld bring the plates they would read it but the Lord had forbid it and he returned to me and gave them to me to translate and I said I cannot for I am not learned but the Lord had prepared Spectacles for to read the Book therefore I commenced translating the cher- -acters and thus the Propicy of Isai^ah was fulfilled which is written in the 29 chapter concerning the book and it came to pass that after we had translated 116 pages that he desired to carry them to read to his friends that peradventure he might convince them of the truth therefore I inquired of the Lord and the Lord said unto me that he must not take them and I spake unto him (Martin) the word of the Lord

and he said inquire again and I inquired again
and also the third time and the Lord said unto
me let him go with them only he shall covenant
with me that he will not shew them to only but
four persons and he covenanted with the Lord that he
would do according to the word of the Lord therefore
he took them and took his journey unto his friends
to Palmira Wayn County & State of New York and he
brake the covenant which he made before the
Lord and the Lord suffered the writings to
fall into the hands of wicked men and Martin
was chastened for his transgression and I also was
chastened also for my transgression for asking
the Lord the third time wherefore the Plates were
taken from me by the power of God and
I was not able to obtain them for a season—
and it came to pass after much humility and
affliction of Soul I obtained them again when
Lord appeared unto a young man by the name
of Oliver Cowdry and I shewed unto him the
plates in a vision and also the truth of the
work and what the Lord was about to do through
me his unworthy servant therefore he was desirous
to come and write for me to translate now my
wife had written some for me to translate and
also my Brother Samuel H Smith but we
had become reduced in property and my wives
father was about to turn me out off doors &
I had not where to go and I cried unto the
Lord that he would provide for me to accomplish the work whereunto he had commandn
-ded me

HISTORY, 1834–1836

Source Note

JS, History, [Dec. 1834–May 1836?]; handwriting of Warren Parrish, Warren Cowdery, Frederick G. Williams, and Oliver Cowdery; includes genealogical and financial tables; 154 pages; verso of JS History, 1838–1856, vol. A-1, CHL. Includes redactions, use marks, and archival marking.

Large blank book composed of ruled paper printed with forty horizontal lines in (now faint) blue ink. The text block includes thirty gatherings of various sizes, each about a dozen leaves per gathering, and originally had 384 interior leaves cut to measure 13⅝ × 9 inches (35 × 23 cm). The text block, which was conserved in the late twentieth century, was probably originally sewn on recessed cords and was apparently also glued on leather tapes. The binding features false bands. The endpapers were single-sided marbled leaves featuring a traditional Spanish pattern with slate blue body and black and red veins. The block was bound to pasteboard covers, probably with a hollow-back ledger binding, making a book measuring 14¼ × 9½ × 2½ inches (36 × 24 × 6 cm). The boards were bound in brown suede calfskin. At some point, blind-tooled decorations were made around the outside border and along the board edges and the turned-in edges of the inside covers.

Oliver Cowdery began the text of the document on the thirteenth page of the text block, numbering it as page 9. Cowdery set aside pages 9–16 for genealogical tables for the members of the church presidency. He inscribed the page numbers, table headings, and column and row ruling for the tables in red ink with a quill pen. The content of the tables was inscribed in ink that is now brown with a quill pen, as was the rest of the history. Cowdery inscribed journal-like entries for 5 and 6 December 1834 on pages 17–20. Pages 21–45 are blank except for page numbering. Frederick G. Williams and Warren Parrish copied Cowdery's 1834–1835 historical articles, published serially in the *Latter Day Saints' Messenger and Advocate,* onto pages 46–103. A passage that Parrish missed while copying the first installment of the Cowdery history is supplied on a slip of paper attached to page 50 with adhesive wafers. On pages 103–104, Parrish copied part of a JS letter, also published in the church newspaper. On pages 105–187, Parrish and Warren Cowdery wrote historical entries based on the entries in JS's 1835–1836 journal. The genealogical table headings written by Oliver Cowdery, the letter headings and closings written by Williams and Parrish, and the datelines written by Parrish and Warren Cowdery are slightly larger than the ordinary script of these individuals. Parrish's datelines also feature a vertical stress that contrasts with the oblique stress of his entry inscriptions. Additionally, in their copying from the *Messenger and Advocate,* Frederick G. Williams and Warren Parrish often used a slightly larger script for words that appear in small caps in the printed version. Although pagination for the 1834–1836 history was inscribed up to page 241, the actual chronicle reaches only to page 187. Oliver Cowdery numbered pages 9–21, Frederick G. Williams numbered pages 22–58, Warren Parrish numbered pages 59–111, and Warren Cowdery numbered pages 112–241. Sometime later, Willard Richards inscribed year and month-and-year headings in black ink on pages 17–20, 46–47, 105–173, and 176–187. Various pages also bear redactions in unidentified handwriting in black and blue pencil.

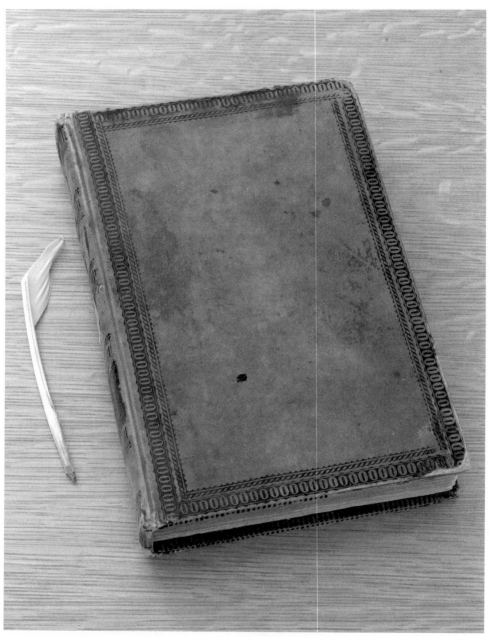

Joseph Smith's 1834–1836 history. Joseph Smith's second history was written in a leather-bound blank book that Smith referred to as his "large journal" (see entry for 29 Oct. 1835, p. 105 herein). The history includes family information for members of the church's presidency, historical entries from December 1834, a transcript of Oliver Cowdery's published history, which describes Joseph Smith's early visions of the angel Moroni, and an adaptation of entries from Smith's second Ohio journal. In 1839, the book was turned over, so that the back cover became the front cover, and was used for the first volume of Joseph Smith's multivolume manuscript history. JS History, 1834–1836, in JS History, vol. A-1, Church History Library, Salt Lake City. (Photograph by Welden C. Andersen.)

In 1839, the book was repurposed for the inscription of a new history. The book was turned over so that the back cover became the front and the last leaf became the first. From this new front of the book, JS's scribes began writing what became the first volume of JS's multivolume manuscript history (the first 61 pages of which are transcribed as "Draft 2" on pages 204–462 herein). That later history filled most of the remaining leaves of the book, running well into the blank pages that were numbered for the 1834–1836 history and up to within five pages of the inscribed entries in the earlier history. However, only numbering on pages 235–241 of the 1834–1836 history were erased (by knife eraser). With the later history's side of the book upward, the spine of the book was labeled as volume "A | 1" of the multivolume history. Archival stickers were also added at some point to the spine and the inside front cover. Two interior leaves are now missing from the initial gathering of the volume and one leaf is missing from the final gathering. The flyleaves and pastedowns were also lost or removed from the book.[1] The volume shows moderate wear, browning, water staining, and brittleness. It has been resewn, rebound, and otherwise conserved.

While the 1834–1836 history was being created, the volume was apparently kept in the homes of JS's scribes.[2] In 1839, scribe James Mulholland converted the book into the first volume of JS's multi-volume manuscript history.[3] In 1842, the church newspaper in Nauvoo, Illinois, began publishing this later history.[4] JS maintained custody of the volume through his later life, as indicated by a note he inscribed memorializing his deceased brother Alvin Smith, which was attached to the verso of the flyleaf preceding the later history. The volume is listed in the first extant Historian's Office inventory, made in Nauvoo in February 1846 by clerk Thomas Bullock, and it is listed in inventories of church records made in Salt Lake City in the second half of the nineteenth century.[5] These and later archival records, as well as archival marking on the volume, indicate continuous institutional custody.

Historical Introduction

JS's 1834–1836 history is a composite historical record consisting of genealogical tables, journal-like entries, and transcripts of newspaper articles. It shifts abruptly in format from one unfinished section to the next. The order of handwriting in the history roughly matches that found in the 1835–1836 journal, and like the journal, the history passed from Oliver Cowdery to Frederick G. Williams to Warren Parrish to Warren Cowdery. Finally, it returned to Parrish. The purpose for which the record was created is unclear, as is the rationale for its differing formats. At the beginning, the 1834–1836 history may have had as much to do with Oliver Cowdery, its first scribe, as with JS. Cowdery was serving at the time as scribe for JS's first Ohio journal. He had transformed that journal into a jointly authored document by writing in the first person plural, making both himself and JS the protagonists. Cowdery made his final entry in the first Ohio journal 5 December 1834, the day he was ordained an assistant president to JS in the general church presidency and

---

1. See JS History, vol. A-1, microfilm, Dec. 1971, CHL. Only one leaf of the original pastedowns and flyleaves is extant. The pastedowns were replaced with undecorated paper in 1994, according to a conservation note on the verso of the extant marbled leaf archived with the volume.

2. See JS, Journal, 29 Oct. 1835 and 25 Jan. 1836, in *JSP*, J1:76–79, 173 (see also entry for 29 Oct. 1835 herein).

3. Jessee, "Writing of Joseph Smith's History," 439–441, 450–451, 464.

4. The serialized publication of this history began in the 15 March 1842 issue of the *Times and Seasons*.

5. "Schedule of Church Records. Nauvoo 1846," [1]; "Historian's Office Catalogue 1858," 2, Historian's Office, Catalogs and Inventories, 1846–1904, CHL.

placed ahead of JS's other assistants. He may have begun the 1834–1836 history in response to his new appointment.

The new record was begun in a massive blank book. Cowdery left the first twelve pages blank, possibly for a title page and other introductory material to be written later. He then inscribed columns and headings on the next eight pages to reserve them for the genealogies of the four members of the new church presidency. On the following page, he began an entry dated 5 December 1834, the same date as his last entry in JS's first Ohio journal.

Just as Oliver Cowdery converted JS's first Ohio journal into a JS-Cowdery journal, he may have conceived of the 1834–1836 history as a record for all four members of the church presidency. Cowdery's entry for 5 December 1834 provided a lengthier and more formal account of his elevation to the church presidency than did JS's first Ohio journal. Regardless of its purpose, however, the daily log was discontinued after two entries.

The next section of the history, begun months later, is a transcript of Oliver Cowdery's series of eight letters on church history published in the *Latter Day Saints' Messenger and Advocate* between October 1834 and October 1835. Frederick G. Williams, who began the transcription, may have begun working under Cowdery's direction, but by 29 October 1835 JS had assumed effective control of the document. JS's journal entry of that date, which notes his employment of Warren Parrish as his scribe, also records that Parrish "commenced writing in my journal a history of my life, concluding President Cowdery 2ᵈ letter to W. W. Phelps, which president Williams had begun."[6]

The final section of JS's history, transcribed by Warren Cowdery and Warren Parrish, is a revised version of JS's daily journal entries from late September 1835 to late January 1836.[7] Warren Cowdery explained that the intention was to provide a "faithful narration of every important item in his every-day-occurrences."[8] The revised entries continue to 18 January 1836. Warren Parrish, the final scribe to write in JS's 1834–1836 history, may have ceased his work in order to embark on a proselytizing mission. However, the reasons for JS's discontinuing the history entirely are not known.

Further information about the different sections of the 1834–1836 history may be found in intratextual notes preceding each section.

As noted above, the first section of the history includes initial work to compile genealogical data for each member of the church presidency. In an 1832 letter to church leaders in Missouri, JS outlined the contents of the church history to be kept by John Whitmer. In addition to an account of "all things that transpire in Zion," JS instructed that the record include the names of those who had formally consecrated their property and received church land. At the second coming of Jesus Christ, he wrote, this record would be used to reward "the Saints whose names are found and the names of their fathers and of their children enroled in the Book of the Law of God."[9] Oliver Cowdery apparently followed this model when he began this new historical record in early December 1834. He reserved the

---

6. JS, Journal, 29 Oct. 1835, in *JSP*, J1:76; see also entry for 29 Oct. 1835 herein. In this case, "my journal" refers to JS's 1834–1836 history, which JS also called his "large journal."

7. JS, Journal, 1835–1836, in *JSP*, J1:61–164.

8. JS History, 1834–1836, p. 94 herein.

9. JS, Kirtland, OH, to William W. Phelps, [Independence, MO], 27 Nov. 1832, in JS Letterbook 1, pp. 1, 3.

Assistants in church presidency, 1834. At the beginning of Joseph Smith's 1834–1836 history, two pages were reserved for family records relating to members of the general church presidency. As recorded in the entry for 5 December 1834, Oliver Cowdery (left) was ordained as an assistant church president under Joseph Smith. Sidney Rigdon (right) and Frederick G. Williams (image on p. 8 herein) had previously been appointed to the church presidency. (Church History Library, Salt Lake City.)

pages at the beginning of the history to record family information for JS, himself, Sidney Rigdon, and Frederick G. Williams, the four members of the general church presidency as designated on 5 December 1834. Inscribing headings to eight pages, Cowdery intended to prepare two genealogical tables for each of the four presidents, one to identify wife and children and the second to identify parents and siblings. The left column lists births and marriages; the column on the right was reserved for deaths. That Cowdery did not create or even leave room for similar tables for the two assistant presidents appointed on 6 December 1834 suggests that he inscribed both the tables and the entry for 5 December between the 5 and 6 December meetings.

——————— ∾ ———————

[*12 pages blank*]

/[10]Genealogy of President Joseph Smith junior.

Joseph Smith junior was born in the town of Sharon, Windsor County Vermont, December 23, A.D. 1805.

Emma Hale was born in the town of Harmony, Susquehanna County, Pennsylvania, July 10, A.D. 1804.

Joseph Smith junior, and Emma Hale, were married in the town of Bainbridge, County of Chenango, New=York, January 18, A.D. 1827.

June 15, 1828, a son was born unto Joseph Smith junior. Harmony, Pennsylvania.   } Died the same hour.

April 30, 1831, a Son and daughter were born unto Joseph Smith jr. in Kirtland, Geauga County, Ohio.   } Lived three hours.

Joseph Smith 3rd was born in Kirtland, Ohio, November 6, 1832.

---

10. TEXT: Oliver Cowdery handwriting begins. The headings designating the genealogy of the presidency are written in larger script in red ink. The information under the headings is separated into two columns and written in ink that is now brown.

Genealogy of President Joseph Smith junior

Joseph Smith [Sen] was born in the town of Topsfield, county of Essex, Massachusetts, July 12, A.D. 1771.

Lucy Mack was born in the town of Gilsom, County of Cheshire New Hampshire, July 8, 1776.

Joseph Smith Sen. and Lucy Mack were married in Tunbridge, Orange Co. Vt. January 24, 1796.

Alvin Smith, born in Tunbridge, Vt. February 11, 1798.   Died in Manchester Ontario Co. N.Y. Nov. 19, 1823. Aged 27 years 9 months 8 days.

Hyrum Smith, born in Tunbridge Vt. February 9, 1800.

Saphrona Smith, born in Tunbridge Vt. May 16, 1803.

Joseph Smith jr, born in Sharon, Windsor Co. Vt. Dec. 23, 1805.

Samuel H. Smith, born Tunbridge Vt. March 13, 1808.

Ephraim Smith, born in Royalton, Windsor Co. Vt. March 13, 1810.   Died Royalton, Vt. March 24, 1810. Aged 12 days.

William Smith, born in Royalton Vt. March 13, 1811.

Katharine Smith, born in Lebanon, Grafton Co. N.H. July 28, 1813.

Don Carlos Smith, born in Norwich, Windsor Co. Vt. March 25, 1816.

Lucy Smith, born in Palmyra, Ontario Co. N.Y. July 18, 1821.

Family information of church presidency. The first section of Joseph Smith's 1834–1836 history was intended for family records of Joseph Smith, Oliver Cowdery, Sidney Rigdon, and Frederick G. Williams, the four members of the general church presidency as designated on 5 December 1834. The column on the left lists births and marriages; the column on the right, deaths. Oliver Cowdery wrote headings reserving two pages for each of the four men, one page to record information about wife and children and one to record information about parents and siblings. Handwriting of Oliver Cowdery. JS History, 1834–1836, p. 10 (transcribed on pp. 30–31 herein), in JS History, vol. A-1 (earliest numbering), Church History Library, Salt Lake City. (Photograph by Welden C. Andersen.)

Joseph S. and Julia Murdock were born in Orange, Cuyahoga Co. Ohio, April 30, 1831, and adopted into Joseph Smith jr's family at the age of nine days.[11]

Joseph S. Murdock died in Hiram, Portage Co. Ohio, March 29, 1832. Age 11 months.

[*15 lines blank*] [p. 9]
Genealogy of President Joseph Smith junior.

Joseph Smith sen. was born in the town of Topsfield, County of Essex, Massachusetts, July 12, A.D. 1772.[12]

Lucy Mack was born in the town of Gilsom [Gilsum], County of Cheshire, New Hampshire, July 8, 1776.[13]

Joseph Smith Sen. and Lucy Mack were married in Tunbridge, Orange Co. Vt. January 24, 1796.

Alvin Smith, born in Tunbridge, Vt. February 11, 1798.

Died in Manchester, Ontario Co. N.Y. Nov. 19, 1825— Aged—27, years—9 months—8 days.[14]

Hyrum Smith, born in Tunbridge Vt. February 9, 1800.

Sophron[i]a Smith, born in Tunbridge Vt. May 16, 1803.

---

11. The autobiographical writings of John Murdock, the biological father of Joseph and Julia Murdock, indicate that the twins were born in Warrensville Township, which bordered Orange Township. The mother of the twins, Julia Clapp Murdock, died in childbirth. (Murdock, Autobiography, 9, 19.)

12. Joseph Smith Sr. was born 12 July 1771. (Topsfield, Essex Co., MA, Records of Birth, Marriage, Death, and Intentions of Marriage, 1677–1833, vol. B, p. 59, microfilm 887,762; Manchester, Hillsborough Co., NH, Town Records, 1746–1868, vol. 1, p. [2], microfilm 15,362, U.S. and Canada Record Collection, FHL.)

13. Lucy Mack Smith was born 8 July 1775. (Gilsum, Cheshire Co., NH, Records of Births, Marriages, and Deaths, 1754–1915, item 2, p. 243, microfilm 2,208,912, U.S. and Canada Record Collection, FHL; JS Family Bible; Lucy Mack Smith, *Biographical Sketches*, 36.)

14. Alvin Smith died 19 November 1823, at age twenty-five, in the Joseph Smith Sr. log home in Palmyra Township, Wayne County, New York. Wayne County was formed from Ontario County in April 1823. (JS History, vol. A-1, miscellaneous papers; Morgan, *Cemetery Records, Palmyra, Wayne, New York*, 2; Joseph Smith Sr., "To the Public," *Wayne Sentinel* [Palmyra, NY], 29 Sept. 1824, [3].)

Joseph Smith jr, born in Sharon, Windsor Co. Vt. Dec. 23, 1805.

Samuel H. Smith, born Tunbridge Vt. March 13, 1808.

Ephraim Smith, born in Royalton, Windsor Co. Vt. March 13, ~~1800~~ 1810.

Died Royalton, Vt. March 24, 1810=Aged—12 days.

William Smith, born in Royalton Vt. [*blank*] March 13, 1811.

Katharine Smith, born in Lebanon, Grafton Co. N.H. July 28, 1813.

Don Carlos Smith, born in Norwich, Windsor Co. Vt. March 25, 1816.

Lucy Smith, born in Palmyra, Ontario Co. N.Y. July 18, 1821.

[*9 lines blank*] [p. 10]

Genealogy of President Oliver Cowdery.

Oliver Cowdery was born in the town of Wells, Rutland Co. Vermont, Friday, October 3, 1806.

Elizabeth Ann Whitmer was born in the town of Fayette, Seneca County, New=York, Sunday, January 22, 1815.

Oliver Cowdery and Elizabeth Ann Whitmer were married in Kaw Township, Jackson Co. Missouri, [Zion] Dec. 18, 1832.

⟨Maria Cowdery was born in Kirtland, Geauga County, Ohio, fifteen (15) minutes past 9 o'clock A.M. Friday, August 21, 1835.⟩

[*27 lines blank*] [p. 11]

Genealogy of President ~~Sidney Rigdon~~ Oliver Cowdery.

[*remainder of page blank*] [p. 12]

Genealogy of President Sidney Rigdon.

[*remainder of page blank*] [p. 13]

Genealogy of President Sidney Rigdon.
[*remainder of page blank*] [p. 14]
Genealogy of President Frederick G. Williams.
[*remainder of page blank*] [p. 15]
Genealogy of President Frederick G. Williams.
[*remainder of page blank*] [p. 16]

——————— ✌ ———————

Editorial Note

As explained previously, Oliver Cowdery apparently wrote the entry for 5 December 1834 sometime between the meeting held that evening and the related meeting held the following day. This promptness suggests that Cowdery's entry for the 6 December 1834 meeting was likewise written the day of that meeting or shortly thereafter. The blank pages between the 6 December entry and the next section of the history were likely reserved for further historical entries, but no similar contemporaneous entries were made here or anywhere else in the history.

——————— ✌ ———————

Chapter 1.

5 December 1834 • Friday

Friday Evening, December 5, 1834. According to the direction of the Holy Spirit, President Smith, assistant Presidents, [Sidney] Rigdon and [Frederick G.] Williams, assembled for the purpose of ordaining ⟨first⟩ High Counsellor [Oliver] Cowdery[15] to the office of assistant President of the High and Holy Priesthood in the Church of the Latter-Day Saints.

It is necessary, for the special benefit of the reader, that he be instructed ⟨into, or⟩ concerning the power and authority of the above named Priesthood.

First. The office of the President is to preside over the whole Chu[r]ch; to be considered as at the head; to receive revelations for the Church; to be a Seer, ~~and~~ Revelator ⟨and Prophet—⟩ having all the gifts of God:— ~~having~~ taking ⟨Moses⟩ for an ensample. Which is ~~Second.~~[16] the office and station of the above

---

15. Cowdery was designated the first speaker of the Kirtland high council at that body's organizational meeting held 17 February 1834, after the members "cast lots or ballot, to ascertain who should speak first." JS's journal entry for 5 December 1834, also in Cowdery's handwriting, states that the church presidency assembled "to converse upon the welfare of the church." (Minute Book 1, 17 Feb. 1834; JS, Journal, 5 Dec. 1834, in *JSP*, J1:47.)

16. TEXT: Cowdery may have originally inscribed "Second" after writing "gifts of God" above, and then canceled "Second" and added the text after "gifts of God".

December 1834

Chapter 1.

17

Friday Evening, December 5, 1834.

According to the direction of the Holy Spirit, President Smith, assistant Presidents, Rigdon and Williams, assembled for the purpose of ordaining first High Counsellor Cowdery to the office of assistant President of the High and Holy Priesthood in the Church of the Latter Day Saints.

It is necessary, for the special benefit of the reader, that he be instructed concerning the power and authority of the above named Priesthood.

First. The office of the President is to preside over the whole Church; to be considered as at the head; to receive revelations for the Church; to be a Seer, and Revelator and Prophet, having all the gifts of God: taking Moses for an ensample. Which is the office and station of the above President Smith, according to the calling of God, and the ordination which he has received.

Second. The office of Assistant President is to assist in presiding over the whole church, and to officiate in the absence of the President, according to his rank and appointment, viz: President Cowdery first; President Rigdon Second, and President Williams Third, as they were severally called. The office of this Priesthood is also to act as Spokesman—taking Aaron for an ensample.

The virtue of the above Priesthood is to hold the keys of the Kingdom of heaven, or the Church militant.

The reader may further understand, that the reason why High Counsellor Cowdery was not previously ordained to the Presidency, was, in consequence of his necessary attendance in Zion, to assist W. W. Phelps in conducting the printing business; but that this promise was made by the angel while in company with President Smith, at the time they received the office of the lesser priesthood. And further: The circumstances and situation of the Church requiring, Presidents Rigdon and Williams were previously ordained, to assist President Smith.

After this short explanation, we now proceed to give an account of the acts, promises, and blessings of this memorable Evening:

First. After assembling, we received a rebuke for our former low, uncultivated, and disrespectful manner of communication and salutation, with, and unto each other, by the voice of the Spirit, saying unto us: Verily condemnation resteth upon you, who are appointed to lead my Church, and to be saviors of men: And also upon the church: And there must needs be a repentance and a reformation among you, in all things, in your ensamples before the Church, and before the world, in all your manners, habits and customs, and salutations one toward another—rendering unto every man the respect due the office, and calling, and priesthood, whereunto I the Lord have appointed and ordained you. Amen.

Journal-like entries in history. The events of 5 and 6 December 1834 were recorded by Oliver Cowdery beginning on page 17 of the 1834–1836 history. On these days, the general presidency of the church, which consisted of Joseph Smith, Sidney Rigdon, and Frederick G. Williams, was enlarged by the addition of Oliver Cowdery, Hyrum Smith, and Joseph Smith Sr. as assistant presidents. The assembled leaders also received "reproof and instruction." Handwriting of Oliver Cowdery. JS History, 1834–1836, p. 17 (transcribed on pp. 32–35 herein), in JS History, vol. A-1 (earliest numbering), Church History Library, Salt Lake City. (Photograph by Welden C. Andersen.)

President Smith, according to the calling of God, and the ordination which he has received.[17]

Second. The office of Assistant President is to assist in presiding over the whole chu[r]ch, and to officiate in the abscence of the President, according to ~~their~~ ⟨his⟩ rank and appointment, viz: President Cowdery, first; President Rigdon Second, and President Williams Third, as they ⟨were⟩ ~~are~~ severally called. The office of this Priesthood is also to act as Spokesman—taking Aaron for an ensample.[18]

The virtue of ~~this~~ the ⟨above⟩ Priesthood is to hold the keys of the kingdom of heaven, or the Church militant.[19]

The reader may further understand, that ~~Presidents~~ ⟨the⟩ reason why ~~President~~ ⟨High Counsellor⟩ Cowdery was not previously ordained ⟨to the Presidency,⟩ was, in consequence of his necessary attendance in Zion, to assist Wm W. Phelps in conducting the printing business; but that this promise was made by the angel while in company with President Smith, at the time they recievd the office of the lesser priesthood.[20] And further: The circumstances and situation of the Church requiring, Presidents Rigdon and Williams were previously ordained, to assist President Smith.

After this short explination, we now proceed to give an account of the acts, promises, and blessings of this memorable Evening:

First. After assembling, we received a rebuke for our former low, uncultivated, and disrespectful manner of communication, and salutation, with, and unto each other, by the voice of the Spirit, saying unto us: Verily, condemnation resteth upon you, who are appointed to lead my Chu[r]ch, and to be saviors of men:[21] and also upon the church: And there must needs be a repentance and a

---

17. JS's early revelations identified him as a Moses-like prophet. (See Book of Mormon, 1830 ed., 66–68 [2 Nephi 3:6–25]; Revelation, Sept. 1830–B, in Doctrine and Covenants 51:1–2, 1835 ed. [D&C 28:1–7]; and Revelation, 24 Feb. 1834, in Doctrine and Covenants 101:3, 1844 ed. [D&C 103:16].)

18. Aaron was chosen as spokesman for Moses. JS's revelations earlier identified an Aaron-like role for Cowdery. (See Exodus 4:10–16; Book of Mormon, 1830 ed., 67 [2 Nephi 3:17–18]; and Revelation, Sept. 1830–B, in Doctrine and Covenants 51:2, 1835 ed. [D&C 28:3].)

19. The "Church militant" refers to "the Church on earth considered as warring against the powers of evil," as opposed to the "church triumphant," the part of the church that has "overcome the world, and entered into glory." ("Church Militant," in *Oxford English Dictionary*, 2:404.)

20. JS later recounted that he and Cowdery received the lesser priesthood from John the Baptist on 15 May 1829 and that the angelic visitor instructed that Cowdery be made second elder, next to JS as first elder. JS and Cowdery were acknowledged in these positions at the organization of the church. (JS History, vol. A-1, pp. 292–294 herein [Draft 2]; Articles and covenants, 10 Apr. 1830, in Doctrine and Covenants 2:1, 1835 ed. [D&C 20:2–3].)

21. A revelation earlier in 1834 stated that the Lord's people "were set to be a light unto the world, and to be the saviors of men." (Revelation, 24 Feb. 1834, in Doctrine and Covenants 101:2, 1844 ed. [D&C 103:9]; compare Obadiah 1:21.)

refor[m]ation among you, in all things, in your ensamples before the Chuch, and before the world, in all your manners, habits and customs, and salutations one toward another—rendering unto every man the respect due the office, ~~and~~ calling, and priesthood, whereunto I the Lord have appointed and ordained you. Amen. [p. 17]

It is only necessary to say, relative to the foregoing reproof and instruction, that, though it was given in sharpness, it occasioned gladness and joy, and we were willing to repent and reform, in every particular, according to the instruction given. It is also proper to remark, that after the reproof was given, we all confessed, voluntarily, that such had been the manifestations of the Spirit a long times since; in consequence of which the rebuke came with greater sharpness.

Not thinking to evade the truth, or excuse, in order to escape censure, but to give proper information, a few remarks relative to the situation of the Chuch previous to this date, is necessary. Many, on hearing the fulness of the gospel, embraced it with eagerness; ⟨yet,⟩ at the same time were unwilling to forego their former opinions and notions relative to Church government, and the rules and habits proper for the good order, harmony, peace, and beauty of a people destined, with the protecting care of the Lord, to be an ensample and light of the world. They did not dispise government; but there was a disposition to organize that government according to their own notions, or feelings. For example: Every man must be subjected ⟨to⟩ wear a particular fashioned coat, hat, or other garment, or else an accusation was brought that we were fashioning after the world. Every one must be called by their given name, without respecting the office or ordinance to which they had been called: Thus, President Smith was called Joseph, or brother Joseph; President Rigdon, brother Sidney, or Sidney, &c. This manner of address gave occasion to the enemies of the truth, and was a means of bringing reproach upon the Cause of God. But in consequence of former prejudices, the Church, many of them, would not submit to proper and wholesome order.[22] This proceeded from a spirit of enthusiasm, and vain ambition—a desire to compel others to come to certain rules, not dictated by the will of the Lord; or a jealous fear, that, were men called by thier respective titles, and the ordinance of heaven honored in a proper manner, some were in a way to be exalted above others, and their form of government disregarded. In fact, the true principle of honor in the Church of the Saints, that the more a man is exalted, the more humble he will be, if actuated by the Spirit of the Lord, seemed to have been overlooked; and the fact,

---

22. A number of religious groups growing out of the Radical Reformation adopted plain dress and common address as modes of class leveling. (See, for example, Scott, *Why Do They Dress That Way?*, 52.)

that the greatest is least and servant of all, as said our Savior,[23] never to have
been thought of, by numbers. These facts, for such they were, when viewed in
their proper light, were sufficient, of themselves to cause men to humble themselves before the Lord; but when communicated by the Spirit, made an impression upon our hearts not to be forgotten. [p. 18]

Perhaps, an arrangement of this kind in a former day would have occasioned some unpleasant reflections, in the minds of many, and at an ~~early~~
⟨earlier⟩ period, in this church, others to have forsaken the cause, in consequence of weakness, and unfaithfulness; but that the leaders of the church
should wait so long before stepping forward according ⟨to⟩ the manifestation of
the Spirit, deserved a reproof. And that the church should be chastened, for
their uncultivated manner of salutation, is also just. But to proceed with the
account of the interview.

After addressing the throne of mercy,[24] President Smith laid hands upon
High Counsellor Cowdery, and ordained him to the Presidency of the High
priesthood in the Church, saying:

Brother, In the name of Jesus Christ of Nazareth, who was crucified for the
sins of the world, that we through the virtue of his blood might come to
the Father,[25] I lay my hands upon thy head, and ordain thee a President of the
high and holy priesthood, to assist in presiding over the Chu[r]ch, and bearing
the keys of this kingdom—[26] which priesthood is after the order of Melchizedek— which is after the order of the Son of God—[27] And now, O Father,
wilt thou bless this thy servant with wisdom, knowledge, and understanding—
give him, by the Holy Spirit, a correct understanding of thy doctrine, laws, and
will— Commune with him from on high— let him hear thy voice, and receive
the ~~ministries~~ ministring of the holy angels— deliver him from temptation,
and the power of darkness— deliver him from evil,[28] and from those who may
seek his destruction,— be his shield, his buckler, and his great reward—[29]

---

23. See Matthew 20:26–27; and Revelation, 9 May 1831, in Doctrine and Covenants 17:6, 1835 ed.
[D&C 50:26].

24. See Hebrews 4:16.

25. See Revelation, 2 Jan. 1831, in Doctrine and Covenants 12:1, 1835 ed. [D&C 38:4].

26. See Matthew 16:19; Revelation, 15 Mar. 1832, in Doctrine and Covenants 79:1, 1835 ed. [D&C 81:2];
and Revelation, 8 Mar. 1833, in Doctrine and Covenants 84:1–3, 1835 ed. [D&C 90:1–6].

27. See Psalm 110:4; Book of Mormon, 1830 ed., 260 [Alma 13:18]; and Vision, 16 Feb. 1832, in Doctrine
and Covenants 91:5, 1835 ed. [D&C 76:57].

28. See Matthew 6:13.

29. See Genesis 15:1; Psalm 91:4; and Revelation, 7 Dec. 1830, in Doctrine and Covenants 11:4, 1835 ed.
[D&C 35:14].

endow him with power from on high,[30] that he may write, preach, and proclaim the gospel to his fellowmen in demonstration of the Spirit and of power—[31] may his feet never slide— may his heart never feint— may his faith never fail. Bestow upon him the blessings of his fathers Abraham, Isaac, Jacob, and of Joseph— Prolong his life to a good old age, and bring him in peace to his end, and to rejoice with thy saints, even the sanctified, in the celestial kingdom;[32] for thine is the kingdom, the power, and the glory, forever. Amen.[33]

Presidents Rigdon, and Williams, confirmed the ordinance and blessings by the laying on of hands and prayer, after which each were blessed with the same blessings and prayer.

Much light was communicated to our minds, and we were instructed into the order of the Church of the saints, and how they ought to conduct in respecting and reverencing each other. The praise of men, or the honor of this world, is of no benefit; but if a man is respected in his calling, and considered to be a man of righteousness, the truth may have an influence, many times, by which means they may teach the gospel with success, and lead men into the kingdom of heaven. [p. 19]

6 December 1834 • Saturday

On Saturday, December 6, Presidents Smith, [Oliver] Cowdery, and [Sidney] Rigdon assembled with High Counsellors Joseph Smith sen. Hyrum Smith, and Samuel H. Smith,[34] in company with Reynolds Cahoon, Counsellor to the Bishop, High Priest William Smith, and ⟨Elder⟩ Don C[arlos] Smith.

The meeting was opened by prayer, and a lengthy conversation held upon the subject of introducing a more refined order into the Church. On further reflection, the propriety of ordaining others to the office of Presidency of the high priesthood was also discussed, after which High Counsellor Hyrum Smith was ordained ⟨to⟩ the Presidency under the hands of President Smith,

---

30. See Luke 24:49; Revelation, 2 Jan. 1831, in Doctrine and Covenants 12:7, 1835 ed. [D&C 38:32]; Revelation, Feb. 1831–A, in Doctrine and Covenants 14:4, 1835 ed. [D&C 43:15–16]; and Revelation, 22 June 1834, in Doctrine and Covenants 102:10, 1844 ed. [D&C 105:33].

31. Cowdery had a special calling to be a preacher and teacher to the church. (See Revelation, Sept. 1830–B, in Doctrine and Covenants 51:1–2, 1835 ed. [D&C 28:1–4].)

32. See 1 Corinthians 15:40–41; Vision, 16 Feb. 1832, in Doctrine and Covenants 91:5, 1835 ed. [D&C 76:50–70]; and Revelation, 27 and 28 Dec. 1832, in Doctrine and Covenants 7:4–5, 1835 ed. [D&C 88:17–22].

33. See Matthew 6:13; and Revelation, 30 Oct. 1831, in Doctrine and Covenants 24:1, 1835 ed. [D&C 65:6].

34. Joseph Smith Sr. and Samuel Smith were original members of the Kirtland high council, created 17 February 1834. Hyrum Smith was added to the council 24 September 1834, taking Sylvester Smith's place. (Minutes, 17 Feb. 1834, in Doctrine and Covenants 5:1, 1835 ed. [D&C 102:2]; Minute Book 1, 24 Sept. 1834.)

and High Counsellor Joseph Smith sen. under the hands of President Rigdon. The others present were blessed under the hands of Presidents J. Smith jr. Cowdery, and Rigdon, and the meeting closed, after a happy season, ~~of~~ and a social intercourse upon the great subject of the gospel and the work of the Lord in this day./[35] [24 lines blank] [p. 20] [pages 21–45 blank]

———— ☙ ————

Editorial Note

The following section includes transcripts of eight letters Oliver Cowdery wrote in 1834 and 1835 regarding JS's visions of an angel and his discovery of the gold plates of the Book of Mormon. Cowdery addressed the letters to William W. Phelps and published them as a series in the *Latter Day Saints' Messenger and Advocate* between October 1834 and October 1835. The titles and formatting employed in this history are similar to those in the published series of articles, indicating that the Cowdery letters were copied into the history from the *Messenger and Advocate,* not from a manuscript version of the letters. Frederick G. Williams could have begun the transcription in JS's history as early as 6 December 1834, the date of Cowdery's last historical entry in the preceding section of the history. However, Cowdery probably gave the history to Williams around 2 October 1835, when he gave Williams JS's journal. On 29 October 1835, JS retrieved the history from Williams and delivered it to Warren Parrish, who continued copying the Cowdery letters. It is likely that Parrish finished copying the letters by early April 1836, when he gave JS's journal (and presumably the 1834–1836 history along with it) to Warren Cowdery.[36]

In the first letter, Oliver Cowdery recounted his experiences with JS beginning when the two first met in April 1829. The letter includes an account of the vision he and JS had of John the Baptist, who gave them the authority to baptize. After composing this letter, but before its publication, Cowdery developed a new history-writing plan: he decided that in subsequent letters he would relate the "full history of the rise of the church," beginning with JS's early life and visions. As editor of the *Messenger and Advocate,* Cowdery prefaced the published version of the first letter with an explanation (also transcribed into the history) of the new plan. Although he had no firsthand knowledge of church history prior to April 1829, Cowdery assured his readers that "our brother J. Smith Jr. has offered to assist us. Indeed, there are many items connected with the fore part of this subject that render his labor indispensible." Some passages in the ensuing narrative seem to have been related to Cowdery by JS, since Cowdery recounted events in which only JS participated.

Cowdery composed the letters to inform the Latter-day Saints of the history of their church, but he also wrote for the non-Mormon public. Employing florid romantic language, frequent scriptural allusions, and much dramatic detail, he clearly intended to present a rhetorically impressive account of early Mormon history. He placed the rise of the church in a dispensational framework, characterizing the time between the end of the New Testament and JS's early visions as a period of universal apostasy. He included the revivalism of various

---

35. TEXT: Oliver Cowdery handwriting ends.
36. See JS, Journal, 1 and 2 Apr. 1836, in *JSP,* J1:216–217.

denominations during the Second Great Awakening, which JS experienced in his youth, as an example of the doctrinal confusion and social disharmony present in Christendom. Throughout the series of letters, he defended JS's character and that of the Smith family, and his explicitly apologetic statements include apparent allusions to both Alexander Campbell's *Delusions* (1832) and Eber Howe's *Mormonism Unvailed* (1834).

Beginning in the third letter, Cowdery provided the most extensive account of the origins of the Book of Mormon published up to that time. He related JS's initial visions of the angel Moroni and, using biblical prophecies, elaborated on the angel's message concerning the gathering of Israel in the last days in preparation for the Millennium. Cowdery continued his narrative up to, but did not include, JS's receiving the gold plates in September 1827.

The transcription of the Oliver Cowdery letters into JS's history was evidently conceived in terms of the entire series, not as a piecemeal copying of the individual letters. As noted above, Cowdery probably gave the "large journal" containing the history begun in 1834 to Williams in October 1835, the month of the *Messenger and Advocate* issue in which his final installment was published.[37] By the time Williams received the history, Cowdery may have already written the final letter; he had at least conceived of it as the final installment in his series. With the serialized Cowdery letters complete or nearing completion, the new history kept in the "large journal" could serve as a repository—more permanent than unbound newspapers—for a copied compilation of the entire series.

/[38]The following communication was designed to have been published in the last No. of the star; but owing to a press of other matter it was laid over for this No. of the Messenger and ad[v]ocate.[39] Since it was writen, upon further reflection, we have thought that a full history of the rise of the church of the Latter Day Saints, and the most interesting parts of its progress, to the present time, would be worthy the perusal of the Saints.— If circumstances admit, an article on this subject will appear ~~on~~ in each subsequent No. of the Messenger and advocate, until the time when the church was driven from Jackson Co. Mo. by a lawless banditti; & such other remarks as may be thought appropriate and interesting.

That our narrative may be correct, and particularly the introduction, it is proper to inform our patrons, that our brother J. Smith Jr. has offered to assist us. Indeed, there are many items connected with the fore part of this subject

---

37. The October issue, like many issues of the early Mormon newspapers, was published late. It includes a letter dated 7 November, so it could not have been published before then. (Noah Packard, Kirtland, OH, 7 Nov. 1835, Letter to the editor, *LDS Messenger and Advocate,* Oct. 1835, 2:208.)

38. TEXT: Frederick G. Williams handwriting begins. This introductory note and the letter that follows were published in *LDS Messenger and Advocate,* Oct. 1834, 1:13–16.

39. The *Latter Day Saints' Messenger and Advocate* succeeded *The Evening and the Morning Star* as the official church newspaper. (Crawley, *Descriptive Bibliography,* 1:32–34, 47–51.)

that render his labor indispensible. With his labor and with authentic documents now in our possession, we hope to render this a pleasing and agreeable narrative, well worth the examination and perusal of the Saints.—⁴⁰

To do ⟨Justice to⟩ this subject will require time and space: we therefore ask the forbearance of our readears, assuring them that it shall be founded upon facts.

Norton, Medina Co. Ohio, Sabbath evening, September 7, 1834.

Dear Brother,— Before leaving home, I promised, if I tarried long, to write; and while a few moments are now allowed me for reflection, asside from the cares and common conversation of my friends in this place, I have thought that were I to communicate them to you, might, perhaps, if they should not prove especially beneficial to yourself, by by confirming you in the faith of the gospel, at least be interesting, since it has pleased our heavenly Father to call us both to rejoice in the same hope of eternal life. And by giving them publicity, some thousands who have embraced the same covenant, may learn something more particular upon the rise of ~~the~~ this church, in this last time. And while the gray evening is fast changing into a settled darkness, my heart responds with the happy millions who are in the presence of the Lamb, and are past the power of temptation, in rendering thanks, though feebly, to the same parent.

Another day has passed, into that, to us boundless ocean Eternity! where nearly six thousand years have gone before; and what flits across the mind like an electric shock is, that it will never return! [p. 46] Whether it has been well improved or not; whether the principles emenating from HIM who "hallowed" it, have been observed; or whether, like the common mass of time, it has been heedlessly spent, is not for me to say—one thing I can say—it can never be recalled!—it has rolled in to assist in filling up the grand space decreed in the mind of its Author, till nature shall have ceased her work, and time its accustomed revolutions—when its lord shall have completed the gathering of his elect, and with them enjoy that sabbath which shall never end!

On Fryday, the 5ᵗʰ, in company with our brother Joseph Smith Jr. I left Kirtland for this place (New Portage,) to attend the conference previously appointed. To be permited, once more, to travel with this brother, occasions reflections of no ordinary kind. Many have been the fatiagues and privations

---

40. One of the "authentic documents" Cowdery relied on may have been JS's circa summer 1832 history. The volume that includes the 1832 history also includes letters copied in by Cowdery—meaning Cowdery had access to JS's history—and passages of Cowdery's letters appear to have been informed by the contents and even wording of JS's earlier work. (See JS Letterbook 1, pp. 62–65, 89; see also Anderson, "Circumstantial Confirmation of the First Vision," 394–398.)

which have fallen to my lot to endure, for the gospel's sake, since 1828[41] with this brother. Our road has frequently been spread with the "fowlers snare," and our persons saught with the eagerness, of the savage's ferocity, for innocent blood, by men, either heated to desperation by the insenuation of those who professed to be "guides and way marks," to the kingdom of glory, or the individuals themselves!— This, I confess, is a dark picture to spread before our patrons, but they will pardon my plainness when I assure them of the truth, In fact, God has so ordered, that the reflections which I am permited to cast upon my past life, relative to a knowledge of the way of salvation, are rendered "doubly endearing." Not only have I been graciously preserved from wicked and unreasonable men, with this our brother, but I have seen the fruit of perseverance in proclaiming the everlasting gospel, immediately after it was declared to the world in these last days, in a manner not to be forgotten while heaven gives my common intellect. And what serves to render the reflection past expression on this point is, that from his hand I received baptism, by the direction of the angel of God—the first received into this church, in this day.

Near the time of the setting of the sun, sabbath evening, April 5th. 1829, my natural eyes for the first time beheld this brother. He then resided in Harmony, susquehanna county Penn. On monday the 6th. I assisted him in aranging some business of a temporal nature,[42] and on tuesday the 7th. commenced to write the book of Mormon.[43] These were days never to be forgotten—to ⟨sit⟩ ~~assist~~ under the ~~voice~~ sound of a voice dictated by the inspiration of heaven, awakened the utmost gratitude of this bosom! Day after day I continued, uninterrupted, to [p. 47] write from his mouth, as he translated with the Urim and Thummim, or, as the Nephites should have said, ["]Interpreters,"[44] the history, or reccord, called "the book of Mormon.["]

To notice, in few words, the interesting account given by Mormon, and his faithful son Moroni, of a people once beloved and favored of heaven, would supercede my present design: I shall therefore defer this to a future period, and as I said in the introduction, pass more directly to some few incidents immediately connected with the rise of this church, which may be entertaining to

41. In the next paragraph, Cowdery stated that he first met JS on 5 April 1829. Here Cowdery may have been tracing his belief in JS's mission and some of the hardships associated with that belief to the period when he boarded with JS's family in Manchester, New York, beginning in fall 1828.

42. The business transacted on 6 April included JS purchasing fourteen acres of land from his father-in-law, Isaac Hale. (Isaac Hale to JS, Agreement, Harmony, PA, 6 Apr. 1829, JS Collection, CHL.)

43. Cowdery was the principal scribe for both the surviving portions of the original Book of Mormon manuscript and the copy made for the printer.

44. See Book of Mormon, 1830 ed., 172–173, 328, 546 [Mosiah 8:13; Alma 37:21, 24–25; Ether 4:5].

some thousands who have stepped forward, amid the frowns of biggots and the callumny of hypocrites, and embraced the gospel of Christ.

No ~~men~~ ⟨man⟩ in their sober senses, could translate and write the directions given to the Nephites, from the mouth of the saviour of the precise manner in which men should build up his church, and especially, when corruption had spread an uncertainty over all forms and systems practiced among men without desiring a privilege of showing the willingness of the heart by being burried in the Liquid grave, to answer a "good concience by the resurection of Jesus Christ.["]⁴⁵

After writing the account given of the savior's ministry to the remnant of the seed of Jacob, upon this continent,⁴⁶ it was easily to be seen, as the prophet said would be, that darkness covered the earth and gross darkness the minds of the people.⁴⁷

On reflecting further, it was as easily to be seen, that amid the great strife and noise concerning religeon, none had authority from God to administer the ordinances of the gospel For, the question might be asked, have men authority to administer in the name of Christ, who deny revelation? when his testamony is no less then the spirit of prophecy? and his religeon based, built, and sustained by immediate revelations in all ages of the world, when he has had a people on earth? If these facts were burried, and carefully concealed by men whose craft would have been in danger, if once permitted to shine in the faces of men, they were no longer to us; and we only waited for the commandment to be given, "arise and be baptized."⁴⁸

This was not long desired before it was realized. The Lord, who is rich is [in] mercy, and ever willing to answer the consistent prayer of the humble, after we had called upon him in a fervent manner, aside from the abodes of men, condescended to [p. 48] manifest to us his will. On a sudden, as from the midst of eternity, the voice of the redeemer spake peace to us, while the vail was parted and the angel of God came down clothed with glory, and delivered the anxiously looked for message, and the keys of the gospel of repentance!—⁴⁹ What Joy! what wonder! what amazement! while the world were wracked and distracted—while millions were grouping [groping] as the blind for the ~~world~~ wall, and while all men were resting upon uncertainty, as a general mass, our eyes beheld—our ears heard. As in the "blaze of day;" yes more—above the

---

45. See 1 Peter 3:21.

46. This narrative is given in the Book of Mormon, 1830 ed., 476–509 [3 Nephi 11–27].

47. See Isaiah 60:2.

48. See Acts 22:16.

49. JS later recorded these 15 May 1829 events in JS History, vol. A-1, pp. 292–296 herein (Draft 2), where he identified the angel as John the Baptist.

glitter of the may sun beam, which then shed its brilliancy over the face of nature! Then his voice, though mild, pierced ~~the~~ to the center, and his words, ["]I am thy fellow servant," dispelled every fear. We listened—we gazed—we admired! Twas the voice of the angel from glory—twas a message from the Most High! and as we heard we rejoiced, while his love enkindled upon our souls, and we were ~~wrapt~~ in the vision of the Almighty! Where was room for doubt? No where: uncertainty had fled, doubt had sunk, no more to rise, while fiction and deception had fled forever!

But, dear brother think further think for a moment, what Joy filled our hearts, and with what surprise we must have bowed, (for who would not have bowed the knee for such a blessing?) when we received under his hand the holy priesthood, as he said, ["]upon ⟨you⟩ my fellow servants, in the name of Messiah I confer this priesthood, and this authority, which shall remain upon earth, that the sons of Levi may yet offer an offering into the Lord in righteousness!"[50]

I shall not attempt to paint to you the feelings of this heart, nor the majestic beauty and glory which surrounded us on this occasion; but you will believe me when I say, that earth, nor men, with the eloquence of time cannot begin to clothe language in as interesting and sublime a manner as this holy personage. No; nor has this earth power to give the Joy, to bestow the peace, or comprehend the wisdom which was contained in each sentence as they were delivered by the power of the holy spirit! Man may deceave his fellow man; deception may follow deception, and the children of the wicked one may have power to seduce the foolish and untaught, till naught but fiction feeds the many, and the fruit of falshood carries in its current the giddy to the grave; but one touch [p. 49] with the finger of his love, yes, one ray of glory from the upper world, or one word from the mouth of the savior, from the bosom of eternity strikes it all into insignifficance, and blasts it forever from the mind! The assurence that we were in the presence of an angel; the certainty that we heard the voice of Jesus, and the truth unsullied as it flowed from a pure personage, dictated by the will of God, is to me, past description, and I shall ever look upon this expression of the Saviors goodness with wonder and thanksgiving while I am

---

50. JS recounted that the angel's words were "untill the sons of Levi do offer again an offering unto the Lord in righteousness." Cowdery later recalled, "I was present with Joseph when an holy angle from god came down from heaven and confered, or restored the Aaronic priesthood. And said at the same time that it should remain upon the earth while the earth stands." (JS History, vol. A-1, p. 292 herein [Draft 2]; Miller, Journal, 21 Oct. 1848.)

permited to tarry, and in those mansions where perfection dwells and sin never comes, I hope to adore in that day which shall never cease![51]

To day the church in this place assembled, and were addressed on the great and important subject of salvation by brother Jared Carter, followed by brother Sidney Rigdon. The cheering truths ably any [and] eloquently advanced by these brethren were like "apples of gold. in baskets of silver."—[52]

⟨*⟩⟨*The saints listened with attention, after which bread was bro◊ken, and we offered another memorial to our Lord that we remembered him.⟩[53] I must close for the present: my candle is quite extinguished. And all nature seems locked in silence, shrouded in darkness, and enjoying that repose so necessary to this life. But the period is rolling on when night will close, and those who are found worthy will inherit that city where neither the light of the sun nor moon will ⟨be⟩ necessary! "for the glory of God will ~~be~~ bright in[54] it, and the Lamb will be the light thereof."[55]

O[liver] Cowdery.

To W[illiam] W. Phelps, Esqr.

P.S. I shall write you again on the subject of the Conference. ⟨O.C.⟩ I will hereafter give you a full history of the rise of this church, up to the time stated in my introduction; which will necessarily embrace the life and character of this brother. I shall therefore leave thy [the] history of baptism, &c. till its proper place.

Letter II.[56]

To W[illiam] W. Phelps, Esqr.

Dear Brother:—

In the Last Messenger and Advocate I promised to commence a more particular or minute history of the rise and progress of the church of the Latter Day Saints; and publish for the benefit of enquirers and all who are disposed to learn. There are certain facts relative to the works of God [p. 50] worthy the

---

51. In the *LDS Messenger and Advocate*, an asterisk appears at this point, which keys to a paragraph at the end of the letter. In the 1834–1836 history, it constitutes the last two sentences of the postscript, beginning "I will hereafter give you a full history."

52. See Proverbs 25:11.

53. TEXT: This sentence was published in its proper place in the *LDS Messenger and Advocate,* but Frederick G. Williams passed over it during transcription into the 1834–1836 history. To correct the oversight, the sentence was inserted on a slip of paper, measuring 1⅞ × 7⅝ inches (5 × 19 cm), attached with adhesive wafers to the page. A mark in the original manuscript keys the insertion to this point in the transcript. Handwriting of Warren Parrish.

54. For "bright in," *LDS Messenger and Advocate* has "lighten."

55. See Revelation 21:23.

56. Oliver Cowdery, "Letter II," *LDS Messenger and Advocate,* Nov. 1834, 1:27–32.

consideration and observance of every individual, and every society:— They are that he never works in the dark—his works are always performed in a clear, intelligible manner: and another point is, that he never works in vain. This is not the case with men; but might it not be? When the Lord works, he accomplishes his purposes, and the effects of his power are to be seen afterward. In view of this, suffer me to make a few remarks by way of introduction, The works of man may shine for a season with a degree of brilliancy, but time changes their comp[l]exion; and whether it did or not, all would be the same in a little space, as nothing except that which was erected by the hand which never grows weak, can remain when corruption is consumed.

I shall not be required to adorn and beautify my narrative with a relation of the faith of Enoch, and those who assisted him to build up Zion, which fled to God[57]—on the mountains of which was commanded the blessing, life forever more—to be held in reserve to add another ray of glory to the grand retinue, when worlds shall rock from their base to their center; the nations of the righteous rise from the dust, and the blessed millions of the church of the first born shout his tri[u]mphant coming, to receive his kingdom, over which he is to reign till all enemies are subdued. Nor shall I write the history of the Lords church raised up according to his own instruction to Moses and Aaron; of the perplexities and discouragements which came upon Israel for their transgressions, their organization upon the land of Canaan, and their overthrow and dispersion among all nations, to reap the reward of their eniquities, to the appearing of the Great Shepherd, in the flesh.

But there is, of necessity a uniformity so exact; a manner so precise, and ordinances so minute, in all ages and generations whenever God has established his church among men, that should I have occasion to recur to either age, and particularly to that characterized by the advent of the Messiah, and the ministry of the apostles of that church; with a cursory view of the same till it lost its visibility on earth; was driven into darkness, or till God took the holy priesthood unto himself wher it has been held in reserve to the present century, as a matter of right [p. 51] in this free country, I may take the privilege. This may be doubted by some—indeed by many—as an admission of this point would overthrow the popular systems of the day. I cannot reasonably expect, then, that the large majority of professors will be willing to listen to my argument for a moment, as a careful, impartial, and faithful investigation of the doctrines which I believe to be correct, and the principles cherished in my

---

57. Genesis 5:24 says of Enoch, "God took him"; JS's revision of the Bible adds that "God received it [Zion] up into his own bosom." (Old Testament Revision 1, p. 20 [Moses 7:69].)

bosom—and believed by this church—by every honest man must be admited as truth.

Of this I may say as Tertullian said to the emperor when writing in defence of the saints in his day: "Whoever looked well into our religeon that did not embrace it?"[58]

Common ~~understanding~~ undertakings and plans of men may be overthrown or destroyed by opposition. The systems of this world may be exploded or annihilated by oppression or falshood; but it is the reverse ~~of~~ ⟨with⟩ pure religeon. There is a power attendant on truth that all the arts and designs of men cannot fathom; there is an increasing influence which rises up in one place the moment it is covered in another, and the more it is traduced, and the harsher the means employed to effect its extinction, the more numerous are its votaries.— It is not the vain cry of "delusion" from the giddy multitude;[59] it is not the snears of biggots; it is not the frowns of zealots, neither the rage [of][60] princes, kings, nor emperors, that can prevent its influence.

The fact is as Tertullian said, no man ever looked carefully into its co[n]sistency and propriety without embracing it. It is impossible: That light which enlightens man, is at once enraptured: that intelligence which existed before the world was, will unite, and that wisdom in the Divine economy will be so conspicuous, that it will be embraced, it will be observed, and it must be obeyed!

Look at pure religion whenever it has had a place on earth, and you will always mark the same characteristics in all its features. Look at truth (without which the former could not exist,) and the same pecularities are apparent. Those who have been guided by them have always shown the same principles; and those who were not, have as uniformly sought to destroy their influence.

Religion has had its friends and its enemies; its advocates and its opponents. But the thousands of years which have [p. 52] come and gone, have left it unaltered; millions who have embraced it, and are now enjoying that bliss held forth in its promises, have left its principles unchanged, and its influence upon the honest heart, unweakened. The many oppositions which have encountered it; the millions of calumnies, the numberless reproches, and the myriads of falshoods, have left its fair form unimpaired, its beauty untarnished, and its excellence as excellent; while its certainty is the same, and its foundation upheld by the hand of God!

---

58. Cowdery provides a translation of "Quis non, ubi requisivit, accedit?" (Tertullian, *Apologeticus,* 50.15.)

59. This is probably an allusion to Alexander Campbell, "Delusions," *Millennial Harbinger,* 7 Feb. 1831, 85–96; see also Campbell, *Delusions,* 5–16.

60. Omitted word supplied from *LDS Messenger and Advocate.*

One peculiarity of men I wish to notice in the early part of my narrative.— So far as my acquaintance and knowledge of men and their history extends, it has been the custom of every generation, to boast of, or extol the acts of the former.

In this respect I wish it to be distinctly understood that I mean the righteous,—those to whom God communicated his will. There has ever been an apparent blindness common to men, which has hindred their discovering the real worth and excellence of individuals while residing with them; but when once deprived of their society, worth and councel, they are ready to exclaim, "how great and inestimable were their qualities, and how precious is their memory."

The vilest and most corrupt are not exempted from this charge: even the Jews, whose former principles had become degenerated, and whose religion was a mere show, were found among that class who were ready to build and garnish the sepulchars of the prophets, and condemn their fathers for putting them to death; making important boasts of their own righteousness, and of their assurance of salvation, in the midst of which they rose up with one consent, and treacherously and shamefully betrayed, and crucified the savior of the world! ~~and~~ No wonder that the enquirer has turned aside with disgust, nor marvel that God has appointed a day when he will call the nations before him, and reward every man according to his works!

Enoch walked with God, and was taken home with out tasting death.— Why were not all converted in his day and taken with him to glory? Noah, it is said, was perfect in his generation:[61] and it is plain that he had communion with his maker, and by his direction accomplished a work the parallel of which is not to be found in the annals of the world! Why were not the world converted, that the flood might have been ~~destroyed~~ stayed? Men, from the days of our father Abraham, have talked, boasted, and extolled his faith: and he is even represented in the scriptures:— ["]The father of [p. 53] the faithful."[62] Moses talked with the Lord face to face; received the great moral law, upon the bases of which those of all civillized governments are founded; led Israel forty years, and was taken home to receive the reward of his toils—then Jacob could realize his worth. Well was the question asked by our lord, "How can the children of the bride chamber mourn while the bridegroom is with them"?[63]

It is said, that he travelled and taught the righteous principles of his kingdom three years, during which he chose twelve men, and ordained them

---

61. See Genesis 6:9.
62. See Galatians 3:7–9; and Genesis 22:16–18.
63. See Matthew 9:15.

apostles, &c. The people saw and heard—they were particularly benefited, many of them, by being healed of infirmities, and diseases; of plagues, and devils: they saw him walk upon the water, they saw the winds and waves calmed at his command; they saw thousands fed to the full with a pittance, and the very powers of darkness tremble in his presence—and like others before them considered it as a dream, or a common occurrence, till the time was fulfilled, and he was offered up. Yet while he was with them he said you shall desire to see one of the days of the Son of Man, and shall not see it,[64] He knew calamity would fall upon that people, and the wrath of heaven overtake them to their overthrow, and when that devoted city was surrounded with armies, well may we conclude that they desired a protector possessing sufficient power to lead them to some safe place aside from the tumult of a seige.

Since the apostles fell asleep all men who profess a belief in the truth of their mission, extol their virtues and celebrate their fame. It seems to have been forgotten that they were men of infirmities and subject to all the feelings, passions, and imperfections common to other men. But it appears, that they as others were before them, are looked upon as men of perfection, holiness, ~~and~~ purity, and goodness, far in advance of any since. So were the characters of the prophets held in the days of the apostles. What can be the difference in the reward, whether a man died for righteousness' sake in the days of Abel, Zecharias, John the twelve apostles chosen at Jerusalem, or since? Is not the life of one equally as precious as the other? and is not the truth, Just as true?

But in reviewing the lives and acts of men in past generations, whenever we find a righteous man among them, there always were excuses for not giving heed or credence to his testamony. The people could see his imperfections; or, if no imperfections, supposed ones, and were always ready to frame an excuse upon that for not believeing.— No matter how pure the principles, nor how precious the teachings—an excuse was wanted—and an excuse was had. [p. 54]

The next generation, perhaps, was favored with equally as righteous men, who were condemned upon the same principles of the former while the acts and precepts of the former were the boasts of the multitude; when in reality, their doctrines were no more pure, their exertions to turn men to righteousness no greater, neither their walk any more ~~perfect~~ circumspect—the grave of the former is considered to be holy, and his sepulcher is garnished while the latter is deprived a dwelling among men, or even an existence upon earth! Such is a specimen of the depravity and inconsistency of men, and such has been their conduct toward the righteous in centuries past.

---

64. See Luke 17:22.

When John the son of Zecharias came among the Jews, it is said that he came neither eating bread nor drinking wine. In another place it is said that his meat was locusts and wild honey.[65] The Jews saw him, heard him preach, and were witnesses of the purity of the doctrines advocated—they wanted an excuse, and they soon found one— "He ~~soon found~~ hath a devil!"—[66] And who among all generations, that valued his salvation, would be taught, by or follow one possessed of a devil?

The savior came in form and fashion of a man; he ate, drank, and walked about as a man, and they said "Behold, a man gluttonous, and a wine bibber, a friend of publicans and sinners!"[67] You see an excuse was wanting, but not long wanting till it was found—who would follow a disscipated leader? or who, among the righteous Pharisees would acknowledge a man who would cond[e]scend to eat with publicans and sinners? This was too much—they could not endure it. An individual teaching the doctrines of the kingdom of heaven, and declaring that that kingdom was nigh, or that it had already come, must appear different from others, or he could not be received. If he were athirst he must not drink, if faint he must not eat, and if weary he must not rest, because he had assumed the authority to teach the world righteousness, and he must be different in manners, and in constitution, if not in form, that all might be attracted by his singular appearance: that his singular demeanor might gain the reverence of the people, or he was an imposter—a false teacher—a wicked man—a sinner—and an accomplice of Beelzebub, the prince of devils!

If singularity of appearance, or difference of manners would command respect, certainly John would have been reverenced, and heard. To see one coming from the wilderness, clad with camels' hair, drinking neither wine nor strong drink, nor yet eating common food, must have awakened the curiosity of the curious, to the fullest extent. But there was one peculiarity in this man common to every righteous man before him, for which the people hated him, and for which he lost his life—he taught holiness, proclaimed [p. 55] repentance and baptism for the remission of sins, warned the people of the consequences of eniquity, and declared that the kingdom of heaven was at hand—All this was too much! To see one dressed so rediculously eating no common food, neither drinking wine like other men; stepping in advance of the learned and reverend Pharisees, wise doctors, and righteous scribes, and declaring at the same time, that the Lords kingdom would soon appear, could not be borne—he must not

---

65. See Matthew 3:4.
66. See Matthew 11:18.
67. See Luke 7:34.

teach—he must [not][68] assume—he must not attempt to lead the people after him—"He hath a devil!"

The Jews were willing, (professedly so) to believe the ancient prophets, and follow the directions of heaven as delivered to the world by them; but when one came teaching the same doctrine, and proclaiming the same things, only that they were nearer, they would not hear. Men say if they could see they would believe, but I have thought the reverse, in this respect—If they cannot see they will believe.

One of two reasons may be assigned as the cause why the messengers of truth have been rejected—perhaps both. The multitude saw their imperfections, or supposed ones, and from that framed an excuse for rejecting them, or else in consequence of the corruption of their own hearts, when reproved, were not willing to repent, but saught to make a man an offender for a word:[69] or for wearing camels hair, eating locusts, drinking wine, or showing friendship to publicans and sinners!

When looking over the sacred scriptures we seem to forget that they were given through men of imperfections, and subject to passions. It is a general belief that the ancient proptets [prophets] were perfect—that no stain, or blemish ever appeared upon their characters while on earth, to be brought forward by the opposer as an excuse for not believing. The same is said of the apostles; but James said that Elias [Eligah] was a man subject to like passions as themselves, and yet he had that power with God that in answer to his prayer it rained not on the earth by the space of three years and a half.[70]

There can be no doubt but those to whom he wrote looked upon the ancient prophets as a race of beings superior to any in those days; and in order to be constituted a prophet of God, a man must be perfect in every respect.—

The idea is, that he must be perfect according to their signification of the word. If a people were blessed with prophets, they must be the individuals who were to prescribe the Laws by which they must be governed, even in their private walks. The generation following were ready to suppose, that those men who believed the word of God were as perfect as those to whom it was delivered supposed they must be, and were as forward to prescribe the rules by which they were governed, or rehearse laws and declare them to be the governing principles of the prophets, as though they themse[l]ves held the keys of the mysteries of ~~the~~ heaven, and had searched the archives of the generations of the world.

---

68. Omitted word supplied from *LDS Messenger and Advocate*.
69. See Isaiah 29:21.
70. See James 5:17.

You will see that I have made mention of the Messiah, of his mission into [p. 56] the world, and of his walk and outward appearance, but do not understand me as attempting to place him on a level with men, or his mission or [on]⁷¹ a parallel with those of the prophets and apostles—far from this. I view his mission such as none other could fill; that he was offered without spot to God a propitiation for our sins; that he rose triumphant and victorious over the grave, and him that has ⟨the⟩ power of death.—

This man could not do— It required a perfect sacrafice—man is imperfect— It required a spotless offering—man is not spotless— It required an infinite atonement—man is mortal!

I have, then as you will see, made mention of our Lord, to show that individuals teaching truth, /⁷²whether perfect or imperfect have been looked upon as the worst of men. and that even our Saviour, the great Shepherd of Israel was mocked and derided, and placed on a parallel with the prince of devils; and the prophets and apostles, though at this day, looked upon as perfect as perfection, were concidered the basest of the human family by those among whom they lived. It is not rumor, though it is wafted by every gale, and retriated [reiterated] by every zephyr, upon which we are to found our judgments of ones merits or demerits: If it is we erect an altar upon which we sacrafice the most perfect of men, and establish a criterion by which the "vilest of the vile" may escape censure.

But lest I weary you with too many remarks upon the history of the past, after a few upon the propriety of a narative of the description I have proposed, I shall proceed.—Editor.

Letter III.⁷³

To W[illiam] W. Phelps Esqr.

Dear Brother:—

after a silence of another month, agreeabley to my my promise I proceed upon the subject I proposed in the first No. of the Advocate. Perhaps an apology for brevity may not be improper, here, as many important incidents consequently transpiring in the organization and ~~establishment~~ ⟨establishing⟩ of a society like the one whose history I am about to give to the world, are overlooked or lost, and soon buried with those who were the actors, will prevent my giving those minute and particular reflections which I have so often wished migh[t] have characterized the "Acts of the apostles," and the ancient Saints.

---

71. Correction supplied from *LDS Messenger and Advocate*.
72. TEXT: Frederick G. Williams handwriting ends; Warren Parrish begins.
73. Oliver Cowdery, "Letter III," *LDS Messenger and Advocate*, Dec. 1834, 1:41–43.

But such facts as are within my knowledge, will be given without any reference to inconsistencies, in the minds of others [p. 57] or impossibilities, in the feelings of such as do not give credence to the system of salvation and redemption so clearly set forth and so plainly written over the face of the sacred scriptures:

Upon the propriety, then, of a narative of this kind, I have briefly to remark: It is known to you, that this church has suffered reproach and persecution, from a majority of mankind who have heard but a rumor, since its first organization. and further, you are also conversant with the fact, that no sooner had the messengers of the fulness of the gospel began to proclaim its heavenly precepts, and call upon men to embrace the same, than they were vilified and slandered by thousands who never saw their faces, and much less knew aught derogatory of their characters, moral or religious—upon this unfair and unsaint like manner of procedure they have been giving in large sheets their own opinions of the incorrectness of our system, and attested volum[e]s of our lives and characters. Since, then, our opposers have been thus kind to introduce our cause before the public, it is no more than just that a correct account should be given; and since they have invariably sought to cast a shade over the truth, and hinder its influence from gaining ascindency, it is also, proper that it should be vindicated, by laying before the world a correct statement of of events as they have transpired from time to time.

Whether I shall succeed so far in my purpose as to convince the publick of the incorrectness of those scurulous reports which have inundated our land, or even but a small portion of them, will be better ascertained when I close than when I commence; and I am content to submit it before the candid for perusal, & before the Judge of all for inspection, as I most assuredly believe that before Him I must stand and answer for the deeds transacted in this life.

Should I, however, be instrumental in causing a few to hear before they judge, and understand both sides of this matter before they condemn, I shall have the satisfaction of seeing them embrace it as I am certain that one is the inevitable fruit of the other.

But to proceede:

You will recollect that I informed you, in my letter published in the first No. of the Messenger and Advocate, that this history would necessarily embrace the life and character of our esteemed friend and brother, J. Smith jr. one of the presidents of this church, and for information on that part of the [p. 58] subject, I refer you to his communication of the same, published in this paper.[74] I shall, therfore, pass over that till I come to the 15th year of his life.

---

74. JS to Oliver Cowdery, Kirtland, OH, *LDS Messenger and Advocate,* Dec. 1834, 1:40.

It is necessary to premise this account by relating the situation of the public mind relative to religion, at this time: one Mr. [George] Lane a presiding Elder of the Methodist church, visited Palmyra, and vicinity. Elder Lane was a talented man possessing a good share of literary endowments, and apparent humility. there was a great awakening, or excitement raised on the subject of religion and much enquiry for the word of life. Large additions were made to the Methodist, Presbyterian, and Baptist churches. Mr. Lane's manner of communication was peculiarly calculated to awaken the intellect of the hearer, and arouse the sinner to look about him for safety—much good instruction was always drawn from his discourses on the scriptures, and in common with others, our brother's mind became awakened.

For a length of time the reformation seemed to move in a harmonious manner, but, as the excitement ceased, or those who had expressed anxieties, had professed a belief in the pardoning influence and condescension of the Saviour a general strugle was made by the leading characters of the different sects, for prosolytes. Then strife seemed to take the place of that apparent union and harmony which had previously characterized the moves and exhortations of the old professors, and a cry—I am right—you are wrong—was introduced in their stead.

In this general strife for followers, his mother, one sister, and two of his natural brothers, were persuaded to unite with the Presbyterians.[75] This gave opportunity for further reflection; and as will be seen in the sequel, laid a foundation, or was one means of laying a foundation for the attestation of the truths, or professions of truth, contained in that record called the word of God.

After strong solicitations to unite with one of those different societies, and seeing the apparent proselyting disposition manifested with equal warmth from each, his mind was led to more seriously contemplate the importance of a move of this kind. To profess godliness without its benign influence upon the heart, was a thing so foreign from his feelings, that his spirit was not at rest day nor night. To unite with a society professing to be built upon the only sure founda[p. 59]tion, and that profession be a vain one, was calculated, in its verry nature, the more it was contemplated, the more to arouse the mind to the serious consequ[e]nces of moving hastily, in a course fraught with eternal realities. To say he was right, and still be wrong, could not profit; and amid so many, some must be built upon the sand.

---

75. These family members were JS's mother, Lucy Mack Smith, and his siblings Sophronia, Hyrum, and Samuel. JS later indicated this was in 1820. Lucy wrote that their affiliation began following the death of son Alvin Smith in November 1823. (JS History, vol. A-1, p. 208 herein [Draft 2]; Lucy Mack Smith, History, 1844–1845, bk. 4, [7]–[8]; Backman and Allen, "Membership of Certain of Joseph Smith's Family," 482–484; "Records of the Session of the Presbyterian Church in Palmyra," 29 Mar. 1830.)

In this situation where could he go? if he went to one he was told they were right, and all others were wrong—if to another, the same was heard from those: All professed to be the true church; and if not they were certainly hypocritical, because, if I am presented with a system of religion, and enquire of my teacher whether it is correct, and he informs me that he is not certain, he acknowledges at once that he is teaching without authority, and acting without a commission! If ~~one~~

If one profess a degree of authority or preference in consequence of age or right, and that superiority was without evidence, it was insufficient to convince a mind once aroused to that degree of determination which at that time operated upon him. And upon fa[r]ther reflecting, that the Saviour had said that the gate was strait and the way narrow that lead to life eternal, and that few entered there; and the way was broad, and the gate wide which lead to destruction, and that many crowded its current,[76] a proof from some source was wanting to settle the mind and give peace to the agitated bosom. It is not frequent that the minds of men are exercised with proper determinations relative to obtaining a certainty of the things of God.— They are too apt to rest short of that assurance which the Lord Jesus has so freely offered in his word to man, and which so beautifully characterizes his whole plan of salvation, as revealed to us.

Letter IV.[77]

To W[illiam] W. Phelps, Esqr.

Dear Brother:—

In my last, published in the 3ᵈ No. of the Advocate I apologized for the brief manner in which I should be obliged to give, in many instances, the history of this church. Since then yours [p. 60] yours of Christmas has been received,[78] It was not my wish to be understood that I could not give the leading items of every important occurrence. at least so far as would effect my duty to my fellowmen, in such as contained important information upon the subject of doctrine, and as would render it intelligbly plain; but as there are, in a great house, many vessels, so in the history of a work of this magnitude, many items which would be interesting to those who follow, are forgotten. In fact, I deem every manifestation of the Holy Spirit, dictating the hearts of the saints in the way of righteousness, to be of importance, and this is one reason why I plead an apology.

---

76. See Matthew 7:13–14.
77. Oliver Cowdery, "Letter IV," *LDS Messenger and Advocate,* Feb. 1835, 1:77–80.
78. See William W. Phelps, "Letter No. 4," *LDS Messenger and Advocate,* Feb. 1835, 1:65–67.

wish to be understood that I could not give the leading items of every important occurrence, at least so far as would effect my duty to my fellowmen, in such as contained important information upon the subject of doctrine, and as would render it intelligibly plain; but as there are, in a great house, many vessels, so in the history of a work of this magnitude, many items which would be interesting to those who follow, are forgotten. In fact, I deem every manifestation of the Holy Spirit, dictating the hearts of the saints in the way of righteousness, to be of importance, and this is one reason why I plead an apology.

You will recollect that I mentioned the time of a religious excitement, in Palmyra and vicinity to have been in the 15th year of our brother J. Smith Jr's, age—that was an error in the type —it should have been in the 17th.— You will please remember this correction, as it will be necessary for the full understanding of what will follow in time. This would bring the date down to the year 1823.

I do not deem it to be necessary to write further on the subject of this excitement. It is doubted by many whether any real or essential good ever resulted from such excitements, while others advocate their propriety with warmth.

The mind is easily called up to reflection upon a matter of such deep importance, and it is just that it should be; but there is a regret occupying the heart when we consider the deep anxiety of thousands, who are lead away with a vain imagination, or a groundless hope, no better than the idle wind or the spider's web.

But if others were not benefited, our brother was urged forward and strengthened in the determination to know for himself of the certainty and reality of pure and holy religion.— And it is only necessary for me to say, that while this excitement continued, he continued to call upon the Lord in secret for a full manifestation of divine approbation, and for, to him, the all important information, if a Supreme being did exist, to have an assurance that he was accepted of him. This, most assuredly, was correct— it was right. The Lord has said, long since, and his word remains steadfast, that to him who knocks it shall be opened, & whosoever will, may come and partake of the waters of life freely.

To deny a humble penitent sinner a refreshing draught from this most pure of all fountains, and most desirable of all refreshments, to a thirsty soul, is a matter for the full performance of which the sacred record stands pledged. The Lord never said—"Come unto me, all ye that labor, and are heavy laden, and I will give you rest," to turn a deaf ear to those who were weary, when they call upon him. He never said, by the mouth of the prophet—"Ho, every one that thirsts, come ye to the waters," without passing it as a firm decree, at the same time, that he that should after come, should be filled with a joy unspeakable. Neither did he manifest by the Spirit to John upon the isle—"Let him that is athirst, come," and command him to send the same abroad, under any other consideration, than that "whosoever would, might take the water of life freely," to the remotest ages of time, or while there was a sinner upon his footstool.

These sacred and important promises are looked upon in our day as being given, either to another people, or in a figurative form, and consequently require *spiritualizing*, notwithstanding they are as conspicuously plain, and are meant to be understood according to their *literal* reading, as those passages which teach us of the creation of the world, and of the decree of its Maker to bring its inhabitants to judgment. But to proceed with my narrative.—

On the evening of the 21st of September, 1823, previous to retiring to rest, our brother's mind was unusually wrought up on the subject which had so long agitated his mind—his heart was drawn out in fervent prayer, and his whole soul was so lost to every thing of a temporal nature, that earth, to him, had lost its charms, and all he desired was to be prepared in heart to commune with some kind messenger who could communicate to him the desired information of his acceptance with God.

At length the family retired, and he, as usual, bent his way, though in silence, where others might have rested their weary frames "locked fast in sleep's embrace;" but repose had fled,

Historical letters copied into history. Between October 1834 and October 1835, the *Latter Day Saints' Messenger and Advocate* published a series of eight letters on church history by Oliver Cowdery. In an unusual instance of a printed original serving as a source for a handwritten document, the letters were copied into Joseph Smith's 1834–1836 history. The text that corresponds with this newspaper page is on pages 54–57 herein. Oliver Cowdery, "Letter IV," *LDS Messenger and Advocate,* Feb. 1835, 1:78. (Church History Library, Salt Lake City. Photograph by Welden C. Andersen.)

You will recolect that I mentioned the time of a religious excitement, in Palmyra and vicinity to have been in the 15th year of our brother J. Smith jr's age—that was an error in the type—it should have been in the 17th.—

You will please remember this correction, as it will be necessary for the full understanding of what will follow in time. This would bring the date down to the year 1823.[79]

I do not deem it to be necessary to write further on the subject of this excitement. It is doubted by many whether any real or essential good ever resulted from such excitements, while others advocate their propriety with warmth.

The mind is easily called up to reflection upon a matter of such deep importance, and it is just that it should be; but there is a regret occupying the heart when we consider the deep anxiety of thousands, who are lead away with a vain imagination, or a groundless hope, no better than the idle wind or the spider's web.

But if others wer not benefited, our brother was urged forward and strengthened in the determination to know for himself of the certainty and reality of pure and holy religion.— And it is only necessary for me to say, that while this excitement continued, he continued, he continued to call upon the Lord in secret for a full manifestation of divine approbation, and for, to him the all important information if a Supreme being did exist, to have an assurance that he was accepted of him. This, most assuredly, was correct—it was right. The Lord has said, long since, and his word remains steadfast, that to him who knocks it shall be opened, & whosoever will, may come and partake of the waters of life freely.[80]

To deny a humble penitent sinner a refreshing draught from [p. 61] this most pure of all fountains, and most desirable of all refreshments, to a thirsty soul, is a matter for the full performance of which the sacred record stands pledged. The Lord never said— "Come unto me, all ye that labor, and are heavy laden, and I will give you rest," to turn a deaf ear to those who were weary, when they call upon him. He never said, by the mouth of the prophet "Ho, every one that thirsts, come ye to the waters," without passing it as a firm decree, at the same time, that he that should after come, should be filled with

---

79. Cowdery may have used the editorial interjection regarding an "error in the type" to effect a change in plans between the third and fourth letters. The narrative in the previous letter appears to be setting the stage for a recital of JS's earliest vision, the theophany JS described in the circa summer 1832 history. However, after changing the date, Cowdery recast the revivalism described in "Letter III" as the background for the 1823 visitation of the angel who directed JS to the gold plates. (See JS History, ca. summer 1832, pp. 10–13 herein.)

80. See Matthew 7:7; and Book of Mormon, 1830 ed., 339 [Alma 42:27].

joy unspeakable. Neither did he manifest by the Spirit to John upon the isle—
"Let him that is athirst, come," and command him to send the same abroad,
under any other consideration, than that "whosoever would, might take of the
water of life freely," to the remotest ages of time, or while there was a sinner
upon his footstool.[81]

These sacred and important promises are looked upon in our day as being
given, either to another people, or in a figurative form, and consequently
require spiritualizing, notwithstanding they are as conspicuously plain, and are
meant to be understood according to their literal reading, as those passages
which teaches us of the creation of the world, and of the decree of its Maker to
bring its inhabitants to judgment. But to proceed with my narrative.—

On the evening of the 21st of September, 1823, previous to retiring to rest,
our brother's mind was unusually wrought up on the subject which had so long
agitated his mind—his heart was drawn out in fervent prayer, and his whole
soul was so lost to every thing of a temporal nature, that earth, to him, had lost
its charms, and all he desired was to be prepared in heart to commune with
some kind messenger who could communicate to him the desired information
of his acceptance with God.[82]

At length the family retired, and he, as usual, bent his way, though in
silence, where others might have rested their weary frames "locked fast in sleep's
embrace;" but repose had fled, and accustomed slumber had spread her refreshing hand over others beside him—he continued still to pray—his heart,
though once hard and obdurate, was softend, and that mind which had often
flitted, like the "wild bird of passage," had settled upon a determined basis not
to be decoyed or driven from its purpose.

In this situation hours passed unnumbered—how many or how few I
know not, neither is he able to inform me; but supposes it must have been
eleven or twelve, and perhaps later, as the noise and bustle of the family, in
retiring, had long since [p. 62] ceased.— While continueing in prayer for a
manifestation in some way that his sins were forgiven; endeavouring to exercise
faith in the scriptures, on a sudden a light like that of day, only of a purer and
far more glorious appearance and brightness, burst into the room.— Indeed to
use his own description, the first sight was as though the house was filled with
consuming and unqu[e]nchable fire. This sudden appearance of a light so
bright, as must naturally be expected, occasioned a shock or sensation, visible

81. See Matthew 11:28; Isaiah 55:1; and Revelation 22:17.

82. For JS's accounts of this experience, see JS History, ca. summer 1832, pp. 13–14 herein; JS, Journal,
9–11 Nov. 1835, in *JSP*, J1:87–88 (see also later version, pp. 116–117 herein); JS History Drafts, 1838–ca. 1841,
pp. 220–233 herein; JS, "Church History," pp. 494–495 herein; and JS, "Latter Day Saints," pp. 508–509
herein.

to the extremities of the body. It was, however, followed with a calmness and serenity of mind, and an overwhelming rapture of Joy that surpassed understanding, and in a moment a personage stood before him.[83]

Notwithstanding the room was previously filled with light above the brightness of the sun, as I before describe⟨d,⟩ yet there seemed to be an additional glory surrounding or accompanying this personage, which shone with an increased degree of brilliancy, of which he was in the midst; and though his countenance was as lightning, yet it was of a pleasing, inocent and glorious appearance, so much so, that every fear was banished from the heart, and nothing but calmness pervaded the soul.

It is no easy task to describe the appearance of a messenger from the skies—indeed, I doubt their being an individual clothed with perishable clay, who is capable to do this work. To be sure, the Lord appeared to his apostles after his resurrection, and we do not learn as they were in the least difficultied to look upon him; but from John's description upon Patmos, we learn that he is there represented as most glorious in appearance; and from other items in the sacred scriptures we have the fact recorded where angels appeared and conversed with men, and there was no difficulty on the part of the individuals, to endure their presence; and others where their glory was so conspicuous that they could not endure. The last description or appearance is the one to which I refer, when I say that it is no easy task to describe their glory.

But it may be well to relate the particulars as far as given[.] The stature of this personage was a little above the common size of men in this age; his garment was perfectly white, and had the appearance of being without seam. [p. 63]

Though fear was banished from his heart, yet his surprise was no less when he heard him declare himself to be a messenger sent by commandment of the Lord, to deliver a special message and to witness to him that his sins were forgiven, and that his prayers were heard; and that the scriptures might be fulfilled, which say— "God has chosen the foolish things of the world to confound the things which are mighty; and base things of the world, and things which are despised, has God chosen; yea, and things which are not, to bring to nought things which are that no flesh should glory in his presence. Therefore, says the Lord, I will proceed to do a marvelous work among this people, even a marvelous work and a wonder; the wisdom of their wise shall perish, and the understanding of their prudent shall be hid; for according to his covenant which he made with his ancient saints, his people, the house of Israel must

83. Cowdery in "Letter VI" identified this angelic visitor as Moroni, the last ancient American prophet to write in the Book of Mormon. (JS History, 1834–1836, p. 71 herein; see also [JS], Editorial, *Elders' Journal,* July 1838, 42–44.)

come to a knowledge of the gospel, and own that Messiah whom their fathers rejected, and with them the fulness of the Gentiles be gathered in, to rejoice in one fold under one Shepherd".[84]

"This cannot be brought about untill first certain preparatory things are accomplished, for so has the Lord purposed in his own mind. He has therefore chosen you as an instrument in his hand to bring to light that which shall perform his act, his strange act, and bring to pass a marvelous work and a wonder. Wherever the sound shall go it shall cause the ears of men to tingle, and wherever it shall be proclaimed, the pure in heart shall rejoice, while those who draw near to God with their mouths, and honor him with their lips, while their hearts are far from him, will seek its overthrow, and the destruction of those by whose hands it is carried. Therefore, marvle not if your name is made a derission, and had as a by-word among such, if you are the instrument in bringing it, by the gift of God, to the knowledge of the people."

He then proceeded and gave a general account of the promises made to the fathers, and also gave a history of the aborigenes of this country, and said they were literal descendants of Abraham. He represented them as once being an enlightned and intelligent people, possessing a correct knowledge of the gospel, and the plan of restoration and redemption. He said this history [p. 64] was written and deposited not far from that place, and that it was our brother's privilege, if obedient to the commandments of the Lord, to obtain and translate the same by the means of the Urim and Thummim, which were deposited for that purpose with the record.

"Yet," said he, "the scriptures must be fulfilled before it is translated, which says that the words of a book, which were sealed, were presented to the learned; for thus has[85] God determined to leave men without excuse, and show to the meek that his arm is ⟨not⟩ shortned that it cannot save."[86]

A part of the book was sealed, and was not to be opened yet. The sealed part, said he, contains the same revelation which was given to John upon the isles of Patmos, and when the people of the Lord are prepared, and found worthy, then it will be unfolded unto them.[87]

---

84. See 1 Corinthians 1:27–29; Isaiah 29:14; and John 10:16.

85. TEXT: "has" possibly written over "had".

86. See Isaiah 29:11–12, 59:1.

87. The Book of Mormon promises that "the things which this Apostle of the Lamb [John] shall write, are many things which thou hast seen; and, behold, the remainder shalt thou see." A similar statement concerning visions being recorded and then sealed up appears later in the Book of Mormon: "And when the Lord had said these words, the Lord shewed unto the brother of Jared all the inhabitants of the earth which had been, and also all that would be; and the Lord withheld them not from his sight, even unto the ends of the earth: . . . And the Lord said unto him, Write these things and seal them up, and I will shew

On the subject of bringing to light the unsealed part of this record, it may be proper to say, that our brother was expressly informed, that it must be done with an eye single to the glory of God; if this consideration did not wholly characterize all his procedings in relation to it, the adversary of truth would overcome him, or at least prevent his making that proficiency in this glorious work which he otherwise would.

While describing the place where the record was deposited, he gave a minute relation of it, and the vision of his mind being opened at the same time, he was permitted to view it critically; and previously being acquainted with the place, he was able to follow the direction of the vision, afterward, according to the voice of the angel, and obtain the book.

I close for the present by subscribing myself as ever, your brother in Christ

Oliver Cowdery

Letter V.—[88]

To W[illiam] W. Phelps, Esqr.

Dear Brother:—

Yours of the 6th ult. is received and published in this No.[89] It contains so many questions, that I have thought I would let every man answer [p. 65] for himself; as it would occupy a larger space to answer all of them than would be proper to devote at this time. When I look at the world as it is, and view men as they are, I am not much surprised that they oppose the truth as many, perhaps, and indeed, the more I see the less I marvle on this subject. To talk of heavenly communications, angels' visits, and the inspiration of the Holy Spirit, now, since the apostles have fallen asleep, and men interpret the word of God without the aid of either the Spirit or angels, is a novel thing among the wise, and a piece of blasphemy among the craft-men. But so it is, and it is wisdom that it should be so, because the Holy Spirit does not dwell in unholy temples, nor angels reveal the great work of God to hypocrites. You will notice in my last, on rehearsing the words of the angel, where he communicated to our brother—that his sins were forgiven, and that he was called of the Lord to bring to light, by the gift of inspiration, this important inteligence, an item like the following— "God has chosen the foolish things of the world, and things which are dispised, God has chosen;"[90] &c. This, I conceive to be an important item— Not many mighty and noble, were called in ancient times, because

---

them in mine own due time unto the children of men." (Book of Mormon, 1830 ed., 34, 545 [1 Nephi 14:24; Ether 3:25, 27].)

88. Oliver Cowdery, "Letter V," *LDS Messenger and Advocate,* Mar. 1835, 1:95–96.

89. William W. Phelps, "Letter No. V," *LDS Messenger and Advocate,* Mar. 1835, 1:81–82.

90. See 1 Corinthians 1:27–29, also quoted in Cowdery's previous letter, pp. 58–59 herein.

they always knew so much that God could not teach them, and a man that would listen to the voice of the Lord and follow the teachings of heaven, always was despised, and concidered to be of the foolish class— Paul prooves this fact, when he says, ["]we are made as the filth of the world—the off-scouring of all things unto this day."[91]

I am aware, that a rehearsal of visions of angels at this day, is as inconsistent with a portion of mankind as it formerly was, after all the boast of this wise generation in the knowledge of the truth: but there is a uniformity so complete, that on the reflection, one is led to rejoice that it is so.

In my last I gave an imper[f]ect description of the angel, and was oblieged to do so, for the reason, that my pen would fail to des[c]ribe an angel in his glory, or the glory of God. I also gave a few sentences which he uttered on the subject of the gathering of Israel. &c.

Since writing the former, I have thought it would, perhaps, be interesting to give something more full on this important subject, as well as a revelation of the gospel. That these holy personages should feel a deep interest in the accomplis[p. 66]hment of the glorious purposes of the Lord, in his work in the last days, is consistent, when we view critically, what is recorded of their sayings in the holy Scriptures.

You will remember to have read in daniel— "And at that time, [the last days] shall Michael stand up, the great prince, who stands for the children of thy people"; and also in Revelations— "I am thy fellow servant, and of thy brethren the prophets." Please compare these sayings with that singular expression in Heb. "Are they [angels] not all ministering Spirits, sent forth to minister for them who shall be heirs of salvation?"[92] And then let me ask nine questions: first

Are the angels now in glory, the former prophets and servants of God? secondly: Are they brethren of those who keep his commandments on earth? and thirdly have brethren & fleshly kindred, in the Kingdom of God, feelings of respect and condescension enough to speak to each other, though one may be in heaven and the other on the earth?

Fourthly: If angels are ministering spirits, sent forth to minister for those who shall be heirs of salvation, will they not minister for those heirs? and fifthly, if they do, will any one know it?

Sixthly: will Michael, the archangel, the great prince, stand up in the last days for Israel? Seventhly: will he defend them from their enemies? Eightly, will he lead them, as they were once lead; and ninthly, if so, will he be seen?

91. See 1 Corinthians 4:13.
92. See Daniel 12:1; Revelation 22:9; and Hebrews 1:13–14.

These questions I leave without answering, because the reasoning is so plain, and so many might be brought, that, they must be at hand in the heart and mind of every saint. But to the gospel, and then to the gathering?

The great plan of redemption being prepared before the fall of man, and the salvation of the human family being as precious in the sight of the Lord at one time as at another, before the Messiah came in the flesh and was crucifyed, as after the gospel was preachd, and many were found obedient to the same. This gospel being the same from the beginning, its ordinances were also unchangable. Men were commanded to repent and be baptised by water in the name of the Lord: and were then blessed with the Holy Spirit. The Holy Spirit being thus given, men were enabled to look forward to the time of the coming of the Son of Man, and to rejoice in that day, because through that sacrifice they looked for a remission of their sins, and for their redemption. [p. 67]

Had it not been for this plan of salvation, which God devised before the fall, man must have remained miserable forever, after transgressing the first commandment, because, in consequence of that transgression he had rendered himself unworthy [of] the presence of his Maker. He being therefore cast out, the gospel was preached, and this hope of eternal life was set before him, by the ministering of angels who delivered it as they were commanded.

Not only did the ancients look forward to the time of the coming of the Messiah in the flesh, with delight, but there was another day for which they sought, and for which they prayed. Knowing, as they did, that the fall had brought upon them death, and that man was sensual and evil, they longed for a day when the earth might again rest, and appear as in the beginning—when evil might be unknown upon its face, and all creation enjoy one undisturbed peace for a thousand years.

This being sought for in faith, it pleased the Lord to covenant with them to roll on his purposes untill he should bring it to pass—and though many generations were to be gathered to their fathers, yet the righteous, those who should, in their lives, embrace the gospel, and live obedient to its requirements, rise and inherit it during this reign of peace.

From time to time the faithful servants of the Lord have endeavored to raise up a people who should be found worthy to inherit this rest; (for it was called the rest of the righteous or the day of the Lord's rest, prepared for the righteous;) but were not able to sanctify them, that they could endure the presence of the Lord, excepting Enoch, who, with his people, for their righteousness, were taken into heaven, with a promise that they should yet see that day when the whole earth should be covered with glory.

Moses labored diligently to effect this object, but in consequence of the transgressions and rebellions of the children of Israel, God swore in his wrath that they should not enter into his rest; and in consequence of this decree, and their transgressions since, they have been scattered to the four winds, and are thus to remain till the Lord gathers them in by his own power.[93]

To a remnant of them the gospel was preachd by the [p. 68] Messiah in person, but they rejected his voice, though it was raised daily among them. The apostles continued to hold forth the same; after the crucifixion & resurection of the Lord Jesus, untill they would hear it no longer; and then they were commanded to turn to the Gentiles.

They however labored faithfully to turn that people from error; that they might be the happy partakers of mercy, and save themselves from the impending storm that hung over them. They were commanded to preach Jesus Christ night and day—to preach through him the resurection from the dead—to ~~preach~~ declare that all who would embrace the gospel, repent and be baptized for the remission of their sins, should be saved—to declare that this was the only sure foundation on which they could build and be safe—that God had again visited his people in consequence of his covenant with their fathers, and that if they would, they might be the first who should receive these glad tidings, and have the unspeakable joy of carrying the same to all people; for before the day of rest comes, it must go to all nations, kindred and toungs.

But in consequence of their rejecting the gospel, the Lord suffered them to be again scattered; their land to be wasted and their beautiful city to be troden down of the Gentiles, untill their time should be fulfilled.

In the last days, to fulfill the promises to the ancient prophets, when the Lord is to pour out his Spirit upon all flesh, he has determined to bring to light his gospel, to the Gentiles, that it may go to the house of Israel. This gospel has been perverted and men have wandered in darkness. That commission given to the apostles at Jerusalem, so easy to be understood, has been hid from the world, because of evil, and the honest have been lead by the designing, till there are none to be found who are practising the ordinances of the gospel, as they were anciently delivered.

But the time has now arived, in which, according to his covenants, the Lord will manifest to the faithful that he is the same to-day, and forever, and that the cup of suffering of his people, the house of Israel, is nearly fulfilled; and that the way may be prepared before their face he will bring to the knowledge of the people the gospel, as it ~~is~~ was preached [p. 69] by his servants on this land, and manifest to the obedient the truth of the same, by the power of the Holy Spirit; for the time is near when his sons and daughters will prophesy,

---

93. Compare Revelation, 22 and 23 Sept. 1832, in Doctrine and Covenants 4:4, 1835 ed. [D&C 84:23–24].

old men dream dreams, and young men see vissions, and those who are thus favored will be such as embrace the gospel as it ~~is~~ was delivered in old times, and they shall be blessed with signs following.[94]

Farther on the subject of the gathering of Israel.— This was perfectly understood by all the ancients prophets. Moses prophesied of the affliction which should come upon that people even after the coming of the Messiah, where he said: and evil will befall you in the latter days; ⟨because ye will do evil in the sight of the Lord⟩ to provoke him to anger through the work of your hands.[95] connecting this with a prophecy in the song which follows; which was given to Moses in the tabernacle—remembering the expression—"in the latter days"—where the Lord foretels all their evil, and their being received to mercy, to such as seek the peace of Israel much instruction may be gained. It is as follows:—

["]I will heap mischiefs upon them; I will spend my arrows upon them. They shall be burnt with hunger, and devoured with burning heat: I will also send the teeth of beasts upon them, with the poison of serpents of the dust. The sword without, and terror within, shall destroy both the young man and the virgin, the suckling with the man of gray hairs."[96]

But after all this, he will judge their enemies and avenge them of theirs; for he says:

"if I whet my glettering sword, and my hand take hold on judgment, I will render vengance to my enemies, and will reward them that hate me. I will make my arrows drunk with blood, and my sword shall devour flesh."[97]

After all this—after Israel has been restored, and afflicted and his enemies have also be[e]n chastised, the Lord says: ["]Rejoice O ye nations, with his people: for he will avenge the blood of his servants, and will render vengance to his adversaries, and will be merciful unto his land and to his people."[98]

I will give a fu[r]ther detail of the promises to Israel, hereafter, as rehearsed by the angel. Accept assurance of my esteem as ever. [p. 70]

Letter VI.[99]

To W[illiam] W. Phelps, Esqr.

Dear Sir:—

Yours of the 24[th] February is received and inserted in this No. of the

---

94. See Psalm 144:12; Joel 2:28; and Acts 2:17.

95. See Deuteronomy 31:29.

96. See Deuteronomy 32:23–25.

97. See Deuteronomy 32:41–42.

98. See Deuteronomy 32:43.

99. Oliver Cowdery, "Letter VI," *LDS Messenger and Advocate*, Apr. 1835, 1:108–112.

Advocate[100] When reviewing my letter No. 3, I am lead to conclude, that some expressions contained in it are calculated to call up past scenes, and perhaps, paint them to the mind, in a manner differently than otherwise were it not that you can speak from experiance of their correctness.

I have not space you know, to go into every particular item noticed in yours, as ⟨that⟩[101] would call my attention too far or too much, from the great object lying before me,— the history of this church;— but one expression, or quotation contained in your last strikes the mind (and I may add—the heart,) with so much force, that I cannot pass without noticing it: It is a line or two from that little book contained in the Old Testament, called "Ruth." It says:

["]Entreat me not to leave thee, or to return from following after thee: for whither thou goest, I will go; and where thou lodgest, I will lodge, thy people shall be my people, and thy God my God."[102]

There is a something breathed in this, not known to the world. The great, as many are called, may profess friendship, and covenant to share in each other's toils, for honors and riches of this life, but it is not like the sacrifice offered by Ruth. She forsook her friends, she left her nation, she longed not for the altars of her former gods, and why? because Israels God was God indeed? and by joining herself to Him a reward was offered, and an inheritance promised with him when the earth was sanctified, and peoples, nations and toungs serve him acceptably? And the same covenant of Ruth's, whispers the same assurance in the same promises, and the same knowled[g]e of the same God.

~~There is a something breathed in this, not known to the world. The great, as many are called, may~~

I gave, in my last, a few words, on the subject of a few items, as spoken by the angel at the time the knowledge of the record of the Nephites was communicated to our [p. 71] brother, and in consequence of the subject of the gospel and that of the gathering of Israel's being so connected, I found it difficult to speak of the one without mentioning the other; and this may not be improper, as it is evident, that the Lord has decreed to bring forth the fulness of the gospel in the last days, previous to gathering Jacob, but a preparatory work, and the other is to follow in quick succession.

This being of so much importance, and of so deep interest to the sainst [saints], I have thought best to give a farther detail of the heavenly message,

---

100. William W. Phelps, "Letter No. 6," *LDS Messenger and Advocate,* Apr. 1835, 1:97. The printed letter is dated 21 February.

101. TEXT: Insertion possibly in another (unidentified) hand.

102. See Ruth 1:16.

and if I do not give it in the precise words, shall strictly confine myself to the facts in substance.

David said, (Ps. C.) make a joyful noise unto the Lord, all ye lands, that is, all the earth. Serve the Lord with gladness: come before his presence with singing.[103] This he said in view of the glorious period for which he often prayed, and was anxious to behold, which he knew could not take place untill the knowledge of the glory of God covered all lands, or all the earth. Again he says, (Ps. 107) O give thanks unto the Lord, for he is good: For his mercy endureth forever. Let the redeemed of the Lord say so, whom he has redeemed from the hand of the enemy; and gathered out of the lands from the east, and from the west from the north and from the south.— They wandered in the wilderness in a solitary way; they found no city to dwell in. Hungry and thirsty, their souls fainted in them. Then they cried unto the Lord in their trouble, and he delivered them out of their distresses; and led them in the right way that they might go to the city of habitations.[104]

Most clearly was it shown to the prophets,[105] that the righteous should be gathered from all the earth: He knew that the children of Israel were led from Egypt, by the right hand of the Lord, and permitted to possess the land of Canaan, though they were rebellious in the desert but the farther knew, that they were not gathered from the east, the west, the north and the south, at that time; for it was clearly manifested that the [p. 72] Lord himself would prepare a habitation, even as he said, when he would lead them to a city of refuge In that, David saw a promise for the righteous, [see 144. Ps] when they should be delivered from those who oppressed them, and from the hand of strange children, or the enemies of the Lord; that their sons should be like plants grown up in their youth, and their daughters like corner-stones, polished after the similitude of ⟨a⟩ beautiful palace. It is then that the sons and daughters shall prophesy, old men dreams dreams, and young men see visions.[106] At that time the garners of the righteous will be full, affording all manner of store. It was while contemplating[107] this time, and viewing this happy state of the righteous, that he further says: The Lord shall reign forever, even thy God, O Zion, unto all generations—Praise ye the Lord![108]

Isaiah who was on the earth at the time the ten tribes of Israel were led away captive from the land of canaan, was shown, not only their calamity and

---

103. See Psalm 100:1–2.

104. See Psalm 107:1–7.

105. *LDS Messenger and Advocate* has "prophet."

106. See Psalm 144:12; Joel 2:28; and Acts 2:17.

107. TEXT: "contemplating" possibly written over "contemplation".

108. See Psalm 146:10.

affliction, but the time w[h]en they were to be delivered. After reproving them for their corruption and blindness, he prophesies of their dispersion. He says, Your country is desolate, your cities are burnt with fire: Your land strangers devour in your presence and it is thus made desolate, being overthrown by strangers. He further says while speaking of the iniquity of that people. Thy princes are rebellious and companions of thieves: every one loves gifts, and follows after rewards: They judge not the fatherless, neither does the cause of the widow come unto them. Therefore, says the Lord, the Lord of hosts, the mighty One of Israel, Ah, I will ease me of my adversaries, and avenge me of my enemies.[109] But after this calamity has befallen Israel, and the Lord has poured upon them his afflicting judgments, as he said by the mouth of Moses— I will heap mischiefs upon them I will spend my arrows upon them.— They shall be afflicted with hunger, and devoured with burning heat, and with bitter distruction: I will also send the teeth of beasts upon them, with the poison of serpents of the earth— he will also fulfill this [p. 73] further prediction uttered by the mouth of Isaiah. I will turn my hand upon thee, and purely purge away thy dross, and take way all thy tin: and I will restore thy judges as at the first, and thy counsellors as at the beginning: afterward you shall be called, the city of righteousness, the faithful city.[110] Then will be fulfilled, also, the sayings of David: And he led them forth by the right way, that they might go to a city of habitation.[111]

Isaiah continues his prophecy concerning Israel, and tells them what would be done for them in the last days; for thus it is written: The word that Isaiah the son of Amos saw concerning Juda and Jerusalem. And it shall come to pass in the last days, that the mountain of the Lord's house shall be established in the top of the mountains, and shall be exalted above the hills;— and all nations shall flow unto it. And many people shall go and say, come ye, and let us go up to the mountain of the Lord's Lord, to the house of the God of Jacob; and he will teach us of his ways and we will walk in his paths; for out of Zion shall go forth the law, and the word of the Lord from Jerusalem.— And he shall judge among the nations, and shall rebuke many people: and they shall beat their swords into ploughshares, and their spears into pruning hooks: nation shall not lift up the sword against nation, neither shall they learn war any more. And the Lord will creat[e] upon every dwelling place of his people in Zion, and upon their assemblies, a cloud and smoke by day, and the shining of a flaming fire by night: for upon all the glory shall be a defence, or above, shall

---

109. See Isaiah 1:7, 23–24.
110. See Isaiah 1:25–26.
111. See Psalm 107:7.

be a covering and a defence. And there shall be a tabernacle for a shadow in the day-time from the heat, and for a place or refuge, and for a covert from storm and from rain.[112] And his people shall dwell safely, they shall possess the land forever, even the land which was promised to their fathers for an everlasting inheritance: for behold, says the Lord by the mouth of the prophet: The day will come that I will sow the house of Israel with the seed of man, and with the seed of beast. And it shall come to pass, that like as I have watched over them, to pluck up, and to break down, and ⟨and to throw down and to destroy and⟩ to afflict; so will I watch over them, to [p. 74] build and to plant, says the Lord.[113]

For this happy situation and blessed state of Israel, did the prophets took [look],[114] and obtained a promise, that, though the house of Israel and Juda, should violate the covenant, the Lord in the last days would make with them a new one: not according to the one which he made with their fathers in the day that he took them by the hand to lead them out of the land of Egypt; which said the Lord, my covenant they broke, although I was a husband and a father unto them: but this shall be the covenant that I will make with the house of Israel: After those days, says the Lord, I will put my law in their inward parts, and will write it in their hearts; and I will be their God, and they shall be my people.[115]

For thus says the Lord, I will bring again the captivity of Jacob's tents, and have mercy on his dwelling places; and the city shall be builded upon her own heap, and the palace shall remain after the manner there of. And out of them shall procede thanksgiving, and the voice of them that make merry:— and I will multiply them and they shall not be few; I will also glorify them and they shall not be small. Their ~~and they shall~~ children also shall be as afore time, and their congregation shall be established before me, and I will punish all that opress them. Their nobles shall be of themselves, and their governor shall procede from the midst of them.[116]

At the same time, says the Lord, will I be the God of all the families of Israel, and they shall be my people; I will bring them from the north country, and gather them from the coasts of the earth; I will say to the north Give up, and to the south, Keep not back:— bring my sons from far, and my daughters from the ends of the earth.[117]

---

112. See Isaiah 2:1–4, 4:5–6.

113. See Jeremiah 31:27–28.

114. Correction supplied based on *LDS Messenger and Advocate.*

115. See Jeremiah 31:32–33.

116. See Jeremiah 30:18–21.

117. See Jeremiah 31:1, 8; and Isaiah 43:6.

And in those days, and at that time, says the Lord though Israel and Juda have been driven and scattered, they shall come together, they shall even come weeping: for with supplications will I lead them: they shall go and seek the Lord their God. They shall ask the way to Zion, with their faces thitherward, [p. 75] and say, Come, and let us join ourselves to the Lord, in a perpetual covenant that shall not be forgotten; and ~~watchman~~ ⟨watchmen⟩ upon Mount Ephraim shall say, arise, and let us go up to Zion, unto the holy Mount of the Lord our God; for he will teach us of his ways, and instruct us to walk in his paths. That the way for this to be fully accomplished, may be prepared, the Lord will utterly destroy the toung of the Egyptian sea, and with his mighty wind shake his hand over the river[,] smite it in its seven streams, and make men go over dry-shod. And there shall be a high way for the remnant of his people, which shall be left, from Assyria; like as it was to Israel when they came up out of the land of Egypt.[118]

And thus shall Israel come: not a dark corner of the earth shall remain unexplored, nor an Island of the seas be left without being visited; for as the Lord has ~~said~~ removed them into all corners of the earth, he will cause his mercy to be as abundantly manifested in their gathering as his wrath in their dispersion, untill they are gathered according to the covenant.

He will, as he said by the prophet, send for ~~them~~ many fishers and they shall fish them; and after will I send for many hunters, who shal hunt them; not as their enemies have to afflict, but with glad tidings of great joy, with a message of peace, and a call for their return.[119]

And it will come to pass, that though the house of Israel has forsaken the Lord, and bowed down and worshiping other gods, which were no gods, and been cast out before the face of the world, they will know the voice of the Shepherd when he calls upon them this time; for soon his day of power comes, and in it his people will ~~rejoice~~ be willing to harken to his counsel; and even now are they already beginning to be stired up in their hearts to search for these things, and are daily reading the anci[e]nt prophets, and are marking[120] the times, and seasons of their fulfilment. Thus God is preparing the way for their return.

But it is necessary that you should understand, that what is to be fulfilled in the last days, Is not [p. 76] only for the benefit of Israel, but the Gentiles, if they will repent and embrace the gospel, for they are to be remembered also in

---

118. See Jeremiah 31:9, 50:4–5, 31:6; and Isaiah 2:3, 11:15–16.

119. See Jeremiah 16:16; Nahum 1:15; Romans 10:15; Book of Mormon, 1830 ed., 260 [Alma 13:22]; and Revelation, Sept. 1830–F, in Doctrine and Covenants 53:2, 1835 ed. [D&C 31:3].

120. TEXT: Possibly "making" revised to "marking".

the same covenant, and are to be fellow heirs with thee seed of Abraham, inasmuch as they are so by faith—for God is no respecter to persons. This was shown to Moses, when he wrote— Rejoice, O ye nations, with his people![121]

In consequence of the transgression of the Jews at the coming of the Lord, the Gentiles were called into the kingdom, and for this obediance, are to be favored with the gospel in its fulness first, in the last days; for it is written The first shall be last, and the last first.[122] Therefore, when the fulness of the gospel, as was preached by the rigteous, upon this land, shall come forth, it shall be declared to the Gentiles first, and whoso will repent shall be delivered, for they shall understand the plan of salvation and restoration for Israel, as the Lord manifested to the ancients.— They shall be baptised with water and with the Spirit— they shall lift up their hearts with joy and gladness, for the time of their redemption shall also roll on, and for their obediance to the faith they shall see the house of Jacob come with great glory, even with songs of everlasting joy, and with him partake of salvation.

Therefore, as the time draws near when the sun is to be darkened, the moon turned to blood, and the stars fall from heaven, the Lord will bring to the knowledge of his people his commandments and statutes, that they may be prepared to stand when the earth shall reel to and fro as a drunken man, earthquakes cause the nations to tremble, and the destroying angel goes forth to waste the inhabitance at noon-day: for so great are to be the calamities which are to come upon the inhabitants of the earth, before the coming of the Son of Man the second time, that w[h]oso is not prepared cannot abide; but such as are found faithful, and remain, shall be gathered with his people and caught up to meet the Lord in the clouds, and so shall they inherit eternal life.[123]

I have now given you a rehearsal of what was communicated to our brother, when he was directed to go and obtain [p. 77] the record of the Nephites. I may have missed in arrangement in some instances, but the principle is preserved, and you will be able to bring forward abundance of corroborating scripture upon the subject of the gospel and of the gathering.

You are aware of the fact, that to give a minute rehearsal of a lengthy interview with a heavenly messenger, is verry difficult unless one is assisted immediately with the gift of inspiration. There is another item I wish to notice on the subject of visions. The Spirit you know, searches all things, even the deep things of God. When God manifests to his servants those things that are to

---

121. See Deuteronomy 32:43.

122. See Matthew 19:30; and Book of Mormon, 1830 ed., 137 [Jacob 5:63].

123. See Matthew 24:29; Isaiah 24:20; 1 Thessalonians 4:17; and Revelation, Sept. 1830–A, in Doctrine and Covenants 10:4–5, 1835 ed. [D&C 29:14–21].

come, or those which have been, he does it by unfolding them by the power of
that Spirit which comprehends all things, always; and so much may be shown
and made perfectly plain to the understanding in a short time, that to the
world, who are ocupied all their life to learn a little, look at the relation of it,
and are disposed to call it false. You will understand then, by this, that while
those glorious things were being rehearsed, the vision was also opened, so that
our brother was permitted to see and understand much more full⟨y⟩ and
perfect⟨ly⟩ than I am able to communicate in writing. I know much may ⟨be⟩
conveyed to the understanding in writing, and many marvellous truths set
forth with the pen, but after all it is but a shadow, compared to an open vision
of seeing, hearing and realizing eternal things. And if the fact was known, it
would be found, that of all the heavenly communications to the ancients, we
have no more in comparison than the alphabet to a quarto vocabulary. It is
said, and I believe the account, that the Lord showd the brother of Jared
(Moriancumer) all things which were to transpire from that day to the end of
the earth, as well as those which had taken place.[124] I believe that Moses was
permitted to see the same, as the Lord caused them to pass, in vission before
him as he stood upon the mount;[125] I believe that the Lord Jesus told many
things to his apostles which are not written, and after his ascension unfolded
all things unto them; I believe that Nephi, the son of Lehi, whom the Lord
brought out of Jerusalem, saw the same; I believe that the twelve upon this
continent, whom the Lord chose to preach his gospel, when he came down to
manifest to this branch of the house of Israel, [p. 78] that he had other sheep,
who should hear his voice, were also permitted to behold the same mighty
things transpire in vision before their eyes; and I believe that the angel Moroni,
whose words I have been rehearsing, w[h]o communicated the knowledge of
the record of the Nephites, in this age, saw also, before he hid up the same
unto the Lord, great and marvelous things, which were to transpire when the
same should come forth; and I also believe, that God will ⟨give⟩ line upon line
precept upon precept to his saints, until all these things will be unfolded to
them, and they finally sanctified and brought into the Celestial glory, where
tears will be wiped from all faces, and sighing and sorrowing flee away!

May the Lord preserve you from evil and reward you richly for all your
afflictions, and crown you in his kingdom. Amen.

Accept, as ever, assurances of the fellowship and esteem of your unworthy
brother in the gospel.

---

124. See Book of Mormon, 1830 ed., 545 [Ether 3:25–26].
125. See Old Testament Revision 1, pp. 1–2 [Moses 1:8, 27–29].

Letter VII.[126]

To W[illiam] W. Phelps, Esqr.

Dear Brother:—

Circumstances having heretofore intervened to prevent my addressing you previously upon the history of this church you will not attribute the neglect to any want on my part, of a disposition to prosecute a subject so dear to me and so important to every saint, living as we do in the day when the Lord has began to fulfill his covenants to his long-dispersed and afflicted people.

Since my last yours of May and June have been received.[127] It will not be expected that I shall digress so far from my object, as to go into particular explanations on different items contained in yours; but as all men are deeply interested on the great matter of revelation, I indulge a hope that you will present such facts as are plain and uncontrovertible, both from our former scriptures and the book of Mormon, [p. 79] to show that such is not only consistent with the character of the Lord, but absolutely necessary to the fulfilment of that sacred volume, so tenaciously admired by professors of religion—I mean that called the bible.

You have, no doubt, ase well as myself, frequently heard those who do not pretend to an "experimental" belief in the Lord Jesus, says, with those who do, that, (to use a familiar phrase,) "any tune can be played upon the bible:"— What is here meant to be conveyed, I suppose, is, that proof can be adduced from that volum[e], to support as many different systems as men please to choose: one saying this is the way, and the other, this is the way, while the third says, that it is all false, and that he can "play this tune upon it." If this is so, alas for our condition: admit this to be the case, and either wicked and designing men have taken from it those plain and easy items,[128] or it never came from Deity, if that Being is perfect and consistent in his ways.

But although I am ready to admit that men, in previous generations, have with polluted hands and corrupt hearts, taken from the sacred oracles many precious items which were plain of comprehension, for the main purpose of building themselves up in the trifling things of this world, yet, when it is carefully e[x]amined a straight forward consistency will be found, sufficient to check the vicious heart of man and teach him to revere a word so precious, handed down to us from our fathers, teaching us that by faith we can approach the same benevolent Being, and receive for ourselves a sure word of prophecy,

---

126. Oliver Cowdery, "Letter VII," *LDS Messenger and Advocate,* July 1835, 1:155–159.

127. See William W. Phelps, "Letter No. 7," *LDS Messenger and Advocate,* May 1835, 1:114–115; and William W. Phelps, "Letter No. 8," *LDS Messenger and Advocate,* June 1835, 1:129–131.

128. See Book of Mormon, 1830 ed., 30 [1 Nephi 13:26].

which will serve as a light in a dark place,[129] to lead to those things within the vail, where peace, righteousness and harmony, in one uninterrupted round, feast the inhabitants of those blissful regions in endless day.

Scarce can the reflecting mind be brought to contemplate these scenes, without asking, for whom are they held in reserve, and by whom are they to be [p. 80] enjoyed? Have we an interest there? Do [*illegible*][130] our fathers, who have waded through affliction and adversity, who have been cast out from the society of this world, whose tears have, times without number, watered their, furrowed faces, while mourning over the corruption of their fellow-men, an inheritance in those mansions? If so, can they without us be made perfect?[131] Will their joy be full till we rest with them? And is their efficacy and virtue sufficient, in the blood of a Saviour, who groaned upon Calvary's summit, to expiate our sins and cleans us from all unrighteousness? I trust, that as individuals acquainted withe the gospel, through repentance, baptism and keeping the commandments of that same Lord, we shall eventually, be brought to partake in the fulness of that which we now only participate—the full enjoyment of the presence of our Lord.

Happy indeed, will be that hour to all saints, and above all to be desired, (for it never ends,) when men will again mingle praise with those who do always behold the face of our Father who is in heaven.

You will remember that in my last I brought my subject down to the evening, or night of the 21st of September, 1823, and gave an outline of the conversation of the angel upon the important fact of the blessings, promises and covenants to Israel, and the great manyifestations of favor to the world, in the ushering in of the fulness of the gospel, to prepare the way for the second advent of the Messiah, when he comes in the glory of the Fathers with the holy angels.

A remarkable fact is to be noticed with ⟨regard⟩ to this vision. In ancient times the Lord warned some of his servants in dreams: for instance, Joseph, the husband of Mary, was warned in a dream to take the young child and his mother, and flee into Egypt: also, the wise men were warned of the Lord in a dream not to return to Herod; and when "out of ⟨Egypt⟩ the Son was called" the angel of the Lord appeard in a dream to Joseph again: [p. 81] also he was warned in a dream to turn aside into the parts of Galilee.[132] Such were the manifestations to Joseph, the favoured descendant of the father of the faithful

---

129. See 2 Peter 1:19.
130. TEXT: Possibly "~~we~~".
131. See Hebrews 11:40.
132. See Matthew 2:12–13, 22.

in dreams, and in them the Lord fulfilled his purposes: But the one of which I have been speaking is what would have been called an open vision. And though it was in the night, yet it was not a dream. There is no room for conjecture in this matter, and to talk of deception would be to sport with the common sense of every man who knows when he is awake, when he sees and when he does not see.

He could not have been decieved in the fact that a being of some kind appeared to him; and that it was an heavenly one, the fulfillment of his words, so minutely, up to this time, in addition to the truth and word of salvation which has been developed to this generation, in the book of Mormon, ought to be conclusive evidence to the mind of every man who is priveleged to hear of the same. He was awake, and in solem prayer, as you will bear in mind, when the angel made his appearance; from that glory which surrounded him the room was lit up to a perfect brilliancy, so that darkness wholly disappeared: he heard his words with his ears, and recieved a joy and happiness indiscribable by hearing that his own sins were forgiven, and his former transgressions to be remembered against him no more, if he then continued to walk before the Lord according to his holy commandments. He also saw him depart, the light and glory withdraw, leaving a calmness and peace of soul past the language of man to paint—was he deceived?

Far from this; for the vision was renewed twice before morning, unfolding farther and still farther the mysteries of godliness and those things to come. In the morning he went. to his labour as us[u]al, but soon the vision of the heavenly messenger was renewed, [p. 82] instructing him to go immediately and view those things of which he had been informed, with a promise that he should obtain them if he followed the directions and went with an eye single to the glory of God.

Accordingly he repaired to the place which had thus been described. But it is necessary to give you more fully the express instructions of the angel, with regard to the object of this work in which our brother had now engaged— He was to remember that it was the work of the Lord, to fulfil certain promises previously made to a branch of the house of Israel, of the tribe of Joseph, and when it should be brought forth must be done expressly with an eye, as I said before, single to the glory of God, and the welfare and restoration of the house of Israel.

You will understand, then, that no motive of a pecuniary, or earthly nature, was to be suffered to take the lead of the heart of the man thus favoured. The allurements of vice, the contaminating influence of wealth, without the direct guidance of the Holy Spirit, must have no place in the heart nor be suffered to take from it that warm desire for the glory and kingdom of the Lord, or instead of obtaining, disapointment and reproof would most assuredly follow. Such was the instruction and this the caution.

Alternately, as we could naturally expect, the thought of the previous vision was ruminating in his mind, with a reflection of the brightness and glory of the heavenly messenger; but again a thought would start across the mind on the prospects of obtaining so desirable a treasure—one in all human probility sufficient to raise him above a level with the common earthly fortunes of his fellow men, and relieve his family from want, in which, by misfortune and sickness they were placed.

It is verry natural to suppose that the mind would revolve upon those scenes which had passed, when those who had acquired a little of this world's goods, by industry and economy, with the blessings of health or friends, or by art and intrigue [p. 83] from the pockets of the day-labourer, or the widow and the fatherless, had passed by with a stif neck and a cold heart, scorning the virtuous because they were poor, and Lording over those who were subjected to suffer the miseries of this life.

Alternately did these, with a swift reflection of the words of the holy messenger,—"Remember, that he who does this work, who is thus favored of the Lord, must do it with his eye single to the glory of the same, and the welfare and restoration of the scattered remnants of the house of Israel"—rush upon his mind with the quickness of electricity. Here was a strugle indeed; for when he calmly reflected upon his errand, he knew that if God did not give, he could not obtain; and again, with the thought or hope of obtaining, his mind would be carried back to its former reflections of poverty, abuce,— wealth, grandure and ease, until before arriving at the place described, this wholly occupied his desires; and when he thought upon the fact of what was previously shown him, it was only with an assurance that he should obtain, and accomplish his desires in relieving himself and friends from want.

A history of the inhabitants who peopled this continent, previous to its being discovered to Europeans by Columbus, must be interesting to every man; and as it would develope the important fact, that the present race were descendants of Abraham, and were to be remembered in the immutable covenant of the Most High to that man, and be restored to a knowledge of the gospel, that they, with all nations might rejoice, seemed to inspire further thoughts of gain and income from such a valuable history. Surely, thought he every man will sieze with eagerness, this knowledge, and this incalculable incom[e] will be mine. Enough to raise the expectations of any one of like inexperience, placed in similar circumstances. But the important point in this matter is, that man does not see as the Lord, neither are his purposes like his.

The small things of this life are but dust in comparison with salvation [p. 84] and eternal life.

~~Alternately did these,~~ It is sufficient to say that such were his reflections during his walk of from two to three miles: the distance from his father's house to the place pointed out. And to use his own words it seemed as though two invisible powers were influencing or striving to influence his mind—one with the reflection that if he obtained the object of his pursuit, it would be through the mercy and condescention of the Lord, and that every act or performance in relation to it, must be in strict ~~according~~ accordance with the instruction of that personage, who communicated the inteligence to him first; and the other with the tho'ts and reflections like those previously mentioned— contrasting his former and present circumstances in life with those to come. That precious instruction recorded on the sacred page—pray always—which was expresly impressed upon him, was at length entirely forgotten, and as I previously remarked, a fixed determination to obtain and agrandize himself, ocupied his mind when he arrived at the place where the record was found.

I must now give you some description of the place where, and the manner in which these records were deposited.

You are acquainted with the mail road from Palmyra, Wayne Co. to Canandaigua, Ontario Co. N.Y. and also, as you pass from the former to the latter place, before arriving at the little village of Manchester, say from three to four, or about four miles from Palmyra, you pass a large hill on the east side of the road. Why I say large, is because it is as large perhaps, as any in that country. To a person acquainted with this road, a description would be unnecessary, as it is the largest and rises the highest of any on that rout. The north end rises quite sudden until it assumes a level with the more southerly extremity, and I think I may say an elevation higher than at the south a short distance, say half or three fourths of a mile. As you pass toward canandaigua it lessens gradually until the surface assumes [p. 85] ~~a level with the more southerly extremity, and I think I may,~~ its common level, or is broken by other smaller hills or ridges, water courses and ravines. I think I am justified in saying that this is the highest hill for some distance round, and I am certain that its appearance, as it rises so suddenly from a plain on the north, must attract the notice of the traveller as he passes by.

At about one mile west rises another ridge of less height, running parallel with the former, leaving a beautiful vale between. The soil is of the first quality for the country, and under a state of cultivation, which gives a prospect at once imposing, when one reflects on the fact, that here, between these hills, the entire power and national strength of both the Jaredites and Nephites were destroyed.

By turning to the 529th and 530th pages of the book of Mormon[133] you will read Mormon's account of the last great struggle of his people, as they were encamped round this hill Cumorah. (it is printed Camorah, which is an error.) In this vally fell the remaining strength and pride of a once powerful people, the Nephites—once so highly favored of the Lord, but at that time in darkness, doomed to suffer extermination by the hand of their barbarous and uncivilized brethren. From the top of this hill, Mormon, with a few others, after the battle, gazed with horror upon the mangled remains of those who, the day before, were filled with anxiety, hope or doubt. A few had fled to the South, who were hunted down by the victorious party, and all who would not deny the Saviour and his religion, were put to death. Mormon himself, according to the record of his son Moroni, was also slain.

But a long time previous to this disaster it appears from his own account, he foresaw approaching destruction. In fact, if he perused the records of his fathers, [p. 86] which were in his possession, he could have learned that such would be the case. Alma, who lived before the coming of the Messiah, prophesies this.[134] He, however, by divine appointment, abridged from those records, in his own style and language, a short account of the more important and prominent items, from the days of Lehi to his own time, after which he deposited, as he says, on the 529th page, all the records in this same hill, Cumorah and after gave his small record to his son Moroni, who, as appears from the same, finished, after witnessing the extinction of his people as a nation.

It was not the wicked who overcame the righteous; far from this: it was the wicked against the wicked, and by the wicked the wicked were punished.—[135] The Nephites who were once enlightened, had fallen from a more elevated standing as to favour and privilege before the Lord in consequence of the righteousness of their fathers, and now falling below, for such was actually the case, were suffered to be overcome, and the land was left to the possession of the red men, who were without inteligence, only in the affairs of their wars; and having no records, only preserving their history by tradition from father to son, lost the account of their true origin, and wandered from river to river, from hill to hill, from mountain to mountain, and from sea to sea, till the land was again peopled, in a measure, by a rude, wild, revengful, warlike and barbarous race.— Such are our indians.

---

133. Now Mormon chap. 6.
134. See Book of Mormon, 1830 ed., 348–349 [Alma 45:9–14].
135. See Book of Mormon, 1830 ed., 525 [Mormon 4:5].

This hill, by the Jaredites, was called Ramah: by it, or around it pitched the famous army of Coriantumr their tents.[136] Coriantumr was the last king of the Jaredites The opposing army were to the west, and in this same vally, and near by, from day to day, did that mighty race spill their blood, in wrath, contending, as it were, brother against brother, and father, against son. In this same spot, in full view from the top of this same hill, one may gaze with astonishment upon the ground which was twice covered with the dead and dying of our fellow men. Here may be seen where once sunk to nought the pride and strength of two mighty nations; and here [p. 87] may be contemplated, in solitude, while nothing but the faithful record of Mormon and Moroni is now extant to inform us of the fact, scenes of misery and distress—the aged, whose silver locks in other places and at other times would command reverence; the mother, who in other circumstances would be spared from violence; the infant, whose tender cries would be regarded and listened to with a feeling of compassion and tenderness; and the virgin, whose grace, beauty and modesty, would be esteemed and held inviolate by all good men and enlightened and civilized nations, alike disregarded and treated with scorn!—in vain did the hoary head and man of gray hairs ask for mercy; in vain did the mother plead for compassion; in vain did the helpless and harmless infant weep for verry anguish, and in vain did the virgin seek to escape the ruthless hand of revengeful foes and demons in human form—all alike were trampled down by the feet of the strong, and crushed beneath the rage of battle and war! Alas, who can reflect upon the last struggles of great and populous nations, sinking to dust beneath the ⟨hand of Justice and retribution without⟩ weeping over the corruptions of the human heart, and sighing for the hour when the clangor of arms shall no more be heard, nor the calamities of contending armies no more experience⟨d⟩ for a thousand years? Alas, the ~~calamities~~ calamity of war, the extinction of nations,[137] the ruin of kingdoms, the fall of empires and the disolution of governments! O the misery, distress and evil attendant on these! Who can contemplate like scenes without sorrowing, and who so destitute of commiseration as not to be pained that man has fallen so low, so far beneath the station in which he was created?

In this vale lie commingled, in one mass of ruin the ashes of thousands, and in this vale was destined to consume the fair forms and vigerous systems of tens of thousands of the human race—blood mixed with blood, flesh with flesh, bones with bones and dust with dust! When the vital spark which [p. 88] animated their clay had fled, each lifeless lump lay on one common level—

---

136. See Book of Mormon, 1830 ed., 571 [Ether 15:11].
137. TEXT: Possibly "nation⟨s⟩".

cold and inanimate. Those bosoms which had burned with rage against each other for real or suposed injury, had now ceased to heave with malice; those arms which were, a few moments before nerved with strength, had alike become paralized and those hearts which had been fired with revenge, had now ceased to beat, and the head to think—in silence, in solitude, and in disgrace alike, they have long since turned to earth, to their mother dust, to await the august, and to millions, awful hour, when the trump of the Son of God shall echo and reecho from the skies, and they come forth, quickened and immortalized, to not only stand in each other's presence, but before the bar of him who is Eternal!

with sentiments of pure respect, I conclude by subscribing myself, your brother in the gospel,

Oliver Cowdery.

Letter VIII.[138]

Dear Brother,—

In my last I said I should give, partially, a "description of the place where, and the manner in which these records were deposited:" the first promise I have fulfilled, and must proceed to the latter:

The hill of which I have been speaking, at the time mentioned, presented a varied appearance: the north end rose suddenly from the plain, forming a promontory without timber, but covered with grass. As you passed to the south you soon came to scattering timber, the surface having been cleared by art or by wind; and a short distance further left, you are surrounded with the common forest of the country. It is necessary to observe, that even the part cleared was only occupied for pasturage, its steep ascent and narrow summit not admitting the plow of the husbandman, with any degree of [p. 89] ease or profit. It was at the second mentioned place where the record was found to be deposited, on the west side of the hill, not far from the top down its side; and when myself visited the place in the year 1830, there were several trees standing: enough to cause a shade in summer, but not so much as to prevent the surface being covered with grass—which was also the case when the record was first found.

Whatever may be the feeling of men on the reflection of past acts which have been performed on certain portions or spots of this earth, I know not, neither does it add or diminish to nor from the reality of my subject. When Moses heard the voice of God, at the foot of Horeb, out of the burning bush, he was commanded to take his shoes off his feet, for the ground on which he

---

138. Oliver Cowdery, "Letter VIII," *LDS Messenger and Advocate*, Oct. 1835, 2:195–202.

stood was holy. The same may be observed when Joshua beheld the "Captain of the Lord's host" by Jericho— And I confess that my mind was filled with many reflections; and though I did not then loose my shoe, yet with gratitude to God did I offer up the sacrifice of my heart.

How far below the surface these records were placed by Moroni, I am unable to say; but from the fact they had been some fourteen hundred years buried, and that too on the side of a hill so steep, one is ready to conclude that they were some feet below, as the earth would naturally wear more or less in that length of time. But they being placed toward the top of the hill, the ground would not remove as much as at two-thirds, perhaps. Another circumstance would prevent a wearing away of the earth: in all probability, as soon as timber had time to grow, the hill was covered, after the Nephites were destroyed, and the roots of the same would hold the surface. However, on this point I shall leave every man to draw his own conclusion, and form his own speculation, as I only promised to give a description of the place at the time the records were found [p. 90] in 1823.—[139] It is sufficient for my present purpose, to know, that such is the fact: that in 1823, yes, 1823, a man with whom I have had the most intimate and personal acquaintance, for almost seven years, actually discovered by the vision of God, the plates from which the book of Mormon, as much as much as it is disbelieved, was translated! Such is the case, though men rack their verry brains to invent falshood, and then waft them upon every breeze, to the contrary notwithstanding.

I have now given sufficent on the subject of the hill Cumorah—it has a singular and imposing appearance for that country, and must ex[c]ite the curiosity curious enquiry of every lover of the book of Mormon: though I hope never like Jerusalem and the sepulcher of our Lord, the pilgrims. In my estimation, certain places are dearer to me for what they now contain than for what they have contained. For the satisfaction of such as believe I have been thus particular, and to avoid the question being a thousand times asked, more than any other cause, shall procede and be as particular as heretofore. The manner in which the plates were deposited:

First, a hole of sufficient depth, (how deep I know not) was dug. At the bottom of this was laid a stone of suitable size, the upper surface being smooth. At each edge was placed a large quantity of cement, and into this cement, at the four edges of this stone, were placed, erect, four others, their bottom edges resting in the cement at the outer edges of the first stone. The four last named, when placed erect, formed a box, the corners, or where the edges of the four came in contact, were also cemented so firmly that the moisture from without

139. TEXT: Possibly "1825 1823".

was prevented from entering. It is to be observed, also, that the inner surface of the four erect, or side stones was smoothe. This box was sufficiently large to admit a breast-plate, such as was used by the ancients to defend the chest, &c. from the arrows and weapons of their enemy. From the bottom of the box, or from the breast-plate, arose three small pillars composed of the same description of cement used on the edges; and upon these three pillars was [p. 91] placed the record of the children of Joseph, and of a people who left the tower far, far before the days of Joseph, or a sketch of each, which had it not been for this, and the never failing goodness of God, we might have perished in our sins, having been left to bow down before the altars of the Gentiles and to have paid homage to the priests of Baal! I must not forget to say that this box, containing[140] the record was covered with another stone, the bottom surface being flat and the upper, crowning. But those three pillars were not so lengthy as to cause the plates and the crowning stone to come in contact. I have now given you, according to my promise, the manner in which this record was deposited;[141] though when it was first visited by our brother, in 1823, a part of the crowning stone was visible above the surface while the edges were concealed by the soil and grass, from which circumstances you will see, that however deep this box might have been placed by Moroni at first, the time had been sufficient to wear the earth so that it was easily discovered when once directed, and yet not enough to make a perceivable difference to the passer-by. So wonderful are the works of the Almighty, and so far from our finding out are his ways, that one who trembles to take his holy name into his lips, is left to wonder at his exact providences, and the fulfilment of his purposes in the event of times and seasons.

A few years sooner might have found even the top stone concealed, and discouraged our brother from attempting to make a further trial to obtain this rich treasure, for fear of discovery; and a few latter might have lef[t] the small box uncovered, and exposed its valuable contents to the rude calculations and vain speculations of those who neither understand common language nor fear God.

But such would have been contra[r]y to the words of the ancients and the promises made to them: and this is why I am left to admire the works and see the wisdom in the designs of the Lord [p. 92] in all things manifested to the eyes of the world: they show that all human inventions are like the vapors, while his word endures forever and his promises to the last generation.

---

140. TEXT: Possibly "~~containes~~ containing".

141. JS's later account of his first visit to Cumorah, including a description of the box and its contents, is found in JS History, vol. A-1, pp. 232–234 herein (Draft 2).

Having thus digressed from my main subject to give a few items for the special benefit of all, it will be necessary to return, and proceed as formerly.—

And if any suppose I have indulged too freely in reflections, I will only say that it is my opinion, were one to have a view of the glory of God which is to cover Israel in the last days, and know that these, though they may be thought small things, were the beginning to effect the same, they would be at a loss where to close, should they give a moment's vent to the imaginations of the heart

You will have woundered, perhaps, that the mind of our brother should be occupied with the thoughts of the goods of this world, at the time of arriving at Cumorah, on the morning of the 22nd of September, 1823, after having been rapt in the visions of heaven during the night, and also seeing and hearing in open day; but the mind of man is easily turned, if it is not held by the power of God through the prayer of faith, and you will remember that I have said that two invisible powers were operating upon his mind during his walk from his residence to Chumorah, and that the one urging the certainty of wealth and ease in this life, had so powerfully wrought upon him, that the great object so carefully and impressively ⟨named by the angel had entirely⟩ gone from his recollection that only a fixed determination to obtain now urged him forward. In this, which occasioned a failure to obtain, at that time, the record, do not understand me to attach blame to our brother: he was young, and his mind easily turned from correct principles, unless he could be favoured with a certain round of experience. And yet, while young, untraditionated and ⟨un⟩taught in the systems of the world, he was in a situation to be lead into the great work of God, and be qualified to [p. 93] perform it in due time.

After arriving at the repository, a little exertion in removing the soil from the edges of the top of the box, and a light pry, brought to his natural vision its contents. No sooner did he behold this sacred treasure than his hopes were renewed, and he supposed his success certain; and without first attempting to take it from its long place of deposit, he thought, perhaps, there might be something more, equally as valuable, and to take only the plates, might give others an opertunity of obtaining the remainder, which could he secure, would still add to his store of wealth. These, in short, were his reflections, without once thinking of the solemn instruction of the heavenly messenger, that all must be done with an express view of glorifying God.

On attempting to take possession of the records a shock was produced upon his system, by an invisible power, which deprived him in a measure, of his natural strength. He desisted for an instant, and then made another attempt, but was more sensibly shocked than before. What was the occasion of this he knew not—there was the pure unsulied record, as had been described—

he had heard of the power, of enchantment, and a thousand like stories, which held the hidden treasures of the earth, and suposed that physical exertion and personal strength was only necessary to enable him to yet obtain the object of his wish. He therefore made the third attempt with an increased exertion, when his strength failed him more than at either of the former times, and without premeditation he exclaimed, "why can I not obtained this book?" ["]because you have not kept the commandments of the Lord", answered a voice, within a seeming short distance. He looked, and to his astonishment, there stood the angel who had previously given him the directions concerning this matter. [p. 94] In an instant, all the former instructions, the great inteligence concerning Israel and the last days, were brought to his mind: he thought of the time when his heart was fervently engaged in prayer to the Lord, when his spirit was contrite, and when his holy ~~message~~ messenger, from the skies unfold[ed] the wonderful things connected with this record. He had come, to be sure, and found the word of the angel ~~fully~~ fullfilled concerning the reality of the record but he had failed to remember the great end for which they had been kept, and in consequence could not have power to take them into his possession and bear them away.

At that instant he looked to the Lord in prayer, and as he prayed darkness began to disperse from his mind and his soul was lit up as it was the evening before, and he was filled with the Holy Spirit; and again did the Lord manifest his condescension and mercy: the heavens were opened and the glory of the Lord shone round about and rested upon him. While he thus stood gazing and admiring, the angel said, "Look!" and as he thus spake he beheld the prince of darkness, surrounded by his innumerable train of associates.

All this passed before him, and the heavenly messenger said, "All this is shown, the good and the evill, the holy and impure, the glory of God and the power of darkness, that you may know hereafter the two powers and never be influenced or overcome by that wicked one Behold, whatever entices and leads to good and to do good, is of God, and whatever does not is of that wicked one,[142] It is he that fills the hearts of men with evil, to walk in darkness and blaspheme God; and you may learn from henceforth, that his ways are to destruction, but the way of holiness is peace and rest. You now see why you could not obtain this record; that the commandment was strict, and that if ever these sacred things are obtained they must be by prayer and faithfulness in obeying the Lord. They are not deposited here for [p. 95] the sake of accumulating gain and wealth for the glory of this world: they were seald by the prayer of faith, and because of the knowledge which they contain they are of

---

142. See Book of Mormon, 1830 ed., 577–578 [Moroni 7:13–14].

no worth among the children of men, only for their knowledge. On them is contained the fulness of the gospel of Jesus Christ, as it was given to his peopel on this land, and when it shall be brought forth by the power of God it shall be carried to the Gentiles, of whom many will receive it, and after will the seed of Israel be brought into the fold of their Redeemer by obeying it also. Those who kept the commandments of the Lord on this land, desired this at his hand, and through the prayer of faith obtained the promise, that if their descendants should transgress and fall away, that a record might be kept and in the last days come to their children. These things are sacred, and must be kept so, for the promise of the Lord concerning them must be fulfilled. No man can obtain them if his heart is impure, because the⟨y⟩ contain that which is sacred; and besides, should they be entrusted in unholy hands the knowledge could not come to the world, because they cannot be interpreted by the learning of this generation; consequently, they would be considered of no worth, only as precious metal. Therefore, remember, that they are to be translated by the gift and power of God. By them will the Lord work a great and a marvelous work: the wisdom of the wise shall become as nought, and the understanding of the prudent shall be hid,[143] and because the power of God shall be displayed those who profess to know the truth but walk in deceit, shall tremble with anger; but with signs and with wonders, with gifts and with healings, with the manifestations of the power of God, and with the Holy Ghost, shall the hearts of the faithful be comforted. You have now beheld the power of God manifested and the power of Satan: you see that there is nothing that is desirable in the works of darkness; that they cannot [p. 96] bring happiness; that those who are overcome therewith are miserable, while on the other hand the righteous are blessed with a place in the kingdom of God where joy unspeakable surrounds them. There they rest beyond the power of the enemy of truth, where no evil can disturb them. The glory of God crowns them, and they continually feast upon his goodness and enjoy his smiles. Behold, notwithstanding you have seen this great display of power, by which you may ever be able to detect the evil one, yet I give unto you another sign, and when it comes to pass then know that the Lord is God and that he will fulfil his purposes, and that the knowledge which this record contains will go to every nation, and kindred and toung, and people under the whole heaven.— This is the sign: When these things begin to be known, that is, when it is known that the Lord has shown you these things, the workers of iniquity will seek your overthrow: they will circulate falshoods to destroy your reputation, and also will seek to take your life; but remember this, if you are faithful, and shall hereafter continue to keep

---

143. See Isaiah 29:14.

the commandments of the Lord, you shall be preserved to bring these things forth; for in due time he will again give you a commandment to come and take them. When they are interpreted the Lord will give the holy priesthood to some, and they shall begin to proclaim this gospel and baptize by water, and after that they shall have power to give the Holy Ghost by the laying on of their hands. Then will persecution rage more and more; for the iniquities of men shall be rev[e]aled, and those who are not built upon the Rock will seek to overthrow this church; but it will inecrease the more opposed, and spread farther and farther, increaseing in knowledge till they shall be sanctified and receive an inheritance where the glory of God will rest upon them; and when this takes place, and all things are prepared, the◊[144] ten tribes of Israel will be revealed in the north country, whither they have been for a long season; and when this is fulfilled will be brought to pass that saying of the prophets—'And the Redeemer shall come to Zion, and unto them that turn from transgression in [p. 97] Jacob, saith the Lord'[145]—But, notwithstanding the workers of iniquity shall seek your destruction the arm of the Lord will be extended, and you will be borne off conqueror if you keep all his commandments. Your name shall be known among the nations, for the work which the Lord will perform by your hands shall cause the rightious to rejoice and the wicked to rage: with the one it shall be had in honor, and with the other in reproach; yet, with these it shall be a terror because of the great and marvelous work which shall follow the coming forth of this fulness of the gospel. Now, go thy way, rem[em]bering what the Lord has done for thee, and be diligent in keeping his commandments, and he will deliver thee from temptations and all the arts and devises of the wicked one.— Forget not to pray, that thy mind may become strong, that when he shall manifest unto thee, thou mayest have power to escape the evil, and obtain these precious things." Though I am unable to paint before the mind, a perfect description of the scenery which passed before our brother, I think I have said enough to give you a field for reflection which may not be unprofitable. You see the great wisdom in God in leading him thus far, that his mind might begin to be more matured, and thereby be able to judge correctly, the spirits. I do not say that he would not have obtained the record had he went according to the direction of the angel—I say that he would; but God knowing all things from the beginning, began thus to instruct his servant. And in this it is plainly to be seen that the adversary of truth is not sufficient to overthrow the work of God. You will remember that I said, two invisible powers were operating upon the mind of our brother while going to Cumorah. In

---

144. TEXT: Possibly "then" or "these".
145. See Isaiah 59:20.

this, then, I discover wisdom in the dealings of the Lord: it was impossible for any man to translate the book of Mormon by the gift of God, and endure the afflictions, and [p. 98] temptations, and devices[146] of satan, without being overthrown unless he had been previously benefited with a certain round of experience: and had our brother obtained the record the first time, not knowing how to detect the works of darkness, he might have been deprived of the blessings of sending forth the word of truth to this generation. Therefore, God knowing that satan would thus lead his mind astray, began at that early hour, that when the full time should arive, he might have a servant prepared to fulfill his purpose. So, however afflicting to his feelings this repuls[e] might have been, he had reason to rejoice before the Lord and be thankful for the favors and mercies shown; that whatever other instruction was necessary to the accomplishing[147] this great work, he had learned, by experience, how to discern betwen the spirit of Christ and the spirit of the devil.

From this time to September, 1827, few occurrences worthy of note transpired. As a fact to be expected, nothing of importance could be recorded concerning a generation in darkness.— In the mean time our brother of whom I have been speaking, passed the time as others, in laboring for his suport. But in consequence of certain fals[e] and slanderous reports which have been circulated, justice would require me to say something upon the private life of one whose character has been so shamefully traduced. By some he is said to have been a lazy, idle, vicious, profligate fellow.[148] These I am prepared to contradict, and that too by the testimony of many persons with whom I have been intimately acquainted, and know to be individuals of the strictest veracity, and unquestionable integrity. All these strictly and virtually agree in saying, that he was an honest, upright, virtuous, and faithfully industrious young man. And those who say to the contrary can be influenced by no other motive than to destroy the reputation of one who never injured any man in either property or person

While young, I have been informed he was afflicted with sickness;[149] but I have been told by those [p. 99] for whom he has labored, that he was a young man of truth and industrious habits. And I will add further that it is my conviction, if he never had been called to the exalted station in which he now

---

146. TEXT: Possibly "~~devil~~ devices".

147. TEXT: Possibly "~~accomplishmet~~ accomplishing".

148. Probably an allusion to the affidavits published the previous year in Howe, *Mormonism Unvailed,* chap. 17.

149. When about seven years old, JS contracted typhoid fever and suffered a severe inflammation in his leg, requiring surgery. (JS History, vol. A-1, 131; Lucy Mack Smith, History, 1844–1845, bk. 2, [11]–bk. 3, [2]; Wirthlin, "Nathan Smith.")

occupies, he might have passed down the stream of time with ease and in respectability, without the foul and hellish toung of slander ever being employed against him. It is no more than to be expected, I admit, that men of corrupt hearts will try to traduce his character and put a spot upon his name; indeed, this is according to the word of the angel; but this does not prohibit me from speaking freely of his merits, and contradicting those falshoods—I feel myself bound so to do, and I know that my testimony, on this matter, will be received and believed while those who testify to the contrary are crumbled to dust, and their words swept away in the general mass of lies when God shall purify the earth!

Connected with this, is the character of the family: and on this I say as I said concerning the character of our brother—I feel myself bound to defend the innocent always when oportunity offers. Had not those who are notorious for lies and dishonesty, also assailed the character of the family I should pass over them here in silence; but now I shall not forbear. It has been industriously circulated that they were dishonest, deceitful and vile.[150] On this I have the testimony of responsible persons, who have said and will say, that this [is][151] basely false; and besides, a personal acquaintance for seven years, has demonstrated that all the difficulty is, they were once poor, (yet industrious,) and have now, by the help of God, arisen to note, and their names are like to, (indeed they will,) be handed down to posterity, and had among the righteous.— They are industrious, honest, virtuous and liberal to all. This is their character; and though many take advantage of their liberality, God will reward them; but this is the [p. 100] fact, and this testimony shall shine upon the records of the saints, and be ⟨recorded on the archives of heaven to be⟩ read in the day of eternity, when the wicked and perverse, who have vilely slandered them without cause or provocation, reap their reward with the unjust, where there is weeping, wailing and gnashing of teeth!— if they do not repent.

Soon after this visit to Cumorah, a gentleman from the south part of the State, (Chenango County,) employed our brother as a common laborer, and accordingly he visited that section of ⟨the⟩ country; and had he not been accused of digging down all, or nearly so the mountains of Susquehannah [Susquehanna], or causing others to do it by some art of nicromancy, I should leave this, for the present, unnoticed. You will remember, in the mean time, that those who seek to vilify his character, say that he has always been notorious for his idleness. This gentleman, whose name is Stowel [Josiah Stowell],

---

150. For examples of such characterizations of the Smith family, see Howe, *Mormonism Unvailed,* 11–12, 248–249, 257–258, 261.

151. Omitted word supplied from *LDS Messenger and Advocate.*

resided in the town of Bainbridge, on or near the head waters of the Susquehannah river. Some forty miles south, or down the river, in the town of
Harmony, Susquehannah county, Pa. is said to be a cave or subteraneous recess,
whether entirely formed by art or not I am uninformed, neither does this matter; but such is said to be the case,— where a company of Spaniards, a long
time since, when the country was uninhabited by white setlers, excavated from
the bowels of the earth ore, and coined a large quantity of money; after which
they secured the cavity and evacuated, leaving a part still in the cave, purposing
to return at some distant period. A long time elapsed and this account came
from one of the individuals who was first engaged in this ⟨mining⟩ buisness.
The country was pointed out and the spot minutely described. This I believe, is
the substance, so far as my memory serves, though I shall not pledge my verasity
for the correctness of the account as I have given.—

Enough however, was credited of the Spaniards story, to ex[c]ite the belief
of many that there was a fine sum of the precious metal lying coined in this
subteraneous vault, among whom was [p. 101] our employer; and accordingly
our brother was required to spend a few months with some others in excavat-
ing the earth, in pursuit of this treasure.[152]

While employed here he became acquainted with the family of Isaac Hale,
of whom you read in several of the productions of those who have sought to
destroy the validity of the book of Mormon.[153] It may be necessary hereafter,
to refer you more particularly to the conduct of this family, as their influence
has been co[n]siderably exerted to destroy the reputation of our brother, probably because he married a daughter of the same, contrary to some of their
wishes, and in connection with this, to certain statements of some others of the
inhabitants of that section of count[r]y.[154] But in saying this I do not wish to be
understood as uttering aught against Mrs. Smith, (formerly Emma Hale.) She
has most certainly evinced a decidedly correct mind and uncommon ability
of talent and judgment, in a manifest willingness to fulfill, on her part, that
passage in sacred writ,—"and they twain shall be one flesh",[155]—by accompanying her husband, against the wishes and advise of her relatives, to a land
of strangers: and however I may deprecate their actions, can say in justice, her
character stands as fair for morality, piety and virtue, as any in the world.
Though you may say, this is a digression from the subject proposed, I trust I

152. JS and others attempted to locate the treasure in October and November 1825. (JS History, vol.
A-1, pp. 234–236 herein [Draft 2].)

153. An affidavit sworn by Isaac Hale, dated 20 March 1834, was published in Howe, *Mormonism
Unvailed*, 262–266.

154. Correction supplied based on *LDS Messenger and Advocate*.

155. See Genesis 2:24.

shall be indulged, for the purpose of ~~satisfaction~~ satisfying many, who have heard so many slanderous reports that they are ⟨led to believe them true because they are⟩ not contradicted; and besides, this generation are dertermined to oppose every item in the form or under the pretence of revelation, unless it comes throug[h] a man who has always been more pure than Michael the great prince; and as this is the fact, and my opposers have put me to the necessity, I shall be more prolix, and have no doubt, before I give up the point, shall prove to your satisfaction, and to that of every man, that the translator of the book of Mormon is worthy the appelation of a seer and [p. 102] a prophet of the Lord. In this I do not pretend that he is not a man subject to passions like other men, beset with infirmities and encompassed with weaknesses; but if he is, all men were so before him, and a pretence to the contrary would argue a more than mortal, which would at once destroy the whole system of the religion of the Lord Jesus; for he anciently chose the weak ~~things~~ to overcome the strong, the foolish to confound the wise, (I mean considered so by this world,) and by the foolishness of preaching to save those who believe.[156]

On the private character of our brother I need add nothing further, at present, previous to his obtaining the records of the Nephites, only that while in that country, some verry officious persons complained of him as a disorderly person, and brought him before the authorities of the ~~country~~ county; but there being no cause of action he was honorably acquited.[157] From this time forward he continued to receive instructions concerning the coming forth of the fulness of the gospel, from the mouth of the heavenly messenger, until he was directed to visit again the place where the records was deposited.

For the present I close, with a thankful heart that I am permitted to see thousands rejoicing in the assurance of the promises of the Lord, confirmed unto them through the obediance of the everlasting covenant.

As ever your brother in the Lord Jesus

Oliver Cowdery

To W[illiam] W. Phelps.

———— ∾ ————

Editorial Note

It is unclear why Warren Parrish began transcribing the following letter into JS's history. He transcribed fewer than three paragraphs before canceling the entry. The letter,

156. See 1 Corinthians 1:21, 27–28.

157. Cowdery here referred to an 1826 hearing in South Bainbridge, New York, in which JS was charged with disorderly conduct related to his activities as a "glass looker." (See Hill, "Joseph Smith and the 1826 Trial"; and Madsen, "Joseph Smith's 1826 Trial.")

copied from the November 1835 issue of the *Latter Day Saints' Messenger and Advocate,* was
the second in a series of three letters in which JS provided instruction for traveling elders.
After copying the first few paragraphs of the published letter, Parrish discontinued the task
and wrote "Error" across the text three times. Parrish's transcription was made after the
November issue was published[158] and apparently before early April 1836, when Warren
Parrish probably transferred custody of the 1834–1836 history to Warren Cowdery along
with JS's journal.[159]

———— ✑ ————

[160]To the Elders of the Church of the Latter Day Saints

At the close of my letter in the September No. of the "Messenger and
Advocate," I promise to continue the subject there commenced: I do so with a
hope that it may be a benefit and a means of assistance to the elders in their
labours, while [p. 103] they are combatting the prejudices of a crooked and
perverse generation, by having in their possession, the facts of my religious
principles, which are misrepresented by almost all those whose crafts are in
danger by the same; and also to aid those who are anxiously inquiring, and
have been excited to do so from rumor, in accertaining correctly, what my
principles are.

I have been drawn into this course of proceding, by persecution, that is
brought upon us from false rumor, and misrepresentations concerning my
sentiments.

But to proceed, in the letter alluded to. The principles of repentance and
baptism for the remission of sins, are not only set forth, but many passages of
scriptures, were quoted, clearly illucidating the subject; let me add, that I do
positively rely upon the truth and veracity of those principles inculcated in the
new testament; and then pass from the above named items, on to the item or
subject of the gathering, and show my views upon this point: which is an item
which I esteem to be of the greates[t] importance to those who are looking for
salvation in this generation, or in these what may be called "the latter times,"/[161]
[*14 lines blank*] [p. 104]

---

158. The November issue of the *LDS Messenger and Advocate* included a letter dated 18 November,
so it must have been published after that date. (Orson Pratt, Kirtland, OH, 18 Nov. 1835, Letter to the
editor, *LDS Messenger and Advocate,* Nov. 1835, 2:223–224.)

159. See JS, Journal, 1 and 2 Apr. 1836, in *JSP,* J1:216–217.

160. TEXT: Warren Parrish canceled this line and the following three paragraphs by writing "Error"
diagonally through the text, twice on page 103 and once on page 104. The passage was copied from JS,
"To the Elders of the Church of Latter Day Saints," *LDS Messenger and Advocate,* Nov. 1835, 2:209–212.

161. TEXT: Warren Parrish handwriting ends.

——— ⟨⟩ ———

Editorial Note

The blank lines following Warren Parrish's abandoned transcript of JS's letter to church elders suggest a new direction in the 1834–1836 history. The final section of the history, a daily narrative beginning with the 22 September 1835 entry and ending abruptly with the 18 January 1836 entry, was begun by Warren Cowdery and continued by Warren Parrish. It is a polished version of JS's second Ohio journal, a document written mostly by scribes but apparently dictated by JS.[162] Although Cowdery and Parrish adhered closely to their journal source, they occasionally went beyond the making of a mere clerical copy. They changed the journal's first-person narrative to third-person and altered the tone or emphasis of several passages. In particular, Parrish took the opportunity to fill in the details of events he had witnessed, especially when those details enhanced the image of JS in his prophetic role. Where differences between journal and history are significant, they are noted herein. Selected annotation from *The Joseph Smith Papers, Journals, Volume 1: 1832–1839* also appears here; for more complete annotation, see pages 52–223 of that volume.

It is clear that this section of the history was intended to be a more refined and permanent document than the journal. The messy wipe erasures, roughly executed knife erasures, and other forms of revision in the journal contrast with the careful erasures and insertions found in this section of the history, and the introductory paragraph to the revised entries expresses the importance of providing a polished historical account of JS's life for future generations. Although Warren Cowdery probably composed this introductory explanation, he attributed ultimate authorship of the history to JS, referring to him not only as "the subject of this narrative" but also as "our author."

Warren Cowdery began transcribing JS's 1835–1836 journal into the history after he received the journal from Warren Parrish in early April 1836.[163] The journal entries from which Cowdery and Parrish drew covered the period when JS and the Latter-day Saints anticipated the completion of the House of the Lord in Kirtland, the solemn assembly to be held therein, and the promised "endowment of power from on high." These late March events were recorded in JS's journal; however, the history carries the narrative only up through mid-January. Cowdery's pagination of the book indicates the intent to adapt more of JS's journal than was accomplished; he numbered the pages of the blank book up to 241, which was ultimately 107 pages further than he wrote and 54 pages further than Parrish wrote.

——— ⟨⟩ ———

162. See Historical Introduction to JS, Journal, 1835–1836, in *JSP*, J1:56.

163. Parrish did not give the journal to Cowdery before 1 April 1836, the date of the last entry Parrish wrote. Cowdery presumably received the journal soon after that date, as he wrote the journal entries for 2 and 3 April 1836. In early April, Parrish was preparing to leave Kirtland to proselytize, like many others who were recently "endowed" at the solemn assembly held in the House of the Lord in Kirtland for that purpose. Parrish's mission departure, however, was delayed until May, and it was probably during this delay that Parrish retrieved the journal and history from Cowdery and used the journal to write the entries dated 18 November 1835–18 January 1836 in the history. (JS, Journal, 1, 2, and 3 Apr. 1836, in *JSP*, J1:216–222; Woodruff, Journal, 19 Apr. and 27 May 1836.)

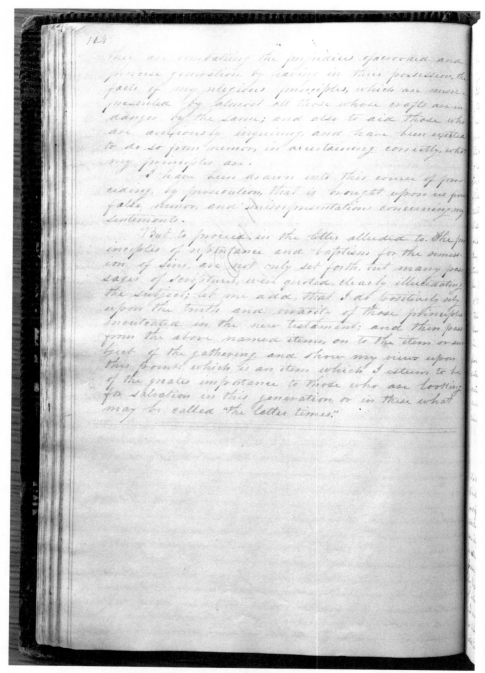

104

they are combating the prejudices of a crooked and perverse generation by having in their possession, the facts of my religious principles, which are misrepresented by almost all those whose crafts are in danger by the same; and also to aid those who are anxiously inquiring, and have been excited to do so from rumor in ascertaining correctly, what my principles are.

I have been drawn into this course of proceeding, by persecution, that is brought upon us from false rumor and misrepresentation concerning my sentiments.

But to proceed in the letter alluded to. The principles of repentance and baptism for the remission of sins, are not only set forth, but many passages of scriptures were quoted clearly illucidating the subject; let me add, that I do positively rely upon the truth and veracity of those principles inculcated in the new testament; and then pass from the above named items, on to the item or subject of the gathering and show my views upon this point: which is an item which I esteem to be of the greatest importance to those who are looking for salvation in this generation, or in these what may be called "the latter times."

Format changes in 1834–1836 history. Pages 104 and 105 reflect a deliberate change in the format of the 1834–1836 history. Scribe Warren Parrish discontinued copying Joseph Smith's letter "To the Elders of the Church" from the November 1835 *LDS Messenger and Advocate* and then wrote "Error" diagonally through the text. On the next page, in the handwriting of Warren Cowdery, is an announcement of a "different form" for the history—a "faithful narration of every important item"

September 1835   104

Here the reader will observe that the narrative assumes a
different form. The subject of it becoming daily more and more
noted, the writer deemed it proper to regret to give a clear simple and
faithful narration of every important item in his every-day
occurrences. Therefore he trusts that to the man of God, no apol-
=ogy will be necessary for such a course, especially when he takes
into consideration that he writes not so much for the benefit
of his cotemporaries as for that of posterity. The candid reflec-
=ting mind will also realize how highly we all estimate every
species of intelligence or correct information we can obtain
relative to the ancient Prophets & Apostles, through whom the
Most High condescended to reveal himself to the children of men.
Such revelations, therefore, as may at any time be given through
him will be inserted, and the characters of other men, from
their necessary connexion with him, will in some instances
be plainly portrayed, but the digression from the main thread
of the narrative, when short, will, the writer trusts, constitute
that pleasing variety, those lights and shades, that picture of
human life on which the eye rests with most pleasure,
The ear, and the mind of both reader and hearer, will be relieved
from that formal sameness, or tiresome monotony, that char-
=acterize a dull tale of no merit, and enable future gen-
=erations, to duly appreciate the claims the subject of this
narrative may have had, on his cotemporaries for their implicit
reliance on what he taught them,

           Sept 22d 1835
This day he labored with his friend and brother in the Lord, Oliver
Cowdery in obtaining and writing blessings. They were thronged a
part of the time with company, so that their labor was rather
retarded, but they obtained many precious things and their souls
were blessed to that degree that they were constrained to cry out
in ecstacy, O Lord, may thy Holy Spirit be with thy servants
forever. Amen.   Sept. 23. This day he was at home, wri-
=ting blessings for his beloved brethren. He was hindered by multitudes
of visitors, but remarked, that the Lord had blessed their souls this day.
and may God grant to continue his mercies unto my house this night
for Christ's sake. This day his soul had desired the salvation of
brother Ezra Thayer. His soul was also drawn out in love for brother

in Joseph Smith's life. Beginning with the entry for 22 September 1835, the history is based on
Smith's 1835–1836 journal. Handwriting of Warren Parrish and Warren Cowdery. JS History, 1834–
1836, pp. 104–105 (transcribed on pp. 90–95 herein), in JS History, vol. A-1 (earliest numbering),
Church History Library, Salt Lake City. (Photographs by Welden C. Andersen.)

/[164]Here the reader will observe, that the narrative assumes a different form. The subject of it becoming daily more and more noted, the writer deemed it proper to give a plain, simple, yet faithful narration of every important item in his every-day-occurrences. Therefore, he trusts, that to the man of God, no apology will be necessary for such a course: especially when he takes into consideration, that he writes, not so much for the benefit of his co[n]temporaries as for that of posterity. The candid, reflecting mind will also realize, how highly we all estimate every species of intelligence or correct information we can obtain relative to the ancient Prophets & Apostles, through whom the Most-High condescended to reveal himself to the children of men. Such revelations, therefore, as may at any time be given through him will be inserted, and the characters of other men, from their necessary connexion with him, will in some instances be plainly pourtrayed; but the digression from the main thread of the narrative, when short, will, the writer trusts, constitute that pleasing variety, those lights and shades, that picture of human life on which the eye rests with most pleasure. The ear, and the mind of both reader and hearer, will be relieved from that formal sameness, or tiresome monotony, that characterize a dull tale of no merit, and enable future generations, to duly appreciate the claims the subject of this[165] narrative may ⟨have⟩ had, on his co[n]temporaries for their implicit reliance on what he taught them.

22 September 1835 • Tuesday

Sept. 22[d.] 1835 This day he labored, with his friend and brother in the Lord, Oliver Cowdery, in obtaining and writing blessings.[166] They were thronged a part of the time with company, so that their labor was rather retarded; but they obtained many precious things and their souls were blessed, to that degree, that they were constrained to cry out in ecstacy, O. Lord, may thy Holy Spirit, be with thy servants forever. Amen.

Sept. 23 [22],[167] This day he was at home, writing blessings for his beloved brethren. He was hindered by multitudes of visitors, but remarked, that the Lord had blessed their souls, this day, and may God grant to continue his mercies unto my house this night for Christ's sake. This day his soul ~~brethren~~ had

---

164. TEXT: Warren Cowdery handwriting begins.

165. TEXT: Possibly "~~the~~ this".

166. The phrase "his friend and brother in the Lord" is not in the corresponding entry of the 1835–1836 journal. On this date, 22 September, JS dictated blessings for David Whitmer, John Whitmer, John Corrill, and William W. Phelps. (See *JSP*, J1:61n30.)

167. In the 1835–1836 journal, JS wrote this paragraph and the following two entries in his own hand. Because the entry follows Oliver Cowdery's entry dated 22 September, JS mistakenly dated his own entry 23 September; the events described here occurred on the twenty-second.

desired the salvation of brother Ezra Thayer. His soul was also drawn out in love[168] for brother [p. 105] Noah Packard, who came to his house and loaned the Chapel Committee,[169] one thousand dollars, for the building of the house of the House of the Lord in this place. O may God bless him an hundred fold, even of this worlds goods, for this act of virtuous liberality. He then as if soliloquizing, writes in his journal. My heart is full of desire this day, to be blessed of the God of Abraham, with prosperity, until I shall be able to pay all my debts, for it is the delight of my soul to be honest, O Lord, that thou knowest right well! help me, and I will give to the poor.

23 September 1835 • Wednesday

September 23ᵈ This day three of his brethren, (viz.) Wm. John & Joseph Tibbits [Tippets] called on him to bid him farewell, having set out on a journey to Missouri, the place designated by the Lord, for the gathering of the Saints in these last days,[170] A number of brethren came in to pray with them. Brother David Whitmer took the lead and truly prayed in the spirit, and to use the expression of the subject of our narrative, a glorious time succeeded his prayer; joy filled our hearts and we blessed them & bid them God speed. We promised them a safe journey and bid them adiue for a season. O may God grant them long life and good days. These blessings I ask for them, in the name of Christ, Amen.

24 September 1835 • Thursday

September 24ᵗʰ· This day the High Council of the Church met at his house to take into consideration the afflictions of Zion, and to devize means for her redemption. It was the voice of the Spirit of the Lord, that a petition be sent to the governor of the state of Missouri,[171] praying for his assistance in his official

---

168. This sentiment is not found in the 1835–1836 journal entry, which notes only, "Also Brother Noah, Packard. Came to my house." (*JSP*, J1:62.)

169. In June 1833, Hyrum Smith, Reynolds Cahoon, and Jared Carter were appointed as a committee to direct the construction of the House of the Lord in Kirtland. (Minute Book 1, 6 June 1833.)

170. The corresponding entry in the 1835–1836 journal specifies that Missouri was "designated for Zion." On 28 November 1834, the Kirtland high council met to consider a letter from church members in Essex County, New York, presented by John and Joseph Tippets. The letter listed money and property totaling $848.40 collected to purchase land in Missouri. The two men were advised to remain in Kirtland during the winter and lend part of their money to the church there. At a high council meeting on 24 August 1835, the Tippetses were counseled to resume their journey to Missouri in the fall. This entry marks their departure. (*JSP*, J1:62; Minute Book 1, 28 Nov. 1834 and 24 Aug. 1835; see also Revelation, 20 July 1831, in Doctrine and Covenants 27:1, 1835 ed. [D&C 57:2].)

171. Daniel Dunklin, governor of Missouri 1832–1836.

capacity, in restoring those to their possessions in Jackson County, who had previously been driven from them by a lawless mob.[172]

The brethren had a good time, and covenanted to struggle for this, their favorite object, until death dissolve this union; and if one falls, the rest are not to abandon the pursuit, but struggle on, until the ultimate object is attained, which, they prayed that God would grant unto them, in the name of Jesus Christ.

September 24ᵗʰ ⟨25ᵗʰ⟩[173] He drew an article for his brethren to sign who were willing to go next Spring and assist in the redemption of Zion.[174] He felt to ask God in the name of Jesus, that eight hundred or one thousand men, well armed would volunteer to accomplish that great work.

25 September 1835 • Friday

September 25ᵗʰ This day he remained at home, and nothing of note transpired during the day. [p. 106]

26 September 1835 • Saturday

September 26ᵗʰ This evening, the "Twelve,["] having returned from the East in the morning,[175] he met them, and conversed upon some matters of difficulty

172. The petition, dated 10 September 1834, was apparently circulated among the Saints and by 30 December 1835 was forwarded to Governor Daniel Dunklin from Kirtland, Ohio, with several hundred signatures attached. The corresponding entry in JS's 1835–1836 journal describes this petition more forcefully: "we petition to the Governer that is those who have been driven out should do so to be set back on their Lands next spring and we go next season to live or dy in Jackson County." In a November 1834 message to the Missouri legislature, Daniel Dunklin made reference to the "outrages" committed against the Mormons and noted that "these unfortunate people are now forbidden to take possession of their homes." A copy of Dunklin's speech arrived in Kirtland in mid-December 1834, reviving hopes that Latter-day Saint losses might be redressed. Following this news, JS counseled the church members in Missouri to "make but little or no stir in that region, and cause as little excitement as possible and endure their afflictions patiently until the time appointed—and the Governor of Mo. fulfils his promise in setting the church over upon their own lands." (Petition to Daniel Dunklin, 10 Sept. 1834, copy, William W. Phelps, Collection of Missouri Documents, CHL; JS History, vol. B-1, 559, 563; Whitmer, History, 79, in *JSP*, H2:88.)

173. JS's 1835–1836 journal has "24ᵗʰ." (*JSP*, J1:64.)

174. This action reflects JS's firm intention to return to Missouri in spring 1836 with an armed expedition to repossess Mormon property. For John Whitmer's description of this meeting, see Whitmer, History, 81, in *JSP*, H2:90.

175. On 12 March 1835, less than a month after it was organized, the Quorum of the Twelve was appointed to a mission to the eastern states to "hold conferences in the vicinity of the several branches of the Church for the purpose of regulating all things necessary for their welfare." The Twelve left 4 May 1835. Six of the Twelve also crossed into Upper Canada and convened a conference at West Loughborough. (Quorum of the Twelve Apostles, Record, 12 Mar. and 4 May 1835; see also Esplin, "Emergence of Brigham Young," 163–170.)

which were resting between some of them and President S[idney] Rigdon, and all things were settled satisfactorily.[176]

27 September 1835 • Sunday

September 27th. He attended meeting: Brethren, Thomas B. Marsh, David W. Patten, Brigham Young & Heber C. Kimball[177] preached, and broke bread. The Lord condescended to pour out his spirit, and the souls of his servants were edified.[178]

28 September 1835 • Monday

September 28th. High Council met and tried F. G[ladden] Bishop: he was reproved, repented, and was reordained. Lorenzo Lewis was tried for fornication and cut off from the church.[179]

29 September 1835 • Tuesday

29th. High Council met to day and tried brother Allen Avery, who on an investigation was acquitted from any charge.[180] P[hineas] H. Young was also tried and acquitted.[181] Lorenzo Young was also tried, confessed his error and was forgiven.[182] In all these cases, the subject of this narrative acted on the part of the defence for the accused, to plead for mercy. The Lord appeared to bless his soul, and the council was also greatly blessed. He congratulated himself that much good would result from the two days he had been laboring in church business.

---

176. A month and a half earlier, on 4 August 1835, JS and the council of church presidents met to consider charges against members of the Twelve for their conduct while proselytizing in the eastern states. (See *JSP*, J1:66n39.)

177. These were the four oldest members of the Quorum of the Twelve. At this time, seniority in the quorum was based on age. (JS History, vol. B-1, 589.)

178. JS's 1835–1836 journal has "my soul was edified." (*JSP*, J1:66.)

179. Bishop was charged with "advancing heretical doctrines which were derogatory to the character of the Church." Lewis's partial confession was judged unsatisfactory. (Minute Book 1, 28 Sept. 1835.)

180. Avery was charged with rebelling against the decision of the Missouri elders council to take away his elder's license. However, Avery came forward and "complied with the requisitions of the council," and he was restored to his office. (Minute Book 1, 29 Sept. 1835.)

181. Phineas Young was charged with "unchristian like conduct" in connection with his sale and distribution of a handful of copies of the Book of Mormon during his 1835 proselytizing journey. (Minute Book 1, 29 Sept. 1835.)

182. Lorenzo Young was charged by William W. Phelps with teaching that "poor men ought not to raise up seed or children" but that they might be permitted to marry. After Young "made an humble acknowledgement," the charge was dismissed. (Minute Book 1, 29 Sept. 1835.)

30 September 1835 • Wednesday

30<u>th</u> He stayed at home and visited many who came to enquire after the work of the Lord.

1 October 1835 • Thursday

October first, He stayed at home and labored on the Egyptian Alphabet in company with his brethren O[liver] Cowdery & W[illiam] W. Phelps. The System of Astronomy was unfolded.[183]

2 October 1835 • Friday

Oct. 2<u>d</u> He wrote a letter to be published in the Messenger & Advocate[184]

3 October 1835 • Saturday

3<u>d</u> He attended, and held a High Council in the case of Elder John Gould. for giving cridence [credence] to false and slanderous reports, instigated and propagated to injure brother Sidney Rigdon, also to investigate the case of Dean Gould, son of John Gould, for threatning S. Rigdon and other Elders. After due reflection on the part of the accused, they both confessed. and were acquitted. In the afternoon of the same day, he waited on the Twelve, most of them at his own house, exhibited to them the ancient records in his possession,[185] and gave explanations of the same. This day he obsirved, passed off with the blessings of the Lord.

4 October 1835 • Sunday

Sunday October 4<u>th</u> He started early in the morning with one of his brethren, by the name of John Carrill [Corrill], to hold a meeting in Perry. When about a mile from home, they saw two deer which gave a turn to their thoughts upon the subject of the Creation of God. [p. 107] They conversed freely upon many topicks, the day passed off in a very agreeable manner, and the Lord blessed their souls. When they arrived at Perry they were disappointed of a

183. Possibly refers to the astronomical material in three "Egyptian alphabet" documents. Astronomical material also appeared in JS's published "Book of Abraham," related to his obtaining Egyptian papyri in July 1835. (Kirtland Egyptian Papers, ca. 1835–1836, 3, 4, 5, CHL; "The Book of Abraham," *Times and Seasons,* 1 Mar. 1842, 3:703–706; 15 Mar. 1842, 3:719–722; 16 May 1842, 3:783–784 [Abraham 1–5]; see also JS History, vol. B-1, 622; *JSP,* J1:57; and Gee, "Eyewitness, Hearsay, and Physical Evidence," 197–203.)

184. This was the first in a series of three letters written by JS and published in successive issues of the *LDS Messenger and Advocate* to give instruction for traveling elders. (JS, "To the Elders of the Church of Latter Day Saints," *LDS Messenger and Advocate,* Sept. 1835, 1:179–182; see also Nov. 1835, 2:209–212; and Dec. 1835, 2:225–230.)

185. In July 1835, JS purchased a number of Egyptian mummies and papyri from a traveling exhibitor. (See *JSP,* J1:57.)

meeting, through some mismanagement, but they conversed freely with Corrill's relatives, which apparently allayed much prejudice in their minds. He truly felt to ask the Lord to have mercy on their souls.

5 October 1835 • Monday

Monday Oct. 5th. He returned home, and being much fatigued, from riding in the rain, he spent the remainder of the day in reading & meditation. In the evening he attended a High Council of the twelve Apostles. He had, as he stated, a glorious time, and gave them many instructions concerning their duties for time to come. He told them it was the will of God that they should take their families to Missouri next season, also that they should attend[186] the solemn assembly of the first Elders, for the organization of the school of the Prophets, attend to the ordinance of washing of feet,[187] and prepare their hearts in all humility for an endowment with power from on high. To this they all assented with one accord, and appeared to be grea[t]ly rejoiced. He felt to pray God to spare the lives of these twelve to a good old age, for Christ, the Redeemer's sake. Amen.

6 October 1835 • Tuesday

Tuesday October 6th. He staid home, and Elder [blank] [blank] Stevens came to his house and loaned F. G. Williams and Co. six hundred dollars, which greatly relieved the Company from its pecuniary embarrassments.[188] May God bless and preserve his soul forever. In the afternoon he called to visit his father, who was very sick, with a fever: he was some better toward evening and the subject of this memoir spent the rest of the day in reading and meditation

---

186. At this point, JS's 1835–1836 journal has "this fall." (*JSP*, J1:68.)

187. A December 1832 revelation announced the formation of the School of the Prophets, whose candidates would "be received by the ordinance of the washing of feet." The school was organized in 1833, but foot washing ceased after the initial school term. The Elders School, a successor to the School of the Prophets, was organized in 1834 and again on 3 November 1835. JS frequently referred to the Elders School as the School of the Prophets. After the House of the Lord was completed and dedicated, the anticipated solemn assembly was finally held, which included the ordinance of foot washing. (Revelation, 27 and 28 Dec. 1832 and 3 Jan. 1833, in Doctrine and Covenants 7:44–45, 1835 ed. [D&C 88:136–139]; JS, Journal, 29 and 30 Mar. 1836, in *JSP*, J1:211–216.)

188. F. G. Williams & Co., the church printing arm, had recently published the first edition of the Doctrine and Covenants, was printing three newspapers, and was preparing the church's first hymnal. By October 1835, the expenses outlaid for these projects brought the company close to economic collapse. (Crawley, *Descriptive Bibliography*, 1:47–53, 54–59; Cook, *Law of Consecration*, 47–50.)

7 October 1835 • Wednesday

Wednesday 7ᵗʰ He went to visit his father and found him very low: he administred some mild herbs to him, agreeably to the commandment of the Lord to his servants in these last days.[189] and earnestly prayed that God would have mercy upon him & restore him immediately to health, for Christ the Redeemer's sake. This day his own natural brother, Hyrum Smith and Newel K. Whitney set out in the Stage for the City of Buffalo, in the State of New York, to purchase goods to replenish the Store called the committee store. May the Lord be propitious, grant them health strength, a prosperous journey and a safe, expeditious return to the bosom of their families and society of their friends.

He here pronounced a blessing and a prophecy upon N. K. Whitney He said blessed of the Lord is brother Whitney, even the Bishop of the Church of Latter-Day Saints,[190] for the Bishoprick shall never be [p. 108] taken away from him while he liveth. and the time cometh when he shall overcome all the narrow-mindedness of his heart, and all his covetous desires that so easily beset him. He shall deal with a liberal hand to the poor, the needy, the sick and afflicted the widow and the fatherless. Marvelously and miraculously shall the Lord his God provide for him, even, that he shall be blessed with a fulness of the good things of this earth, and his seed after him from generation to generation. And it shall come to pass, that according to the measure that he metes out with a liberal hand unto the poor, so shall it be measured to him again by the hand of his God, even an hundred fold. Angels shall guard his habitation, and protect the lives of his posterity; and they shall become very numerous on the earth. Whomsoever he blesseth, shall be blessed and whosoever. he curseth shall be cursed. When his enemies seek to hurt or destroy him, let him rise up and curse them and the hand of God shall be upon his enemies in judgement: They shall be utterly confounded and brought to desolation. Therefore, he shall be preserved unto the utmost, for his life shall be precious in the sight of the Lord. He shall rise up and shake himself as a Lion. As a Lion riseth out of his nest and roareth until he shaketh, the hills, as a Lion goeth forth among the lesser beasts, so shall the goings forth of him be whom the Lord hath anointed to exalt the poor and humble the rich. Therefore, his name shall be on high and his rest among the sanctified.[191]

---

189. Apparently a reference to Revelation, 9 Feb. 1831, in Doctrine and Covenants 13:12, 1835 ed. [D&C 42:43]; or Revelation, 27 Feb. 1833, in Doctrine and Covenants 80:2, 1835 ed. [D&C 89:10].

190. Whitney was bishop of the church in Kirtland; Edward Partridge held the same office for the church in Missouri. (See *JSP*, J1:69n54.)

191. The corresponding entry in the 1835–1836 journal ends with an additional sentence: "this afternoon recommenced translating the ancient reccords." (*JSP*, J1:71; see also Historical Introduction to JS, Journal, 1835–1836, in *JSP*, J1:57.)

8 October 1835 • Thursday

Thursday 8ᵗʰ· He staid at home and attended his sick father with anxiety; nothing worthy of notice transpired.

9 October 1835 • Friday

Friday 9ᵗʰ This day passed much as the preceding, he waited on his father, and nothing occurred worthy of notice.

10 October 1835 • Saturday

Saturday 10ᵗʰ visited the house of his father and found him failing very fast.

11 October 1835 • Sunday

Sabbath 11ᵗʰ· Visited his father again, who was very sick. While the subject of this narrative was in secret prayer in the morning, the Lord said, my servant, thy father shall live. He waited on him all this day, with his desires raised to God in the name of Jesus Christ, that he would restore to health again, that he might be blessed with his company and advise, esteeming it one of the greatest earthly blessings to be favored with the society of parents, whose mature years and experience, render them capable of giving [p. 109] the most salutary advice. At evening David Whitmer came and united with J. Smith Junʳ· in calling on the Lord in mighty prayer, in the name of Jesus Christ. and laid their hands on him and rebuked the disease, and God heard and answered ~~our~~ ⟨their⟩ prayer to the great joy and satisfaction of ~~our~~ their souls His aged sire arose, dressed himself, shouted and praised the Lord. He [JS] called his Brother Wm. [Smith] who had retired to rest, that he might join with them in songs of praise to the Most High.

12 October 1835 • Monday

Monday Oct. 12ᵗʰ He rode to Willoughby (a small village about two miles and a half from Kirtland)[192] in company with his wife, to purchase goods at W. Lyon's[193] Store. On his return he found a Mr. Bradley, who had been thrown from his waggon, lying across the road, and apparently much injured by his fall.

---

192. This parenthetical information about Willoughby, Cuyahoga County, Ohio, does not appear in the 1835–1836 journal.

193. Probably Windsor Lyon.

13 October 1835 • Tuesday

Tuesday 13ᵗʰ He visited his father, who was very much recoverd from his sickness; indeed, so much so as to cause his friends to marvel at the might, power, and condescension of God in answering prayer in his behalf.

14 October 1835 • Wednesday

Wednesday 14 He was at home through the day.

15 October 1835 • Thursday

Thursday. 15ᵗʰ· He labored in his father's orchard,[194] gathering fruit.

16 October 1835 • Friday

Friday 16ᵗʰ· He was called into the printing office to settle some difficulties which had occurred in it. At evening of the same day he baptized Ebenezer Robinson,[195] and his own words in his journal, are ["]the Lord poured out his spirit upon us and we had a good time["]

17 October 1835 • Saturday

Saturday 17ᵗʰ· He called his family together, arranged some of his domestic concerns, and dismissed his boarders.[196]

18 October 1835 • Sunday

Sunday 18ᵗʰ· He attended meeting in the Chapel, confirmed several who had been baptized, and blessed several children, with the blessings of the new and everlasting covenant. Elder P[arley] P. Pratt preached in the fore-noon and John F. Boynton in the afternoon. It was truly an interesting time.[197]

19 October 1835 • Monday

Monday 19ᵗʰ· He was at home and exhibited the Egyptian Records of antiquity to a number of persons who called to see them.

---

194. An apple orchard. (*JSP*, J1:72.)

195. Although he worked in the printing office and had boarded with JS, Robinson did not become a member of the church until this day. Robinson later recalled that he requested baptism during lunchtime and, after finishing work for the day, went to the east branch of the Chagrin River for the ordinance. (Ebenezer Robinson, "Items of Personal History of the Editor," *The Return*, May 1889, 74.)

196. JS was boarding men who worked in the printing shop. (See *JSP*, J1:72n58.)

197. John Whitmer described this 18 October meeting and the reassuring prophecies spoken by JS on that occasion. (Whitmer, History, 81–82, in *JSP*, H2:90.)

20 October 1835 • Tuesday

Tuesday 20ᵗʰ He was at home during the day, but preached in the school house in the evening.

21 October 1835 • Wednesday

Wednesday 21ˢᵗ He was at home during the day and nothing of much moment transpired.

22 October 1835 • Thursday

Thursday 22ᵈ He was at home attending to his domestic concerns.

23 October 1835 • Friday

Friday 23ᵈ He was at home. Nothing worthy of note occurred.[198] [p. 110]

24 October 1835 • Saturday

Saturday 24ᵗʰ· Mr. Goodrich and his lady called on him to see the ancient Egyptian Records, and also went to Doct. F[rederick] G. Williams, to see the Mummies. Brethren Hawks & Carpenter from Michigan called and tarried with him over the sabbath. and attended meeting

25 October 1835 • Sunday

Sunday 25ᵗʰ· He attended meeting. President S[idney] Rigdon preached in the forenoon and Elder Lyman Johnson in the afternoon; after which, Elder S. Brownson [Seymour Brunson] joined brother Wm. Perry and Sister Eliza Brown in matrimony,[199] and the subject of this narrative blessed them with long life and prosperity in the name of Jesus Christ. At evening he attended a prayer meeting, opened it and exhorted his brethren and sisters about an hour. The Lord poured out his spirit, and some glorious things were spoken in the gift of tongues, and interpreted concerning the redemption of Zion.

26 October 1835 • Monday

Monday 26ᵗʰ· Went to Chardon to attend the County Court, in company with three of his Brothers, (viz.) Hyrum, Samuel & Carloss [Don Carlos Smith]. His Brother Samuel was summoned before this court for not doing

---

198. A prayer meeting was held this day. The text of the prayer appears following the entry for 27 November 1835 herein.

199. Brunson, who had obtained a license in Jackson County, Ohio, to solemnize weddings, may have been the only Latter-day Saint with such a license at this time. (Bradshaw, "Joseph Smith's Performance of Marriages in Ohio," 40.)

Military duty[200] and was fined because they had not their conference minutes with them, for testimony to prove that F[rederick] G. Williams was clerk of the conference. This testimony, they would have carried with them, had it not been for the neglect of their Council, or Lawyer,[201] who did not notify them that it was necessary to his success in the suit. This act of the Attorney, he felt as did his brethren, was a want of fidelity to his client, apparent indeed, and a base insult practiced upon him on account of his religious faith, that the ungodly might have an unlawful power over him, and trample him and our feelings under their unhallowed feet. In consequence of this omission of duty a fine of twenty dollars including costs, was imposed upon his brother, and to cancel it and the expenses attending the suit he was obliged to sell his cow. The subject of this narrative, felt to say in the name of Jesus Christ, that the money thus unjustly taken, shall be a testimony against them, and canker their flesh as fire.

27 October 1835 • Tuesday

Tuesday 27th In the morning he was called at to his Brother Samuel Smith's to visit his wife,[202] who was confined and in a dangerous situation. His brother Carloss [Don Carlos Smith] went to Chardon after Doctor F[rederick] G. Williams.[203] He went himself out into the field and bowed in mighty prayer before the Lord, beseeching him in the name of Jesus Christ in her behalf. The word of the Lord came unto him, saying, my servant Frederick shall come and[204] deal prudently, and my mine handmaiden shall be delivered of a living child and be spared. [p. 111] The Doctor came in about an hour; and in the course of two hours after she was safely delivered.[205] Thus what God had manifested to him, was fulfilled every whit. On the evening of the same day he preached in the school-house to a crowded congregation.

---

200. As in other states, in Ohio the state militia act required free, white, adult male citizens to serve in the state militia. Fines were levied for failure to attend training. However, the law exempted mail carriers, sailors at sea, and, as in most states, clergymen. In this appeal to the county court of common pleas, where he was fined an additional twenty dollars for not bringing the necessary documentation, Samuel Smith argued that he met the legal requirements of an acting minister. (See *JSP*, J1:75n62.)

201. Benjamin Bissell.

202. Mary Bailey Smith.

203. The 1835–1836 journal notes that Don Carlos Smith took one of JS's horses for the trip. (*JSP*, J1:75.)

204. The 1835–1836 journal here includes "shall have wisdom given him to." (*JSP*, J1:75.)

205. The infant was Susanna Bailey Smith, the couple's first child.

28 October 1835 • Wednesday

Wednesday 28ᵗʰ He was at home during the day employed in d[o]mestic concerns.

29 October 1835 • Thursday

Thursday 29ᵗʰ· Warren Parrish began to write for him at $15.00 per month, and received $16.00 in advance out of the Store, known by the name of the Committe Store. His father & mother Smith visited at his house this day. Bishop E[dward] Partridge returned this day from a long journey to the East.[206] It is proper here to note that his clerk, W. Parrish, agreed, subsequently to board himself, for which he was to have four dollars more per month, making $19. The subject of this memoir was then summoned to appear before the High Council of the Church, which was then setting to give his testimony in the case of David Elliott who was arraigned before that tribunal for whipping his own daughter unreasonably. His testimony was in Elliott's favor.[207] He then returned to his writing room, thence to Dr. William's [Frederick G. Williams's] after his large journal[208] and on returning, he made some observations to his scribe relative to the plan of a city which is to be built up hereafter on on this ground consecrated for a stake of Zion.[209] It is proper here to notice that during his absence at the Doctor's Bishop E. Partridge came in, accompanied with President W[illiam] W. Phelps. He was much rejoiced to see them.[210] He returned home and his scribe commenced writing, in his journal a history of his life: concluding President O[liver] Cowdery's 2ᵈ letter to W. W. Phelps, which, President Williams had begun.[211] Bishop [Newel K.] Whitney and his wife[212] with his father & mother called to see him. The Bishop's parints had

206. On 2 June 1835, Partridge left with Isaac Morley for a fund-raising mission to the East. (Partridge, Journal, 2 June 1835.)

207. The high council met at Edmund Bosley's home in Kirtland. William Smith brought charges against both David and Mary Cahoon Elliott for whipping and beating David's teenage daughter from an earlier marriage. The discipline had caused public commotion in Willoughby, where the Elliotts lived. JS had visited with the daughter and her parents in their home, and he testified that "the girl was in the fault, and that the neighbors were trying to create a difficulty." (Minute Book 1, 29 Oct. 1835.)

208. The "large journal" referred to here is the present history; Frederick G. Williams had begun the copying of the Oliver Cowdery letters published in the *LDS Messenger and Advocate.* After he was hired, Warren Parrish finished copying in the Cowdery letters. (See pp. 38–39 herein.)

209. Maps dating from 1833 and 1837 depict Latter-day Saint plans for major expansion in the city of Kirtland. The first map shows 49 square plots, each subdivided into 20 lots; the latter has 225 plots similarly divided. (Plats of Kirtland, OH, ca. 1833, ca. 1837, CHL.)

210. The corresponding journal entry also notes that they "examined the mumies." (*JSP,* J1:76.)

211. Parrish's handwriting begins on page 57 of the 1834–1836 history (p. 51 herein).

212. Elizabeth Ann Smith Whitney.

but recently come from the East,[213] and had called to make some enquiry concerning the coming forth of the Book of Mormon. Bishop Partridge and some
others came in; and he then set down and related to them the history of the
coming forth of the Book, the administration of the Angel to him and the rudiments of the Gospel of Christ. They appeared to be well satisfied, and he
expected to baptize them in in a few days, at least, such were his feelings
although they made no request of that kind at the time of the interview. He
then Went to the Council in the case of Elliott where he had previously been
called as testimony. The Presidency adjourned, and on his return Elder
J[ohn F.] Boynton, observed that long debates were indulged.[214] He replied
[p. 112] that it was generally the case that too much altercation was indulged on
both sides, and their debates protracted to an unprofitable length. He was now
called to his supper. After being seated around the table, Bishop Whitney
observed to Bishop Partridge, that the thought had just occurred to his mind,
that perhaps, in about one year from that time they might be seated together,
around a table in the land of Zion. His wife[215] observed, on hearing this remark, she hoped it might be the case, that not only they, but the rest of the
company present might be seated around a table in that land of promise. The
same sentiment was reciprocated by the company round the table, to which his
full soul seemed to respond his hearty amen, praying God to grant it in the
name of Jesus Christ. After supper he went again to the High Council, accompanied at this time, with his wife, and some others that belonged to his household. He was solicited to take a seat with the Presidency, and preside in the
case of Sister [Mary Cahoon] Elliott. He did so, his mother was mother was
called as testimony and began to relate circumstances that had previously been
brought before the church and settled. He objected against such testimony.
The Complainant, Wm. Smith arose and accused him of invalidating or
doubting his mother's' testimony, which he had not done, nor had he any
desire to do so.[216] He told his Brother Wm. he was out of place and asked him
to set down: but he refused; the request was repeated and W<u>m</u>. became
enraged. He was finally ordered to set down, but said he would not, unless he

---

213. Samuel and Susanna Kimball Whitney arrived from Marlborough, Windham County,
Vermont.

214. For "indulged," the 1835–1836 journal has "had." (*JSP*, J1:77.)

215. That is, JS's wife, Emma Smith.

216. The official minute entry for this date indicates that William Smith also brought a second
charge, against Mary Cahoon Elliott only, for "abusing said E[lliott]s daughter as referred to before, and
also abusing the rest of her children." That JS agreed to preside in the case indicates his approval of considering the new charges. JS ruled that his mother, Lucy Mack Smith, was out of order in presenting testimony about matters that had already been resolved by the high council earlier in the day. (Minute
Book 1, 29 Oct. 1835.)

was knocked down. By this time he (President J. S. J$^{unr.}$) became wounded and agitated in his feelings on account of the wilful and wicked stubbornness of his brother Wm.[217] and was about to leave the house; But his aged father who was present, requested him not to do so. He hearkened to his advice, the house was brought to order, after much debate upon the subject and the council resumed business. Brother Elliot & his wife were both acquitted of the charges against them.[218]

30 October 1835 • Friday

Friday 30th He was at home. This day M̲r̲. Francis Porter, a member of the Methodist Episcopal church from Jefferson County N.Y. called to make some inquiry about lands in this place, whether there are any farms for sale that are valuable, and whether a member of our church could move into this vicinity and enjoy his own possessions and property without making it common stock.

He had been requested to do so by some brethren, who live in LeRay, Jefferson County N. Y. He [JS] replied that he had a valuable farm joining the Temple lot that He would sell, and that there are other lands for sale in this place, that there is no commonstock business, among us, and that [p. 113] every man enjoys his own property; or he can if he is be disposed consecrate liberally or illiberally to support the poor & needy or to the building up of Zion,[219] He also inquired how many members there were in this church. He was told there were about five or six hundred who communed at our chapel and that perhaps, there were one thousand in this vicinity.[220]

At evening the subject of this narrative was presented with a letter from his brother Wm. Smith, the purport of which was that that he was censured by the brethren, in consequence of what took place in the council the preceding evening: he also wished to have the cause of censure removed to the satisfaction and understanding of all, that he might not unjustly be censured or made to

---

217. Descriptions of JS as "wounded" and William's actions as "wilful and wicked" are scribal elaborations not found in the 1835–1836 journal.

218. Minutes of the council state that the Elliotts made confession after the council heard new evidence presented by a "Sister Childs" who had lived in the Elliott home. They were "forgiven, and . . . restored to fellowship." (Minute Book 1, 29 Oct. 1835.)

219. Prior to their 1830 conversion to Mormonism, followers of Sidney Rigdon in Kirtland established a communal society featuring group ownership of property. An 1831 JS revelation mandated establishing a new basis for economic reorganization that featured individual stewardships rather than common ownership. (See *JSP*, J1:79n72.)

220. Approximately nine hundred to thirteen hundred Latter-day Saints, including children, lived in Kirtland Township at this time, with two hundred or more in the surrounding area. (Backman, *Heavens Resound*, 139–140.)

suffer in his feelings.[221] He then considered that he had been materially injured. He (J.S. [Jnr.]) replied that he thought they parted with the best of feelings, and that he was not accountable for the dissatisfaction of others. Wm. was invited by Joseph, to call and talk with him, assuring him that he would converse in the spirit of meekness on the subject, and give him all the satisfaction he could. This reply was by letter and a copy retained.

31 October 1835 • Saturday

Saturday 31[st] In the morning his Brother Hyrum Smith called in and said he had been much trou[b]led all night, and had not slept any. He said something was wrong, and while they were conversing his brother Wm. [Smith] came in according to his (Joseph's) request last night. His brother Hyrum observed that he must go to the Store. He was invited by Joseph to stay; he replied that he could go and do his business and return: He did so, and during his absence Wm. introduced the subject of their difficulties at the council.[222] Joseph told him he did not want to converse upon that subject until Hyrum returned. He soon came in, and it was proposed to relate the ocurrences of the Council before named, and wherein he (Joseph) had done wrong he would confess it and ask his forgiveness; and then he (Wm.) should relate his story and make confession wherein he had done wrong, and then leave it to brother Hyrum Smith & brother [Warren] Parrish to decide the matter between them, and he would agree to the decision and be satisfied therewith. Wm. observed that he had not done wrong and that Joseph was always determined to carry every point whether right or wrong, and, therefore, he could not stand [p. 114] an equal chance with him. This was truly an insult. It was indirectly accusing him of wilful stubbornness and wicked obstinacy:[223] however he did not reply to him in a harsh manner, knowing his brother's irascible disposition, but tried to reason with him and show him the propriety of a compliance with his request. He finally succeeded with the assistance of his brother Hyrum, in obtaining his assent to the proposition. he had made. He, (Joseph) then related the circumstances as they occurred, and wherein he had done wrong he confessed it and asked him to forgive him. Wm. then made his statements justifying himself, wholly not only in transgressing the rules of the council, but in treating the Presidency[224] with utter contempt. After he had closed, brother

---

221. In place of "might not unjustly be censured or made to suffer in his feelings," the 1835–1836 journal has "may not be censured unjustly, concidering that his cause was a just one." (*JSP*, J1:79.)
222. See entry for 29 Oct. 1835 herein.
223. "It was indirectly accusing him of wilful stubbornness and wicked obstinacy" is a scribal addition not found in the 1835–1836 journal.
224. For "Presidency," the journal has "authority of the Presidency." (*JSP*, J1:80.)

Hyrum began to make some remarks in the spirit of meekness. Wm. became enraged, Joseph now joined his br. Hyrum in trying to calm the stormy feelings of Wm. But, neither neither reason nor argument were of any avail. He insisted that they intended to add abuse to injury. His passion increased; he arose abruptly and said he wanted no more to to do with them or the church and they might take his license for he would have nothing to do with them. He rushed out of the door in a fit of rage,[225] his brothers trying to prevail on him to stop, but all their entreaties had no effect to soften his heart or subdue his passion. He went away in a rage and soon sent his license to his brother Joseph. He appeared to be under the influence of the Adversary of righteousness,[226] and consequently, to spread the leaven of iniquity among the brethren of the Church. He succeeded in ~~prejudiced~~ prejudicing the mind of his brother Samuel [Smith]. He was also soon heard in the highway exclaiming against his br. Joseph; which would make his enemies to greatly rejoice. Where the matter would end he knew not, but he prayed God to forgive them, and give them humility and unfeigned repentance. The feelings of his heart he could not express. on that occasion. He could prevail nothing with them; he could only pray his Heavenly Father to open their eyes that they may discover where they stand, and extricate themselves from the snare into which they had fallen.

After dinner he in company with his wife, children and brother Carloss [Don Carlos Smith] and some others rode out on a visit to brother [Shadrach] Roundys who lived near the village of Willoughby in Cayahoga [Cuyahoga] County. He expressed himself as having had an agreeable visit, and as soon as he returned, he was called upon to baptize. Mr. Samuel Whitney, wife and daughter.[227] After baptizm, he with others returned to their [p. 115] house and offered our thanks to the Most High. While in prayer he obtained an evidence that his brother W^m. would return to the church and confess[228] the wrong he had done.

1 November 1835 • Sunday

Sabbath Nov. 1st Verily, thus saith the Lord unto his servant Joseph Smith J^{unr.} mine anger is kindled against my servant Reynolds Cahoon, because of his iniquities, his covetous and dishonest principles, in himself and family; and

---

225. The phrase "in a fit of rage" does not occur in the corresponding journal entry.

226. This statement does not appear in the journal.

227. Kirtland bishop Newel K. Whitney's parents, Samuel and Susanna Kimball Whitney, had recently arrived in Kirtland. Their daughter Caroline probably arrived with them. (Entry for 29 Oct. 1835 herein; Marlboro, Windham Co., VT, Vital Records, 1768–1857, vol. 1, p. 44, microfilm 28,528, U.S. and Canada Record Collection, FHL; Obituary for Caroline Whitney Kingsbury, *The Wasp*, 29 Oct. 1842, [3].)

228. For "confess," the 1835–1836 journal has "repair." (*JSP*, J1:81.)

⟨if⟩ he doth not purge them away and set his house in order, ⟨~~chastizement awaiteth him~~⟩ therefore, if he repent not chastizement awaiteth him, even as it seemeth good in my sight.[229] Therefore go and declare unto him this word. He (the subject of this narrative) went immediately and delivered this message according as the Lord had commanded him. He even, called him in, and read what the Lord had said concerning him. He acknowledged that it was verily so, and expressed much humility. He then went to meeting. Elder Carrill [John Corrill] preached a fine discourse[.] In the P. M. President Wm. W. Phelps continued the services of the day by reading the 5.th. chapter of Matthew, also the law regulating the High Council[230] and made some remarks upon them. The eucharist was administred, he (Joseph) then confirmed a number who had been baptized, and blessed a number of children in the name of Jesus Christ, with the new and everlasting Covenant Notice was then given that the Elder's school would commence the next day. He then dismissed the meeting.

2 November 1835 • Monday

Monday morning Nov. 2.d He was engaged in regulating the affairs of the school. He then had his team harnessed, and he, S[idney] Rigdon O[liver] Cowdery, F[rederick] G. Williams, his Scribe,[231] and a number of others, went to Willoughby to hear Doct. Piexotto [Daniel Peixotto] deliver a lecture on the theory and practice of Physic.[232] They called at Mr. [Nathan] Cushman's had their horses put in the stable, took dinner, attended the lecture and was treated with marked respect, throughout. They then returned home. Lyman Wight came in to the place to day from Zion[233] & George [A.] Smith & Lyman Smith

---

229. Less than three months earlier, on 10 August 1835, JS brought charges against Cahoon in a high council meeting for having "failed to do his duty in correcting his children, and instructing them in the way of truth & righteousness." The council agreed with the charges, and Cahoon "confessed the correctness of the decision, and promised to make public acknowledgement before the church." (Minute Book 1, 10 Aug. 1835.)

230. See Minutes, 17 Feb. 1834, in Doctrine and Covenants 5, 1835 ed. [D&C 102].

231. Warren Parrish.

232. Peixotto, a public health advocate of national prominence, had revised George Gregory's medical textbook, *Elements of the Theory and Practice of Physic,* and had recently moved from New York City to become a professor at the newly established Willoughby Medical College in Willoughby, Ohio. (George Gregory, *Elements of the Theory and Practice of Physic, Designed for the Use of Students* [New York: M. Sherman, 1830]; *History of Geauga and Lake Counties, Ohio,* 40; "Peixotto," in *Jewish Encyclopedia,* 9:583.)

233. Wight had traveled from Clay County, Missouri, to Kirtland, where he attended the Elders School. He was among the earliest group called by JS to travel to Kirtland to be endowed with "power from on high." (Minute Book 2, 23 June 1834.)

from the East.[234] ~~They~~ The question was then agitated, Which[235] should go to New-York to make arrangements respecting a book-bindery. The question was at length referred to him for a decision. The word of the Lord came thus unto him, saying, It is not my will that my servant, Frederick should go to New York, but inasmuch as he wishes to go and visit his relatives, that he may warn them to flee the wrath to come let him go and see them, for that purpose, and let that be his only business. And behold in this thing he shall be blessed [p. 116] with power to overcome their prejudices. Verily thus saith the Lord, Amen.[236]

3 November 1835 • Tuesday

Tuesday 3ᵈ Thus came the word of the Lord unto him concerning the, Twelve,

> behold they are under condemnation because they are not suf-
> ficiently humble, in my sight, and in consequence of their covetous
> desires, in that they have not dealt equally with each other, in the
> division of the monies which came into their hands, nevertheless some
> of them dealt equally, therefore, they shall be rewarded. But verily I say
> unto, you they must all humble themselves before me, before they will
> be accounted worthy to receive an endowment, to go forth in my name
> unto all nations. As for my servant William [Smith], let the Eleven
> humble themselves in prayer and in faith and wait on me in patience
> and my servant William shall return and I will make him a polished
> shaft in my quiver, in bringing down the wickedness and abominations
> of men and there shall be none mightier than he in his day and
> generation, nevertheless, if he repent not speedily, he shall be brought
> low and shall be chastened, and sorely for all his iniquity which he has
> committed against me. Nevertheless the sin which he hath sinned
> against me, is not even now more grievous than the sin with which my
> Servant David W. Patten, my Servant Orson Hyde, and my Servant
> Wm. E. MᶜLel[l]in, have sinned against me, and the residu are not
> sufficiently humble before me. Behold the parable which I spake
> concerning a man having twelve sons. For what man among you

---

234. Five months earlier, on 5 June 1835, JS's cousin George A. Smith departed with Lyman Smith on a proselytizing mission to Ohio, Pennsylvania, and New York. ("Sketch of the Auto Biography of George Albert Smith," 13, Historian's Office, Histories of the Twelve, ca. 1858–1880, CHL.)

235. That is, either Frederick G. Williams or Oliver Cowdery. (JS, Journal, 2 Nov. 1835, in *JSP*, J1:82.)

236. Oliver Cowdery soon left for New York City to "purchase a book-binding establishment and stock, and also a quantity of Hebrew books for the school." He returned within the month. (Oliver Cowdery, Kirtland, OH, to Warren Cowdery, [Freedom, NY], 22 Nov. 1835, in Cowdery, Letterbook, 63; entry for 20 Nov. 1835 herein.)

having twelve Sons and is no respecter to them and they serve him
obediently and he saith unto the one be thou clothed in robes and sit
thou here, and to the other be thou clothed in rags and sit thou there.
And looketh upon his sons and saith I am just.[237] Ye will answer and
say no man, and ye answer truly. Therefore, ⟨verily⟩ thus saith the Lord
your God. I appointed these 'Twelve' that they should be equal in their
ministry and in their portion, and in their evangelical rights.
Wherefore they have sinned a very grievous sin, inasmuch as they have
made themselves unequal. and have not hearkned unto my voice.
Therefore, let them repent speedily and prepare their hearts for the
solemn assembly, and for the great day which is to come. Verily thus
saith the Lord. Amen.[238] [p. 117]

He then went to assist in organizing the Elders school: called to order and
made some appropriate remarks on the object of the school, and the great
necessity there was of rightly improving time and reigning up our minds to a
sense of the great object that lies before us, (viz.) That glorious endowment that
God has in store for the faithful. He then dedicated the school in the name of
the Lord Jesus, Christ. After the school was dismissed, he attended a patriarchal meeting at his brother Samuel's Smith's. his wife's parents[239] were blessed,
also his own child. and named Susanna.[240] At evening he preached in the
school house to a crowded congregation.

4 November 1835 • Wednesday

Wednesday Nov. 4 He was at home in the morning, but attended school,
during the school hours; made good progress in studies. In the evening he lectured. on Grammar at home. On this day King Follet[t] arrived in this place
from Zion.

---

237. See Revelation, 2 Jan. 1831, in Doctrine and Covenants 12:5, 1835 ed. [D&C 38:26].

238. A revelation concerning the Quorum of the Twelve and a charge given to its members soon
after its founding warned against disunity and inequality. The twelve apostles met with JS nine days later.
Tension between the apostles and other church leaders had been partially resolved more than a month
earlier on their return but was not fully resolved for weeks to come. (Instruction on priesthood, ca. Apr.
1835, in Doctrine and Covenants 3:11–12, 1835 ed. [D&C 107:27–33]; entries for 26 Sept. and 12 Nov. 1835
and 16 Jan. 1836 herein.)

239. Samuel Smith's parents-in-law, Joshua and Susannah Boutwell Bailey.

240. On the birth of Samuel's daughter Susanna Bailey Smith, see entry for 27 Oct. 1835 herein. In
blessing the infant, Joseph Smith Sr. evidently gave her a name. Rather than having their infants baptized
and christened, Latter-day Saints were directed to bring their children "unto the elders before the church,
who are to lay their hands upon them in the name of Jesus Christ, and bless them in his name." (Articles
and covenants, 10 Apr. 1830, in Doctrine and Covenants 2:20, 1835 ed. [D&C 20:70–71]; see also Book of
Mormon, 1830 ed., 581 [Moroni 8:10–11].)

5 November 1835 • Thursday

Thursday— 5[th.] He attended school. This day Isaac Morley came in from the East. He was called in the morning to visit Thomas Burdick, who was sick. He took his scribe[241] with him and they prayed for, and laid their hands upon him in the name of the Lord Jesus The disease was rebuked. Wm. E. M[c·]Lel[l]in and Orson Hyde came in and desired to hear the revelation concerning the "Twelve"[242] His Scribe read it to them: They expressed some little dissatisfaction but after examining their own hearts, they acknowledged it to be the word of the Lord, and said they were satisfied. After School Elder Brigham Young came in and being one of the 'Twelve' he desired also to hear it read. After hearing it he appeared perfectly satisfied. In the evening he [JS] lectured on Grammar.

6 November 1835 • Friday

Friday 6[th.] He was at home in the morning, but attended school during the school hours of the day. spent the evening at home. It may not be improper here to remark that in the morning he was introduced to a man from the East. After hearing the name, Joseph Smith, he remarked that he was nothing but a man. i[n]timating by this expression that he had imbibed the idea, that a person through whom the Lord revealed himself, must be something more than a man. He appeared to have forgotten that all the ancient Prophets were but men, particularly what St. James said of the Prophet, Elias, that he was a man of like passions as we are, yet he had that power with God, that he prayed that it might not rain on the earth, and it rained not for three years and six months. And again in answer to his prayer, the Lord gave rain and the earth brought forth her fruits.[243] Indeed, such is the [p. 118] darkness and ignorance of this generation, that it is a thing incredible that a man should have any intercourse with his Maker.

7 November 1835 • Saturday

Saturday 7[th.] He spent the day at home attending to his domestic concerns. The word of the Lord came unto him, saying, behold I am well pleased with my servant, Isaac Morley and my Servant Edward Partridge, because of the integrity of their hearts in laboring in my vineyard for the salvation of the souls

---

241. Warren Parrish.
242. The revelation included a rebuke of McLellin and Hyde. (See entry for 3 Nov. 1835 herein.)
243. See James 5:17–18.

of men.[244] Verily I say unto you their sins are forgiven them; Therefore, say unto them in my name, that it is my will that they should tarry for a little season and attend the school, and also the Solemn assembly for a wise purpose in me, even so. Amen.

8 November 1835 • Sunday

Sunday 8ᵗʰ. He went to meeting in the morning at the usual hour. In the fore noon Z[erubbabel] Snow preached a very interesting discourse. In the after noon J[oseph] Young preached; and after preaching Isaac Hill came forward to make some remarks, by way of confession. He had previously been excommunicated from the Church, for lying, and for an attempt to seduce a female. His confession was not satisfactory to the mind of the subject of these memoirs. John Smith then rose and made some remarks, touching the proceedings of the High Council in the case of said Hill. He observed that the council decided, that he should make a public confession of his crime and have it published in the Messenger & Advocate. He proposed that Mr. Hill should now make his confession before the congregation, and then immediately observed that he had forgiven Mr. Hill. which seemed rather to militate against the statement he first made, which doubtless was rather to be attributed to an error of the head than the heart.[245] President S[idney] Rigdon then arose and made some remarks in opposition to those made by the preceding speaker,[246] and were directly calculated to destroy his influence and bring him into disrepute in the eyes of the Church. This was not right; he also misrepresented Mʳ. Hill's case and spread darkness rather than light upon the subject. A vote of the Church was then called on his case and he was restored without any further confession; that he should be received into the Church by baptism, which was administered accordingly. After he (J. S.) came home from meeting, he took up a labor with his Uncle John Smith, and convinced him that he was wrong in some of his remarks respecting I. Hill, and he confessed it. He then went and labored with President Rigdon, and succeeded also in convincing him of his error, which [p. 119] he confessed. The word of the Lord then came unto

---

244. Partridge and Morley had departed on a fund-raising mission to the East almost five months earlier. Partridge returned to Kirtland on 29 October 1835, and Morley on 5 November 1835. They were among a group of Missouri church leaders whom JS appointed in June 1834 to travel to Kirtland to receive the endowment of "power from on high." (Entries for 29 Oct. and 5 Nov. 1835 herein; Partridge, Journal, 2 June and 29 Oct. 1835; Minute Book 2, 23 June 1834.)

245. For "which doubtless was rather to be attributed to an error of the head than the heart," the 1835–1836 journal has "this I attributed to an error in judgment not in design." (*JSP*, J1:86.)

246. For "made some remarks in opposition to those made by the preceding speaker," the 1835–1836 journal has "verry abruptly militated against the sentiment of Uncle John." (*JSP*, J1:86.)

him that President Wm. W. Phelps and President J[ohn] Whitmer were under condemnation before the Lord for their errors.[247] He also commenced a labor with J. Carrill [John Corrill] for not partaking of the Sacrament, and he made his confession. He also reproved his wife for leaving the meeting before Sacrament she made no reply but manifested contrition by weeping.

9 November 1835 • Monday

Monday Nov. 9th After breakfast Mary Whitiker[248] came in and wished to see him; her request was granted. She gave a relation of her grievances which, for the time being, were unfathomable, and if true they were sorrowful indeed. He prayed his Heavenly Father to bring the truth of her case to light, that the reward due to evil doers may be given them, and that the afflicted and oppressed, may be delivered. While sitting in his house this morning between the hours of ten an[d] eleven, a man came in and introduced himself to him calling himself Joshua, the Jewish Minister,[249] His appearance was something singular, having, a beard about three inches in length which is quite grey. his hair was also long and considerably silvered with age. He had the appearance of a man about 50 or 55 years old. He was tall and straight, slender frame, blue eyes, thin visage, and fair complexion. He wore a green frock coat and pantaloons of the same color. He had on a black fur hat with a narrow brim. When speaking he frequently shuts his eyes and exhibits a kind of scowl upon his countenance. He (Joseph) made some inquiry after his name, but, received no definite answer. The conversation soon turned upon the subject of Religion, and after the subject of this narrative had made some remarks concerning the bible, he commenced giving him a relation of the circumstances, connected with the coming forth of the Book of Mormon, which were nearly as follows. Being wrought up in my mind respecting the subject of Religion, and looking at the different systems taught the children of men, I knew not who was right or who was wrong, but considered it of the first importance to me that I should be aright right, in matters of so much moment, matter involving eternal consequences. Being thus perplexed in mind I retired to the silent grove. and there bowed down before the Lord, under a realizing sense, (if the bible be true) ask and you shall receive, knock and it shall be opened, seek and you shall find, and again, if any man lack wisdom, let [him ask][250] of God who giveth to all

247. For "errors," the 1835–1836 journal has "iniquities." Phelps later inserted in the journal that "they made satisfaction the same day."
248. The 9–11 November 1835 entry in JS's journal gives the name as "Whitcher." (*JSP*, J1:87.)
249. Robert Matthews, more commonly known as the Prophet Matthias.
250. Omitted words supplied from the corresponding journal entry. (See *JSP*, J1:87.)

men liberally & upbraideth not.[251] Information was what I most desired, [p. 120] ~~with age. He had~~ at this time. and with a fixed determination to obtain it, I called on the Lord for the first time in the place above stated, or in other words, I made a fruitless attempt to pray My tongue seemed to be swoolen in my mouth, so that I could not utter. I heard a noise behind me like some one walking towards me: I strove again to pray, but could not; the noise of walking seemed to draw nearer; I sprang upon my feet and looked round, but saw no person, or thing that was calculated to produce the noise of walking. I kneeled again, my mouth was opened and my tongue loosed; I called on the Lord in mighty prayer. A pillar of fire appeared above my head; which presently rested down upon me, and filled me with unspeakable joy. A personage appeared in the midst of this pillar of flame, which was spread all around and yet nothing consumed. Another personage soon appeared like unto the first: he said unto me thy sins are forgiven thee. He testified also unto me that Jesus Christ is the son of God. I saw many angels in this vision. I was about 14 years old when I received this first communication.[252] When I was about 17 years I had another vision of angels; in the night season, after I had retired to bed; I had not been asleep, but was meditating upon my past life and experience. I was well aware I had not kept the commandments, and I repented heartily for all my sins and transgressions, and humbled myself before him, whose eye surveys all things at a glance. All at once the room was illuminated above the brightness of the sun; An Angel appeared before me; his hands and feet were, naked, pure and white; he stood betwen the floors of the room, clothed with purity inexpressible.[253] He said unto me I am a Messenger sent from God, be faithful and keep his commandments in all things. He told me also of a sacred record which was written on plates of gold. I saw in the vision the place where they were deposited. He said to me the Indians were the literal decendants of Abraham. He explained many of the prophecies to me; one of which I will mention, which is in Malachi 4ᵗʰ chapter. Behold, the day of the Lord cometh ⟨⟨(&c⟩ He also informed me that the Urim & Thummim was hid up with the record, and that God would give me power to translate it with the assistance of this instrument;

251. See Matthew 7:7–8; and James 1:5.

252. For JS's other accounts of this vision, see JS History, ca. summer 1832, pp. 11–13 herein; JS History Drafts, 1838–ca. 1841, pp. 210–215 herein; JS, "Church History," p. 494 herein; and JS, "Latter Day Saints," p. 508 herein.

253. JS identified this angel as Moroni, the last ancient American prophet to write in the Book of Mormon. ([JS], Editorial, *Elders' Journal,* July 1838, 42–44; see also Oliver Cowdery, "Letter VI," *LDS Messenger and Advocate,* Apr. 1835, 1:112 [see also later version, p. 71 herein]; and Revelation, ca. Aug. 1830, in Doctrine and Covenants 50:2, 1835 ed. [D&C 27:5]. JS's other accounts of this experience are found in JS History, ca. summer 1832, pp. 13–14 herein; JS History Drafts, 1838–ca. 1841, pp. 220–233 herein; JS, "Church History," pp. 494–495 herein; and JS, "Latter Day Saints," pp. 508–509 herein.)

he then gradually vanished out of my sight or the vision closed. while meditating on what I had seen, The Angel appeared to me again, and related the, [p. 121] same things and much more, also the third time bearing the same tidings and departed. During the time I was in this vision I did not realize any thing around me, except what was shown to me in this communication. After the vision had all passed, I found that it was nearly day light; The family soon arose, and got up also. On that day while in the field at work with my father, he asked me if I was sick, I replied, I had but little strength. He told me to go to the house. I started and went part of the way, and was finally deprived of my strength and fell; but how long I remained I do not know. The Angel came to me again and commanded me to go and tell my father what I had seen & heard. I did so. The old man wept and told me that it was a vision from God, and to attend to it. I went and found the place where the plates were, according to the direction of the Angel, I also saw them and the Angel as before. The powers of darkness strove hard against me. I called on God. The Angel told me, that the reason why I could not obtain the plates at this time, was because I was under transgression, but to come again in one year from that time. I did so but did not obtain them, also the third and the fourth year the last of which time I obtained them, and translated them into ⟨the⟩ english language by the gift and power of God and have been preaching it ever since.

While President Smith was relating this brief history of the establishment of the Church of Christ in these last days, Joshua seemed to be highly entertained. After he had gone through he observed to him (Joshua) that the hour of worship and time to dine had now arrived, and asked him to tarry, to which he consented, After dinner the conversation was resumed, & Joshua proceeded to make some remarks on the Prophecies as follows. He observed that he was aware that, he (Joseph) could bear stronger meat than many others, therefore he should open his mind the more freely. Daniel has told us that he is to stand in his proper lot in the latter days. According to his vision he had a right to shut it up and also to open it again after many days, or in the latter times.[254] Daniel's image whose head was gold, and body, arms legs and feet were composed of the different materials described in his vision, represents the different governments [p. 122]

The golden head was to represent Nebuchadnezzar, King of Babylon; the other parts other kings and forms of government,[255] which I shall not now mention in detail, but confine my remarks more particularly to the feet of the

---

254. See Daniel 12:4.

255. Matthews drew on Daniel 2, a Bible chapter that was also important in early Latter-day Saint eschatology. (Whittaker, "Book of Daniel in Early Mormon Thought," 158–166.)

image. The policy of the wicked spirit is to seperate what God has joined together, and unite what he has seperated, which he has succeded in doing to admiration, in the present state of society, which is like unto iron & clay. There is confusion in all things both political and religious and notwithstanding all the efforts that are made to bring about a union, society remains disunited, and all attempts to unite it are as fruitless as to attempt to unite it are as ⟨it are as⟩ fruitless as to attempt to unite iron and clay.

The feet of the image is the government of these United-States. Other nations ⟨& kingdoms⟩ are looking up to her for an example of union, freedom and equal rights, and, therefore, worship her like as Daniel saw in the vision, although they are beginning to lose confidence in her, on seeing the broils and discord that distract her political and religious horizons. This image is characteristic of all governments and institutions, or most of them; as they begin with a head of gold and terminate in the conte[m]ptible feet of iron and clay. They make a splendid appearance at first, promising much more than they can perform, and finally end in degradation and sink in infamy. We should not only start to come out of Babylon, but we should leave her entirely, lest we be overthrown in her ruins. We should, therefore, keep on improving and reforming. Twenty four hours for improvement now, is worth as much as a year was, a hundred years ago. The spirit of the Fathers was cut down, or those that were under the altar, are now rising, this is the first resurrection. the Elder that falls first will rise last. We should not form any opinion only for the present, and leave the result of futurity with God. I have risen up out of obscurity, but was looked up to, when but a youth in temporal things. It is not necessary that God should give us all things at first, or in his first commission to us, but in his second John Saw the Angel deliver the gospel in the last days,[256] which would not be necessary if it were already in the world: This expression would be inconsistent, The small lights that God has given are sufficient to lead us out of Babylon [p. 123] and when we get out we shall have the greater light. He told Joshua that he did not perfectly[257] understand him concerning the resurrection, and wished him to be more explanatory on that subject: he replied that he did not feel impressed by the spirit to unfold it further at that time, but perhaps, he might at some other time.— President Smith then withdrew to do transact some business with a gentleman that had called to see him.

Joshua informed W[arren] Parrish[,] Smith's scribe that he was born in the Town of Cambridge Washington County in the state of New York. He said that all the Rail-Roads, Canals and other improvements, are performed by

256. See Revelation 14:6.
257. The word "perfectly" does not appear in the 1835–1836 journal.

spirits of the resurrection. The silence, spoken of by John the Revelator, he said, which is to be in Heaven for the space of half an hour,[258] is between 1830 & 1851, during which time the judgements of God will be poured out: After that time there will be peace.

Curiosity to see a man that was said to be a Jew, induced many to call during the day, and more particularly at evening. Suspicions were entertained that said Joshua was none other ~~that~~ than the noted Matthias of New York City, about whom, so much had been said in the public prints on account of the trials he underwent in that place before courts of justice, The crimes alledged against him were murder, manslaughter, contempt of Court, and whipping his daughter, for the two last of which he was found guilty was imprisoned and came out about four months since After some equivocating he confessed that he was really Matthias.[259] After supper it was proposed that Matthias should deliver a lecture to those present, He did so sitting in his chair He commenced, by saying, God said let there be light and there was light, which he dwelt upon through his discourse. He made some very excellent remarks but his mind was evidently filled with darkness. After he dismissed his meeting & the congregation dispersed, he conversed freely upon the circumstances that tra[n]spired in New York.

His name is Robert Matthias [Matthews]. He says that Joshua is his priestly name. During all this time no one contradicted his sentiments. The object of President Smith, was to draw out all he could concerning his faith. The next morning——

10 November 1835 • Tuesday

[*illegible*][260] Tuesday 10ᵗʰ He [JS] resumed the conversation and desired him [Robert Matthews] to enlighten his mind with his views respecting the [p. 124] resurrection. He says he possesses the spirit of his fathers, that he is the literal decendant of Matthias the Apostle, who was chosen in the place of Judas that fell.[261] and that his spirit is resussitated in him, and that ~~the~~ this is the way or scheme of Eternal life; this transmigration of soul or spirit from Father to Son.

---

258. See Revelation 8:1.

259. In April 1835, Matthews was tried in White Plains, New York, and acquitted of murder and manslaughter, but he was charged with contempt of court for shouting during the proceedings. He was then immediately tried for an alleged assault on his daughter, Isabella Laisdell, and found guilty. He was sentenced to jail for three months on the assault charge and for thirty days for contempt of court. Newspapers covering this widely publicized case expressed astonishment over Matthews's light sentence. (Johnson and Wilentz, *Kingdom of Matthias*, 144–165.)

260. TEXT: Possibly "~~February~~".

261. See Acts 1:15–26.

He told Matthias that his doctrine was of the Devil. That he in reality was possessed of a wicked and deformed spirit. Notwithstanding, he professed to be the spirit of truth itself,[262] and said also that he possessed the soul of Christ. He tarried until the next day.

11 November 1835 • Wednesday

Wednesday 11th. After breakfast Joshua [Robert Matthews] was told that his God was the Devil and could stay no longer, but he must depart, and so for once says the subject of these memoirs I cast out the Devil in bodily shape.[263]

Here it may not be improper to mention that on the 9th A[lvah] Beaman came to ask advice relative to purchasing land. in this place or in Missouri.[264] As he could not arrange his business to go to Missouri next spring he was advized to buy and settle here until he arrange his mind and then go to Zion if he chose to do so,[265] President Smith was at home this day except during school hours. He spent the evening around his own fireside teaching his family the science of grammar. The weather was now cold, the wind high and it commenced snowing.

12 November 1835 • Thursday

Thursday 12th He attended school again during the school hours. Rain and snow continued to fall. The snow by that time was about one inch in depth. the wind high and the weather extremely unpleasant. The laborers who had commenced finishing the out-side of the Lord's House were obliged to break off from their business on the 11th. at the commencement of this storm. The job of finishing the out side of the House was let to A[rtemus] Millet & L[orenzo] Young for $1000. They progressed rapidly, in it. Jacob Bump has the Job of plastering the inside throughout for $1500. He commenced on the 9th. and still continues, the inclemency of the weather ⟨to the contrary⟩ notwithstanding. This evening (12) President Smith met with a council of the "Twelve" by their request. Nine of them were present. Council opened by singing and prayer and he then remarked to them nearly as follows: I am happy in the enjoyment of this opportunity in meeting this council on this occasion. I am satisfied that [p. 125]

---

262. On Matthews's claim to be "the spirit of truth," the same spirit that was once within the New Testament apostle Matthias, see Johnson and Wilentz, *Kingdom of Matthias,* 94–95.

263. The corresponding journal entry also states, "& I believe a murderer." On parting, Matthews and JS apparently shared a mutual contempt. (*JSP,* J1:95; see also "Prophet Catch Prophet," *Painesville [OH] Telegraph,* 20 Nov. 1835, 3.)

264. The 1835–1836 journal also includes "whether it is best for him to purchase in this vicinity and move into this church, or not." (*JSP,* J1:95.)

265. The corresponding entry in JS's journal ends, "I advised him to come here, and settle untill he could move to Zion." (*JSP,* J1:95.)

the spirit of the Lord is here, and I am satisfied with all the [brethren present]²⁶⁶ and I need not say to you that you have my utmost confidence, and that I intend to uphold you to the uttermost, for I am well aware that you have to sustain my character against the vile calumnies and reproaches of this ungodly generation, and that you delight in so doing. Darkness prevails; it is in a great degree now as it was when Christ was about to be crucified. The powers of darkness strove to obscure the glorious sun of righteousness, that then began to dawn upon the world, and was soon to burst in great blessings upon the heads of the faithful; and let me tell you, brethren, That great blessings await is us at this time, and will soon be poured out upon us if we are faithful in all things: for we are even entitled to greater blessings than they were, because they had the person of Christ with them to instruct them in the great plan of salvation. His personal presence we have not, therefore we need the greater faith on account of our peculiar circumstances. I am determined to do all I can to uphold you. Although I may do many things inadvertantly that are not right in the sight of God. You want to know many things that are before you, that you may know how to prepare yourselves for the great things that God is about to bring to pass. But there is one great deficiency or obstruction in the way, that deprives us of the greater blessings, and in order to make the foundation of this church complete, and permanent, we must remove this obstruction, which is to attend to certain duties to which we have not attended. I supposed I had established this church on a permanent foundation when I went to Missouri. and indeed I did so, for if I had been taken away it would have been enough.²⁶⁷ But as I yet live, therefore, God requires more at my hands. The item to which I wish the more particularly to cite your minds this night is the ordinance of washing of feet, This we have not done as yet, but it is as necessary now as it was in the days of the Saviour,²⁶⁸ and we must have a place prepared that we may attend to this ordinance, aside from the world,²⁶⁹ We have not desired

266. Omitted words supplied from the corresponding journal entry. (See *JSP*, J1:96.)

267. Before leaving on the 1834 military expedition to Missouri, JS established a "high council" for governance over the stake in Kirtland. While in Missouri in July, he similarly organized a high council. In Missouri he also appointed David Whitmer, William W. Phelps, and John Whitmer as a local presidency to preside over the high council, as well as designating David Whitmer as a potential successor in the office of general church president. JS remarked on that occasion that "if he should now be taken away that he had accomplished the great work which the Lord had laid before him." (Minute Book 2, 3 and 7 July 1834 and 15 Mar. 1838.)

268. See John 13:4–17; compare New Testament Revision 2, part 2, p. 117 [Joseph Smith Translation, John 13:10].

269. Though JS instituted the washing of feet in the 1833 School of the Prophets, he now prepared to introduce the practice in connection with the House of the Lord. (See Revelation, 27 and 28 Dec. 1832 and 3 Jan. 1833, in Doctrine and Covenants 7:44–46, 1835 ed. [D&C 88:137–141].)

much from the hand of the Lord. with that faith and obedience that we ought. Yet we have enjoyed great blessings, but we are not so sensible of them as we should be [p. 126] When or where has God suffered one of the witnesses or first Elders of this church to fall? Amidst all the calamities and judgements that have befallen the inhabitants of the earth, his Almighty arm has sustained us. Men & Devils have raged but they have raged in vain. We must have all things prepared and call our solemn assembly as the Lord has commanded us, that we may be able to accomplish his great work. It must be done in God's own way, The House of the Lord must be prepared and the solemn assembly be called and organized in it, according to the order of the House of God: & in it we must attend to the ordinance of washing of feet. This ordinance was never intended for any but official members: it is calculated to unite our hearts, that we may be one in feeling & sentiment, and that our faith may be strong so that Satan can not overthrow us, nor have any power over us. The endowment about which you are so anxious, you cannot comprehend now, nor could the Angel, Gabriel explain it to the understanding of your dark minds, but strive to be prepared in your hearts, be faithful in all things, that when we meet in the solemn assembly, that is, such as God shall name out of all the official members, will meet, and we must be clean every whit. Let us be faithful and silent, brethren, and if God gives you a manifestion keep it to yourselves, be watchful and prayerful and you shall have a prelude of those joys that God will pour out on that day. Do not watch for iniquity in each other, if you do, you will not get an endowment, for God will not bestow it on such: but if we are faithful, and live by every word that proceeds forth from the mouth of God I will venture to prophecy that we shall get a blessing that will be worth our grateful acknowledgements and everlasting remembrance. If we should live as long as John the Revelator[270] our blessings will be such as we have not realized before, nor in this generation.

The order of the House of God has been, and ever will be the same, even after Christ comes, and after the termination of the Thousand years it will be the same, and we shall finally enter the celestial kingdom of God and enjoy it forever.

You need an endowment, brethren, in order that you may be prepared and able to overcome all things, and then those who reject your testimony will be damned. The sick will be healed, the lame made to walk the deaf to hear and the blind to see through your instrumentality.[271] But let me tell you, that you

270. Jesus told John that he would "tarry till" the Second Coming. (John 21:20–24; see also Account of John, Apr. 1829–C, in Doctrine and Covenants 33, 1835 ed. [D&C 7].)
271. See Mark 16:14–18; compare Book of Mormon, 1830 ed., 514 [4 Nephi 1:5].

will not have power after the endowment, to heal those who have not faith, nor to benefit them. [p. 127] for you might as well expect to benefit a Devil in Hell as such an one. Such ones are possessed of his spirit and are willing to keep it, for they are habitations of Devils and are only fit for his society. But when you are endowed and prepared to preach the Gospel to all nations, kindreds & tongues in their own languages, you must faithfully warn all, bind up the law and seal up the testimony,[272] and the destroying angel will follow close at your heels and execute his tremendous mission upon the children of disobedience, and destroy the workers of iniquity:[273] while the Saints will be gathered out from among them, and stand in holy places[274] ready to meet the Bride-Groom when he comes.[275]

I feel disposed to speak a few words more to you, my brethren, concerning the endowment, all who are prepared and are sufficiently pure to abide the presence of the Lord, will see him in the solemn assembly.[276]

The brethren expressed their gratification for the instructions he had given them. He closed by prayer, returned home and retired to rest.

13 November 1835 • *Friday*

Friday Nov. 13th He attended school During school hours. After school a Mr. Messenger [George Messinger Jr.] of Bainbridge Chenango County N.Y. came in to make some inquiry about H[ezekiah] Peck's family. Messenger was a Universalian Minister,[277] and the conversation was soon turned upon Religion. He [went][278] with him to President [Sidney] Rigdon's and spent the evening in conversation. Preached the gospel to him, bore testimony to him of

---

272. See Isaiah 8:16; and Revelation, 27 and 28 Dec. 1832 and 3 Jan. 1833, in Doctrine and Covenants 7:23, 1835 ed. [D&C 88:84].

273. See Revelation, 27 Feb. 1833, in Doctrine and Covenants 80:3, 1835 ed. [D&C 89:21].

274. See, for example, Matthew 24:15; and Revelation, 16 and 17 Dec. 1833, in Doctrine and Covenants 97:5, 1835 ed. [D&C 101:22].

275. See, for example, Matthew 25:1–13; and Revelation, Oct. 1830–B, in Doctrine and Covenants 55:3, 1835 ed. [D&C 33:17].

276. See Revelation, 2 Nov. 1831, in Doctrine and Covenants 25:3, 1835 ed. [D&C 67:10]; and Matthew 5:8.

277. Messinger was a preacher for the First Universalist Society of Smithville Flats, Chenango County, New York. The Peck family, converts from Chenango County, New York, were living at this time in Clay County, Missouri, where Hezekiah was a Latter-day Saint priest. (Smith, *History of Chenango and Madison Counties, New York,* 303–304; Chenango Co., NY, Deed Records, 1798–1905, vol. TT, pp. 225–226, 20 Mar. 1833, microfilm 818,137, U.S. and Canada Record Collection, FHL; George Messinger Jr., South Bainbridge, NY, to S. Presson Landers, Prompton, PA, 1 Aug. 1837, Andover-Harvard Theological Library, Cambridge, MA; Whitmer, History, 80, in *JSP,* H2:89–90.)

278. Omitted word supplied from the corresponding journal entry. (See *JSP,* J1:99.)

what they had seen & heard. He attempted to raise some objections, but the force of truth bore him down, and he was silent although unbelieving

14 November 1835 • Saturday

Saturday 14ᵗʰ Thus ~~saith~~ came the word of the Lord unto me saying:

> Verily thus saith the Lord unto my servant Joseph concerning my servant Warren [Parrish], behold, his sins are forgiven him because of his desires to do the works of righteousness, therefore, inasmuch as he will hearken unto my voice, he shall be blessed with wisdom and with a sound mind, even above his fellows. Behold, it shall come to pass in his day that he shall see great things shew forth themselves ~~in him~~ unto my people; he shall see much of my ancient records and shall know of hidden things, and shall be endowed with a knowledge of hidden languages, and if he desires, and shall [p. 128] seek it at my hand. he shall be privileged with writing much of my word as a scribe unto me for the benefit of my people.
>
> Therefore, this shall be his calling until I shall order it otherwise in my wisdom: and it shall be said of him in a time to come, behold Warren, the Lord's Scribe, for the Lord's Seer whom he hath appointed in Israel. therefore, if he will keep my commandments he shall be lifted up at the last day, even so. Amen.

A gentleman called this afternoon, by the name of Erastus Holmes of Newbury Clemon [Clermont] Co. Ohio, to make inquiry about the establishment of the Church of the Latter Day Saints, and to be instructed more perfectly in the doctrine & principles of it. He (Smith) commenced and gave him a brief relation of his experience while in his youthful days, say from the age of six years up to the time he received the first visitation of Angels which was when he was about 14 years old.[279] He also gave him an account of the revelations he ~~had~~ afterward received concerning the coming forth of the Book of Mormon, and a succinct account of the rise and progress of the church up to this date. He listened very attentively and seemed highly gratified. and expressed a

---

279. JS may have recounted the traumatic leg operation he underwent at age seven, as he did in a later history. His recounting of "the first visitation of Angels" corresponds with the vision he described earlier in the week to Robert Matthews, wherein he saw two "personage[s]" and "many angels" when he "was about 14." (JS History, vol. A-1, 131nA; entry for 9 Nov. 1835 herein; compare JS History, ca. summer 1832, pp. 12–13 herein; and JS History, vol. A-1, p. 214 herein [Draft 2].)

determination to unite with the Church. He truly appeared to be a sincere inquirer after truth, which rendered his society endearing.[280]

15 November 1835 • Sunday

Sunday 15th. He, (President Smith) and his friend, [Erastus] Holmes, of whom mention has been made above, went to meeting, which was held in the School-house.[281] President [Sidney] Rigdon preached on the subject of men's being called to preach the gospel and their qualifications &c. He was happy in the delivery, and in his peculiar, entertaining manner gave an interesting, instructing discourse.[282] Holmes appeared to be well satisfied. He has been a member of the Methodist Church and was excommunicated for receiving the Elders of the Church of the Latter-Day-Saints into his house. In the afternoon before partaking of the Sacrament, the case of Isaac Hills [Hill], an offending brother, was called up & agitated. This case was settled after much controversy and Hills retained in the Church by his making a humble acknowledgement before the Church, and consenting to have his confession published in the Messenger & Advocate.[283] Sacrament was then admininstered and congregation [p. 129] dismissed at a late hour.

16 November 1835 • Monday

Monday Nov. 16th. President Smith was at home this day and dictated a letter for the Messenger & Advocate.[284] also one to Harvey Whitlock. Elders, [Alvah] Beaman, Strong[285] & others called to see him in the course of the day.

Here follows the Copy of a long letter from H. Whitlock.[286]

---

280. In place of this sentence, the 1835–1836 journal has "he is a verry candid man indeed and I am much pleased with him." (*JSP*, J1:100.)

281. The 1835–1836 journal notes, "on account of the Chappel not being finished plastering." (*JSP*, J1:100.)

282. In place of the previous sentence, the 1835–1836 journal has "we had a fine discourse it was verry interesting indeed." (*JSP*, J1:100.)

283. Hill's case was first heard the previous Sunday. His confession was never published. (Entry for 8 Nov. 1835 herein.)

284. This was the second in a series of three letters written by JS and published in successive issues of the *LDS Messenger and Advocate* providing instruction for traveling elders. The second letter concerns the gathering of Israel in the last days to Zion, the New Jerusalem, and admonishes elders to proselytize only with the permission of heads of households.[a] Warren Parrish copied a portion of this letter into the present history.[b] (a. JS, "To the Elders of the Church of Latter Day Saints," *LDS Messenger and Advocate*, Nov. 1835, 2:209–212; see also Sept. 1835, 1:179–182; and Dec. 1835, 2:225–230. b. JS History, 1834–1836, p. 90 herein.)

285. Probably Ezra Strong. (Minute Book 1, 7 Mar. 1835; Elder's certificate for Ezra Strong, 31 Mar. 1836, in Kirtland Elders' Certificates, 33.)

286. Written 28 September 1835, as noted in JS's response below.

Dear Sir,

Having a few leisure moments, I have at last concluded to do what my judgement has long dictated would be right, but the allurements of many vices, have long retarded the hand, that would wield the pen, that would make intelligent the communication that I wish to send you. And even now, that ambition which is a prevailing and pre-dominant principle among the great mass of natural men, forbids that plainness of sentiment with which I wish to write. For know assuredly, Sir, to you I wish to unbosom the secrets of my heart, as before the Omnicient Judge of all the earth.

Be not surprized when I declare unto you, as the Spirit will bear record, that my faith is firm and unshaken in the things of the Everlasting Gospel as it is proclaimed by the servants of the Latter-Day-Saints.

Dear brother Joseph (if I may be allowed the expression) when I consider the happy times, the peaceful moments, and pleasant seasons, I have enjoyed with you and this people; contrasted with my now degraded state, together with the high and exalted station, I have held before God:[287] and the abyss into which I have fallen. is a subject that swells my heart too big for utterance, and language is overwhelmed with feelings, and looses its power of description. And as I desire to know the will of God concerning me I believe it is my duty to make known unto you my real situation. I shall, therefore, dispassionately, proceed to give a true and untarnished relation; I need not tell you that in former times I have preached the word, and endeavored to be instant in Season and out of season, to reprove rebuke exhort, and faithfully discharge that trust reposed in me. But, Oh! with what grief, and lamentable sorrow & anguish do I have to relate that I have fallen from that princely station whereunto our God has called me. Reasons why are unnecessary. May the fact suffice, and believe me when I tell you I have sunk myself (since my last separation from this Body) [p. 130] in crime of the deepest dye, and that I may the better you to understand what my real sins are, I will mention, (although pride forbids it) some that I am not guilty of. My hands have not been stained with innocent blood, neither have I lain couched around the cottages of my fellow men to seize and carry off the booty; nor have I slandered my neighbor, nor born false testimony, nor taken unlawful hire, nor oppressed the widow nor fatherless, neither have I persecuted the saints. But my hands are swift to do iniquity and my feet are fast

---

287. Whitlock was ordained a high priest in 1831. (Minute Book 2, 3 June 1831.)

running in the paths of vice and folly, and my heart, quick to devise wicked imaginations. Nevertheless I am impressed with the sure thought that I am fast hastening to a whole world of disembodied beings, without God and with but one hope in the world: which is to know that to err is human, but, to forgive is Divine. Much I might say in relation to myself and the original difficulties with the Church, which I will forbear and inasmuch as I have been charged with things that I was not guilty of, I am now more than doubly guilty, and am now willing to forgive and forget, only let me know that I am within the reach of mercy. If I am not I have no reflections to cast, but say that I have sealed my own doom and pronounced my own sentence. If the day is passed by with me may I here beg leave to entreat of those who are toiling up the rugged asscent, to make their way to endless felicity, and delight to stop not for anchor here below, follow not my example, but steer your course onward in spite of all the combined powers of earth and Hell, for know that one mistep here is only retrievable by a thousand groans & tears before God. Dear brother Joseph, let me entreat you on the reception of this letter, as you regard the salvation of my soul, to inquire at the hand of the Lord in my behalf for I this day in presence of God, do covenant to abide the word that may be given. for I am willing to receive any chastisement that the Lord sees I deserve. Now hear my prayer & suffer me to break forth in the agony of my soul. O ye, angels, that surround the throne of God. Princes of Heaven, that excell in strength, ye who are clothed with transcendent brightness, plead O plead for one of the most wretched of the sons of men. O Ye Heavens whose azure arches rise immensely high, and stretch immeasurably wide grand amphitheatre of nature, throne of the Eternal God, bow to hear the prayer of a poor wretched bewildered way wanderer to ~~the~~ eternity. O, Thou Great Omnicient & omnipresent [p. 131] Jehovah, Thou who sitteth upon the throne before whom all things are present, Thou Maker, Moulder and Fashioner of all things, visible and invisible, breathe I O breathe into the ears of thy servant, the Prophet, words suitably adapted to my case and situation. Speak once more Make known thy will concerning me, which favors I ask in the name of the Son of God, Amen.

N.B. I hope you will not let any business hinder you from answering this letter in haste.

Yours Respectfully
Harvey Whitlock

To Joseph Smith

Kirtland Nov. 16ᵗʰ 1835

Brother Harvey Whitlock,

I have received your letter ⟨of⟩ the 28ᵗʰ. of Sept. 1835 and I have read it twice, and it gave sensations that are better imagined than described. let it suffice that I say the very flood-gates of my heart were broken up: I could not refrain from weeping. I ~~think~~ ⟨thank⟩ God that it has entered into your heart to return to the Lord and to his people, if it so be that he will have mercy upon you.

I have inquired of the Lord concerning your case. These words came to me.

Verily thus saith the Lord unto you: Let him who was my servant Harvey, return unto me, and unto the bosom of my church, and forsake all the sins, wherewith he has offended against me, and pursue from hencforth a virtuous and upright life, and remain under the directions of those I have appointed to be pillars, and heads of my Church, and behold saith the Lord your God, his sins shall be blotted out from under Heaven, and shall be forgiven from among men, and shall not come up in mine ears nor be recorded as a memorial against him. but I will lift him up as out of deep mire, and he shall be exalt[ed] upon the high places, and shall be county [counted]²⁸⁸ worthy to stand among princes, and shall yet be made a polished shaft in my quiver, of bringing down the strong hold of wickedness among those who set themselves up on high. that they may take council against me and against my anointed ones, in the [p. 132] last days.

Therefore let him prepare himself speedily and come unto you, even to Kirtland, and inasmuch as he shall hearken to all your council, from henceforth he shall be restored, unto his former state and shall be saved unto the uttermost, even as the Lord your God liveth, Amen.

Thus you see, my dear brother, the willingness of our Heavenly Father to forgive sins and restore to favor, all those who are willing to humble themselves before him and confess their sins and forsake them, and return to him with full purpose of heart. acting no hypocrisy to serve him to the end.

Marvel not that the Lord has condescended to speak from the Heavens and give you instructions, whereby you may learn your duty, he has heard your prayers and witnessed your humility, and holds forth

---

288. Word correction supplied from the corresponding journal entry. (See *JSP*, J1:104.)

the hand of paternal affection for your return, The angels rejoice over you while the saints are willing to receive you again into fellowship.

I hope on the receipt of this you will lose no time in coming to Kirtland, for if you get here in season you will have the privilege of attending the school of the Prophets, which has already commenced, and also receive instruction in doctrine and principle from those whom God has appointed, whereby you may be qualified to go forth and declare the true doctrines of the Kingdom according to the mind and will of God. And when you come to Kirtland, it will be explained to you why God has condescended to give you a revelation according to your request.

Please give my respects to your family and be assured I am yours in the new and everlasting covenant.[289]

Joseph Smith Jun[r].

On the same evening (viz.) the 16[th]. a council was called at his house, to advise with Alvah Beaman on the subject of his moving to Missouri. The subject of these memoirs had previously told him that the Lord had said that he had better go next Spring, however, to gra[t]ify him a council was called. It met agreeably to his request. President D[avid] Whitmer arose after the council was ready to proceed to business, and observed that the spirit manifested to him that it was his duty to go,[290] and others also bore the same testimony.

The same night (16) he (J. S. Jun[r].) received the word of the Lord, on the case of Erastus Holmes who called on the 14 [p. 133] [*illegible*] to He had desired him to inquire at the hand of the Lord whether it was his duty to be baptized here or wait till he returned home: The Word of the Lord came to him (J. S. Jun[r]) that Mr. Holmes had better not be baptized here, and that he had better not return by water also that there were three men seeking his destruction, and to beware of his enemies.

17 November 1835 • Tuesday

Tuesday Nov 17[th.] He exhibited the Alphabet of the ancient Egyptian Records[291] to <u>Mr</u>. [Erastus] Holmes & some others, went with him to

---

289. Two and a half months later, church leaders resolved that Whitlock be "restored to the church in full fellowship on his being rebaptized and after be ordained to the High Priest-hood." (Minute Book 1, 30 Jan. 1836.)

290. See entry for 11 Nov. 1835 herein. Whitmer presided over the Latter-day Saints in Missouri. (Minute Book 2, 3 July 1834.)

291. Possibly the "Egyptian alphabet" that JS, Oliver Cowdery, and William W. Phelps apparently worked on seven weeks earlier. (See entry for 1 Oct. 1835 herein; see also Kirtland Egyptian Papers, ca. 1835–1836, 4, CHL.)

F[rederick] G. Williams' to see the Mummies, after which he (Holmes) to[ok] leave, by giving the parting hand and started for home, being strong in the faith of the Gospel of Christ, and apparently determined to obey its requirements.[292]

He, of whom we write more particularly, returned home after his friend Holmes had taken leave, and spent the day in comparing and dictating letters. In the evening he preached at the school House, from thence he went home and retired to rest.

18 November 1835 • Wednesday

Wednesday 18[th.] He was at home in the A.M. until about 11, o clock, at which time, he set out with his wife, mother and his scribe[293] to go to Preserved, Harris'. He had been requested to attend at said Harris' and by a request of the family and preach the funerel Sermon of Harris' father.[294] The congregation were very attentive. We returned after meeting, to his own house, having had a pleasant ride ⟨al⟩though the weather was cool, and the occasion of his ride a melancholy one.

In the evening Bishop [Newel K.] Whitney, his wife, father, mother and Sister in law came to visit him in[295] and gave him & his wife a pressing invitation to go with them on visit to his father Smith's /[296]When we they arived we they found that some of the young Eldr's were about engaging in a debate upon the subject of miracles.[297]

After an interesting debate of three hours or more, during which time much talent was displayed, it was decided by the presidents of the school in the negative: Which was a righteous decision.

He discovered in this investigation to[o] much warmth manifested, to[o] much zeal for mastery, to[o] much of that enthusiasm that characterizes a lawyer at the bar, who is determined on victory[298] right or wrong.

---

292. There is no evidence that Holmes joined the church.

293. Warren Parrish.

294. Nathan Harris, father of Preserved and Martin Harris, died the day before at Mentor, Geauga County, Ohio. (Tuckett and Wilson, *Martin Harris Story,* 178.)

295. Whitney was accompanied by his wife, Elizabeth Ann Smith Whitney; his parents, Samuel Whitney and Susanna Kimball Whitney; and probably Eve Doane Whitney, wife of Newel Whitney's brother Samuel Whitney, who also lived in Kirtland during this time. (Geauga Co., OH, Probate Court, Marriage Records, vol. B, p. 132, 26 July 1829, microfilm 873,461; Geauga Co., OH, Duplicate Tax Records, 1816–1850, Tax Record for 1835, pp. 18–19, microfilm 506,578, U.S. and Canada Record Collection, FHL.)

296. TEXT: Warren Cowdery handwriting ends; Warren Parrish begins.

297. According to the corresponding entry in JS's journal, "the question was this; was or was it not the design of Christ to establish his gospel by miracles." (*JSP,* J1:106.)

298. For "on victory," the 1835–1836 journal has "to defend his cause." (*JSP,* J1:106.)

He therefore ⟨availed⟩ himself of this favourable opportunity to drop a few words upon this subject by way of advise, that they might improve their minds, and cultivate their powers of intilect in a proper manner, that they might not incur the displeasure of heaven, that they should [p. 134] handle sacred things very sacredly; and with due deference to the opinions of others, and with an eye single to the glory of God.

19 November 1835 • Thursday

Thursday 19th. In company with Dr. F[rederick] G. Williams he went to see how the workmen prospered in finishing the house of the Lord.[299]

On his return he met with br's Lloyd & Lorenzo Lewis[300] who he had been informed were much dissatisfied; but found that this was not the fact, as touching the faith of the church but with the conduct of some of the members. He returned home and spent the day in translating the Egyptian records. The weather is warm & pleasant.

20 November 1835 • Friday

Friday 20th[301] He continued translating & made rapid progress At evening Pres. [Oliver] Cowdery returned from New York, bringing ~~with him~~ a quantity of Hebrew books, for the benefit of the school, he presented ~~me~~ him with a Hebrew bible, lexicon & Grammar, also a Greek & English lexicon.—[302] Pres. Cowdery had a prosperous journey, according to the prayers of the saints

21 November 1835 • Saturday

Saturday 21st. He spent the day at home, in examining & studying his Hebrew books.—[303] At evening he met with the class to make some arangments about a teacher, it was decided by the voice of the school that we would send to New York for a Jew, to teach us the Hebrew language, having asertained that

---

299. The 1835–1836 journal also states: "the masons on the inside had commenced puting on the finishing coat of plastureing." (*JSP,* J1:107.)

300. Lorenzo Lewis was excommunicated almost two months earlier. (Entry for 28 Sept. 1835 herein.)

301. JS's journal here notes, "in morning at home: the weather is warm but rainy." (*JSP,* J1:107.)

302. The Hebrew Bible referred to here is probably Augustus Hahn, ed., *Biblia Hebraica,* 2nd ed. (Leipzig: Caroli Tauchnitz, 1833). The grammar is likely Moses Stuart, *A Grammar of the Hebrew Language,* 5th ed. (Andover, MA: Gould and Newman, 1835). The lexicon referred to is probably Josiah W. Gibbs, *A Manual Hebrew and English Lexicon Including the Biblical Chaldee. Designed Particularly for Beginners,* 2nd ed. (New Haven, CT: Hezekiah Howe, 1832). The 1835–1836 journal specifies the English lexicon as "Websters English Lexicon," referring to a reprinting of Noah Webster's 1828 *American Dictionary of the English Language.* (See *JSP,* J1:107n159.)

303. The corresponding journal entry states that JS also studied "the hebrew alphabet." (*JSP,* J1:107.)

Dr. Piexotto [Daniel Peixotto] was not qualified to give us the knowledge we wished to acquire.[304]

22 November 1835 • Sunday

Sunday 22^ond. He ~~went~~ attended meeting at the usual hour:[305] Eldr. Simeon Carter preach[ed] from Math. 7th ch.—[306] At our evening meeting Eldr. Jackson Squires who had withdrawn from the church made application to return, to the fold of Christ. We organized into a regular council,[307] and after much altercation upon the subject, & keen rebuke Eldr. Squires was restored by the voice of the council & church, and the clerk ordered to give him his licence.—[308] On this night we had a snow storm

23 November 1835 • Monday

Monday 23^d. Several brethren called to converse with him & see the records. To day he received a letter from Jared Carter. His leasure moments he devoted to study, meditation, & prayer.[309]

24 November 1835 • Tuesday

Tuesday 24th. He spent the A.M. in instructing those that called to inquire respecting the things of God in the last days. In the P.M. he translated some of the ancient manuscripts.—[310] This evening he had an invitation to attend a wedding, at his brother Hyrum Smith's, to solemnize the rights of matrimony between Newel Knights [Knight] & Lydia Goldthwait [Goldthwaite Bailey]. His wife & some others accompanied [p. 135] him[.] when they arived, they found a respectable company assembled, the interview was opened by singing & prayer, Pres. Smith then requested the bridegroom, & bride, to arise & join hands, and then proceeded to make some remarks, upon the subject of mariage as follows; that it was an institution of heaven first solemnized in the garden of

304. The 1835–1836 journal specifies that the school would seek to "get released from the engagement we had made with Doct. Piexotto." (*JSP*, J1:107.)

305. Ten o'clock. (See entry for 13 Dec. 1835 herein.)

306. The 1835–1836 journal here includes "President [Sidney] Rigdon's brother in Law & Some other relatives were at meeting, in the after noon the meeting was held in the School-house." (*JSP*, J1:109.)

307. The corresponding journal entry also states that "Sylvester Smith was chosen Clerk." (*JSP*, J1:109.)

308. Squires had joined the Methodists for a time. At this council, JS spoke on the "impropriety of turning away from the truth" and Sidney Rigdon spoke on the "folly of fellowshiping any doctrine or spirit aside from that of Christ." (Minute Book 1, 22 Nov. 1835.)

309. The corresponding entry in JS's 1835–1836 journal also notes, "This has been a stormy day." (*JSP*, J1:109.)

310. JS's 1835–1836 journal more specifically identifies these as the "Egyptian, records." (*JSP*, J1:109.)

Eden by God himself, by the authority of the everlasting priesthood.[311] The following is in substance the ceremony delivered on that occasion— ~~You~~ calling them by name you covenant to be eachothers companions during your lives, and discharge the the duties of husband & wife in all respects, to which they gave their assent. He then pronounced them husband & wife in the name of God with many blessings,[312] after which he dismissed the audiance & returned home— The weather is freezing cold and snow on the ground

25 November 1835 • Wednesday

Wednesday 25th. Nov. He spent the day in translating.— To day Eldrs. Harvey Redfield & Jesse Hitchcock arived here from Missouri; the latter says that he has no doubt, but that a dose of poison was administered to him in a boll of milk[313] by the hand of an enemy, with the intention to kill him. It sickened him & he vomited it up, & thus the Lord verified his word ~~to him~~ and delivered him. "If they drink any deadly thing it shall not hurt them."[314]

26 November 1835 • Thursday

Thursday 26th. We spent the day in transcribing Egyptian characters from the papyrus.[315] Our br. at this time is labouring under a severe affliction in concequence of a violent cold. may the Lord deliver him from his indisposition, that he may the more successfully persue the avocation, where unto God has called him.[316]

27 November 1835 • Friday

Friday 27th. He was severely afflicted with his cold, yet able to attend to his domestic concerns, & determined to overcome in the name of the Lord Jesus. He spent the day in reading Hebrew at home. Eldr. [Warren] Parrish his scribe being indisposed in concequence of having taken cold called on Pres. J. Smith

---

311. According to the 1835–1836 journal, JS stated "that it was necessary that it should be Solemnized by the authority of the everlasting priesthood." (*JSP,* J1:110.)

312. The 1835–1836 journal specifies that JS blessed the couple with "the blessings that the Lord confered upon adam & Eve in the garden of Eden; that is to multiply and replenish the earth, with the addition of long life and prosperity." This is the first known wedding performed by JS; ten more followed over the next two months. (*JSP,* J1:110; see also 110n163.)

313. From this point to the end of the entry, the journal notes only, "but God delivered him." (*JSP,* J1:110.)

314. See Mark 16:18.

315. The transcriptions made this day may have been the manuscripts now known as Kirtland Egyptian Papers, ca. 1835–1836, 8–9, CHL. (Gee, "Eyewitness, Hearsay, and Physical Evidence," 196.)

316. This sentence is a scribal addition; in its place, the corresponding entry in the 1835–1836 journal notes that "to day Robert Rathbone [Rathbun Jr.] and George Morey arrived from Zion." (*JSP,* J1:111.)

jun. to pray for & lay hands on him in the name of the Lord; He did so and in return Eldr. Parrish prayed for & laid hands on him, this reciprocal kindness was heard and graciously answered upon both their heads by our Heavenly Father in relieving them from their affliction.[317]

Prayer • 23 October 1835

The following prayer was offered to the God of heaven on the 23[d.] day of October 1835, by the individuals whose names are [p. 136] inserted as follows below. viz Joseph Smith jun., Oliver Cowdery, David Whitmer, Hyrum Smith, John Whitmer, Sidney Rigdon, Samuel H. Smith Frederick G. Williams & W[m] W. Phelps,[318] who assembled on the above mentioned day at 4 oclock P.M. and united in prayer with one, voice before the Lord for the following blessing.

That the Lord will give us means sufficient to deliver us from all our afflictions and difficulties, wherein we are placed by means of our debts; that He will open the way & deliver Zion in the appointed time[319] and that without the shedding of blood; that He will hold our lives precious, and grant that we may live to the common age of man, and never fall into the hands of our enemies nor power of the mob in missouri, nor any other place; that he will also preserve our posterity, that none of them fall even to the end of time; that he will give us the blessings of the earth sufficient to carry us to Zion and that we may purchase inheritances in that land, even enough to carry on and accomplish the work unto which he has appointed us; and also that he will assist all others who desire according to his commandments to go up and purchase inheritances and all this easily & without perplexity and trouble; and finaly that in the end he will save us in his c[e]lestial kingdom. Amen.

Oliver Cowdery   Clerk

---

317. For this entry describing his own interactions with JS, Warren Parrish here expanded the statement that he previously wrote as scribe for the 1835–1836 journal: "and in return I asked him to lay his hands on me & we were both relieved." (*JSP,* J1:111.)

318. The assembled group constituted the full membership of the church presidencies from both Ohio and Missouri, except for Joseph Smith Sr., for whom his son Samuel Smith may have been standing in.

319. In August 1834, JS declared to Missouri church leaders that 11 September 1836 was the "appointed time for the redemption of Zion." (JS, Kirtland, OH, to Lyman Wight et al., Missouri, 16 Aug. 1834, in JS Letterbook 1, p. 86.)

28 November 1835 • Saturday

Saturday 28ᵗʰ· He spent the morning in comparing & correcting[320] his journal.— Eldr. Josiah Clark called this morning to ⟨see⟩ him, he lives in Camel [Campbell] County, Kentucky, about 3 miles above Cincinnati,[321] he had been bitten by a mad dog some three or four years since, & had spent much upon physician's and received some benefit by so doing; but is much afflicted notwithstanding; he came here that he might receive the benefit of the united prayers of the church; accordingly we prayed for and laid our hands on him in the name of the Lord Jesus Christ, & anointed him with oil, & rebuked his affliction praying our Heavenly Father to hear and answer our prayers according to our faith in him, even so, Amen. [p. 137]

29 November 1835 • Sunday

Sunday Nov. 29ᵗʰ· This morning he went to meeting at the usual hour Eldr. Isaac Morley[322] occupied the desk in the A.M. & Bp. Edward Partri[d]ge in the P.M. Their discourses were well adapted to the times in which we live, and the circumstances, under which we are placed; their words were truly words of wisdom "like apples of gold in pictures of silver,"[323] spoken in the unaffected simple accents of a child; yet sublime as the voice of an angel. The saints appeared to be much pleased with the beautiful discourses of these two fathers in Israel. After these servises closed, three of the Zion brethren[324] came forward and received their blessing. Solon Foster was ordained to the office of an Eldr. The Lord's supper was then administered, and the meeting closed. Our brother returned home and spent the evening in his family circl, around the social fire side.— The weather continues cold and stormy.

30 November 1835 • Monday

Monday morning 30ᵗʰ· The snow continues falling and is already sufficiently deep to make good sleighing This is uncommon for this country, at this season of the year. He spent the day in writing, or in other words dictating a letter for the Messenger & Advocate on the subject of the gathering in the last

---

320. For "comparing & correcting," the 1835–1836 journal has only "compareing." (*JSP*, J1:112.)

321. Here the 1835–1836 journal continues: "I am conciderably recovered from my cold, & I think I shall be able in a few days to translate again, with the blessing of God.— The weather is still cold and stormy, the snow is falling, & winter seems to be closing in, all nature shrinks before the chilling blast's of rigid winter." (*JSP*, J1:112.)

322. Morley served as one of Edward Partridge's counselors in the Missouri bishopric. They had recently served a mission together in the eastern states. (See 114n244 herein.)

323. See Proverbs 25:11.

324. Veterans of the 1834 expedition to Missouri. (See "Camp of Israel," in Glossary.)

days from Matthew 13th ch.³²⁵ This afternoon Henry Capron called to see him Mr. Capon is an old acquaintance of his from Manchester NewYork. He showed him the ancient records and explained them to him.

1 December 1835 • Tuesday

Tuesday December 1st. ³²⁶ This is a delightful morning indeed; Pres. Joseph made preperations to ride to Pain[e]sville, his wife & children with some others of his household, accompanied him. When we were passing through Mentor street, we overtook two men with a team, & politely asked them to let us pass; they granted our request, and as we passed them, they abruptly bawled out to Pres. Smith do you get any revelations lately, with an addition of blackguard & vulgarity, to us uninteligable. This is a fair specimine of the character of the inhabitants of Mentor; who have rendered themselves notorious, for mobing & persecuting the saints;³²⁷ [p. 138] and are ready to scandalize, & traduce, the characters of men, who never laid a straw in their way, and, in fact men whose faces they never saw, and against whom they cannot bring an accusation either of a temporal or spiritual nature; except our firm belief in the fulness of the gospel. And we were led to marvle at the longsuffering, and great condesention of our Heavenly Father, in permitting these ungodly wretches to possess this goodly land, which is indeed as beautifully situated, & and its soil as fertile, as any in this region of country, and its inhabitants wealthy, even blessed, above measure in temporal things; and feign would God bless them with spiritual blessings, even eternal life, were it not for their evil hearts of unbelief, and we are inclined to mingle our cries with the souls of those saints, who have suffered the like treatment before us; whose souls are under the altar, praying for vengance upon those who dwell upon the earth.³²⁸

---

325. This was the third in a series of three letters written by JS and published in successive issues of the *LDS Messenger and Advocate* to provide instruction for traveling elders. (JS, "To the Elders of the Church of Latter Day Saints," *LDS Messenger and Advocate*, Dec. 1835, 2:225–230; see also Sept. 1835, 1:179–182; and Nov. 1835, 2:209–212.)

326. In the 1835–1836 journal, the 1 December 1835 entry consists of the following: "at home spent the day in writing, for the M[essenger] & Advocate, the snow is falling and we have fine sleighing." The entry here for 1 December corresponds to the entry dated 2 December in the 1835–1836 journal. (*JSP*, J1:113.)

327. The passage from "who have rendered" to this point is a scribal elaboration not found in the 1835–1836 journal. Before joining with the Latter-day Saints, Sidney Rigdon led the Reformed Baptist congregation in Mentor, some of whom now deeply resented the new religion that had taken Rigdon and many from the neighboring Kirtland congregation. On Mentor-based opposition to the Mormons in 1835, see Adams, "Grandison Newell's Obsession," 170–173.

328. See Revelation 6:9–10.

And we rejoice in our hearts, that the time is at hand when those who persist in wickedness, will be swept from the earth with the besom of distruction,[329] and the earth become an inheritance for the poor & the meek.—[330]

When we [*illegible*] arived at Painsville we called at sister Harriet How[e']s, and lef Mrs. Smith & family to visit while we rode into town ~~to do some buisiness;~~ we called on br. H[orace] Kingsbury, and ~~after~~ also at the bank, and at various other places,[331] and after accomplishing our buisiness we returned & dined with sister How; & took the parting hand & returned home. We had a fine ride, and agreeable visit; the sleighing is good and weather pleasant.

2 December 1835 • *Wednesday*

Wednesday 2ᵒⁿᵈ· [332] Nothing of much importance transpired, suffice it to say that he of whom we write, spent the day in the society of his family, manageing his domestic concerns, visiting, & receiving visitors, and instructing such, as desired a knowledge of the things of God.

3 December 1835 • *Thursday*

Thursday 3ᵈ· He was at home, and indited a letter to David Dort[,] Rochester Michigan; also another [p. 139] to Almira Scob[e]y[,] Liberty Clay county Missouri.[333] At evening he & his wife were invited to attend a wedding at Thomas Carrico [Jr.]'s to solemnize the rights of matrimony between Eldr. W[arren] Parrish, & Martha H. Raymond; when we arived we found a very pleasant & respectable company waiting: We opened our interview by singing & prayer; Pres. Smith then delivered an appropriate address upon the subject of matrimony; he then invited the parties who were to be joined in wedlock to arise, and solemnized the institution in a brief, & explicit manner, and pronounced them husband & wife in the name of God according to the articles &

---

329. See Isaiah 14:23. A besom is a broom, especially one made of twigs.

330. See Matthew 5:5; and Revelation, 27 and 28 Dec. 1832 and 3 Jan. 1833, in Doctrine and Covenants 7:4, 1835 ed. [D&C 88:17].

331. The passage "and also at the bank, and at various other places" does not appear in the 1835–1836 journal.

332. The content of this entry does not appear in the journal; as noted above, most of the 2 December journal entry is made up of material that appears here under 1 December. (*JSP*, J1:113.)

333. JS's letters to his maternal cousin Almira Scobey and her sister's husband David Dort remain unlocated. He may have written to encourage them to move to Kirtland, where both apparently settled in 1836. (See Minutes, *LDS Messenger and Advocate*, Mar. 1837, 3:477; and Cumming and Cumming, *Pilgrimage of Temperance Mack*, 21.)

covenants of the church of Latterday Saints;[334] closed by singing & prayer, took some refreshment and retired, having spent the evening agreeably.

4 December 1835 • Friday

Friday 4[th.] To day he got a note of three hundred & fifty dollars discounted at Pain[e]sville bank[335] by giving the following names with his own.— viz. F G. Williams &co. N[ewel] K. Whitney J[ohn] Johnson & Vinson Knights [Knight]. He settled with Eldr. Knights & paid him two hundred & fifty dollars:[336] He also settled with his brother Hiram [Hyrum] Smith; & has the means to pay a debt due Job Lewis, which he has been much perplexed about;[337] and he feels hartily to thank God, that He has thus graciously smiled upon him, & blessed him with such a multiplicity of blessings, & thus far crowned our feeble efforts with success:[338] And we ask our Heavenly Father in the name of Jesus Christ, to enable us to extricate ourselves, from all embarasments whatever, that we may not be brought into disrepute in any respect; that our enemies may not have any power over us.— He spent the day at home, devoted some time in studying the Hebrew language.— This has been a warm & rainy day; the snow is melting fast.—

This evening a Mr. John Hol[l]ister of Portage County Ohio called to see Pres. Smith upon the all important subject of religion; said Holister is a member of the close communion baptist church,[339] he said that his object in calling on us, was to enquire concerning our faith, [p. 140] having heard many reports of an unfavourable character, he desired now to know the truth of the matter.

He appeared to be an honest inquirer. Pres. Smith spent the evening with him, in conversation, & found him to be a candid man; but without any

---

334. The term "articles and covenants" applied originally to the statement of church principles and practices dated 10 April 1830 and approved at the church conference held 9 June 1830. It refers here to the recently published Doctrine and Covenants, which compiled revelations and statements of belief such as the new article on marriage. (Minute Book 2, 9 June 1830; "Marriage," ca. Aug. 1835, in Doctrine and Covenants 101, 1835 ed.; see also Minute Book 1, 17 Aug. 1835.)

335. Apparently the Bank of Geauga, founded in 1831. The 1835–1836 journal further describes this transaction: "we drew, three hundred and fifty Dollars, out of Painsvill Bank, on three months credit." (*History of Geauga and Lake Counties, Ohio*, 216; *JSP*, J1:115.)

336. The 1835–1836 journal gives this amount as $245. (*JSP*, J1:115.)

337. In March 1834, Lewis evidently loaned JS or the church approximately one hundred dollars, which JS hoped to pay back at the end of 1835. JS had not paid Lewis by May 1836. (Minute Book 1, 23 May 1836.)

338. The passage from "that He has thus graciously smiled" to this point is not found in the journal.

339. Closed Communion Baptists took the sacrament of the Lord's Supper only with other Baptists. (Jeter, *Baptist Principles Reset*, chap. 13.)

peculiarities about him except his simplicity, he tarried over night [with][340] us, and acknowledged in the morning, that although he had thought that he knew something about religion, he was now convinced, that he knew but little, which was the greatest trait of wisdom which he displayed.

5 December 1835 • Saturday

Saturday 5th. This morning the weather is cold & the snow is gently dropping from the heavens, & there is a prospect of sleighing again.— Presdts. [Oliver] Cowdery & [Frederick G.] Williams called and spent the fore noon in studying Hebrew with us.— our author Pres. Smith is labouring under a slight indisposition of health; but after taking a little repose, he resumed his wonted cheerfulness and throug[h] the blessings of God was abled to attend to his business. on this day he received a letter from Reuben McBride dated at Villanovia [Villanova] NewYork, and another from Parley [P.] Pratt's mother in law,[341] dated at Herkimer Co. N.Y. of no consequ[e]nce as to what it contained but cost us 25 cents for postage; he mentioned this because it [is][342] a common occurrence, and he is subjected to a great expense in this way, by those who he knows nothing about, only that they are destitute of good manners, for if people wish to be benefited by his counsel & instruction, common respect, and good breeding would dictate them to pay the postage on their letters.

6 December 1835 • Sunday

Sunday 6th. He as usual attended meeting, being ever constant at the shrine of public & private devotion, setting an example of unremitting, & untiring zeal and piety teaching, & enforcing, both by precept, and example, the principles, & doctrines, of the holy religion he professes.[343]

Eldr. Gideon Carter occupied the desk in the morning and delivered an interesting discourse. In the P.M. an exhortation was delivered, and the Lords supper administered. br. Draper came forward to make a [p. 141] confession for having left the meeting abruptly as we were about to partake of the Lord's supper and disturbed the peace & quiet of the congregation. But his confession was not satisfactory, it seemed to be affected and superficial: He was therefore delivered over to the bufitings of satan until he should [humble][344] himself before the Lord, & repent of his sins and confess them before the church.

---

340. Omitted word supplied from the corresponding journal entry. (See *JSP*, J1:115.)

341. Thankful Cooper Halsey.

342. Omitted word supplied from the corresponding journal entry. (See *JSP*, J1:116.)

343. This paragraph is a scribal elaboration by Warren Parrish; the 1835–1836 journal has only "went to meeting at the us[u]al hour." (*JSP*, J1:116.)

344. Omitted word supplied from the corresponding journal entry. (See *JSP*, J1:116.)

7 December 1835 • Monday

Monday 7[th.] Received a letter from Milton Holmes and was much rejoiced to hear of his prosperity in proclaiming the gospel in the west;[345] he wrote him a letter in which he requested br. Holmes to return to this place:— spent the day in reading Hebrew— Mr. John Hollister called to take the parting hand with Pres. Smith and remarked that he had been in darkness all his days, but had now found the true light and intended to obey it; a number of brethren also call[ed] this evening to see the ancient records, which he exibited & explained to their satisfaction.

8 December 1835 • Tuesday

Tuesday 8[th.] He spent the day in his family circle, receiving & waiting upon those who called to visit him; his few leisure moments he devoted to study.[346]

This evening as usual, he preach[ed] at the school house had great liberty in speaking. the power of God in a ~~powerful~~ ⟨wonderful⟩ manner rested upon the audiance.[347] After the servises closed Eldr. [Leonard] Rich proposed to the brethren, to assist Pres. Smith in getting his supply of wood for the winter, to which they cheerfully assented, and fixed on tomorrow. for the day.[348]

9 December 1835 • Wednesday

Wednesday 9[th.] At home. This morning the south wind blows strong and chilly, ~~and~~ the sky is overcast and the clowds portend a storm at hand.

Eldr. [Noah] Packard called and made our author, a present of a twelve dollar note, which he held against him;[349] Eldr. James Aldrich also sent him a note of twelve dollars by the hand of Eldr. J[esse] Hitchcock.—[350] Also the brethren whose names are written below opened their hearts in great liberality

---

345. This entry may refer to Holmes's letter of 2 November 1835 reporting his preaching throughout 1835 in Tennessee and Illinois and his success in baptizing over forty people. (Milton Holmes, Hamilton Co., IL, 2 Nov. 1835, Letter to the editor, *LDS Messenger and Advocate,* Jan. 1836, 2:255.)

346. The corresponding journal entry specifies that JS read Hebrew with Oliver Cowdery, Frederick G. Williams, Hyrum Smith, and Orson Pratt. (*JSP,* J1:117.)

347. In place of the previous sentence, the 1835–1836 journal has "the congregation, were attentive." (*JSP,* J1:117.)

348. In place of this sentence, the 1835–1836 journal notes only the following: "after the servises closed the brethren proposed to come and draw wood for me." (*JSP,* J1:117.)

349. The 1835–1836 journal continues, "and may God bless him for his liberality." In the largely barter economy, debts were often recorded on handwritten scraps of paper. These notes became a sort of scrip and circulated until retired by cash, labor, or barter. As in this case, the debt could be settled by the creditor's presenting his copy of the note as a gift to the debtor. (*JSP,* J1:117; see also McCabe, "Early Ledgers and Account Books," 5–12.)

350. The 1835–1836 journal continues, "and may God bless him, for his kindness to me." (*JSP,* J1:117.)

& paid him at the Committee's store [p. 142] the sums set oposite their respective names, as follows.

John Carrill [Corrill] $5.00
Levi Jackman 3.25
Elijah Fordham 5.25
James Emmett. 5.00
Newel Knights [Knight]. 2.00
Truman Angell 3.00
Wm. Felshaw 3.00
Emer Harris 1.00
Truman Jackson 1.00
Samuel Rolph [Rolfe] 1.25
Elias Higby [Higbee] 1.00
Albert Brown 3.00
Wm. F. Cahoon 1.00
Harlow Crozier 50
Salmon Gee 75
Harvey Stanley 1.00
Zemira Draper 1.00
George Morey 1.00
John Rudd [Jr.] 50
Alexander Badlam [Sr.] 1.00
Warren Parrish . . . . — 5.00[351]

My[352] heart swells with gratitude inexpressible when I realize the great condescension of my Heavenly Father in opening the hearts of these my beloved brethren to administer so liberally, to the wants of the servant, of the Most High; and we hear him breaking forth in the the following accents of prayer and praise to God.— I ask the[e] my Heavenly Father in the name of Jesus to smile propiciously upon these my brethren and multiply blessings without number upon their heads.— and bless me O Lord [with][353] great grace and wisdom from heaven, and dispose of me to the best advantage for the benefit of my brethren and the building up of thy kingdom on the earth; and whether in life, or in death, in prosperity, or in adversity, in time, or in eternity,[354] I say in my heart, O Lord, let me enjoy the society of such brethren.— To day

---

351. The 1835–1836 journal does not record a contribution from Parrish.

352. This paragraph alternates between referring to JS in the first person and in the third person.

353. Omitted word supplied from the corresponding journal entry. (See *JSP*, J1:118.)

354. For "in prosperity, or in adversity, in time, or in eternity," the 1835–1836 journal has "whether my days are many or few." (*JSP*, J1:118.)

Eldr Tanner[355] brought him half of a fatned hog for the benefit of his family; and a few days since Eldr. [Shadrach] Roundy presented him with a quarter of beef; thus we se[e] the word of the Lord verified, that He will not se[e] the righteous forsaken, nor his seed beging bread.[356]

10 December 1835 • Thursday

Thursday 10th. A delightful morning indeed, and fine sleighing: This morning the brethren met according to previous arangement, to chop & draw wood for him, and have been very active, and industrious and have probably supplied him with wood for the winter; for which kindness his heart swells [p. 143] with gratitude, which flow forth in blessings upon the heads of his brethren, in substance as follows.[357]

I am sincerely thankful to each and every one of you my brethren, for this testimony of your respect and goodness manifested toward me; and in the name of Jesus christ I invoke the rich benediction of heaven to rest upon them, & their families, and I ask my Heavenly Father to preserve their health's, that they may [have][358] strength of body, to persue successfully, their several avocations in life, & the use and activity of their limbs; also power of intelect & sound minds, that they may treasure up wisdom understanding & inteligence above measure, that they may readily desern between the righteous & the wicked between him that serveth God & him that serveth him not; and be preserved from plagues pestilence and famine, from the power of the destroyer that that wicked one touch them not, and give unto them wisdom & strength, to elude the grasp of all their enemies, that they may be able to counteract the designs & purposes of ~~evil~~ ⟨wicked⟩ ~~designing~~ men and prepare ~~them, O God~~ way before them, O God that they may journey to the land of Zion and be established on their inheritances, to enjoy undisturbed peace and happiness for ever, and ultimately be crowned with everlasting life in the celestial kingdom of God, which favours, & blessings I ask in the name of Jesus of Nazereth Amen.[359] This after noon he was called in company with Pres. D[avid] Whitmer

---

355. Probably John Tanner.

356. See Psalm 37:25. Instead of quoting this scripture, the 1835–1836 journal has "and may all the blessings, that are named above, be poured upon their heads, for their kindness toward me." (*JSP,* J1:118.)

357. The passage from "his heart swells" to this point is not found in the 1835–1836 journal.

358. Omitted word supplied from the corresponding journal entry. (See *JSP,* J1:119.)

359. Omitted here is a paragraph from the 1835–1836 journal: "I would remember Elder Leonard Rich who was the first one that proposed to the brethren, to assist me, in, obtaining wood for the use of my family, for which I pray my heavenly Father, to bless him with all the blessings, named above, and I shall ever remember him with much gratitude, for this testimony, of benevolence and respect, and thank the great I am, for puting into his heart, to do me this kindness, and I say in my heart, I will trust in thy

to visit sister Angeline Works,[360] they found her ver[y] sick and much deranged;[361] they prayed for and laid hands on her in the name of the Lord that
she might be restored to her senses and healed; the former, was immediately
done, but the latter was progressive, she was much better when we left.—
[*illegible*] On their returned they[362] found the brethren engaged in extinguish-
ing a fire that had broken out, in a board kiln near the chapel; after contending
with this distructive [p. 144] element, for about one hour they succeeded in
conquering it. there was a large quantity of lumber in the kiln, three forths of
which, was consumed, the committee have sustained a very conciderable loss
by this fire.

There was about 200 brethren engaged on this occasion who deserve much
credit for the activity & interest they manifested.— The finishing of the house
of the Lord, will necessarily be protracted, on account of this accident, as the
lumber that was lost, was designed for that purpose.[363] This evening a number
of brethren called at Pres. Smith's to see the ancient manuscripts and were
much pleased with their interview.

11 December 1835 • Friday

Friday morning 11th. A fire broke out in a shoemaker's shop owned by
Orison [Orson] Johnson, but was soon extinguished by the active exertions of
the brethren; on it's appearance the family were much alarmed, the shop being
connected with their dwelling house; they carried their furniture into the
streets, but not much damage was sustained. This is a pleasant morning, the
atmosphere is serene & healthy;[364] our author spent the day at home in reading,
meditation, and prayer, and instructing those who called for advise. To day
Eldr. Daily & wife[365] lef for home.

12 December 1835 • Saturday

Saturday 12th. He devoted the morning to reading; At about 12 oclock a
number of young persons called to see the Egytian records, he resquested his
scribe (W[arren] Parrish) to exibit them; he did so, one of the young ladies who

---

goodness, and mercy, forever, for thy wisdom and benevolence O Lord is unbounded and beyond the
comprehension; of men and all of thy ways cannot be found out." (*JSP,* J1:119.)

360. The 1835–1836 journal notes that Works lived "at Elder Booths," possibly referring to Lorenzo
Dow Booth, a member of the First Quorum of the Seventy. (*JSP,* J1:119; Record of Seventies, bk. A, 4.)

361. According to the 1835–1836 journal, Works was "so much deranged, that She did not, recognize
her friends, and intimate acquaintences." (*JSP,* J1:119.)

362. TEXT: Possibly "~~we~~ they".

363. The previous sentence does not appear in the 1835–1836 journal.

364. The 1835–1836 journal also notes that "their is a prospect of a thaw." (*JSP,* J1:120.)

365. Probably Moses and Almira Barber Daley.

had been examining them, was asked by the subject of this narative, if the manuscripts had the appearance of Antiquity, to which she replied with an air of contempt in the negative: on hearing this he was surprised at the ignorance she manifested, and very justly remarked to her that she was an anomaly in creation, for all the wise and learned that had ever examined them, without hesitation pronounced them ancient: He further observed that it was downright ignorance, bigotry, superstition, & wickedness, that caused her to make the remark and that it was worthy of record, for after generations to gaze upon, because it is a fair specimine of the [p. 145] prevailing spirit of the times; showing that priestcraf[t] has it's victims, also in this age, like those in ages past, that would not believe, though one should rise from the dead. This evening he attended a debate at his brother Wm. Smith's; The question propounded was as follows.— Was it, or was it not, necessary for God to reveal himself to man to render them happy. He (Joseph) was on the affirmative, and the last one to speak on that side of the question: But while listning [to] the ingenious arguments of the contending parties, he & Eldr. Carrill [John Corrill] (who was his opponent in this debate) was called away to visit the sick, and neither of them had the opportunity of speaking on that occasion.[366]

13 December 1835 • Sunday

Sunday morning 13ᵗʰ· At the usual hour, viz. 10. oclock he attended meeting at the school-house on the flats. Eldr. Jesse Hitchcock preached a very feeling discourse indeed; in the after noon Eldr. Peter Whitmer [Jr.] related his experiance, after which Pres. F[rederick] G. Williams, related his also; they both spoke of many things connected with the rise and progress of this church of Christ, which were highly interesting and the saints listned with attention. After these servises closed, the sacrament of the Lord's supper was administered, under the superintendance of Pres. David Whitmer, who presided over the meeting during the day. Pres. Joseph (our author) then made some remarks respecting prayer meetings, and our meeting was brought to a close by invoking heavens blessings upon the audiance.

He returned home and ordered his horses saddled and himself, & Scribe rode to br. Mr. Jennings where he had been envited to solemnize the marriage contract, between br. Mr. Ebenezer Robinson, & sister Miss. Angeline Works.[367] After these ceremonies were concluded we rode to Mr. [Isaac] Mc Withy's the

---

366. With Corrill, JS again called on Angeline Works. According to the journal, they "went and prayed for and layed hands on her in the name of Jesus Christ, She appeard to be better." (*JSP*, J1:121.)

367. The journal continues, "Miss Works had so far recoverd from her illness, that she was able to sit in her easy chair while I pronounced the mariage ceremony." (*JSP*, J1:121.)

distance of about 3 miles from town, where he had been solicited to attend and join in marrage Mr. E[dwin] Webb & Miss E A. Mc Withy [Eliza Ann McWethy]: The parents and many of the connexions of both parties were present, with a large and respectable company of friends, who were invited as [p. 146] guests: The necessary arangements were made, and the company came to order, and the Groom & Bride with their attendants politely came forward and and took their seats; our interview was then opened by singing & prayer, & having been invited to make some preliminary remarks upon the subject of matrimony, he delivered an interesting lecture of about 40 minutes in length, during which time all present appeared highly gratified with the exception of two individuals who manifested a spirit of grovling contempt, which he was constrained to reprove and sharply rebuke. He then sealed the matrimonial ceremony in the name of God and pronounced the blessings of heaven upon the heads of the young pair, praying that they may be blessed with long life & prosperity, and ultimately with everlasting life in the kingdom of God.[368]

a sumptuous feast was then spread and the company were invited to seat themselves at the table two by two, male, and female, commencing with the eldest, and the interview throughout was conducted with propriety & decorum; and our hearts were made to rejoice while together and cheerfulness smiled on every countinanc we spent the evening agreeably, until the tolling 9 oclock, announced to us that the time to retire, had arived: We pronounced a blessing upon the company and returned home.—

To day the board-kiln took fire again, in concequence of bad management.[369]

14 December 1835 • Monday

Monday 14th. This morning a number of brethren from New York called to visit him, and see the records. Eldr. [Martin] Harris also returned this morning from visiting his family who live in Palmyra N. Y. also a brother [Frazier] Eaton of the same place a very worthy brother made him a visit.

Sister Harriet How[e] of Pain[e]sville also visit[ed] us to day.— after dinner Pres. Smith & his family attended a funeral at Sylvester Smith's who had lost his youngest child.—[370] This evening [met][371] agreeably to [p. 147] previous notice, to make arrangements to guard against fire, and organized a company

---

368. In place of this passage beginning "praying that they may be blessed," the 1835–1836 journal has "we then closed by returning thanks." (*JSP*, J1:122.)

369. The phrase "in concequence of bad management" does not appear in the 1835–1836 journal.

370. Sylvester M. Smith, no relation to JS, died of whooping cough at the age of two months. (Obituary for Sylvester M. Smith, *LDS Messenger and Advocate*, Dec. 1835, 2:240.)

371. Omitted word supplied based on the corresponding journal entry. (See *JSP*, J1:122.)

for that purpose, they also counseled on others. affairs of a temporal nature.—
To day Samuel Branum [Brannan], called at his house much afflicted with a
swelling on his arm;[372] he had been prayed for, but lacked faith to be healed,
and at this time his pain was intolerable; Sister Emma Smith (wife of our
author) who is ever ready to alleviate the distresses of the afflicted, administered to ~~him~~ his swolen ~~arm,~~ limb such applications as occured to her mind,
and succeeded, in checking the inflamation, and his arm was saved, and
restored to health, through the blessings of God. He (Joseph) spent the ⟨day⟩ at
home in reading, and waiting upon friends who called to see him.

15 December 1835 • Tuesday

    Tuesday 15th. Spent the day at home, and as usual was blessed with much com-
pany, some of which called to see the records.—[373] This afternoon Eldr. Orson
Hyde handed a letter to him, the purport of which is that, he is dissatisfied
with the committee[374] as it respects their dealing with him in merchandise;
that they do not deal as liberally with him as they do with ⟨Eldr.⟩ Wm. Smith,
he also requested him (Joseph) to reconcile the revelation given to the 12, since
their return from their eastern mission.—[375] That unless these things with others named in the letter alluded to, could be reconciled to his mind, his honour
would not stand united with them. This I believe is the amount of Eldr. Hydes
letter, although much was written, in justification of the course he had taken.
On reading this letter his feelings were inexpressible, knowing that he had
dealt in righteousness with him in all things; and endeavoured to promote his
happiness and well being, and do him good, as much as lay in his power.

    He was therefore concious that the reflections cast upon him by Eldr. Hyde
were ungrateful, & unjust, and founded in jealousy; that the [p. 148] adversary
of righteousness, is striving, with his subtle devises and evil influence, to
destroy him by causing a division among the 12. Apostles that God has chosen
in these last days, to open the gospel kingdom among all nations, kindred,
toungs, and people. But with his usual descission of mind and firm reliance on
Him, who possesses all wisdom, & knows the thoughts & intents of every

---

372. Starting at this point, the corresponding sentence in the 1835–1836 journal concludes as follows:
"which was occasioned by a bruise on his elbow, we had been called to pray for him and anoint him with
oil, but his faith was not sufficient to effect, a cure, and my wife prepared a poultice of herbs and applyed
to it and he tarryed with me over night." (*JSP*, J1:122.)

373. At this point, the corresponding 1835–1836 journal entry states: "Samuel Brannum [Brannan],
is verry sick in consequence of his arm, it being much inflamed." (*JSP*, J1:122.)

374. The committee overseeing temple construction consisted of Hyrum Smith, Reynolds Cahoon,
and Jared Carter. For the text of the Hyde letter, see entry for 17 Dec. 1835 herein.

375. The revelation of 3 November 1835 named Hyde as having sinned against the Lord. (See entry
for 3 Nov. 1835 herein.)

heart, we hear him making the following appeal to the throne of grace,[376] that God may deliver him (Eldr. Hyde) from the power of that wicked one, that his faith fail not in this hour of temptation, & darkness, and prepare him, with the rest of his fellow labourers in the vinyard of the Lord, to receive an induement, in the habitation of the most High, as God shall see fit, to call them into the solemn assembly of the saints, from time to time, until his kingdom becomes universal, and time is no more

16 December 1835 • Wednesday

Wednesday morning 16[th.] The weathere is extremely cold.— This morning he went to the council room,[377] to lay before the presidency the letter that he received from Eldr. O[rson] Hyde, but when he arived he found that he had lost it said letter, he made search for it in vain, however he related the substance of it to that body; but they had not time to attend to it on account of other business; and accordingly laid it over ⟨until⟩ monday evening following.— He returned home. Eldr.s Mc Lellen [William E. McLellin] [Brigham] Young & [Jared] Carter call[ed] to visit him he was much pleased with the interview; he exhibited, & explained the Egytian records to them, and many things concerning the dealings of God, with the ancients especially the system of astronomy as taught by Abraham, which is contained upon these manuscripts;[378] they were much gratified with this inteligence.— This evining he went to his brother Wm. Smith's to take part in the debate, that was commenced on last Saturday evening, upon the question before named, viz. was it necessary for God to reveal himself to the world &c. [p. 149] after the debate was concluded, and a descision given in favour of the affirmative,[379] some altercation was had upon the impropriety of continuing the school. He and his brother Hyrum Smith were decidedly of the opinion that it would not result in good. Their brother Wm. strenuously opposed them and insisted on having another question propounded,[380] asserting that he was in his own house and should insist on continuing the school regardless of consequences, and at length he became much inraged especially at his brother Joseph, and committed

---

376. Instead of the passage from "kindred, toungs, and people" to this point, JS's journal has "but I pray my Heavenly Father in the name of Jesus of Nazareth." (*JSP,* J1:123.)

377. The council room was "in the printing office" on the second floor of the schoolhouse. (Entry for 14 Jan. 1836 herein.)

378. Compare entry for 1 Oct. 1835 herein. For "especially the system of astronomy as taught by Abraham," the 16 December 1835 journal entry has "and the formation of the planetary System." (*JSP,* J1:124.)

379. JS argued the affirmative side of the debate over whether it was "necessary for God to reveal himself to man to render them happy." (Entry for 12 Dec. 1835 herein.)

380. That is, a new topic was proposed for debate in the next session.

violence upon his person, and others who interfered to stay him, in his wicked course. After his passion had abated a little, and his stormy feelings were partialy tranquilized Joseph, returned home, grieved beyond expr[e]ssion, at ⟨the⟩ wickedness of his brother, who Cain like had sought to kill him, and had conciderably wounded him,[381] notwithstanding the exertions of his brothren to prevent it; nevertheless he prayed God to forgive him inasmuch as he would heartily repent and humble himself before the Lord.

17 December 1835 • Thursday

Thursday 17th. This morning he was very unwell on account of the unhappy occurrence that took place on the preceeding evening at his brother Williams [William Smith's];— Eldr. [Orson] Hyde called and presented him with a copy of the letter that he handed him on last tuesday, which he had lost; the following is a true copy.

Dec. 15th 1835
Pres. Smith
Sir you may esteem it a novel circumstance to receive a written communication from me at this time.

My reasons for writing are the following. I have some things which I wish to communicate to you, and feeling a greater liberty to do it by writing alone by myself I take this method; and it is generally the case that you are thronged with [p. 150] business, and not convenient to spend much time in conversing upon subjects of the following nature.

Therefore let these excuses paliate the novelty of the circumstance and patiently hear my recital. after the committee had received their store of fall & winter goods, I went to Eldr. [Reynolds] Cahoon and told him that I was destitute of a cloak and wanted him to trust me until spring for materials to make one.

He told me that he would trust me until Jany. but must then have his pay, as the payments for the goods become due at that time. I told him that I knew not from whence the money would come and I could not promise it so soon. But in a few ~~days~~ weeks after I unexpectedly obtained the money to buy a cloak, and applyed immediately to Eldr. C. for one and told him that I had the cash to pay for it, but he said that the materials for cloaks were all soald, and that he could not accommodate me; and I will here venture a guess, that he has not

---

381. The passage "who Cain like had sought to kill him, and had conciderably wounded him" is not found in the corresponding journal entry.

realized the cash for one cloak pattern. A few weeks after this I called on Eldr. Cahoon again and told him that I wanted ~~some~~ cloth for some shirts, to the amount of four or five dollars, I told him that I would pay him in the spring and sooner if I could; he let me have it. Not long after, my school was established, and some of the hands who laboured on the house attended, and wished to pay me at the committees store for their tuition. I called at the store to see if any negotiation could be made and they take me off where I owed them; but no such negotiation could be made. These with some other circumstances of like character called for the following reflections. In the first place I gave the committee two hundred & seventy five dollars in cash, besides some more, and during the last season have traveled through the middle and eastern States, to support and uphold the Store,[382] and in so doing, have reduced myself to nothing in a pecuniary point. ~~of~~ Under these circumstances [p. 151] this establishment refused to render me that ~~assistance~~ accommodation which a worldlings establishment would have gladly done, and one too which never received a donation from me, nor in whose favour I never raised my voice, or exerted my influence.

But after all this, thought I, it may be right, and I will be still,— until not long since I asertained that Eldr. Wm. Smith could go to the Store and get whatever he pleased, and no one to say why do ye so; until his account has amounted to seven hundred dollars or there abouts, and that he was a silent partner in the concern,[383] yet not acknowledged as such, fearing that his creditors would make a haul upon the Store. While we were abroad this last season we strained every nerve to obtain a little something for our families, and regularly divided the monies equally for ought that I know, not knowing that William had such a fountain at home, from whence to draw his support. I then called to mind the revelation in which myself, Mc Lellen [William E. McLellin], & Patten [David W. Patten], were chastned,[384] and also the ~~revelation~~ quotation in that revelation of the parable of the twelve sons;

---

382. During their recent five-month mission, Orson Hyde and his colleagues in the Quorum of the Twelve were assigned to solicit funds for the House of the Lord, for Zion, and for church publications. Hyde obviously considered the temple committee store an integral part of the financing of temple construction. (JS, Kirtland, OH, to the Quorum of the Twelve Apostles, 4 Aug. 1835, in JS Letterbook 1, pp. 90–93.)

383. Ira Ames, the store clerk, later listed William Smith among the building committee members. (Ames, Autobiography, 1836.)

384. This revelation is copied in the 3 Nov. 1835 entry herein.

as if the original meaning refered directly to the twelve Apostles of the church of Latter day Saints. I would now ask if each one of the twelve, has not an equal right to the same accomodations from that Store, provided they are alike faithful? If not with such a combination mine honour be not thou united. If each one has the same right, take the basket off from our noses or put one to Williams nose; or if this cannot be done, reconcile the parable of the twelve sons, with the superior priviliges that William has. Pardon me if I speak in parables or in parody.

A certain shepherd had twelve Sons and he sent them out one day to go and gather his flock which were scattered upon the mountains and in the valleys afar off. They were all obediant to their fathers mandate; and at evening they returned with the flock. And one Son received wool [p. 152] enough to make him warm and comfortable; and also received of the flesh and milk of the flock.

The other eleven received not so much as one kid to make merry with their friends.

These facts with some others, have disqualified my mind for studying the Hebrew language at present, and believing as I do, that I must sink or swim, or in other words take care of myself; I have thought that I should take the most efficient means in my power to get out of debt; and to this end I proposed taking the school. But if I am not thought competent to take the charge of it, or worthy to be placed in that station, I must devise some other means to help myself, althoug[h] having been ordained to that office under your own hands, with a promise that it should not be taken from me.—

conclusion of the whole matter is such, I am willing to continue, and do all I can, provided we can share equal benefits one with the other, and upon no other principles whatever. If one has support from the "public crib" let them all have it. But if ~~I am willing~~ one is pinched, I am willing to be, provided we are all alike.

If the principles of impartiality and equality can be observed by all, I think that I will not peep again

If I am damned it will be for doing what I think is right. There has been two applications made to me, to go into business, since I talked of taking the School. But it is[385] in the world, and I had rather remain in Kirtland, if I can consistently

All I ask is <u>Right</u>

---

385. TEXT: Possibly "~~in~~ is".

I am Sir with Respect
Your ob^t. Servt.
Orson Hyde

To President J. Smith jr
Kirtland Geauga Co.

Ohio [p. 153]

Eldr. O. Hyde called and read the foregoing letter himself and Pres. Smith explained upon the objections named in it, and satisfied his mind upon every objectionable point, and Eldr. Hyde remarked after they had got through, that he was more than satisfied, with his explannations, and would attend the Hebrew School, and on parting gave him his hand, with every expression of friendship that a gentleman and a christian could manifest; which our author reciprocated with cheerfulness, declareing at the same time, that he entertained the best of feelings for him, and most cordially forgave him the ingratitude, which was manifested in his letter, knowing that it was for want of correct information, that his mind was disturbed as far as his reflections related to ~~me~~ Joseph. But the committee had not dealt, in righteousness with him in all things; but all is now amicably adjusted and setled, and no hardness exists between ~~us~~ them.

This evening his father & mother called to see him upon the subject of the difficulty that transpired at their house on wednesday evening, between him and his brother William. They were sorely afflicted in mind, and almost heart broken on the account of that occurrence. The subject of our narative conversed with his parents and convinced them that he was not to ⟨be⟩ blame[d] for taking the course he did with his brother William on that occassion. But that he had acted in righteousness with him in all things.

He invited his parents to come and live with him, which they concented to do, as soon as it is practicable.

18 December 1835 • Friday

Friday morning 18th. He was at home; his brother Hyrum [Smith] called to see him, and read a letter that he received from William [Smith], in which he asked his (Hyrum's) forgiveness for the abuse he offered him at the debate. He tarried most of the fore noon and conversed freely with Joseph upon the subject of the difficulty existing between him [p. 154] and their brother William. He said he was perfectly satisfied with the course Joseph had taken, with his brother William, in rebukeing him in his wickedness. But he is deeply wounded in his feeling on account of the conduct of William and although he ⟨feels⟩ all the tender sympathy and fine feelings, of a brother toward him, yet he can but look upon his conduct, as an abomination in the sight of God: And said Joseph, (as his brother Hyrum took the parting hand with him,) I could pray in my heart that all my brethren were like unto my ~~brother~~ beloved brother Hyrum, for truly he possesses ~~he~~ ⟨the⟩ mildness of a lamb, and the integrity of a Job; and in short the meek and quiet spirit, of Jesus Christ; and I love him with that love, that is stronger than death, for I never had occasion to rebuke him, nor he me, which he declared when he left me to day.

The following is a copy of a letter from Eldr. William Smith

December 18th 1836 [1835]

Br. Joseph— Though I do not know but I have forfeited all right and title to the word brother in consequence of what I have done, for I concider myself, that I am unworthy to be called one, after coming to myself, and reflecting upon what I have been doing, I feel as though it was my duty, to make an humble confession to you, on account of what took place at my house the other evening but I shall [leave][386] this part of the subject for the present. I was called to an account yesterday by the quorum of the 12, for my conduct; or in other words they desired to know my mind and determinations and what I intended to do. I told them that on reflection upon the many difficulties that I had had, with the church & the much disgrace I had brought upon myself in consequence of my bad conduct; and also that my health would not admit of my going to school, to make any preperation for the induement, and that I was not able to travel; therefore it would be better for them to appoint one in my stead, that would be better able to fill that important station than myself: And by doing [p. 155] this they throw me into the hands of the church, and leave me where I was before I was chosen among the twelve.

Then I would not be in a situation to bring so much disgrace upon the casuse [cause], when I fell into temptations. And perhaps by this means I might obtain salvation. You know dear brother my passions and the danger of falling from so high a station: And therefore I chose to withdraw from the office of the Apostleship, while there is salvation for me, and remain a member in the church. I feel afraid if I do not, it will be worse for me some other day.

And again my health is poor and it is necessary that the office should not be idle. And again I say, you know my passions and I am fearful that it will be worse for me by, and by; do so, if the Lord will

---

386. Omitted word supplied from the corresponding journal entry. (See *JSP*, J1:129.)

have mercy on me, and let me remain a member in the church, and travel & preach, when I am able. do not think that I am your enemy, for what I have done. perhaps the inquiry may arise in your mind, why I do not rem[em]ber the many good deeds you have done for me; or if I do remember them, why it is that I should treat you so basely.— when I reflect upon the injuries I have done you, I must confess that I cannot account for my conduct. I feel truly sorry for what I have done and humbly ask your forgiveness. I have not confidence as yet, to come and see you, for I feel ashamed of what I have been doing; and as I feel now I feel as though all the confession that I could make verbally, or by writing, would not be sufficient to atone for my transgression. Be this as it may, I am willing to make all the restitution you shall require, if I can stay in the church as a member, I will try to make all the satisfaction I possibly can.

Yours with respect
William Smith

P.S. do not cast me off, but strive to save me in the church as a member: I do heartily repent of what I have done to you, and ask your forgiveness.— I consider my transgression the other evening, of no small magnitude. But it is done and I cannot help it now— I know brother Joseph you are always willing to forgive; but I sometimes think when I reflect upon the many injuries I have done you [p. 156] as though a confession was not sufficient; but have mercy on me this once, and I will try to do so no more.

The quorum[387] of the 12, called a council yesterday and sent for me, and I went over. This council was called together without my knowledge, or concent.—[388] Yours

W^{m.} S.

Letter to William Smith • 18 or 19 December 1835

Kirtland Friday December 18th. 1836 [1835]
Answer to the foregoing letter. A Copy
Br. William
Having received your letter I now procede to answer it. I shall first proceed to give a brief narration of my feelings and emotions, since the night I first came to the knowledge of your having a debating-School

---

387. TEXT: "quorum" possibly written over "12".
388. For "without my knowledge, or concent," the 1835–1836 journal has "by themselves and not by me." (*JSP*, J1:131.)

at your house; which was at the time I called with Bishop [Newel K.] Whitney & family—[389] This was the first that I knew any thing about it, and from that time I took an interest in them; and was delighted with it, and formed a determination to attend the school for the purpose of obtaining [information],[390] and with the idea of imparting the same, through the assistance of the spirit of the Lord; if by any means I should have faith to do so, and with this intent I went to the School on Wednesday night. Not with the idea of breaking up the school; neither did it enter into my heart, that there was any wrangling or jealousy's in your heart, against me.

However previous to my leaving home there were feelings of solemnity rolling across my heart, which were unaccountable to me. These feelings continued by times to depress my spirits, and seemed to manifest that all was not right, even after the school commenced, and during the debate. Yet I strove to believe that all would work together for good. I was pleased with the arguments, & ingenuity manifested and did not feel to cast any reflections, upon any one that had spoken. But I felt that it was the duty of old men that set as presidents, to be as grave at least as young men. And that it was our duty to smile at solid arguments, and sound reasoning; and be impressed with solemnity, which should be expressed in our countinance [p. 157] when folly, and that which militates against truth and righteousness, rears it[s] deformed head.

Therefore in the spirit of my calling, and in view of the authority of the priesthood which has been confered upon me, it was my duty to reprove whatever I considered to be wrong; fondly hoping in my heart, that all parties, would think it right; and therefore humble themselves, that satan might not take the advantage of us, and hinder the progress of our school.— Now brother William I want you should bear with me, notwithstanding my plainness.

I would say to you then, that my feeling[s] were grieved when you interupted Eldr. Mc Lellen [William E. McLellin] in his speech. I thought that you should have considered your relation to him in your Apostleship: And not have manifested any divission of sentiment, between you & him, for the surrounding multitude to take the advantage of.

---

389. See entry for 18 Nov. 1835 herein.
390. Omitted word supplied from the corresponding journal entry. (See *JSP*, J1:131.)

Therefore by way of entreaty, on account of the anxiety I had for you, & your influence ⟨& welfare⟩ in society, I said unto you do not have any feeling, or something to that amount.—

Why I am thus particular, is that if you have misunderstood my feeling⟨s⟩³⁹¹ or motives toward you; you may be corrected. But to proceed.— After the school was ~~commenced~~ closed brother Hyrum [Smith] requested the privilege of speaking; you objected. However you said if he would not abuse the school, he might speak, observing at the same time that you would not allow any man to abuse the School in your house. You had no reason dear brother to suspect that Hyrum would abuse the School.

Therefore my feelings were mortified, at those unnecessary observations. I undertook to reason with you; but you manifested an inconsiderate and stubborn spirit: I then dispared of benefiting you on the account of the spirit you manifested; which drew from me the expression that you was as ugly as the devil.

Father then commanded silence and I formed the de[te]rmination to obey his mandate, and was about to leave the house, with the impression that you was under the influence of a wick[ed] spirit [p. 158] you replyed that you, would say what you pleased, in your own house. Father replyed say what you please; but let the rest hold their toungs. Then a reflection rushed through my mind of the anxiety and care I had for you, and your family, in doing what I did in finishing your house and providing flower [flour] for your family &c. And also father had possession in the house as well as yourself. And when at any time have I transgressed the commandments of my father or sold my birth-right? that I should not have ⟨the⟩ privilege of speaking in my father's house, or in other words in my fathers family, or in your house, (for so we will call it; and so it shall be,) that I should not have the privilege of reproving a younger brother?

Therefore I said I will speak for I built the house, and it is as much mine as yours, or something to that effect, (I should have said that I helped to finish the house.) I said it merely to show that it was not the right spirit, that would rise up for trifling matters, and undertake to put me to silence.

I saw that your indignation was kindled against me, and you made towards me; I was not then to be moved, and I thought to pull off my loose coat, least it should tangle me, and you be left to hurt me. But

---

391. TEXT: Possibly "feelings" (with plural in original inscription).

not with the intention of hurting you. But you was to[o] soon for me; and having once fallen into the hands of a mob and wounded in my side, and now into the hands of a brother, my side gave way: and after having been rescued from your grasp, I left your house, with feelings that were indiscribable. The scenery had now changed and all those fond expectations, that I had cherished (when going to your house,) of brotherly kindness, charity forbearance, and natural affection, that binds us in duty, not to make eachother an offender for a word.

But alas! abuse, anger, malice, hatred, and rage, are heaped upon me, by a brother; and with marks of violence upon my body, with a lame side,[392] I left your habitation bruised and wounded; and not only oppressed with these, but more severely so in mind being born down under the reflection of my disappointment. I returned home, not able to sit down or rise up without help. But through the blessing of God I am [p. 159] now better.— I have received your letter and perused it with care; I have not entertained a feeling of malice against you; I am older than yourself, and have endured more suffering, having been marred by mobs, with the labour's of my calling, with a series of persecution and injuries, continually heaped upon me, all serve to debiletate my system. And it may be that I cannot boast of being stronger than you: If I could, or could not, would this be an honour, or dishonour to me? If I like David could boast of slaying a Goliath, who defied the armies of the living God; or like Paul, of contending with a Peter face to face,[393] with sound and iresistable arguments, it might be an honour. But to mangle the flesh or seek revenge upon one who never done you any wrong, cannot be a source of sweet reflection to you, nor me, neither to our honerable father & mother, brothers & sisters. And when we reflect upon the care and unremitting diligence our parents have wached over us by night, & by day, and how many hours of sorrow, and painful anxiety they have spent over our cradles and by our bedsides, in sickness and in health. How careful ought we to be of their feelings in their old age? It surely cannot be a source of sweet reflection to us, to say or do any thing that would bring down their grey hairs with sorrow to the grave. In your letter you asked my forgiveness, which I readily grant; but it seems to me that you still retain an idea that I have ~~done~~ given you reason to be angry, or dissatisfied with me.

---

392. The remainder of this sentence does not appear in the corresponding 1835–1836 journal entry.
393. See Galatians 2:11.

Grant me the privilege then of saying, that however hasty, or harsh, I might have spoken at any time to you, it has been for the express purpose of endeavouring to warn exhort, admonish & rescue you from falling into difficulties & sorrows which I foresaw that you were plunging yourself, by giving way to that wicked spirit, which you call your passion⟨'s⟩, which you should curb and break down, and put under your feet, which if you do not, you never can be saved, (in my view) in the kingdom of God.

The Lord requires the will of his creatures to be swallowed up in his will. [p. 160]

You desire to remain in the church, but to forsake your Apostleship This permit me to tell you is a stratigem of the evil one. When he has gained one advantage, he lays a plan for another; but by rising up and maintaining your Apostleship and by making one tremendious effort, you may overcome your passions and please God. And by forsakeing your apostleship, you say that you are not willing to make that sacrafice that God requires at your hand. And by so doing you ⟨will⟩ incur his displeasure, and without pleasing God, do not think that it will be any better for you. When a man falls one step he must regain that step, or fall another[.] he then has still more to regain or eventually all is lost.

I desire brother William that you would humble yourself. I feel for you, and freely forgive you all; and you know my unshaken and unchangable disposition, I know in whom I trust, I stand upon the rock, the floods cannot, no they shall not overthrow me. You know the doctrine I teach is true, and you know that God has blessed me, I brought salvation to my fathers house, as an instrument in the hand of God, when they were in a miserable situation. You also know that it is my duty to admonish you when you do wrong. This liberty I shall always take, and you shall have the same privilege,— I take the privilege to admonish you because of my birthright, and I grant you the privilege because it is my duty to be humble and receive rebuke, and instruction from a brother or a friend.

As it regards what course you shall persue hereafter I do not pretend to say; I leave you in the hands of God and his church. Make your own decision, I will do you good although you marr me, or slay me; by so doing my garments shall be clear of your sins. And if at any time you should consider me to be an impostor, for heavens sake leave me in the hands of God, and not think to take vengance upon me yourself.— Tyrany, userpation, and to take men's rights, ever has been, and ever shall be, banished from my heart.— And now may God have mercy upon my fathers house; may God [p. 161] take away enmity, from between me, and them and may all blessings be restored, and the past errors be forgotten forever, may humble repentance bring us both to thee O God, and under thy power and protection, and to a crown to enjoy the society of father, mother, Alvin, Hyrum, Sophronia, Samuel, Catharine [Katharine], Carloss [Don Carlos], Lucy, the Saints and all the sanctified in peace forever, is the prayer of

Your brother
Joseph Smith Jun.

To Wm. Smith—

19 December 1835 • Saturday

Saturday Dec. 19ᵗʰ· He was at home and wrote the above letter, or rather indited[394] it, to his brother William[395] concerning whom he had many solemn feelings and he prayed hartily, that the Lord ~~will~~ cast him not off, but that he may return to the God of Jacob & magnify his apostleship and calling, may this be his happy lot for the Lord of Glory sake, Amen.

20 December 1835 • Sunday

Sunday 20ᵗʰ· He spent the day at home, in the society of his family, with whom he enjoyed great comfort & satisfaction. He also had many serious reflections, which were profitable.— br's Palmer, & [Jonathan] Taylor, called to day to see him, to whom he exhibited the sacred records, to their joy, and satisfaction, and for whom he prayed as follows,— O may God have mercy upon thes[e] men, and keep them in the way of everlasting life in the name of Jesus Christ, Amen.

21 December 1835 • Monday

Monday morning 21ˢᵗ· He spent this day in endeavouring to treasure up wisdom, & knowledge for the benefit of my [his] calling; The day passed off very pleasantly, for which, his soul flowed out in thankfulness to the Lord for his mercy and blessings to himself, & family, in sparing their lives, and administering to all their wants; O continue thy parental care over him, & his family, for Jesus sake.

---

394. TEXT: Possibly "~~dictated~~ indited".

395. In the 1835–1836 journal, the remainder of the corresponding entry and the three following entries are in JS's own hand. JS may have taken over the writing because of the illness of his scribe Warren Parrish. (See entry for 22 Dec. 1835 herein.)

22 December 1835 • Tuesday

Tuesday 22nd He continued his studies at home, [p. 162] with his heart raised in prayer to the Lord to give him learning, especially a knowledge of languages, and endue him with qualifications, to magnify, and adore, his great and exalted name. This evening he delivered an address, to the church, the Lord blessed him with utterance & power; and the saints were edified.— His scribe[396] being indisposed at this time, in consequence of a cold, he prayed thus for him.— O may God heal him, for his kindness to me, O my soul be thou greatful to him, & bless him, and he shall be blessed of God forever; I believe him to be a faithful friend of mine, therefore my soul delighteth in him, Amen.

Joseph Smith Junr.

23 December 1835 • Wednesday

Wednesday 23^d. He spent the fore noon at home, in studying the Greek language, and in waiting upon brethren who called to visit him;—[397] in the afternoon, in company with ~~Pres O Cow~~ Eldr. Leonard Rich, he called at Pres. O[liver] Cowdery'[s] to visit his relatives; but had not a very agreeable visit, for he found them filled with prejudice against the work of the Lord, and their minds blinded with superstition and ignorance.

24 December 1835 • Thursday

Thursday 24th. Spent the A.M. at home, in reading, meditation, & prayer,[398] in the P.M. he assisted in laying out a road across his farm. The commissioner who had been appointed by the County court superintended the same.[399]

25 December 1835 • Friday

Friday 25th. Dec. This Christmas-day, he spent at home in his family circle, and injoyed great satisfaction and comfort, for which he blessed the name of the Lord of Host's; For the privilege of spending this day of the year, in the bosom of his family; he had not enjoyed for a long time before.

---

396. Warren Parrish.

397. The 1835–1836 journal notes that JS exhibited the Egyptian papyri to these visitors. (*JSP*, J1:135.)

398. The phrase "in reading, meditation, & prayer" does not appear in the corresponding 1835–1836 journal entry.

399. The county board of commissioners had appointed a surveyor, Levi Edson, and a committee of three others to lay out the road. (Geauga Co., OH, Board of Commissioners, Road Records, 1806–1884, vol. C, pp. 327–328, Mar. 1836, microfilm 887,929, U.S. and Canada Record Collection, FHL.)

26 December 1835 • Saturday

Saturday 26ᵗʰ· To day in company with Pres. F[rederick] G. Williams & Eldr. W[arren] Parrish, who were convened at his own house he commenced regularly, & systematically, to study the venerable Hebrew language; we had paid some little attention to it before.——⁴⁰⁰ Eldr. Lyman Sherman called and requested the word of the Lord, throug[h] his servant Joseph, our author; he (Sherman,) said that he had been wrought upon for a long time to make known [p. 163] his feelings to him, (Joseph) with an assurance from the Lord that he would give him a revelation which should make known his duty.⁴⁰¹

The following is a revelation⁴⁰² given to Lyman Sherman Through Joseph Smith Jun. this 26ᵗʰ· day of Dec. 1835

Verily thus saith the Lord unto you my servant Lyman, your sins are forgiven you because you have obeyed my voice in coming up hither this morning to receive counsel of him whom I have appointed.

Therefore let your soul be at rest concerning your spiritual standing and resist no more my voice, and arise up and be more careful henceforth in observing your vows, which you have made, and do make, and you shall be blessed with exceeding great blessings. Wait patiently until the time when the solemn assembly shall be called, of my seventy,⁴⁰³ then you shall be rem[em]bered⁴⁰⁴ with the first of mine elders and receive right by ordination with the rest of mine elders whom I have chosen.

Behold this is the promise of the father unto you, if you continue faithful; and it shall be fulfilled upon you in that day that you shall have right to preach my gospel, wheresoever I shall send you from henceforth from that time. Therefore strengthen your brethren⁴⁰⁵ in all

---

400. The previous sentence is an expansion of "commenced studeing the Hebrew Language in company with bros Parish & Williams," as written in the corresponding 1835–1836 journal entry. (*JSP*, J1:137.)

401. The 1835–1836 journal also includes these sentences: "last evening a brother from the east called upon me for instruction whose name is Jonathan Crosby also in the course of the day two gentlemen called upon me while I was cutting wood at the door and requestd an interview with the heads of the church which I agreed to grant to them on Sunday morning the 27 Insᵗ." The journal entry for the following day reported that the "two gentlemen" failed to keep their appointment, causing JS to conclude that "they were trifling characters." (*JSP*, J1:137–138.)

402. Now D&C 108.

403. The copy of this revelation found in JS's journal has "servants" instead of "seventy." (See *JSP*, J1:138.)

404. TEXT: Possibly "numbered", as in the corresponding journal entry. (See *JSP*, J1:138.)

405. Here the history omits "in all your conversation," which appears in the corresponding journal entry. (*JSP*, J1:138.)

your exhortations, in all your prayers, and in all your doings, and behold, and lo, I am with you forever, Amen.

27 December 1835 • Sunday

Sunday morning 27ᵗʰ· At ⟨the⟩ usual hour he attended meeting at the school-house. Pres. [Oliver] Cowdery delivered a very able discourse,[406] which was edifying to the saints, and calculated to administer grace to all enquiring minds. In the after part of the day Pres. Hyrum Smith, & Bish. Partrige [Edward Partridge] delivred each, a short an[d] interesting lecture; after which the sacrament of the Lord's supper was administered and our meeting dismissed.

28 December 1835 • Monday

Monday morning 28ᵗʰ· Having prefered a charge against Eldr. Almon Babbit[t], for traduceing his character, he was called before the high council with his witnesses, & substantiated his charges [p. 164] against him; and Eldr. Babbit in part acknowledged his fault, but not satisfactory to the council, and after parleying with him a long time, and granting him every indulgence that could be required in righteousness, the council adjourned without obtaining a full confession from him.[407]

On this day the quorum of the seventy met, to render an account of their travels and ministry, since they were ordained to the apostleship. The meeting was interesting indeed, and his heart was made glad while he listened to the relations of those, who had been labouring in the vinyard of the Lord with such marvelous success, and he prayed God to bless them with an increas of faith, and power, and keep them all with the indurance of faith, in the name of Jesus christ to the end

29 December 1835 • Tuesday

Tuesday 29ᵗʰ· At about 10. oclock A.M. in company with his wife, & father & mother, (who had come to live with him,)[408] ~~also his scribe accompanied them. A large~~ he went to br. Oliver Olneys, to attend a blessing meeting;[409] his

---

406. The remainder of this sentence is not found in the 1835–1836 journal.

407. JS asked for an investigation "that my character and influence may be preserved as far as it can in righteousness." Babbitt had been complaining that JS "got mad" after losing an argument at the debating school. Five days later, Babbitt acknowledged that he was in error and was restored to fellowship. (Minute Book 1, 28 Dec. 1835; entry for 2 Jan. 1836 herein; Minute Book 1, 2 Jan. 1836.)

408. Twelve days earlier, JS invited his parents to move into his house from the home they shared with William Smith. (Entry for 17 Dec. 1835 herein.)

409. That is, a patriarchal blessing meeting.

scribe also accompanied them. After the company had assembled and were seated, his father Joseph Smith Sen. (who is ordained to the office of a patriarch in the church of Latterday Saints, to confer blessings by the spirit of prophecy.)[410] arose and made some preliminary remarks which were very applicable to the occasion; a hymn was then sung, after which he opened the meeting, by an able address, to the throne of grace. Fifteen persons came forward and received, each, a patriarchal blessing under his hands, as the spirit gave utterance[411]

The servises then were closed, as they commenced viz. by singing & prayer. A table was then spread and crowned with the bounties of the earth; and after invoking the benediction of heaven upon the rich repast, we fed sumptuously upon the same, and suffice it to say, that we had a glorious meeting, throughout, and he was highly pleased with the harmony and decorum that existed among the brethren and sisters. We returned home at evening. He then repaired to the School-house where [p. 165] he preached to a crowded audiance, who listened with attention while he delivered a lecture of about 3, hours in length; he had great liberty in speaking.

We were afterwards informed that there were, some persons present, who are of the calvinistic faith; if so we have no doubt but some of our authors sayings set to them like a garment that, was well fited, as he exposed their craft, and abominations, to a nicety, and that too, in the language of the scriptures. And his prayer to God is that it may be like a nail in a sure place, driven by the Master of assemblies.[412]

To day Col. Chamberlain's Son called to see him, a respectable gentleman.[413]

30 December 1835 • Wednesday

Wednesday 30th. He spent the day in reading hebrew at the council room, with his scribe, in whose company he delighted, & who had sufficiently recovered his health, to attend to his usual avocation.[414]

---

410. This parenthetical comment does not appear in the corresponding 1835–1836 journal entry.

411. Among those who received blessings at this time were Lyman Wight, Ezra Hayes, and George Morey. (Patriarchal Blessings, 1:29–30, 37.)

412. See Ecclesiastes 12:11; and Isaiah 22:23–25.

413. The phrase "a respectable gentleman" does not occur in the corresponding 1835–1836 journal entry. "Col. Chamberlain's Son" refers to Lee, Lorenzo, or Jacob Chamberlain. (Seneca Co., NY, Surrogate's Court, Probate Records, vol. E, pp. 8–9, 14 Nov. 1855, microfilm 843,630, U.S. and Canada Record Collection, FHL; Porter, "Study of the Origins," 272, 315–316.)

414. Warren Parrish discontinued writing in JS's journal after inscribing the first part of the entry for 19 December 1835. Frederick G. Williams penned the entries for 23 to 26 December, and Parrish resumed his duties as scribe beginning with the 27 December journal entry.

31 December 1835 • Thursday

Thursday 31ˢᵗ. After attending to his domestic concerns, he retired to the council room, in the ~~post office~~ printing office, in order to persue his studies.

The council of the twelve convened in an upper room under the same roof, and sent for him and some of the rest, of the ⟨first⟩ presidency to meet with them, to take into consideration the subject of the council, that is to be holden on Saturday next, and to make some arangments respecting it.— In the afternoon he attended at the Lord's House to give some directions concerning, the finishing of the upper rooms, and more especially the west room which he intends occupying for a translating room which will be prepared this week.

1 January 1836 • Friday

Friday morning January 1ˢᵗ. 1836.— On the introduction of the newyear, his heart is filled with greatful praise to God, for his kind care that has been over him and his family in preserving their lives while another year has rolled away. They have been sustained and upheld in the midst of a wicked, and pervers generation and exposed to all the afflictions temptations and miseries that are incident to human life; for which [p. 166] he felt to humble himself, as it were in dust and ashes before the Lord.— But notwithstanding the gratitude that filled his heart, on retrospecting the past year, with the multiplied blessings that have crowned his head; his heart is pained, and his peace distrubed when he reflects upon the difficulties that exists in his fathers family

The Devil has made a violent attack upon his brother William Smith & his brother in law Calvin Stoddard,[415] and the powers of darkness seem to hover over their minds and obscure the light of truth: And not only theirs but a gloomy shade appears to be cast over the minds of some more of his brothers & Sisters,[416] which prevents them from seeing thing as they really are. And the powers of earth & hell seem combined to overthrow us, and the church by causing a division in his fathers family. Indeed the adversary is bringing into requisition all his subtlety to prevent the saints from being endued; by causing divisions among the twelve, also among the seventy, and bickerings & jealousies among the Elders, & official members, and thus the leaven of iniquity foments & spreads among the lay members of the church.— But Joseph determined in his heart, that no exertion on his part should be wanting to adjust,

---

415. Tension surfaced between JS and William Smith in late October and erupted again in a mid-December confrontation. Stoddard, the husband of JS's sister Sophronia, was censured sometime before 7 March 1836, when he made a confession in his elders quorum; on 26 October 1836, his church standing was restored. (See entries for 29, 30, and 31 Oct. 1835; 16, 17, 18, and 19 Dec. 1835 herein; see also Kirtland Elders Quorum, "Record," 7 Mar. and 26 Oct. 1836.)

416. The 1835–1836 journal has "my ~~my parents and somee of my~~ brothers and sisters." (*JSP*, J1:140.)

Exterior of House of the Lord, Kirtland, Ohio. Circa 1875. (Courtesy Community of Christ Library-Archives, Independence, MO. Stereograph by W. A. Faze.)

and amicably dispose of, and settle, all family difficulties on this day; that the ensuing year, & years, be they many, or few, may be spent in righteousness before the Lord. And he declared that he feels confident, that the cloud will burst, and satan's kingdom be laid in ruins, with all his black designs; and the saints come forth like gold seven times tried in the fire,[417] being made perfect throug[h] temptations & sufferings: and the blessings of heaven, & earth, will be multiplied upon our heads, which may God grant for his Sons sake, Amen.

This morning his brother Wm. Smith called to see him upon the subject of their difficulties; they retired to a private room with their father, ~~and~~ their uncle John Smith, their brother Hyrum Smith, & Eldr. Martin Harris;[418] their aged father then opened the interview by prayer [p. 167] after which he expressed his feelings on the occasion in a very feeling and pathetic manner; even with all the sympathy of a father whose feelings were deeply wounded on account of the difficulty that was existing in his family: and while he was speaking the spirit of God rested down upon them in mighty power and their hearts melted down in contrition and humility before the Lord. William made an humble confession and asked his brother Joseph's forgivness for having abused him; and wherein Joseph had been out of the way he asked his forgiveness, and indeed the spirit of confession, and forgiving, was mutual among us all, and we entered into a covenant with eachother, before the Lord, & the Holy Angels, and the brethren present, to strive from hence forward, to build eachother up in righteousness in all things, and not listen to evil reports concerning eachother; but like brethren of the same household, go to eachother with our grievances in the spirit of meekness and be reconciled, and strive to promote our own happiness, and the happiness of our fathers family, & the happiness of our own families, and in short the happiness, and well being of all. His wife, mother and scribe, was then called in to partake of our joys to whom we related the covenant we had entered into, and while gratitude swelled our bosoms, tears flowed from our eyes.— Joseph was then requested to close our interview, which he did by prayer, and truly it was a time of rejoicing, and ⟨a⟩ jubillee to his fathers family.

2 January 1836 • Saturday

Saturday Jany 2ond. A council had been called to set in judgment, on a complaint prefered against Eldr. Wm. Smith, by Eldr. Orson Johnson.[419] At 9. oclock

---

417. See Zechariah 13:9.

418. Harris, apparently brought in as a neutral mediator, was a friend of the family from their New York days. (Lucy Mack Smith, History, 1844–1845, bk. 5, [8]; bk. 6, [3].)

419. Johnson brought charges against William Smith of "unchristian like conduct in speaking disrespectfully of President Joseph Smith Junr and the revelations & commandments given through him" and

this morning agreeably to previous arangments, Pres. Smith attended this council. The council organized and proceeded to business: but before entering on the trial, his brother William arose and humbly confessed the charges prefered against him, and the forgiveness of the council, and the whole congregation. A vote was then called to know whether his confession was sattisfactory, and whether the [p. 168] brethren would extend the hand of fellowship to him again. With cheerfulness the whole congregation raised their hands to receive him.— Eldr. Almon Babbit[t] also confessed the charge which our author had prefered, ~~against~~ and sustained against him, before a previous council,[420] and was received into fellowship; and some other business was transacted in harmony and union and a mutual good feeling seemed to prevail among the brethren, and our hearts were made glad on the occasion, and there was joy in heaven and our souls magnifyed the Lord for his goodness and mercy manifested to us. The council adjourned by prayer

3 January 1836 • Sunday

Sunday morning 3ᵈ· He attended meeting at the usual hour. President [Sidney] Rigdon delivered an interesting lecture upon the subject of revelation,—[421] in the P.M. he (Joseph) confirmed about 10 or 12 individuals who had been baptized, among whom was M[arvel] C. Davis who had previously belonged to the church.[422] His brother William made his confession to day, the church cheerfully forgave, and cordially received him into fellowship again:— The Lord supper was administered and William gave out an appointment to preach in the evening at early candlelight, and preached accordingly. This has been a day of rejoicing to him, of whom we write; the cloud that has been hanging ove[r] his mind has burst with great blessings upon his head and satan has been foiled in his attempts to destroy him and the church by causing divisions & jealousy's to arise in the hearts of some of the brethren, and we unitedly thank our Heavenly Father for the union and harmony that now exists in the church.

"for attempting to inflict personal violence" on him. These charges arose from William Smith's assault on JS two weeks earlier. Six of the seven most senior members of the Quorum of the Twelve sat on this high council to consider the charges against their fellow quorum member. (Minute Book 1, 29 Dec. 1835; entry for 16 Dec. 1835 herein; Minute Book 1, 2 Jan. 1836.)

420. See Minute Book 1, 28 Dec. 1835 and 2 Jan. 1836.

421. TEXT: Possibly "revelations".

422. Davis's rebaptism followed church discipline that occurred sometime after 17 August 1835, when he served as a substitute high council member. (Minute Book 1, 17 Aug. 1835.)

4 January 1836 • Monday

Monday 4ᵗʰ· He met in the west school-room in the chape[l], to assist in organizeing the Hebrew class. Dr. Piexotto [Daniel Peixotto] who had engaged to teach our Hebrew school agreed to wait on us to day, and deliver his introductory lecture.— yesterday he sent word to us that he could not come until Wednesday next; a vote was called to know wether the class would submit to such treatment or not, and carried in the negative⁴²³ [p. 169] Eldr. Sylvester Smith was appointed to inform the said Dr. Piexotto that his servises were not wanted;⁴²⁴ and Eldr's Wm. McLellen [William E. McLellin], & Orson Hyde were appointed by the voice of the school to go to Hudson Seminary,⁴²⁵ to hire a teacher and notwithstanding our disapointment we concluded to go on with our school and do the best we can until we can obtain a teacher. By the voice of the class Pres. Joseph Smith Jun. was solicited to take charge of school for the time being, to which he concented.— This being the first day that this room⁴²⁶ was occupied, we thought meet to dedicate it to God, which was solemnized by the venerable patriarch Joseph Smith Sen.— This evening we met at the chapel to make arangements for a singing school; after some altercation, a judicious arangement was entered into, and a committe of 6 was chosen to take charge of the singing department.

This is a rainy unpleasant time, and the roads are extremely mudy.

5 January 1836 • Tuesday

Tuesday 5ᵗʰ· He attended the Hebrew school, & made several divisions in the class, had some debate with Eldr. Orson Pratt respecting the Hebrew pronunciations which was unpleasant, he manifested a stubourn spirit, which grieved Joseph much.

---

423. After retaining Peixotto, the school sought to be released from its agreement with him. Peixotto apparently did not release the school from its agreement yet failed to appear as scheduled. (See entry for 21 Nov. 1835 herein.)

424. The letter has not been located, but Peixotto's 5 January letter of reply and Warren Parrish's 11 January rejoinder were transcribed into the 1835–1836 journal. The entirety of Peixotto's letter and part of Parrish's response were also copied into this history. (JS, Journal, 18 Jan. 1836, in *JSP*, J1:161–164; see also entry for 18 Jan. 1836 herein.)

425. Western Reserve College at Hudson, Portage County (now Summit County), Ohio. (See Perrin, *History of Summit County*, 450–453.)

426. This was the westernmost of the five rooms on the third story of the House of the Lord, which JS intended to use as a translating room. (Robison, *First Mormon Temple*, 55, figs. 4–7; see also entry for 31 Dec. 1835 herein.)

6 January 1836 • Wednesday

Wednesday 6ᵗʰ· At 9 oclock AM. he repaired to the school room, and spent most of the fore noon in setling the difficulty that took place the preceeding day between him and Eldr. [Orson] Pratt, and after much controversy he [Pratt] confessed his fault and asked the forgiveness of the whole school, which was cheerfully, & readily granted by all.— Eldr. McLellen [William E. McLellin] returned from Hudson and reported to the school that he had engaged a man to teach 40 schollars for the term of 7 weeks at 320 Dollars, to commence about fifteen days from this time. His name is Joshua Seixas a Jew by birth & education[427] and highly celebrated as a Hebrew teacher, and proposes to give us sufficient knowledge of the language to read and translate it, in the above mentioned time;[428] or at least to those who attend to his instruction and diligently apply themselves to study [p. 170]

At a conference held at the schoolhouse on Saturday the 2ⁿᵈ Insᵗ· the following individuals were appointed by the voice of the conference to be ordained to the office of Eldrs, in the church of Latter day Saints.— They were ordained under the hands of Pres. J. Smith Jr.—viz.

Vincent [Vinson] Knight	Hyram Dayton
Thomas Grover	Samuel James
Elisha [Elijah] Fordham	John Herrott [Herritt][429]

7 January 1836 • Thursday

Thursday 7ᵗʰ·— He attended a sumptuous feast at Bp. N[ewel] K. Whitneys; this feast was after the order of the Son of God, the lame, the halt, & blind were invited according to the instructions of the Saviour.[430] Our

---

427. McLellin hired Joshua Seixas, a member of a prominent New York Jewish family, who had taught Hebrew in connection with several educational institutions. Seixas's Hebrew textbook was organized for a six-week curriculum. As noted in the journal, Seixas commenced classes 26 January. (Goldman, "Joshua/James Seixas," 73–77; Seixas, *Hebrew Grammar,* iv; JS, Journal, 26 Jan. 1836, in *JSP,* J1:173; see also F. C. Waite, Cleveland, OH, to Joseph L. Rubin, Washington DC, 19 Oct. 1933, in Milton V. Backman, Ohio Research Papers, ca. 1975, CHL; and Snow, "Who Was Professor Joshua Seixas?")

428. The remainder of this sentence is not found in the 1835–1836 journal.

429. The journal also notes that Sidney Rigdon served as clerk. Only Knight, Grover, and Dayton are mentioned in the official minutes. The proceedings to which this entry refers may have taken place during an additional meeting held that day for which no original minutes are extant. (*JSP,* J1:145; Minute Book 1, 2 Jan. 1836.)

430. See Luke 14:12–14. As bishop in Ohio, Whitney had an ecclesiastical responsibility to administer to the poor. According to Elizabeth Ann Smith Whitney, this feast for the poor continued over the next three days, 7–9 January, with "Joseph and his two Counselors being present each day, talking, blessing, and comforting the poor." ([Elizabeth Ann Smith Whitney], "A Leaf from an Autobiography," *Woman's Exponent,* 1 Nov. 1878, 83; Whitney, "Aaronic Priesthood," 129–130; see also entry for 9 Jan. 1836 herein.)

meeting was opend by singing and prayer,[431] the Bishops father & mother[432] were bless[ed], and several others with a patriarchal blessing.

We then received a bountiful refreshment furnished by the liberality of the Bishop; the company was large and respectable. Before we parted the Lord poured out his spirit upon us in mighty power, and some of the songs of Zion were sung, and our hearts were made glad while partaking of an antipast[433] of those joys that will be poured upon the heads of the saints when they are gathered together upon mount Zion, to enjoy eachothers society forever; even all the blessings of heaven and earth, where there will be none to molest or make us afraid.—[434] He returned home and spent the evening in the bosom of his family.

8 January 1836 • Friday

Friday 8th He spent the day in the Hebrew School, and made rapid progress in his studies, and advanced the students in theirs.

9 January 1836 • Saturday

Saturday 9th. While at school in the A.M. he received the following note.—

> Thus saith the voice of the Spirit to me if thy brother Joseph Smith Jun. will attend the feast at thy house this day at 12 oclock, the poor & lame will rejoice at his presence, & also think themselves honoured
> Yours in friendship & love
> N[ewel] K. Whitney
9th Jany 1836 [p. 171]

He dismissed his class in order to comply with the Bp's. request, his wife, father, & mother accompanied him. A large company assembled, and a number were blessed under the hands of the patriarch,[435] ⟨&⟩ indeed the Lord blessed us all, we had a good time. He spent the evening at home.

10 January 1836 • Sunday

Sunday 10th. He attended meeting; Eldr. Wilber [Wilbur] Denton & Eldr. J. [Wilkins Jenkins] Salisbury preached in the fore noon:— In the P.M. his

---

431. According to the 1835–1836 journal entry, the prayer was offered by Joseph Smith Sr. (*JSP*, J1:146.)

432. Samuel and Susanna Kimball Whitney.

433. "A foretaste; something taken before the proper time." ("Antepast," in *American Dictionary*, 39.)

434. This phrasing appears throughout the Old Testament, as in, for example, Micah 4:2–4 and Zephaniah 3:13.

435. Joseph Smith Sr.

brother's Samuel & Carloss [Don Carlos] Smith delivered each a discourse; all
these young Eldr's did well concidering their advantages & experiance and bid
fair to make useful men in the vinyard of the Lord. The Lords supper was
administered and the meeting dismissed. At the intermission to day three were
received into the church by baptism.[436]

11 January 1836 • Monday

Monday morning 11ᵗʰ˙ There being no school to day he injoyed the sweets
of the social fireside with his family; however many brethren visited him
among whom was Alva Beeman [Alvah Beman] of Gennessee [Genesee] Co.
New York, who had come to attend the solemn assembly.— I delight (says
Joseph) in the society of my friends & brethren & pray that the blessings of
heaven and earth may be multiplied upon their heads.

12 January 1836 • Tuesday

Tuesday Jany. 12ᵗʰ˙ To day he called on the presidency of the church and
made arangements to meet tomorrow at 10 oclock A.M. to take into concider-
ation the subject of the Solemn Assembly. This after noon a young man called
to see the Egyptian records and on viewing them, he expressed great satisfaction and appeared very anxious to know how to translate them.— also a man
was introduced to him by the name of Russel Wever [Russell Weaver] from
Cambray Niagary [Cambria, Niagara] Co. New York; This man is a preacher
in the Christian or Unitarian church. Mr. Wever remarked that he had but few
minutes to spend with me,[437] we imediately entered into conversation, and had
some little debate upon the subject of prejudice, but soon came [p. 172] to an
understanding, he spoke of the gospel and said he believed it, adding at the
same time that it was ~~the power~~ good tidings of great joy.— Pres. Smith
replyed that it was one thing to proclaim good tidings, and another to tell
what those tidings consisted in; he [Weaver] waived the conversation and
retired.— He was introduced by Joseph Rose

13 January 1836 • Wednesday

Wednesday 13ᵗʰ˙ At 10 oclock A.M. he met in council with all the presidency of Kirtland, & Zion, together with their counsellors, (or their legal

---

436. The 1835–1836 journal entry notes that Martin Harris performed these baptisms. (See *JSP*,
J1:147.)

437. That is, JS.

representatives),[438] the presidents of the seventy and many of the Eldr's. of the church of Latterday Saints, came to order and sung Adam-ondi-Ahman[439] and opened by prayer offered up by Joseph Smith Sen. Pres. Joseph Smith Jun. presided on the occasion.— The council being thus organized and opened, he arose and made some preliminary remarks in general terms to[u]ching the authoritys of the church; also laying before them the business of the day, which was to supply some deficiencies in the several quorums, which were occasioned by the calling of the twelve & ~~seventies~~ ⟨seventy⟩ &c. After some altercation upon the subject as to the most proper manner to proceed Eldr. Vinson Knight was nominated and seconded to fill the bishops quorum in Kirtland

The vote of the presidency was called and carried ~~in the~~ unanimously,— vote of the high council of Zion was then called & carried also,— vote of the twelve was called and carried,— vote of the council of the Seventy was called and carried,— vote of the bishop of Zion & his council was called & carried, and Eldr. Knight was received by the unanimous voice & consent of all the authoritys of the church as a counsellor in the bishops council in Kirtland to fill the place of Hyrum Smith who is ordained to the presidency.—[440] Eldr. Knight was then ordained under the hands of Bp. N[ewel] K. Whitney to the office of a councillor also to the high priesthood.— Council adjourned for one hour, by sing[ing] come let us rejoice in the day of salvation &c.—[441] Council assembled at 1, oclock P.M. and proceeded to business— John P. Greene was nominated & seconded, as councilor in the high council of Kirtland to fill the place of O[liver] Cowdery who is ordained to the presidency—[442] a vote was called of the several quorums in their respective order and carried unanimously [p. 173]

---

438. For "their counsellors, (or their legal representatives)," the 1835–1836 journal has "all their councilors that could be found in this place however some of the councellors were absent, both of Kirtland and Zion." (*JSP*, J1:148.)

439. The text of this hymn was written by William W. Phelps, a member of the Missouri presidency in attendance at this council. (Hymn 23, *Collection of Sacred Hymns* [1835], 29–30; see also "Adam-ondi-Ahman," in Glossary.)

440. The corresponding journal entry reads: "who is ordained to the Presidency of the high council of Kirtland." In the period during which this entry was made, members of the presidency of the church were also the presidency of the Kirtland high council. The terminology may have been in transition. (*JSP*, J1:148; see also J1:148n259.)

441. The text of this hymn was also written by William W. Phelps. (Hymn 18, *Collection of Sacred Hymns* [1835], 24–25.)

442. The corresponding journal entry reads: "who is elected to the presidency of the high council in this place." JS ordained Cowdery "assistant President of the High and Holy Priesthood, . . . to assist in presiding over the whole chu[r]ch" a year earlier. (*JSP*, J1:149; entry for 5 Dec. 1834 herein.)

Eldr. Thomas Grover was nominated & seconded to supply the place of Eldr. Luke Johnson[443] in the high council of Kirtland, vote called and carried unanimously.

Eldr. Noah Packard was nominated & seconded to supply the place of ⟨Eldr.⟩ Sylvester Smith[444] in the high council of Kirtland, vote call[ed] of the respective authorities and carried unanimously.

Eldr. Joseph Kingsbury was nominated & seconded to fill the place of Eldr. Orson Hyde[445] in the high council of Kirtland, vote called and carried unanimously Eldr. Samuel James was nominated & seconded to supply the place of Joseph Smith Sen.—[446] vote called and carried unanimously.

The newly elected counsellors were then called forward and ordained in order as they were elected under the hands of Presidents J. Smith Jn S[idney] Rigdon & H. Smith to the office of high priests and counsellors in the high council of Kirtland the Stake of Zion.

Many great and glorious blessings were pronounced upon the heads of these councillors by Pres. Rigdon who was mouth on the occasion.—[447] Next proceeded to supply the deficiencies in the Zion high council. Eldr's Alva Beeman [Alvah Beman] & Isaac Mc Withy were nominated & seconded to fill the places of Eldrs. John Murdock and Solomon Hancock[448] for the time being.— vote was called and carried unanimously:[449]

Eldr. Nathaniel Milliken, & Thomas Carrico [Jr.], were nominated & seconded to serve as door keepers in the house of the Lord, vote called and carried unanimously by the whole assembly. Presdt's J. Smith Jn., S. Rigdon, W[illiam] W. Phelps, D[avid] Whitmer, & H. Smith, were nominated &

---

443. Johnson, an original member of the Quorum of the Twelve, was ordained an apostle eleven months earlier. (Minute Book 1, 14 Feb. 1835.)

444. The 1835–1836 journal specifies the reason that a replacement was needed for Sylvester Smith: he was "ordained to the presidency of the Seventy." Smith was ordained more than ten months earlier. Minutes of the council clarify that Packard replaced not Sylvester Smith but Hyrum Smith, who was called to the Kirtland high council on 24 September 1834 to replace Sylvester Smith, who had been dropped from the council at that day's meeting. (*JSP*, J1:149; JS History, vol. B-1, 578; Minute Book 1, 24 Sept. 1834 and 13 Jan. 1836.)

445. The 1835–1836 journal specifies that Hyde was "chosen and ordained one of the twelve." This ordination took place eleven months earlier. (*JSP*, J1:149; Minute Book 1, 15 Feb. 1835.)

446. Joseph Smith Sr. was appointed to the presidency a year earlier. Though he continued to serve as a council member, his advancement was recognized in council minutes by placing "President" after his name. (Entry for 6 Dec. 1834 herein; Minute Book 1, 18 Jan. 1835.)

447. For synopses of the blessings, see Minute Book 1, 13 Jan. 1836.

448. According to the 1835–1836 journal, Murdock and Hancock were absent from this meeting. (See *JSP*, J1:150.)

449. A week earlier, a council at Kirtland permanently replaced five other members of the Missouri high council, four of whom had been called to the Quorum of the Twelve. (Minute Book 2, 6 Jan. 1836.)

seconded to draft rules & regulations to govern the house of the Lord; vote was called and carried by the unanimous voice of the whole assembly.

The question was then agitated whether whispering should be allowed in our councils & assemblies; a vote was called and carried unanimously in the negative, that not only whispering, but loud talking shall be prohibited in our assemblies except by those who are called upon, or ask permission to speak [p. 174] upon any consideration whatever; and that no man shall be interupted while speaking unless he is speakin out of place, and every man shall be allowed to speak in his turn.— Eldr. N. Milliken refused to serve as door-keeper in the house of the Lord on account of his ill health and was released by the voice of the Assembly.

Pres. S. Rigdon made a request to have some of the presidency pray for & lay hands upon him and rebuke a severe affliction with which he was afflicted in his face, chiefly nights;— Presdts H. Smith & D. Whitmer, prayed for & laid hands on him and rebuked his affliction in the name of the Lord Jesus, the whole assembly responded Amen. Eldr. D[avid] W. Patten also made a request in behalf of his wife, our author, offered up a prayer in her behalf, ⟨&⟩ the whole assembly responded Amen. The minuets of the council were read[450] and council adjourned until Friday 15th. Inst. at 9. oclock A.M. at the school room in the upper part of the Chapel.— Pres. Rigdon arose and made some very appropriate remarks touching the enduement and dismissed ~~by~~ the assembly by prayer

W[arren] Parrish   <u>Scribe</u>

This (says Joseph) has been one of the best days I ever spent, there has been an entire unison of feeling expressed in all our proceedings during this days and it has been good for us to be here, in this heavenly place in Christ Jesus, and although much fatigued with the labours of the day; yet my spiritual reward has been very great.— He returned home and spent the evening.

14 January 1836 • Thursday

Thursday 14th.— At 9 oclock A.M. he met the Hebrew class at the school-room in the Chapel and made some arangments about our anticipated teacher Mr. J[oshua] Seixas.— He then repaired to the council room in the printing office, to meet with his colleagues who were appointed with himself to draft ~~resolutions~~ rules & regulations to be observed in the house of the Lord in

---

450. Minute Book 1, 13 Jan. 1836.

Kirtland, built by the church of latter day saints in the year of our Lord 1834,[451] as follows.— [p. 175]

1ˢᵗ It is according to the rules & regulations of all regularly and legal organized bodies to have a president to keep order.

2ᵒⁿᵈ· The body thus organized are under obligations to be in subjections to that authority.

3ᵈ· When a congregation assembles in this house they shall submit to the following rules that due respect may be paid to the order of worship. viz.

1ˢᵗ· No man shall be interupted who is appointed to speak by the permission of the church, by any disorderly person or persons in the congregation, by whispering, by laughing, by talking, by manaceing gestures, by getting up and running out in a disorderly manner, or by offering indignity to the manner of worship, or the religion, or to any officer of said church while officiateing in his office in any wise whatever, by any display of ill manners, or ill breeding, from old, or young, rich, or poor, male or female, bond or free, black or white, believer or unbeliever, and if any of the above insults are offered such measures will be taken as are lawful to punish the aggressor, or aggressors and eject them out of the house.

2ᵒⁿᵈ· An insult offered to the presiding Eldr. of said church shall be concidered an insult to the whole body, also an insult offered to any of the officers of said church while officiateing shall be considered an insult to the whole body.—

3ᵈ· All persons are prohibited from going up the stairs in times of worship.

4ᵗʰ· All persons are prohibited from exploreing the house except waited upon by a person appointed for that purpose.

5ᵗʰ· All persons are prohibited from going into the several pulpits except the officers who are appointed to officiate in the same.

6ᵗʰ· All persons are prohibited from cutting, marking, or maring, the inside, or outside of the house, with a knife pencil or any other instrument whatever, under pain of such penalty as the law shall inflict.

---

451. The foundation and walls of the House of the Lord were built in 1834, completing the major structural stonework and masonry. Roofing and finishing work continued in 1835 and 1836. (See Corrill, *Brief History,* 21, in *JSP,* H2:151; see also Robison, *First Mormon Temple,* 78–81, 149–157.)

7th. All children are prohibited from assembling in [p. 176] the house above, or below, or any ~~where~~ part of it, to play or for recreation at any time, and all parents guardians or mastures [masters], shall be ameniable for all damage that shall accrue in consequence of their children.

8th.— All persons whether believers or unbelievers shall be treated with due respect by the authorities of the church.

9th. No imposition shall be practiced upon any member of the church by depriving them of their rights in the house.

council adjourned sine die.— Our author returned home this afternoon Pres. O[liver] Cowdery returned from the City of Columbus the metropolis of this State (Ohio).[452]

At evening himself & wife were invited to attend on a matrimonial occasion at Mrs. [Catherine Noramore] Wilcox where he was solicited to solemnize the marriage contract between Mr. John Webb & Mrs. Catharine Wilcox; also Mr. Thomas Carrico [Jr.] & Miss. Eliza[be]th Baker, at the same place. The crowded assembly were seated, and the interview opened by singing & prayer suited to the occasion; after which he made some remarks in relation to the duties that are incumbent on husbands & wives; in particular the great importance there is in cultivating the pure principles of the institution in all its bearings and relations to each other and society in general.— He then invited them to arise and join hands, and pronounced the ceremony according to the rules & regulations of the Church of Latterday Saints;[453] and pronounced such blessings upon their heads as the Lord put into ~~their~~ his heart; even the blessings of Abraham Isaac & Jacob, and dismissed by singing and prayer.— We then took some refreshment and our hearts were made glad with the fruit of the vine. This is according to the pattern set us by ~~the~~ our Saviour himself whene he graced the marriage in Cana of Gallilee and turned the water into wine that they might make themselves joyful,[454] and we feel disposed to patronize all the institutions of heaven. Pres. Smith took leave of the audiance and retired.

15 January 1836 • Friday

Friday 15th. Jany.— At 9. oclock A.M. he met in council agreeably to adjournment, at the council room in the Chapel, & organized the authorities of the church agreeable to their respective offices in the same. He then made

---

452. Cowdery had been in Columbus to serve as a delegate from Geauga County to the state Democratic Party convention. (Cowdery, Diary, 8–9 Jan. 1836.)

453. "Marriage," ca. Aug. 1835, in Doctrine and Covenants 101, 1835 ed.

454. See John 2:1–11.

[p. 177] some observations respecting the order of the day and the great ~~importance~~ responsibility we are under, to transact all our business in righteousness before the Lord, inasmuch as our descisions will have a bearing upon all mankind and upon all generations to come. The song Adam Ondi Ahman was sung & council opened by prayer; & proceeded to business by reading the rules & regulations to govern the house of the Lord, as drafted by the committee chosen for that purpose. The vote of the presidency was called upon these rules; some exceptions were taken by Pres. O[liver] Cowdery which he withdrew on an explanation, and the vote passed unanimously.— The subject was then laid before the high council of Kirtland and after some altercation their vote was called and unanimously passed in favour of the rules.— The investigation was then thrown before the high council of Zion; some inquiry was made upon some particular items, which were soon settled, and their vote called and passed unanimously in favour of them.— The quorum of the twelve investigated the subject next, and their vote called & unanimously passed in favour of them.— Council adjourned for one hour.

1. oclock P.M. council called to order & proceeded to business. The subject of the rules & regulations to govern the house of the Lord, came next in order before the quorum of the seventy, their vote called and carried unanimously.

The question was then thrown before the bishop in Kirtland & his councillors, their vote called & carried in the affirmative.— The above named bill having now passed unanimously through all the quorums, in their order, it is received & established as a law to govern the house of the Lord in Kirtland.— In the investigation which has been had today upon the above mentioned subject; he (Joseph) saw that many who had deliberated upon it, were darkened in their minds respecting it; which drew forth the following remarks from him, concerning the privileges of the authorities of the church; that they should each speak in his turn, and in his place, and in his time & season, that their may be perfect order in all things, and that every man before he makes an objection to any item that is thrown before them for their consideration, should be certain that he [p. 178] can throw light upon the subject, rather than spread darkness, and that his objection be founded in righteousness: Which may be done, by applying ourselves diligently to study & know the mind & will of the Lord; whose spirit always makes manifest, and demonstrates to the understanding of all who are in possession of its benign influence.

Eldr. Carloss [Don Carlos] Smith was nominated & seconded to be ordained president of the high priesthood to preside over that quorum in

Kirtland,[455] a vote was called of all the respective quorums and unanimously passed.

Eldr. Alva Beeman [Alvah Beman] was nominated and seconded to officciate as president of the Eldrs. in Kirtland;[456] The vote of the several authorities was call[ed], and unanimously passed.

William Cowdery [Jr.] was nominated & seconded to officiate as president over the priests of the Aaronic priesthood in Kirtland the vote of the assembly was called beginning at the bishops council and passing through the several authorities until it come to the first presidency and received their sanction having been carried unanimously in all the other quorums.

Oliver Olney was nominated & seconded to preside over the teachers in Kirtland; the vote was call[ed] and unanimously passed through all the assembly.

Ira Bond was nominated and seconded to preside over the deacons in Kirtland;— vote called & passed unanimously.

Eldr. Carloss Smith was called forward to the seat of the presidency and ordained to the office whereunto he had been elected; and many blessings pronounced upon his head, by Joseph Smith Sen. S[idney] Rigdon & H[yrum] Smith who were appointed to ordain him.

Eldr. Beeman also received his ordination & blessings under the hands of the presidency.

Bishop N[ewel] K. Whitney & his councillors then proceeded to ordain those that had been elected to fill the several quorums of the Aaronic priesthood; & pronounced such blessings upon their heads, as the Lord put into their hearts.

Next proceeded to appoint door keepers to serve in the house of the Lord. The officers of the several quorums were nominated & seconded, and vote carried, that each should [p. 179] serve in his turn as doorkeeper in the Lords house.— also Nathaniel Milliken, Thomas Carrico [Jr.], Samuel Rolph [Rolfe], & Amos R. Orton were elected to the office of doorkeepers.[457]

Nominated & seconded that the presidency of the high council hold the keys of the inner & outer courts of the Lords house in Kirtland, except the key

---

455. The 1835–1836 journal clarifies that Don Carlos Smith was also nominated to be ordained a high priest on this occasion.

456. The 1835–1836 journal records this remark from Beman: "Brethren you know that I am [you are] young and I am old and ignorant and kneed much instructions, but I wish to do the will of the Lord." (*JSP*, J1:155.)

457. Milliken had recently declined to serve as a doorkeeper and was released from this duty. (Entry for 13 Jan. 1836 herein.)

to one of the vestrys, which is to be held by the bishopric of the Aaronic priesthood.— The vote of the assembly called & carried unanimously.

Nominated & seconded that John Carrill [Corrill] be appointed to take immediate charge of the house of the Lord in Kirtland[458] The vote of the assembly called & passed unanimously.

Pres. Rigdon then arose and delivered his charge to the assembly; his remarks were few and appropriate.

Council adjourned by prayer.—

W[arren] Parrish   Scribe

16 January 1836 • Saturday

Saturday morning 16[th.]— By request he met with the council of the twelve, in company with his colleagues F[rederick] G. Williams & S[idney] Rigdon.— council organized and opened by singing & prayer offered up by Thomas B. Marsh president of the twelve. He arose and requested the privilege in behalf of his colleagues of speaking, each in his turn until they all had spoken without being interupted; which was cheerfully granted by the presidency.— Eldr. Marsh proceeded to unbosom his feelings touching the mission of the twelve; but more particularly respecting a certain letter which they received from the presidency of the high council in Kirtland, while they were attending a conference in the State of Maine.[459] He also cast some reflections on the account of the twelve having been placed in our council on friday last, below the high councils of Kirtland & Zion having been previously placed in our assemblies next [to] the presidency.— He also remarked that their feelings were hurt on account of some remarks made by Pres. H[yrum] Smith on the trial of Glad[d]en Bishop who had been previously tried before the council of the twelve while on their mission in the east;[460] who had by their request thrown his case before the high council in Kirtland for investigation; And from some remarks made by the presidency the twelve drew the conclusion that their proceedings [p. 180] with him were in some degree discountinanced.

---

458. Corrill was earlier appointed to oversee "the finishing of the Lord's house." On this occasion, he was charged with enforcing the rules of conduct for the House of the Lord. (Corrill, *Brief History,* 22, in *JSP,* H2:153; Minute Book 1, 15 Jan. 1836.)

459. As reported in Quorum of the Twelve Apostles, Record, the quorum held conferences in Maine on 21 and 28 August 1835. The letter in question is JS, Kirtland, OH, to the Quorum of the Twelve Apostles, 4 Aug. 1835, in JS Letterbook 1, pp. 90–93. It conveyed reprimands and instructions to the Twelve from a high council consisting of the Kirtland and Missouri presidencies and others, and was signed by JS as moderator. Regarding the term "presidency of the high council in Kirtland," see *JSP,* J1:148n259.

460. See entry for 28 Sept. 1835 herein.

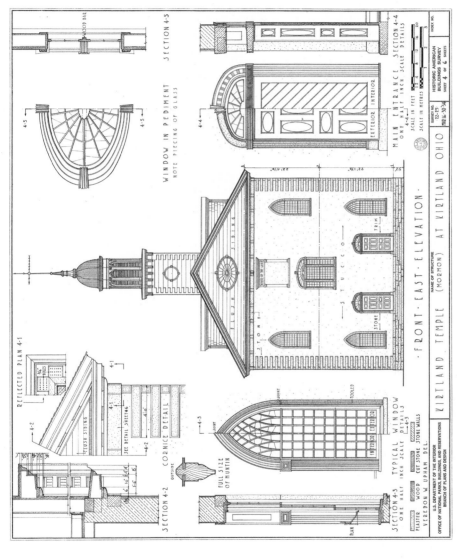

Architectural details of House of the Lord, Kirtland, Ohio. 1934. Veredon W. Upham documented design elements of the Kirtland temple in a series of drawings commissioned by the Historic American Buildings Survey. The architectural historian Elwin C. Robison has described the building as "a mixture of Georgian, Federal, Greek Revival, and Gothic elements." (Robison, *First Mormon Temple*, 16–17; image courtesy Library of Congress, Washington DC.)

Eldr. Marsh then gave way to his brethren and they arose and spoke in turn until they had all spoken acquiessing in the observations of Eldr. Marsh and made some additions to his remarks as follows,— That the letter in question which they received from the presidency, in which two of their number were suspended,[461] and the rest severely chastened, and was upon testimony that was unwarantable also that particular stress, was laid upon a certain letter which the presidency had received from Dr. Warren A. Cowdery of Freedom New York, in which he prefered charges against the twelve which were false; and upon which the presidency had acted, in chastning them.[462]

And therefore the twelve had come to the conclusion that the presidency had lost confidence in them; and that whereas the church in Kirtland had caressed them at the time of their appointment to the apostleship; they now treated them coolly and appeared to have lost confidence in them also.— They spoke of their having engaged in the work, or at least some of them almost from it's commencement and had borne the burden in the heat of the day, and passed through many trials, & hardship, and that the presidency ought not to suspect their fidelity nor loose confidence in them, neither to have chastened them upon such testimony as was lying before them.

They also urged the necessity of an explanation upon the letter which they received from the presidency, and the propriety of their having information as it respects their duties authority &c. That they might come to understanding. in all things, that they might act in perfect unison and harmony before the Lord and be prepared for the enduement.— Also that the twelve had prefered a charge against Dr. Cowdery for his unchristian conduct, which the presidency had disregarded.— also that Pres. O[liver] Cowdery on a certain occasion, made use of language to one of the twelve that was unchristian, and unbecoming any man; and that they would not submit to such treatment.

The remarks of all the twelve, were made in a very forcible, determined, & explicit manner; yet cool, & deliberate. [p. 181]

Pres. Smith arose and observed that to the twelve, that the presidency had sat and heard them patiently, and in their turn should expect to be heard patiently by them— also.— And first he remarked that it was necessary that the twelve should state whether they were determined to persevere in the work of the Lord, whether the presidency are able to satisfy them or not.— The president of the twelve call[ed] a vote of his quorum, upon this question, which

---

461. William E. McLellin and Orson Hyde.

462. Warren Cowdery was president of the conference at Freedom, Cattaraugus County, New York, which the Quorum of the Twelve visited on their 1835 mission to the East. Cowdery had faulted the Twelve for not following JS's commission to raise money for building the House of the Lord. (JS, Kirtland, OH, to the Quorum of the Twelve Apostles, 4 Aug. 1835, in JS Letterbook 1, pp. 90–93.)

was unanimously carried in the affirmative. Our author then assured them that he had not lost confidence in them, and that they had no reason to suspect his confidence; and that he would be willing to be weighed in the scale of truth to day, with them in this matter, and risk the event in the day of judgment.

And as it respects the chastning contained in the letter in question, which he acknowledged might have been expressed in language to[o] harsh; which was not intentional, and therefore I ⟨he⟩ asked their forgivness in as much as he had injured their feelings in concequence of it.— But nevertheless said he the letter that Eldr. Mc Lellen [William E. McLellin] sent back to Kirtland, while the twelve were at the east, was harsh also and he was willing to set the one against the other.[463] He next proceeded to explain the subject of the duty of the twelve, which is next the and their authority; which is next to that of the first presidency; and that the organization of the council on the 15th Inst, on which occasion the high council of Kirtland was seated next [to] the presidency; was because the business to be transacted on that day, was business that particularly related to that body.— Not because they were first in office; therefore the arrangement was most judicious that could be made on that occasion.

And furthermore he observed that the twelve are not subject to any other authority in the church, except the first presidency.[464] He also remarked to the twelve that he did not countinance the harsh language of Pres. Cowdery to them; neither did he countinance it in himself, nor any other man; although he had sometimes indulged in it, & spoken to[o] harsh from the impuls of the moment, and wherein he had [p. 182] wounded their feelings by so doing, he asked their forgiveness.— For said he I truly love you brethren, with a perfect love, and will hold you up with all my heart, in all righteousness before the Lord, & before all men.— be assured brethren I am willing to stem the torrent of all opposition in your behalf, in storms, in tempests, in thunder, in lightning, by sea & by land, in the wilderness, among fals brethren, or mobs, or wherever God in his providence may call me for your support or defence, and I am determined that neither hights, nor depths, principalities, nor powers, things present, or to come, nor any other creature shall seperate me from you.[465] And I will now covenant with you before God this day that I will not listen to nor credit any derogatory report against any of you, to condemn you upon any testimony beneath the heavens, save that which is infalable, until I can see you face to face and know of a surety of the things whereof you are accused.

---

463. McLellin had criticized a coeducational school that Sidney Rigdon was conducting in Kirtland. (JS, Kirtland, OH, to the Quorum of the Twelve Apostles, 4 Aug. 1835, in JS Letterbook 1, pp. 90–93; see also *JSP*, J1:66n39.)

464. JS's journal specifies: "viz. myself S. Rigdon and F G. Williams." (*JSP*, J1:158.)

465. See Romans 8:38–39.

I believe you to be men of God, therefore I place unlimited confidence in you.[466] And I ask the same confidence on your part brethren, when I tell you any thing, for I will not declare any thing to you, that I do not know to be truth. But I have allready consumed more time in my remarks than I intended when I arose, and I will now give way to my colleagues.— Pres. Rigdon arose and acquiessed in what Pres. Smith had said & acknowledged to the twelve that he had not done as he ought in not attending to the charges that were put into his hands by them against Doct. W. A. Cowdery, he frankly acknowl- edged ~~his duty~~ that he had neglected his duty in that thing for which he asked their forgiveness, and pledged himself to attend to it immediately if they desired him to do so. Pres. Rigdon also observed to the twelve that if he had at any time spoken ~~to~~ or reproved to[o] harsh, and had injured their feelings in consqence thereof, he asked their forgivness.

Pres. F G. Williams arose and acquiessed in the sentiments expressed by Presdt's. Smith & Rigdon [p. 183] and said many good things.

The Pres. of the twelve then called a vote of that body to know whether they were perfectly satisfied with the explanation which ~~we had given~~ had been given them, and whether they would enter into the covenant which the presi- dency proposed to make with them; which was most readily manifested in the affirmative, by raising their hands to heaven, in testimony of their willingness and desire to enter into this covenant and their entire satisfaction with the explanation of the presidency upon all the difficulties that were on their minds.— The presidency, scribe, & twelve, all took eachother by the hand in confirmation of the covenant they had mutually entered into, and there was a perfect unison of feeling expressed, and their hearts overflowed with blessings which they pronounced upon eachothers heads as the spirit gave them utter- ance; may God enable them all to perform their vows & covenants with eachother in all fidelity & righteousness before Him, that their influence may be felt among the nations of the earth in mighty power, even to rend the king- doms of darkness in sunder, and triumph over priestcraft and spiritual wicked- ness in high places, & break in pieces all kingdoms that are opposed to the kingdom of Christ, and spread the light & truth of the everlasting gospel from the rivers to the ends of the earth.[467]

Eldr. Beeman [Alvah Beman] called upon Pres. Smith for counsel upon the subject of his returning; he desired to know whether it would be wisdom

---

466. For the previous sentence, the 1835–1836 journal has "I do place unlimited confidence in your word for I believe you to be men of truth." (*JSP*, J1:159.)

467. See Daniel 2:45; Zechariah 9:10; and Revelation, 30 Oct. 1831, in Doctrine and Covenants 24:1, 1835 ed. [D&C 65:2].

for him to go before the Solemn Assembly or not. The subject was laid before the council, who advised Eldr. Beeman to tarry until after the assembly

Council adjourned by singing & prayer.

W[arren] Parrish   Scribe

17 January 1836 • Sunday

Sunday morning January 17th Pres. Smith attended meeting at the usual hour, a large congregation assembled; he [p. 184] proceeded to organize the several quorums present; first the presidency, then the twelve, & all of the seventy who were present, also the counsellors of Kirtland, & Zion.

Pres. S[idney] Rigdon then arose and remarked to the audiance that instead of preaching as usual the time would be occupied by the quorums in speaking each in his turn, until they had all spoken commencing with the presidency. The Lord poured out his spirit upon the congregation, as the brethren began to confess their faults one to another, & tears flowed from our eyes, & some of our hearts were to[o] big for utterance; (to use the language of our author,) the gift of toungs came upon us like the rushing mighty wind, and my soul was filled with the glory of God.— In the P.M. Pres. Smith joined three couple in the bonds of matrimony,[468] in the publick congregation; the Lord's supper was administered and the congregation dismissed.—[469] Pres. Smith was then envited to attend a feast at Eldr. [William] Cahoon's which was prepared on the occasion, and had a good time while partaking of the rich repast that was spread before us; and verily said he, it is good for brethren to dwell together in unity, it is like the dew upon the mountains of Israel where the Lord commanded blessings even life for ever more.—[470] He returned home and spent the evening.

18 January 1836 • Monday

Monday 18th— He attended the Hebrew school;— On this day the Eldrs was removed into an upper room in the Lord's house prepared for that purpose[471]

---

468. The corresponding entry in the 1835–1836 journal names the couples who were married: William F. Cahoon and Miranda Gibbs, Harvey Stanley and Lerona Cahoon, and Tunis Rappleye and Louisa Cutler. (*JSP*, J1:161.)

469. The 1835–1836 journal notes that the congregation at the wedding was "so dense that it was verry unpleasant for all." Cahoon later recalled, "I should suppose what with the people in the Church & outside as well there was 3000 people assembled." (*JSP*, J1:161; Cahoon, Autobiography, 44–45.)

470. See Psalm 133:1–3.

471. The Elders School moved from the schoolroom below the printing office to the third floor of the House of the Lord, in the room adjoining the westernmost room where the Hebrew School met. (See entry for 4 Jan. 1836 herein; compare JS, Journal, 18 Jan. 1836, in *JSP*, J1:161; and JS History, vol. B-1, 693.)

Copy of a Letter from Doct. Piexotto [Daniel Peixotto] to his scribe

Willoughby Jany 5th. 1836.

To Eldr. W[arren] Parrish
Sir

I have received an <u>open</u> note[472] from Mr. Sylvester Smith informing me that your school concidered itself dissolved from all engagements with me, for this I was [p. 185] not unprepared. But he adds that I must excuse him for saying that I appear to be willing to trifle with you in regard to appointments, time, &c—

This insinuation is unworthy of me beneath my sence of honour, and I could hope unwaranted by any mean suspicion of your whole body.— I wrote for books to New York by Mr. [Oliver] Cowdery,— not but ~~what~~ I could have taught the rudiments without them,— but because I wished to make my instructions philosophically availing as well as mere elementary. In this object ⟨I⟩ thought myself confirmed by <u>you</u>; my books have not come as yet & are probably lost—of the pecuniary value I seek not.— I borrowed a book of Eldr. [John F.] Boynton & told him believing him to be responsible that wednesday would be best for me to deliver a publick lecture owing to my engagements here. I here was <u>officially</u> informed when the school was to be <u>opened</u> by me.— The addition of insult to abuse may be gratifying to small minds, mine is above it, scorns and repud[i]ates it—

I am very respectfully
Your very obt. Servt.
Daniel L M. Piexotto

The answer

Kirtland Jany 11th. 1836

Dr. Piexotto
Sir

I received yours of the 5th Inst. in which you manifested much indignation and concidered your <u>honour</u> highly insulted by us as a body, if not by me as an individual, and deprecated our conduct because we informed you that you appeared willing to trifle with us, as

472. The seal on the letter was apparently opened prior to Peixotto's receipt. In his reply, Warren Parrish included the following postscript: "The note that we sent you, was well sealed when it was put into the hands of the messenger; which you informed me you recieved open." (Warren Parrish, Kirtland, OH, to Daniel Peixotto, [Willoughby, OH], 11 Jan. 1836, in *JSP,* J1:164.)

it respects our engagements with you to teach our Hebrew class. I have acted in this matter as agent for the school; the time agreed upon for you to commence, was not to be protracted, at farthest later than [p. 186] Dec. 15th. & the class have ever till now, considered themselves bound by the engagements I made with you.— When [Oliver] Cowdery & myself called, you set a time that you would come to Kirtland & have our agreement committed to writing, but did not come, some were displeased, I excused you; some days elapsed & we heard nothing from you: at length Dr. [Frederick G.] Williams called & you specified another time that you would come, which is some 2, or 3, weeks since, the class were again disappointed, again I plead an excuse for you; on last saturday week (the 2^{ond.} Inst.) our class met and agreed to organize on Monday morning the 4th Inst. at 9 oclock A.M. and by the voice of the school I was appointed to wait on you, and advertize your <u>honour</u> that we were ready, and should expect you to attend at that hour; presuming that you would be ready at that late period to fulfill your engagements if you ever intended to; and accordingly I called, and informed you of the arangements we had made, but on account of your arangements at the medical university I was willing to exceed my instructions, and let you name the hour that you would wait on us on that day, which was at 4. oclock P.M.[473] [*18 lines blank*] [p. 187]

---

473. TEXT: Pages 186 and 187 bear stains from a smaller loose sheet that was housed for some time between these pages. Warren Parrish left off transcribing JS's journal into the history without copying in the remainder of his own 11 January 1836 letter to Daniel Peixotto. For the remainder of the letter, see *JSP*, J1:163–164.

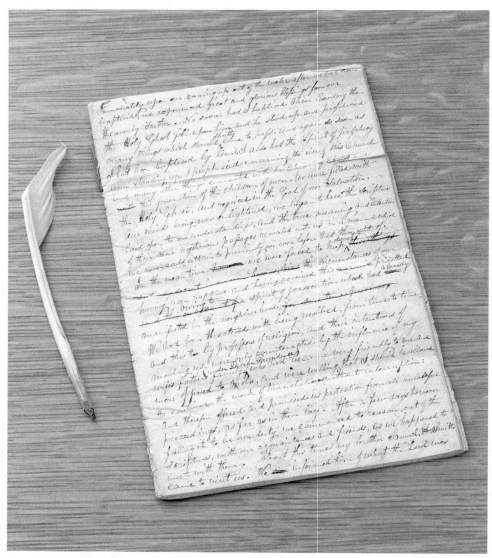

History drafted in 1839 (Draft 1). James Mulholland inscribed this draft of Joseph Smith's history on a loose gathering of pages. The opening words are "Immediately upon our coming up out of the water," referring to the baptisms of Joseph Smith and Oliver Cowdery on 15 May 1829. This abrupt beginning suggests that the manuscript picks up where an earlier history, no longer extant, left off. JS History, 1839, Church History Library, Salt Lake City. (Photograph by Welden C. Andersen.)

HISTORY DRAFTS, 1838–CIRCA 1841

Source Notes

DRAFT 1

JS, History, [ca. June–Oct. 1839], draft; handwriting of James Mulholland; twenty-five pages; CHL. Includes file notes.

This draft history was inscribed in a makeshift gathering of nine loose leaves measuring 12⅜ × 15¾ inches (31 × 40 cm), folded in half to form eighteen unlined leaves measuring 12⅜ × 7⅞ inches (31 × 20 cm). The loose leaves are held together by a piece of string threaded through two holes in the upper half of the center fold of the leaves. Other holes in the folds indicate that additional sewing was in place at some earlier time. The eighteen-leaf gathering was used circa July 1833 as part of an effort to index JS's revision of the Bible.[1] Frederick G. Williams inscribed the first page of the gathering with the title "Scriptures on Covenants", followed by five lines of references from JS's revision of Genesis. This entire page was lined in graphite by Frederick G. Williams. A remnant of a wafer is also found on the upper left corner of this original first page, indicating that it may have been attached to a book or that another document was attached to the page. At some point, apparently in preparation to be used for the history draft, the fold of the gathering was inverted so that the original first and last pages became the center of the gathering (pages 18 and 19) and the original center spread became the first page and last page. James Mulholland inscribed the history draft on twenty-five pages of the gathering, leaving eleven pages blank.

After its inscription in 1839, the whereabouts of this text for the remainder of the nineteenth century are unknown, though it presumably remained in church custody. The document was not listed on any of the known early Church Historian's Office inventories, which did not detail all holdings. The first known listing of the history draft is in the inventory from circa 1905.[2] The document is also listed on a 1970 inventory of papers of Joseph Fielding Smith, who had served as church historian and recorder of The Church of Jesus Christ of Latter-day Saints since 1921, perhaps indicating that the document had been in his possession for some time.[3] The draft history became part of the First Presidency's papers when Smith became president of the church in 1970, and it remained there until it was transferred in 2010 to the Church History Library.

DRAFT 2

JS, History, [ca. June 1839–ca. 1841]; handwriting of James Mulholland and Robert B. Thompson; sixty-one pages; in JS History, 1838–1856, vol. A-1, CHL. Includes redactions, use marks, and archival marking.

---

1. See Jensen, "Ignored and Unknown Clues of Early Mormon Record Keeping," 147–154.
2. "Contents of Box No. Two," Joseph Fielding Smith, Papers, 1893–1973, CHL.
3. "Inventory of President Joseph Fielding Smith's Safe," 23 May 1970, First Presidency, General Administration Files, CHL.

First volume of 1838–1856 history (including Draft 2). This book, originally a blank volume with lined pages, was first used to inscribe Joseph Smith's 1834–1836 history. In 1839, scribe James Mulholland turned it over, so that the back cover became the front cover, and began inscribing what became the first volume of the multivolume manuscript history, using material written in 1838. The spine of the book (see inset) was later labeled volume "A-1" of the series. JS History, vol. A-1, Church History Library, Salt Lake City. (Photographs by Welden C. Andersen.)

Large blank book composed of ruled paper printed with forty horizontal lines in (now faint) blue ink. The text block includes thirty gatherings of various sizes, each about a dozen leaves per gathering, and originally had 384 interior leaves cut to measure 13⅝ × 9 inches (35 × 23 cm). The text block, which was conserved in the late twentieth century, was probably originally sewn on recessed cords and was apparently also glued on leather tapes. The binding features false bands. The endpapers were single-sided marbled leaves featuring a traditional Spanish pattern with slate blue body and veins of black and red. The block was bound to pasteboard covers, probably with a hollow-back ledger binding, making a book measuring 14¼ × 9½ × 2½ inches (36 × 24 × 6 cm). The boards were bound in brown suede calf-skin. At some point, blind-tooled decorations were made around the outside border and along the board edges and the turned-in edges of the inside covers.

The volume was originally used for JS's 1834–1836 history, comprising 154 pages.[4] It was subsequently turned upside down so the back cover became the front cover, and on the new first page, James Mulholland began copying the history that had been begun by the church presidency in 1838. He left the first seventeen lines blank, presumably to create a large title when the work was complete, although a title was never added. Because the volume had been turned upside down, the unlined top margin became the bottom margin and there was no longer any top margin. Mulholland inscribed pages 2–19 beginning at the head of the page; then, beginning with page 20, he left the line at the top of the page blank, effectively creating a top margin. He also inscribed one line of text below the lowest printed line at the foot of the page, in the original top margin. Starting on page 13, he penciled in a horizontal line at the bottom of each page to ensure straight text on this last line. Mulholland inscribed 59 pages in all. Robert B. Thompson, who replaced Mulholland as scribe, commenced on page 60 and wrote for sixteen pages, the first two pages of which are included in the transcript herein. Thompson maintained the blank upper margin, but instead of filling in the lower margin as Mulholland had done, he left the space blank. In addition, he created a left margin on each page by penciling in a vertical line. Both Mulholland and Thompson numbered the pages as they inscribed them. At a later time, Willard Richards inserted headings giving the year, or the month and year, narrated on each page.[5] The volume includes 553 pages of the history inscribed beginning in 1839, followed by sixteen pages of addenda that were recorded by Charles Wandell and Thomas Bullock. Four blank pages separate the addenda from the end of the 1834–1836 history. Multiple layers of emendations and other later marks accumulated as the history was created, revised, and published. The transcript here presents the initial text, along with only those revisions made to it by the first two scribes, Mulholland and Thompson.

With the later history's side of the book upward, the spine of the book was at some point in time labeled as volume "A | 1" of the multivolume history. Archival stickers were also added at some point to the spine and inside front cover. Two interior leaves are now missing from the initial gathering of the volume and one leaf is missing from the final gathering. The original flyleaves and pastedowns were also removed.[6] The volume shows moderate wear, browning, water staining, and brittleness. It has been resewn, rebound, and otherwise conserved.

In the first half of the 1840s, the volume was in the possession of church scribes and printers while JS's history was updated and prepared for publication, which was begun in the church newspaper in Nauvoo, Illinois, in the 15 March 1842 issue. JS maintained custody of the volume through his later life, as indicated by a note he inscribed memorializing his deceased brother Alvin Smith, which was attached to the verso of the front flyleaf. The volume is listed in the first extant Historian's Office inventory, made in Nauvoo in February 1846 by clerk Thomas Bullock, and it is listed in inventories of

---

4. See pp. 23–25 herein.

5. Of the excerpt transcribed here, manuscript pages 1–9, 18, 19, and 36 do not have a heading.

6. See JS History, vol. A-1, microfilm, Dec. 1971, CHL. Only one leaf of the original pastedowns and flyleaves is extant. The pastedowns were replaced with undecorated paper in 1994, according to a conservation note on the verso of the extant marbled leaf archived with the volume.

Joseph Smith's 1838–circa 1841 history (Draft 3). In about 1841, at Joseph Smith's request and possibly with his assistance, Howard Coray drafted a revised version of the history begun in 1838. His source was the text in the large bound volume later labeled "A-1," which was in turn a copy of material drafted in 1838 (no longer extant) and of a draft dating from 1839. Handwriting of Howard Coray. JS History, 1838–ca. 1841, Church History Library, Salt Lake City. (Photograph by Welden C. Andersen.)

church records made in Salt Lake City in the second half of the nineteenth century.[7] These and later archival records, as well as archival marking on the volume, indicate continuous institutional custody.

DRAFT 3

JS, History, [ca. 1841], draft; handwriting of Howard Coray; 102 pages and one attached slip; CHL.

Howard Coray inscribed two copies of a new draft of JS's history in about 1841. The earlier draft copy is the document transcribed herein. At the bottom of page 1 of the later fair copy is an inscription in the handwriting of Howard Coray identifying it as the second copy, and similar inscriptions are found on the last page of each bifolium of the fair copy. In addition to the draft copy and the fair copy, there is a four-page partial copy, also in the handwriting of Howard Coray, that corresponds to text on pages 13–16 of both the draft and fair copies.[8]

The draft copy contains twenty-five bifolia (making one hundred pages) and a final loose leaf. Pages 1–92 measure from 12½ to 12⅝ inches high and 7⅝ inches across (32 × 19 cm); pages 93–102 measure 12 × 7⅝ inches (30 × 19 cm). The larger pages are lined with between thirty-four and thirty-eight blue horizontal lines, and the shorter pages contain thirty-eight blue horizontal lines; most of the ruling throughout the manuscript is now faint or completely faded. Page numbering appears at the top center of each page. Embossed in the upper left corner of the first recto side of many bifolia is a decorative star and "D & J. Ames Springfield", the insignia of a Springfield, Massachusetts, paper mill firm established by brothers David and John Ames in 1828.[9]

The draft was inscribed in ink that is now brown. It includes several graphite insertions in Coray's handwriting. Quill and steel pens were used interchangeably for inscription. The paper is cream colored and yellowed at the edges, with some foxing. The first page and last page of the draft exhibit moderate wear. Ink was spilled on the gutter edge of the stacked manuscript, slightly staining many bifolia. At one time the manuscript was sewn together, as evidenced by a single needle hole in the upper left corner of each bifolium. A slip of paper containing a handwritten insertion was pinned to page 36. The lower left corner of the final leaf (page 101) was torn off, and it was subsequently reattached to the page with a straight pin.

Offsetting, a characteristic of iron gall ink corrosion, is present throughout the manuscript. The offsetting pattern indicates that at some point after the composition process, the bifolia were opened and laid flat on each other, then folded together to form temporary gatherings. The manuscript was put into three such groups, comprising pages 1–60, 61–92, and 93–100. The bifolia were subsequently reordered to create a normal pagination sequence. The purpose of these temporary gatherings is unknown. Coray's fair copy of the history has an offsetting pattern comparable to the draft, though pages 9–20 and 81–88 bear sequential offsetting, meaning these pages were not overlaid as elsewhere. The fair copy ends after one hundred pages and does not include the material on pages 101–102 of the draft copy.

Howard Coray's handwriting style varies throughout both the draft copy and the fair copy. The handwriting varies to such an extent that the manuscripts could be mistaken for the work of two scribes. However, evidence such as letter combinations, letter formation within words and lines of text, and consistent misspelling of specific words indicates that both manuscripts were inscribed entirely by Coray.

The draft copy was created from both dictation and copying. Evidence of dictation, including absence or excess of punctuation as originally inscribed (the latter possibly signaling pauses by the

---

7. "Schedule of Church Records. Nauvoo 1846," [1]; "Historian's Office Catalogue 1858," 2, Historian's Office, Catalogs and Inventories, 1846–1904, CHL.

8. The four-page fragment contains a copy of Revelation, July 1828 [D&C 3], and is housed in Revelations Collection, CHL. As explained later, the text in the draft copy and fair copy match page for page, so each page begins at the same point. The fragment is not a page-for-page copy, though the first and third pages begin at the same point as do pages 13 and 15 of the other two copies.

9. Whiting, "Paper Making in New England," 309; Gravell et al., *American Watermarks,* 235.

speaker) and misspellings indicative of misheard phonemes, is found on manuscript pages 1–8, 17–22, 27–28, 57–58, and 77–78. At other points in the manuscript, Coray faithfully reproduced paragraph breaks and end-of-sentence blank spaces occurring in the large history volume (his source for the draft), suggesting that these portions of the draft were copied rather than dictated. Where the blank spaces signal breaks in the narrative, they have been transcribed herein as paragraph breaks.

At an unknown time, the draft and the fair copy were gathered with other papers, wrapped in brown paper, and tied with string. The other papers in the bundle included the "Book of Commandments and Revelations" (Revelation Book 1), notes on JS's boyhood leg operation in the handwriting of Willard Richards, and historical material by Edward Partridge, which was situated between the draft and the fair copy of Coray's work.[10] It is unclear how or why these different records became associated with each other. At some point, a cream-colored slip of paper measuring 3⅞ × 8 inches (5 × 20 cm) was attached to the bundle. The slip contains a note written in black and red ink by Historian's Office clerk Robert L. Campbell and signed in red ink by Howard Coray: "Two copies of the first hundred pages of Dft. Mss. History of Joseph Smith[.] These hundred pages of History were written by me, under Joseph the Prophet's dictation. Dr Miller helped me a little in writing the same. (Historians office, 1869.) H. Coray". This note was taped over a penciled notation in the handwriting of Joseph Fielding Smith: "Book of Commandments MS Early history (H. Coray) MS". Smith began working at the Church Historian's Office in 1901. Other filing notations were made in the mid-1980s to identify and distinguish the various documents in the bundle.

The custodial history of Coray's two copies of the 1838–circa 1841 history is uncertain between their creation and the 1846 Latter-day Saint exodus from Nauvoo, Illinois, though they likely remained in the possession of JS, his office staff, and subsequent church leadership. The Church Historian's Office inventory from 1846 lists "Rough Book.— Revelation History &c.," possibly referring to the grouping of Revelation Book 1, Coray's draft and fair copy, and miscellaneous historical material.[11] A "Ms. History of Jos. Smith (2 copies of the first 100 pages)" is listed with the manuscript "Book of Commandments and Revelations" in a Church Historian's Office inventory from 1858.[12] Both history copies were presumably among manuscript material in the possession of church historian and recorder Joseph Fielding Smith, who held that office from 1921 to 1970, since they became part of the First Presidency's papers when Smith became president in 1970.[13] Both copies of the history were then transferred, along with Revelation Book 1 and the other historical materials in the bundle, from the First Presidency's office to the Church History Library in 2005.

Historical Introduction

This section presents in parallel columns three early drafts of the history begun by JS in 1838. The history designated Draft 1 is a twenty-five page manuscript written in James Mulholland's handwriting in 1839. Draft 2, inscribed by James Mulholland and Robert B. Thompson from 1839 to about 1841, consists of the first sixty-one pages of the manuscript

10. Revelation Book 1 is reproduced in *JSP*, MRB:3–405. Portions of the Partridge materials were published in the 1839–1840 *Times and Seasons* series "A History, of the Persecution, of the Church of Jesus Christ, of Latter Day Saints in Missouri," reproduced in *JSP*, H2:206–229.

11. "Schedule of Church Records. Nauvoo 1846," [1], Historian's Office, Catalogs and Inventories, 1846–1904, CHL.

12. "Contents of the Historian and Recorder's Office. G. S. L. City July 1858," [5], Historian's Office, Catalogs and Inventories, 1846–1904, CHL.

13. A 1970 inventory confirms that material authored by Howard Coray was grouped with Revelation Book 1 and was in the possession of Joseph Fielding Smith later in his life. ("Inventory of President Joseph Fielding Smith's Safe," 23 May 1970, First Presidency, General Administration Files, CHL.)

history later labeled volume "A-1" of JS's multivolume history. Draft 3 is a 102-page document penned by Howard Coray in about 1841.

The production of these history drafts was part of an evolutionary process in JS's history writing. Dean C. Jessee has observed that "although Mormon record keeping was inaugurated by the [6 April] 1830 revelation, details for carrying out that commandment were largely hammered out on the anvil of experience."[14] By 1838, JS had in his possession historical narratives covering the period from his birth to early 1829 and from 22 September 1835 to 18 January 1836, but this accumulated historical material lacked continuity and a consistent methodology. In earlier histories, JS and his assistants tried several different approaches. The circa summer 1832 history, for example, included significant experiences but gave only a brief narrative; the 1834–1836 history included genealogies, minute-like entries, transcripts of the published installments of a serialized history, and slightly revised copies of journal entries, all potentially significant resources for a history but lacking in connective material. JS had also assigned John Whitmer to write a church history in 1831, but Whitmer was excommunicated in 1838 and declined to make his work available to the church.[15] It was in the context of these inadequate and unavailable records that JS and Sidney Rigdon began a new history project. On 27 April 1838, they began a "history of this Church from the earliest perion [period] of its existance up to this date."[16] No manuscript of their 1838 effort is known to have survived, but drafts written after 1838, including the documents presented here, incorporated the 1838 work and presumably followed its format.

Serious problems in Missouri made it difficult to continue work on the history after early 1838. Armed conflict broke out between the Mormon settlers and their Missouri neighbors, and on 27 October 1838, Governor Lilburn W. Boggs ordered that the Saints "must be treated as enemies and must be exterminated or driven from the state if necessary for the public peace."[17] JS and other church leaders were taken captive within a few days, and for six months JS remained a prisoner in Missouri. By the time he escaped his captors, the Saints had left Missouri and begun to settle in Illinois. JS arrived in Quincy, Illinois, on 22 April 1839, and within a few weeks again turned his attention to the history of the church.[18]

Draft 1

The history drafted in 1839 was inscribed by James Mulholland, who began writing for JS on 3 September 1838. In addition to his work on the history, Mulholland served as a scribe for patriarchal blessing records, JS's second letterbook, and JS's journals. After an interruption of his clerical work brought on by JS's Missouri imprisonment, Mulholland "commenced again to write for the Church" on 22 April 1839.[19] JS's journal noted that JS

14. Jessee, "Reliability of Joseph Smith's History," 27; see also Revelation, 6 Apr. 1830, in Doctrine and Covenants 46:1, 1835 ed. [D&C 21:1].

15. See Historical Introduction to Whitmer, History, in *JSP*, H2:9–10.

16. JS, Journal, 27 Apr. 1838, in *JSP*, J1:260.

17. Lilburn W. Boggs, Jefferson City, MO, to John B. Clark, Fayette, MO, 27 Oct. 1838, Mormon War Papers, MSA.

18. JS, Journal, 16 Apr. and 10–14 June 1839, in *JSP*, J1:336, 340.

19. Mulholland, Journal, 22 Apr. 1839.

"began to study & prepare to dictate history" on 10 June and that he dictated history while Mulholland wrote on 11–14 June.[20] During JS's 15–26 June absence from Commerce while visiting his brothers William and Don Carlos, Mulholland remained in Commerce, "writing history" on three days and "studying for history" for part of another day.[21] Work done by Mulholland in JS's absence may have included organizing sources from which to compile history, drafting the history itself from other sources, or making a clean draft of the history, as explained in the next section. After JS returned, he dictated history to Mulholland on three additional days.[22] Mulholland mentioned in his journal spending several more days writing for the church, without specifying which project he was working on.[23]

Because the history produced by JS and Sidney Rigdon in 1838 is not extant, it is impossible to know the exact relationship between that work and the extant versions of JS's history presented here. It is probable, however, that Draft 1 represents the resumption of the historical narrative at the point where the now-lost 1838 manuscript ended. The extant draft picks up the narrative at the baptism of JS and Oliver Cowdery and covers the publication of the Book of Mormon, the organization of the Church of Christ, and events later in 1830. The narrative covering mid-April through August 1830, much of which involved Newel Knight as either a participant or an eyewitness, is relatively detailed. It was likely during work on this portion of the history that, according to JS's journal, JS was "assisted by Br Newel Knight."[24]

When James Mulholland created the twenty-five-page Draft 1, it appears he began with an outline, identifying revelations, events, and other pieces of information and leaving blank space between these notations to be filled in later with connective narrative supplied by JS, Knight, or other sources. Beginning on the second page, Mulholland named particular revelation texts from the 1835 edition of the Doctrine and Covenants that were to be inserted into the history, but he did not copy the full texts from the Doctrine and Covenants into this draft. The revelations served as the initial threads around which JS wove his dictated narrative. Beginning with page 9 of Draft 1, following the notation to insert the title page of the Book of Mormon, the inscription pattern becomes much more complex. It appears that at this point, Mulholland began to write in dates of conferences, names of individuals baptized, and other key details, leaving large blank spaces between. This procedure for creating the history was not without drawbacks. When Mulholland came back and composed text or transcribed JS's dictation to fill in the details, the narrative sometimes exceeded the reserved space, forcing Mulholland to squeeze extra lines of text onto the page. At other times the inserted narrative fell short of filling in all the blank space set aside for it. False starts are evident throughout much of the middle portion of the draft history.

JS's work on the history was interrupted in early July 1839 when a malaria epidemic in Commerce and vicinity required JS and Emma Smith to attend to the sick for an extended

---

20. JS, Journal, 10, 11, and 12–14 June 1839, in *JSP*, J1:340; see also Mulholland, Journal, 10–15 June 1839.
21. Mulholland, Journal, 17–20 June 1839.
22. JS, Journal, 3 and 4–5 July 1839, in *JSP*, J1:345; Mulholland, Journal, 3–6 July 1839.
23. See Mulholland's journal entries from July to October 1839.
24. JS, Journal, 4–5 July 1839, in *JSP*, J1:345.

period.[25] Mulholland continued to work on JS's history until at least 26 July. Many of the entries in his personal journal that mention "writing for the Church" may refer to additional work on the history. Mulholland's tenure as a scribe was cut short when he died on 3 November 1839, possibly the victim of a stroke.[26]

DRAFT 2

After JS concluded his dictation of history on 5 July 1839, James Mulholland devoted some of his time to inscribing the history compiled to that point into a large manuscript book. He began this new draft of the history in the back of the volume in which the 1834–1836 history had been inscribed, turning it over so the back cover became the front cover. Serving as principal sources for this version of the history were the manuscript that JS, Sidney Rigdon, and George W. Robinson had created in Missouri in 1838, and Draft 1. Textual evidence that the nonextant 1838 material was used when composing Draft 2 is found in the second paragraph of the latter, which situates the composition in "the eighth year since the [1830] organization of said Church," and a later passage that gives the date of composition as "the Second day of May, One thousand Eight hundred and thirty eight."[27] Starting at 15 May 1829, the remainder of the text in Mulholland's handwriting is a copy of Draft 1. Although the first seven pages of Draft 1 match Draft 2 quite closely, the two versions are markedly less similar after that point. This contrast may indicate that an intermediate draft of the history was made beginning at about page 7 of Draft 1 and that Mulholland copied the text from this intermediate draft, not directly from Draft 1.

Mulholland inscribed pages 1–59 in the large history volume. After his death in November 1839, Robert B. Thompson served as scribe for the history. Little is known about the circumstances surrounding Thompson's inscription, totaling only sixteen pages, in the large history volume. The transcript of Draft 2 presented herein ends on page 61 of the manuscript volume, after the first two pages of Thompson's inscription, to correspond with the end of Draft 3; the other fourteen pages in his hand give a biographical sketch of Sidney Rigdon, including a brief narrative of his conversion to Mormonism. Because the majority of the pages in Thompson's hand deal with Rigdon's life before joining the church, Rigdon was likely consulted for this portion of the narrative.

The opening statement of the draft in the large manuscript volume refers to defamation and persecution to which the Latter-day Saints and JS in particular had been subjected, and it characterizes such maltreatment as one motivation for telling the story of the church and its founder: "Owing to the many reports which have been put in circulation by evil disposed and designing men," JS proclaimed, the history was designed to "disabuse the publick mind, and put all enquirers after truth into possession of the facts" and set the record straight "in relation both to myself and the Church." This introduction was written not long after JS had fled Kirtland, Ohio, for Far West, Missouri, under threat of several lawsuits; thus, when he began the history in summer 1838 he was especially motivated to justify himself and the church in light of what he considered a long history of persecution. Such

---

25. See JS, Journal, 8 July–28 Sept. 1839, in *JSP*, J1:348–352.

26. Emma Smith, Nauvoo, IL, to JS, Washington DC, 6 Dec. 1839, Charles Aldrich Autograph Collection, State Historical Society of Iowa, Des Moines.

27. JS History, vol. A-1, pp. 204, 238 herein (Draft 2).

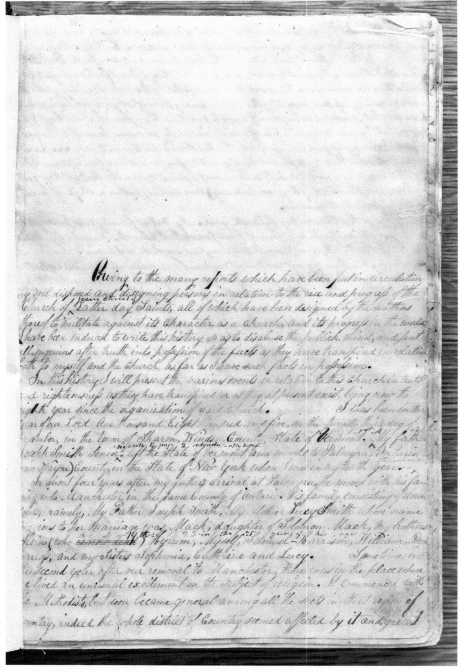

First page of large history volume (Draft 2). When he began inscribing Joseph Smith's history into a large volume in 1839, James Mulholland left the top half of the first page blank, perhaps intending to provide a large title for the manuscript at a later time. The revisions evident on this page were made in about 1842 by Willard Richards. Handwriting of James Mulholland, with redactions in handwriting of Willard Richards. JS History, vol. A-1, [1] (transcribed on pp. 204–208 herein), Church History Library, Salt Lake City. (Photograph by Welden C. Andersen.)

an introduction may also have been written as a more general response to the accumulated negative reports transmitted orally and in the press beginning in JS's youth and continuing throughout the 1830s.[28]

After briefly narrating JS's birth and early years, Draft 2 proceeds immediately to the circumstances that culminated in his first vision of Deity in the spring of 1820, followed closely by the visitations of an angel in 1823 and JS's commission to retrieve a sacred record buried nearby. JS's religious mission is the primary focus; his personal affairs, like his marriage to Emma Hale, whom he met while employed in digging for a rumored silver mine, are discussed only briefly and in the context of that mission.

Following JS's recitation of his retrieval of the ancient record, the beginnings of his translation thereof, and the loss of the translation manuscript, James Mulholland began including the full texts of JS's revelations, which became a major element of the account. The revelations were integrated into the history starting with July 1828, and they generally appear in chronological order. Mulholland copied the revelations into the history from the 1835 edition of the Doctrine and Covenants, rather than from earlier versions. Many of JS's early revelations underwent significant updating and expansion in order to suit rapidly changing circumstances after the organization of the Church of Christ in 1830, so the inclusion of the 1835 version of revelations into a narrative covering events before 1835 introduced numerous anachronisms. Significant instances of anachronism are identified in the annotation of the text herein.

Additionally, the narrative itself, composed beginning in 1838, necessarily reflects the perspective of JS and his collaborators at the time of its production, thus inadvertently introducing terminology and concepts that were not operative a decade earlier in the period the narrative describes. Examples include using later priesthood nomenclature such as "Aaronic" and "Melchizedek" and calling the church JS established "the Church of Jesus Christ of Latter Day Saints," a name not designated until 1838. Such usage makes it difficult to trace the details of the unfolding of church governance and doctrine in the faith's dynamic early years. Readers wishing to more fully understand these issues may consult the revelation texts and other documents found in the Documents series of *The Joseph Smith Papers*.

While much of the narrative is anchored by documents, particularly published revelations, JS and his associates were dependent upon unrecorded memories for the balance of the historical account found in Draft 2. JS used collective memory and oral recollections of fellow participants, such as Newel Knight, to reconstruct the events of early church history. Such reminiscences formed the basis for not only factual details in the history but likely for quotations as well, such as long portions of the report of the 1830 trial proceedings in South Bainbridge and Colesville, New York (pages 398–412 herein). JS evidently had to

---

28. Although the history was begun in 1838, it is possible that the preamble in the first paragraph was added in 1839 when James Mulholland wrote Draft 2. If so, the concern with negative publicity may also have been a reaction to the widespread news of the Mormon conflict in Missouri in fall 1838 and JS's imprisonment, or to the growing number of publications critical of JS and the church since 1838. See, for example, Origen Bacheler, *Mormonism Exposed, Internally and Externally* (New York, 1838), and La Roy Sunderland's eight-part series published in the Methodist *Zion's Watchman* from 13 January to 3 March 1838 and republished in pamphlet form as *Mormonism Exposed and Refuted* (New York: Piercy & Reid, 1838).

rely on his own memory and that of others to provide some extensive quotations, such as the words of the angel Moroni during his first appearance to JS (pages 220–232 herein) and the remarks scholars in New York City made to Martin Harris when he showed them characters copied from the gold plates (pages 240–244 herein). Lists of persons baptized may have come from records no longer extant or possibly from eyewitnesses consulted for the production of the history.

The manuscript itself was a dynamic text, emended at several times by various scribes. Revisions made in the hand of James Mulholland at the time of inscription or shortly after are included in the transcript herein. Later changes in the hand of Willard Richards, made beginning in December 1842, are not incorporated into the transcript, although substantial changes are described in annotation. Thus, the transcript of Draft 2 presents the history in an early stage, before changes were made by Richards and others, and it approximates the state of the history when Howard Coray used it for a new history draft in about 1841.

Draft 3

Howard Coray, a recent convert to Mormonism from Perry, Illinois, met JS while visiting Nauvoo in April 1840. In his autobiography, written in the early 1880s, Coray recalled the clerical work he undertook after meeting JS:

> The Prophet, after looking at me a little and asking me some questions, wished to know whether it would be convenient for me to come to Nauvoo, and assist, or rather clerk for him. As this was what I desired, I engaged at once to do so; and, in about 2 weeks thereafter, I was busily employed in his office, copying a huge pile of letters into a book—correspondence with the Elders as well as other persons, that had been accumulating for some time. [. . .]
>
> I finished the job of copying letters. I was then requested by bro. Joseph to undertake, in connection with E[dwin] D. Woolley, the compilation of the Church History. This I felt to decline, as writing books was something, in which I had had no experience. But bro. Joseph insisted on my undertaking it, saying, if I would do so, it would prove a blessing to me as long as I should live. His persuasive arguments prevailed; and accordingly in a short time, bro. Woolley and myself, were busily engaged in compiling the church history. The Prophet was to furnish all the materials; and our business, was not only to combine, and arrange in cronological order, but to spread out or amplify not a little, in as good historical style as may be. Bro. Woolley's education, not being equal to mine, he was to get the matter furnished him in as good shape as he could; and my part was to go after him, and fix his up as well as I could, making such improvement and such corrections in his grammar and style as I might deem necessary. On seeing his work, I at once discovered, that I had no small job on my hands, as he knew nothing whatever of grammar; however, I concluded to make the best I could of a bad job, and thus went to work upsetting and recasting; as well a[s] casting out not a little. Seeing how his work was handled, he became considerably discouraged; and rather took offence at the way and manner in which I was doing things, and consequently soon withdrew from the business.

Howard Coray. 1893. This photograph, taken at the 1893 World's Fair in Chicago, shows Howard Coray with grandchildren Eppie and Sidney Coray (seated) and step-grandchildren Laban and Elizabeth Harding. Coray served as a scribe for Joseph Smith's history in the early 1840s. (Church History Library, Salt Lake City.)

Immediately after bro. Woolley left, I succeeded in obtaining the services of Dr. Miller, who had written for the press, and was considerably accustomed to this kind of business. Now I got on much better. I continued until we used up all the historical matter furnished us by the Prophet. And, as peculiar circumstances prevented his giving attention to his part of the business we of necessity discontinued our labors, and never resumed this kind of business again.[29]

Although Coray's copying work in JS's 1838–1843 letterbook and other records has long been noted,[30] no manuscript evidence of his work on JS's history was located until 2005, when two manuscripts in Coray's hand were identified among documents in the possession of the First Presidency of The Church of Jesus Christ of Latter-day Saints. These two manuscripts consisted of a new draft (here designated Draft 3) of the material Mulholland and Thompson had written in the first sixty-one pages in JS's large history volume, and a fair copy that incorporated the revisions Coray made in his earlier draft.

However, Coray's autobiographical recollection of his work on JS's history does not seem to match the two manuscripts identified in 2005. Whereas the autobiography refers to "writing books" and to assembling in chronological order a "compilation" of "materials" furnished by JS, the two extant Coray manuscripts are lightly edited copies of work already drafted by James Mulholland and Robert B. Thompson in a single original source. Furthermore, the existing manuscripts do not contain the handwriting of Edwin D. Woolley. In producing Draft 3, Coray made some editorial changes to the history, but his work could not be described as "writing books" and certainly not as a "compilation." Coray's autobiographical account of his work more likely refers to a different, probably earlier assignment for which no related document has been located. Perhaps the assignment given to Coray, Woolley, and "Dr. Miller" was to create rough draft notes comparable to the outline prepared by Mulholland in Draft 1 and those later prepared by William W. Phelps and successors as work on the multivolume manuscript history continued. Coray indicated that work began on the compilation task in about December 1840 and terminated when they exhausted their supply of documents from JS.[31]

In 1869 Coray signed a statement that was later attached to the paper wrapper that enclosed his two drafts: "These hundred pages of History were written by me, under Joseph the Prophet's dictation. D[r] Miller helped me a little in writing the same. (Historians office, 1869)."[32] If by "dictation" Coray meant that he transcribed as JS spoke, it seems more likely to be a description of JS's involvement in the history draft presented here than of the role JS played in the compilation project Coray described in his autobiography. In the latter project, according to Coray, JS only supplied materials and gave general instructions. If the

---

29. Coray, Reminiscences, 17, 19–20.

30. See Jessee, "Writing of Joseph Smith's History," 452–453, 463.

31. Coray, Reminiscences, 19. In Coray's account, he was assigned to the history after he completed an assignment to copy correspondence. The last two items in Coray's handwriting found in JS's letterbook were a 19 October 1840 letter and an undated letter most likely written in early December 1840. (JS Letterbook 2, pp. 188–196.)

32. The identity of "Dr. Miller," mentioned in this note and in Coray's autobiography, is unknown. It is possible Coray misidentified the "doctor" who assisted in writing the history. (Coray, Reminiscences, 19.)

statement was accurate in that sense, it suggests that JS read aloud from Draft 2 in the large manuscript volume, directing editorial changes as he read. Several passages of Draft 3 contain evidence of dictation, but the history itself includes no indication of who was dictating the text.

Coray's history draft includes departures from the earlier drafts which, though minor, show an intention to refine the story by imposing certain editorial preferences. Coray deleted passages that seemed to be defensive, to plead the cause of the Saints, or to play on the reader's sympathies—a list of grievances, for example, or complaints against individuals. The draft often softened wording about the persecution of JS, as can be seen in the omission of the first paragraph of Draft 2. Also, whereas the latter specifies that Methodists and Presbyterians treated JS and other Saints without respect, Coray's draft avoided naming the denominations. Additionally, Draft 3 employs more moderate language in describing opposition to JS in New York, avoiding the word "mob" and glossing over accounts of violence. Many times narrative details that added verisimilitude to previous versions were deleted. For example, when Coray copied the section recounting Martin Harris's carrying a sample of Book of Mormon characters to New York City, he omitted details such as Harris placing the certificate of authenticity from Charles Anthon in his pocket, then retrieving it at Anthon's request (pages 241–245 herein).

The document presented in this volume is the first of two manuscripts Coray completed. This earlier draft shows the original creation as well as revisions Coray made before inscribing the second, cleaner copy. A four-page partial copy, corresponding to text on pages 13–16 of the draft and the fair copy, is also extant.[33] The Coray manuscripts exhibit notable variations in handwriting style. A careful comparison of the style shifts, spelling idiosyncrasies, and letter formations, however, reveal that both the earlier draft and fair copy are entirely in Coray's handwriting. His work is clearly based on Draft 2; Coray's versions could not have been written before Draft 2 because he incorporated emendations made in the latter.[34] The fair copy of Coray's work, which may be read online at josephsmithpapers.org, includes few changes other than those Coray marked in his rough draft, and none are of a substantive nature.

CONCLUSION

Although the identification of handwriting—that of Howard Coray, for example, in Draft 3—tends to link a document firmly to one or more particular scribes, the documents that have survived are only a part of what once existed. It is not possible to know the clerical or creative work that may lie behind a document in Coray's hand, or in the hand of any other scribe. Thus some individuals who contributed to the history necessarily remain uncredited.

---

33. See Revelation, July 1828, in Revelations Collection, CHL [D&C 3]. The four-page fragment implements corrections made to both the draft and fair copies, but the punctuation more closely matches the latter. Unlike page endings in the fair copy, the page endings in the fragment do not match those of the draft copy.

34. Examples of emendations made in the large history volume that also appear in Coray's adaptation include revisions regarding JS's marriage to Emma Hale (pp. 236–237 herein); Martin Harris's explanation to Anthon that the plates were sealed and that he was forbidden to bring them (pp. 244–245 herein), and Mulholland's loose note, later pinned into the large history volume, giving JS's description of the hill where the gold plates were obtained (pp. 232–233 herein).

Likewise, the relationship of author and scribe was conflated, making it difficult to distinguish between JS's contribution and that of his scribes. For example, in Draft 1, it is ultimately unclear how much influence James Mulholland had with respect to the composition of the historical narrative; he may have directed the initial outline of the history with JS filling in the details later, or JS may have dictated the framework to Mulholland himself. The full extent of the contribution by scribes is impossible to determine, but understanding the composition of JS's history requires in turn an understanding that scribes and others shared with JS some authorial responsibility for the various drafts.

The three documents presented here show an early trajectory of the history, when JS was more involved in its production than at later phases. The early history drafts—all created as a first-person record in JS's voice, arranged chronologically—helped establish a methodology followed by those who worked on the official history over the next two decades. For whatever reason, JS ultimately preferred the draft found in the large history volume to the version Coray produced, and the "History of Joseph Smith," published in the *Times and Seasons* beginning 15 March 1842, followed Draft 2, not Coray's work. Thus bypassed, Coray's history work is an artifact demonstrating a course JS considered following for his history but then abandoned. Instead, Willard Richards and later scribes continued inscribing and revising the history in the large manuscript volume, and that version, eventually comprising six manuscript volumes and a fair copy in a second set of volumes, served as the source for subsequent publications.[35] Work on this history continued after JS's death and after the Latter-day Saint migration to the intermountain West, finally concluding in 1856.

The extant drafts of the history written from 1838 to circa 1841 are presented here in parallel columns to facilitate comparison. The transcripts of Draft 1 and Draft 3 include minimal bracketed clarifications and only annotation that relates to textual aspects of those drafts; Draft 2 includes more complete bracketed clarifications (such as expanding incomplete names) and carries the historical annotation. Such editorial inclusions at times require that vertical white space be introduced in a column to maintain parallel texts. These blank spaces are also found where a given draft does not include material corresponding to other drafts, and may signal where the text was cut, expanded, revised, rearranged, or reformatted as new drafts were produced. When blank space is introduced in the middle of a paragraph, the text resumes without an opening indention. Because Draft 1 begins with the 15 May 1829 baptism of JS and Oliver Cowdery, rather than at JS's birth, the first column is blank for the first several pages.

---

35. See "Joseph Smith's Historical Enterprise," xxxi–xxxii herein. The entirety of the multivolume history will be published at josephsmithpapers.org.

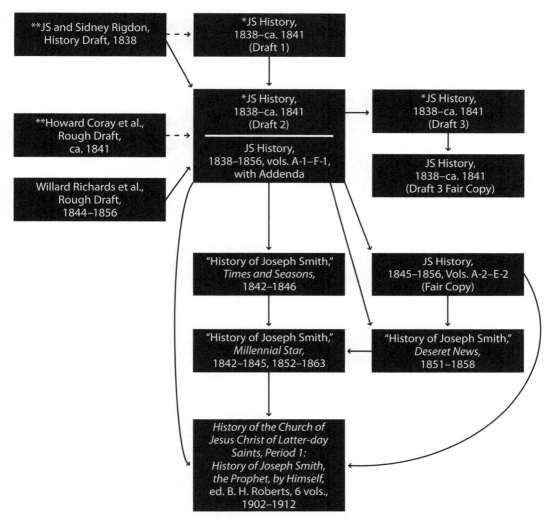

Filial relationships among manuscript and published versions of Joseph Smith's 1838–1856 history. An asterisk (*) indicates documents transcribed herein. Double asterisks (**) indicate nonextant documents. An arrow from one document to another indicates that the former was a source text for the latter. A dashed arrow indicates a possible source. As explained in the historical introduction to the 1838–circa 1841 history, Draft 2 constitutes the first sixty-one pages of JS History, volume A-1, as it appeared circa 1841, before later redactions.

Draft 1

Draft 2

[17 lines blank]

/³⁶Owing to the many reports which have been put in circulation by evil disposed and designing persons in relation to the rise and progress of the Church of Latter day Saints, all of which have been designed by the authors thereof to militate against its character as a church, and its progress in the world; I have been induced to write this history so as to disabuse the publick mind, and put all enquirers after truth into possession of the facts as they have transpired in relation both to myself and the Church as far as I have such facts in possession.

In this history I will present the various events in relation to this Church in truth and righteousness as they have transpired, or as they at present exist, being now the eighth year since the organization of said Church.

I was born in the year of our Lord One thousand Eight hundred and five, on the twenty third day of December, in the town of Sharon, Windsor County, State of Vermont.³⁷ My father Joseph Smith Senior³⁸ left the State of Vermont and moved to Palmyra, Ontario, (now Wayne) County, in the State of New York when I was in my tenth year.³⁹

In about four years after my father's arrival at Palmyra, he moved with his family into Manchester in the same County of Ontario.⁴⁰ His family consisting of eleven souls, namely, My Father Joseph Smith, My Mother Lucy Smith whose name previous to her marriage was Mack, daughter of Solomon Mack, my brothers Alvin (who is now dead) Hyrum, Myself, Samuel Harrison, William, Don Carloss [Carlos], and my Sisters Soph[r]onia, Cathrine [Katharine] and Lucy.

Draft 3

I was born in the town of Sharon. Windsor Co., Vt. on the 23. day of Dec. in the year of our Lord, 1805.

When I was 10 years old my Father, Joseph. Smith Senr. emigrated to Palmyra, Ontario C̶o̶ (now Wayne.) Co, N, Y, After residing there about four years. he removed with his Family, to Manchester, in the same County. His Family at this time consisted of a̶b̶o̶u̶t̶ Eleven Souls, viz Joseph Smith. Senr.— his consort Lucy S̶m̶i̶t̶h̶ whose maiden name was Mack. (daug[h]ter of Solomon Mack. of [*blank*].) my Brothers; H̶y̶r̶a̶m̶ Alvin. (now deceased.) Hyrum. myself. Samuel. Harrison. William. ⟨and⟩ Don—Carlos. my Sisters. Sophronia, Catherine and Lucy,

NOTES

36. TEXT: James Mulholland handwriting begins.

37. A later redaction here by Willard Richards points to "Note A," which he penned by December 1842 on pages 131–132 of the manuscript book. The note describes JS's contraction of typhoid fever as a child, a leg infection that ensued, and the operation he underwent to remove pieces of the bone. The note also recounts the difficult journey JS made with his mother and siblings to join his father, who had relocated to Palmyra, New York. A transcript of this note may be found as part of the complete transcript of JS's multivolume history at the Joseph Smith Papers website, josephsmithpapers.org.

38. A later redaction here by Willard Richards points to "Note E page 2. adenda." The relevant note is actually note C, which was written in the handwriting of Charles Wandell in the "Addenda" section following page 553 of the manuscript book. The note provides birth information for JS's paternal ancestors. A transcript of this note may be found as part of the complete transcript of JS's multivolume history at josephsmithpapers.org.

39. Joseph Smith Sr. left Vermont in late summer or early fall 1816, when JS was ten years old. The rest of the Smith family joined him in Palmyra in early 1817, shortly after JS turned eleven. (Palmyra, NY, Record of Highway Taxes, 1817, Copies of Old Village Records, 1793–1867, microfilm 812,869, U.S. and Canada Record Collection, FHL; Lucy Mack Smith, History, 1844–1845, bk. 3, [3]–[6]; JS History, vol. A-1, 131–132.)

40. Lucy Mack Smith stated that two years after they arrived in Palmyra, or by 1819, the Smiths settled on the Palmyra side of the Palmyra-Farmington township line and began clearing land for a farm on the Farmington side. The eastern part of Farmington, which included the Smith farm, was divided off and became Manchester Township in 1822. The Smiths did not actually move across the township line onto their Manchester farm until they completed their frame house in late 1825. (Lucy Mack Smith, History, 1844–1845, bk. 3, [7]–[8]; Bushman, *Rough Stone Rolling*, 32–34; Porter, "Study of the Origins," 38–43, 76–77.)

Draft copy and fair copy of 1838–circa 1841 history. Howard Coray inscribed two copies of the history draft in about 1841. The draft copy (left), reproduced herein as "Draft 3," includes insertions and deletions that show the revision process. The changes marked in the earlier copy were incorporated into

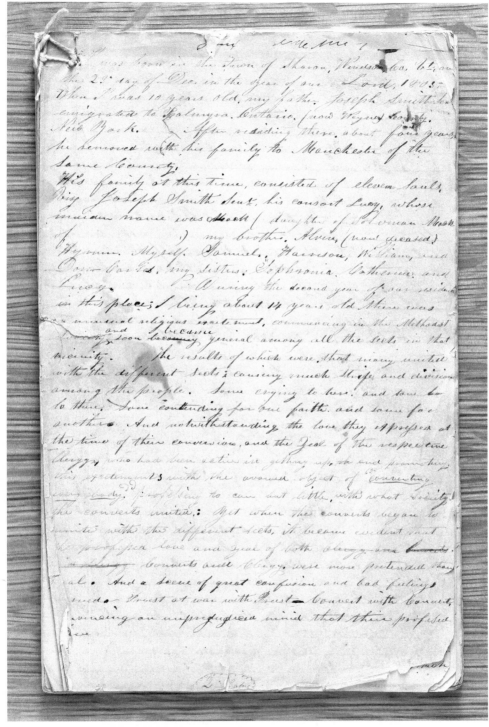

the fair copy (right). Handwriting of Howard Coray. JS History, 1838–ca. 1841, p. 1 (transcribed on pp. 205–209 herein); JS History, 1838–ca. 1841 (fair copy), p. 1, Church History Library, Salt Lake City. (Photographs by Welden C. Andersen.)

Draft 1   **Draft 2**

Sometime in the second year after our removal to Manchester, there was in the place where we lived an unusual excitement on the subject of religion. It commenced with the Methodist,[41] but soon became general among all the sects in that region of country, indeed the whole district of Country seemed affected by it and great [p. [1]] multitudes united themselves to the different religious parties, which created no small stir and division among the people, Some Crying, "Lo here" and some Lo there. Some were contending for the Methodist faith, Some for the Presbyterian, and some for the Baptist; for notwithstanding the great love which the converts to these different faiths expressed at the time of their conversion, and the great Zeal manifested by the respective Clergy who were active in getting up and promoting this extraordinary scene of religious feeling in order to have every body converted as they were pleased to call it, let them join what sect they pleased[.][43] Yet when the Converts began to file off some to one party and some to another, it was seen that the seemingly good feelings of both the Priests and the Converts were ~~mere pretence~~ more pretended than real, for a scene of great confusion and bad feeling ensued; Priest contending against priest, and convert against convert so that all their good feelings one for another (if they ever had any) were entirely lost in a strife of words and a contest about opinions.

I was at this time in my fifteenth year. My Fathers family was proselyted to the Presbyterian faith and four of them joined that Church, Namely, My Mother Lucy, My Brothers Hyrum, Samuel Harrison, and my Sister Sophonia.[44]

During this time of great excitement my mind was called up to serious reflection

Draft 3

During the Second year of our residence ~~in this place an unusual excite of religion commenced in the Methodist Church and soon~~ in this ⟨place. I being about 15 years old.⟩ there was an unusal religious excitement. Commencing in the Methodist ~~Church~~ ⟨Society⟩ ~~and~~ ⟨and⟩ soon became⟨ing⟩ general among all ⟨the sects⟩ in that vicinity, The results of which. were that ~~multitudes~~ ⟨many⟩ united with the different Sects. ~~which cre caused~~ causing much strife and division among the people, Some crying lo here, and some lo ~~hence~~[42] there. some contending for one faith, and some for another.

And notwithstanding the love ~~which~~ they expressed. at the time of their conversion. and the zeal of the respective clergy. who had been active in getting up. and promoting this excitement. with the avowed object of "converting every body;" professing to care but little, ⟨with⟩ what ~~church~~ ⟨Society⟩ the converts united; ~~themselves.~~ ~~Yet~~ Yet when the converts began to unite ~~themselves~~ with the different sects. it became evident. that the professed love. and zeal. of both converts and Priests. were more pretended than real, And a scene of great confusion. and bad feelings. ensued—Priest at war with Priest—convert with convert—convincing and unprejudiced mind. that their professed love [p. 1] and zeal. were lost in a strife of words. and contest of opinions.

During this excitement, I made it an object of much study and reflection. Although my

NOTES

41. Methodists held camp meetings at Palmyra in June 1818 and at Oaks Corners, near Vienna and within six miles of Palmyra, in July 1819. (Latimer, *Three Brothers,* 12; Peck, *Early Methodism,* 502; Staker, *Hearken, O Ye People,* 128–130.)

42. TEXT: "hence" written over "there" and then canceled.

43. TEXT: The right edge of the page is damaged, obscuring end punctuation.

44. Lucy Mack Smith and three of her children, Hyrum, Sophronia, and Samuel, attended the Western Presbyterian Church in Palmyra. Lucy wrote that their affiliation began following the death of her son Alvin in November 1823, or near the end of JS's eighteenth year. (Lucy Mack Smith, History, 1844–1845, bk. 4, [7]–[8]; see also "Records of the Session of the Presbyterian Church in Palmyra," 10 Mar. 1830.)

Draft 1   **Draft 2**

and great uneasiness, but though my feelings were deep and often pungent, still I
kept myself aloof from all these parties
though I attended their several meetings as
occasion would permit. But in process of
time my mind became somewhat partial to
the Methodist sect, and I felt some desire
to be united with them, but so great was
the confusion and strife amongst the different denominations that it was impossible
for a person young as I was and so unac-
quainted with men and things to come to
any certain conclusion who was right and
who was wrong.

My mind at different times was greatly
excited ~~for~~ the cry and tumult were so great
and incessant. The Presbyterians were most
decided against the Baptists and Methodists, and used all their powers of either reason or sophistry to prove their errors, or at
least to make the people think they were in
error. On the other hand the Baptists and
Methodists in their turn were equally Zealous in endeavoring to establish their own
tenets and disprove all others.

In the midst of this war of words, and
tumult of opinions, I often said to myself,
what is to be done? Who of all these parties
are right? Or are they all wrong together?
and if any one of them be right which is it?
And how shall I know it?[45]

While I was laboring under the extreme difficulties caused by the contests of
these parties of religionists, I was one day
reading the Epistle of James, First Chapter
and fifth verse which reads, "If any of you
lack wisdom, let him ask of God, that
giveth to all men liberally and upbraideth
not, and it shall be given him.["] Never did
any passage of scripture come with more
power to the heart of man that this did at
this time to mine. It seemed to enter with
great force into every feeling of my heart. I

Draft 3

feelings were deeply interested. still I kept myself aloof from all parties. In process of time, however. I became partial, to the Mithodist⟨s⟩ ~~Chursociety~~ I and I felt some desire to unite ⟨with⟩ them. But the confusion and strife rendered it impossible. for a person of my age. and ~~little acqu of my~~ limited acquaintance with men and things. to determine, who were right. & who wrong.

NOTES

45. In his circa summer 1832 history, JS recounted that by the time of his vision he had already concluded that the world lay in apostasy and that "there was no society or denomination that built upon the gospel of Jesus Christ as recorded in the new testament." (JS History, ca. summer 1832, pp. 11–12 herein.)

While in this situation. I often said to myself. what is to be done. ~~who~~ ⟨which⟩ of all these are right. or are they all wrong ~~together~~. If any of them are right. which is it. and how shall I know it.

While in this state of perplexity. I was one day reading the Epistle of St. James. 1st chapter. fifth ver. where. I found the following ~~the~~ words. If any of you lack wisdom. let him ask of God. that giveth to all men liberally. and upbraideth not. and it shall be given him.

Never did any passage of scripture. make a deeper impression. on the heart of man ~~than This~~ than was made on mine. by this. Knowing as I did. that I needed wisdom from <u>God.</u> & unless I obtained it. I

Draft 1   **Draft 2**

reflected on it again and again, knowing
that if any person needed wisdom from
God, I did, for how to act I did not know
and unless I could get more wisdom than I
then had [I] would never know, for the
teachers of religion of the different sects
understood the same [p. 2] passage of
Scripture so differently as ⟨to⟩ destroy all
confidence in settling the question by an
appeal to the Bible. At length I came to the
conclusion that I must either remain in
darkness and confusion or else I must do as
James directs, that is, Ask of God. I at last
came to the determination to ask of God,
concluding that if he gave wisdom to them
that lacked wisdom, and would give liberally and not upbraid, I might venture. So in
accordance with this my determination to
ask of God, I retired to the woods to make
the attempt. It was on the morning of a
beautiful clear day early in the spring of
Eighteen hundred and twenty.[46] It was the
first time in my life that I had ⟨made⟩ such
an attempt, for amidst all ⟨my⟩ anxieties I
had never as yet made the attempt to pray
vocally.

　　After I had retired into the place where
I had previously designed to go, having
looked around me and finding myself
alone, I kneeled down and began to offer
up the desires of my heart to God, I had
scarcely done so, when immediately I was
⟨siezed⟩ upon by some power which entirely overcame me and ⟨had⟩ such astonishing influence over me as to bind my
tongue so that I could not speak. Thick
darkness gathered around me and it seemed
to me for a time as if I were doomed to
sudden destruction. But exerting all my
powers to call upon God to deliver me out
of the power of this enemy which had
siezed upon me, and at the very moment
when I was ready to sink into despair and

Draft 3

could not ⟨detirmne⟩ ~~assertain~~ which were right. And the teachers of the different sects, interpreted this passage ~~of scripture.~~ so as ⟨to⟩ destroy all confidence. in settling the question by an appeal to the Bible. ~~this~~ ⟨thus⟩ ~~compelled~~ ⟨compelling⟩ me to conclude that I must remain in darkness. or do as James directs. which is to "ask of God". At length I came to the conclusion, to ask of him for wisdom, believing that he "that giveth ~~giveth~~ to all men". liberally and upbraideth not. would not refuse to verify his promise to me, [p. 2]

Accordingly I retired into the woods, to make the attempt. It was on the morning of a clear and beautiful day, early in the spring of Eighteen hundred and twenty. ~~It~~ ⟨and it⟩ was the first time that I ever made such an effort; for amidst all my anxieties. I had as yet never made the attempt to pray vocally. After arriving at the place where I had previously designed to go I looked around me. and finding myself alone, kneeled down. and began to offer up ⟨to God.⟩ the desires of my heart. I had scarcely done so, when I was immediately seized upon, by some power which entirely overcame me, and had such astonishing influence over me, as to bind my tongue ~~so~~ ⟨so as to⟩ ~~depriving~~ ⟨deprive⟩ me of ~~the power of~~ speech— Thick darkness gathered around me, and for a time it seemed that I were doomed to distruction. But exerting every energy to call upon God. to deliver me out of the power of this enemy; at the ~~very~~ moment when I was sinking ~~into~~ dispair and abandon myself to distruction. ⟨an⟩ not ~~a~~ imaginary. but to the ~~power~~

46. JS History, ca. summer 1832, p. 12 herein, indicates that this event occurred "in the 16th year of my age," or 1821.

Draft 1   **Draft 2**

abandon myself to destruction, not to an imaginary ruin but to the power of some actual being from the unseen world who had such a marvelous power as I had never before felt in any being. Just at this moment of great alarm I saw a pillar ⟨of⟩ light exactly over my head above the brightness of the sun, which descended ~~gracefully~~ gradually untill it fell upon me. It no sooner appeared than I found myself delivered from the enemy which held me bound. When the light rested upon me I saw two personages (whose brightness and glory defy all description) standing above me in the air. One of ⟨them⟩ spake unto me calling me by name and said (pointing to the other) "This is my beloved Son, Hear him."

My object in going to enquire of the Lord was to know which of all the sects was right, that I might know which to join. No sooner therefore did I get possession of myself so as to be able to speak, than I asked the personages who stood above me in the light, which of all the sects was right, (for at this time it had never entered into my heart that all were wrong) and which I should join. I was answered that I must join none of them, for they were all wrong, and the Personage who addressed me said that all their Creeds were an abomination in his sight, that those professors were all corrupt, that "they draw near to me ~~to~~ with their lips but their hearts are far from me, They teach for doctrines the commandments of men, having a form of Godliness but they deny the power thereof."[48] He again forbade me to join with any of them and many other thing[s][49] did he say unto me which I cannot write at this time.[50] When I came to myself again I found myself lying on ⟨my⟩ back looking up into Heaven.[51] Some few days later after I had this vision I happened to be in company

Draft 3

⟨influence⟩ of some being from the unseen world. who had such marvelous power as this. Just at this moment of alarm, I saw a pillar of light. over my head, ~~exceeding the brightn~~ ⟨far more bright and dazling than the sun in his meridian splendor⟩[47] the brightness of which. exceeded that of the sun; which gradually decended untill it fell upon me. and I found myself. delivered from the enemy which held me bound. When the light rested upon me I saw two personages. (whose brightness and glory defy all description.) standing above in the air. One of them called me by name. ⟨and⟩ said (pointing to the other) this is my beloved son hear him.

My object ~~in going~~ was to assertain. which of the sects were right. that I might join it. ⟨Consequently⟩ as soon as possible. I asked the Personages who stood in the light; Which [p. 3] of the sects were right. (for I supposed that one of them were so.) and which I should join. I was answered "join none of them; they ~~are~~ all are wrong—their creeds are an abomination in my sight— those professors are all corrupt—they draw near ⟨to⟩ me with their lips. but their hearts are far from me.— They teach for doctrine. the commandments of men. having a form of Godliness. but they deny the power thereof". He again borfade [forbade] me to join any of them; and many other things. did he say unto me; which I cannot write at this time.

When I came to myself ~~again~~, I was lying on my ~~my~~ back, looking up into heaven. A few days after this, I happened to be in company, with one of the Methodist

47. TEXT: Insertion in graphite.

48. See Isaiah 29:13; Matthew 15:9; and 2 Timothy 3:5.

49. TEXT: "thing[*edge worn*]".

50. For JS's other accounts of this vision of Deity, see JS History, ca. summer 1832, pp. 11–13 herein; JS, Journal, 9–11 Nov. 1835, in *JSP*, J1:87– 88 (see also later version, pp. 115–116 herein); JS, "Church History," p. 494 herein; and JS, "Latter Day Saints," p. 508 herein.

51. A later redaction here by Willard Richards points to note "B," which he penned on pages 132–133 of the manuscript book on 2 December 1842. The note describes JS's interaction with his mother following the vision, when he told her, "I have learned for myself that Presbyterianism is not true." A transcript of this note may be found as part of the complete transcript of JS's multivolume history at josephsmithpapers.org. (Richards, Journal, 2 Dec. 1842.)

Draft 1   **Draft 2**

with one of the Methodist Preachers who
was very active in the before mentioned religious excitement[52] and conversing with
him on the subject of religion I took occasion to give him an account of the vision
which I had had. I was greatly surprised at
his behaviour, he treated my communication not only lightly but with great contempt, saying it was all of the Devil, that
there was no such thing as visions or revelations in these days, that all such things
had ceased with the [p. 3] apostles and that
there never would be any more of them.

I soon found however that my telling
the story had excited a great deal of prejudice against me among professors of religion and was the cause of great persecution
which continued to increase and though I
was an obscure boy only between fourteen
and fifteen years of age and my circumstances in life such as to make a boy of no
consequence in the world, Yet men of high
standing would take notice sufficiently to
excite the public mind against me and create a hot persecution, and this was common ⟨among⟩ all the sects: all united to
persecute me. It has often caused me serious reflection both then and since, how
very strange it was that an obscure boy of a
little over fourteen years of age and one too
who was doomed to the necessity of obtaining a scanty maintainance by his daily
labor should be thought a character of sufficient importance to attract the attention
of the great ones of the most popular sects
of the day so as to create in them a spirit of
the bitterest persecution and reviling. But
strange or not, so it was, and was often
cause of great sorrow to myself. However it
was nevertheless a fact, that I had had a
Vision. I have thought since that I felt
much like as Paul did when he made his
defence before King Aggrippa and related

Draft 3

preachers. who had been very active in the before mentioned excitement; whilst conversing with him on the subject of religion. I gave him an account of the vision which I had ~~I~~ seen, I was greatly surprised at the manner he treated my communication; avowing it to be of the Devil; that there could be no visions or revelations from God in these days: that they had ceased with the Apostles. and never would be restored again. I soon found that a relation of ~~the~~ this fact excited the prejudice of the professors of religion. and caused them to persecute me.

Although an obscure boy. ⟨about⟩ fifteen years old. my circumstances ~~in life~~ being such as to make me of but little consequence in the world. Yet men of high standing. endeavored to excite the publick mind ⟨against me.⟩ ~~against me~~ and cause the sects to unite in persecuting me.

52. In an 1834 account, Oliver Cowdery mentioned Methodist preacher George Lane in connection with religious excitement in Palmyra and vicinity in "the 15th year" of JS's life. Cowdery subsequently revised the dating to "the 17th" year. Although there is no recorded statement from JS mentioning Lane specifically, the latter's assignments and travels between July 1819 and July 1825 placed him in close enough proximity to Palmyra and Manchester that he would have had numerous opportunities for contact with JS. (Oliver Cowdery, "Letter III," *LDS Messenger and Advocate,* Dec. 1834, 1:42 [see also later version, p. 53 herein]; Oliver Cowdery, "Letter IV," *LDS Messenger and Advocate,* Feb. 1835, 1:78 [see also later version, p. 56 herein]; Porter, "Reverend George Lane," 328–339.)

Draft 1	**Draft 2**
	the account of the Vision he had when the saw a light and heard a voice,[53] but still there were but few who beleived him, some said he was dishonest, others said he was mad, and he was ridiculed and reviled, But all this did not destroy the reality of his vision. He had seen a vision he knew he had, and ⟨all⟩ the persecution under Heaven could not make it otherwise, and though they should persecute him unto death Yet he knew and would know to his latest breath that he had both seen a light and heard a voice speaking unto him and all the world could not make him think or believe otherwise. So it was with me, I had actualy seen a light and in the midst of that light I saw two personages, and they did in reality speak ⟨un⟩to me, or one of them did, And though I was hated and persecuted for saying that I had seen a vision, Yet it was true and while they were persecuting me reviling me and speaking all manner of evil against me falsely for so saying, I was led to say in my heart, why persecute for telling the truth? I have actually seen a vision, "and who am I that I can withstand God"[54] Or why does the world think to make me deny what I have actually seen, for I had seen a vision, I knew it, and I knew that God knew it, and I could not deny it, neither dare I do it, at least I knew that by so doing ⟨I⟩ would offend God and come under condemnation.
	I had now got my mind satisfied so far as the sectarian world was concerned, that it was not my duty to join with any of them, but continue as I was untill further directed, for I had found the testimony of James to be true, that a man who lacked wisdom might ask of God, and obtain and not be upbraided. I continued to pursue my common avocations in life untill the twenty first of September, One thousand

Draft 3

NOTES

53. See Acts 26:12–18.
54. See Acts 11:17.

My mind was now satisfied. that it was my duty to join none of the sects. but to continue as I was, untill further directed. I had found the testimony of James ~~true~~ to be true; that a man lacking wisdom might ⟨ask of God.⟩ ~~call upon~~ [p. 4] and obtain it and not be upbraided. I continued to pursue my common avocasions in life. until the 21ˢᵗ sep.ᵗ. 1823. suffering severe persecusion from both religious & irreligious;

Draft 1   **Draft 2**

Eight hundred and twenty three, all the
time suffering severe persecution at the
hand of all classes of men, both religious
and irreligious because I continued to affirm that I ⟨had⟩ seen a Vision.

During the space of time which intervened between the time I had the vision
and the year Eighteen hundred and twenty
three, (having been forbidden to join any
of the religious sects of the day, and being
of very tender years and persecuted by
those who ought to have been my friends,
and to have treated me kindly [p. 4] and if
they supposed me to be deluded to have
endeavoured in a proper and affectionate
manner to have reclaimed me) I was left to
all kinds of temptations, and mingling
⟨with⟩ all kinds of society I frequently ⟨fell⟩
into many foolish errors and displayed the
weakness of youth and the corruption of
human nature which I am sorry to say led
me into divers temptations to the gratification of many appetites offensive in the
sight of God.⁵⁵ In consequence of these
things I often felt condemned for my
weakness and imperfections; when on the
evening of the above mentioned twenty
first of september, after I had retired to my
bed for the night I betook myself to prayer
and supplication to Almighty God for forgiveness of all my sins and follies, and also
for a manifestation to me that I might
know of my state and standing before him.
For I had full confidence in obtaining a divine manifestation as I had previously had
one. While I was thus in the act of calling
upon God, I discovered a light appearing
in the room which continued to increase
untill the room was lighter than at noon-
day ~~and~~ ⟨when⟩ immediately a personage
⟨appeared⟩ at my bedside standing in the
air for his feet did not touch the floor.
He had on a loose robe of most exquisite

Draft 3

because I asserted the truth of what I had seen.

Professors of religion neglecting to obey the precepts of the ~~religion~~ ⟨Saviour;⟩ ~~which they professed inasmuch as~~ instead of extending towards me that kindness of demeanor. which my extreme youth demanded. and endeavoring ~~in kindness and~~ with affection. to win me back from my fanaticism and delusion: (as they were pleased to term it.) ~~they~~ heaped upon me bitter persecutions. and revilings. Consequently I was Subject to all kinds of temptations. and mingling with all kinds of company. I ~~frequently~~ fell into ~~my~~ many errors. ~~and displayed the weak~~ (~~evinced~~ evincing the weakness of youth and corruptions of human nature.) which were offensive in the sight of God. ~~In co.~~ In consequence of which, I often felt condemned; for ~~these~~ ⟨this⟩ my imperfection and weakness. On ⟨the evening of⟩ the above mentioned. 21ˢᵗ of Sep.ᵗ. after I ~~had~~ retired to rest, I betook myself to prayer and supplication. to Almighty God; asking forgivness for all my sins. and follies. also for a manifestation of my state and standing before him; still having full confidence. that my prayer would be answered. as it had previously been. While in the act of calling upon God. I discovered a light in the room. which continued to increase untill it exceeded that of the sun at mid.-day. when a person appeared at my bed side. standing in the air. for his feet did not touch the floor; having on a robe of most exquisite whiteness. exceeding anything I had ever seen. nor do I believe. that any earthly thing could [p. 5] be made so exceedingly white. and briliant.

NOTES

55. A later redaction here by Willard Richards points to "Note C," which he penned on page 133 of the manuscript book on 2 December 1842. A transcript of the note, which explains that JS's sins were of a minor nature, may be found as part of the complete transcript of JS's multivolume history at josephsmithpapers.org. This insertion was written after the *Times and Seasons* began publishing JS's history in March 1842 and does not appear in that publication. (Richards, Journal, 2 Dec. 1842.)

Draft 1   **Draft 2**

whiteness. It was a whiteness beyond
any⟨thing⟩ earthly I had ever seen, nor do I
believe that any earthly thing could be
made to appear so exceedinly white and
brilliant, His hands were naked and his
arms also a little above the wrist. So also
were his feet naked as were his legs a little
above the ankles. His head and neck were
also bare. I could discover that he had no
other clothing on but this robe as it was
open so that I could see into his bosom.
Not only was his robe exceedingly white
but his whole person was glorious beyond
description, and his countenance truly like
lightning. The room was exceedingly light,
but not so very bright as immediately
around his person. When I first looked
upon him I was afraid, but the fear soon
left me. He called me by name and said
unto me that he was a messenger sent from
the presence of God to me and that his
name was Nephi.[56] That God had a work
for me to do, and that my ⟨name⟩ should be
had for good and evil among all nations
kindreds and tongues. or that it should be
both good and evil spoken of among all
people. He said there was a book deposited
written upon gold plates, giving an account
of the former inhabitants of this continent
and the source from whence they sprang.
He also said that the fullness of the everlasting Gospel was contained in it as delivered by the Saviour to the ancient inhabitants. Also that there were two stones in
silver bows and these put into a breast plate
which constituted what is called the Urim
& Thummin deposited with the plates, and
that was what constituted seers in ancient
or former times[57] and that God ⟨had⟩ prepared them for the purpose of translating
the book. After telling me these things he
commenced quoting the prophecies of the
Old testament, he first quoted part of the

Draft 3

His hands and arms were naked. alittle above the wrist. so also ⟨were⟩ his feet and legs alittle ab[o]ve the ancles; his head and neck were also bare. I could discover that he had no other clothing but the robe. as it was open so that I could see his bosom. Not only was his robe exceedingly white; but his whole person was glorious beyond ◊discription. and his countenance truly like lightning. The room was exceedingly light but not so much so as immediately around his person When I first looked upon ⟨him⟩ it̶ I was afraid; but the fear soon left me: calling me by name, ⟨he⟩ said. t̶h̶a̶t̶ he was a messenger. sent from the presence of God to me. and that his name was Nephi.— that he had a work for me to do that my name should be had for good and evil. among all nations. kindreds. & tongues— that there was a book deposited: written upon gold plates, giving an account of the former inhabitants of this Continent. as well as their origin— that the fullness of the everlasting Gospel as delivered by the Savior. to ⟨the⟩ ancient inhabitants. was contained in them— that there were two stones in silver bows. and these (stones fastened to a brest plate.) constitutes what is called the Urim & Thummin. deposited with the Plates. the possession. and use of which. constituted seers in ancient times— that God had prepared them for the purpose of translating the book!

After telling me these things. he commenced quoting the prophecies of the old testament. He first quoted part of the f̶i̶r̶s̶t̶

56. A later redaction in an unidentified hand changed "Nephi" to "Moroni" and noted that the original attribution was a "clerical error." Early sources often did not name the angelic visitor, but sources naming Moroni include Oliver Cowdery's historical letter published in the April 1835 *LDS Messenger and Advocate;* an expanded version of a circa August 1830 revelation, as published in the 1835 edition of the Doctrine and Covenants; and a JS editorial published in the *Elders' Journal* in July 1838.[a] The present history is the earliest extant source to name Nephi as the messenger, and subsequent publications based on this history perpetuated the attribution during JS's lifetime.[b] (*a.* Oliver Cowdery, "Letter VI," *LDS Messenger and Advocate,* Apr. 1835, 1:112 [see also later version, p. 71 herein]; Revelation, ca. Aug. 1830, in Doctrine and Covenants 50:2, 1835 ed. [D&C 27:5]; [JS], Editorial, *Elders' Journal,* July 1838, 42–44. *b.* See "History of Joseph Smith," *Times and Seasons,* 15 Apr. 1842, 3:753–754; and "History of Joseph Smith," *LDS Millennial Star,* Aug. 1842, 3:53–54. For JS's other accounts of this experience, see JS History, ca. summer 1832, pp. 13–14 herein; JS, Journal, 9–11 Nov. 1835, in *JSP,* J1:88–89 [see also later version, pp. 116–117 herein]; JS, "Church History," pp. 494–495 herein; and JS, "Latter Day Saints," pp. 508–509 herein.)

57. See Book of Mormon, 1830 ed., 172–173, 546 [Mosiah 8:13–17; Ether 4:5], where the instrument is referred to as "interpreters."

Draft 1	Draft 2

Draft 1

Draft 2

third chapter of Malachi and he quoted also the fourth or last chapter of the same prophecy though with a little variation from the way it reads in our Bibles. Instead of quoting the first verse as reads in our books he quoted it thus, "For behold the day cometh that shall burn as an oven, and all the proud ⟨yea⟩ and all that do wickedly shall burn as stubble, for ⟨they⟩ that cometh shall burn them saith the Lord of hosts, that it shall leave them neither root nor branch." And again he quoted the fifth verse thus, "Behold I will reveal unto you the Priesthood by the hand of Elijah the prophet before the coming of the great and dreadful day of the Lord." He also quoted the next verse differently, [p. 5] "And he shall plant in the hearts of the Children the promises made to the fathers, and the hearts of the children shall turn to their fathers, if it were not so the whole earth would be utterly wasted at his coming." In addition to these ~~quotations~~ he quoted the Eleventh Chapter of Isaiah saying that it was about to be fulfilled. He quoted also the third chapter of Acts, twenty second and twenty third verses precisely as they stand in our new testament, He said that that prophet was Christ, but the day had not yet come when "they who would not hear his voice should be cut off from among the people," but soon would come.

He also quoted the second chapter of Joel from the twenty eighth to the last verse. He also said that this was not yet fulfilled but was soon to be. And he further stated the fullness of the gentiles was soon to come in.[58] He quoted many other passages of scripture and offered many explanations which cannot be mentioned here. Again he told me that when I got those plates of which he had spoken (for the time that they should be obtained was not yet

Draft 3

⟨third⟩ Chapter of Malachi. He also quoted
the fourth or last chap^r of the same prophecy; though with a little variation [p. 6]
from the way it reads in our Bible Instead
of quoting the first verses as it reads in ⟨the
present translation⟩ ~~our~~ book, he ⟨rendered
it⟩ ~~quoted~~ as follows. For behold the day
cometh that shall burn as an oven. and all
the proude, yea and all that do wickedly.
shall burn as stubble, for they that cometh
shall burn them. saith the Lord of Hosts.
that it shall leave them neither root nor
branch. Then quoting the fifth verse thus;
Behold I will reveal unto you the priesthood. by the hand of Elijah the prophet.
before the coming of the great and dreadful day of the Lord. quoting the next verse
in this manner; And he shall plant in the
hearts of the children the promises made to
the fathers. and the hearts of the children
shall turn ~~the~~ to their fathers; if it were not
so. the whole earth would be utterly wasted
at his coming. Then he ~~quoted~~ quoted the
Elevnth Chap of Is[ai]ah. Saying. "it is
about to be fulfilled". He then quoted the 3^d
Chap^r of Acts. as ~~they~~ ⟨it⟩ reads in ⟨the⟩ ~~our~~
new Testament saying. that. the Prop[h]et
spoken of was Christ; and that the day
would soon come. when they who would
not hear his voice would be cut off from
among the people.

He then qu[o]ted the 2^d· Chap^r· of Joel. saying. that this was not yet fullfilled. but
soon would be— That the fullness of ⟨the⟩
Gentiles was soon to come in;— ~~he~~ ⟨He⟩
~~quoting~~ ⟨quoted⟩ many other passages.
and ⟨made⟩ many explanations. which cannot be mentioned here.— That when I
should get those plates of which he had
spoken. (for the time had not yet arrived
when they should appear.) ~~I should not
show them~~ [p. 7] if I showed them. [59](either

58. See Romans 11:25; see also Revelation,
ca. 7 Mar. 1831, in Doctrine and Covenants 15:4,
1835 ed. [D&C 45:28].

59. TEXT: Coray inserted this opening parenthesis at a later time. The original opening parenthesis (after "either") was not canceled, but
lines extending to the right from the inserted
parenthesis enclose "either the", effectively over-
riding the original parenthesis.

Draft 1   **Draft 2**

fulfilled) I should not show ⟨them⟩ to any person, neither the breastplate with the Urim and Thummin only to those to whom I should be commanded to show them, If I did I should be destroyed. While he was conversing with me about the plates the vision was opened to my mind that I could see the place where the plates were deposited and that so clearly and distinctly that I knew the place again when I visited it.

After this ~~conversation~~ communication I saw the light in the room begin to gather immediately around the person of him who had been speaking to me, and it continued to do so untill the room was again left dark except just round him, when instantly I saw as it were a conduit open right up into heaven, and he ascended up till he entirely disappeared and the room was left as it had been before this heavenly light had made its appearance.

I lay musing on the singularity of the scene and marvelling greatly at what had been told me by this extraordinary messenger, when in the midst of my meditation I suddenly discovered that my room was again beginning to get lighted, and in an instant as it were, the same heavenly messenger was again by my bedside. He commenced and again related the very same things which he had done at his first visit without the least variation which having done, he informed me of great judgements which were coming upon the earth, with great desolations by famine, sword, and pestilence, and that these grievous judgments would come on the earth in this generation: Having related these things he again ascended as he had done before.

By this time so deep were the impressions made on my mind that sleep had fled from my eyes and I lay overwhelmed in

Draft 3

(the br[e]ast plate with the Urim & Thummin ⟨and⟩ plates.) to any person save those
to whom I should be commanded to show
them; I should be destroyed.— While he
was conversing ~~the~~ with me. the vision was
opened so that I could see the place where
the plates were deposited so clearly and distinctly. that I knew the place when I visited
it.

Then the light in the room ~~began to~~
gather⟨ed⟩ around him, who had spoken.
until the room was left dark, except immediately around his person; when instantly I
saw an aperture open up into Heaven. and
he asscended up. disappearing from my
sight; leaving the room as dark as it was
previous to ⟨his⟩ ~~His~~ appearance.

While Meditating upon this wonderful vision. ~~and~~ ⟨being⟩ much surp[r]ised at what
this messenger had told me; I discovered
that my room was again suddenly illuminated. and the same messenger standing
before me. He again related the same without any vairation. Then informed me of
great judgments which were coming upon
the world. desolations by famine sword and
pestilence. should visit the earth in this
generations; Having related these things he
disappeared as before,—

The impressions on my mind were of such a
nature, that I could not possibly sleep. but
lay obsorbed in astonishment. ~~and surprise~~

8

if I should them, (either (the brast plate with the
Urim & Thummim and plate.) to any person save
those to whom I should be commanded to show
them, I should be distroyed.— While he was convers=
ing with me, the vision was opened so that I could
see the place where the plates were deposited so clearly
and distinctly, that I knew the place when I visited
it. Then the light in the room began
to gather around him who had spoken
until the room was left dark except
immediately around his person; when
instantly I saw an aperture open up into
Heaven, and he ascended up, disap=
=pearing from my sight; leaving the room
as dark as it was previous to his appearance
While meditating upon this wonderful mis=
=ion. and being much surprised at what this mess=
=enger had told me; I discovered that my
room was again suddenly illuminated.
and the same messenger standing before
me. He again related the same without
any variation. Then informed me of great
judgments which were coming upon the world des=
olations by famine, sword and pestilence, should
visit the earth in this generation. Having related
these things he disapeared as before.— The imp=
ressions on my mind were of such a nature, that
I could not possibly sleep but lay absorbed in
astonishment, ~~and which~~ at what I had seen
and heard.— What was my surprise to again
behold the same Messenger at my bed side
and hear him rehearse the same things as
before, adding a caution to me that Satan
would tempt me, (because of the indigence
of my father's family) to enrich myself with
the plates. This he forbid me, saying, that I

having no other in view. and influenced by
no other motive than the building up of his kingdom. otherwise, I could not get them. When he
again ascended up into heaven, and was left
to wonder upon, the what I had seen

Immediately after the third departure of
the Messenger. the cock crew. and I found
day was approaching. So that our interviews
must have lasted the whole night. I shortly
after rose from my bed. and went to the
usual labors of the day; but found my strength so exhausted. as to render me entirely unable to labor; My father who. was with me,
discovered my weakness; and told me to go
home. In attempting to do so. while getting over
the fence. my strength entirely failed me; and
I fell helpless on the ground. for a time unc-
onscious of any thing: The first that I can recollect. was a voice. calling me by name. I
looked and beheld the same Messenger. standing over me surrounded by light as before

He again related all that he had spoken the previous night. and commanded me to
tell my father of the vision and commandments I had received. I returned back
to the field. and rehearsed to my father.
the whole matter; He replied to me that it
was of God. advising me to obey the commandments I had received. I then
went to the place where the Messenger told
me the plates were deposited. and owing
to the distinctness of the vision I had concerning it. I knew the place the instant
I arrived there. Convenient to the village
of Manchester, Ontario, Co. N.Y. stands.

example of the abrupt shifts in handwriting style found throughout the manuscript. Handwriting of Howard Coray. JS History, 1838–ca. 1841, pp. 8–9 (transcribed on pp. 225–233 herein), Church History Library, Salt Lake City. (Photographs by Welden C. Andersen.)

Draft 1   **Draft 2**

astonishment at what I had both seen and
heard:

But what was my surprise when again
I beheld the same messenger at my bedside,
and heard him rehearse or repeat over
again to me the same things as before and
added a caution to me, telling me that
Satan would try to tempt me (in consequence of the indigent circumstances of
my father's family) to get the plates for the
purpose of getting rich, This he forbid me,
saying that I must have no other object in
view in getting the plates but to glorify
God, and must not be influenced by any
other motive but that of building his kingdom, otherwise I could not get them. After
this third visit he again ascended up into
heaven as before and I was again left to ponder on the [p. 6] strangeness of what I had
just experienced, when almost immediately
after the heavenly messenger had ascended
from me the third time, the cock crew, and
I found that day was approaching so that
our interviews must have occupied the
whole of that night. I shortly after arose
from my bed, and as usual went to the necessary labors of the day, but in attempting
to labor as at other times, I found my
strength so exhausted as rendered me entirely unable. My father who was laboring
along ⟨with⟩ me discovered something to
be wrong with me and told me to go home.
I started with the intention of going to the
house, but in attempting to cross the fence
out of the field where we were, my strength
entirely failed me and I fell helpless on the
ground and for a time was quite uncon-
scious of any thing. The first thing that I
can recollect was a voice speaking unto me
calling me by name. I looked up and beheld the same messenger—standing over
my head surrounded by light as before.

Draft 3

at what I had seen and heard. What was
my surprise to again behold the same
Messenger at my bed-side and hear him re-
hears the same things as before, adding a
caution to me that satan would tempt me.
(because of the indigance of my father's
family.) to enrich myself with the plates;
This he forbid me. saying. that I [p. 8] must
have no object in view. and ⟨be⟩ influenced
by no other motive. than the building up
of his kingdom. otherwise. I could not get
them. When he again ascended up into
heaven, and ⟨I⟩ was left to wonder upon ~~the~~
~~results of~~ what I had seen.

Immediately after the third departure
of the Messenger. the cock crew. ~~I~~ and I
found day was approaching. so that our interviews must have lasted the whole night.
~~A~~ I shortly ~~time~~ after rose from my bed.
and went to the usual labors of the day; but
found my strength so exhausted. as to render me entirely unable to ⟨labor;⟩ ~~so to do~~
My father who. was with me, discovered
my weakness; and told me to go home. In
attempting to do so. while getting over the
fence. my strength entirely failed me; and I
fell helpless on the ground. for a time un-
conscious of any thing: The first that I can
recollect. was a voice. calling me by name.
I looked and beheld the same Messenger.
standing over me surrounded by light as
before

Draft 1

Draft 2

He then again related unto me all that he
had related to me the previous night, and
commanded me to go to my father and tell
him of the vision and commandments
which I had received.

I obeyed. I returned back to my father
in the field and rehearsed the whole matter
to him. He replyed to me, that it was of
God, and to go and do as commanded by
the messenger. I left the field and went to
the place where the messenger had told
me the plates were deposited, and owing to
the distinctness of the vision which I had
had concerning it, I knew the place the instant that I arrived there.⟨*⟩ ⟨⟨*⟩Convenient
to the ~~little~~ village of Manchester, Ontario
County, New York, Stands a hill of considerable size, and the most elevated of any in
the neighborhood, On the west side of this
hill not far from the top⟩[60] Under a ~~stound~~
stone of considerable size, lay the plates deposited in a stone box, This stone was thick
and rounding in the middle on the upper
side, and thinner towards the edges, so that
the middle part of it was visible above the
ground, but the edge all round was covered
with earth. Having removed the earth ~~off
the edge of the stone,~~ and obtained a lever
which I got fixed under the edge of the
stone, and with a little exertion raised it up,
I looked in and there indeed did I behold
the plates, the Urim and Thummin and
the Breastplate as stated by the messenger
The box in which they lay was formed by
laying stones together in some kind of cement, in the bottom of the box were laid
two stones crossways of the box, and on
these stones lay the plates and the other
things with them. I made an attempt to
take them out but was forbidden by the
messenger[62] and was again informed that
the time ⟨for⟩ bringing them forth had not
yet arrived, neither would untill four years

Draft 3

He again related all that he had spoken the previous night. and commanded me to tell my father of the vision and commandments, I had received—

I returned back to the field. and rehearsed to my father the whole matter: He replied to me that it was of God. advising me to obey the commandments I had received— I then ~~went~~ went to the place where. the Messenger told me the plates were deposited. and owing to the distinctness of the vision I had concerning it; I knew the place the instant I arrived there.— Convenient to the vilage of Manchester, Ontario. Co.. N. Y. stands. [p. 9] a hill of considerable size. and ⟨the⟩ most elevated of any in the neighbourhood; on the west side of ~~this hill.~~ ⟨which⟩ near the top under a ⟨large⟩ stone ~~of large size.~~ lay the plates deposited in a stone box— This stone. was rounding. thiner at the edges than in the middle which was visible above the ground—

Having removed the earth which covered the thin edge of the stone. I fixed a lever under it. ~~and ⟨raised it.⟩ with little~~ and raised it with ⟨a⟩ little exertion—I looked in there[61] indeed did I behold the plates. with the Urim & Thummin. & the breast plate— The box in which they ~~lay~~ were ⟨placed⟩ was formed of stones, laid in some kind of cement— In the bottom of the box. were ~~two~~ transversed stones. on which lay the plates &c. I made ⟨an⟩ ~~en◊◊~~ attempt to take them. but was forbidden ⟨by the Messenger.⟩ as the time for bringing them forth. had not yet arrived; neither would ⟨it⟩ untill four years had expired: but he told me to visit the ~~plats~~ place. in one year from that time. and that he would ⟨be⟩

NOTES

60. TEXT: James Mulholland inscribed this insertion on a loose slip of paper, which was pinned to this page of the manuscript. On the opposite side of the slip he made another asterisk and wrote, "I mentioned to President Smith that I considered it necessary that an explanation of ⟨the location of⟩ the place where the box was deposited would be required in order that the history be satisfactory. J, M,".

61. TEXT: Or "then".

62. In 1835, Oliver Cowdery wrote that JS was "sensibly shocked" each time he attempted to remove the plates from their repository. (Oliver Cowdery, "Letter VIII," *LDS Messenger and Advocate,* Oct. 1835, 2:198 [see also later version, p. 82 herein]; see also Knight, Reminiscences, 1; and Lucy Mack Smith, History, 1844–1845, bk. 5, [5].)

Draft 1   **Draft 2**

from that time, but he told me that I
should come to that place precisely in one
year from that time, and that he would
there meet with me, and that I should continue to do so untill the time should come
for obtaining the plates. Accordingly as I
had been commanded I went at the end of
each year, and at each time I found the
same messenger there and received instruction and intelligence from him at each of
our interviews respecting what the Lord
was going to do, and how and in what
manner his kingdom was to be conducted
in the last days.

As my father's worldly circumstances
were very, ⟨limited⟩ we were under the necessity of laboring with our hands, hiring
by days works and otherwise as we could
get opportunity[.] sometimes we were at
home and some times abroad and by continued labor were enabled to get a comfortable maintenance.

In the year Eighteen hundred and
twenty four my fathers family met with a
great affliction by the death of my eldest
brother Alvin.[63] In the month of October
Eighteen hundred and twenty five I hired
with an old Gentleman, by name of Josiah
Stoal [Stowell] [p. 7] who lived in Chenango
County, State of New York. He had heard
something of a silver mine having been
opened by the Spaniards in Harmony,
Susquahanah [Susquehanna] County, State
of Pensylvania, and had previous to my hiring with him been digging in order if possible to discover the mine.[64] After I went to
live with ⟨him⟩ he took me among the rest
of his hands to dig for the silver mine, at
which I continued to work for nearly a
month without success in our undertaking,
and finally I prevailed with the old gentleman to cease digging after it. Hence arose

Draft 3

with me and I should continue to do so until permitted to obtain them. Accordingly I went at the end of each year ⟨&⟩ found the Messenger there. receiving instruction, and inteligence. from him of what the Lord was going to do; and how his kingdom was to be conducted. in the last days

NOTES

63. Alvin Smith died 19 November 1823. (Morgan, *Cemetery Records, Palmyra, Wayne, New York,* 2; Patriarchal Blessings, 1:1; Joseph Smith Sr., "To the Public," *Wayne Sentinel* [Palmyra, NY], 29 Sept. 1824, [3].)

64. According to Oliver Cowdery, Stowell hoped to discover a substantial quantity of coins said to have been minted by Spaniards from ore they had mined in the vicinity and left in a "subterraneous vault." (Oliver Cowdery, "Letter VIII," *LDS Messenger and Advocate,* Oct. 1835, 2:201 [see also later version, p. 88 herein].)

In the year 1824. my father's family. met with a great affliction. in the death of my eldest brother— In Oct. the following year. I. hired to Josiah Stoal. an elderly Gent. risiding in Chenanga Co. N. Y.

He had heard something of a silver mine. in Harmony [p. 10] Susquehannah, Co, Pa. which had been discovered by the Spaniards. and had previous to my hiring with him. been endeavouring to find it: He placed me with the rest of his hands. digging for silver: At which. I continued to work. nearly a month, without success; when I prevailed with the old ~~gentlemen~~ gentleman to ⟨abandon⟩ ~~cease~~ the undertaking. ⟨T⟩hence arose the very prevalent story. of my having been a <u>money digger</u>—

Draft 1   **Draft 2**

the very prevalent story of my having been
a money digger.[65]

 During the time that I was thus employed I was put to board with a M[r] Isaac
Hale of that place, 'Twas there that I first
saw my wife, (his daughter) Emma Hale.
On the eighteenth of January Eighteen
hundred and twenty seven we were married while yet I was employed in the service
of M[r] Stoal. Owing to my still continuing
to assert that I had seen a vision, persecution still followed me, and so much was my
wife's father excited, that he was greatly opposed to our being married,[66] in so much
that he would not suffer us to be married at
his house, I was therefore under the necessity of taking her elsewhere, so we went,
and were married at ~~M[r] St~~ the house of M[r]
~~Stoal~~ ⟨Squire Tarbill [Zechariah Tarble].[67]
in South Bainbridge. Chenango County.
New York⟩. Immediately after my marriage
I left M[r] Stoals, and went to my father's
and farmed with him that season.

 At length the time arrived for obtaining the plates, the Urim and Thummin and
the breastplate, ~~In~~ ⟨On⟩ the twenty second
day of September, One thousand Eight
hundred and twenty seven, having went as
usual at the end of another year to the place
where they were deposited, the same heavenly messenger delivered them up to me
with this charge that I should be responsible for them. That if I should let them go
carelessly or ⟨through⟩ any neglect of mine
I should be cut off, but that if I would use
all my endeavours to preserve them untill
⟨he⟩ (the messenger) ~~called~~ should call for
them, they should be protected.

 I soon found out the reason why I had
received such strict charges to keep them
safe and why it was that the messenger
had said that when I had done what was
required at my hand, he would call for

Draft 3

While ~~being the~~ thus employed. I boarded
with Mʳ· Isaac Hale. where I first saw my
wife. (~~his daughter~~ Emma Hale.). On the
eighteenth ⟨day⟩ of Jan. 1827. we were married. I being yet in the employ of Mʳ· Stoal—

Persecution still followed me, and Mʳ·
Hale & family were very much opposed ~~of~~
⟨to⟩ ~~an intermarriage with me~~ ⟨to the intended marriage⟩. I was therefore under the
necessity. of taking her elsewhare: so we
went and were married. at the house of a
Esq Tarbill. in south. bainbridge. Chenango.
Co.. N Y ~~I~~ Immediately after my marriage. I
returned to my father's·. and farmed with
him that season—

At length the time arrived for obtaining the plates. Urim & Thummin. &
Breast plate.

On the 22ᵈ· day of Sepᵗ·. ~~1820~~⁶⁸ 1827.
having went as usual to the place where
they were deposited. the same havenly
Messenger delivered them up to me. with
the charge. that I should be responsible for
them—that if I should let them go carelessly. or through neglect. I should be cut
off. But if I should use all my endeavouers.
to preserve them. until he should call for
them. they should be protected. ~~the~~ The
reason why I had received such charges
soon became evident. [p. 11]

NOTES

65. JS acknowledged receiving wages of fourteen dollars per month from Stowell for his
assistance in treasure seeking. Additionally, JS
and his father purportedly were parties to a contract regarding shares in the distribution of any
valuables they found.ᵃ Several of JS's neighbors
recounted his participation in treasure-seeking
activities between 1823 and 1826 in locations rang-
ing from the Palmyra-Manchester area to
Harmony.ᵇ (*a.* [JS], Editorial, *Elders' Journal,* July
1838, 42–44; Isaac Hale et al., Agreement,
Harmony, PA, 1 Nov. 1825, in "An Interesting
Document," *Salt Lake Daily Tribune,* 23 Apr.
1880, [4]. *b.* Trial proceedings, Bainbridge, NY,
20 Mar. 1826, State of New York v. JS [J.P. Ct.
1826], in "The Original Prophet," *Fraser's Magazine,* Feb. 1873, 229–230; "Mormonism—No. II,"
Tiffany's Monthly, July 1859, 164; see also
Bushman, *Rough Stone Rolling,* 48–52.)

66. Isaac Hale wrote later that he told JS his
reasons for refusing to consent to the marriage,
"some of which were, that he was a stranger, and
followed a business that I could not approve,"
apparently referring to JS's involvement with treasure seeking. (Isaac Hale, Affidavit, 20 Mar. 1834,
in Howe, *Mormonism Unvailed,* 263.)

67. Porter, *Study of the Origins,* 75, 86n40.

68. TEXT: Possibly "~~1829~~".

Draft 1   **Draft 2**

them, for no sooner was it known that I
had them than the most strenious exertions
were used to get them from me.[69] Every
stratagem that could be ~~resorted~~ invented
was resorted to for that purpose. The persecution became more bitter and severe than
before, and multitudes were on the alert
continualy to get them from me if possible
but by the wisdom of God they remained
safe in my hands untill I had accomplished
by them what was required at my hand,
when according to arrangement the messenger called for them, I delivered them up
to him and he has them in his charge untill
this day, being the Second day of May,
One thousand Eight hundred and thirty
eight.[70]

The excitement however still continued, and rumour with her thousand tongues
was all the time employed in circulating
tales about my father's family and about
myself. If I were to relate a thousandth part
of them it would fill up volumes. The persecution however became so intolerable
that I was under the necessity of leaving
Manchester and going with my wife
⟨to⟩ Susquahanah County in the State of
Pensyllvania.[72] While preparing to start
(being very poor and the persecution so
heavy upon us that there was no probability that we would ever be otherwise) in
the midst of our afflictions we found a
friend in a Gentleman by name of Martin
Harris, who came to us and gave me fifty
dollars [p. 8] to assist us in our affliction,[73]
Mᵣ Harris was a resident of Palmyra township Wayne County in the State of New
York and a farmer of respectability. By this
timely aid was I enabled to reach the place
of my destination in Pensylvania, and immediately after my arrival there I commenced copying the characters of ~~all~~ the

Draft 3

No sooner was it known. that I had them than the most strenuous exertions. were made. to get them from me. persicution became more bitter; & multitudes were on the alert. to get them from me.— But by the wisdom of God. they remained safely in my hands. until. I accomplished all that was required, when the Messenger called for them, I delivered them to him in whose charge they ⟨now⟩ are now kept.

The excitement still continued. and rumor with her thousand tongues was busy in circulating them tales. about myself. and father's family.— and persecution. became so intolerable. that I was compeled to leave Manchester. and go to Susquehannah. Co. P^a.— While preparing to start. (being very poor.) in the midst of our afflictions. we found a friend in a Gen^t by the name of Martin Harris; who presented me^{71} with fifty dollars who Mr Harris was a farmer of respectibility. residing in Palmira. Wayne. Co. N Y. who presented me with fifty dollars, to assist us in our afflictions; by the assistance of which. I was enabled to reach to reach the place of my destination. in P^a, and commenced copying the characters of the plates.—

NOTES

69. Lucy Mack Smith related that JS hid the plates in the woods the day he obtained them and that a few days later, after retrieving them from their hiding place, he was attacked three times while carrying them home. Subsequently, she wrote, two more unsuccessful attempts were made to take the plates from the Smith property in Manchester. (Lucy Mack Smith, History, 1844–1845, bk. 5, [6], [12]; bk. 6, [2].)

70. JS worked on the initial composition of this text in late April and early May 1838, and James Mulholland incorporated the 1838 work into Draft 2 in 1839. (See JS, Journal, 30 Apr.–4 May 1838, in *JSP*, J1:263–264.)

71. TEXT: "me" written over "us" and then canceled with the rest of the passage.

72. Lucy Mack Smith indicated that in response to a request from JS and Emma Smith to the Hales, Emma's brother Alva Hale came to Manchester to help the couple move to Harmony, Pennsylvania. (Lucy Mack Smith, History, 1844–1845, bk. 6, [6].)

73. According to Lucy Mack Smith, JS asked her to approach Harris for financial assistance to enable JS to continue translation work. JS was preparing to move to Harmony when Harris met him and Alva Hale at a "public house" and gave him a bag of silver valued at fifty dollars "to do the Lords work with." In a later interview, Harris was quoted as saying that he encouraged JS to move to Harmony, paid JS's debts, and "furnished him money for his journey." (Lucy Mack Smith, History, 1844–1845, bk. 6, [3], [6]; "Mormonism— No. II," *Tiffany's Monthly,* July 1859, 170.)

Draft 1   **Draft 2**

plates. I copyed a considerable number of
them and by means of the Urim and Thummin I translated some of them which I did
between the time I arrived at the house of
my wife's father in the month of December,
and the February following. Some time in
this month of February the aforementioned
Mr Martin Harris came to our place, got
the characters which I had drawn off of the
plates and started with them to the City of
New York.[74] For what took place relative to
him and the characters I refer to his own
account of the circumstances as he related
them to me after his return which was as
follows. "I went to the City of New York
and presented the Characters which had
been translated, with the translation thereof, to Professor Anthony [Charles Anthon]
a gentleman celebrated for his literary attainments. Professor Anthony stated that
the translation was correct, more so than
any he had before seen translated from the
Egyptian.

I then shewed him those which were
not yet translated, and he said that they
were Egyptian, Chaldeak, Assyriac, and
Arabac, and he said that they were true
characters. He gave me a certificate certifying to the people of Palmyra that they were
true characters and that the translation of
such of them as had been translated was
also correct.

I took the Certificate and put it into
my pocket, and was just leaving the house,
when Mr Anthony called me back and
asked me how the young man found out
that there were gold plates in the place
where he found them. I answered that an
Angel of God had revealed it unto him. He
then said to me, let me see that certificate,
I accordingly took it out of my pocket and
gave it [to] him when he took it and tore it
to pieces, saying that there was no such

Draft 3

I copied quite a number of them—and ⟨translated them⟩ by the assistance. of the Urim & Thummin— Sometime in the month Feb. M⁻ Harris came, to our place. got the characters. and ⟨carried⟩ ~~started with~~ them to the City. of N. Y.

On his return. he gave me the following particulars.

"I went to the City of N. Y. and presented the characters. and the translation of them. to Professor Anthony. ~~a Gent~~ celebrated for his literary attainments. Proⁿ· Anthony [p. 12] stated, that the translation was ⟨more⟩ correct. ~~more so~~ than any he had before seen. translated from the Egytian.

I then showed him those which were not translated, and he said that they were Egyptian, Chaldean, Assyric, &~~and~~ Arabic, and that they were true characters.

He gave me a cirtificate. that they were true characters, and that the translation was correct.—

I took the certificate and was leaving the house, when ⟨he⟩ ~~M⁻ Anthony~~ called me back, and asked me how the Young man. ascertained that the gold plates, were in the place where he found them. I answered that an Angel of God had revealed it to him. He then said, let me see that certificate; I accordingly gave it to him; when he tore it in pieces. saying, there is now no such thing. as the ministering of Angles, and that if I would bring the plates to him.

74. Although this account does not indicate why Harris took the sample to New York City, other narratives suggest that his errand was to explore the possibilities for obtaining a translation and that JS began translating only after Harris returned without finding a translator. (Knight, Reminiscences, 3; Lucy Mack Smith, History, 1844–1845, bk. 6, [7]; JS History, ca. summer 1832, p. 15 herein.)

Martin Harris. Circa 1870s. In February 1828, Joseph Smith gave Martin Harris a transcript of characters from the gold plates and his translation of them, which Harris took to New York to show scholars. (Church History Library, Salt Lake City.)

Charles Anthon. Circa 1855–1865. Martin Harris met with Charles Anthon, professor of classical studies and literature at Columbia College. Harris's report of the meeting was included in Joseph Smith's history; see page 240 herein. (Courtesy Library of Congress, Washington DC.)

Draft 1   **Draft 2**

thing now as ministring of angels, and that
if I would bring the plates to him, he would
translate them.⟨*⟩ ⟨I informed him that
part of the plates were sealed, and that I
was forbidden to bring them, he replied
"I cannot read a sealed book".⟩ I left him
and went to D͏ͬ Mitchel [Samuel Mitchill]
who sanctioned what Professor Anthony
had said respecting both the Characters
and the translation."[75]

M͏ͬ Harris having returned from this
tour he left me and went home to Palmyra,
arranged his affairs, and returned again to
my house about the twelfth of April,
Eighteen hundred and twenty eight, and
commenced writing for me while I translated from the plates, which we continued
untill the fourteenth of June following, by
which time he had written one hundred
and sixteen ⟨pages⟩ of manuscript on fools-
cap paper.[76]

Some time after M͏ͬ Harris had began
to write for me, he began to tease me to
give him liberty to carry the writings home
and shew them, and desired of me that I
would enquire of the Lord through the
Urim and Thummin if he might not do so.
I did enquire, and the answer was that he
must not. However he was not satisfied
with this answer, and desired that I should
enquire again. I did so, and the answer was
as before. Still he could not be contented
but insisted that I should enquire once
more. ~~after~~ After much solicitation I again
enquired of the Lord, and permission was
granted him to have the writings on certain conditions, which were, that he shew
them only to his brother. Preserved Harris,
his own wife [Lucy Harris Harris], his father [Nathan Harris], and his mother
[Rhoda Lapham Harris], and a M͏ͬˢ [Mary
(Polly) Harris] Cobb a sister to his wife. In
accordance with this last answer I required

Draft 3

he would translate them. I informed him that part of the plates were sealed, and that I was forbidden to bring them.— He replied. "I cannot read a sealed book".— I left him, and went to Doc^t. Mitchell, who sanctioned, all that Pro. Anthony had said. respecting the characters & translations ~~of the plates~~.

M^r. Harris having returned ~~from his tour~~, went home to Palmira. ~~and~~ arranged his affairs, and returned again about the twelvth of April, 1828. and commenced writing, while I translated: which we continued, until the 14th of June; ~~at~~ having written. 216—pages of manuscript, on fools cap paper—

Sometime after M^r. Harris began to write, ~~for me~~ he requested me to give him liberty. [p. 13] to carry the writings home. and exhibit them. and desired me to enquire of the Lord, through the Urim & Thummin; if he might do so. I did enquire, and the answer was, that he must not.

He was not sattisfied with this answer, and desired, that I would enquire again. I did so, and the answer was as before.—

Still he could not be contented. and insisted. that I should enquire. once more.

After much solicitation, I again enquired of the Lord; and permission was granted. ~~was granted~~ on certain conditions:— which were that he should show them, only to his brother, (Preserved Harris,) his own wife, his father, his Mother, and ~~a~~ Mrs Cobb, a Sister of his wife. In accordance with this last answer, I required of him. that he should bind himself, in a covenant to me, in the most solemn manner;

NOTES

75. The origin of the Harris account quoted here is unknown. In none of the earlier accounts of this episode was there an indication that Harris took a copy of JS's translation of the characters to Anthon or Mitchill. Journalist James Gordon Bennett produced the earliest known written account of what Harris said about his trip to New York. According to Bennett, Harris told lawyer Charles Butler that Anthon "said that he did not know what language they were" and referred Harris to Mitchill. The latter "compared them with other hieroglyphics—thought them very curious—and they were the characters of a nation now extinct which he named." Harris then revisited Anthon, "who put some questions to him and got angry with Harris."^a According to two later accounts by Anthon, Mitchill referred Harris to Anthon, who concluded that the story of the gold plates was "a scheme to cheat the farmer of his money" and declined to give Harris a written statement.^b (a. Arrington, "James Gordon Bennett's 1831 Report on 'the Mormonites,'" 355; see also [James Gordon Bennett], "Mormon Religion— Clerical Ambition—Western New York—The Mormonites Gone to Ohio," *Morning Courier and New-York Enquirer* [New York City], 1 Sept. 1831, [2]; and Bennett, "Read This I Pray Thee," 212– 216. b. Charles Anthon, New York, to Eber D. Howe, Painesville, OH, 17 Feb. 1834, in Howe, *Mormonism Unvailed,* 270–272; Charles Anthon, New York, to Thomas Winthrop Coit, New Rochelle, NY, 3 Apr. 1841, in Clark, *Gleanings by the Way,* 233–238.)

76. Emma Smith later stated that she also served as a scribe for the translation of the Book of Mormon, as did her brother Reuben Hale. Their inscriptions were likely included in this earliest manuscript, along with Harris's. On the length of the manuscript, see 15n59 herein. (Joseph Smith III, "Last Testimony of Sister Emma," *Saints' Herald,* 1 Oct. 1879, 289–290.)

Draft 1   **Draft 2**

of him that he should bind himself in a
covenant to me [p. 9] in the most solemn
manner that he would not do otherwise
than had been directed. He did so. He
bound himself as I required of him, took
the writings and went his way.[77]

Notwithstanding however the great
restrictions which he had been laid under,
and the solemnity of the covenant which
he had made with me, he did shew them to
others and by stratagem they got them
away from him, and they never have been
recovered nor obtained back again untill
this day.[78]

In the mean time while Martin Harris
was gone with the writings, I went to visit
my father's family at Manchester. I continued there for a short season and then
returned to my place in Pensylvania.[79]
Immediately after my return home I was
walking out a little distance, when Behold
the former heavenly messenger appeared
and handed to me the Urim and Thummin
again (for it had been taken from me in
consequence of my having wearied the Lord
in asking for the privilege of letting Martin
Harris take the writings which he lost by
transgression) and I enquired of the Lord
through them and obtained the folowing
revelation.

Revelation to Joseph Smyth jr, given
July 1828 concerning certain manuscripts
on the first part of the book of Mormon
which had been taken from the possession of Martin Harris.[80]

The works, and the designs, and the
purposes of God, cannot be frustrated
neither can they come to nought, for
God doth not walk in crooked: ⟨paths:⟩
neither doth he turn to the right hand
nor to the left; neither doth he vary from
that which he hath said: therefore his

Draft 3

that he would do as directed— He bound himself, as I required of him. took the writings, and went his way.

Notwithstanding the great restrictions, that had been laid upon him; and the solemn covenent, which he had made with me; he did show them to others; and by stratagem, they were taken from him: and they never have been recovered—

In the meantime, I went to visit my father's family, at Manchester, After returning to my place in Pᵃ·, I was walking out, when behold the former heavenly Messenger appeared, to and handed to me the Urim & Thummin again, (for they had been taken from me because of having wearied. the Lord in asking, that Martin Harris might take the writings, that ⟨which⟩ he lost by transgression)— [p. 14] And I enquired of the Lord. through them, and obtained the following Revelation.

The works, and the designs. and the purposes, of God cannot be frustrated; neither can they come to nought: for God does doth not walk in crooked paths, neither doth he turn to the right hand, or to the left; neither doth he vary from that which he hath said: therefore

NOTES

77. Lucy Mack Smith said that Harris "bound himself in a written covenant of the most solemn nature." (Lucy Mack Smith, History, 1845, 127.)

78. In his preface to the first edition of the Book of Mormon, JS wrote: "I would inform you that I translated, by the gift and power of God, and caused to be written, one hundred and sixteen pages, the which I took from the Book of Lehi, which was an account abridged from the plates of Lehi, by the hand of Mormon; which said account, some person or persons have stolen and kept from me, notwithstanding my utmost exertions to recover it again." (Preface to Book of Mormon, 1830 ed., iii.)

79. According to Lucy Mack Smith's account, JS traveled from Harmony to Manchester to ascertain why Harris had not returned to Harmony or communicated with JS after an absence of "nearly three weeks." JS returned to Harmony after learning that Harris lost the Book of Mormon manuscript. (Lucy Mack Smith, History, 1845, 127.)

80. Revelation, July 1828, in Doctrine and Covenants 30, 1835 ed. [D&C 3]. James Mulholland copied this revelation—and all revelations he inscribed in Draft 2 of the history—from the 1835 edition of the Doctrine and Covenants.

Draft 1   **Draft 2**

paths are strait and his course is one eternal round.

Remember remember that it is not the
work of God that is frustrated, but the
work of men: for although a man may
have many revelations, and have power
to do many mighty works, yet, if he
boasts in his own strength, and sets at
nought the counsels of God, and follows
after the dictates of his own will, and
carnal desires, he must fall and incur the
vengeance of a just God upon him.

Behold, you have been entrusted with
these things, but how strict were your
commandments; and remember, also,
the promises which were made to you, if
you did not transgress them; and behold
how oft you have transgressed the commandments and laws of God, and have
gone on in the persuasions of men: for
behold you should not have feared man
more than God, although men set at
nought the councils of God, and despise
his words, yet you should have been
faithful and he would have extended
his arm, and supported you against all
the fiery darts of the adversary; and he
would have been with you in every time
of trouble.

Behold thou art Joseph, and thou wast
chosen to do the work of the Lord, but
because of transgression, if thou art not
aware thou wilt fall, but remember God
is merciful: therefore repent of that
which thou hast done, which is contrary
to the commandment which I gave you,
and thou art still chosen and art again
called to the work: except thou do this,
thou shalt be delivered up and become as
other men, and have no more gift.

And when thou deliveredst up that
which God ⟨gave⟩ thee sight and power

Draft 3

his paths are straight, and his course ~~is~~ ⟨is⟩ one eternal round.

Remember, remember, that it is not the work of God, that is frustrated, but the works of men: for although a man may have many revelations. and have power to do many mighty works,— Yet if he boast in his own strength. and set at nought, the counsels of God; and follow after the dictates of his own will, and carnal desires. he must fall and incur the vengeance of a just God ~~upon him~~.

Behold you have been intrusted, with these things; but how strict were your commandments, ~~and remember.~~ and remember also. the promises, ~~that~~ which were made ~~un~~to you, if you did not transgress them; and behold how oft you have transgressed the commandments, and laws of God: and have gone on in the persuasions of men; for behold you should not fear~~ed~~ men. more than God; although men set at nought the counsels of God; and despise his words: yet you should have been faithful, and he would have extended his arm, and supported you, against all the fiery darts of the. Adversary; and he would have been with you. in every time of trouble.

Behold thou art Joseph. and thou wast chosen to do the work of the Lord; but because [p. 15] of transgression, if thou art not ⟨cautious⟩ ~~aware~~, thou wilt fall; but remember God is merciful. Therefore repent of that which thou hast done. which is contrary to the commandment. which I gave, and thou art still chosen. and art again called, to the work. Except thou do this, thou shalt be delivered up, and become as other men. ~~and have no more~~ ⟨having no⟩ gift.

And when thou deliverdest up, that which God gave ~~you~~ thee sight and power

Draft 1   **Draft 2**

to translate, thou deliveredst up that
which was sacred, into the hands of a
wicked man, who has set at nought the
counsels of God, and has broken the most
sacred promises, which were made before
God, and depended upon his own judgment, [p. 10] a[nd] [boas]ted in his ow[n]
wisdom and this is the reason why thou
has[t][81] lost thy privileges for a season,
for thou hast suffered the counsel of thy
director to be trampled upon from the
beginning.

Nevertheless my work shall go forth,
for, inasmuch as the knowledge of a
Saviour has come unto the world,
through the testimony of the jews, even
so shall the knowledge of a Saviour come
⟨un⟩to my people; and to the Nephites,
and the Jacobites, and the Josephites,
and the Zoramites, through the testimony of their fathers; and this testimony
shall come to the knowledge of the
Lamanites, and the Lemuelites, and the
Ishmaelites, who dwindled in unbelief
because of the iniquities of their fathers,
whom the Lord has suffered to destroy
their brethren the Nephites, because of
their ~~unbelief~~ iniquities and their abominations: and for this very purpose are
these plates preserved which contain
these records, that the promises of the
Lord might be fulfilled, which he made
to his people; and that the Lamanites
might come to a knowledge of their
fathers, and that they might know the
promises of the Lord, and that they
might believe the gospel, and rely upon
the merits of Jesus Christ, and be glorified through faith in his name; and that
through their repentance they might be
saved:

}Amen.

Draft 3

to translate; thou deliverdest up that which was sacred, into the hands of ⟨a⟩ wicked man; who has set at nought the counsels of God; and broken the most sacred promises, which were made before God, and depended upon his own judgment. and boasted in his own wisdom; and this is the reason why thou hast lost thy privileges for a season; for thou hast suffered the counsel of thy director, to be trampled upon from. the beginning.

Nevertheless my work shall go forth, for inasmuch as the knowledge of a Saviour, has come unto ⟨the world,⟩ through the testimony of the Jews; even so shall the knowledge of a Saviour. come unto my people, and to the Nephites, and to the Jacobites, and the Josephites, and the Zoramites, through the testimony of their fathers, and this testimony shall come ~~unto~~ the knowledge, of ⟨the⟩ Lamanites, and the Lemulites, and the Ishmaelites, who ⟨dwindled⟩ ~~dwindled~~ in unbelief, because of the iniquities, of their father's, whom the Lord has suffered to destroy their bretheren, the Nephites, because of their eniquities, and abominations; & for this very purpose, are these plates preserved, containing these records; that the promises of the Lord might be fulfilled, which he made to his people; and that the Lamenites, might come to a knowledge of their fathers, and that they might know the prom[i]ses of the Lord; and that they ~~might~~ believe the Gospel, and rely on the merits, of[82] Jesus Christ, and be glorified through faith in his name, and that through their repentance, they might be saved. [p. 16]

NOTES

81. TEXT: The previous four sets of brackets supply text obscured by residue from the adhesive wafers explained in 253n83 herein. Text supplied based on the 1835 edition of the Doctrine and Covenants.

82. TEXT: The remaining text on this page was written vertically up the left margin, possibly to keep the text of the revelation on one page.

Draft 1

Draft 2

After I had obtained the above revelation, both the plates, and the Urim and Thummin were taken from me again, but in a few days they were returned to me.⟨***⟩ ⟨when I enquired of the Lord, and the Lord said thus unto me⟩ ⟨***⟩[83]

⟨*** Revelation given to Joseph Smith Jr May 1829 informing him of the alteration of the manuscript of the forepart of the Book of Mormon.

1 Now, behold I say unto you, that because you delivered up those writings which you had power given ⟨unto⟩ you to translate, by the means of the Urim and Thummin, into the hands of a wicked man, you have lost them; and you also lost your gift at the same time, and your mind became darkened; nevertheless, it is now restored unto you again, therefore see that you are faithful and continue on unto the finishing of the remainder of the work of translation as you have begun: do not run faster, or labor more than you have strength and means provided to enable you to translate, but be diligent unto the end: pray always, that you may come off conqueror; yea, ~~and~~ that you may conquer Satan, and that you may escape the hands of the servants of Satan, that do uphold his work. Behold they have sought to destroy you; yea, even the man in whom you have trusted, has sought to destroy you. And for this cause I said, that he is a wicked man, for he has sought to take away the things wherewith you have been intrusted and he has also sought to destroy your gift, and because you have delivered the writings into his hands, behold wicked men have taken them from you: therefore, you have delivered them up: yea, that which was sacred unto wickedness. And behold Satan has put it

Draft 3

After I had obtained the above revelation, both the plates and the Urim and Thummin were taken from me again; but in a few days they were returned to me, when I enquired of the Lord. and ~~the Lord~~ ⟨he⟩ said thus unto me.

1 Now ~~I~~ Behold I say unto you, that because you delivered up those writings which you had power given unto you to translate, by the means of the Urim and Thummin; into the hands of a wicked man, you have lost them, and you also lost your gift at the same time, and your mind became darkened; nevertheless it is now restored to you again. Therefore see that you are faithful and continue on unto the finishing of the remainder of the work of translation. as you have begun; Do not run faster or labor more than you have strength and means provided ~~you~~ to enable you to translate, but be diligent unto the end; pray always that you may come off conquerer, yea that you may conquer Satan and that you may escape the hands of the Servants of Satan. that do uphold his works. Behold they have sought to destroy you, yea even the man in whom you have trusted has sought to destroy you; And for this cause I said ⟨~~that~~⟩ 'he is a wicked man,['] for he has sought to take away the things wherewith you have been intrusted; and he has also sought to destroy your gift, and because you have delivered the writings into his hands, behold wicked men have taken them from you: Therefore you have delivered them up, yea; that which was sacred unto wickedness. And behold satan has put it

NOTES

83. TEXT: The asterisks key to a four-page insertion attached by six adhesive wafers to the top of page 11 of Draft 2. The four pages are transcribed herein immediately following the inserted asterisks. The insertion is in the handwriting of James Mulholland and contains a copy of Revelation, ca. Apr. 1829, in Doctrine and Covenants 36, 1835 ed. [D&C 10]. At the top of the first page of the insertion, Mulholland noted where in the manuscript this text was to be inserted: "N.B. This Revelation will read, after the interlined words in page 11 & line 17ᵗʰ—." The text, which he copied from the 1835 edition of the Doctrine and Covenants, includes numerous changes in wording from earlier versions of the revelation. Mulholland's insertion of the revelation at this point and his contextualization of its receipt—an explanation apparently composed under the direction of JS—contradict the May 1829 dating of the revelation given in both the 1833 Book of Commandments and the 1835 Doctrine and Covenants and repeated here. Since the first two pages of the revelation are missing from the earliest extant copy of the revelation, in Revelation Book 1, it is impossible to know what specific date may have been listed in that source, but it was situated among revelations dated April 1829, and the index of Revelation Book 1 gives the year as 1829. Although the brief explanation that Mulholland penned in the history suggests that the revelation originated in summer 1828, content analysis suggests that at least some of the material originated in about April 1829. (Doctrine and Covenants 36, 1835 ed.; Book of Commandments 9; Revelation Book 1, pp. 11–12, 207, in *JSP*, MRB:13–15, 385 [D&C 10].)

Composition of Joseph Smith's history in large volume (Draft 2). Residue from six adhesive wafers is found at the top of page 11 of the large history manuscript. The flour-based adhesives originally secured a four-page insertion to the page, and asterisks indicate where the material was to be inserted. The insertion, written by James Mulholland, was a copy of a circa April 1829 revelation (now D&C 10) directing Joseph Smith not to retranslate the portion of the gold plates for which the original translation had been lost. The revelation copy, which matches the text found in the 1835 edition of the Doctrine and Covenants, was later separated from the history but is still archived with the volume. Handwriting of James Mulholland. JS History, vol. A-1, p. 11 (transcribed on pp. 250–252 herein), Church History Library, Salt Lake City. (Photograph by Welden C. Andersen.)

Revision pinned in 1838–circa 1841 history draft (Draft 3). Howard Coray pinned a slip of paper to page 36 of the history he inscribed. The slip of paper noted that when Joseph Smith and Oliver Cowdery discussed the nascent Latter-day Saint movement with Samuel Smith, they appealed to the Bible for support—a detail Coray had not included in the original draft of the adaptation. An asterisk on the manuscript page (obscured in the photograph by the slip of paper) indicates where the insertion was to be placed in the history. The phrase appears in its proper place in Coray's fair copy. Handwriting of Howard Coray. JS History, 1838–ca. 1841, p. 36 (transcribed on pp. 297–299 herein), Church History Library, Salt Lake City. (Photograph by Welden C. Andersen.)

Draft 1   **Draft 2**

into their hearts to alter the words which
you have caused to be written, or which
you have translated, which have gone out
of your hands; and behold I say unto
you, that because they have altered the
words, they read contrary ~~to~~ from that
which you translated and caused to be
written; and on this wise the devil has
sought to lay a cunning plan, that he
might destroy this work; for he has put it
into their hearts to do this, that by lying
they may say they have caught you in the
words which you have pretended to
translate.

2 Verily I say unto you, that I will not
suffer that Satan shall accomplish his
evil design in this thing, for behold he
has put it into their hearts to get thee to
tempt the Lord thy God, in asking to
translate it over again, and then behold
they say, and think in their hearts, we
will see if God has given him power to
translate, if so he will also give him power
again; and if God giveth him power
again [p. [1]] or if he translate again, or
in other words, if he bringeth forth the
same words, behold we have altered
them: therefore they will not agree, and
we will say that he has lied in his words,
and that he has no gift, and that he has
no power: therefore we will destroy him,
and also the work, and we will do this
that we may not be ashamed in the end,
and that we may get glory of the world.

3 Verily, verily I say unto you, that
Satan has great hold upon their hearts
he stirrith them up to iniquity against
that which is good, and their hearts are
corrupt and full of wickedness and
abominations, and they love darkness
rather than light because their deeds are
evil: therefore they will not ask of me.
Satan stirreth them up, that he may lead

Draft 3

into their hearts to alter the words,
which you have caused to be written, or
which you have translated; which have
gone out of your hands, and behold I say
unto you that because they have altered
the words they read contrary from that
which you translated. [p. 17] and caused
to be written; and on this wise the Devil
has sought to lay a cunning plan, that he
might destroy this work; for he has put it
into their hearts to do this, that by lying,
they may say, they have caught you in
the words which you have pretended to
translate.

2 Verily, I say unto you that I will not
suffer that Satan shall accomplish his
evil design in this, thing, for behold he
has put it into their hearts to get theee to
tempt the Lord thy god, in asking to
translate it over again; and then behold
they say and think in their Hearts, we
will see if god has given him power to
translate; if so he will give him power ~~to
translate~~ again, or if he translate again,
or in other words, if he bring⟨eth⟩ forth
the same words; behold we have altered
them, therefore they will not agree, <u>and
we</u> will say that he has lied in his <u>words</u>,
and that he has no gift, and that he has
no power: therefore ⟨we⟩ will destroy
him, ⟨and⟩ also the work; and we will do
this, that we may not be ashamed in the
end, and that we may get glolry of the
world.

3 Verily, verily. I say unto you, that
Satan has great hold upon their hearts;
he stireth them up to iniquity against
that which is good, and their hearts are
corrupt and full of wickedness, and
abomanations, and they love darkness
rather than light. because their deeds are
evil; therefore they will not ask of me.
Satan Stireth them up, that he may lead

Draft 1   **Draft 2**

their souls to destruction. And thus he
has laid a cunning plan, thinking to destroy the work of God, but I will require
this at their hands, and it shall turn to
their shame and condemnation in the
day of judgement; yea, he stirreth up
their hearts to anger against this work,
yea, he saith unto them, deceive and lie
in wait to catch, that ye may destroy: behold this is no harm, and thus he flattereth them and telleth them that it is no
sin to lie, that they may catch a man in a
lie, that they may destroy him, and thus
he flattereth them and leadeth them
along, untill he draggeth their souls
down to hell; and thus he causeth them
to catch themselves in their own snare;
and thus he goeth up and down, to and
fro in the earth, seeking to destroy the
souls of men.

4 Verily, verily I say unto you, wo be
unto him that lyeth to decieve because
he supposeth that another lieth to
decieve, for such are not exempt from
the justice of God.

5 Now behold they altered those
words, because Satan saith unto them,
He hath deceived you: and thus he flattereth them away to do iniquity, to get
thee to tempt the Lord thy God.

6 Behold I say unto you, that you shall
not translate again those words which
have gone forth out of your hands; for
behold they shall not accomplish their
evil designs in lying against those words.

For behold, if you should bring forth
the same words, they will say, that you
have lied; that you have pretended to
translate, but that you have contradicted
yourself: and behold they will publish
this, and Satan will harden the hearts of
the people to stir them up to anger

Draft 3

their souls to destruction. And thus he
has laid a cunning ~~palan th~~ plan, thinking to destroy the work of God; but I
will requ[i]re this at their hands, and it
shall turn to their shame and condemnation in the day of judgement. Yea he
stireth up their hearts, to anger against
this work; yea he saith unto them decieve,
and lie in wait to catch that ⟨~~ye may
decieve~~⟩ ~~you may decieve~~ ye may destroy:
behold this is no harm, and thus he f[l]at-
tereth them, and telleth them that it is
no sin to lie that they may catch a man
in a lie. that they may destroy him; and
thus ~~he~~ he flattereth them ~~also~~ and leadeth them along, until he drageth their
souls down to hell, and thus he causeth
them to catch themselves in their own
Snare, and thus he goeth up and down
to and fro, in the earth, seeking to destroy the souls of men.

4 Verily, Verily, I say unto you, wo be
unto him that [p. 18] lyeth to deceive,
because he supposeth that another lyeth
to decieve; for such are not exempt from
the Justice of God.

5 Now behold they altered those
words. because satan saith unto them;
He hath decieved you, and thus he flattereth them away to do iniquity, to get
thee to tempt the Lord thy God.

6 Behold I say unto you, that you shall
not translate again those words which
have gone forth out of ⟨your⟩ ~~your~~ hands,
for behold they shall not accomplish
their evil designs in lying against those
words, for behold if you ⟨should⟩ bring
forth the same words they will say that
you have lied, that you have pretended to
translate, but that you have contradicted
yourself. And behold they will publish
this, and satan will harden the hearts of
the people, to stir them up to anger

Draft 1   **Draft 2**

against you, that they will not believe
my words. Thus Satan thinketh to over-
power your testimony in this generation;
that the work may not come forth in this
generation: but behold here is wisdom,
and because I shew unto you wisdom,
and give you commandments concerning these things, what you shall do, shew
it not unto the world untill you have accomplished the work of translation.

7 Marvel not that I said unto you here
is wisdom, show it not unto the [p. [2]]
world that you may be preserved. Behold
I do not say that you shall not show it
unto the righteous, but as you cannot
always judge the righteous, or as you
cannot always tell the wicked from the
righteous, therefore I say unto you, hold
your peace untill I shall see fit to make all
things known unto the world concerning the matter.

8 And now verily I say unto you, that
an account of those things that you have
written, which have gone out of your
hands, are engraven upon the plates of
Nephi: yea, and you remember, it was
said in those writings, that a more particular account was given of these things
upon the plates of Nephi.

9 And now, because the account
which is engraven upon the plates of
Nephi, is more particular concerning the
things which in my wisdom I would
bring to the knowledge of the people in
this account therefore you shall translate the engravings which are on the
plates of Nephi down even till you come
to the reign of King Benjamin, or untill
you come to that which you have translated, which you have retained, and behold you shall publish it as the record of
Nephi, and thus I will confound those
who have altered my words. I will not

Draft 3

against you, that they will not beli[e]ve
my words: Thus satan thinketh to over-
power your testimony in this generation,
that the work may not come forth in this
Generation; but behold here is wisdom,
and because I show unto you wisdom,
and give you commandments concerning these things. what you shall do; show
it not unto the world, until you have accomplished the work of translation.

7 Marvel not that I said unto you, here
is wisdom, show it not unto the world;
that you may be preserved. Behold I
do not say that you shall not show it
unto the rightious, but as you cannot
always judge the righteous. or as you
cannot always tell the wicked from the
righteous; therefore, I say unto you, hold
your peace until I shall see fit to make all
things known unto the world; concerning ⟨this⟩ matter.

8 And now verily, I say unto you, that
an account of those things that you have
written, which have gone out of your
hands, are engraven upon the plates of
Nephi; Yea and you remember it was
said in those writings, that a more particular account was given of these things
upon the plates of Nephi.

9 And now because ~~of~~ the account.
which is engraven upon the plates of
Nephi, is more particular concerning the
things which in my wisdom I would
bring to the knowledge of the people; in
this account therefore, you Shall translate the engravings [p. 19] which are on
the plates of Nephi, down even till you
come to the reign of King Benjamin, or
until you come to that which you have
translated ⟨that⟩ ~~which~~ you have retained:
and behold you shall publish it as the record of Nephi, and thus I will confound
those who have altered my words. I will

Draft 1   **Draft 2**

that suffer that they shall destroy my
work; yea, I will show unto them that
my wisdom is greater than the cunning
of the devil.

10 Behold they have only got a part, or
an abridgement of the account of Nephi.
Behold there are many ~~writings~~ things
engraven on the plates of Nephi, which
do throw greater views upon my gospel,
therefore, it is wisdom in me, that you
should translate this first part of the engravings of Nephi, and send forth in this
work. And behold all the remainder of
this work does contain all those parts
of my gospel which my holy Phrophets,
yea and also my disciples desired in their
prayers should come forth unto this people. And I said unto them, that it should
be granted unto them according to their
faith in their prayers; yea, and this was
their faith, that my gospel which I gave
unto them, that they might preach in
their days might come unto their brethren, the Lamanites, and also all that
had become Lamanites, because of their
dissensions.

11 Now this is not all, their faith in
their prayers were, that this gospel
should be made known also, if it were
possible that other nations should possess this land, and thus they did leave a
blessing upon this land in their prayers,
that whosoever should believe in this
gospel, in this land, might have eternal
life; yea, that it might be free unto all of
whatsoever nation, kindred, tongues[84] or
people, they may be.

12 And now behold according to their
faith in their prayers, will I bring this
part of my gospel to the knowledge of
my people. Behold I do not bring it to
destroy that which they have received,
but to build it up.

Draft 3

not suffer that they shall destroy my work, yea I will show unto them, that my wisdom is greater than the cunning of the Devil.

10 Behold they have only ~~gotten~~ a part ~~of~~ or an abridgement, of the account of Nephi; behold there are many things engraven on the plates of Nephi, which do throw greater views upon my gospel; therefore it is wisdom in me, that you should translate this first part of the engravings of Nephi, and send forth in this work: And behold all the remainder of this work, does contain all those parts of my gospel, which my holy prophets, yea and also my disciples desired in their prayers should come forth unto this people; and I said unto them, that it should be granted unto them, according to their faith in their prayers; yea and this was their faith; that my gospel which I gave unto them that they might preach ~~in~~ in their days, might come unto their bretheren, the Lamanites; and also all that had become Lamanites, because of their dessentions.

⟨11⟩ Now this is not all; their faith in their prayers were, that this Gospel should be made known also, If it were possible that other nations should possess this Land; and thus they did leave a blessing upon this land in their praye[r]s, that whosoever should beleve in this Gospel, in this land, might have eternal life. Yea that it might be free unto all, of whatsoever nation, kindred, tounge, or people, they may be.

12 And now behold, according to their faith in their prayers, will I bring this part of my gospel to the knowledge of my p[e]ople; behold I do not bring it to destroy what they have recieved but to build it up. [p. 20]

84. TEXT: Possibly "tongue,". The 1835 edition of the Doctrine and Covenants has "tongue".

Draft 1   **Draft 2**

13 And for this cause have I said, if this generation harden not their hearts, I will establish my Church among them. Now I do not say ⟨*⟩ [p. [3]]⁸⁵ * this to destroy my church, but I say this to build up my Church, therefore whosoever belongeth to my Church need not fear, for such shall inherit the kingdom of heaven: but it is they who do not fear me, neither keep my commandments, but buildeth up Churches unto themselves, to get gain; yea, and all those that do wickedly and buildeth up the kingdom of the devil; yea, verily, verily I say unto you that it is they that I will disturb, and cause to tremble and shake to the Centre.

14 Behold I am Jesus Christ, the son of God: I came unto my own and my own received me not. I am the light which shineth in the darkness, and the darkness comprehendeth it not. I am he who said, other sheep have I which are not of this fold, unto my disciples, and many there were that understood me not.

15 And I will shew unto this people, that I had other sheep, and that they were a branch of the house of Jacob: and I will bring to light their marvelous works, which they did in my name, yea, and I will also bring to light my gospel which was ministered unto them, and behold they shall not deny that which you have recieved, but they shall build it up, and shall bring to light the true points of my doctrine: yea, and the only doctrine which is in me; and this I do, that I may establish my gospel, that there may not be so much contention: yea, Satan doth stir up the hearts of the people to contention, concerning the points of my doctrine; and in these things they do err, for they do wrest the scriptures, and do not understand them: therefore

Draft 3

13 And for this cause have I said, if this generation harden not their hearts, I will establish my church among them. Now I do not say this to destroy my Church, but I say this to build up my church: Therefore whosoever belongeth to my church, need not fear, for such shall inherit the kingdom of heaven; but it is those who do not fear me; neither keep my commandments, but build up churches unto themselves, to get gain; yea, and all those that do wickedly, and build up the kingdom of the devil; Yea verily, verily, I say unto you, that it is those, whom I will disturb, and cause to to tremble; and shake to the center.

14 Behold, I am Jesus Christ the Son of God. I came unto my own, but my own recieved me not. I am the light; that shineth in darkness, and the darkness comprehendeth it not. I am he who said, other sheep have I, who are not of this fold unoto my disciples; and many there were, that understood ~~me not~~ me not

15 And I will shew unto this people, that I had other Sheep, and that they were a branch of the house of Jacob, and I will ~~will~~ bring to light their ~~marvellous~~ marvellous works, which they did in my name; yea ~~&,~~ and I will also bring to light my gospel, which was ministered unto them; and behold they shall not deny what you have received, but shall build it up, and bring to light the true points of my doctrine. Yea and the only doctrine which is in me. and this I do. that I may establish my gospel. that there may not be so much contention. Yea Satan doth stir up the hearts of the people. to contention, concerning the points of my doctrine; and in these things they do err, for they do wrest the Scriptures, and do not understand them. Therefore,

NOTES

85. TEXT: The text on the fourth page of the insertion (described in 253n83 herein) is upside down relative to the text on the third page. The asterisks at the bottom of page 3 and the top of page 4 were likely intended to indicate continuity.

Draft 1   **Draft 2**

I will unfold unto them this great mystery, for behold I will gather them as a hen gathereth her chickens under her wings, if they will not harden their hearts: yea, if they will come, they may, and partake of the waters of life freely.

16 Behold this is my doctrine: whosoever repenteth and cometh unto me, the same is my Church: whosoever declareth more or less than this the same is not of me, but is against me: therefore, he is not of my Church.

17 And now behold whosoever is of my church, and endureth of my church to the end, him will I establish upon my rock, and the gates of hell shall not prevail against them.

18 And now remember the words of him, who is the life and the light of the world, your Redeemer, your Lord and your God. Amen. [4 lines blank] [p. [4]])[86]

I did not however go immediately to translating, but went to laboring with my hands upon a small farm which I had purchased of my wife's father, in order to provide for my family.[87] In the month of February, Eighteen hundred and twenty nine my father came to visit us at which time I received the following revelation for him.

Revelation to Joseph Smith Sen.[r.] given February 1829.[88]

Now, behold, a marvellous work is about to come forth among the children of men, therefore, O ye that embark in the service of God, see that you serve him with all your heart, might, mind and strength, that you may stand blameless before God at the last day: therefore, if ye have desires to serve God, ye are called to the work, for behold the field is white already to harvest, and lo, he that thrusteth in his sickle with his might,

Draft 3

I will unfold unto them. ~~the~~ this great [p. 21] mystery; for behold, I will gather them, ⟨as⟩ a hen gathereth her chickens under her wings, if they will not harden their hearts: Yea if they will come they may, and partake of the waters of Life freely.

16 Behold this is my doctrine. whosoever repenteth and cometh unto me, the same is my Church; whosoever declareth more or less than this, the same is not of me, but is against me; therefore he is not of my Church.

17 And now behold whosoever is of my Church, and endureth of my church to the end, him will I establish upon my rock, and the gates of hell Shall not prevail against him. And now remember the words of him, who is the life and the light of the world; your Redeemer, your Lord, and your God— Amen

I did not, however immediately commence translating, but tilled a small farm, which I purchased of my father in law; to provide for my family, In the month of Feb. 1829, my father came to visit ~~me~~ me, at which time I recieved the following Revelation for him.

Now behold, a marvelous work, is about to come forth among the children of men; therefore, O ye that embark in the service of God, see that you serve him with all your heart, might, mind, and strength; that you may stand blameless before God at the last day. Therefore if ye have desires to serve God, ye are called to work. for behold the field is white all ready to harvest and lo he that thrusteth in his Sickle with his might,

NOTES

86. TEXT: This is the final page of the long insertion described in 253n83 herein.

87. JS purchased about thirteen acres of land in Harmony, Pennsylvania, from Isaac Hale. (Isaac Hale to JS, Agreement, Harmony, PA, 6 Apr. 1829, JS Collection, CHL; Isaac and Elizabeth Hale, Indenture, 25 Aug. 1830, JS Collection, CHL.)

88. Revelation, Feb. 1829, in Doctrine and Covenants 31, 1835 ed. [D&C 4].

Draft 1   **Draft 2**

the same layeth up in store that he perish
not, but bringeth salvation to his soul,
and faith, hope, ~~and~~ charity, and love,
with an eye single to the glory of God,
qualifies him for the work.

Remember faith, virtue, knowledge,
temperance, patience, brotherly kindness, Godliness, charity, humility, diligence.— Ask and ye shall recieve, knock
and it shall be opened unto you. Amen.

The following I applied for at the request of the aforementioned Martin Harris
and obtained.

Revelation given March, 1829.[89]

Behold I say unto you, that as my servant Martin Harris has desired a witness
at my hand, that you, my servant Joseph
Smith Jr., have got the plates of which
you have testified and borne record that
you ⟨have⟩ received of me: and now behold, this shall you say unto him, He
who spake unto you, said unto you, I the
Lord am God, and ~~gave~~ ⟨have given⟩
these things unto you my servant Joseph
Smith Jr. and ⟨have⟩ commanded you
that you shall stand as a witness of these
things, and I have caused you that you
should enter into a cove[p. 11]nant with
me that you should not shew them except to those persons to whom I command you; and you have no power over
them except I grant it unto you. And you
have a gift to translate the plates; and
this is the first gift that I bestowed upon
you, and I have commanded you that
you pretend to no other gift untill my
purposes is fulfilled in ~~you~~ this; for I will
grant unto you no other gift untill it is
finished.

Verily I say unto you, that wo shall
come unto the inhabitants of the earth if
they will not hearken unto my words: for

Draft 3

the same layeth up in Store that he perish not but bringeth Salvation to his soul
and faith hope charity, and Love with
[p. 22] an eye single to the glory of God;
Qualifies him for the work. Remember,
faith, virtue, knowledge, Temperance,
patience, brotherly kindness, godliness,
Charity, humility, diligence— Ask and
ye shall recieve, knock and it shall be
opened ⟨un⟩to you.

Amen.

At the request of the afore mentioned
Martin Harriss, I applied for the following
Revelation for him.

Behold I say unto you, that as my servant Martin Harris, has desired a witness
at my hand that you, my Ser^t· Joseph
Smith J^r· have the plates of which you
have testified & borne record, that you
have recieved of me; & now behold, this
shall you say unto him, he who spake
unto you said; I, the Lord am God, and
have given these things unto you my
serv^t· Joseph Smith J^r· and have commanded you, that you shall stand as a
witness of these things; & I have caused
you, that you should enter into a covenant with me, that you should not show
them except to those persons to whom I
commanded you. & you have no power
over them, except I grant unto you, and
you have a gift to translate the plates,
and this is the first gift I have bestowed
upon you; and I have commanded you,
that you pretend to no other gift, until
my purpose is fulfilled in this, for I will
grant unto you no other gift until it is
finished.

Verily, I say unto you, that wo shall
come unto the inhabitants of the earth, if
they will not harken unto my words; for

NOTES

89. Revelation, Mar. 1829, in Doctrine and
Covenants 32, 1835 ed. [D&C 5].

Draft 1   **Draft 2**

hereafter you shall be ordained and go
forth and deliver my words unto the
children of men, Behold if they will not
believe my words, they would not believe
you, my servant Joseph, if it were possible that you could show them all these
things which I have committed unto
you. O this unbelieving and stiffnecked
generation mine anger is kindled against
is kindled a them.

Behold, verily I say unto you I have reserved those things which I have entrusted unto you, my servant Joseph, for
a wise purpose in me, and it shall be
made known unto future generations;
but this generation shall have my word
through you; and in addition to your testimony, the testimony of three of my servants whom I shall call and ordain, unto
whom I shall show these things:[90] and
they shall go forth with my words that
are given through you, yea, they shall
know of a surety that these things are
true: for from heaven will I declare it
unto them: I will give them power that
they may behold and view these things
as they are; and to none else will I grant
this power, to receive this same testimony,
among this generation, in this, the beginning of the rising up, and the coming
forth of my church out of the wilderness—clear as the moon, and fair as the
sun, and terrible as an army with banners. And the testimony of three witnesses will I send forth of my word; and
behold whosoever believeth on my words
them will I visit with the manifestation
of my spirit, and they shall be born of
me, even of water and of the spirit.

And you must wait yet a little while;
for ye are not yet ordained—and their
testimony shall also go forth unto the
condemnation of this generation if they

Draft 3

hereafter you shall be ordained, and go
forth and deliver my words unto the
children of men Behold if they will not
beleive my words, they would not beleive
you my servant Jos^e. [p. 23] if it were possible, that you could show them all these
things which I have committed unto
you. O this unbelieving and stiffed necked
generation, mine anger is kindled against
them.— Behold, verily, I say unto you I
have reserved these things, which I have
entrusted unto you, my servant Joseph
for a wise purpose in ⟨me⟩ me; and it
shall be made known unto future generations, but this generation shall hear
⟨hav⟩ my word through you, and in addition to your testimony, the testimony of
three of my Servants, whom I shall call,
and ordain. I shall show these things,
and they shall go forth, with my words
that are given through you, yea they
shall know of a surety that these things
are true; for from heavn will I declare it
unto them. I will give ⟨you⟩ power to behold and view these things as they are,
and to none else will I grant this power.
to reciev this same testimony among this
generation, in this the beginning of the
rising up, and the coming forth of my
chu[r]ch out of the wilderness. Clear as
the moon, fair as the Sun, and terrible, as
an ⟨army⟩ army with banners; and the testimony of three wittnesse, will I send
forth with of my word, and behold whosoever believeth on my words, them will
I visit, with the manifestation of of my
spirit, and they shall be born of me of
the water and of the Spirit: and you must
wait yet a little while, for ye are not yet
ordained, and ⟨their⟩ bear testimony
unto shall also go forth unto the condemnation, of this generation, if they
harden their hearts against them; for a

NOTES

90. The Book of Mormon referred to three
future witnesses who were to see the plates. (Book
of Mormon, 1830 ed., 110, 548 [2 Nephi 27:12;
Ether 5:2–4].)

Draft 1

Draft 2

harden their hearts against them: for a desolating scourge shall go forth among the inhabitants of the earth, and shall continue to ⟨be⟩ poured out, from time to time, if they repent not, untill the earth is empty, and the inhabitants there- of are consumed away, and utterly con- sumed ⟨destroyed⟩ by the brightness of my coming. Behold, I tell you these things even as I also told the people of the destruction of Jerusalem, and my word shall be verified at this time as it hath hitherto been verified.

And now I command you, my servant Joseph, to repent and walk more up- rightly before me, and yield to the per- suasions of men no more; and that you be firm in keeping the commandments wherewith I have commanded you, and if you do this, behold I grant unto you eternal life, even if you should be slain.

And now again I speak unto you my servant Joseph, concerning the man that desires the witness: Behold I say unto him he exalts himself and does not hum- ble himself sufficiently before me: but if he will bow down before me, and hum- ble himself in mighty prayer and faith, in the sincerity of his heart, then will I grant unto him a view of the things which he desires to see. And then he shall say unto the people of this generation, behold I have seen the things which the Lord has shewn to Joseph Smith jr and I [p. 12] know of a surety that they are true for I have seen them: for they have been shown unto me by the power of God and not of man. And I the Lord command him, my servant Martin Harris that he shall say no more unto them concerning these things, except he shall say, I have seen them and they have been shown unto me by the power of God: And these

Draft 3

desolating scourge shall go forth, among the inhabitants of the earth, and shall continue to be poured out ~~if they re~~ from time to time, if they repent not. untill the earth is empty and the inhabitants thereof are consumed away, and utterly destroyed, by the [p. 24] brightness of my coming; behold I tell you these things even as I also told the people, of the destruction of Jerusalem; and my words shall be verified at this time, as it hath hitherto been.

And now I command you my Servant Joseph, to repent and walk more uprightly before me, and yield to the pursuasions of men no more; and that you be firm in keeping the command⟨ment⟩s wherewith I have commanded you, and if you do this, behold I grant unto you eternal life, even if you should be slain. And now ~~again~~ again, I speak unto you my se[r]vant Joseph, concerning the man, who desires the witness. Behold, I say unto him, he exalts himself and does not humble himself sufficiently before me, but if he will bow down before me, and humble himself in mighty prayer and faith, in the cincerity of his heart; then will I grant unto him a view of the things which he desires to see, and then he shall say unto the people of this generation, behold I have seen the things which the lord has shown to Joseph Sm[i]th J^r; and I know of a surety that they are true, for I have seen them, they have been shown unto me by the power of ⟨~~and~~⟩ god ⟨and⟩ not of man. And I the the lord command him my se[r]vant Martin Harriss, that he shall say no more unto them concerning these things, except he shall say, I have seen them, and they have been shown unto me by the

Draft 1   **Draft 2**

are the words which he shall say. But if
he deny this he will break the covenant
which he has covenanted with me, and
behold he is condemned. And now except he humble himself and acknowledge unto me the things ~~the things~~ that
he has done which are wrong, and covenant with me, that he will keep my commandments, and exercise ~~in me~~ faith in
me, behold I say unto him, he shall have
no such views; for I will grant unto him
no views of the things of which I have
spoken. And if this be the case I command you, my servant Joseph, that you
shall say unto him that he shall do no
more, nor trouble me any more concerning this matter.

And if this be the case, behold I say
unto thee Joseph, when thou hast translated a few more pages thou shalt stop
for a season, even untill I command thee
again, then thou mayest translate again.
And except thou do this, behold, thou
shalt have no more gift, and I will take
away the things which I have entrusted
with ~~you~~ ⟨thee⟩. And now because I foresee the lying in wait to destroy thee: yea
I foresee that if my servant Martin
Harris, humbleth not himself, and receive a witness from my hand that he
will fall into transgression; and there are
many that lie in wait to destroy thee
⟨from⟩ off the face of the earth: and for
this cause that thy days may be prolonged, I have given unto thee the⟨se⟩
commandments; yea, for this cause I have
said, stop and stand still until I command thee, and I will provide means
whereby thou mayest accomplish the
thing which I have commanded thee;
and if thou art faithful in keeping my
commandments, thou shalt be lifted up
at the last day. Amen.

Draft 3

power of god. And these are the words which he shall say; but if he deny this, he will break the covenant which he has made with me, and behold he is condemned. And now except he humble himself and acknowledge unto me the things that he has done that are wrong; and covenant with me, that he will keep my commandments, and exercise faith in me, behold. I Say unto him he shall have no such views; for I will grant unto him no views of the things of which I [p. 25] have spoken. And if this be the case I command you my se[r]vant Joseph, that you shall say unto him that he shall do no more, nor trouble me any more concerning this matter; and if this be the case behold I say unto thee Joseph. when thou hast translated a few more pages, thou shalt stop for a season, even until I command thee again, then thou mayest translate again. and except thou do this, behold thou shalt have no more gift, and I will take away the th[i]ngs which I have entrusted with thee, and now because I foresee the lying in wait to destroy thee; yea I foresee that if my Se[r]vant Martin Harriss, humbleth ~~not~~ not himself, and recieve ⟨a⟩ witness from my hand, that he will fall into transgression, and there are many that lie in wait to destroy thee. from off the face of the Earth; and for this cause ⟨that⟩ thy days may be prolonged, I have given unto thee these commandments. Yea for this cause, I have said stop and stand still, until I command thee, and I will provide means whereby thou mayest accomplish the thing which I hav commanded thee. and if thou art faithful, ~~on~~ in keeping my Commandments, thou shalt be lifted up at the last day.

Amen.

Draft 1   **Draft 2**

On the fifth day of Aprile Eighteen
hundred and twenty nine Oliver Cowdery
came to my house, untill when I had never
seen him. He stated to me that having been
teaching school in the neighborhood where
my father resided, and my father being one
of those who sent to the school, he had
went to board for a season at my father's
house,[92] and while there the family related
to him the circumstance of my having received the plates, and accordingly he had
came to make enquiries of me.

Two days after the arrival of Mr Cowdery (being the seventh of April) I commenced to translate the book of Mormon
and he commenced to write for me, which
having continued for some time I enquired
of the Lord through the Urim and Thummin and obtained the following revelation.

Revelation given April 1829, to Oliver
Cowdery and Joseph Smith J^r.[93]

A great and marvelous work is about
to come forth unto the children of men:
behold I am God, and give heed unto my
word, which is quick and powerful,
sharper than a two edged sword, ~~to dividing asunder of the joints~~ to the dividing asunder of both joints and marrow:
therefore give heed unto my words.

Behold the field is white already to
harvest, therefore whoso desireth to reap,
let him thrust in his sickle with his
might and reap while the day lasts, that
he may treasure up for his soul everlasting salvation in the kingdom of God:
yea who[p. 13]soever will thrust in his
sickle and reap, the same is called of
God, therefore, if you ⟨will⟩ ask of me
you shall receive; if you ⟨will⟩ knock ~~and~~
it shall be opened unto you. Now as you
have asked, behold I say unto you, keep
my commandments, and seek to bring
forth and establish the cause of Zion:

Draft 3

On the fifth day of April. 1829, Olive Cowdry cam[e] to my house. (untill which time I had never seen him) and stated to me that having been teaching school, in the neighbourhood where my father resided, and ⟨learning⟩ from ~~him~~ some of the family, ~~learning~~[91] that I had received the plates, ~~and~~ now came to make inquiries of me,

Two days after the arrival of M^r. Cowdry, I commenced translating the Book of Mormon: and he commenced writing for me; which having [p. 26] continued for some time. I enquired of the Lord through the Urim & Thummin, and obtained the following Revelation.

A great and marvelous work, is about to come forth unto the children of men; behold I am god, and give heed unto my word, which is quick and powerful, sharper than a two edged Sword, to the dividing assunder of both joints and marrow: therefore give heed unto my words.

behold the field is white allready to harvest, therefore whoso desireth to reap, let him thrust in his sickle with his might, and reap while the day lasts, that he may treasure up for his soul, everlasting salvation, in the kingdom of God. Yea whoso[e]ver will thrust in his sickle, and reap, the same is called of god, therefore if you will ask of me, you shall recieve; if you will knock, it shall be opened unto you; now as you have asked, behold I say unto you, keep my commandments, and seek to bring forth, and establish the cause of Zion. Seek not for

NOTES

91. TEXT: "learned" changed to "learning" and then canceled.

92. JS's siblings Katharine, Don Carlos, and Lucy Smith were probably among the 107 pupils who were enrolled in the Joint District 11 school in Manchester, where Cowdery taught. (See Report to New York common schools superintendent, 1 July 1829, microfilm, Manchester, NY, Public School Records, 1828–1915, BYU.)

93. Revelation, Apr. 1829–A, in Doctrine and Covenants 8, 1835 ed. [D&C 6].

Draft 1   **Draft 2**

seek not for riches but for wisdom, and
behold the mysteries of God shall be
unfolded unto you, and then shall you
be made rich. Behold he that hath eternal life is rich. Verily, verily I say unto
you, even as you desire of me, so shall it
be unto you; and if you desire, you shall
be the means of doing much good in this
generation. Say nothing but repentance
⟨un⟩to this generation, keep my commandments and assist to bring forth my
work according to my commandments,
and you shall be blessed.

Behold thou hast a gift, and blessed
art thou because of thy gift. Remember
it is sac[r]ed and cometh from above: and
if thou wilt inquire, thou shalt know
mysteries which are great and marvelous: therefore thou ⟨shalt⟩ exercise thy
gift, that thou mayest find out mysteries,
that thou mayest bring many to the
knowledge of the truth; yea, convince
them of the error of their ways. Make
not thy gift known unto any save it be
those of who are of thy faith. Trifle not
with sacred things. If thou wilt do good,
yea and hold out faithful to the end,
thou shalt be saved in the kingdom of
God, which is the greatest of all the gifts
of God; for there is no gift greater than
the gift of salvation.

Verily verily I say unto thee, blessed art
thou for what thou hast done, for thou
hast enquired of me, and behold as often
as thou hast enquired, thou hast received
instruction of my Spirit. If it had not been
so, thou wouldst not have come to the
place where thou art at this time.

Behold thou knowest that thou hast inquired of me and I did enlighten thy
mind and now I tell thee these things,
that thou mayest know that thou hast
been enlightened by the Spirit of truth;

Draft 3

riches, but for wisdom; and behold the
mysteries of God, shall be unfolded unto
you, and then Shall you be made rich;
behold he that hath eternal life, is rich.
Verily, Verily, I say unto you even as you
desire of me, so shall it be unto you; and
if you desire you shall be the means of
doing much good. in this generation. Say
nothing but repentance, unto this generation; keep my commandments, and
assist to bring forth my work, according
to my commandments; you Shall be
blest. Behold thou hast a gift, and blessed
art thou because of thy gift; remember
it is sacred and cometh from above and
if thou wilt inquire, thou shalt know
mysteries, which are great and marvellous: therefore thou shalt exercise thy
gift, [p. 27] that thou mayest find out
mysteries; that thou mayest bring many
to the knowledge to of the truth, yea,
convince them of the errors of their ways.
Make not thy gift known unto any, save
it be those who are of thy faith; trifle not
with sacred things. if thou wilt do good;
yea, and hold out faithful to the end,
thou shalt be saved in the kingdom of
god, which is the greatest of all the gifts
of god; for there is no gift greater than
the gift of salvation.

Verily Verily I say unto thee blessed art
thou for what thou hast done for thou
hast enquired of me and behold as often
as thou hast enqu[i]red thou hast recievid
instruction of my spirit if it had not been
so thou wouldst not have come to the
place where thou art at this time behold
thou knowest thou hast enquired of me
and I did enlighten thy mind and now I
tell thee these things that thou mayest
know that thou hast been enlightened by
the spirit of truth yea I tell thee that thou

Draft 1

Draft 2

yea, I tell thee, that thou mayest know that there is none else save God, that knowest thy thoughts and the intents of thy heart: I tell thee these things as a witness unto thee, that the words or the work which thou hast been writing is true.

Therefore be diligent, stand by my servant Joseph faithfully in whatsoever difficult circumstances he may be, for the word's sake. Admonish him in his faults and also receive admonition of him. Be patient; be sober; be temperate: have patience, faith, hope and charity.

Behold thou art Oliver, and I have spoken unto thee because of thy desires; therefore, treasure up these words in thy heart. Be faithful and diligent in keeping the commandments of God, and I will encircle thee in the arms of my love.

Behold I am Jesus Christ, the Son of God. I am the same that came unto my own and my own received me not.— I am the light which shineth in darkness, and the darkness comprehendeth it not.

Verily, verily I say unto you, if you desire a further witness, cast your mind upon the night that you cried unto me in your heart, that you might know concerning the truth of these things; did I not speak peace to your mind concerning the matter? What greater witness can you have than from God? And now behold you have received a witness, for if I have told you things which no man knoweth, have you not received a witness? And behold I grant unto you a gift, if you desire of me, to translate even as my servant Joseph.

Verily, verily I say unto you, that there are records which contain much of [p. 14] my gospel, which have been kept back because of the wickedness of the people; and now I command you, that if you

Draft 3

mayest know that there is none else save
god that knowest thy thoughts and
intents of thy hearts I ⟨tell⟩ thee these
things as a witness unto thee that the
words or the work which thou hast
been writing is true Therefore be diligent
stand by my sevent [servant] Joseph
faithfully in whatsoever difficult circumstances he may be for the words sake admonish him in his faults and also recieve
admonition of him be patient be sober
and be temperate have patience faith
hope and charity behold tho[u] art oliver
and I have spoken unto thee because of
thy desires therefore treasure up these
words in thy heart be faithful and diligent in keeping the commandments of
god and I will encircle thee in the arms
of my love behold I am jesus Christ the
son of god I am the same that came unto
my own [p. 28] and my own recieved me
not. I am the light that shineth in darkness but the darkness comprehendeth it
not Verily verily I say unto you if you desire a further witness cast your mind
upon the night that you cried unto me in
your heart that you might know concerning the truth of these things did I
not speak peace unto your mind concerning the matter what greater witness
can you have ~~then~~ ⟨than⟩ from God and
now behold you have reccieved a witness
for if I have told you things which no
man knoweth have you not reci^d. a witness and behold I grant unto you a gift if
you desire of me to translate even as my
servant Joseph

Verily Verily I say unto you ⟨that⟩ there
are records ~~⟨which⟩~~ that contain much of
my Gospel which have been kept back
because of the wickedness of the people
and now I command you that if you

Draft 1   **Draft 2**

have good desires, a desire to lay up treasures for yourself in heaven, then shall
you assist in bringing to light, with your
gift, those parts of my scriptures which
have been hidden because of iniquity.

And now behold I give unto you, and
also unto my servant Joseph the keys of
this gift, which shall bring to light this
ministry: and in the mouth of two or
three witnesses, shall every word be established.

Verily, verily I say unto you, if they
reject my words, and this part of my gospel and ministry, blessed are ye, for they
can do no more unto you than unto me;
and if they do unto you even as they have
done unto me, blessed are ye, for you
shall dwell with me in glory: but if they
reject not my words, which ⟨shall⟩ be established by the testimony which shall be
given, blessed are they; and then shall ye
have joy in the fruit of your labours.

Verily, verily I say unto you, as I said
unto my disciples, where two or ~~there~~
three are gathered together in my name,
as touching one thing, behold there will
I be in the midst of them, even so am I in
the midst of you. Fear not to do good my
sons, for whatsoever ye sow, that shall
ye also reap: therefore if ye sow good,
ye shall also reap good for your reward:

Therefore fear not little flock, do good,
let earth and hell combine against, ⟨you⟩
for if ye are built upon my rock, they
cannot prevail. Behold I do not condemn
you, go your ways and sin no more: perform with soberness the work which I
have commanded; ⟨you⟩ look unto me
in every thought, doubt not, fear not:
behold the wounds which pierced my
side, and also the prints of the nails in
my hands and feet: be faithful; keep my

Draft 3

have good desires a desire to lay up treasures for yourself in heaven then shall
you assist in bringing to light with your
gift those parts of my scriptures which
have been hidden because of iniquity
and now behold I give unto you and also
my servant Joseph the keys of this gift
which shall bring to light this ministry

   and in the mouth of two or three witnesses shall every word be established.

   Verily Verily I say unto you if they
regect my word and this part of Gospel
and my ministry blessed are ~~you~~ ⟨ye⟩ for
they can do no more unto you than unto
me and if they do unto you even as they
have done unto me blessed are ye for ~~ye~~
you shall dwell with me in glory But if
they reject not my words which shall be
established by the testimony which shall
be given blessed are they and then shall
ye have joy in the fruit of your labours.

   Verily verily I say unto you [p. 29] as I
said unto my disciples where two or three
are gathered in my name as touching one
thing behold there will I be in the midst
of them even so ~~will~~ ⟨am⟩ I ~~be~~ in the
midst of you Fear not to do good my
sons for whatsoever ye sow that shall ~~you~~
⟨ye⟩ also reap therefore if you sow good
you shall also reap good for your reward—

   Therefore fear not little flock do good
let earth and hell combine against you
for if ye are built on my rock they cannot
prevail ~~against you~~ Behold I do not condemn you go your way and sin no more
perform with soberness the work wich I
have commanded you look unto me in
every thought doubt not fear not Behold
the wounds which pierced my side and
also the prints of the nails ~~which are~~ in
my hands and feet be faithful keep my

Draft 1   **Draft 2**

commandments, and ye shall inherit the kingdom of heaven. Amen.

After we had received this revelation he (Oliver Cowdery) stated to me that after he had gone to my father's to board, and after the family communicated to him concerning my having got the plates, that one night after he had retired to bed, he called upon the Lord to know if these things were so, and that the Lord had manifested to him that they were true, but that he had kept the circumstance entirely secret, and had mentioned it to no being, so that after this revelation having been given, he knew that the work was true, because that no ~~mortal~~ being living knew of the thing alluded in the revelation but God and himself.

During the month of April I continued to translate, and he to write with little cessation, during which time we received several revelations. A difference of opinion arising between us about the account of John the Apostle, mentioned in the new testament, John, twenty first chapter and twenty second verse, whether he died, or whether he continued; ~~We~~ we mutually agreed to settle ⟨it⟩ by the Urim and Thummin, and the following is the word which we received.

A Revelation given to Joseph Smith jr, and Oliver Cowdery in Harmony Pensylvania April 1829. when they desired to know whether John, the beloved disciple, tarried on earth.—

Translated from parchment, written and hid up by himself.[94]

And the Lord said unto me, John, my beloved, what desirest thou? For if you ask what you will, it shall be granted unto you. And I said unto him, Lord, give me power over [p. 15] death, that I may live and bring souls unto thee. And the Lord

Draft 3

commandments and ye shall inherit the Kingdom of heaven, Amen,

After we had rec^d· this Revelation Oliver Cowdry stated that after having been told by some of my father's family that I had the plates he retired to rest and called upon the Lord asking him if these things were so and that the Lord had manifested to him that they were true—that he had divulged this to no one consequently he knew this work to be true because none but himself and God knew of the thing alluded to in the Revelation

During the month of April we continued to translate and write during which ~~we~~ time we received several Revelations— A difference of opinion arising between us relative to the account of John the Apostle mentioned in the New Testament John 21st & 22^d ver[se] whether he died or continued we mutually agreed to settle it by the Urim & Thummin & the following [p. 30] is the word that we received

And the Lord said unto me John my beloved what desirest thou for if you ask what you will it shall be granted unto you and I said ~~Lord~~ unto him Lord give me power over death—that I may live and bring souls to thee.

NOTES

94. Account of John, Apr. 1829–C, in Doctrine and Covenants 33, 1835 ed. [D&C 7].

Draft 1   **Draft 2**

said unto me, Verily, verily I say unto
thee, because thou desiredst this, thou
shalt tarry untill I come in my glory, and
shall prophesy before nations, kindreds,
tongues and people.

And for this cause the Lord said unto
Peter, If I will that he tarry till I come,
what is that to thee? For he desiredst of
me that he might bring souls unto me;
but thou desiredst that thou might
speedily come ~~into my kingdom~~ unto me
in my kingdom. I say unto thee, Peter,
this was a good desire, but my beloved
has desired, that he might do more, or a
greater work, yet among men than what
he has before done; yea he has undertaken a greater work; therefore, I will
make him as flaming fire and a ministring angel: he shall minister for those
who shall be heirs of salvation who dwell
on the earth; and I will make thee ~~a~~ ⟨to⟩
minister for him and for thy brother
James: and unto you three I will give this
power and the keys of this ministry untill I come.
Verily I say unto you, ye shall both
have according to your desires, for ye
both joy in that which you have desired.
Whilst continuing the work of translation during ~~this~~ ⟨the⟩ month of April; Oliver Cowdery became exceedingly anxious
to have the power to translate bestowed
upon him and in relation to this desire the
folowing revelations were obtained.
Revelation given April 1829.[95]
Oliver Cowdery, verily, verily I say
unto you that assuredly as the Lord liveth
who is your God and your Redeemer,
even so sure shall you receive a knowledge of whatsoever things you shall ask
in faith, with an honest heart, believing
that you shall recieve a knowledge con-

Draft 3

And the Lord said unto me Verily Verily I say unto ~~you~~ thee ~~thou~~ because thou desiredst this thou shalt tarry until I come in my glory and shall prophesy before nations kindreds tongues & people.

And for this cause the Lord said unto Peter ~~If~~ if I will that he tarry till I come what is that to thee— For he desired of me that he might bring souls unto me; but thou desiredst that thou might speedily come unto me in my kingdom—

I say unto thee Peter this was a good desire, but my beloved has desired that he might do more or a greater work yet among men than what he has done yea he has undertaken a greater work; therefore I will make him a flaming fire and a ministering angel— He shall be a minister to those who ⟨shall be⟩ ~~are~~ heirs of salvation who dwell on the earth; I will make thee to minister for him and for thy brother James: and unto you three will I give this power and the keys of this ministery untill I come—

Verily Verily I say unto you ye shall both have according to your desires for ye both joy in that which you have desired.

Whilst continuing the work of translation, (during this month of April,) Oliver Cowdry become exceedingly anxious to have ~~the~~ power to translate bestowed upon him, and in relation to this desire the following ⟨Revelation⟩ ~~translation~~ was obtained—

Oliver Cowdry verily, verily I say [p. 31] that assuredly as the Lord liveth who is your God and your Redeemer even so sure shall you receive a knowledge of whatsoeve[r] ~~you~~ things you shall ask in faith with an honest heart beleiving ⟨that⟩ you shall receive a knowledge con-

NOTES

95. Revelation, Apr. 1829–B, in Doctrine and Covenants 34, 1835 ed. [D&C 8].

Draft 1   **Draft 2**

cerning the engravings of old records,
which were ancient which contain those
parts of my scripture of which have been
spoken, by the manifestation of my
spirit; yea, behold I will tell you in your
mind and in in your heart by the Holy
Ghost, which shall come upon you, and
which shall dwell in your heart.

Now behold this is the Spirit of Revelation: behold this is the Spirit by which
Moses brought the children of Israel
through the red sea on dry ground:
therefore this is thy gift; apply unto it
and blessed art thou, for it shall deliver
you out of the hands of your enemies,
when, if it were not so, they would slay
you and bring your soul to destruction.

O remember these words, and keep my
commandments.— Remember this is
your gift. Now this is not all y̶o̶u̶r̶ ⟨thy⟩
gift: for you have another gift, which is
the gift of Aaron:[96] behold it has told you
many things: behold there is no other
power save the power of God, that can
cause this gift of Aaron to be with you;
therefore, doubt not, for it is the gift of
God, and you shall hold it in your hands,
and do marvelous works; and no power
shall be able to take it away f̶r̶o̶m̶ out of
your hands: for it is the work of God.
And therefore whatsoever you shall ask
me to tell you by that means, that will I
grant unto you, and you shall have
knowledge concerning it: remember,
that without faith you can do nothing.
Therefore ask in faith. Trifle not i̶n̶ ⟨with⟩
these things: do not ask for that which
you ought not ask that you may know
the mysteries of God, and that you may
translate and [p. 16] receive knowledge
from all those ancient records which
have been hid up, that are sacred, and
according to your faith shall it be done

Draft 3

cerning the engravings of old records which contain those parts of my scriptures that have been spoken ⟨of⟩ by the manifestation of my spirit; yea behold I will tell you in your mind and in your heart by the Holy Ghost which shall come upon you and which shall dwell in your heart— Now behold this is the spirit of revelation. Behold this is the spirit which brought the children of Israel through the red sea on dry ground; therefore this is thy gift

Apply unto it and blessed art thou for it shall deliver you out of the hands of your enemies when if it were not so they would slay you and bring your soul to destruction.

O remember these words and keep my commandments. Remember this is your gift. Now this is not all thy gift, for you have another ~~person~~ gift which is that of Aaron: Behold it has told you many things. Behold there is ~~another~~ ⟨no other⟩ power save the power of God that can cause this gift ⟨of Aaron⟩ to be with you. Therefore doubt not for it is the gift of God and you shall hold it in your hands and do marvelous works; and no power shall be able to take it out of your hands, for it is the work of God. And therefore whatsoever you shall ask me to tell you by that means I will grant unto you and you shall ⟨have⟩ knowledge concerning it. Remember that without faith you can do nothing; therefore ask in faith. Trifle not with these things; do not ask for what you ought not to that you may know the mysteries of God [p. 32] and that you may translate and receive knowledge from all those ancient records which have been hid up that are sacred and according to your faith shall it be done unto you

96. An earlier version of this revelation specified this as "the gift of working with the ~~sprout~~ rod." (Revelation Book 1, p. 13, in *JSP*, MRB:17.)

Draft 1   **Draft 2**

unto you. Behold it is I that have spoken
it: and I am the same who spake unto
you from the beginning. Amen.

Revelation given to Oliver Cowdery,
April 1829.[97]

Behold I say unto you, my son, that because you did not translate according to
that which you desired of me, and did
commence again to write for my servant
Joseph Smith jr even so I would that ~I~
you should continue untill you have finished this record, which I have intrusted
unto him: and then behold, other records have I, that I will give unto you
power that you may assist to translate.

Be patient my son, for it is wisdom in
me, and it is not expedient that you
should translate at this present time.
Behold, the work which you are called to
do, is to write for my servant Joseph; and
behold it is because that you did not continue as you commenced, when you
began to translate, that I have taken away
this privilege from you. Do not murmur
my son, for it is wisdom in me that I have
dealt with you after this manner.

Behold you have not understood, you
have supposed that I would give it unto
you, when you took no thought, save it
was to ask me; but behold I say unto you,
that you must study it in your mind; then
you must ask me if it be right, and if it is
right, I will cause that your bosom shall
burn within you: therefore, you shall feel
that it is right; but if it be not right, you
shall have no such feelings, but you shall
have a stupor of thought, that shall cause
you to forget the thing which is wrong:
therefore you cannot write that which is
sacred, save it be given you from me.

Now if you had known this, you could
have translated; nevertheless, it is not expedient that you should translate now.

Draft 3

Behold it is I that have spoken it, and I am the same who spoke unto you from the beginning. Amen,

Revelation to O. Cowdry

April 1829

Behold I say unto you my son that because you did not translate according to that which you desired of me, and did commence again for my servant Joseph Smith J^r· even so I would that you continue until you have finished this record which I have entrusted unto him.

And then behold other records have I that I will give you power to assist in translating them— Be patient my son for it is wisdom in me and it is not expedient that you should translate at this present time. Behold the work which you are called to do, is to write for my servant Joseph; and behold it is because you did not continue as you commenced to when you began to translate that I have taken away this privilege from you

Do not murmur my son for it is wisdom in me that I have dealt with you after this manner. Behold you have not understood—you have supposed that I would give it unto you when you took no thought save it was to ask me; but behold I say unto you that you must study it in your mind[98] then you must ask me if it be right. and if [it] is right I will cause that your bosom shall burn within you: Therefore you shall feel that is it is right. But if it be not right you shall have [p. 33] no such feelings but you shall have a stupor of thought that shall cause you to forget the thing wich is wrong; therefore you cannot write that which is sacred save it be given you from me.

Now if you could had known this could you could have translated; Nevertheless it is not expedient that you should

97. Revelation, Apr. 1829–D, in Doctrine and Covenants 35, 1835 ed. [D&C 9].
98. TEXT: Possibly "minds".

Draft 1	**Draft 2**

Behold it was expedient when you commenced but you feared, and the time is past, and it is not expedient now: for do you not behold that I have given unto my servant Joseph sufficient strength, whereby it is made up? and neither of you have I condemned.

Do this thing which I have commanded you, and you shall prosper. Be faithful and yield to no temptation. Stand fast in the work ~~wherein~~ wherewith I have called you, and a hair of your head shall not be lost, and you shall be lifted up at the last day. Amen.

We still continued the ⟨work of⟩ translation, when in the ensuing month (May, Eighteen hundred and twenty nine) we on a certain day went into the woods to pray and inquire of the Lord respecting baptism for the remission of sins as we found mentioned in the translation of the plates.[99] While we were thus employed praying and calling upon the Lord, a Messenger from heaven, descended in a cloud of light, and having laid his hands upon us, he ordained us, saying unto us; "Upon you my fellow servants in the name of Messiah I confer the priesthood of Aaron, which holds the keys of the ministring of angels and of the gospel of repentance, and of baptism by immersion for the remission of sins, and this shall never be taken again from the earth, untill the sons of Levi do offer again an offering unto the Lord in righteousness."[100] He said this Aaronic priesthood[101] had not [p. 17] the power of laying on of hands, for the gift of the Holy Ghost, but that this should be conferred on ⟨us⟩ hereafter and he commanded us to go and be baptized, and gave us directions that I should baptize Oliver Cowdery, and afterward that he should baptize me. ~~and that I should be~~

Draft 3

translate now.

Behold it was expedient ~~when~~ when you commenced but you feared and the time is past, and it is not expedient now; for do you not behold that I have given unto my servant Joseph sufficient strength whereby it is made up and neither of you have I condemned.

Do this thing which I have commanded you and you shall prosper. Be faithful and yield to no temptation. Stand fast in the work wherewith I have called you and a hair of your head shall not be lost and you shall be lifted up at the last day amen

We still continued the work of translation and in the ensuing month (May 1829) on a certain day we went into the woods to pray and inquire of the Lord respecting baptism for the remission of sins spoken of in the translation of the Plates.

While we were thus praying & calling upon the Lord a Messenger decended in a cloud ⟨of light ~~from~~⟩ from heaven and having laid his hands upon us ordained us saying upon you my fellow servants in the name of the Messiah I confer the Priesthood of Aaron which holds the keys of the ministering of Angels and ~~of~~ the Gospel of repentence and baptism by immersion for the remission of sins and this shall never be taken from the earth until the sons of Levi do ~~offer~~ [p. 34] again make an offering unto the Lord in righteousness". He said this Aronic Priesthood had not the power of the laying on of hands for the gift of the Holy Ghost but ~~this~~ ⟨that⟩ should be confered upon us at some future time. He also commanded us to go and be baptized— that I should baptize Oliver—Cowdry and that he should then baptize me

NOTES

99. Oliver Cowdery indicated specifically that the impetus for seeking further information about baptism was the translation of "the account given of the savior's ministry to the remnant of the seed of Jacob, upon this continent." This account, found in the Book of Mormon, 1830 ed., 472–510 [3 Nephi 9–28], includes several passages concerning baptism. (Oliver Cowdery, Norton, OH, to William W. Phelps, 7 Sept. 1834, *LDS Messenger and Advocate,* Oct. 1834, 1:15 [see also later version, p. 42 herein].)

100. The earliest known account of this event, written by Oliver Cowdery, gives the angel's statement thus: "Upon you my fellow servants, in the name of Messiah I confer this priesthood and this authority, which shall remain upon the earth, that the sons of Levi may yet offer an offering unto the Lord in righteousness." (Oliver Cowdery, Norton, OH, to William W. Phelps, 7 Sept. 1834, *LDS Messenger and Advocate,* Oct. 1834, 1:16 [see also later version, p. 43 herein]; see also Malachi 3:3.)

101. Use of the term "Aaronic priesthood" in an 1829 context is anachronistic. The term first appears in JS's written record in a document dated circa April 1835. An earlier revelation of September 1832 referred to "the lesser priesthood which priesthood was confirmed upon Aaron and his Sons." (Instruction on priesthood, ca. Apr. 1835, in Doctrine and Covenants 3:1, 2, 8, 1835 ed. [D&C 107:1, 6, 13–14]; Revelation, 22 and 23 Sept. 1832, in Revelation Book 1, pp. 150–151, in *JSP,* MRB:277–279 [D&C 84:30].)

Draft 1

Draft 2

~~called the first elder of the Church and he the second.~~

Accordingly we went and were baptized, I baptized him first, and afterwards he baptized me, after which I laid my hands upon his head and ordained him to the Aaronick priesthood, and afterward he laid his hands on me and ordained me to the same priesthood, for so we were commanded.[102]

The messenger who visited us on this occasion and conferred this priesthood upon us said that his name was John, the same that is called John the Baptist in the new Testament, and that he acted under the direction ⟨of⟩ Peter, James, and John, who held the keys of the priesthood of Melchisedeck,[103] whi[c]h priesthood he said should in due time be conferred on us. ⟨And that I should be called the first Elder of the Church and he the second.⟩

It was on the fifteenth day of May, Eighteen hundred and twenty nine that we were baptized; ~~under~~ and ordained under the hand of ~~that~~ ⟨the⟩ Messenger.[104]

Immediately upon our coming up out of the water after we had been baptized, we experienced great and glorious blessings from our Heavenly Father. No sooner had I baptized Oliver Cowdery than the Holy Ghost fell upon him and he stood up and prophecied many things which should ⟨shortly⟩ come to pass. And again so soon as I had been baptized by him, I also had the Spirit of prophecy when standing up I prophecied concerning the rise of this Church and many other things connected with the Church ~~of Christ~~ and ~~with~~ this generation of the children of men. We were filled with the Holy Ghost, and rejoiced in the God of our Salvation. Our minds being now enlightened, we began to have the scriptures laid open to our understandings,

Immediately upon our coming up out of the water after we had been baptized we experienced great and glorious blessings from our Heavenly Father.

No sooner had I baptized Oliver Cowdery than the Holy Ghost fell upon him and he stood up and prophecied many things which should shortly come to pass: And again so soon as I had been baptized by him, I also had the Spirit of Prophecy, when standing up I prophecied concerning the rise of this church, and many other things connected with the Church and this generation of the children of men. We were filled with the Holy Ghost, and rejoiced in the God of our Salvation.

Our minds being now enlightened, we began to have the Scriptures laid open to

Draft 3

He also said that his name was John; the same that was called John the Baptist in the new Testament—that he acted under the direction of Peter, James & John who held the keys of the priesthood of Melchisedeck which should in due time be confered upon us—

Accordingly we went and wer baptized ~~and ordained~~ as directed by the Messenger ~~on the (15 day of~~ (May ⟨15⟩ 1829)

Immediately upon our coming up out of the water we experienced great and glorious blessings from our heavenly Father

~~no~~ No sooner had I baptized Oliver Cowdry than the Holy Ghost fell upon him and he stood up and prophesied many things which should shortly come to pass. ~~again so~~

I also had the spirit of propesy and standing up ~~I~~ prophesied concerning the ⟨rise⟩ ~~Church~~ rise of the church and many things connected with it and this generation of the children of men We were filled with the Holy-Ghost and rejoiced in the God of our Salvation. Our minds being now enlightened we began to have the scriptures laid open to our understanding

102. Lucy Mack Smith indicated that a revelation through the Urim and Thummim commanded JS and Cowdery "to repair to the water, and attend to the ordinance of baptism," which they then did. (Lucy Mack Smith, History, 1845, 144.)

103. The Book of Mormon and JS's revision of Genesis chapter 14 stated that Melchizedek was a high priest, but the earliest record of JS using Melchizedek's name as a title for a higher priesthood is dated February 1832. (Vision, 16 Feb. 1832, in Revelation Book 2, p. 5, in *JSP*, MRB:423 [D&C 76:57]; see also Book of Mormon, 1830 ed., 260 [Alma 13:14–18]; and Old Testament Revision 1, pp. 33–34 [Joseph Smith Translation, Genesis 14:18, 27–28].)

104. Oliver Cowdery's report of these events was copied into JS's 1834–1836 history. (See pp. 42–43 herein.)

Draft 1

and the true meaning and intention of their more mysterious passages revealed unto us, in a manner which we never could attain to previously, nor ever before had thought of. In the mean time ~~however~~ we were forced to keep ⟨secret⟩ ~~these things entirely secret in our own bosoms, viz:~~ the circumstances of our having been baptized and having received this ~~aaronic~~ priesthood. ~~And this on account of~~ ⟨owing to⟩ a spirit of persecution ~~who~~ which had ~~been~~ ⟨already⟩ manifested itself in the neighborhood, ~~for some time previous.~~ We had been threatened with being mobbed, from time to time and this too by professors of religion, and their intentions of mobbing us, were only counteracted by the influence of my wife's father's family, ⟨⟨under Divine Providence⟩⟩ who had became very friendly to me and were opposed to mobs, and were willing that I should be allowed to continue the work of ~~translating~~ ⟨translation⟩ without interruption: And therefore offered and promised us protection from all unlawful proceedings, as far as in them lay. After a few days however feeling it to be our duty we commenced to reason, out of the scriptures, with our acquaintances and friends, as we happened to meet with them. About this time my brother Samuel, H. Smith came to visit us. We ~~soon~~ informed him of what the Lord was [p. [1]] about to do for the Children of men, And to reason with him out of the Bible, we also showed him ~~the~~ ⟨that⟩ part of the work which we had translated, and laboured to persuade him concerning the Gospel of Jesus Christ which was now about to be revealed in its fullness. He however was not very easily persuaded of these things, but after much enquiry and explanation he retired to the woods, in order that by secret and fervent prayer he might obtain of a merciful God,

Draft 2

our understandings, and the true meaning and intention of their more mysterious passages revealed unto us, in a manner which we never could attain to previously, nor ever before ⟨had⟩ thought of.

In the meantime we were forced to keep secret the circumstances of our having been baptized, and having received this priesthood; owing to a spirit of persecution which had already manifested itself in the neighborhood. We had been threatened with being mobbed, from time to time, and this too by professors of religion, and their intentions of mobbing us, were only counteracted by the influence of my wife's father's family (under Divine Providence) who had became very friendly to me and were opposed to mobs; and were willing that I should be allowed to continue the work of translation without interruption: And therefore offered and promised us protection from all unlawful proceedings as far as in them lay.

After a few days however, feeling it to be our duty, we commenced to reason out of the scriptures, with our acquaintences and friends, as we happened to meet with them. About this time my brother, Samuel, H. Smith ~~cam◊~~ came [p. 18] to visit us. We informed him of what the Lord was about to do for the children of men; and to reason with him out of the Bible: We also showed him that part of the work which we had translated, and labored to persuade him concerning the Gospel of Jesus Christ which was now about to be revealed in it's fulness.

He was not however very easily persuaded of these things, but after much enquiry and explanation, he retired to the woods, in order that by secret and fervent

Draft 3

and the true meaning of the more misterious passages of were revealed to us in a manner we had never before thought of—

In the mean time we were forced to [p. 35] keep our baptism and ordination a secret owing to a spirit of persecution already too prevalent in the neighbourhood, Mobs had threatened us from time to time and that to composed ⟨too,⟩ of <u>professors of religion</u> from which we were only preserved under divine Providence by the influence of my father in law's ⟨and⟩ family who had now become very friendly and were anxious that I should continue the work of translation without interuption and were determined to protect us.

After a few days feeling it our duty we began to reason out of the scriptures with our acquaintances and friends in accordance with our holy calling.

About this time my brother Samuel H Smith visited us, We informed him of what the Lord was about to do for the children of men and reasoned with him out of the Bible and laboured labouring to convince him of the truth of the Gospel now about to be revealed in its fullness⟨*⟩. ⟨*Appealing to Holy Bible for the truth of the doctrines we advanced⟩[105] ⟨taking the acknowledged[106] the bible for our guide⟩ Not being very easily convinced of these things he retired into the woods that by secret and fervent prayer he might obtain ⟨wisdom⟩ of a benevolent God wisdom that he might judge

105. TEXT: This insertion was inscribed on a slip of paper that was pinned to page 36 of Draft 3. A mark in the original inscription keys to the slip of paper.

106. TEXT: "acknowledged" was canceled when initially inserted and then canceled a second time with the rest of the passage.

Draft 1

wisdom to enable him to judge for himself: The result was that he obtained revelation for himself sufficient to convince him of the truth of our assertions to him, and on the [*blank*] day of that same month in which we had been baptized and ordained, Oliver Cowdery baptized him, and he returned to his father's house greatly glorifying and praising God, being filled with the Holy Spirit.

Not many days afterwards, my brother Hyrum Smith came to us to enquire concerning these things when ~~upon~~ ⟨at⟩ his earnest request, I enquired of the Lord through the Urim and Thummin, and received for him the folowing.

Revelation given to Hyrum Smith, at Harmony Susquehanah County, Pensylvania May, 1829.

Book of Covenants page 167[109]

Draft 2

prayer he might obtain of a merciful God, wisdom to enable him to judge for himself: The result was that he obtained revelation for himself sufficient to convince him of the truth of our assertions to him and on the [*blank*][107] day of that same month in which we had been baptized and ordained; Oliver Cowdery baptized him, And he returned to his father's house greatly glorifying and praising God, being filled with the Holy Spirit.

Not many days afterwards, my brother Hyrum Smith came to us to enquire concerning these things, when at his earnest request, I enquired of the Lord through the Urim and Thummin, and received for him the following

Revelation given to Hyrum Smith, at Harmony, Susquehanah [Susquehanna] County, Pensylvania. May 1829.[108]

1 A great and marvelous work is about to come forth among the children of men: behold I am God and give heed to my word, which is quick and powerful, sharper than a two edged sword, to the dividing asunder of both joints and marrow: therefore, give heed unto my word.

2 Behold the field is white already to harvest, therefore, whoso desireth to reap let him thrust in his sickle with his might, and reap while the day lasts, that he may treasure up for his soul everlasting salvation in the kingdom of God; yea, whosoever will thrust in his sickle and reap, the same is called of God: therefore, if you will ask of me, you shall receive; if you will knock it shall be opened unto you.

3 Now as you have asked, behold I say unto you keep my commandments, and seek to bring forth and establish the cause of Zion. Seek not for riches, but for wisdom, and behold the mysteries of

Draft 3

for himself[.] The result was that he ~~was~~ ⟨became⟩ convinced by revelation of the truth of the doctrines we presented to him. In accordance with the commands of the Gospel he was baptized by O. Cowdry and returned home greatly blessed praising God ⟨and⟩ ~~being~~ filled with the holy ⟨Ghost⟩ ~~Spirit~~

Shortly after my brother Hyrum Smith came enquiring ⟨after⟩ ~~for~~ these things At his earnest request I inquired of the Lord through the Urim & Thummin and received for him the following ~~to Rev~~^{n.} ⟨Revelation⟩ [p. 36]

A great and marvellous work, is about to come forth among the children of men; behold I am God and give heed to my word, which is quick and powerful. sharper than a two edged sword, to the dividing asunder of both joints and marrow: therefore give heed to my word

2 Behold the field is white allready to harvest; therefore whoso desireth to reap, let him thrust in his sickle. with all his might and reap while the day lasts, that he may treasure up for his soul everlasting salvation in the kingdom of God: yea ~~whoso will~~ whosoever will thrust in his sickle and reap, the same is called of God: therefore if you will ask of me you shall recieve; if you will knock it shall be opened unto you.

3. Now as you have asked, behold I say unto you, keep my comandments, and seek to bring forth, and establish, the cause of Zion. Seek not for riches, but for wisdom. and behold the mysteries of

107. This blank was later filled by the insertion "twenty fifth" in what appears to be the handwriting of Thomas Bullock, who began clerking in JS's office on 16 June 1844 and was Willard Richards's main scribe for JS's history in 1845. Lucy Mack Smith indicated that Samuel Smith accompanied Oliver Cowdery on his initial trip to Harmony and that Samuel was baptized the same day that JS and Oliver Cowdery "received authority to baptize." (Lucy Mack Smith, History, 1844–1845, bk. 8, [3]–[4]; see also Jessee, "Writing of Joseph Smith's History," 456–458.)

108. Revelation, May 1829–A, in Doctrine and Covenants 37, 1835 ed. [D&C 11].

109. TEXT: James Mulholland inscribed an embellished circle around this reference, presumably to indicate the intent to supply text from the 1835 edition of the Doctrine and Covenants.

Draft 1   **Draft 2**

God shall be unfolded unto you, and
then shall you be made rich; behold he
that hath eternal life is rich.

4 Verily, verily I say unto you, even as
you desire of me, so shall it be done unto
you; and, if you desire you shall be the
means of doing much good in this generation.[110] Keep my commandments, and
assist to bring forth my work according
to my commandments, and you shall be
blessed.

5 Behold thou hast a gift, or thou shalt
have a gift if thou wilt desire of me in
faith with an honest heart, believing in
the power of Jesus Christ, or in my power
which speaketh unto thee: for behold it
is I that speaketh: behold I am the light
which shineth in the darkness, and by
my power I give these words unto thee.

6 And now, verily, verily I say unto
thee, put your [p. 19] trust in that spirit
which leadeth to do good: yea, to do
justly; to walk humbly; to judge righteously; and this is my Spirit.

7 Verily, verily I say unto you, I will
impart ⟨unto⟩ you of my spirit, which
shall enlighten your mind, which shall
fill your soul with joy, and then shall you
know, or by this shall ye know, all things
whatsoever you desire of me, which is
pertaining unto things of righteousness,
in faith believing in me that you shall
receive.

8 Behold I command you, ~~that you~~
that you need not suppose that you are
called to preach untill you are called: wait
a little longer, untill you shall ~~receive~~
⟨have⟩ my word, my rock, my church, and
my gospel, that you may know of a surety
my doctrine; and then behold, according
to your desires, yea, even according to
your faith; shall it be done unto you.

Draft 3

God shall be unfolded unto you, and then shall you be made rich; behold he that hath eternal life is rich

4 Verily verily I say unto you. even as ~~I desire~~ you desire of me, shall it be done unto you: and if you desire, you shall be the means of doing much good in this generation. Keep my commandments, and assist to bring forth my work, according to my, work, according to my commandments, and you shall be blessed

5 Behold thou hast a gift. or thou shalt ~~a~~ have a gift, if thou wilt desire of me ~~with faith~~ in faith with an honest heart, believing in the power of Jesus Christ; or in my power who speaketh unto thee: for behold it is I that speaketh; behold I am the light which Shineth in ⟨the⟩ darkness. and by my power. I give these words unto thee.

~~6~~ 6 And now, verily, verily. I say unto thee put your trust in that spirit which leadeth to do good; yea, to do justly, to walk humbly, to Judge righteously; and this is my spirit

7 Verily verily I say unto you, I will impart unto you of my Spirit, which shall enlighten your mind, which Shall [p. 37] fill your soul with Joy. and then shall you know. or by this shall ye know all things whatsoever you desire of me, which is pertaining unto things of righteousness in faith believing in me that you shall recieve ~~8~~

8 Behold I command you that you need not suppose that you are called to preach untill you are called: wait a little longer untill you shall have my word my rock my church and my Gospel that you may have of a surety my doctrine and then behold according to your desires yea even according to your faith shall it be done unto you,

NOTES

110. The 1835 edition of the Doctrine and Covenants here includes, "Say nothing but repentance unto this generation." James Mulholland apparently missed this sentence when copying the revelation into the history. (Doctrine and Covenants 37:4, 1835 ed. [D&C 11:9].)

Draft 1   **Draft 2**

9 Keep my commandments; hold your peace; appeal unto my spirit: yea, cleave unto me with all your heart, that you may assist in bringing to light those things of which have been spoken: yea, the translation of my work: be patient untill you shall accomplish it.

10 Behold this is your work, to keep my commandments: yea, with all your might, mind and strength: seek not to declare my word, but first seek to obtain my word, and then shall your tongue be loosed; then if you desire, it you shall have my Spirit, and my word: yea the power of God, unto the convincing of men: but now hold your peace; study my word, which hath gone forth among the children of men; and also study my word which shall come forth among the children of men; or that which is now translating; yea, untill you have obtained all which I shall grant unto the children of men in this generation; and then shall all things be added thereunto.

11 Behold thou art Hyrum; my son, seek the kingdom of God, and all things shall be added according to that which is just. Build upon my rock, which is my gospel; deny not the spirit of revelation, nor the spirit of prophecy, for wo unto him that denieth these things: therefore treasure up in your hearts untill the time which is in my wisdom, that you shall go forth: behold I speak unto all who have good desires, and have thrust in their sickles to reap.

12 Behold I am Jesus Christ, the son of God: I am the life and the light of the world: I am the same who came unto my own, and my own received me not: but

Draft 3

9 Keep my commandments, hold your peace, appeal unto my spirit; yea cleave unto me with all your heart, that you may assist in bringing to light those things, of which have been spoken: yea the translation of my work. Be patient until you shall accomplish it.

10. Behold this is your work, to keep my commandments; yea with all your might mind and strength. Seek not to declare my word, but first seek to obtain it my word, and then shall your tongue be loosed; then if you desire you shall have my spirit, and my word; yea the power of God unto the convincing of men

But now hold your peace Sutdy [Study] my word wich hath gone forth among the children of men. And also study my word which shall come forth among the children of men or that which is now translating yea until you shall obtain all that I shall grant unto the children of men in this generation and then shall all things be added thereunto

11 Behold thou art Hyrum my son seek the Kingdom of God and all things shall be added according to that which is just, Build upon [p. 38] my rock which is my Gospel; deny not the spirit of revelation nor the spirit of prophecy for wo unto him that denieth these things; Therefore treasure up in your heart until the time which is in my wisdom that you shall go forth.

Behold I speak unto all who shall have good desires, and have thrust in their sickels to reap.

Behold I am Jesus Christ the Son of God I am the life and the light of the world I am the same who came unto my own and my own received me not:

Draft 1

About the same time, ~~with my brother Hyrum~~ came an old Gentleman to visit us. of whose name I wish to make honorable mention; Mr Joseph Knight Senr of Cole'sville, Broom County, Pen, who having heard of the manner in which we were occupying our time, very kindly and considerately brought us, a quantity of provisions, in order that we might not be interrupted in the work ⟨of translation⟩ by the want of such necessaries of life. And I would just mention [p. [2]] here (as in duty bound) that he several times afterwards brought us supplies, (a distance of ⟨at⟩ least thirty miles) which enabled us to continue the work, when otherwise we must have relinquished it for a season. Being very anxious to know his duty, as to this work, I enquired of the Lord for him, and obtained as follows.

Revelation given to Joseph Knight Senr at Harmony, Susquehanah County Pensylvania May 1829.

Book of Covenants Page ~~167~~ 169[114]

Draft 2

verily, verily I say unto you, that as many as receiveth me, them will I give power to become the sons of God, even to them that believe on my name. Amen.

About the same time came an old Gentleman to visit us, of whose name I wish to make honorable mention; Mr Joseph Knight Senr. of Colesville, Broom[e] County, Penn;[111] who having heard of the manner in which we were occupying our time, very kindly and considerately brought us, a quantity of provisions, in order that we might not be interrupted in the work of translation, by the want of such necessaries of life:[112] and I would just [p. 20] mention here (as in duty bound) that he several times brought us supplies (a distance of at least thirty miles) which enabled us to continue the work when otherwise we must have relinquished it for a season. Being very anxious to know his duty as to this work, I enquired of the Lord for him, and obtained as follows.

Revelation given to Joseph Knight Senr. at Harmony Susquehanah County, Pennsylvania. May 1829.[113]

1 A great and marvelous work is about to come forth among the children of men: behold I am God, and give heed to my word, which is quick and powerful, sharper than a two edged sword, to the dividing asunder of both joints and marrow: therefore give heed unto my word.

2 Behold the field is white already to harvest, therefore whoso desireth to reap let him thrust in his sickle with his might, and reap while the day lasts, that he may treasure up for his soul everlasting salvation in the kingdom of God: yea, whosoever will thrust in his sickle and reap, the same is called of God: therefore ~~knock~~ if you will ask of me you

Draft 3

but verily verily I say unto you that as many as receiveth me to them will I give power to become the sons of God even to them that believe in my name. Amen.

About this time came an old Gen^t. to visit us of ⟨whom⟩ ~~whose name~~ I wish to make honorable mention M^r. Jo^s. Knights senior of Colesvill Broom Co, P^a. who having heard of the manner in which we were occupying our time very kindly ~~and consideratel~~ brought us a quantity of provisions that we might continue ~~the translation~~ translating ⟨without⟩ ~~un~~interupted ⟨from⟩ ~~by~~ the want of ~~the~~ necessaries of life. Being very anxious to know his duty relative to this work I enquired of the Lord and obtained for him the following Revelation

1 A great and marvelous work is about to come forth among the childdren of men. Behold I am God and give heed ~~unto~~ my word which ⟨is⟩ quick and powerful sharper than a two edged sword to the dividing assunder ⟨of⟩ both joints and marrow therefore give heed unto my word

2 Behold the field is white already to harvest therefore whoso desireth to reap [p. 39] let him thrust in his sickle with his might and reap while the day lasts that he may treasure up for his soul everlasting salvation in the kingdom of God Yea whosoever will thrust in his sickle and reap the same is called of God therefore if you will ask of me you shall

NOTES

111. Actually New York.
112. Knight recalled that he bought and provided to JS "a Barral of Mackrel and some lined paper for writing[,] . . . nine or ten Bushels of grain and five or six Bushels taters and a pound of tea." (Knight, Reminiscences, 6.)
113. Revelation, May 1829–B, in Doctrine and Covenants 38, 1835 ed. [D&C 12].
114. TEXT: James Mulholland inscribed an embellished circle around this reference, presumably to indicate the intent to supply text from the 1835 edition of the Doctrine and Covenants.

Draft 1

Draft 2

shall receive; if you knock it shall be opened unto you.

3 Now as you have asked, behold I say unto you, keep my commandments and seek to bring forth and establish the cause of Zion.

4 Behold I speak unto you, and also to all those who have desires to bring forth and establish this work, and no one can assist in this work, except he shall be humble and full of love, having faith, hope and charity, being temperate in all things, whatsoever shall be intrusted to his care.

5 Behold I am the light and the ~~light~~ ⟨life⟩ of the world, that speaketh these words: therefore, give heed with your might, and then you are called.

Amen.

Shortly after ~~my having commenced~~ ⟨commencing⟩ to translate, I became acquainted with ~~the f~~ Mr Peter Whitmer ~~Senʳ~~ of ⟨Fayette⟩ Seneca County, New York and also with ⟨some of⟩ his family. In the beginning of the month of June, his Son David Whitmer came to the place where we were residing, ⟨and brought⟩ with ⟨him⟩ a two horse waggon, for the purpose, of ~~prevailing upon~~ ⟨having⟩ us ~~to~~ accompany him to his father's place, ⟨and there remain untill we finished the work⟩ He proposed that we should ~~go~~ have our board free of charge, and the assistance of one of his brothers to write for me, as also his own assistance when it might answer. Having much need of such timely aid in ~~such~~ an undertaking so arduous, and being informed that the people in the neighborhood were anxiously waiting ~~to g~~ the opportunity to enquire into these things. We ~~consented~~ accepted the invitation, and accompanied Mʳ Whitmer to his father's house, and there ~~remained~~ ⟨resided⟩ untill

Shortly after commencing to translate, I became acquainted with Mʳ Peter Whitmer [Sr.] of Fayette, Seneca County New York, and also with some of his family. In the beginning of the month of June, his son, David Whitmer came to the place where we were residing, and brought with him a two horse waggon, for the purpose of having us accompany him to his father's place and there remain untill we should finish the work.[115] He proposed that we should have our board free of charge, and the assistance of one of his brothers to write for me, as also his own assistance when convenient.

Having much need of such timely aid in an undertaking so arduous, and being informed that the people of the neighborhood were anxiously ~~the~~ awaiting the opportunity to enquire into these things; we accepted the invitation and accompanied Mʳ Whitmer to his father's house, and there resided [p. 21] untill the translation was finished, and the copyright secured.

Draft 3

recieve if you knock it shall be opened unto you.

3 Now as you have asked behold I say unto you keep my commandments and seek to bring forth and establish the cause of Zion.

4 Behold I speak unto you and also all those who have desires to bring forth and establish this work and no one can assist in this work except he shall be humble and full of love having faith hope and charity being temperate in all things whatsoever shall be intrusted to his care—

5 Behold I am the ⟨light⟩ ~~life~~ and the ~~light~~ ⟨life⟩ of the world that speaketh these words therefore give heed with your might and then you are called Amen.

~~Shortly after com~~

In the beginning of June a son of Peter Whitmer of Fayett Seneca Co. N.Y. with whom I had formed an acquaintance ~~some~~ shortly after commencing the translation came to the place where we were ⟨living⟩ ~~residing~~ with a carriage to take us to his father's residence there to remain until we should finish the work. He proposed to ⟨gratuitously⟩ give us our board and the assistance of one of his brothers to write ~~for me~~ as well as his own when convenient ~~free of c◊ a~~

Having ~~much~~ need of such ~~kindly~~ ⟨timely⟩ aid and being informed ~~by~~ that the people of the neighbourhood were anxious to inquire into these things we accepted the invitation and accompanied him home where we remained [p. 40] until the translation was completed and copy richt secured

NOTES

115. JS probably became acquainted with the Whitmer family through his parents, who visited the Whitmers before visiting JS in Harmony in the fall of 1828, and through Oliver Cowdery, with whom David Whitmer visited while on "a business trip to Palmyra" in 1828. David Whitmer later wrote that Cowdery wrote him three letters from Harmony in April and May 1829, the third "telling me to come down into Pennsylvania and bring him and Joseph to my father's house, giving as a reason therefore that they had received a commandment from God to that effect." (Lucy Mack Smith, History, 1845, 151; "Mormonism," *Kansas City [MO] Daily Journal,* 5 June 1881, [1].)

Draft 1

the translation was finished, and the copy
right secured. Upon our arrival, we found
Mr Whitmer's family very anxious concerning the work, and very friendly towards
ourselves. They continued so, boarded and
lodged us according to ~~the~~ proposal, and
John Whitmer, in particular, assisted [p. [3]]
us very much in writing ~~&c~~ during the remainder of the work. ~~The family in~~ in the
mean time ~~however~~ David, John and Peter
Whitmer became ~~very zealous in the cause~~
⟨our zealous friends and assistants in the
work,⟩ and ⟨being⟩ anxious to know their
respective duties, and ⟨having⟩ desired with
much earnestness that I should enquire of
the Lord concerning them I did so through
the means of the Urim and Thummin and
obtained for them the following revelations, in succession.——

3 revelations, Book of Covenants
Page 169[117]

Draft 2

Upon our arrival, we found Mr Whitmer's family very anxious concerning the
work, and very friendly towards ourselves.
They continued so, boarded and lodged us
according to proposal, and John Whitmer,
in particular, assisted us very much in writing during the remainder of the work.[116]

In the meantime, David, John, and
Peter Whitmer Jr became our zealous
friends and assistants in the work; And
being anxious to know their respective duties, and having desired with much earnestness that I should enquire of the Lord
concerning them, I did so, through the
means of the Urim and Thummin and obtained for them in succession the folowing
Revelations.

Revelation given to David Whitmer,
at Fayette, Seneca County
New York. June 1829.[118]

1 A great and marvelous work is about
to come forth unto the children of men:
behold I am God, and give heed to my
word, which is quick and powerful,
sharper than a two edged sword, to the
dividing asunder of both joints and marrow: therefore give heed unto my word.

2 Behold the field is white already to
harvest, therefore whoso desireth to reap
let him thrust in his sickle with his
might and reap while the day lasts, that
he may treasure up for his soul everlasting salvation in the kingdom of God:
yea, whosoever will thrust in his sickle
and reap, the same is called of God:
therefore, if you will ask of me you shall
receive; if you will knock it shall be
opened unto you.

3 Seek to ~~establish~~ bring forth and establish my Zion. Keep my commandments in all things, and if you keep my

Draft 3

116. David Whitmer recalled later that Christian Whitmer and Emma Smith were scribes for the Book of Mormon at Fayette, in addition to Oliver Cowdery, who inscribed most of the extant text (about a fourth of the original manuscript). Based on an analysis of the extant manuscript, John Whitmer also served as scribe for several pages. Additionally, unidentified handwriting in the manuscript may be that of Martin Harris. It is not known whether other sribes helped with the nonextant portion of the original manuscript. (James H. Hart, "About the Book of Mormon," *Deseret News,* 9 Apr. 1884, 190; see also Skousen, *Original Manuscript,* 13–14; and Jessee, "Original Book of Mormon Manuscript," 272–278.)

117. TEXT: James Mulholland inscribed a partial embellished circle around this reference, presumably to indicate the intent to supply text from the 1835 edition of the Doctrine and Covenants.

118. Revelation, June 1829–A, in Doctrine and Covenants 39, 1835 ed. [D&C 14].

In the mean time, David, John, and Peter, Whitmer Jr. sons of Peter Whitmer Senr. became our zealous friends and assistants in the work; and being very anxious to know the will of the Lord concerning them after much solicitation I enquired of the Lord through the Urim and Thummin and recieved the following Revelations

1 A great and marvellous work is about to come forth unto the children of men: behold I am God and give heed unto my word, which is quick and powerful, sharper than a two edged sword, to the dividing assunder of both joints and marrow: therefore give heed unto my word.

2 Behold the field is white already to harvest. therefore whoso desireth to reap. let him thrust in his sickle with his might. and reap while the day lasts, that he may treasure up for his soul everlasting salvation in the kingdom of god: Yea, whosoever will thrust in his sickle and reap, the same is called of god: therefore if ~ye~ you will ask of me you shall recieve, if you will knock it shall be opened unto you.

3 Seek to bring forth and establish my Zion. Keep my commandments and endure to the end, & you shall have eternal

Draft 1   **Draft 2**

commandments, and endure to the end,
you shall have eternal life; which gift is
the greatest of all the gifts of God.

4 And it shall come to pass, that if you
shall ask the father in my name, in faith
believing, you shall receive the Holy
Ghost, which giveth utterance, that you
may stand as a witness of the things of
which you shall both hear and see; and
also, that you may declare repentance
unto this generation.

5 Behold I am Jesus Christ the son of
the living God, who created the heavens
and the earth, a light which cannot be
hid in darkness: wherefore, I must bring
forth the fulness of my gospel from the
Gentiles unto the house of Israel. And
behold thou art David, and thou art
called to assist: which thing if ye do, and
are faithful ye shall be blessed both spiritually and temporally, and great shall be
your reward. Amen.

Revelation given to John Whitmer, at
Fayette, Seneca County, New York, June
1829.[119]

1 Hearken my servant John, and listen
to the words of Jesus Christ, your Lord
and your Redeemer, for behold I speak
unto you with sharpness and with power,
for mine arm is over all the earth, and I
will tell you that which no man knoweth
save me and thee alone: for many times
you have desired of me to know that which
would be of most worth unto you.

2 Behold, blessed are you for this thing,
and for speaking my words which I have
given [p. 22] you, according to my commandments.

3 And now behold I say unto you, that
the thing which will be of the most
worth to unto you, will be to declare repentance unto this people, that you may
bring souls unto me, that you may rest

Draft 3

life, which gift is the greatest of all the gifts of God

4 And it shall come to pass that if you shall ask the the father in my name. in faith believing; you shall recieve the Holy Ghost, which giveth utterance, that you may stand as a witness of the things which you shall both hear and see; and ~~shall~~ that you may declare repentance ⟨unto⟩ ~~to~~ this generation

5 Behold I am Jesus Christ the sun of the living God. who created the heavens and the earth, a light which cannot be hid in darkness: wherefore I must bring forth the fulness of my gospel from the Gentiles unto the House of Israel. And behold thou art David and thou art called to assist: which thing if ye do, and are [p. 41] faithful ye shall be blessed both spiritulally and temporally and great shall be your reward Amen

1 Hearken my servent John, and listen to the words of Jesus Christ. your Lord and your Redeemer, for behold I speak ⟨un⟩to you with Sharpness and with power, for mine arm is over ~~you~~ all the earth. and I will tell you that which no man knoweth save me and thee alone: for many times you have desired of me to know that which would be of most worth unto you

2 Behold, blessed are you for this thing. and for speaking my words ~~wich~~ which I have given you according to my commandments

3 And now behold. I say unto you that the thing which will be of the most worth unto you, will be to declare repentance unto this people, that you may bring souls unto me. that you may rest

NOTES

119. Revelation, June 1829–C, in Doctrine and Covenants 40, 1835 ed. [D&C 15].

Draft 1

We found the people ~~in general of Fayette~~ ⟨of⟩ Seneca Co. in general, friendly, and disposed to enquire in to the truth of these strange matters, which now began to be noised abroad. Many opened their houses ⟨to us,⟩ in order that we might have an opportunity of meeting with their friends for the purpose of instruction, and explanation. We met with many willing to hear us, and wishful to find out the truth as it is in Christ Jesus, and apparently willing to obey the ~~truth~~ ⟨Gospel⟩ when once, fairly convinced and satisfied in their own minds; and in this same month ⟨(June)⟩ of June, My Brother Hyrum Smith, ~~and~~ David Whitmer and Peter Whitmer Jr

Draft 2

with them in the kingdom of my Father. Amen.

Revelation given to Peter Whitmer Jr at Fayette, Seneca County, New York. June 1829.[120]

1 Hearken my servant Peter, and listen to the words of Jesus Christ, your Lord and your Redeemer, for behold I speak unto you with sharpness and with power, for mine arm is over all the earth, and I will tell ⟨thee⟩ that which no man knoweth save ~~thee~~ ⟨me⟩ and thee alone: for many times you have desired of me to know that which would be of the most worth unto you

2 Behold, blessed are you for this thing, and for speaking my words which I have given you according to my commandments:

3 And now behold I say unto you, that the thing which will be of the most worth unto you, will be to declare repentance unto this people, that you may bring souls unto me, that you may rest with them in the kingdom of my Father. Amen.

We found the people of Seneca County in general friendly and disposed to enquire into the truth of these strange matters which now began to be noised abroad: Many opened their houses to us in order that we might have an opportunity of meeting with our friends for the purposes of instruction and explanation. We met with many from time to time, who were willing to hear us, and wishful to find out the truth as it is in Christ Jesus, and apparently willing to obey the Gospel when once fairly convinced and satisfied in their own minds; and in this same month of June, my brother Hyrum Smith, David Whitmer, and Peter Whitmer Jr were

Draft 3

with them in ~~my~~ the kingdom of my Father

120. Revelation, June 1829–D, in Doctrine and Covenants 41, 1835 ed. [D&C 16].

1 Harken my Servant Peter and listen to the words of Jesus Christ your Lord and your Redeemer for behold I speak unto you with sharpness and power for mine arm is over all the earth and I will tell thee what no man knoweth save me and thee alone for many times you have desired of me to know that which would be of the most worth unto you

2 Behold blessed are you for this thing, and for speaking my words which I have given you according to my commandments

3 And now behold—I say unto you that the thing which will be of the most worth unto you will be to declare repentance unto this people that you may bring souls unto me that you may rest with them in the kingdom of my Father, amen. [p. 42]

We found the people of Seneca Co, in the main friendly and disposed to inquire into the truth of these strange things which were being noised abroad and many opened their houses to us so that we might have an opportunity of meeting with our friends and obtain instruction— We met from time to time at this place and found ~~mayny~~ m[a]ny that were willing to hear us and anxious to find out truth as in Christ Jesus and apparently willing to obey the Gospel. In this month (June) David Whitmer Peter Whitmer J[r.] and my brother Hyrum were baptized in Seneca Lake

Draft 1

were baptized, the two former by myself, and the latter by Oliver Cowdery. From this time forth, many became believers, and were baptized whilst we continued to instruct and persuade as many as ~~expressed desires~~ applied for information, In the course of the work of translation, ⟨we⟩ ~~became~~ we ascertained that ~~this~~ ⟨three⟩ ⟨work⟩ especial witness[es] were to be provided by the Lord, to whom he would grant, that they should ~~have a~~ see the plates from which this work, (The Book of Mormon) should be translated, and that these witness[es] should bear ~~testimony of the same publickly to~~ record of the same [p. [4]] as will be found recorded Book of Mormon Page [*blank*] second Edition and Page [*blank*] first edition——

~~almost~~ So soon as we had made this discovery, it ⟨almost immediately⟩ occurred to, Oliver Cowdery David Whitmer and the aforementioned Martin Harris who had came to see us, and make enquiry how we got along with our work— ⟨of translation;⟩ that they would have me enquire of the Lord, to know if they might not obtain of him to be allowed to be these three witnesses and ~~at length~~ ⟨finally⟩ they became so very solicitous, and teazed me so much almost without intermission for some time, that I at length complied, and through the Urim and Thummim I obtained ⟨of the Lord⟩ for them the fowlowing

Revelation to Oliver Cowder &c, Book
Covenants Page 171

Draft 2

baptized, ⟨in Seneca lake⟩ the two former by myself; the latter by Oliver Cowdery—

From this time forth many became believers, and were baptized, whilst we continued to instruct and persuade as many as ⟨applied⟩ for information.[121]

In th[e] course of the work of translation, we ascertained that three special witnesses were to be provided by the Lord, to whom he would grant, that they should see the plates from which this work (the Book of Mormon) should be translated, and that these witnesses should bear record of the same; as will be found, recorded, Book of Mormon First edition Page [*blank*] and second edition Page [*blank*].[122]

Almost immediately after we had made this discovery, it occurred to Oliver Cowdery, David Whitmer, and the aforementioned Martin Harris (who had came to enquire after our progress in the work) that they would have me enquire of the Lord, to know if they might not obtain of him to be these three special witnesses; and finally they became so very solicitous, and teazed me so much, that at length ⟨I⟩ complied, and through the Urim and Thummin, I obtained of the Lord for them the folowing Revelation. [p. 23]

Revelation to Oliver Cowdery, David Whitmer, and Martin Harris, at Fayette, Seneca County, New York, June 1829. Given previous to their viewing the plates containing the Book of Mormon.[123]

1 Behold I say unto you, that you must rely upon my word, which if you do with full purpose of heart, you shall have a view of the plates, and also the breastplate, the sword of Laban, the Urim and

Draft 3

From this time ~~henceforth~~ many became believers and were baptized whilst we continued to instruct those ~~as many as~~ ⟨who⟩ applied for information.

We had learned during the work of translation that the Lord would provide three special witnesses to whom he would show the plates from which the Book of Mormon was translated that they (the witnesses) should bear record of the same see Book of Mormon 1st Edition page [*blank*] second edition

Immediately after we had made this discovery it occured to Oliver Cowdry David Whitmer and Martin Harris (the latter having come to ~~inquire~~ ascertain our progress in the work) that the Lord would permit them to become these witnesses accordingly they became very solicitous that I should inquire of the Lord respecting it which I did and obtained the following Revelation [*5 lines blank*] [p. 43] [*4 lines blank*]

1 Behold I say unto you that you must rely upon my word which if you do with full purpose of heart. you shall have a view of the plates and also the breast plate the sword of Laben the Urim and

NOTES

121. The Reverend Diedrich Willers reported from Fayette that by June 1830 the "Mormonites" had baptized Lutherans, Presbyterians, Baptists, and members of the German Reformed Church in that vicinity, amounting to perhaps "at least 100 persons." (Diedrich Willers, Fayette, NY, to L. Mayer and D. Young, York, PA, 18 June 1830, in Quinn, "First Months of Mormonism," 331.)

122. See Book of Mormon, 1830 ed., 110–111, 548; and Book of Mormon, 1837 ed., 118, 577–578 [2 Nephi 27:12–14; Ether 5:2–4].

123. Revelation, June 1829–E, in Doctrine and Covenants 42, 1835 ed. [D&C 17].

Draft 1   **Draft 2**

Thummin which were given to the brother of Jared on the mount, when he talked with the Lord face to face, and the miraculous directors which were given to Lehi while in the wilderness, on the borders of the red sea; and it is by ⟨your⟩ faith that you shall obtain a view of them; even by that faith which was had by the prophets of old.

2 And after that you have obtained faith and have seen them with your eyes, you shall testify of them by the power of God; and this you shall do that my servant Joseph Smith jr, may not be destroyed, that I may bring about my righteous purposes unto the children of men in this work. And ye shall testify that you have seen them, even as my servant Joseph Smith Jr has seen them, for it is by my power that he has seen them, and it is because he had faith: and he has translated the book, even that part which I have commanded him, and as your Lord and your God liveth it is true.

3 Wherefore you have received the same power, and the same faith, and the same gift like unto him; and if you do these last commandments of mine, which I have given you, the gates of hell shall not prevail against you; for my grace is sufficient for you: and you shall be lifted up at the last day.— And I, Jesus Christ, your Lord and your God, have spoken it unto you, that I might bring my righteous purposes unto the children of men. A[men.][125]

Not many days after the above revelation was given, we four, viz; Martin Harris, ⟨David Whitmer⟩ Oliver Cowdery and

Not many days after the above commandment was given, we four, viz Martin Harris, David Whitmer, Oliver Cowdery

Draft 3

Thummin which were given to the brother of Jared on the mount when he talked with the Lord face to face and the miraculous directions which were given to Lehi while in the wilderness on the borders of the red sea and it is by your faith that you shall obtain a view of them even by that faith which was had by the Prop[h]ets of old.

2 And after that you have obtained faith and have seen them with your Eyes you shall testify of them by the power of God And this you shall do that my Servant Joseph Smith Jr. may not be destroyed that I may bring about my righteous purposes unto the children of men in this work. And ye shall testify that ye have seen them ~~with your eyes you shall testify of them by the power of God~~ even as my Servant Joseph Smith Jr. has seen them for it is by my power that he has seen them and it is because he hath faith and he hath translated the book even that part which I have commanded him and as your Lord and your God liveth it is true

3 Wherefore you have received the same power and the same faith and the same gift like unto him and if you do these last commandments of mine which I have given you the gates of hell shall not prevail against you for my grace is sufficient for you and you shall be lifted up at the last day ⟨and⟩ I ~~am~~ Jesus Christ your Lord and your God [p. 44]

~~Revelation To Joseph Smith Junr given to July 1828 concerning the plates~~[124]

have spoken it unto you that I might bring about my righteous purposes unto the children of men Amen

Not many days after the above commandment was given we retired into the woods, to obtain by fervent and humble

NOTES

124. This canceled passage is the introduction to the revelation found on manuscript page 10 of Draft 2 (p. 246 herein).

125. TEXT: "A[*page torn*]". Missing text supplied based on the 1835 edition of the Doctrine and Covenants.

Draft 1

myself, agreed to retire into the woods, and try to obtain by ~~faithful, and~~ fervent and humble prayer, the fulfillment of the promises given in ~~the~~ this revelation (that they should have a view of the plates &c,) we accordingly made choice of a ~~retired~~ piece of woods convenient, to ~~Fat[her]~~ Mʳ Whitmer's ⟨house⟩ to which we retired and, having knelt down, we began to pray in much faith, to Almighty God, to bestow upon us a realization of those promises. ~~It was deci~~[128] ~~had been arranged by us pre~~ according to previous arrangement, I commenced by vocal prayer to our Heavenly Father, ~~and in succ~~ and was followed by each of the ~~other three~~ ⟨rest⟩ in succession, we however did not yet receive any answer or manifestation of the divine favour in our behalf. We again observed the same order of prayer each calling on and praying fervently to God in regular rotation. but with the same ⟨unbeneficial⟩ result as before. Upon our again failing, Martin Harris proposed that he should withdraw himself from us believing, as he expressed himself, that his presence was the cause of our not obtaining the object [p. [5]] of our desires at that time. He accordingly withdrew from us, and we k[n]elt down again, and had not been many minutes engaged in prayer when presently we beheld a light above us in the air of exceeding brightness and behold an angel stood before us; in his hands he held the plates which we had been praying ~~to God to~~ ⟨for ~~these~~ those to⟩ have a view of. he turned over the plates one by one so that we could see them, and discern the engravings thereon distinctly, He addressed himself to David Whitmer, and said ~~unto him~~ "David, blessed is ~~God~~ ⟨The Lord⟩, and ~~all those who~~ ⟨he that⟩ keep⟨s⟩ his commandments". When immediately afterwards we heard a voice from out ⟨of⟩ the bright light

Draft 2

and myself, agreed to retire into the woods, and try to obtain by fervent and humble prayer, the fulfilment of the promises given in this revelation; that they should have a view of the pl[a]t[es] &c[,][126] we accordingly made choice of a piece of woods convenient to Mʳ Whitmer's [house],[127] to which we retired, and having knelt down, we began to pray in much faith, to Almighty God to bestow upon us a realization of those promises. According to previous arrangement, I commenced by vocal prayer to our Heavenly Father and was folowed by each of the rest in succession; we did not yet however obtain any answer or manifestation of the divine favour in our behalf.

We again observed the same order of prayer each calling on and praying fervently to God in rotation; but with the same result as before. Upon this our second failure, Martin Harris proposed that he would withdraw himself from us, believing as he expressed himself that his presence was the cause of our not obtaining what we wished for: He accordingly withdrew from us, and we knelt down again, and had not been [p. 24] many minutes engaged in prayer when presently we beheld a light above us in the air of exceeding brightness, and behold, an angel stood before us; in his hands he held the plates which we had been praying for these to have a view of: he turned over the leaves one by one, so that we could see them, and discern the engravings thereon distinctly: He addressed himself to David Whitmer, and said, "David, blessed is the Lord, and he that keeps ~~all~~ his commandments:" when immediately afterwards we heard a voice from out of the bright light above us, saying "These plates have been revealed by the power of God, and they have been translated by the power of

Draft 3

prayer the fulfillment of the promises given in this Revelation ~~that they should have a v~~ According to previous arrangement I commenced by vocal prayer to Almighty God and was followed by each of the others in succession. We did not yet however obtain any manifestation of divine favor.

We again observed the same order of prayer but with the same result as before Upon this second failure Martin Harris proposed to withdraw himself from us fearing that his presence was the cause of our not obtaining what we wished ~~he accordingly withdrew from us~~ ⟨After he had retired⟩ ~~and~~ we bowed ourselves again in prayer and had not been many minutes ⟨so⟩ engaged when we beheld a light of exceeding brightness above us and behold an angel stood before us having in his hands the plates for a view of which we had been praying. He slowly turned ⟨over⟩ the ⟨leaves⟩ ~~leaves over~~ so that we could distinctly see the engravings thereon Addressing himself to David Whitmer said David blessed ⟨be⟩ the Lord and he that keeps his commandments, And immediately after we heard a voice proceeding from the light above us saying "these plates have been revealed [p. 45] by the power of God and they have been translated by the power of God the translation of them which you have seen is correct and I command you to bear record of what you now see and hear—

126. TEXT: "pl[*page torn*]t[*page torn*] &c[*page torn*]". Missing text supplied based on Draft 1.

127. TEXT: Page torn. Missing text supplied based on Draft 1.

128. TEXT: "was deci" was canceled when initially inscribed and then canceled a second time with the rest of the passage.

Draft 1

above us, saying "these plates have been revealed by the power of God, and they have
been translated by the power of God, the
translation of them which you have seen is
correct, and I command ~~to~~ you to bear record of ~~the truth thereof,~~ ⟨what you now see
& hear⟩ ~~Immediately afterwards~~ I ⟨now⟩
~~left these two,~~ David, and Oliver, and went
in pursuit of Martin Harris, whom I found
at a considerable distance fervently engaged in prayer, he soon told me however
that he had not yet prevailed with the
Lord, and earnestly requested of me, to
join him in prayer, ~~to the intention~~ that he
also might realize the same blessings,
which we had just received. we now joined
in prayer, and obtained our desires, for before we had yet finished, the same vision
was opened to our view at least it was,
again to me, and I once more beheld ⟨and
heard⟩ the same things. Whilst at the same
moment, Martin Harris cried out apparently in an extasy of Joy, "'tis enough. 'tis
enough mine eyes have beheld, mine eyes
have beheld", and jumping up he shouted
Hosanna, ~~and~~ blessed God, and otherwise
rejoiced exccceedingly. Having thus, through
the mercy of God, obtained ~~to~~ these glorious manifestations, it now remain[p. [6]]ed
for those three individuals to fulfill the
commandment which they had received to
bear record of these things, in order to accomplish which they drew up and subscribed their names to the folowing document.
The Testimony of three witnesses.

Draft 2

God; the translation of them which you
have seen is correct, and I command you to
bear record of what you now see and hear".—

I now left David and Oliver, and went
in pursuit of Martin Harris, who I found at
a considerable distance fervently engaged
in prayer; he soon told me however that he
had not yet prevailed with the Lord, and
earnestly requested me, to join him in
prayer, that he also might realize the same
blessings which we had just recieved: we
accordingly joined in prayer, and ultimately obtained our desires, for before we
had yet finished, the same vision was
opened to our view; at least it was again to
me, and I once more beheld, and seen, and
heard the same things; whilst at the same
moment, Martin Harris cried out, apparently in an ecstasy of Joy "'Tis enough, 'tis
enough; mine eyes have beheld, mine eyes
have beheld", and jumping up he shouted,
Hosanna, blessing God; and otherwise rejoiced exceedingly. Having thus through
the mercy of God, obtained these glorious
manifestations, it now remained for these
three individuals to fulfil the commandment which they had received, viz: to bear
record of these things; in order to accomplish which, they drew up and subscribed
the following document.[129]

The Testimony of Three Witnesses.
Be it known unto all nations, kindreds,
tongues, and people, unto whom this
work shall come, that we through the
grace of God the Father, and our lord
Jesus Christ, have seen the plates which
contain this record, which is a record of
the people of Nephi, and also of the

Draft 3

129. The earliest copy of the testimony that follows is found in the printer's manuscript of the Book of Mormon, in the handwriting of Oliver Cowdery. Cowdery likely was the author of the statement, given his writing abilities and similarities between the document and Cowdery's 1829 correspondence to JS and Hyrum Smith. The copies of the "Testimony of Three Witnesses" and the "Testimony of Eight Witnesses" that follow match the versions in the second edition of the Book of Mormon. (Book of Mormon, Printer's Manuscript, 463–464, CCLA; "Testimony of Three Witnesses" and "Testimony of Eight Witnesses," in Book of Mormon, 1837 ed., [620]–[621]; see also JS Letterbook 1, pp. 4–9.)

I now went in ⟨Search⟩ ~~pursuit~~ of Martin Harris whom I found at a distance earnestly engaged in prayer from him I learned that he had not yet obtaiined what he wished ⟨and⟩ ~~when~~ I joined with him ⟨in prayer⟩ and ultimately obtained a view of the plates ~~When~~ and ⟨he⟩ ~~Martin Harris~~ cried out in an ecstacy of joy tis enough tis enough mine eyes have beheld mine eyes have beheld and jumping up ~~he~~ shouted hosanna and rejoiced exceedingly having through the mercy of God thus obtained these glorious manifestations It now remained for these individuals to obey the command which they had receivd ⟨Accordingly⟩ They drew ~~up~~ and subscribed to the following ~~document~~ testimony

Be it known unto all nations kindreds tongues and people unto whom this work shall come that we through the grace of God the Father and our Lord Jesus Christ have seen the plates which contain this record which is a record of the people of Nephi and also of the

Draft 1   **Draft 2**

Lamanites, their brethren, and also of
the people of Jared, who came from the
tower of which ~~has~~ hath been spoken;[130]
and we also know that they have been
translated by the gift and power of God,
for his voice hath declared it unto us;
wherefore we know of a surety, that the
work is true. And we also testify that we
have seen the engravings which are upon
the plates; and they have been shewn
unto us by the power of God and not of
man. And we declare with words of soberness, that an angel of God came down
from Heaven, and he brought and laid
before our eyes, that we beheld and saw
the plates, and the engravings thereon;[131]
and we know that it is by the grace of
God the Father, and our Lord Jesus
Christ, that we beheld and bear record
that these things are true; and it is marvelous in our eyes, nevertheless, the voice
[p. 25] of the Lord commanded us, that
we should bear record of it; wherefore, to
be obedient unto the commandments of
God, we bear testimony of these things.

And we know that if we are faithful in
Christ, we shall rid our garments of the
blood of all men, and be found spotless
before the judgement seat of Christ, and
shall dwell with him eternally in the
heavens. And the honor be to the Father,
and to the Son, and to the Holy Ghost,
which is one God. Amen.

                                    Oliver Cowdery
                                    David Whitmer
                                    Martin Harris.

Soon after these things had transpired   Soon after these things had transpired
the following testimony was obtained from   the following additional tes[t]imony was
those whose names are subscribed thereto.   obtained.
"And also the Testimony of Eight   And also the Testimony of Eight
           Witnesses"   Witnesses.

Draft 3

Lamenites their bretheren and also of the people of Jared who came from the tower of which hath been spoken and we also know that they have been ~~spoke by~~ translated by the gift and power of God for his voice hath declared it unto us wherefore we know of a surety that the work is true. And we also testify that we have seen the engravings which are upon the plates and they have been shown to us by the power of God and not of man [p. 46]

And we declare with ⟨words of⟩ soberness that an angel of God came down from heaven and he brought and laid them before our eyes—that we beheld and saw the plates and the engravings thereon and we know that it is by the grace of God the Father and our Lord Jesus Christ that we beheld and bear record that these things are true and it is marvelous in our eyes Nevertheless the voice of the Lord commanded us that we should bear record of it wherefore to be obedient unto the commandments of God we bear testimony of these things

And we know that if we are faithful in Christ we shall rid our garment of the blood of all men and be found spotless before the judgment seat of Christ and shall dwell with him eternally in the heavens. And ⟨the honor⟩ be to the Father and to the son and to the Holy Ghost which is one God. Amen

Oliver Cowdry
David Whitmer
Martin Harris

Soon after these things had transpired the following additional testimony was obtained.

NOTES

130. See Book of Mormon, 1830 ed., 539 [Ether 1:33].

131. David Whitmer told several interviewers in the 1870s and 1880s that he saw additional items on this occasion. Most of these later accounts listed the gold plates, the interpreters or Urim and Thummim, the sword of Laban, the "directors," and additional records; in some Whitmer also mentioned the breastplate. (See, for example, "Interview with David Whitmer," *Deseret News,* 21 Aug. 1878, 461; "Mormonism," *Kansas City [MO] Daily Journal,* 5 June 1881, [1]; and "Letter from Elder W. H. Kelley," *Saints' Herald,* 1 Mar. 1882, 66–69; compare Revelation, June 1829–E, in Doctrine and Covenants 42:1, 1835 ed. [D&C 17:1].)

Draft 1

Draft 2

Draft 1 (right column begins empty until lower section)

Draft 2

Be it known unto all nations, kindreds, tongues, and people, unto whom this work shall come, that Joseph Smith Jr, the translator of this work has shewn unto us, the plates of which hath been spoken, which have the appearance of gold; and as many of the leaves as the said Smith has translated, we did handle with our hands: and we also saw the engravings thereon, all of which has the appearance of ancient work, and of curious workmanship. And this we bear record with words of soberness, that the said Smith has shewn unto us, for we have seen and hefted, and know of a surety, that the said Smith has got the plates of which we have spoken. And we give our names unto the world, to witness unto the world, that which we have seen; and we lie not, God bearing witness of it.

Christian Whitmer	Hiram Page
Jacob Whitmer	Joseph Smith Senr
Peter Whitmer Jr	Hyrum Smith
John Whitmer	Samuel H. Smith.

Draft 1 (continued)

~~During all this time however~~ ⟨Mean time⟩ we continued to translate, ⟨at intervals⟩ when ~~we were~~ not necessitated to attend to the ⟨numerous⟩ ~~enquiries~~ enquirers ~~of the numbers~~ that now began to visit us, some for the sake of finding the truth, others for the purpose of putting hard questions, and trying to confound us. ~~We had several~~ Among these latter class ⟨weree⟩ several learned Priests, ~~to visit us,~~ generally for the purpose of disputation. however the Lords continued to pour out upon us his Holy Spirit and as often as we had need, he gave us in that moment what to say. so that although, unlearned, and inexperienced in religious controversies, yet were we able to confound these learned Rabbi's of the day, whilst at the same time we were enabled, to

Draft 2 (continued)

Mean time we continued to translate, at intervals, when not necessitated to attend to the numerous enquirers, that now began to visit us; some for the sake of finding the truth, others for the purpose of putting hard questions, and trying to confound us, among the latter class, were several learned Priests ⟨who⟩ generally came for the purpose of disputation: However the Lord continued to pour out upon us his Holy Spirit, and as often as we had need, he gave us in that moment what to say; so that although unlearned, and inexperienced in religious controversies, yet were we able to confound those learned Rabbi's of the day, whilst at the same time, we were enabled to convince the honest in heart, that we had obtained (through the mercy

Draft 3

Be it known unto all nations kindreds tongues and people unto whom this work shall come that Joseph Smith Jr. the translator of this work has shewn unto us the plates of which hath been spoken which have the appearance of Gold and as many of the leaves as the said Smith has translated we did handle with our hands, and we also saw the engravings thereon, all of which has the appearance of ancient works and of curious workmanship and this we bear record with words of soberness that the said ⟨Joseph Smith Jr.⟩ has shewn unto ⟨us⟩ for we have seen and hefted and know of a surety [p. 47] that the said Smith has got the plates of which we have spoken And we give our names unto the world to witness unto the world ⟨to witness unto the world⟩ that which we have seen and we lie not God bearing witness of it.

Christian Whitmer	Hiram Page
Jacob Whitmer	Jos. Smith sen
Peter Whitmer	Hyrum Smith
John Whitmer	Saml. H Smith

After this we continued to translate when not attending to the numerous inquirers that now began to visit us some seeking for truth others desiring to confound us with many questions Among the latter were severel learned priests who came to dispute the truth of the word of God. I say dispute because they deny the power of Godliness as it is taught us in his word; however the Lord continued to pour out his Holy Spirit upon us

And as often as we had need he gave us in that moment what to say Although unlearned and inexperienced in religious controversies we were enabled to confound the learned rabbies of the day and at the same time convince the honest in heart that we had obtained through the mercy

Draft 1

convince the honest in heart, that we had
obtained to the true ⟨&⟩ everlasting gospel
of Jesus Christ, so that almost daily we administered the ordinance of baptism for
the remission of sins to such as believed.
We now became anxious to have that
promise ~~which conferred upon~~ ⟨realized to⟩
us, which the angel ~~had~~ that conferred
upon us the Aaronick Priesthood ~~upon us~~.
had given us, viz, that provided we continued faithful, ~~the~~ we should also have the
Melchesidec Priesthood, which holds the
authority of the laying on of hands for
the gift of the Holy Ghost [p. [7]] we had
for some time made this a subject of humble prayer, and at length we got together in
the Chamber of Mr Whitmer's house in
order more particularly to seek of the Lord
information, and if possible obtain what
we now so earnestly desired. ~~We had not
been long~~ After some time spent in solemn
and fervent prayer, the Word of the Lord
came unto us, in the Chamber, commanding us, that I should ordain Oliver Cowdery
to be an Elder in the Church of Jesus
Christ, and that he also should ordain me
to the same office, and that after having
been thus ordained, we should proceed to
ordain others to the same office, according
as it should be made known to us, from
time to time,

~~We~~ also commanding us, that as soon as
practicable we should call together all those
who had already been baptized by us, to
bless bread, and break it with them, also to
take wine, bless it, and drink it with them
doing all these things in the name of the
Lord, but to defer our own ordination untill we had called ~~the Chur~~ together our
brethren and had their sanction, and been
accepted by them as their teachers, after
which we were commanded to proceed to

Draft 2

of God) to the true and everlasting gospel
of Jesus Christ, so that almost daily we
administered the ordinance of Baptism
for the remission of sins, so [to] such as
believed.[132]

We now became anxious to have that
promise realized to us, which the Angel
that conferred upon us the Aaronick
Priesthood [p. 26] had given us, viz: that
provided we continued faithful; we should
also have the Melchesidec Priesthood,
which holds the authority of the laying on
of hands for the gift of the Holy Ghost. We
had for some time made this matter a subject of humble prayer, and at length we got
together in the Chamber of Mr Whitmer
[Peter Whitmer Sr.]'s house in order more
particularly to seek of the Lord what we
now so earnestly desired: and here to our
unspeakable satisfaction did we realize the
truth of the Saviour's promise; "Ask, and
you shall recieve, seek, and you shall find,
knock and it shall be opened unto you;"[133]
for we had not long been engaged in solemn and fervent prayer, when the word of
the Lord, came unto us in the Chamber,
commanding us; that I should ordain
Oliver Cowdery to be an Elder in the
Church of Jesus Christ, and that he also
should ordain me to the same office, ~~accor-
din~~ and then ⟨to⟩ ordain others as it should
be made known unto us, from time to
time: we were however commanded to
defer this our ordination untill, such times,
as it should be practicable to have our
brethren, who had been and who should be
baptized, assembled together, when we
must have their sanction to our thus proceeding to ordain each other, and have
them decide by vote whether they were
willing to accept us as spiritual teachers, or
not, when also we were commanded to
bless bread and break it with them, and to

Draft 3

of God the true and everlasting Gospel of Jesus Christ so that daily we administered the ordinance of baptism for the remission of sins to such as believed.

We ~~now~~ ⟨now⟩ became anxious ~~the~~ that the promise of the Melchisedec priesthood which holds the authority ~~for~~ ⟨of of⟩ the laying on of hands for the gift of the Holy Ghost given us by the angel that confirred upon ⟨us⟩ the Aronick priesthood should ⟨now⟩ be fulfilled. Having for some time made this a subject of prayer we finally met [p. 48] to unitedly ask of the Lord what we so much desired and to our unspeakable satisfaction we realized a fulfillment of our Saviour's promise ask and ye Shall receive Seek and ye shall find Knock and it shall be opened unto you; for we had been engaged in fervent prayer but a short time when the word of the Lord came unto us commanding me to ordain Oliver Cowdry to be an Elder in the Church of Jesus Christ and that he should ordain—me to the same office and then ordain others as it should from time to time be made known unto us.

We were commanded however to defer our ordination until our bretheren who had been and should be baptized were assembled together when we ⟨might⟩ ~~must~~ have their sanction ⟨to⟩ such an ordination and ascertain if they were willing to receive us as spiritual teachers. ~~if so~~ If so we were to bless bread break and eat it with them to take wine bless and drink it with them then proceed to ordain each other according to commandment and such others as

NOTES

132. David Whitmer recalled that about seventy individuals had been baptized by 6 April 1830. (Whitmer, *Address to All Believers in Christ,* 33.)

133. See Matthew 7:7; compare Book of Mormon, 1830 ed., 484, 509 [3 Nephi 14:7, 27:29].

Draft 1

ordain each other and ~~then~~ call out such men as the spirit should dictate unto us, and ordain them, and then attend to the laying on of hands for the Gift of the Holy Ghost,

The following commandment will further illustrate the nature of our calling to this Priesthood as well as others who were yet to be sought after.

Revelation Page 172

Draft 2

take wine, bless it, and drink it with them, afterward proceed to ordain each other according to commandment, then call out such men as the Spirit should dictate, and ordain them, and then attend to the laying on of hands for the gift of the Holy Ghost, upon all those whom we had previously baptized; doing all things in the name of the Lord.

The following commandment will further illustrate the nature of our calling to this Priesthood as well as that of others who were yet to be sought after.

Revelation to Joseph Smith Jr, Oliver Cowdery, and David Whitmer, making known the calling of twelve apostles in these last days, and also instructions relative to building up the Church of Christ, according to the fulness of the gospel: Given in Fayette, Seneca County New York, June 1829.[134]

1 Now behold, because of the thing which you, my servant, Oliver Cowdery have desired to know of me, I give unto you these words: behold I have manifested unto you by my Spirit in many instances, that the things which you have written are true: wherefore you know that they are true; and if you know that they are true, behold I have given unto a you a commandment, that you rely upon the things which are written, for in them are all things written concerning the foundation of my Church, my gospel and my rock; wherefore if you shall build up my Church upon the foundation of my gospel and my [p. 27] rock, the gates of hell shall not prevail against you.

2 Behold the world is ripening in iniquity, and it must needs be, that the children of men are stirred up unto repentance, both the Gentiles, and also the house of Israel: wherefore, as thou hast

Draft 3

the Spirit should dictate and then lay ⟨on⟩ hands for the gift of the Holy Ghost upon all whom we had previously baptized doing all things in the name of the Lord

NOTES

134. Revelation, June 1829–B, in Doctrine and Covenants 43, 1835 ed. [D&C 18].

1 The following Revelation will further illustrate the nature of this priest hood

1 Behold 1 Now behold because of the thing which you my servant Oliver Cowdry has ⟨have⟩ desired to know of me I give unto you the⟨se⟩ words—Behold I have manifested unto you by my spirit in many instances that the things which you have written are true wherefore you know ⟨that⟩ they are true And if you know that they are true behold I have given unto you a commandment that you rely upon the things ⟨which are⟩ written for in them are all things written concerning the foundation of my church my Gospel and my rock. the gates of hell [p. 49] shall not prevail against you.

2 Behold the world is ripening in iniquity and it must needs be that the children of men are stirred up unto repentance both the gentiles and also the house of Israel wherefore as thou hast

Draft 1   **Draft 2**

been baptized by the hand of my servant
Joseph Smith Jr—according to that
which I have commanded him, he hath
fulfilled the thing which I commanded
him. And now marvel not that I have
called him to ~~my~~ mine own purpose;
which purpose is known in me: wherefore
if he shall be diligent in keeping my commandments, he shall be blessed unto eternal life, and his name is Joseph.

3 And now Oliver Cowdery, I speak
unto you, and also unto David Whitmer
by the way of commandment: for behold
I command all men every where to repent, and I speak unto you, even as unto
Paul mine apostle, for you are called
even with that same calling with which
he was called. Remember the worth of
souls is great in the sight of God: for behold the Lord your Redeemer suffered
death in the flesh: wherefore he suffered
the pain of all men, that all men might
repent and come unto him. And he hath
risen again from the dead that he might
bring all men unto him on conditions of
repentance. And how great is his joy in
his soul that repenteth.— Wherefore you
are called to cry repentance unto this
people. And if it ⟨so⟩ be that you should
labour all your days, in crying repentance to this people, and bring save it be
one soul unto me, how great shall be
your joy with him in the kingdom of my
Father.

4 And now if your joy will be great
with one soul, that you have brought
unto me into the kingdom of my Father,
how great will be your joy, if you should
bring many souls unto me? Behold you
have my gospel before you, and my rock
and my salvation: ask the Father in my
name in faith believing that you shall receive, and you shall have the Holy Ghost

Draft 3

been baptized by the hand of my servant
Joseph Smith Jr according to that which
I have commanded him he hath fulfilled
the thing which I have commanded him.
And now marvel not that I have called
him unto ~~my~~ mine own purpose which
purpose is known in me wherefore if he
shall be diligent in keeping my commandments he shall be blessed unto eternal life and his name is Joseph.

3 And now Oliver Cowdry, I speak
unto you and also unto David Whitmer
by the way of commandment for behold
I command ~~every~~ all men every where to
repent and I speak unto you even as unto
Paul mine Apostle for you are called even
with that same calling with which he
was called. Remember the worth of souls
is great in the sight of God for behold the
Lord your Redeemer suffered death in
the flesh wherefore he suffered the pain
of all men that all might repent and
come unto him.

And he hath risen again from the dead
that he might bring all men unto him on
conditions of repentance. And how great
is his joy in the soul that repenteth wherefore you are called to cry repentance
unto this people. And if it ~~should~~ so be
that you should labour all your days in
crying repentance unto this people and
bring save it be one soul unto me how
great shall be your joy with him in the
kingdom of my Father?

4 And now if your joy will be great
with one soul that you have brought
unto me into the kingdom of my Father
how great will be your joy if you should
bring many souls unto me? Behold you
have my Gospel before you and my rock
and my salvation Ask the Father in my
name in faith beleiving [p. 50] that you
shall receive and you shall have the Holy

Draft 1

Draft 2

which manifesteth all things which is
expedient unto the Children of men.
And if you have not faith, hope and
charity, you can do nothing. Contend
against no church, save it be the Church
of the devil. Take upon you the name of
Christ, and speak the truth in soberness,
and as many as repent, and are baptized
in my name, which is Jesus Christ, and
endure to the end, the same shall be
saved. Behold, Jesus Christ is the name
⟨which is⟩ given of the Father, and there
is none other name given whereby man
can be saved: wherefore all men must
take upon them the name which is given
of the Father, for in that name shall they
be called at the last day: wherefore if
they know not the name by which they
are called, they can not have place in the
kingdom of my Father.

5 And now behold there are others
who are called to declare my gospel both
unto Gentile, and unto Jew: yea, even
twelve: and the twelve shall be my disciples, and they shall take upon them my
name, ~~with full purpose of heart:~~ and the
twelve are they, who shall desire to take
upon them my name with full purpose
of heart: and if they desire to take upon
them my name [p. 28] with full purpose
of heart, they are called to go into all the
world, to preach my gospel unto every
creature: and they are they who are ordained of me to baptize in my name, according to that which is written; and you
have that which is written before you:
wherefore you must perform it according
to the words which are written. And now
I speak unto the twelve: Behold my grace
is sufficient for you: you must walk
uprigh[t]ly before me, and sin not. And
behold you are they who are ordained of

Draft 3

Ghost which manifes[t]eth all things which is expedient unto the children of men. And if you have not faith hope and charity you can do nothing. Contend against no church save it be the church of the devil. Take upon you the name of Christ and speak the truth in soberness and as many as repent and are baptized in my name which is Jesus Christ and endure to the end the same shall be saved.

Behold Jesus Christ is the name which is given of the Father and there is none other name given whereby men can be saved. Wherefor all men must take upon them the nam[e] which is given of the Father for in that name shall they be called at the last day. Whrefore if they know not the name by which they are called they cannot have place in the Kingdom of my Father.

5 And now behold there are others who are called to declare my Gospel both unto Gentile and unto Jew yea even twelve and the twelve shall be my disciples and they shall take upon them my name with full purpose of heart and if th[e]y desire to take upon them my name with full purpose of heart they are called to go into all the world to preach my Gospel unto every creature. And they are they who are ordained of me ~~to preach my Gos~~ to baptize in my name according to that which is written before you wherefore you must perform it according to the words which are ~~before you~~ written.

And now I speak unto the twelve Behold my grace is sufficient for you you must walk uprightly before me and sin not. And behold you are they who are ordained of me to ordain priests and

Draft 1   **Draft 2**

me, to ordain priests and teachers to declare my gospel, according to the power
of the Holy Ghost which is in you, and
according to the callings, and gifts of
God unto men: and I Jesus Christ, your
Lord, and your God have spoken it. These
words are not of men, nor of man, but of
me: wherefore, you shall testify they are
of me, and not of man: for it is my voice
which speaketh them unto you: for they
are given by my spirit unto you: and by
my power you can read them one to another: and save it were by my power, you
could not have them: wherefore you can
testify that you have heard my voice, and
know my words.

6 And now behold I give unto you,
Oliver Cowdery, and also unto you
David Whitmer, that you shall search
out the twelve who shall have the desires
of which I have spoken; and by their desires and their works you shall know
them: and when you have found them
you shall shew these things unto them.
And you shall fall down and worship the
Father in my name: and you must preach
unto ~~all~~ the world saying you must repent and be baptized in the name of
Jesus Christ: for all men must repent,
and be baptized; and not only men, but
women, and children who have arriven
to the years of accountability.

7 And now, after that you have received this, you must keep my commandments in all things: and by your hands I
will work a marvelous work among the
children of men, unto the convincing of
many of their sins, that they may come
unto repentance: and that they may
come unto the kingdom of my Father:
wherefore the blessings which I give unto
you, are above all things. And after ⟨that⟩
you have received this, if you keep not

Draft 3

teachers to declare my gospel according
to the power of the Holy Ghost which is
in you and according to the callings and
gifts of God unto men And I Jesus
Christ your Lord and [p. 51] and your
God have spoken it. These words are not
of men nor of man but of me wherefore
you shall testify they are of me and not
of man for it is my voice which speaketh
them unto you for they are given by my
spirit unto you and ~~by~~ by my power you
can read them one to another and save it
were by my power you could not have
them wherefore you can testify that you
have heard my voice and know my
words.

6 And now behold I give unto you
Oliver Cowdry and also unto David
Whitmer that you shall search out the
twelve who shall have the desires of of
which I have spoken and by their desires
and their works you shall know them
and when you have found them you shall
show these things unto them. And you
shall fall down and worship the Father in
my name and you must preach unto the
world saying you must repent and be
baptized and not only men but women
and children who have arriven to the
years of accountability.

7 And now after that you have received this you must keep my commandments in all things and by your hands I
will work a marvelous work among the
children of men unto the convincing of
~~their~~ many of their sins that they may
come unto repentance and that they may
come unto the kingdom of my Father
wherefore the blessings which I give unto
you are above all things. And after that
you have received this if you keep not

Draft 1   **Draft 2**

my commandments, you cannot be saved
in the kingdom of my Father.

Behold I Jesus Christ, your Lord and
your God, and your Redeemer by the
power of my spirit have spoken it. Amen.

We continued to receive instruction
concerning our duties from time to time,
and among ~~the~~ many things the folowing
directions, fixing the time of our anticipated meeting together ⟨for the purpose of
being organized⟩ were given by the Spirit of
prophecy & revelation

In this manner did the Lord continue
to give us instructions from time to time,
concerning ~~our~~ ⟨the⟩ duties which now de-
volved upon us, and among many other
things of the kind, we[135] obtained of him
the folowing, by the Spirit of Prophecy and
revelation; which not only gave us much
information, but also pointed out to us the
precise day upon which, according to his
will and commandment, we should proceed ~~to organize~~ to organize his Church
once again, here upon the earth.[136] [p. 29]

Section 2ⁿᵈ [p. [8]]

1 The rise of the Church of Christ in
these last days, being One thousand eight
hundred and thirty years since the coming of our Lord and Saviour Jesus Christ
in the flesh, it being regularly organized
and established, agreeably to the laws of
our country,[137] by the will and commandments of God in the fourth month, and
on the sixth day of the month which is
called April: which commandments were
given to Joseph Smith Jr who was called
of God, and ordained an apostle of
Jesus Christ, to be the first Elder of this
Church: and to Oliver Cowdery, who was
also called of God, an apostle of Jesus
Christ; to be the second elder of this
Church, and ordained under his hand:
and this according to the grace of our
Lord and Saviour Jesus Christ, to whom
be all glory both now and forever. Amen.

2 After it was truly manifested unto
this first elder that he had received a remission of his sins, he was entangled
again [in] the vanities of the world; but
after repenting, and humbling himself,
sincerely, through faith God ministered

Draft 3

my commandments you cannot be saved in the kingdom of my Father. Behold I Jesus Christ your Lord and your God and your Redeemer by the power of my spirit have spoken it Amen [*4 lines blank*] [p. 52]

In this manner did the Lord continue to give us instruction concerning the duties ~~involve~~ incumbent upon us and among other ⟨things⟩ of the kind we obtained the following by the Spirit of Prophecy and Revelation which not only gave us much information but pointed out the precise day upon which according to his will and commandment we should proceed to organize his church again upon ⟨the⟩ earth

1 The rise of the church of Christ in these last days being one thousand eight hundred and thirty years since the coming of our Lord & and Savior Jesus Christ in the flesh it being regularly organized and established agreeably to the laws of our Country by the will and commandments of God in the fourth month and on the sixth day of the month which is called April: which commandments were given to Joseph Smith Jr. who was called of God and ordained an apostle of Jesus Christ to be the first elder of this church and to Oliver Cowdry who was also called of God an apostle of Jesus Christ to be the second elder of this church and ordained under his hand and this according to the grace of our Lord and Savior Jesus Christ to whom be all glory both now and forever Amen.

2 After it was truly manifested unto this first elder that he had received a remission of his sins he was entangled again in the vanities of the world but after repenting and humbling himself sincerely through faith God ministered

NOTES

135. JS and Oliver Cowdery. (Revelation Book 1, p. 52, in *JSP*, MRB:75.)

136. Articles and covenants, 10 Apr. 1830, in Doctrine and Covenants 2, 1835 ed. [D&C 20]. This document is titled "Church Articles & Covenants" in Revelation Book 1, which indicates that it was "received in Fayette Seneca County New York April 10th. 1830." Its placement at this point in the history narrative, and the statement here that it designated the day on which the church was to be organized, apparently contradict the 10 April 1830 dating. (Revelation Book 1, p. 52, in *JSP*, MRB:75; see also the first volume of the Documents series [forthcoming] for additional analysis.)

137. The church was possibly organized as an unincorporated religious society—a "voluntary association of individuals or families . . . united for the purpose of having a common place of worship, and to provide a proper teacher to instruct them . . . and to administer the ordinances of the church"—and not as a religious corporation. (Tyler, *American Ecclesiastical Law,* 54; see also "Society," in Bouvier, *Law Dictionary,* 2:515; Stott, "Legal Insights into the Organization of the Church in 1830," 122–132; and An Act to Provide for the Incorporation of Religious Societies [5 Apr. 1813], *Laws of the State of New-York* [1813], vol. 2, pp. 212–219.)

Draft 1

Draft 2

unto him by an holy angel, whose countenance was as lightning, and whose garments were pure and white above all
other whiteness; and gave unto him commandments, which inspired him, and
gave him power from on high, by the
means which were before prepared, to
translate the Book of Mormon, which
contains a record of a fallen people, and
the fulness of the Gospel of Jesus Christ
to the Gentiles, and to the Jews also,
which was given by inspiration, and is
confirmed to others by the ministering
of angels, and is declared ⟨un⟩to the world
by them, proving to the world that the
holy Scriptures are true, and that God
does inspire men, and call them to his
holy work in this age and generation, as
well as in generations of old, thereby
showing that he is the same God, yesterday, today, and for ever.— Amen.

3 Therefore having so great witnesses,
by them shall the world be judged, even
as many as shall ~~here~~ hereafter come to a
knowledge of this work; and those who
receive it in faith, and work righteousness,
shall receive a crown of eternal life; but
those who harden their hearts in unbelief,
and reject it, it shall turn to their condemnation, for the Lord God has spoken it;
and we the elders of the Church, have
~~read~~ ⟨heard⟩ and bear witness to the
words of the glorious Majesty on high, to
whom be glory forever and ever. Amen.

4 By these things we know that there
is a God in heaven, who is infinite and
eternal, from everlasting to everlasting,
the same unchangeable God, the framer
of heaven and earth and all things which
are in them, and that he created man
male and female: after his own image,
and in his own likeness created he them,
and gave unto them commandments,

Draft 3

unto him by an holy angel whose countenance was as lightning and whose garments were pure and white above all other whiteness and gave unto him commandments which inspired him and gave him power from on high by the means which were before prepared to translate the book of Mormon [p. 53] which contains a record of a fallen people and the fullness of the gospel of Jesus Christ to the Gentiles and to the Jews also which was given by inspiration and is confirmed to others by the ministering of angels and is declared unto the world by them proving to the world that the holy scriptures are true and that God does inspire men and call them to his holy work in this age and generation as well as in generations of old thereby showing that he is the same God yesterday to day and forever. Amen

3 Therefore having so great witnesses by them shall the world be judged even as many as shall hereafter come to a knowledge of this work and those who receive it in faith and work righteousness shall receive a crown of eternal life but those who harden their hearts in unbelief and reject it, it shall turn to their own condemnation for the Lord has spoken it and we the elders of the church have heard and bear witness to the words of the glorious Magesty on high to whom be glory forever Amen.

4 By these things we know that there is a God in heaven who is infinite and eternal from everlasting to everlasting the same unchangeable God the framer of heaven and earth and all things which are in them and that he created man Male & female after his own image and in his own likeness created he them and gave unto them commandments that

Draft 1

Draft 2

that they should love and serve him the only ~~true and~~ living and true God, and that he should be the only being whom they should worship: but by the transgression of these holy laws, man became sensual and devilish, and became fallen man.

5 Wherefore the Almighty God gave his only begotten Son, as it is written in those scriptures which have been given of him; he suffered temptations but gave no [p. 30] heed unto them; he was crucified, died, and rose again the third day; and ascended into heaven to sit down on the right hand of the Father, to reign with almighty power according to the will of the Father, that as many as would believe and be baptized, in his holy name, and endure in faith to the end should be saved: not only those who believed after he came in the meridian of time in the flesh, but all those from the beginning, even as many as were before he came, who believed in the words of the holy prophets, who spake as they were inspired by the gift of the Holy Ghost who truly testified of him in all things, should have eternal life, as well as those who should come after, who should believe in the gifts and callings of God by the Holy Ghost, which beareth record of the Father, and of the Son, which Father, Son and Holy Ghost are one God, infinite and eternal, without end. Amen.

6 And we know that all men must repent and believe on the name of Jesus Christ, and worship the Father in his name, and endure in faith on his name to the end, or they cannot be saved in the kingdom of God. And we know that justification through the grace of our Lord and Saviour Jesus Christ, is just and true: and we know also, that sanctification through the grace of our Lord

Draft 3

they should love and serve him the only
living and true God and that he should
be the only being whom they should
worship. But by the transgression of
these holy laws man became sensual and
devlish and became fallen man.

5 Wherefore the Almighty God gave
his only begotten son as it is written in
those scriptures which have been given
of him he suffered temptations but gave
no heed unto them; he was crucified deid
and rose again the third day and ascended into[138] heaven to sit down on the
right hand of the Father that as many as
would beleive and be baptized in [p. 54]
his holy name and endure in faith to the
end should be saved not only those who
believed after he came in the meridian of
time in the flesh but all those from the
beginning even as many as were before
he came who believed in the words of
the holy prophets who spake as they were
inspired by the gift of the holy Ghost
who truly testified of him in all things
should have eternal life as well as those
who should come after who should
beleive in the gifts and callings of God
by the Holy Ghost which beareth record
of the Father and of the son which
Father ~~and~~ son and Holy Ghost are one
God infinite and eternal without end
amen.

6 And we know that all men must repent and beleive on the name of Jesus
Christ and worship the Father in his
name to the end or they cannot be saved
in the kingdom of God. And we know
that justification through the grace of
our Lord & Savior Jesus Christ is just
and true to all those who love and serve
God with all their ~~mights~~ minds and
strength but there is a possibility that

138. TEXT: Or "unto".

Draft 1

Draft 2

and Saviour Jesus Christ is just and true, to all those who love and serve God with all their mights; minds, and strength: but there is a possibility that man may fall from grace, and depart from the living God. Therefore let the Church take heed and pray always, lest they fall into temptations; yea, and even let those who are sanctified, take heed also.— And we know that these things are true, and according to the revelations of John, neither adding to, nor diminishing from the prophecy of his book, the holy scriptures, or the revelations of God which shall come hereafter by the gift and power of the Holy Ghost, the voice of God, or the ministering of Angels: And the Lord God has spoken it; and honor, power, and glory, be rendered to his holy name, both now and ever. Amen.

7 And again by way of commandment to the church concerning the manner of baptism. All those who humble themselves before God and desire to be baptized, and come forth with broken hearts and contrite spirits, and witness before the church that they have truly repented of ⟨all⟩ their sins and are willing to take upon them the name of Jesus Christ, having a determination to serve him to the end, and truly manifest by their works that they have received of the spirit of Christ unto the remission of their sins, shall be received by baptism into his church.

8 The duty of the elders, priests, teachers, ⟨deacons,⟩ and members of the church of Christ. An apostle is an elder, and it is his duty[139] to baptize, and to ordain other elders, priests, teachers, and deacons, and to administer bread and wine—the emblems of the flesh and blood of Christ—and to confirm those who are

Draft 3

man may fall from grace and depart from the living God. Therefore let the church take heed and pray always lest they fall into temptations yea and even let those who are sanctified take heed also.— And we know that these things are true and according to the revelations of John neither adding nor diminishing from the prophecy of his book the holy scriptures or the revelations of God which shall come hereafter by the gift and power of the Holy Ghost the voice of God or the ministering of angels: and the Lord God has spoken it and honor power and glory be rendered to his holy name both ⟨now⟩ and ⟨for⟩ ever Amen

7 And again by way of commandment to the church concerning the manner of baptism.

All those who humble themselves before God and desire to be baptized and come forth with broken hearts and contrite spirits and witness before the church [p. 55] that they have repented of all their sins and willing to take upon them the name of Jesus Christ having a determination to serve him to the end and truly manifest by their works that they have received of the spirit of Christ unto the remission of their sins shall be received by baptism into his church

8 The duty of the elders priest teachers deacons and members of the church of Christ

An apostle is an elder and it is his calling to baptize and to ordain others elders priest teachers and deacons and to administer bread and wine—the emblems of the flesh and blood of Christ—and to

139. The 1835 edition of the Doctrine and Covenants, the source for this copy of the articles and covenants, has "calling." (Doctrine and Covenants 2:8, 1835 ed. [D&C 20:38].)

Draft 1

Draft 2

baptized into the Church, by the laying on of hands for the baptism of fire and the Holy Ghost, according to the scriptures; and to teach, expound, exhort, baptize, and watch over the church; and to confirm the Church by the laying on of the hands, and the giving [p. 31] of the Holy Ghost—and to take the lead in all meetings.

9 The elders are to conduct the meetings as they are led by the Holy Ghost, according to the commandments and revelations of God.

10 The priests duty is to preach, teach, expound, exhort, and baptize, and administer the sacrament, and visit the house of each member, and exhort them to pray vocally and in secret, and attend to all family duties: and he may also ordain other priests, teachers, and deacons— and he is to take the lead of meetings when there is no elder present, but when there is an elder present, he is only to preach, teach expound, exhort, and baptize, and visit the house of each member, exhorting them to pray vocally, and in secret, and attend to all family duties. In all these duties the priest is to assist the elder if occasion requires.

11 The teacher's duty is to watch over the Church always, and be with, and strengthen them, and see that there is no iniquity in the church, neither hardness with each other; neither lying, backbiting, nor evil speaking; and see that ~~each member~~ ⟨the church⟩ meet together often, and also see that all the members do their duty—and he is to take the lead of ~~all~~ meetings in the absence of the elder or priest—and is to be assisted always, in all his duties in the church, by the deacons if occasion requires: but neither

Draft 3

confirm those who are baptized into the Church by the laying on of hands for the baptism of fire and the Holy Ghost according to the scriptures and to teach expound exhort baptize and watch over the church and to confirm ⟨those who are baptized into⟩ the church by the laying on of hands and the giving of the Holy Ghost—and to take the lead of all meetings

9 The elders are to conduct the meetings as they are led by the Holy Ghost according to the commandments and revelations of God

10 The priest's duty is to preach teach expound exhort and baptize and administer the sacrament and visit the house of each member and exhort them to pray vocally and in secret, and attend to all family duties: and also ordain other priests teachers and deacons—and he is to take the lead of meetings when there is no elder present but when there is an elder present he is only to preach teach expound exhort and baptize and visit the house of each member exhorting them to pray vocally and in secret and attend to all family duties. In all these duties the priests are to assist the elders if occasion requires.

11 The teacher's duty is to watch over the church always, and be with and strengthen them and see that there is no iniquity in the church neither hardness with each [p. 56] other, neither lying backbiting nor evil speaking and see that the church meet together often and also see that all the members do their duty— and he is to take the leading of meetings in the absence of the elder or priest—and is to be assisted always in all his duties in the church by the deacons if occasion requires: but neither teachers nor deacons

Draft 1   **Draft 2**

teachers nor deacons have authority to
baptize, administer the sacrament or lay
on hands; they are however to warn, expound, exhort, and teach, and invite all
to come to Christ.

12 Every Elder, priest, teacher, or deacon, is to be ordained according to the
gifts and calling of God unto him: and
he is to be ordained by the power of the
Holy Ghost which is in the one that ordains him.

13 The several elders composing this
Church of Christ are to meet in conference once in three months, or from time
to time, as said conferences shall direct or
appoint: and said conferences are to do
whatever Church business is necessary to
be done at the time.

14 The elders are to receive their li-
cences from other elders by vote of the
church to which they belong, or from the
conferences.

15 Each priest teacher or deacon, who
is ordained by a priest, may take a certificate from him at the time, which certificate when presented to an elder shall
entitle him to a license, which shall authorize him to perform the duties of his
calling—or he may receive it from a conference.

16 No person is to be ordained to any
office in this church, where there is a regularly organized branch of the same,
without the vote of that church; but the
presiding elders, travelling bishops, high
counsellors, high priests, and elders, may

Draft 3

have authority to baptize administer the
sacrament or lay on hands they are however to warn expound exhort and teach
and invite all to come unto Christ

12 Every elder priest teacher or deacon
is to be ordained according to the gifts
and callings of God unto him and he is
to be ordained by the power of the Holy
Ghost which is in the one who ordains
him.

13 The several elders composing this
church of Christ are to meet in conference once in three months or from time
to time as said conferences shall direct or
appoint and said conference ~~are~~ is to do
whatever church business is necessary to
be done at the time

~~14 The several elders composing this
church of Christ are to meet in conference once in three months or from time
to time as said conferences shall direct or
appoint and said conferences are to do
whatever Church business is necessary to
be done at the time~~

14 The elders are to recieve their li-
cinses from other elders by vote of the
church to which they belong or from the
conferences

15 Each priest teacher or deacon who
is ordained by a priest may take a certificate from him at the time which certificate when presented to an elder shall
entitle him to a license which shall authorize him to perfo[r]m the duties of his
calling—or he may recieve it from a conference [p. 57]

16 No person is to be ordained to any
office in this church where there is a regularly organized branch of the same
without the vote of that church but the
presiding elders travelling bishops high
counsellors high priests and elders may

Draft 1   **Draft 2**

have the privilege of ordaining, where
there is no branch of the Church, that a
vote may be called.

17 Every president of the high priesthood, (or presiding elder) bishop, high
counsellor, and high priest, is to be ordained by the direction of a high council
or general conference,

18 The ~~duties~~ ⟨duty⟩ of the members
after they are received by [p. 32] baptism:

19 The Elders or priests are to have a
sufficient time to expound all things
concerning the church of Christ to their
understanding, previous to their partaking of the sacrament, and being confirmed by the laying on of the hands of
the elders: so that all things may be done
in order. And the members shall manifest before the Church, and also before
the elders, by a godly walk and conversation, that they are worthy of it, that there
may be works and faith agreeable to the
holy scriptures—walking in holiness before the Lord.

20 Every member of the Church ⟨of
Christ⟩ having children is to bring them
unto the elders before the church, who
are to lay their hands upon them in the
name of Jesus Christ, and bless them in
his name.

21 No one can be received into the
church of Christ unless he has arrived
unto the years of accountability before
God, and is capable of repentance.

22 Baptism is to be administered in
the following manner, unto all those who
repent: The person who is called of God,
and has authority of Jesus Christ to baptize, shall go down into the water with
the person who has presented him or
herself for baptism, and shall say, calling
him or her by name: Having ~~authority of~~
been commissioned of Jesus Christ, I

Draft 3

have the privilige of ordaining where
there is no branch of the church that a
vote may be called

17 Every president of the high priesthood (or presiding elder) bishop. high
counsellor and high priest is to be ordained by the direction of a high counsel
or General Conference

18 The ~~duty~~ duties of members ~~after~~
after they are recieved by babtism

19 The elders or priests are to have a
sufficient time to expound all things
concerning the church of Christ to their
understanding previous to their partaking of the sacrament and being confirmed by the laying on of ⟨the⟩ hands of
the elders ~~of~~ so that all things may be
done in order And the members shall
manifest before the church and also before the elders by a godly ~~was~~ walk and
conversation that they are worthy of it
that there may be works and faith ~~agree-
ably~~ agreeable to the holy scriptures—
walking in ~~holy~~ holiness before the Lord

20 Every member of the church having children is to bring them unto the
elders before the church who are to lay
their hands upon them in the name of
Jesus Christ and bless them in his name

21 No one can be recieved into the
church of Christ unless he has arrived
unto the years of accountability before
God and is capable of repentance

22 Baptism is to be administered in
the following manner unto all those who
repent: The person who is called of God
and has authority from Jesus Christ to
baptize shall go down into the water
with the person who has presented him
or herself for baptism [p. 58] and shall
say calling him or her by name having
been commissioned of Jesus Christ I

Draft 1	Draft 2

Draft 2

baptize you in the name of the Father, and of the Son, and of the Holy Ghost, Amen. Then shall he immerse him or her in the water, and come forth ~~out~~ ⟨again⟩ out of the water.

23 It is expedient that the Church meet together often to partake of bread and wine in remembrance of the Lord Jesus: and the elder or priest shall administer it: and after this manner shall he administer it: he shall kneel with the church, and call upon the Father in solemn prayer, saying, O God, the Eternal Father, we ask thee in the name of thy son Jesus Christ, to bless and sanctify this bread to the souls of all those who partake of it, that they may eat in remembrance of the body of thy son, and witness unto thee O God, the Eternal Father that they are willing to take upon them the name of thy son, and always remember him and keep his commandments which he has given them, that they may always have his Spirit to be with them Amen.

24 The manner of administering the wine: He shall take cup also, and say, O God, the eternal Father, we ask thee in the name of thy son Jesus Christ to bless and sanctify this wine to the souls of all those who drink of it, that they may do it in remembrance of the blood of thy son which was shed for them, that they may witness unto thee O God, the Eternal Father, that they do always remember him, ~~and~~ that they may have his Spirit to be with them. Amen.

25 Any member of the Church of Christ transgressing, or being overtaken in a fault, shall be dealt with as the scriptures direct.

26 It shall be the duty of the several churches composing the Church of Christ, to send one or more of their

Draft 3

baptize you in the name of the Father and of the Son and of the Holy Ghost. Amen. Then shall he immerse him or her in the water and come forth again out of the water.

23 It is expedient that the church meet together often to partake of bread and wine in remembrance of the Lord Jesus, and the elder or priest shall administer it: and after this manner shall he administer it: he shall kneel with the church and call upon the Father in solemn prayer saying O God the eternal Father we ask thee in the name of thy Son Jesus Christ to bless and sanctify this bread to the souls of all those who partake of it that they may eat in remembrance of ~~thy son~~ the body of thy son and witness unto thee O God the eternal Father that they are willing to take upon them ⟨the name⟩ of thy son and always remember him and keep his commandments which he has given them that they may always have his spirit to be with them. Amen

24 The manner of administering the wine. he Shall take the cup also and say O God the eternal Father we ask thee in the name of thy son Jesus Christ to bless and sanctify this wine to the souls of all those who drink ~~it~~ of it that they may do it in remembrance of the blood of thy Son which was shed for them that they may witness unto thee O God the eternal Father that they do always remember him that they may have his spirit to be with them. Amen

25 Any member of the church of Christ transgressing or being overtaken in a fault ~~shalt~~ shall be dealt with as the scriptures direct. [p. 59]

26 It shall be the duty of the several churches composing the church of Christ to send one or more of their

Draft 1

Mean time our translation drawing to a close, we went to Palmyra, and agreed there ⟨with Mʳ⟩ Egbert Granden to print ~~and publish it~~ five thousand ⟨copies⟩ for three thousand Dollars, and about this time secured the copy right. I would mention here also in order to correct a misunderstanding, which has gone abroad concerning the title page of the Book of Mormon, that it is not a composition of mine or of any other man's who has lived or does live in this generation, but that it is a literal translation taken from the last leaf of the plates, on the left hand side of the collection of plates, the language running same as ~~the~~ ⟨all⟩ Hebrew ⟨wr[i]ting⟩ ~~language~~ ⟨in general⟩. And that no error can henceforth

Draft 2

teachers to attend the several conferences held by the elders of the Church; with a list of the names of the several members [p. 33] uniting themselves with the church since the last conference, or send by the hand of some priest, so that a regular list of all the names of the whole church may be kept in a book, by one of the elders, whoever the other elders may appoint from time to time:— And also, if any have been expelled from the church: so that their names may be blotted out of the general church record of names.

27 All members removing from the church where they reside, if going to a church where they are not known, may take a letter certifying that they are regular members and in good standing: which certificate may be signed by any elder or priest, if the ~~person~~ member receiving the letter is personally acquainted with the elder or priest, or it may be signed by the teachers, or deacons of the church.

Mean time our translation drawing to a close, we went to Palmyra, Wayne County, N. Y: Secured the Copyright;[140] and agreed with Mʳ Egbert Grandon [Grandin] to print five thousand Copies, for the sum of three thousand dollars.[141]

I wish also to mention here, that the Title Page of the Book of Mormon is a literal translation, taken from the very last leaf, on the left hand side of the collection or book of plates, which contained the record which has been translated; ~~and not by any means~~ the language of the whole running same as all Hebrew writing in general; and that, said Title Page is not by any means a modern composition either of mine or of any other man's who has lived

Draft 3

teachers to attend the several conferences held by the elders of the church with a list of the names of the several members uniting themselves with the church since the last conference or send by the hand of some priest so that a regular list of all the names of the whole church may be kept in a book by one of the elders who-ever the other elders shall appoint from time to time:— and also if any have been expelled from the church so that their names may be blotted out of the general church record of names.

27 All members removing from the church where they resid[e] if going to a church where they are not known may take a letter certifying that they are reg-ular members and in good standing which certificate may be signed by any elder or priest if the member recieving the letter is personally acquainted with the elder or priest or it may be signed by the teachers or deacons of the church.

Having finished the translation we went to Palmira Wayne Co, N.Y. and se-cured the copy right and engaged M^r. Gilbert Grandon to print 5000 copies for the sum of $3000.

I wish to mention here that the title page of the Book of Mormon is a literal translation taken from the last leaf on the lift hand side of the collection of plates which con-tained the record that has been translated ~~the lan~~ The language of the whole running the same as all Hebrew writings; and that said title page is not a modern composition Therefore in order to correct an error which generally exists concerning it I give below that part of the title [p. 60] page which is a

NOTES

140. The copyright was obtained 11 June 1829. (Copyright for Book of Mormon, retained copy, CHL.)

141. According to Pomeroy Tucker, editor of the *Wayne Sentinel* (which Grandin printed), Grandin initially declined to publish the Book of Mormon but was persuaded after book printer Elihu F. Marshall of Rochester agreed to do so. Martin Harris mortgaged his farm to guarantee payment. (Tucker, *Origin, Rise, and Progress of Mormonism,* 51–53; Martin Harris to Egbert B. Grandin, Indenture, Wayne Co., NY, 25 Aug. 1829, Wayne Co., NY, Mortgage Records, vol. 3, pp. 325–326, microfilm 479,556, U.S. and Canada Record Collection, FHL.)

Draft 1

possibly exist I give here the Title so far as it is a translation.

Title page—

Draft 2

or does live in this generation. Therefore, in order to correct an error which generally exists concerning it, I give below that part of the Title Page of the English Version of the Book of Mormon, which is a genuine and literal translation of the Title Page of the Original Book of Mormon, as recorded on the plates.[142]

The
Book of Mormon
An account written by the hand of Mormon, upon plates, Taken from the plates of Nephi.[143]

Wherefore it is an abridgement of the record of the people of Nephi, and also of the Lamanites; written to the Lamanites, who are a remnant of the house of Israel; and also to Jew and Gentile: written by way of commandment, and also by the spirit of prophecy and of revelation.

Written, and sealed up, and hid up unto the Lord, that they might not be destroyed; to come forth by the gift and power of God unto the interpretation thereof: sealed by the hand of Moroni, and hid up unto the Lord, to come forth in due time by the way of Gentile; the interpretation thereof by the gift of God.

An abridgement taken from the book of Ether, also; which is a record of the people of Jared; who were scattered at the time the Lord confounded the language of the people when they [p. 34] were building a tower to get to Heaven: which is to shew unto the remnant of the house of Israel what great things the Lord hath done for their fathers; and that they may know the Covenants of the Lord, that they are not cast off forever; and also to the convincing of ⟨the⟩ Jew and Gentile that Jesus is the Christ, the Eternal God, manifesting himself unto all nations. And now if there are faults, they are the

Draft 3

genuine and ~~literal~~ ⟨literal⟩ ~~account~~ translation of the title page of the book of Mormon recorded on the plates

142. The following copy of the title page matches
the title page of the 1837 edition of the Book of
Mormon.

143. TEXT: The title is written in larger script,
each line of text taking up two lines of the page.

144. TEXT: The title is written in larger script,
each line of text taking up two lines of the page.

The Book of Mormon
An account written by the hand. of
Mormon upon plates ~~of~~ taken from the
plates of Nephi[144]
Wherefore is an abridgement of the
record of the people of Nephi and also of
the Lamenites written to the Lamenites
who are a remnant of the house of Israel
and also to Jew and Gentile written by
way of commandment and also by the
spirit of prophecy and of revelation.
Written and sealed up and hid up unto
the Lord that they might not be destroyed to come forth by the gift and
power of God unto the interpretation
thereof sealed by the hand of Maroni
and hid up unto the Lord to come forth
in due time by the way of Gentile the
interpretation thereof by the gift of God
An abridgment taken from the book
of Ether also which is a record of the
people of Jared who were scattered at the
time the Lord confounded the language
of the people when they were building a
tower to get to heaven which is to shew
unto the remnant of the house of Israel
what great things the Lord hath done for
their fathers and that they know the covenants of the Lord that they are not cast
off forever and also to the convincing of
the Jew and Gentile that Jesus is the
Christ the eternal God manifesting
[p. 61] himself unto all nations And now
if there are faults they are the mistakes of

Book of Mormon copyright. When Joseph Smith applied for the copyright of the Book of Mormon in June 1829, he used as the book description the text later published as the title page of the first edition. The copyright was filed with the northern New York district court, probably in Utica. Copyright for Book of Mormon, 11 June 1829, retained copy, Church History Library, Salt Lake City.

Emma Smith. Gouache and ink on paper, 12 × 7½ inches. Circa 1842. This profile portrait of Emma Smith in a riding dress was made by Sutcliffe Maudsley, who painted a companion portrait of Joseph Smith on 25 June 1842. Maudsley employed a pantograph, a device that allowed him to reproduce a profile by tracing the shadow of his subject on paper; he then painted in the details. A revelation to Emma Smith was recorded in Joseph Smith's history; see pages 420–424 herein. (Courtesy Church History Museum, Salt Lake City.)

Draft 1   **Draft 2**

mistakes of men; wherefore condemn
not the things of God, that ye may be
found spotless at the judgement seat of
Christ.

(The remainder ⟨(of the Title page)⟩
is of course, modern)

Revelation page 174[145]

A commandment of God and not of
man to Martin Harris, given (Manchester
New York, March, 1830) by him who is
eternal.[146]

1 I am Alpha and Omega, Christ the
Lord: yea, even I am ~~the~~ ⟨He⟩, the beginning and the end, the Redeemer of the
world: I having accomplished and finished the will of him whose I am, even
the Father concerning me: having done
this that I might subdue all things unto
myself: retaining all power, even to the
destroying of Satan and his works at the
end of the world, and the last great day
of judgement, which I shall pass upon
the inhabitants thereof, judging every
man according to his works, and the
deeds which he hath done. And surely
every man must repent or suffer, for I
God am endless: wherefore, I revoke not
the judgements which I shall pass, but
woes shall go forth, weeping, wailing
and gnashing of teeth: yea, to those who
are found on my left hand; nevertheless
it is not written, that there shall be no
end to this torment; but it is written endless torment

2 Again, it is written eternal damnation: wherefore it is more express than
other scriptures, that it might work upon
the hearts of the children of men, altogether for my name's glory: wherefore I
will explain unto you this mystery, for it
is meet unto you, to know even as my
apostles. I speak unto you that are chosen in this thing, even as one, that you
may enter into my rest. For behold, the

Draft 3

men wherefore condemn not the things of God that ye may be found spotless at the judgment seat of Christ.

The remainder of the Title page is of course modern

A commandment of God and not of man to Martin Harris given (Manchester New York March 1830) by him who is eternal

1 I am Alpha and Omega Christ the Lord; yea even I am he the beginning and the Redeemer of the world I having accomplished and finished the will whose I am even the Father concerning me; having done this, that I might subdue all things unto myself: retaining all power even to the destroying of Satan and his works at the end of the world and the last great day of judgment, which I shall pass upon the inhabitants thereof judging every man according to his works and the deeds which he hath done. And surely every man must repent or suffer for I God am endless wherefore I revoke not the judgments which I shall pass. ~~but~~ Woes shall go forth weeping wailing and gnashing of teeth, yea to those who are found on my left hand nevertheless it is not written that there shall be no end to this ~~punishment~~ torment but is written endless torment.

2 Again it is written eternal damnation wherefore it is more express than other scriptures that it might work upon the hearts of the children of men. altogether for my names glory: wherefore I will explain unto you this mystery for it is meet unto you to know even as mine apostles. I speak unto you that are chosen in this thing even as one that you [p. 62] may enter into my rest. For behold

145. TEXT: James Mulholland inscribed this revelation reference and left blank lines to be filled in later. He subsequently inserted the next paragraph (p. 364 herein), which flowed beyond the reserved space and into the space he left after "Revelation Page 177" (p. 364 herein). It is unknown exactly where the insertion ends and the original inscription after "Revelation Page 177" recommences.

146. Revelation, Mar. 1830, in Doctrine and Covenants 44, 1835 ed. [D&C 19]. The index to the earliest compilation of revelations lists the year for this "Revelation to Martin" as 1829. The 1833 Book of Commandments gives a date of March 1830, which was used in all subsequent official publications and which is probably erroneous. In both the Book of Commandments and the 1835 edition of the Doctrine and Covenants, the March 1830 date was put in parentheses, suggesting the editors were uncertain about the date. (Revelation Book 1, p. 207, in *JSP*, MRB:385; Book of Commandments 16; Doctrine and Covenants 44, 1835 ed.; see also discussion of this revelation in the first volume of the Documents series [forthcoming].)

Draft 1   **Draft 2**

mystery of godliness, how great is it? for
behold I am endless, and the punishment which is given at ⟨from⟩ my hand is
endless punishment, for endless is my
name: wherefore

Eternal   ⎫ Endless
punishment   ⎬ punishment
is God's   ⎪ is God's
punishment   ⎭ punishment

wherefore I command you to repent, and
keep the commandments which you
have received by the hand of my servant
Joseph Smith Jr, in my name: and it is by
my almighty power that you have received them: therefore I command you
to repent, repent, lest I smite you by the
rod of my mouth, and by my wrath, and
by my anger, and your sufferings be sore:
how sore you know not! how exquisite
you know not! yea, how hard to bear ye
know not! For behold, I God have suffered these things for all, that they might
not suffer, if they [p. 35] would repent,
but if they would not repent, they must
suffer even as I: which suffering caused
myself, even God, the greatest of all to
tremble because of pain, and to bleed at
every pore, and to suffer both body and
Spirit: and would that I might [not][147]
drink the bitter cup and shrink: nevertheless, glory be to the Father, and I partook
and finished my preparations unto the
children of men: wherefore I command
you again to repent lest I humble you by
my almighty power, and that you confess
your sins lest you suffer these punishments of which I have spoken, of which
in the smallest, yea, even in the least degree you have tasted at the time I withdrew my Spirit. And I command you
that you preach nought but repentance;
and show not these things unto the
world untill it is wisdom in me; for they

Draft 3

the mystery of Godliness how great is it
for behold I am endless and the punishment which is given from my hand is
endless punishment for endless is my
name; wherefore Eternal punishment is
God's punishment: Endless punishment
is God's punishment: wherefore I command you to repent and keep the commandments which you have received by
the hand of my servant Joseph Smith Jr.
in my name: and it is by my Almighty
power that you have received them therefore I command you to repent, repent
lest I smite you by the rod of my mouth
and by my wrath and by my anger and
your sufferings be sore how sore you
know not ⟨how exquisite you know not⟩
yea how hard to bear you know not.

For behold I God have suffered these
things for all that they might not suffer
if they would repent but if they would
not repent they must suffer even as I:
which suffering caused myself even God
the greatest of all to tremble because of
pain and to bleed at every pore and to
suffer both body and spirit and would
that I might not drink the bitter cup and
shrink: nevertheless glory be to the Father
and I partook and finished my preparations unto the children of men wherefore
I command you again to repent lest I
humble you by my almighty power and
that you confess your sins lest you suffer
these punishments of which I have spoken of which in the smallest yea ⟨even⟩ in
the least degree you have tasted at the
⟨time⟩ I withdrew my spirit. And I command you that you preach nought but
repentance and show not these things
unto the world until it is wisdom in me
for they cannot bear meat now but milk

NOTES

147. Omitted word supplied from Doctrine and
Covenants 44:2, 1835 ed. [D&C 19:18].

Draft 1

Draft 2

cannot bear meat now, but milk they must receive: wherefore, they must not know these things lest they perish: learn of me, and listen to my words; walk in the meekness of my Spirit, and you shall have peace in me: I am Jesus Christ: I came by the will of the Father, and I do his will.

3 And again: I command thee, that thou shalt not covet thy neighbor's wife. Nor seek thy neighbor's life. And again: I command thee, that thou shalt not covet thine own property, but impart it freely to the printing of the book of Mormon, which contains the truth and the word of God, which is my word to the Gentile, that soon it may go to the jew, of whom the Lamanites are a remnant: that they may believe the gospel, and look not for a Messiah to come who has already come.

4 And again I command thee, that thou shalt pray vocally as well as in thy heart: yea, before the world, as well as in secret; in public as well as in private. And thou shalt declare glad tidings: yea, publish it upon the mountains, and upon every high place, and among every people that thou shalt be permitted to see. And thou shalt do it with all humility, trusting in me, reviling not against revilers. And of tenets thou shalt not talk, but thou shalt declare repentance and faith on the Savior and remission of sins of by baptism and by fire; yea, even the Holy Ghost.

5 Behold this is a great, and the last commandment which I shall give unto you concerning this matter: for this shall suffice for thy daily walk even unto the end of thy life. And misery thou shalt receive, if thou wilt slight these counsels; yea, even destruction of thyself and property. Impart a portion of thy property;

Draft 3

they must recieve wherefore they must not [p. 63] know these things lest they perish: learn of me and listen to my words walk in the meekness of my spirit and you shall receive peace in me. I am Jesus Christ I came by the will of the Father and I do his will

3 And again I command thee that thou shalt not covet thy neighbour's ~~wife~~ life: And again I say unto thee thou shalt not covet ~~thy~~ thine own property but impart it freely to the printing of the book of Mormon which contains the truth and the word of God which is my word to the Gentiles that soon it may go to the Jews of whom the Lamenites are a ~~remnant~~ remnant that they may beleive the Gospel and look not for a Messiah to come who has already come.

4 And again I command thee ~~thou~~ that thou shalt pray vocally as well as in thy heart yea before the world as well as in secret in publick as well as in private. And thou shalt declare glad tidings yea publish it upon the mountains and upon eve[r]y high place and among every people that thou shalt be permitted to see. And thou shalt do it with all humility trusting in me reviling not against revilers. And of tenets thou shalt not talk but thou shalt declare repentance and faith on the Savior and remission of sins by baptism and by fire yea even the Holy Ghost

5 Behold this is ⟨a⟩ great and the last commandment which I shall give unto you concerning this matter for this shall suffice for thy daily walk, even unto the end of thy ~~days~~ life. And misery thou shalt recieve if thou wilt slight these counsels. yea even destruction of thyself and property. Impart a portion [p. 64] of

Draft 1

Draft 2

yea, even part of thy lands and all save the support of thy family. Pay the debt thou hast contracted with the printer. Release thyself from bondage. Leave thy house and home, except when thou shalt desire to see thy family. And Speak freely to all; yea, preach, exhort, declare the truth, even with a loud voice; with a sound of rejoicing, crying hosanna! hosanna! blessed be the name of the Lord God.

6 Pray always and I will pour out my Spirit upon you, and great shall be your blessing: yea, even more than if you should obtain treasures of the earth, and corruptibleness to the extent thereof. Behold, canst thou read this without rejoicing and lifting up thy heart for gladness: or canst thou run about longer as a blind guide, or canst thou be ~~meek and~~ humble and meek, and conduct thyself wisely before me; yea, come unto me thy Saviour.

Amen. [p. 36]

⟨Whilst the Book of Mormon was in the hands of the printer, we still continued to bear testimony, ~~and preach~~ to such as would hear as far as we had opportunity. ~~And~~ ⟨We⟩ made known also to ~~the~~ ⟨those⟩ ~~members~~ who had already been baptized, that we had received commandment to organize the Church: and ~~according to~~ accordingly ⟨we⟩ met to together, ⟨(being ~~about 30~~ ⟨six⟩ in number) besides a number who were beleiving—met with us⟩ on Tuesday the Sixth day of Aprile ~~in the year of our~~ A.D. ~~A thousand &~~ One thousand, Eight hundred and thirty, and proceeded, as follows, ⟨at the house of the above mentioned Mʳ Whitmers——⟩⟩

Whilst the Book of Mormon was in the hands of the printer,[148] we still continued to bear testimony, and give information, as far as we had opportunity; and also made known to our brethren, that we had received commandment to organize the Church And accordingly we met together for that purpose, at the house of the above mentioned Mʳ Whitmer [Peter Whitmer Sr.] (being six in number)[149] on Tuesday the sixth day of April, AD One thousand, eight hundred and thirty.

Revelation Page 177——[150]

Having opened the meeting by solemn prayer to our Heavenly Father ⟨and the

Having opened the meeting by solemn prayer to our Heavenly Father we proceeded,

Draft 3

thy property yea even part of ⟨with⟩ thy lands and all save the support of thy family. Pay the debt thou hast contracted with the printer. Release thyself from bondage. Leave thy house and home except when thou shalt desire to see thy family. And speak freely to all: yea preach exhort declare the truth even with a loud voice with a sound of rejoicing crying hosanna! hosanna! blessed be the name of the Lord God.

6 Pray always and I will pour out my spirit upon you and great shall be your blessing yea even more than if you should obtain treasures of earth and corruptableness to the extent thereof.

Behold canst thou read this without rejoicing and lifting up thy heart for gladness or canst thou run about longer as a blind guide or canst thou be humble and meek and conduct thyself wisely before me yea come unto me thy Savior. Amen.

We still continued while the book of Mormon was in the hands of the printer to bear testimony of the truth of the gospel delivered to us as ~~opportunity~~ opportunities were presented ~~to us~~ on tuesday the sixth day of April 1830 we met at the house of M^r. Whitmer for the purpose ⟨of⟩ organizing the church ~~of church of Christ~~ of Christ according to commandment.

Having commenced ~~by~~ ⟨with⟩ solemn prayer to our heavenly Father we proceeded

148. The first pages of the manuscript were delivered to printer E. B. Grandin in August or early September 1829. Copies of the book were offered for sale 26 March 1830. (John H. Gilbert, Palmyra, NY, to James T. Cobb, Salt Lake City, Utah Territory, 10 Feb. 1879, in *Theodore Schroeder, Papers;* John H. Gilbert, Memorandum, 8 Sept. 1892, photocopy, CHL; "The Book of Mormon," *Wayne Sentinel* [Palmyra, NY], 26 Mar. 1830, [3].)

149. Variant lists of the six organizers, relying on information from David Whitmer, Brigham Young, and Joseph Knight Jr., provide a total of eleven names, including JS, Oliver Cowdery, Joseph Smith Sr., Hyrum Smith, Samuel Smith, David Whitmer, John Whitmer, Peter Whitmer Sr., Peter Whitmer Jr., Christian Whitmer, and Orrin Porter Rockwell. More than six individuals attended the organizational meeting; David Whitmer recalled that "about 50 members & the 6 Elders were present." (Anderson, "Who Were the Six?," 44–45; Stevenson, Journal, 2 Jan. 1887.)

150. That is, Revelation, 6 Apr. 1830, in Doctrine and Covenants 46, 1835 ed. [D&C 21], copied into drafts 2 and 3 (pp. 368–371 herein).

Draft 1

~~meeting Ch~~ brethren & sisters having by a unamious vote, accepted us as &c⟩ I proceeded to lay my hands upon Oliver Cowdery—and ordained him an Elder of the Church of Jesus Christ of Latter Day Saints, after which he ordained me also to the office of an Elder of said Church.

We then took bread, blessed it, & brake it with them, also wine, blessed it, and drank it with them. We then laid our hands on each individual member of the Church present, to confirm them members of the Church of Jesus Christ, and that they might receive the Holy Ghost, when immediately the Holy Ghost was poured out upon ⟨us all⟩ ~~the whole community~~ ⟨to a gre◊ter or less degree.⟩ ~~in a ⟨very⟩ miraculous manner.~~ ⟨Father Smith [Joseph Smith Sr.] Martin Harris baptized this evening 6th April Mother [Lucy Mack] Smith & Sister Rockwell 2 or 3 days afterwards⟩[152] Some [p. [9]] prophecied, ~~many spoke with new tongues, and~~ ⟨several⟩[153] ~~of our number were ⟨so⟩ completely overpowered for a time, that we were obliged to lay them upon beds &c &c, and when bodily sensibility was restored to them they shouted Hosannas to God and the Lamb—& declared that the Heavens had been opened unto them,~~ ⟨especialy N Knights⟩ ~~that they had seen Jesus Christ sitting at the right hand of the Majesty on high, and many other great and glorious things. Either at this time or very shortly after⟨war[d]⟩ the following were ⟨with others⟩ called to the~~

Draft 2

(according to previous commandment)[151] to call on our brethren to know whether they accepted us as their teachers in the things of the Kingdom of God, and whether they were satisfied that we should proceed and be organized as a Church according to said commandment which we had received. To these they consented by an unanimous vote. I then laid my hands upon Oliver Cowdery and ordained him an Elder of the "Church of Jesus Christ of Latter Day Saints." after which he ordained me also to the office of an Elder of said Church.

We then took bread, blessed it, and brake it with them, also wine, blessed it, and drank it with them. We then laid our hands on each individual member of the Church present that they might receive the gift of the Holy Ghost, and be confirmed members of the Church of Christ. The Holy Ghost was poured out upon us to a very great degree. Some prophesied, whilst we all praised the Lord and rejoiced exceedingly.

Draft 3

(according to previous commandment) to call on our bretheren in order to ascertain ~~whether~~ if ~~they would accept us~~ we would be accepted by them as their ~~spiritual~~ teachers in ~~the~~ things pertaining to the kingdom of God; and were willing to be organized as a church according to the commandment that we had receivd. To these they [p. 65] unanimously consented. I then laid my hands upon Oliver Cowdry and ordained him an elder of the church of Jesus Christ of Latter Day Saints and immediately afterwards he ordained me ⟨also⟩ ~~an elder~~ to the office of an elder of the same church.

We then took bread blessed and broke it with them then took wine blessed and drank it with them. We then laid our hands upon each member of the church present for the reception of the Holy Ghost and to confirm them members of the church of Christ. The Holy Ghost was poured out upon us to a very great degree insomuch that some prophesied whilst all praised the Lord and rejoiced exceedingly.

151. The commandment to which this refers may be "the word of the Lord" that came "in the Chamber" in the home of Peter Whitmer Sr. (JS History, vol. A-1, p. 326 herein [Draft 2].)

152. TEXT: This insertion by James Mulholland runs along the bottom of pages 9 and 10 of Draft 1, with the page break occurring between "April" and "Mother".

153. TEXT: "several" written over "some" and then canceled with the rest of the passage.

Draft 1

priesthood & ordained ⟨to⟩ the respective offices, according as the Spirit made it manifest, viz Joseph Smith Senior, Hyrum Smith, John Whitmer, Peter Whitmer Christian Whitmer Samuel Smith, Martin Harris.

Draft 2

Whilst yet together I received the following commandment.

Revelation to Joseph Smith Jr, Given at Fayette, Seneca Co N Y. April 6th 1830.[154]

1 Behold there shall be a record kept among you, and in it, thou shalt be called a seer, a translator, a prophet, an apostle of Jesus Christ, an elder of the Church through the will of the Father God the Father, and the grace of your Lord Jesus Christ; being inspired of the Holy Ghost to lay the foundation thereof, and to build it up unto the most holy faith; which church was organized and established, in the year of ⟨y⟩our Lord, eighteen hundred and thirty, in the fourth month, and on the sixth day of the month, which is called April.

2 Wherefore, meaning the Church, thou shalt give heed unto all his words, and commandments, which he shall give unto you, as he receiveth them, walking in all holiness before me: for his word ye shall receive, as if from mine own mouth, in all patience and faith; for by doing these things, the gates of hell shall not prevail against thee you: yea, and the Lord God will disperse the powers of darkness from before you; and cause the heavens to shake for your good, and his name's glory.—

For thus saith the Lord God, him have I inspired to move the cause of Zion in mighty power for your good; and his diligence I know, and his prayers I have heard: yea, his weeping for Zion ⟨I⟩ have I seen, and I will cause that he shall

Draft 3

NOTES

154. Revelation, 6 Apr. 1830, in Doctrine and
Covenants 46, 1835 ed. [D&C 21].

Before we ~~disperced~~ ⟨separated⟩ I receivd
the following commandment—
    April 6th 1830

    1 Behold there shall be a record kept
among you and in it thou shalt be called
a seer a translator a a prophet an apostle
of Jesus Christ an elder of the church
through the will of God the Father and
the grace of your Lord Jesus Christ being
inspired of the Holy Ghost to lay the
foundation thereof and to build it up
unto the most holy faith which church
was organized and established in the
year of your Lord ~~one thousand eight
hundred~~ eighteen hundred and thirty in
the fourth month and on the sixth day of
the month which is called April
    2 Wherefore (meaning the church)
thou shalt give heed unto all his words
and commandments which he shall give
unto you as he receiveth them walking
in all holiness before me for his word ye
shall receive as if from mine own mouth
in all patience and faith for by doing
these things the gates of hell shall not
prevail against you: yea and [p. 66] ⟨the⟩
Lord God will disperse the powers of
darkness from before you and cause the
heavens to shake for your good and his
name's glory.— For thus saith the Lord
God him have I inspired to move the
cause of Zion in mighty power for good
and his diligence I know and his prayers
I have heard yea his weeping for Zion I
have seen and I will cause that he shall
mourn for her no longer for his days of

Draft 1

We afterwards called out and ordained ~~Several~~ ⟨some others⟩ of the brethren to the respective offices of the Priesthood, according as the Spirit made manifest unto us. ⟨~~Revelation~~⟩ [155]As may reasonably ⟨be⟩ expected, such scenes as these were calculated, to inspire our hearts with Joy unspeakable, at the same time that we felt ourselves almost over whelmed, with awe and reverence for that Almighty Being, by whose grace we had been called to be instrumental in bringing about for the children of men, the enjoyment of such glorious blessings, as were now at this time poured out upon us. To find ourselves engaged in the very same order of things which ~~were~~ was observed by the Holy Apostles of old, To realize the importance and solemtily [solemnity] of the above mentioned

Draft 2

mourn ⟨for her⟩ no longer, for his days of rejoicing are come unto the remission of his sins [p. 37] and the manifestations of my blessings upon his works.

3 For behold I will bless all those ~~that~~ ⟨who⟩ labour in my vineyard, with a mighty blessing, and they shall believe on his words, which are given through me, by the Comforter, which manifesteth that Jesus was crucified by sinful men for the sins of the world; yea, for the remission of sins unto the contrite heart. Wherefore, it behooveth me, that he should be ordained by you, Oliver Cowdery, mine apostle; this being an ordinance unto you, that you are an elder under his hand, he being the first unto you, that you might be an elder unto this Church of Christ, bearing my name; and the first preacher of this Church, unto the Church, and before the world; yea, before the Gentiles: yea, and thus saith the Lord God, lo, lo, to the Jews also. Amen.

We now proceeded to call out and ordain some others of the brethren to different offices of the Priesthood, according as the Spirit manifested unto us;

Draft 3

rejoicing are come unto the remission of his sins and the manifestations of my blessings upon his ~~words~~ works

3 For behold I will bless all those who labor in my vineyard with a mighty blessing and they shall beleive on his words which are given him through me by the comferter which manifesteth that Jesus was crucified by sinful men for the sins of the world yea for the remissions of sins unto the contrite heart. Wherefore it behooveth me that he should be ordained by you (Oliver Cowdry) mine apostle this being an ordinance unto you that you are an elder under his hand he being the first unto you that you might be an elder unto the church of Christ bearing my name and the first preacher of this church unto the church and before the world yea before the Gentiles: yea and thus saith the Lord God, lo, lo, to the Jews, also Amen

~~We~~ Accordingly ⟨we⟩ proceeded to ordain several of the bretheren to different offices of the priesthood as the spirit revealed to us.

NOTES

155. TEXT: Horizontal lines inserted here and after "cannot be described" (p. 372 herein) separate the two enclosed sentences from the remainder of the text. This marked passage appears at a later point in Draft 2 (p. 390 herein), where it was used to describe the June 1830 church conference.

Draft 1

proceedings, and to witness ⟨& feel⟩ with
our own natural senses, the like glorious
manifestions of the powers of the Priesthood; the gifts and blessings of the Holy
Ghost, ~~which we had often read of as things~~
and the goodness and grace of a merciful
God, unto such as obey the everlasting gospel of our Lord Jesus Christ, combined to
create within use [us] sensations of rapturous gratitude, which may be felt, but cannot be described. After a considerable time
spent in such ⟨a⟩ happy manner, we dismissed; with the pleasing knowledge, that
we now individually were members of—
and had been acknowledged of God, The
~~organized~~ Church of Jesus Christ, organized in [p. [10]] accordance with commandments and revelations, given by him
to ourselves, in these last days; as well as
according to the order of the Church of
Christ, as found recorded in the New
Testament.

Severals persons who attended this
meeting, but who had ⟨not⟩ as yet been
baptized, came forward shortly after, and
were received into the church having on
that occasion got entirely convinced of the
truth of the work. ⟨Among th[e] rest Father
Smith, Martin Harris & Mother Smith⟩

Revelation page 176—& Revelation 178

Draft 2

and after a happy time spent in witnessing and feeling for ourselves the ~~mercies~~
⟨powers &⟩ the blessings of the Holy
Ghost, through the grace of God bestowed
upon us, we dismissed with the pleasing
knowledge that we were now individually,
members of, and acknowledged of God,
"The Church of Jesus Christ," organized in
accordance with commandments and revelations, given by him to ourselves, in these
last days, as well as according to the order
of the Church as recorded ~~of~~ in the New
Testament.

Several persons who had attended the
above meeting, and got convinced of the
truth, came forward shortly after, and were
received into the church, among the rest
My own Father and Mother were baptized
to my great joy and consolation, and about
the same time Martin Harris and a [*blank*]
Rockwell.[156]

Revelation to the Church of Christ,
which was established in these last days,
in the year of our Lord One thousand
eight hundred and thirty: Given ⟨at⟩
Manchester New York, April 1830, in
consequence of some desiring to unite
with the Church without re-baptism,
who had previously been baptized.[157]

1 Behold I say unto you, that all old
covenants have I caused to be done away
in this thing, and this is a new and an
everlasting covenant; even that which

Draft 3

156. Thomas Bullock later filled in the blank space with "Orrin Porter," but Draft 1 noted Orrin Porter Rockwell's baptism as occurring after the June 1830 church conference. (See p. 390 herein.)

157. Revelation, 16 Apr. 1830, in Doctrine and Covenants 47, 1835 ed. [D&C 22].

We here obtained a witness of the blessings and power ~~through~~ ⟨of⟩ the ~~grace o~~ the Holy Ghost bestowed upon us through the grace of God ⟨and⟩ several persons became convinced of the truth and were ⟨afterwards⟩ baptized among whom were my father and mother and we obtained the consolation that we were members of the church of Jesus Christ [p. 67] organized in accordance with the commandments of God and acknowledged by him to be the same as that instituted by Jesus Christ while upon ⟨the⟩ earth

~~About this In the month of April Some time in the same month I received the following revel~~ Some time afterwards in the same month (being the month of April) I received the following revelation given at Manchester N. Y. in consequence of some desiring to unite with the church without rebaptism

1 Behold I say unto you that all old covenants have I caused to [be] done away in this thing and this is a new and an everlasting covenant; even that which

about to do for the Children of men, And to reason with him out of the Bible, we also showed him that part of the work which we had translated, and laboured to persuade him concerning the Gospel of Jesus Christ which was now about to be revealed in its fulness. He however was not very easily persuaded of these things, but after much enquiry and explanation he retired to the woods, in order that by secret and fervent prayer he might obtain of a merciful God, wisdom to enable him to judge for himself: The result was that he obtained revelation for himself sufficient to convince him of the truth of our assertions to him, And on the   day of that Same month in which we had been baptised and ordained, Oliver Cowdery baptised him, And he returned to his father's house greatly glorifying and praising God, being filled with the Holy Spirit. Not many days afterwards, My brother Hyrum Smith came to us to enquire concerning these things when at his earnest request, I enquired of the Lord through the Urim and Thummim, And received for him the following.

Revelation given to Hyrum Smith, at Harmony Susquehanah County, Pensylvania May. 1829.

Book of Covenants page 167

About the same time, with my brother Hyrum came an old Gentleman to visit us. of whose name I wish to make honourable mention; Mr Joseph Knight Senr of Colesville, Broom County, Pen. who having heard of the manner in which we were occupying our time, very kindly and consideratety brought us, a quantity of provisions, in order that we might not be interrupted in the work of translation by the want of such necessaries of life. And I would just mention

Composition of 1839 history draft (Draft 1). The first pages of this early draft of Joseph Smith's history, including page 2 (above), show a straightforward composition process with relatively few revisions. As work on the history progressed, however, it appears that James Mulholland began to outline the narrative, writing in key revelations, events, and dates for several pages and leaving large blank spaces to be filled in later. When he came back and filled in the details, the texture of the document became more compli-

accordance with commandments and revelations, given by him to ourselves, in these last days; as well as according to the order of the Church of Christ, as found recorded in the New Testament.

Severals persons who attended this meeting, but who had not as yet been baptized, came forward shortly after, and were received into the church having on that occasion got entirely convinced of the truth of this work. Among the rest Father Smith, Martin Harris, Revelation page 176 —— & Revelation 178

On Sunday April 11th 1830, we held a public meeting by appointment at Mr Whitmer's Fayette Seneca Co. N. Y —, when Oliver Cowdery preached the first public sermon, which was delivered by any of our Church, we had a crowded audience; And the same day he baptized the following persons viz: Hiram Page, Catherine Page, Christian Whitmer, Anne Whitmer, Jacob Whitmer & Elizabeth Whitmer and Mary Page, And on the 18th of said month Peter Whitmer Senr. Mary Whitmer, William Jolly, Elizabeth Jolly — Vincent Jolly — Richd. B. Peterson, and Elizabeth Ann Whitmer.

June 10th 1830 David Whitmer baptized John Poorman, John Jolly Julia anne Jolly and Harriett Jolly — Jerushee Smith, Katherine Smith — Wm Smith, Don C. Smith, Porter Rockwell, Caroline Rockwell and Electa Rockwell, The last eleven were all baptized in Seneca lake ——

During this month of April, I went on a visit to the residence of Mr Joseph Knight, — of Colesville. Broom Co. N. Y with whom I had been formerly well acquainted, as well as with his family and in the Neighborhood generally — Mr Knight & his family were Universalists — but were as usual glad to see me and very friendly and willing to reason on the Subject of religion, We held several meetings in the neighborhood, we had many friends and some enemies our meetings were well attended however, and many began to pray fervently to Almighty God to give them wisdom to understand the truth; Among those who attended our meetings regularly, was Newel Knight, Son to Joseph Knight, He and I had frequent conversations on this important Subject of the plan of man's eternal Salvation, we had got into the habit of praying much at our meetings

cated, as Mulholland had to squeeze varying amounts of text into the spaces he had reserved for the narrative. One example of the disorderly result is seen on page 11 of the manuscript (above). Handwriting of James Mulholland. JS History, 1839, pp. [2], [11] (transcribed on pp. 296–304, 372–380 herein), Church History Library, Salt Lake City. (Photographs by Welden C. Andersen.)

Draft 1   **Draft 2**

was from the beginning.— Wherefore,
although a man should be baptized an
hundred times, it availeth ~~not~~ him nothing; for you cannot enter in at the strait
gate by the law of Moses, neither by your
dead works; for it is because of your dead
works, that I have caused this last covenant, and this church to be built up unto
me; even as in days of old. Wherefore
enter ye in at the gate, as I have commanded, and seek not to cou[n]sel your
God. Amen.

The following persons being anxious
to know of the Lord what might be their
respective duties, in relation to this work, I
enquired of the Lord and received for them
the following——

Revelation to Oliver Cowdery, Hyrum
Smith, Samuel H. Smith, Joseph [p. 38]
Smith sen, and Joseph Knight Senʳ,
Given at Manchester, New York, April
1830.[158]

1 Behold I speak unto you, Oliver, a few
words. Behold thou art blessed, and art
under no condemnation. But beware of
pride, lest thou shouldst enter into temptation. Make known thy calling unto the
Church, and also before the world; and
thy heart shall be opened to preach the
truth from henceforth and for ever. Amen.

2 Behold I speak unto you Hyrum a
few words: for thou also art under no
condemnation, and thy heart is opened,
and thy tongue loosed; and thy calling is
to exhortation, and to strengthen the
church continually. Wherefore thy duty
is unto the church forever; and this because of thy family. Amen.

3 Behold I speak a few words unto you
Samuel: for thou also art under no condemnation, and thy calling is to exhortation, and to strengthen the church. And

Draft 3

was from the beginning.— Wherefore although a man should be baptized a hundred times it availeth him nothing; for you cannot enter in at the straight gate by the law of Moses neither by your dead works; for it is because of your dead works that I have caused this last covenant and this church to be built up unto me even as in days of old. Wherefore enter ye in at the ~~straight~~ gait, as I have commanded and seek not to councel your God Amen

~~As the~~ At the same time Oliver Cowdry Hyrum Smith, Samuel H. Smith, Joseph Smith sen and Joseph Knight sen being anxious to know their respective duties respecting this work I inquired of the Lord and receivd for them the following revelation

1 Behold I speak unto you Oliver a few words. Behold thou art blessed and art under no condemnation. Beware of pride lest thou shouldst enter into temptation. Make known thy calling unto the church and also before the world; and thy heart shall be opened to preach the truth from henceforth and forever Amen [p. 68]

2 Behold I speak unto you Hyrum a few words for thou also art under no condemnation and thy heart is opened and thy tongue loosed and thy calling is to exhortation and to strengthen the church continually. Wherefore thy duty is unto the church forever and this because of thy family. Amen

3 Behold I speak a few words unto you Sam[l.] for thou also art under no condemnation and thy calling is to exhortation and to strengthen the church. And

158. Revelations, Apr. 1830–A through E, in Doctrine and Covenants 45, 1835 ed. [D&C 23].

Draft 1

On Sunday April 11ᵗʰ 1830, ~~Oliver Cowdery preached at ⟨Mr.⟩~~ ⟨we held a public meeting by appointment at⟩ Whitmer's [*blank*]¹⁵⁹ Fayette Seneca Co. NY—, When Oliver Cowdery preached the first ⟨real⟩ public sermon, which was deliverd by any ~~Elder~~ ⟨member⟩ of our Church, we had a crowded audience, And the same day he baptized the following persons viz: Hiram Page Katharine Page, Christian Whitmer, Anne Whitmer, Jacob Whitmer, & Elizabeth Whitmer and Mary Page, And on the 18ᵗʰ of said month Peter Whitmer Senʳ Mary Whitmer, William Jolly Elizabeth Jolly—Vincent Jolly— Richᵈ· B. Peterson, and Elizabeth Ann Whitmer.

⟨~~Conference Jun 1ʳˢᵗ⟩~~ June 10ᵗʰ 1830 ~~David Whitmer baptized John Poorman, John Jolly Julia Anne Jolly and Harriett Jolly—Jerushee Smith, Kathrine Smith— Wm Smith, Don C. Smith, Porter Rockwell, Caroline Rockwell and Electa~~

Draft 2

thou art not as yet called to preach before the world. Amen.

4 Behold I speak a few words unto you, Joseph: for thou also art under no condemnation, and thy calling also is to exhortation, and to strengthen the Church. And this is thy duty from henceforth and forever. Amen.

5 Behold I manifest unto you Joseph Knight, by these words, that you must take up your cross, in the which you must pray vocally before the world as well as in secret, and in your family, and among your friends, and in all places.— And behold it is your duty to unite with the true Church, and give your language to exhortation continually, that you may receive the reward of the Laborer. Amen.

On Sunday April 11ᵗʰ 1830, Oliver Cowdery preached the first public discourse, that was delivered by any ⟨of⟩ our number. Our meeting was held by previous appointment at the house of Mʳ Whitmer [Peter Whitmer Sr.], Fayette, large numbers of people attended, and the same day the following were baptized; Viz: Hyrum [Hiram] Page, Kathrine [Catherine Whitmer] Page, Christian Whitmer, Anne [Schott] Whitmer[,] Jacob Whitmer, Elizabeth [Schott] Whitmer, and on the 18ᵗʰ D[itt]o Peter Whitmer, Snʳ[,] Mary [Musselman] Whitmer, William Jolly, Elizabeth [Stones] Jolly, Vincent Jolly, Richard B. Peterson¹⁶⁰ and Elizabeth anne Whitmer, all by Oliver Cowdery in Seneca Lake.

Draft 3

thou art not as yet called to preach before the world. Amen

4 Behold I speak a few words unto you Joseph for thou also art under no condemnation and thy calling also is to exhortation and to strengthen the church. And this is thy duty from henceforth and forever Amen

5 Behold I manifest unto you Joseph Knight by these words that you must take up your cross in the which you must pray vocally before the world as well as in secret and in your family and among your friends and in all places.— And behold it is your duty to unite with the true church and give your language to exhortation continually that you may receive the reward of the laborer Amen

On sunday April 11th. 1830 we held a meeting at the house of Mr. Whitmer when Oliver Cowdry delivered the first sermon ever preached by any of us

~~Large~~ Many people were present and the following persons were baptized. viz. Hiram Page, ~~Catharine~~ Katharine Page Christian Whitmer Anne Whitmer Jacob Whitmer Elizabeth Whitmer and on Sunday following Peter Whitmer Jr. Mary [p. 69] Whitmer and Elizabeth Ann Whitmer were also baptized—

NOTES

159. TEXT: It is possible that James Mulholland originally inscribed "Revelation page 176—& Revelation 178 | On Sunday April 11th 1830, Oliver Cowdery preached at Whitmer's" (see Draft 1 text on p. 372 herein) and then left a large blank space to be filled in later, as he had done on page 9 of Draft 2 (see 359n145 herein). If that is the case, then the rest of this paragraph was a later insertion.

160. Nothing further is known about this person. Early in the twentieth century, a redaction to the Journal History of the Church's entry for 18 April 1830 changed the name from Richard B. Peterson to Ziba Peterson, but no primary source supports this change. (Historical Department, Journal History of the Church, 18 Apr. 1830.)

Draft 1

Rockwell, ~~The last eleven were all baptized in Seneca lake~~

During this month of ~~June~~ ⟨April⟩, I went ~~in company with Oliver Cowdery~~ ⟨on a visit⟩ to the residence of Mʳ Joseph Knight's—of Colesville—Broom Co. N.Y with whom I had been formerly well acquainted, as well as with his family and in the Neighborhood generally—Mʳ Knigth & his family were Universalists—but were as usual glad to see ~~us~~ ⟨me⟩ and very friendly and willing to reason on the subject of religion, We held several meetings in the neighborhood, we had many friends and some enemies—our meetings were well ⟨attended⟩ however, and many began to pray fervently to Almighty God to give them wisdom to understand the truth;

Among those who attended our meetings regularly, was Newel Knights, son to Joseph Knights, He and I had frequent conversations on this important subject of the plan of man's eternal salvation, we had got into the habit of praying much at our meetings [p. [11]] And Newel had promised me on a certain day, that he would that evening take up his cross and pray vocally in the meeting the same evening— The evening came, and the meeting was held, but when ~~it came to~~ Newels was asked to pray, he begged to be excused. I tried to prevail upon him and encourage him to pray, ⟨when⟩ ~~he brought up as figure the following, "Suppose that a man travelling along the road, sho~~ he replied that when he got out in the woods by himself he should there take up his cross. I endeavored to persuade him that where so many were ~~there~~, ready & willing to assist him there was the place for him to pray—and that for my part I would & could help him by my faith, provided he would only, make an

Draft 2

During this month of april I went on a visit to the residence of Mr Joseph Knight [Sr.], of Colesville, Broom[e] Co N.Y. with whom and his family I had been previously acquainted, and of whose name I have above mentioned, as having been so kind and thoughtful towards us, while translating the book of Mormon.[161] Mʳ Knights and his family were Universalists, but were willing to reason with me upon ⟨my⟩ religious views, and were as usual friendly and hospitable. We held several meetings in the neighbourhood, we had many friends, and some enemies. Our meetings were well attended, and many began to pray fervently [p. 39] to Almighty God, that He would give them wisdom to understand the truth.

Amongst those who attended our meetings regularly, was Newel Knight son to Joseph Knight.[162] He and I had now many and serious conversations on the important subject of man's eternal salvation: we had got into the habit of praying much at our meetings and Newel had said that he would try and take up his cross, and pray vocally during meeting; but when we again met together, he rather excused himself; I tried to prevail upon him, making use of the figure, supposing that he should get into a mudhole would he not try and help himself out, and that we were willing now to help him out of the mudhole, he replied that provided he had got into a mudhole through carelessness, he would rather wait and get out him self, than have others to help him, and so he would wait untill he should get into the woods by himself, and there he would pray.

Draft 3

During this month I paid a visit to M^r. Joseph Knight of Coles vill Broom County N.Y. with whom I had previously been acquainted and of whom I have before spoken

M^r. Knights and family were Universalists but were willing to reason with me and receive the truth when made known to them— We held several meetings in the neighborhood where we soon found many friends and a few enemies our meetings were well attended and many began to pray to Almighty God for wisdom to understand the truth

one of these was Newel son of Joseph Knights with whom I ~~now~~ had many serious conversations on ⟨the⟩ important subjects of man's eternal salvation. We were in the habit of praying much at our meetings and Newel had become convinced that it was his duty to take up his cross which he avowed a determination to do; but when we again met ~~together~~ he excused himself by saying he would wait until he could retire to the woods and then he would pray

161. See JS History, vol. A-1, p. 304 herein (Draft 2).

162. In July 1839 Newel Knight assisted JS with the dictation of the history. Knight's recollections as an eyewitness may have contributed to the narrative recorded on pages 380–438 herein. (JS, Journal, 4–5 July 1839, in *JSP*, J1:345.)

Draft 1

attempt to pray. He now brought up the follow[ing] figure, Suppose I should be traveling along the road & through carelessness get into a mudhole and a number of men came along, it is natural to expect, that I should be so much ashamed that I would rather wait untill they would go past & then try to get out myself.— To this I replied that provided he should get into a situation of the kind, ~~And~~ that it was most likely he would require help, but that no person would help him out of a mud hole, unless he would show a willingness to Assist himself also. All arguments were however useless, he deferred praying untill next morning—when he then retired into the woods, where according to his own account afterwards he made several attempts to pray, but could scarcely do so, feeling as he said, that he had not done his duty, but that he should have taken up his cross in the presence of others, he began to feel uneasy and felt worse both in mind and body, untill upon reaching his house, his appearance was such as to alarm his wife very much—he requested her to go and bring me to him, I went and found him suffering very much in his mind, and his body acted upon in a most strange manner, His visage and limbs distorted & twisted into every possible shape and appearances, and finally he was caught up off the floor of the apartment and tossed about most fearfully. his situation was soon made known to his neighbors and relatives and in a short time as many as eight or nine grown persons had got together to witness the scene. After he had thus suffered for some time, I succeeded in getting hold of him by the hand, when almost immediately he was able to speak, and requested with great earnestness ~~that~~ I should cast the Devil out of him, that [p. [12]] he knew that he was in him,

Draft 2

Accordingly he deferred praying untill next morning, when he retired into the woods, where (according to his own accoount afterwards) he made several attempts to pray, but could scarcely do so, feeling that he had not done his duty, but that he should have prayed in the presence of others. He began to feel uneasy, and continued to feel worse both in mind and body, untill, upon reaching his own house, his appearance was such as to alarm his wife very much. He requested her to go and bring me to him. I went and found him suffering very much in his mind, and his body acted upon in a very strange manner. His visage and limbs distorted and twisted in every shape and appearance possible to imagine; and finally he was caught up off the floor of the apartment and tossed about most fearfully. His situation was soon made known to his neighbours and relatives, and in a short time as many as eight or nine grown persons had got together to witness the scene. After he had thus suffered for a time, I succeeded in getting hold ⟨of⟩ him by the hand, when almost immediately he spoke to me, and with great earnestness requested of me, that I should cast the Devil out of him, saying that he knew he was in

Draft 3

~~accordingly~~ On the following morning he
retired to the grove where he made several
attempts to pray but could not do so feeling that he had neglected his duty on the
previous evening on his return to the house
his appearance was such as to very much
alarm his wife—having requested his wife
to bring me to him I went and found him
suffering very much in mind and his body
acted upon in a very strange manner his
face and limbs distorted and twisted into
⟨almost⟩ every shape possible and finally he
was raised from the floor by the spirit
which possessed him and tossed about
[p. 70] the room in a most fearful manner.
His neighbors were immediately made acquainted with his situation ~~who~~ and came
to witness this singular scene. After he had
thus suffered sometime I succeeded in getting hold of his hand. when immediately
he requested me to cast the Devil out of
him saying that he knew the devil was in
him and that I could cast him out

Draft 1

and that he also knew that I could cast him out, I replied "If you know that I can, it shall be done". And almost unconsciously I ~~commanded~~ rebuked the Devil, ~~in~~ and commanded him ~~to leave him~~ in the name of Jesus Christ to depart from him. When immediately Newel spoke out and said that he saw the Devil leave him and vanish from his sight— ⟨This was the first miracle wrought in this Church⟩

The scene was now entirely changed, for ~~very~~ ⟨as⟩ soon as the Devil, had departed, from this our friend his countenance became natural, his distortions of body ceased, and almost immediately the Spirit of God descended upon him, to such a degree that the visions of eternity were opened to his view and he beheld great and glorious things—he afterward related his experience of this as follow, "I now began to feel a most pleasing sensation resting upon me, and immediately the visions of Heaven were opened to my view I felt ⟨myself⟩ attracted ~~towards~~ ⟨upwards⟩ ~~it~~, and remained for some time enwrapt ~~in the~~ ⟨in⟩ contemplation in so much that I knew not what was going on in the room, but by and by I felt some weight pressing upon my shoulder and the side of my head, which served to recall ~~my~~ me to a sense of my situation And I found that the Spirit of the Lord had actually lifted me off the floor, ~~and that I had removed the floor of the Chamber above,~~ and that my shoulder & head were pressing against the beams"

Draft 2

him, and that he also knew that I could cast him out. I replied "If you know that I can, it shall be done" and then almost unconsciously I rebuked the devil, and commanded him in the name of Jesus Christ to depart from him; when immediately Newel spoke out and said that he saw the devil leave him and vanish from his sight. This was the first miracle which was done in this Church, ~~and it~~ or by any member of it, and it was done, not by man nor by the power of man, but it was done by God, and by the power of Godliness: Therefore let the honour and the praise, the dominion and the glory be ascribed to the Father, Son, and Holy Spirit for ever and ever Amen.

The scene was now entirely changed for as soon as the devil had departed from our friend, his countenance became natural, his distortions of body ceased, and almost immediately the Spirit of the Lord descended upon him, and the visions of eternity were opened to his view. He afterwards related his experience as follows.

"I now began to feel a most pleasing sensation resting upon me, and immed-[p. 40]iately the visions of heaven were opened to my view. I felt myself attracted upward and remained for some time enwrapt in contemplation in so much that I knew not what was going on in the room. By and by I felt some weight pressing upon my shoulder and the side of my head; which served to recall me to a sense of my situation, and I found that the Spirit of the Lord had actually caught me up off the floor, and that my shoulder and head were pressing against the beams."

Draft 3

I replied if you know that I can it shall be done and almost unconsciously I rebuked the devil and commanded him in the <u>name</u> of <u>Jesus Christ</u>[163] to depart from him and Newel immediately spoke and said that he <u>saw</u> the devil vanish from his sight ~~this~~ This was the <u>first</u> miracle performed in this Church and this was done not by man or the power of man but by the power of <u>God</u>[164] therefore let the glory be asscribed to him.

The scene was now entirely changed. His countenance became natural his distortions of body ceased and the spirit of the Lord descended upon him, ⟨and⟩ the visions of eternity were opened to his view. He afterwards gave us the following relation.

I now began to feel a most pleasing sensation resting upon me, and immediately the visions of heaven ~~of heaven~~ were opened to my view. I felt myself attracted upwards and remained sometime enwrapt in contemplation insomuch that I knew not what was going on in the room.

By and by I felt some weight pressing upon my shoulder and the side of my head, which served to recall me to a sense of my situation. I found that ~~that~~ the spirit of the Lord had actually caught me up off the floor and that my shoulder and head were pressing against the beams. [p. 71]

163. TEXT: Double underlining in original.
164. TEXT: Double underlining in original.

Draft 1

All this was witnessed by many to their great astonishment, and satisfaction when the[y] Saw the Devil thus Cast out of a human being and the power of God and His Holy Spirit thus made manifest.

~~As~~ So soon as consciousness returned, his bodily weakness was such that we were obliged to put him to bed, and wait upon him some time. As may be expected such a scene as this contributed much to make believers of those who witnessed it, and the greater part finally became members of the Church.

I soon after returned to Fayette Seneca Co—and as the Book of Mormon had now been for some time published, we found quite enough to occupy our time, No small stir was created by its appearance great opposition, much persecution, to those who believed in its authenticity was generally the case—but on the other hand, many were friendly and anxious to hear so that we continued to preach and give information as far as in our power,

~~On the day in which the Church~~ [p. [13]] ~~was organized, we had agreed to hold a conference of the Church the first day of June following~~— [*blank*] ~~About~~ ⟨During⟩ the last week of May the above mentioned Newel Knights came to visit us at Fayette and was baptized by ~~Oliver Cowdery~~ ⟨David Whitmer⟩.

On the First day of June the Church met in Conference according to appoint-

Draft 2

All this was witnessed by many, to their great astonishment and satisfaction when ~~thy~~ ⟨they⟩ saw the devil thus cast out; and the power of God and his holy spirit thus made manifest. So soon as consciousness returned, his bodily weakness was such that we were obliged to lay him upon his bed, and wait upon him for some time. As may be expected, such a scene as this contributed much to make believers of those who witnessed it, and finally, the greater part of them became members of the Church.

Soon after this occurrence I returned to Fayette, Seneca County. The Book of Mormon ("The Stick of Joseph in the hands of Ephraim") had now been published for some time, and as the ancient Prophet had predicted of it; "It was accounted as a strange thing."[166] No small stir was created by its appearance; great opposition, ⟨and⟩ much persecution followed the believers of its authenticity;[167] but it had now come to pass that, Truth had sprung out of the earth; and Righteousness had looked down from Heaven,[169] so we feared not our opponents, knowing that we had both Truth and righteousness on our side; that we had both the Father and the Son, because we had the doctrines of Christ and abided in them; and therefore ⟨we⟩ continued to preach and to give information to all who were willing to hear.

During the last week in May the above mentioned Newel Knight came to visit us, at Fayette and was baptized by David Whitmer.

On the first day of June 1830, we held our first ~~conference as an~~[170] conference as

Draft 3

This manifestation of the power of God was witnessed by many to their great astonishment and satisfaction

And as may be expected influenced them to ~~believe of~~ become the members of the church of Christ

Soon after this ~~occurence~~ occurrence I returned to Fayett when[165] I found ~~that~~ that the appearance of the book of Mormon "(The stick of Joseph in the hands of Ephraim")" had created great opposition and persecution to ~~those~~ the believers in its authenticity

But <u>truth</u> had sprung out of the earth and <u>rightiousness</u>[168] had looked down from heaven consequently we feared none of ⟨our⟩ opponents and continued to preach and give information to such as desired. ~~do~~

During the last of May Newel Knight came and was baptized by David Whitmer.

On the first day of June 1830 we held our first conference as an organized Church,

NOTES

165. TEXT: Or "where".

166. See Ezekiel 37:19; and Hosea 8:12.

167. Lucy Mack Smith described persecution of her husband, Joseph Smith Sr., and of her son Samuel in response to publication of the Book of Mormon, and she implied that concerted efforts by neighbors to collect debts allegedly owed by her son Hyrum were not based on purely financial motives. (Lucy Mack Smith, History, 1845, 179–184.)

168. TEXT: "truth" and "rightiousness" have double underlining in original.

169. See Psalm 85:11.

170. TEXT: After reaching the end of the line at "our first", James Mulholland mistakenly inscribed "conference as an" at the beginning of the same line, in the space created by the paragraph indention. He then canceled the three words and continued the inscription on the next line.

Draft 1

ment made on the day of our organization. Our numbers being now about thirty, many however attended who were either believing or wishful to hear.

Having opened by singing and prayer, we partook together of the emblems of the body and blood of our Lord Jesus Christ.

We then ⟨called out &⟩ ordained Severals to ~~the~~ various offices in the Church, and proceeded to confirm a number who had been lately baptized,— The Holy Ghost was poured out upon us in a miraculous manner, many of our number prophecied, others had the heavens opened to their view, whilst several were so overcome that we had to lay them on beds, &c. Amongst the rest, was ~~the afore mentioned~~ ⟨Brother⟩ Newel Knights, who was overcome, and laid on a bed because he was unable to help himself—according to his own relation of his experience, He could not understand why we laid him on the bed, he felt ⟨no sensibility of weakness⟩ ~~strong~~, his heart ⟨was⟩ filled with Love, Glory & pleasure unspeakable, and could (as he thought) discern all that was going on in the room, when all of a sudden, a vision of futurity burst upon him, He saw there ⟨represented⟩ the great work which through my instrumentality was yet to be accomplished, He saw Heaven opened and beheld the Lord Jesus Christ, sitting [at] the right hand of the Majesty on high, and had it made plain to his understanding that the time would come when he should be admitted into his presence to enjoy his society for ever and ever, When their bodily strength returned to them, they shouted Hosannas to God, and the Lamb, & rehearsed the glorious things which they had seen and felt, whilst

Draft 2

an organized Church.[171] Our numbers were about thirty, beside whom, many assembled with us, who were either believers or anxious to learn.

Having opened by singing and prayer, we partook together of the emblems of the body and blood of our Lord Jesus Christ,

we then ~~called~~ proceeded to confirm several who had lately been baptized; after which we called out and ordained severals to the various offices of the Priesthood. Much exhortation and instruction was given; and the Holy Ghost was poured out upon us in a miraculous manner many of our number prophecied, whilst others had the Heavens opened to their view, and were so over come that we had to lay them on beds, or other convenient places: Among the rest was Brother Newel Knights who had to be placed on a bed, being unable to help himself. By his own account of the transaction, He could not understand why we should lay him on the bed, ⟨as⟩ he felt no sensibility of weakness. He felt his heart filled with love, with glory and pleasure [p. 41] unspeakable, and could discern all that was going on in the room, when all of a sudden a vision of futurity burst upon him. He saw there represented, the great work which through my instrumentality was yet to be accomplished. He saw Heaven opened and beheld the Lord Jesus Christ, seated at the right hand of the majesty on high, and had it made plain to his understanding that the time would come whe[n] he would be admitted into his presence to enjoy his society for ever and ever. When their bodily strength was restored to these brethren, they shouted "hosannas to God and the lamb" and rehearsed the glorious

Draft 3

which consisted of about thirty members besides ~~many~~ ⟨others⟩ who attended ~~for the purpose of learning to learn respecting~~ for the purpose of obtaining a knowledge of our doctrine.

Having opened by prayer, ~~and~~ ⟨then and⟩ ~~singing~~ ⟨sung⟩ an appropriate hymn, we partook of the emblems of the body and blood of our Lord Jesus Christ—

We then proceeded to confirm those who had recently been baptized; and ordained several to the various offices of the Priesthood, Much instruction was given at this time and the Holy Ghost in a miraculous manner was poured out upon us some propecied ~~whilst~~ others had the heavens opened to their view and were so overcome that we were ⟨under the necessity of laying⟩ ~~compelled compeled to lay~~ them on beds or other convenient places. ~~Newel Knights was among~~ ⟨one of⟩ ~~those that were put out~~[172] ~~upon beds thus taken care of~~ and among whom was [p. 72] bro^r. Newel Knights. From him we afterwards learned that he felt no weakness but that his heart was filled with love when suddenly a vision of futurity opened to his view he saw heaven opened and beheld the Lord Jesus Christ seated at the right hand of the majesty on high and it was manifested to him that he should be permitted to enter into his presence and enjoy his society for ever and ever

NOTES

171. Minute Book 2 recorded the date as 9 June 1830 and the place as Fayette, Seneca County, New York. (Minute Book 2, 9 June 1830.)

172. TEXT: Or "ont[o]". This word or partial word appears to have been canceled twice, once when originally inscribed and again with the rest of the passage.

Draft 1

yet in the spirit. (Comments)[173] upon the whole we had a [*blank lines*][174] [p. [14]] [*1/4 page blank*]

About this time David Whitmer baptized the following viz: John Poorman, John Jolly, Julia Anne Jolly—and Harriette Jolly Jerushee Smith Kathrine Smith Wm Smith, Don C. Smith—Porter Rockwell—Caroline Rockwell and Electa Rockwell in Seneca Lake.

Immediately after the conference, I ⟨returned to my own house & from thence (in company with my wife) Oliver Cowdery—John Whitmer—⟨&⟩ David Whitmer)⟩ ~~returned~~ journeyed ⟨again⟩ on a visit to Mr Knights' Broom Co. We found a number in the neighborhood still believing and now anxious, to be baptized, accordingly we appointed a meeting on the ⟨next⟩ Sabbath day, intending to attend to the

Draft 2

things which they had seen and felt, whilst they were yet in the Spirit.

Such scenes as these were calculated to inspire our hearts with joy unspeakable, and fill us with awe and reverence for that Almighty Being, by whose grace we had been called to be instrumental in bringing about for the children of men, the enjoyment of such glorious blessings as were now at this time poured out upon us. To find ourselves engaged in the very same order of things, as observed by the holy Apostles of old; To realize the importance and solemnity of such proceedings, and to witness and feel with our own natural senses, the like glorious manifestations of the powers of the Priesthood; the gifts and blessings of the Holy Ghost; and the goodness and condescension of a merciful God, unto such as obey the everlasting gospel of our Lord Jesus Christ, combined to create within us, sensations of rapturous gratitude, and inspire ⟨us⟩ with fresh zeal and energy, in the cause of truth.

Shortly after this conference David Whitmer baptized the following persons in Seneca lake. viz: John Poorman, John Jolly, Julia Anne Jolly—and Harriett Jolly, Jerushee [Jerusha Barden] Smith, Kath[a]rine Smith, William Smith, Don C[arlos] Smith—Peter [Orrin Porter?] Rockwell—Caroline Rockwell and Electa Rockwell.

Immediately after conference, I returned to my own house,[175] and from thence (accompanied by my wife, Oliver Cowdery, John Whitmer and David Whitmer) journeyed again on a visit to Mr Knight [Joseph Knight Sr.]'s of Colesville, Broom Co. We found a number in the neighborhood still believing and now anxious to be baptized.

We appointed a meeting for the Sabbath, and on the afternoon of Saturday we

Draft 3

such scenes as these were calculated to inspire our hearts with joy and awe for that
Almighty Being who in his great wisdom
had called us to be instruments by which
he would bestow ⟨upon this generation⟩ in
these last days the inestimable blessing of
the gospel ~~and its gifts~~ preached in its
fullness.

Shortly after conference David Whitmer
baptized the following persons in Seneca
Lake, viz, John Jolly Julia A Jolly, Harriet
Jolly Jerusha Smith Katharine Smith
William Smith Don-Carlos Smith O. P.
Rockwell Caroline Rockwell and Electa
Rockwell.

Shortly after I (accompanied by my wife)
Oliver Cowdry John Whitmer and David
Whitmer again visited Brown [Broome]
County where we found a number beleiv-
ing the gospel and anxious to obey

We appointed a meeting for following
sabbath and on the afternoon of saturday

NOTES

173. TEXT: Possibly an ink blot rather than a
cancellation.

174. TEXT: This blank space may indicate that
James Mulholland intended to add more narrative
at a later time. In Draft 2, a paragraph at this
point was taken from earlier in Draft 1 (see 371n155
herein). A small scrap of paper affixed to the top
right corner of this page of Draft 1 is inscribed in
Mulholland's hand as follows: "[*page torn*]ag 112
N 2 | [*page torn*] & 181 No 1". These numbers cor-
respond to the page numbers of, respectively, sections 29 and 28 in the 1835 edition of the Doctrine
and Covenants. These revelations both date to
September 1830, providing evidence that Mulholland organized the sections of the Doctrine
and Covenants (which often appear out of chronological order) into a chronological sequence
before putting them into the history.

175. At Harmony, Pennsylvania.

Draft 1

ordinance. On the afternoon previous, we had erected a dam across a stream in order to form a place for baptism, but during the night a mob collected (at the instigation of sectarian Priests of the neighborhood) and tore away our dam, which hindered our intentions of baptizing those who wished at this time,

We however held our meeting, Oliver Cowdery preached, & many of us bore record & testimony to the truth of the book of Mormon, the doctrine of repentance &c Amongst our Audience were those who had torn down our dam the night previous, &¹⁷⁶ seemed wishful to give us trouble, but did not untill after our meeting had been dismissed, when they immediately commenced talking to those who they considered our friends—⟨to try to turn them against us and our doctrines.⟩ [p. [15]]

⟨And⟩ a young woman, ⟨named Emily Coburn⟩ a sister in law to Newel Knight was ~~forcibly~~ taken upon a power of attorney, and ⟨forcibly⟩ carried out of the neighborhood because her relations understood her to be in the way of believing our doctrine.

Draft 2

erected a dam across a stream of water which was convenient, for the purpose of there attending to the ordinance, but during the night a mob collected, and tore down our dam which hindered us of attending to the baptism on the sabbath.

We afterward found out that this mob had been instigated to this act of molestation, by certain Sectarian Priests of the neighborhood, who began to consider their craft in danger, and took this plan to stop the progress of the truth, and the sequel will show how determinedly they prosecuted their opposition, as well as to how little purpose in the end.

The Sabbath arrived and we held our meeting, Oliver Cowdery preached, and others of us bore testimony to the truth of the Book of Mormon, the doctrine of repen[p. 42]tance, baptism for the remission of sins, and laying on of hands for the gift of the Holy Ghost &c &c, amongst our audience were those who had torn down our dam and who seemed wishful to give us trouble, but did not untill after the meeting was dismissed, when they immediately commenced talking to those whom they considered our friends, to try to turn them against us and our doctrines.

Amongst the many present at this meeting was one Emily Coburn sister to the wife¹⁷⁷ of Newel Knight. The Revᵈ Mʳ [John] Shearer, a divine of the presbyterian faith, who had considered himself her pastor,¹⁷⁸ came to understand that she was likely to believe our doctrine, and had a short ⟨time⟩ previous to this, ~~our~~ meeting, came to labor with her, but having spent some time with her without being able to persuade her against us, he endeavored to have her leave her sisters house, and go

Draft 3

erected a dam across ~~the~~ a small stream of water for the purpose of attending to the ordinance of baptism but during the night a mob collected and tore down the dam which ~~prevented us~~ thwarted our intentions.

We afterwards learned that this mob had been influenced by certain sectarian priests ~~who feared~~ ⟨fearing⟩ that their craft was ~~in danger~~ in jeopardy ~~and~~ pursued this [p. 73] ⟨unhallowed⟩ course to stop the progress of truth

~~The sabbath~~ agreeably to appointment ~~in~~ on the sabbath Oliver Cowdry preached and we bore testimony of the truth of the book of Mormon the doctrine of repentance ~~and~~ for the remission of sins and laying on of hands for the gift of the Holy Ghost &c &c.

Among the many present at this meeting was one Emily Coburn sister of Newel Knight's wife who became convinced of the truth ~~as~~ preached by us.

Short time previous to which the Rev. ~~Mr.~~ Shearer who considered himself her pastor made her a visit and endeavored to prevail upon her to leave her sister's house and go with <u>him</u> to her father's who lived several miles from Mr. Knight's to effect this he resorted to stratagem saying that her brothers[179] was waiting at a certain place for

NOTES

176. TEXT: Possibly an ink blot rather than a cancellation.
177. Sarah (Sally) Coburn Knight.
178. John Shearer served as pastor for the Sanford and Colesville Presbyterian churches from 1830 to 1831 with funding from the American Home Missionary Society. Shearer reported Emily Coburn's defection from the Presbyterian church to the society's New York office. (Hotchkin, *History of the Purchase and Settlement of Western New York,* 303; John Shearer, Colesville, NY, to Absalom Peters, New York City, NY, 18 Nov. 1830, in *American Home Missionary Society Papers.*)
179. TEXT: Possibly "brother's".

Draft 1   **Draft 2**

with him to her father's,[180] who lived at a distance of at least [*blank*] miles off: For this purpose he had recourse to stratagem; he told her that one of her brothers was waiting at a certain place, wishful to have her go home with him; he succeeded thus to get her a little distance from the house when, seeing that her brother was not in waiting for her, She refused to go any further with him; upon which he got hold of her by the arm to force her along; but her sister, was soon with them; and the two women were too many for him and he was forced to sneak off without his errand, after all his labor and ingenuity. Nothing daunted however he went to her Father, represented to him something or other, which induced the Old Gentleman to give him a power of Attorney, which, as soon as our meeting was over, on the above named sunday evening, he immediately served upon her and carried her off to her father's residence, by open violence, against her will. All his labor was in vain however, for the said Emily Coburn, in a short time afterwards, was baptized and confirmed, a member of the "Church of Jesus Christ of Latter Day Saints."[181]

Early however on Monday morning we wer on the alert, and got together ~~quite early in the~~ before our enemies were awar[e] we soon repaired the dam, and proceeded to baptize—when the following thirteen persons were baptized for the remission of their sins under the hands of Oliver Cowdery. Viz:

However, early on Monday morning we were on the alert, and before our enemies were aware we had repaired the dam, and proceeded to baptize, when the following thirteen persons were baptized under the hands of Oliver Cowdery viz:

Emma Smith, Hezekiah Peck & wife, Joseph Knights & wife William Stringham & wife Joseph Knights Jr Aron Culver & wife Levi Hall, Polly Knight, ⟨&⟩ Julia Stringham.

Emma Smith, Hezekiah Peck and wife, Joseph Knight [Sr.] and wife—William Stringham and wife—Joseph Knight Jr Aarron [Aaron] Culver and wife—Levi Hale [Hall]—Polly Knight and Julia Stringham.—[182]

Draft 3

her to ⟨accompany him home⟩ ~~go home with him~~ after going a short distance she discovered his falshood and refused to go any further,

Upon this he laid hold of her to compel her to go with him but with the assistance of her sister she ~~compeled~~ ⟨forced⟩ him to desist nothing daunted however he went to her father and by misrepresentations induced the old gentleman to give him a power of attorney which he served on her person at the close of our meeting on the sabbath of which we have spoken and carried her away against her will. ~~however~~ all his labor was in vain for in a short time she was baptized and confirmed a member of the Church of Jesus Christ of Latter Day Saints

Early on the following morning we repaired the dam and baptized the following persons

To wit, Emma Smith Hezekiah Peck and [p. 74] and wife Joseph Knight and wife William Stringham and wife Joseph Knight Jʳ Aaron Culver and wife Levi Hale Polly Knight and Julia Stringham.

NOTES

180. Amariah Coburn.

181. Emily Coburn's later account of these events varied from JS's history on numerous details. According to Coburn, prior to her extended visit with Sally and Newel Knight at Colesville, she had been living at the home of her brother Esick Lyon Coburn at Sanford, about twelve miles from Colesville. An unnamed messenger found Emily among the congregation assembled at the home of Newel Knight and told her that her brother was waiting nearby to talk with her. During Coburn's conversation with her brother, Shearer joined them and attempted to take her to her uncle, who was apparently waiting to escort her back to Sanford. After her father, who was living at Guilford, Chenango County, New York, signed a power of attorney, Coburn was returned to the home of her brother Esick at Sanford. In autumn 1830 Newel and Sally Knight obtained permission from Coburn's parents to take her home to Colesville for another visit. Within a week of her arrival there, Coburn was baptized and confirmed. (Austin, *Life among the Mormons,* 30–31, 40–46, 57.)

182. The women not named are, respectively, Martha Long Peck, Polly Peck Knight, Esther Knight Stringham, and Esther Peck Culver. These baptisms were performed on 28 June 1830 in a stream that flowed from Pickerel Pond, on the farm of Joseph Knight Sr., to the Susquehanna River. Anna Knight DeMille may also have been been baptized at this time. (Berrett, *Sacred Places,* 2:124–125; Porter, "Colesville Branch and the Coming Forth of the Book of Mormon," 372–373.)

Draft 1

Before we had yet finished the baptism of these, the same mob began again to collect together, and shortly after we had done and retired to the house of Joseph Knight, the mob ~~had~~ amounted to about fifty men. They surrounded the House, raging with anger, and apparently wishful to commit violence upon us, some of them asked questions, others threatened us, and annoyed us so much that we thought it wisdom to leave and go to the house of Newel Knight. They followed us there also, and it was with great persevereance and prudence that we were enabled to keep them in bounds ~~untill we succeeded in Confirming those who had been baptized,~~ Some ⟨Numbers⟩ of the brethren had to constantly keep the door and keep them in talk, ⟨&⟩ answer their various and unprofitable questions, so long as they were inclined to stay. I talked to them considerable, but in general to no purpose. We had appointed a meeting on the evening of the same day, for the purpose of confirmations, the time appointed had arrived and our friends had nearly all collected together, when to my surprise I was visited by a constable, and arrested by him, on ⟨a⟩ warrant on a charge of being a disorderly person, of setting the country in an uproar by preaching the Book of Mormon, and various other such like charges. The constable informed me soon after he had arrested me that the plan of those who had got out this warrant, was to get me into the hands of the mob who were now lying in ambust [ambush] for me [p. [16]] but that he was determined to save me from them, as he had found me to be a different kind of person, from what had been represented to him. We ~~got into~~ ⟨had⟩ a waggon to travel in and ~~he~~ I soon found that he had told me the truth in this matter, for not far from

Draft 2

Before the baptism was entirely finished, the mob began again to collect, and shortly after we had retired, they amounted to about fifty men. They surrounded the house of Mr Knight [Joseph Knight Sr.] (where we had retired to) raging with anger and apparently wishful to commit violence upon us. Some asked us questions, others threatened us, so that we thought it wisdom to leave and go to the house of Newel Knight.

There also they followed us, and it was only by the exercise of great prudence on our part, and reliance on our heavenly Father that they were kept [p. 43] from laying violent hands upon us, and so long as they chose to stay, we were obliged to answer them various unprofitable questions, and bear with insults and threatenings without number.

We had appointed a meeting for this evening, for the purpose of attending to the confirmation of those who had been the same morning baptized; the time appointed had arrived, and our friends had nearly all collected together, when to my surprise, I was visited by a constable, and arrested by him on a warrant, on charge of being a disorderly person; of setting the country in an uproar by preaching the Book of Mormon, &c &c.[183] The Constable informed me (soon after I had been arrested) that the plan of those who had got out the warrant, was to get me into the hands of the mob, who were now lying in ambush for me; but that he was determined to save me from them, as he had found me to be a different sort of person from what I had been represented to him.

I soon found that he had told me the truth in this matter, for not far from

Draft 3

Before he had finished the mob began to collect and shortly after we had retired, amounted to upwards of fifty men. They surrounded the house of Mʳ· Knight (where we were) raging with anger some asking us questions others threatning us so that we thought it wise to leave and seek safety in the house of Newel Knight

here they followed us and it was only by the exercise of prudence and reliance upon God that they were kept from laying violent hands upon us yet we could not escape their taunts and insults.

We met ~~on~~ ⟨during⟩ the evening of this day to confirm those who had been baptized when our friends had nearly collected to my surprise I was arrested by a constable on charge of being a disorderly person and setting the country in an uproar by preaching the book of Mormon &c &c The constable informed me that ~~is~~ it was the intention of those who ~~had~~ obtained the warrant to place me in the hands of the mob who were in ambush at a short distance from Mʳ· Knight's: but that he would thwart them in their intentions as he found me a different person from ⟨what⟩ he expected and that my calumniators had done me great injustice.

This I found to be true for we had gone but a short distance when the waggon in which

NOTES

183. The constable was Ebenezer Hatch. Although the formal charge was for being a "disorderly person," Joseph Knight Sr. wrote that the charge was "pertending to see under ground." One of the legal definitions of "disorderly person" was someone "pretending to tell . . . where lost or stolen goods may be found." The charges resembled those filed earlier against JS in a South Bainbridge court proceeding in March 1826. (Trial bill, 1 June 1830, People v. JS [J.P. Ct. 1830], Chenango County Courthouse, Norwich, NY; Ebenezer Hatch, Bill of services, 4 July 1830, Chenango County Historical Society, Norwich, NY; Knight, Reminiscences, 8; Of Disorderly Persons, *Revised Statutes of the State of New-York* [1827–1828], 1:638, part 1, chap. 20, title 5, sec. 1; see also Madsen, "Joseph Smith's 1826 Trial," 91–95.)

Draft 1

Mr Knight's house the waggon was surrounded by the mob, who seemed only to
await some signal from the constable, but
to their great disappointment—he gave the
horse the whip, ~~and left them far behind~~—
and drove me out of their reach, however
whilst we were driving pretty quickly along
one of our wheels came off, which left us
very nearly once more in their power, as
they were in close pursuit, however we
managed to get the wheel on again and
once more left them behind,

he drove on to ⟨a town⟩ ~~what~~ which was
then called south Bainbridge, ⟨in Chenango
Co⟩ where he lodged me for the time being
in an upper room in a Tavern there, and in
order that all might be right with me, and
himself also, he slept ~~all~~ during the night,
with his feet against the door, and a loaded
musket by his side whilst I occupied a bed,
which was [in] the room. have declared
that if we were interrupted, he would fight
for me and defend me as far as in his
power.

A court was here convened on the
[blank] day of [blank] for the purpose of investigating those charges which had been
preferred against me. A great excitement
prevailed, on account of the scandalous
falsehoods which had been circulated, the
nature of which will come out in the sequel. In the mean time ~~we~~ as soon as M^r
Joseph Knights had heard of my arrest, he
immediately repaired to two of his neighbours respectable farmers ⟨viz: Esq. James
Davidson & John Reed men⟩, renowned
for their integrity and well-versed in the
laws of their country, and retained them on
my behalf on the coming trial. At length
the trial commenced amidst a multitude of
spectators who in general evinced a belief
~~of~~ that I was guilty, of all that had been

Draft 2

Mr Knight's house, the waggon in which
we had set out; was surrounded by the
mob, who seemed only to await some signal from the Constable; but to their great
disappointment—he gave the horse the
whip and drove me out of their reach.

Whilst driving along pretty quickly,
one of the waggon wheels came off, which
left us, once more, very nearly surrounded
by them, as they had came on, in close
pursuit; however we ~~now~~ managed to get
the wheel on again and, again left them
behind us.

He drove on to the Town of South
Bainbridge Chenango County, where he
lodged me for the time being, in an upper
room of a Tavern, and in order that all
might be right with himself and with me
also, he slept during the night with his feet
against the door, and a loaded musket by
his side, whilst I occupied a bed which was
in the room, he having declared that if we
were interrupted unlawfully, that he would
fight for me, and defend me as far as in his
power.

On the day following a court was convened for the purpose of investigating
those charges which had been preferred
against me, A great excitement prevailed
on account of the scandalous falsehoods
which had been circulated, the nature of
which will come out in the sequel.

In the mean time, my friend, Joseph
Knight [Sr.], had repaired to two of his
neighbours viz: James Davidson and John
Reid [Reed] Esqrs, (respectable farmers;
men renowned for their integrity, and well
versed in the laws of their country,) and retained them on my behalf during my trial.

At ⟨length⟩ the trial commenced
amidst a multitude of spectators who in
general evinced a belief that I was guilty of
all that had been reported concerning me,

Draft 3

we were riding was surrounded by the mob
~~who~~ that only waited for a preconcerted
signal from [p. 75] the constable but to
their disappointment and my sattisfaction
he put whip to his horse thus placing me
out of their reach

he drove on to the town of South Bainbridge where he lodged me for the time
being in a room of the Hotel and ~~in order~~
to make all things secure he slept during
the night on the floor (while I occupied the
bed) with his feet against the door and a
loaded gun at his side declairing that no
person should unlawfully disturb us with
impunity.

On the following day a court was convened
to investigate the charges prefered against
me
        The falshoods circulated by my ene-
mies caused great excitement among the
people.

In the mean time Joseph Night had secured the services of James Davidson and
⟨John⟩ Reid (respectable farmers men of
well known integrity and well versed in the
laws of their Country) to assist me.

At length the trial commenced amidst a
multitude of spectators who generally believed me to be guilty and were anxious to
see me punished one of the many witnesses

Draft 1

~~hatched~~ reported concerning me. and of course were very zealous that I should be punished, according to my crimes— ⟨among many witnesses⟩ Mr Josiah Stoal, (of whom I have heretofore spoken) was called up and ~~examined~~ ⟨questioned⟩, ⟨nearly⟩ as follows, Did not the prisener Joseph Smith have a horse of you? Ansᵗ Yes, Did ⟨not⟩ he go to you and tell you, that an angel had appeared unto him, and authorized him to get the horse from you. Answer No, he told me no such story [p. [17]] Well! How how had he the horse of you? ⟨Aⁿˢ⟩ He bought him of me, as another man would do. Q. Have you had your pay? Ansᵗ That is not your business.

The question being again put, the witness replied, I hold his note for the price of the horse, which I consider as good as the pay—for I am ⟨well⟩ acquainted with him and know him to be an honest man, and if he wishes—I am ready to let him have another horse on the same terms.

Mʳ Jonathan Thompson was next called up, and examined. Question, Has not Joseph Smith, the prisoner had a yoke of oxen of you, Ansᵗ Yes, Did he not ⟨obtain them by⟩ tell⟨ing⟩ you that he had a revelation to the effect that he was to have them? Ansᵗ No, he did ⟨not⟩ mention a word of the kind concerning the oxen, he purchased them, same as another ~~and~~ man would?

After a few more such attempts, the court was ~~adjourned untill~~ [blank] ⟨detained for a

Draft 2

and of course were very zealous, that I should be punished according to my crimes. Among many witnesses call⟨ed⟩ up against me, was Mʳ Josiah Stoal [Stowell] (of whom I have made mention, as having worked for him some time) and examined to the following effect.—[184]

Q—Did not the prisoner Joseph Smith have a horse of you?

Ansᵗ Yes.

Q—Did not he go to you and tell you, that an angel had appeared unto him, and authorised him to get [p. 44] the horse from you?

Ansᵗ No, he told me no such story.

Q—Well; How ~~did~~ had he the horse of you?

Ansᵗ He bought him of me, as another man would do.

Q— Have you had your pay?

Ansᵗ That is not your business.

The question being again put, the witness replied, "I hold his note for the price of the horse, which I consider as good as the pay—for I am well acquainted with Joseph Smith Jr, and know him to be an honest man; and if he wishes I am ready to let him have another horse on the same terms".[185]——

Mʳ Jonathan Thompson was next called up, and examined—

Q—Has not the prisoner, Joseph Smith Jr had a yoke of oxen of you?

Ansᵗ Yes.

Q—Did he not obtain them of you by telling you that he had a revelation to the effect that he was to have them?

Ansᵗ No, He did not mention a word of the kind concerning the oxen; he purchased them, same as another man would.

After a few more such attempts, the court was detained for a time, in order that

Draft 3

called up against me was M^r. Josiah Stole
(of whom I have heretofore spoken) who
was examined as follows.

Q. Did not the prisoner Joseph Smith
have a horse of you

A. ~~Yes~~ Yes.

Q Did not he go to you and tell you
that an angel had appeared unto him and
authorized him to get the horse from you?

An^s. No, he told me no such story

Q Well how had he the horse of you

Ans He bought ⟨it⟩ of me as another
man would do

Q Que^s. Have you had your pay [p. 76]

Answer. That is not your business.

The question being again put, the witness replied, I hold his note for the price of
the horse which I consider as good as the
pay for I am well acquainted with Joseph
Smith J^r. ⟨I⟩ ~~and~~ know him to be an honest
man; and if he wishes I am ready ~~I~~ to let
him have another horse on the same terms.

Mr Jonathan Thompson was next
called and examenid

Ques Has not the prisoner Joseph
Smith J^r had a yoke of Oxen of you;

Ans yes

Q Did he not obtain them of you by
telling you that he had a revelation to ~~the~~
this effect that he must have them

Ans No he did not mention a word of
the kind concerning the oxen he ⟨pur-
chased them⟩ ~~Bought~~ the same as any other
man would

After a few more such attempts the
court was detained some time to obtain the

NOTES

184. It is not known whether any transcript
of the South Bainbridge or Colesville trial was
available to those compiling JS's history in
Illinois. The only known trial report that predates
the history was published in 1832 and does not
include details found here. (See "Mormonism,"
Morning Star, 16 Nov. 1832, 114.)

185. JS purchased the horse from Josiah Stowell
in October 1829. (JS, Harmony, PA, to Oliver
Cowdery, 22 Oct. 1829, in JS Letterbook 1, p. 9.)

Draft 1

time⟩ in order that two you young women ⟨⟨daughters to Mʳ Stoal⟩⟩ might be sent for, with whom I had ⟨often⟩ kept ⟨often⟩ company; in order if possible to elicit something f̶o̶r̶ from them that might be made a pretext against me. The court again sat, and the ⟨young⟩ Ladies were ⟨separately⟩ examined touching my Character, Conduct, a̶n̶d̶ in general, but particulcarliy as to my behaviour towards them, both in public and in private. When they both bore such testimony in my favor as left my enemies with out a pretext on their account. Several attempts were now made to prove something against me, and even circumstances which ⟨were alleged to have⟩ had taken place in Broom Co were brought forward, but which my lawyers would not admit of being here brought against me. In order therefore that I should if possible be made [to] appear guilty of something. The Court was detained over untill a warrant was obtained from Broom County. and served upon me just immediately after I had been acquitted and set at liberty by this court. The Constable who served this warrant, had no sooner done so than he began to abuse and insult me, and so unfeeling was he with me, that although, I had been kept all the day in court with out any thing to eat since the morning yet he hurried me off to Broom County, a distance of about 15 miles w̶e̶ before he allowed me time ⟨to⟩ eat anything. [p. [18]]

¹⁸⁷⟨about this time we were over against my own house, I wished to be allowed to go t̶o̶ home for the night ⟨offering security for safety—⟩ but would not [*illegible*].⟩ He then took me to a Tavern, and gathered in a number of men who used every means to abuse, ridicule, and insult me. They spit upon me, pointed their fingers at me,

Draft 2

two young women (daughters to Mr Stoal) with whom I had at times kept company; might be sent for, in order, if possible to elicit something from them which might be made a pretext against me. The young Ladies arrived and were severally examined, touching my character, and conduct in general but particularly as to my behaviour towards them both in publick and private, when they both bore such testimony in my favor, as left my enemies without a pretext on their account.—

Several attempts were now made to prove something against me, and even circumstances which were alleged to have taken place in Broom[e] County were brought forward; but these, my lawyers would not here admit of against me, in consequence of which, my persecutors managed to detain the court, untill they had succeeded in obtaining a warrant from Broom Co, and which warrant the[y] served upon me, at the very moment in which I had been acquitted by this court.¹⁸⁶

The constable who served this second warrant upon me, had no sooner arrested me, than he began to abuse and insult me, and so unfeeling was he with me, that although I had been kept all the day in court, without any thing to eat since the morning, yet he hurried me off to Broom Co, a distance of about fifteen miles before he allowed me any t̶h̶i̶n̶g̶ ⟨kind⟩ of food whatever.

He took me to a tavern, and gathered in a number of men, who used every means to abuse, ridicule, and insult me. They spit upon me, pointed their fingers at me, saying prophesy, prophesy, and thus did they

Draft 3

testimony of two Young Ladies ⟨(daughte[r]s of Mr Stoal)⟩ with whom I had associated previous to my marriage They ~~young~~ arrived and testified that I had always treated them with ~~the u~~ respect ~~both in public and in private~~ in ~~publick~~ ⟨Society⟩ as well as when out of ~~Society~~ it

Several attempts were now made to prove things which were <u>said</u> to have been committed in another ⟨Broom⟩ County but my <u>Lawyers</u> (Davidson and Ried) would not permit such a mode of proceedure as this and while those of the prosecution were contending for the admisson of such testimony my persecutors had time to obtain a Warrant from Broom Co. which was served upon my person as soon as this court had acquitted me

The Constable who served this second warrant immediately commenced abusing ~~me~~ and insulting me and although I had ate nothing since morning having been detained in court ~~all~~ during the day yet he hurried me off [p. 77] to Broom Co ⟨a distance of fifteen miles⟩ without permitting me to eat anything ~~at all~~

He took me to a tavern and having collected a number of men commenced abusing me ~~in~~ in every way possible They spit upon ⟨me⟩. pointed their fingers at me saying, 'propecy propecy" and thus did they

186. John Reed, counsel for JS, later recalled that the hearing at South Bainbridge began at about ten o'clock in the morning and concluded at about midnight with an acquittal, but that JS was arrested again and within a half hour was being transported to Colesville. ("Some of the Remarks of John S. Reed," *Times and Seasons,* 1 June 1844, 5:549–552.)

187. TEXT: The following inscription appears at the top of page 19 of Draft 1, in the handwriting of Frederick G. Williams: "Scriptures on Covenants | Genesis | IX Section 20.4. and 21 Par 28th Par | X Section 12 Paragraph, [*blank*] | XI Section 5th Paragraph [*blank*] 8 Par. 9th [*blank*] Par 10th Par [*blank*] 11th Par." This list was composed circa July 1833 as part of an index to JS's Bible revision. The indexing project was discontinued and this gathering of pages was later repurposed for the present history draft. In preparation for the history, the fold of the gathering was inverted so that what had been the first page of the gathering (including this list of scriptures) became page 19 in the center of the gathering.

Draft 1

saying to me, prophesy prophesy, and in many ⟨others⟩ ways did the[y] insult me. I applied for some thing to eat, The constable ordered me some crusts of bread and some water which was the only fare I that night received; ~~and I at length got some respite from my persecutors, being furnished with a bed in the second story of the house,~~

At length the constable and I retired to bed, he made me lie next the wall, and he lay down beside me, ~~and lest I might escape, he~~ ⟨and⟩ put his arms around me, and upon my moving in the least, would clench me fast, fearing I intended to escape from him. Burch, a lawyer for the prosecution[188]

Next day I was brought before the Magis⟨trates⟩[189] Court of Broom Co, and put upon my trial. My former, faithful friends and lawyers were again at my side, my former persecutors were again arrayed against me. ~~Among the latter was one Mr Seymour a zealous professor and advocate of the presbyterian creed,) who had made himself conspicuous against[191] me; and had been all along ⟨both⟩ during the former and present trial.[192]~~ Many witnesses were again called ~~up~~ forward and examined. Some of whom swore to the most palpable falsehoods, and like to the false witnesses which had appeared against me on the former trial, they condradicted themselves, so plainly that the court would not admit their testimony, ~~and after using~~ Others were called who ~~proved~~ ⟨showed⟩ by their zeal that they were willing enough to prove something against me, but all they could do, was to ~~prove~~ tell somethings which

Draft 2

imitate those who crucified the Saviour of mankind, not knowing what they did. We were at this time not far distant from my own house, I wished to be allowed the privilege of spending the night with my wife at home, offering any wished for security, for my appearance, but this was denied me. I applied for something to eat. ~~the~~ The Constable ordered me some crusts of bread, and water, which was the only fare I that night received.

At length we retired to bed; the constable [p. 45] made me lie next the wall; He then laid himself down by me, and put his arm around me; and upon my moving in the least, would clench me fast, fearing that I intended to escape from him: And in this (not very agreeable) manner did we pass the night.—

Next day I was brought before the Magistrate's Court of [*blank*], Broom Co, and put upon my trial.[190] My former faithful friends and lawyers were again at my side, my former persecutors were arrayed against me. Many witnesses were again called forward and examined; some of whom swore to the most palpable falsehoods, and like to the false witnesses which had appeared against me the day previous; they contradicted themselves so plainly, that the Court would not admit their testimony.

Others were called who shewed by their zeal, that they were willing enough to prove something against me; but all they could do, was to tell somethings which some body else had told them. In this

Draft 3

follow the example of those who crucified
our Saviour "not knowing what they did"
We were at this time not far distant from
my own house and I wished to spend the
night ~~the night~~ with my family offering
any amount of security for my appearance
they could ask for but this was denied me
with threats and taunts. On asking for
food the constable ordered some crusts of
bread and cold water which was the only
~~food~~ ⟨sustenance⟩ I recieved that night

At length we retired to bed ~~and~~ the
constable ~~directed~~ directing me to lie next
to the wall and placing himself by my side
put his arm around me and if I moved he
would ~~cling~~ clinch me fast fearing that I
would escape and in this disagreeable
maner I spent the night

Next day I was brought before the
Magistrate Court of Broom Co and put
upon my trial

My former faithful friends again appeared at the bar in my behalf while my
former enemies were still arrayed against
me Many witness were ~~call~~ examined some
of whom swore to the most palpable falsehoods ~~but~~ ⟨and⟩ like those of the day previous ~~and~~ contradicted themselves so often
and so ~~pointedly~~ pointedly that the court
was <u>compelled</u> to see the ~~dishonesty and~~
intriegue and injustice of my persecutors
and influence ⟨it⟩ ~~them~~ to prohibit the ad-
mittance of their testimony

Others evincd their zeal and desire to
convict me of <u>something</u> but all they could
do was to tell someth[i]ng that ~~some some~~
other persons had Said

188. TEXT: James Mulholland inscribed an
embellished circle around "Burch, a lawyer for the
prosecution". Elsewhere in this document, cir-
cling around words indicated the intent to supply
information from an additional source, such as
the 1835 edition of the Doctrine and Covenants;
see, for instance, 299n109 herein.

189. TEXT: "the Magistrates" possibly inserted
over a blank space in the original inscription.

190. This was in Colesville. According to a
report apparently copied from the docket book of
Joel K. Noble, who heard the case as one of three
justices of the peace sitting as a court of special
sessions, JS was charged with "a breach of the
peace, against the good people of the state of New
York, by looking through a certain stone to find
hid treasures, &c." Noble recalled that the trial
occupied twenty-three hours. ("Mormonism,"
Morning Star, 16 Nov. 1832, 114; Joel K. Noble,
Bainbridge, NY, to Jonathan B. Turner, Jacksonville, NY, 8 Mar. 1842, in Vogel, *Early Mormon
Documents,* 4:106–111.)

191. TEXT: "against" written over "in" and then
canceled with the rest of the passage.

192. TEXT: There appear to be two layers of cancellation. The first revised the sentence to read,
"Mr Seymour had made himself conspicuous
against me, during the former trial"; then the
entire passage was canceled.

About this time David Whitmer baptized the following viz:

John Poorman, John Jolly, Julia Anne Jolly — and Harriette Jolly Lerusha Smith Kathrine Smith Wm Smith, Don C Smith Porter Rockwell — Caroline Rockwell and Electa Rockwell in Seneca Lake. —

Immediately after the conference, I (in company with my wife) returned to my own house & from thence Oliver Cowdery — John Whitmer & David Whitmer) journeyed again on a visit to Mr Knights Broom Co. We found a number in the neighbourhood still believing and more anxious, to be baptized, accordingly we appointed a meeting on the next Sabbath day, intending to attend to that ordinance. On the afternoon previous, we had erected a dam across a stream in order to form a place for baptism, but during the night a mob collected (at the instigation of sectarian Priests of the neighbourhood) and tore away our dam, which hindered our intentions of baptizing those who wished at that time; We however held our meeting, Oliver Cowdery preached, & many of us bore record & testimony to the truth of the Book of Mormon, the doctrine of repentance Amongst our Audience were those who had torn down our dam the night previous, & seemed wishful to give us trouble, but did not untill after our meeting had been dismissed, when they immediately commenced talking to those who they considered our friends to try to turn them against us and our doctrines.

Scrap of paper with revelation references (Draft 1). A tiny scrap of paper attached to the top right corner of page 15 in the 1839 history draft contains what at first seem to be cryptic numbers and abbreviations. The numbers correspond to pages in the 1835 edition of the Doctrine and Covenants, arranged on the scrap of paper to be in order of the dates of the revelations referenced on those page numbers. This indicates that James Mulholland may have made a preliminary, chronologically arranged list of revelations to be included in the history (see 391n174 herein). The blank lines at the top of the page may indicate that Mulholland intended to return later and add to the narrative. Handwriting of James Mulholland. JS History, 1839, p. [15] (transcribed on pp. 390–392 herein), Church History Library, Salt Lake City. (Photograph by Welden C. Andersen.)

Reuse of paper for 1839 history draft (Draft 1). At the top of the nineteenth page of the 1839 draft of Joseph Smith's history is found a list of scriptural references under the heading "Scriptures on Covenants." The list, in the handwriting of Frederick G. Williams, was composed in about July 1833 as part of an index to Joseph Smith's Bible revision. The indexing project was discontinued, and the gathering of papers was later used for the 1839 history draft. The insertions and deletions on this page also provide evidence of the complex process of composing the history. Handwriting of Frederick G. Williams and James Mulholland. JS History, 1839, p. [19] (transcribed on pp. 402–408 herein), Church History Library, Salt Lake City. (Photograph by Welden C. Andersen.)

Draft 1

some body else had told them, in this frivolous and vexatious manner did they proceed for a considerable [p. [19]] time, when finally, Newel Knight was called up ~~for~~ ⟨and⟩ examined by Lawyer Seymour, (who was a Presbyterian, ⟨and who had been specially sent for on this occasion—⟩ and had shown great zeal, lest the people should be deluded by me, and false doctrines propagated in the neighborhood.) to the following effect.

What is your name? Ans[t] Newel Knight. Did the prisoner Joseph Smith, Cast the Devil out of you? ⟨Ans[t]⟩ No Sir— Why have not you had the Devil cast out of you? Ans[t] Yes Sir. And had not Joe Smith some hand in its being done! Ans[t] Yes Sir. And did not he cast him out of you? Ans[t] No Sir, it was done by the power of God, and ~~he was~~ Joseph Smith was the instrument made use of on the occasion, He commanded him out of me in the name of Jesus Christ. And are you sure that it was the Devil? Ans[st] Yes Sir. Did you see him after he was cast out of you? Ans[t] Yes sir, I saw him— Pray, what ⟨did⟩ he look like?

(Here one of my lawyers, informed the witness that he need not answer the question The witness replied, I believe I need not answer your last question, but I will do it provided I be allowed to ask you one question first, and you answer me. Viz: Do you

Draft 2

"frivolous and vexatious" manner did they proceed for a considerable time, when finally Newel Knight was called up, and examined by Lawyer [William] Seymour, who had been especially sent for on this occasion. One Lawyer Burch, also was on the side of the prosecution; but M[r] Seymour seemed to ⟨be⟩ a more zealous Presbyterian, and appeared very anxious and determined that the people should not be deluded by any one professing the power of Godliness; and not "denying the power thereof."[193]

So soon as M[r] Knight had been sworn, M[r] Seymour proceeded to interrogate him as follows.

Q—Did the prisoner, Joseph Smith, Jr cast the devil out of you?[194]

Ans[t] No sir.

Q—Why, have not you had the devil cast out of you?

Ans[t] Yes Sir.

~~Q And did he not cast~~ Q—And had not Joe Smith some hand in its being done?

Ans[t] Yes Sir.

Q And did not he cast him out of you?

Ans[t] No Sir it was done by the power of God, and Joseph Smith was the instrument in the hands of God on the occasion; He commanded him out of me in the name of Jesus Christ.

Q, And are you sure that it was the devil?

Ans[t] Yes Sir.

Q Did you see him, after he was cast out of you?

Ans[t] Yes Sir I saw him.

Q Pray, what did he look like?—

(Here one of my lawyers, informed the witness that he need not answer the question,) The witness replied, I believe I need not answer your last question, but I will do it, provided I be allowed to ask you one question first, and you answer me. Viz: Do

Draft 3

At length Newel Knight was examined by Lawyer Seymour ⟨assisted by one Burch⟩ who had been especially sent for on this occasion and ⟨he Seymour⟩ being the more zealous sectarian of the two seemed determined to put a stop to my [p. 78] preaching of the <u>Gospel</u> of Jesus Christ and that the people should not be deluded by one who belevied in the power of Godliness and not denying the power thereof

As soon as Mr Knights had been sworn Mr Seymour proceded to examine him as follows

Ques Did the prisoner Joseph Smith J꜓ cast the Devil out of you;

Ans No Sir

Q Why have you not had the Devil cast out of you

A yes Sir

Q And did not Jo Smith have some hand in it

A Yes Sir

Q. And did not he cast him out of you

A No sir <u>it was done by the power of God</u>[195] and Joseph Smith J꜓ was the <u>instrument</u> in the hands of God on the occasion <u>He commanded him out of me in the name of Jesus Christ</u>[196]

Q. And are you sure it was the Devil

Ans yes sir

Q. Did you see him after he was cast out of you

A Yes sir. I saw him

Q Pray what did he look like

Here one of my Lawyers told the Witness that he need not answer the question

The witness replied I will answer you provided you answer me one question to wit Do you Mr Seymour understand the things of the spirit No. (answered ~~my~~

NOTES

193. See 2 Timothy 3:5.

194. Regarding the exorcism of Newel Knight, see JS History, vol. A-1, pp. 382–384 herein (Draft 2).

195. TEXT: "God" has double underlining in original.

196. TEXT: "Jesus Christ" has double underlining in original.

Draft 1

Mʳ Seymour ~~profess~~ understand the things of the Spirit? Anˢ No I do not pretend to such big things. Well then said Knight, 'Twould be of no use to tell you, what the Devil looked like. for it was a Spiritual sight, and of course you would ⟨not⟩ understand it, were I to tell you of it. The lawyer dropped his head, whilst the loud laugh of the assembled ~~audience~~ ⟨multitude⟩ proclaimed his discomfiture.

Mʳ Seymour now addressed the Court, and in a long & violent harangue endeavored to blacken my character, and bring me out guilty of the charges which had been brought against me, among other things, he brought up the story of my having been a money digger and in this manner proceeded in hopes to influence the court and the people against me. ~~My Lawyers followed in my behalf~~ Mʳ Davidson and Mʳ Reed followed in my behalf, ~~they showed~~ [p. [20]] they held forth in its true colors, the nature of the prosecution, the malignancy of intention, and apparent disposition to persecute their client, rather than to afford him justice. They took up the different arguments which had been brought by the Lawyers for the prosecution and having shewed their utter futility & misapplication. then ~~to h~~ proceeded to scrutinize the evidence which had been adduced, and ⟨each⟩ in his turn, thanked God that He had been engaged in so good a cause as that of defending ~~the Character~~ ⟨cause⟩ of a man, whose character stood ~~the~~ so well the test of such ~~an~~ scrutinizing enquiry. In fact these men (although not regular lawyers) were upon this occasion ~~enabled~~ to put to silence ~~these~~ their opponents—and convince the court that I was innocent. They spoke like men inspired of God, whilst ~~their~~ lawyers who were arrayed against me,

Draft 2

you, Mʳ Seymour, understand the things of the Spirit? No (answered Mʳ Seymour) I do not pretend to such big things. Well then (replied Knight,) it would be of no use to tell you what the devil looked like, for it was a a spiritual sight, and spiritually discerned; and of course you would not understand it, were I to tell you of it.

The Lawyer dropped his head, whilst the loud laugh of the audience proclaimed his discomfiture.

Mʳ Seymour now addressed the court, and in a long and violent harangue endeavored to blacken my character and bring me in guilty of the charges which had been brought against me; among other things, he brought up the story of my having been a money digger, and in this manner proceeded, in hopes to influence the court and the people against me. Mʳ Davidson [p. 46] and Mʳ Reid followed on my behalf. They held forth in true colours, the nature of the prosecution; the malignancy of intention, and the apparent disposition to persecute their client, rather than to afford him justice. They took up the different arguments which had been brought by the lawyers for the prosecution and having shewed their utter futility and misapplication; then proceeded to scrutinise the evidence which had been adduced, and each in his turn, thanked God that He had been engaged in so good a cause, as that of defending a man whose character stood so well the test of such a strict investigation. In fact, these men, (although not regular lawyers) were upon this occasion able to put to silence their opponents, and convince the court that I was innocent.

They spoke like men inspired of God, whilst those who were arrayed against me, trembled under the sound of their voices,

Draft 3

Mr Seymour) Well then it would be of no
use to tell you what the devil looked. like
for it was a spiritual sight and spiritually
discerned and of course you could not understand it were I to tell you of it

The Lawyer dropped his head while the
loud laugh of the audience proclaimed his
discomfeiture [p. 79]

Mr Seymour proceded to address the
court and in a long and violent harrangue
endeavered to blacken my character and influence the court to pronounce me guilty

Mess[r]s Davidson and Reid followed
in my behalf They presented in true colors
the nature of the prosecution the malignancy of the intention and the apparant
disp[o]sition to <u>persecute</u> the defendant
rather than afford him Justice They noticed
the arguments of the prosecution ~~in~~ and in
a masterly and able manner convinced the
court of their utter futility and ⟨in⟩ application They then proceeded to scrutinize the
testimony and each thanked God that he
was ~~engaged~~ engaged in ~~su◊◊ good a cause~~
such a good cause in asmuch as they were
defending a man whos charactor stood the
test of such a strict examination

In fact these men although not regular
Lawyers were able to put to silence two
able Lawyers and convince the court of the
innocence of their client

They spoke like men <u>inspired</u> from on <u>high</u>
and those arrayed against me trembled and
quailed ~~under~~ ⟨before them⟩ ~~while they~~

Draft 1

trembled under their sound of their voice, and quailed before them like criminals before a bar of Justice. The majority of the all who had attended, had now began to see find that nothing could be sustained against me. Even the Constable who had arrested me and who had treated me so badly—now came and apologized to me, and asked my forgiveness of his behaviour towards me. And so far was he changed that he informed me, that the mob were determined; that if the court acquitted me, that they would have me, and rail ride me and tar & feather me, and further told me that he was willing to favor me so, that he would lead me out in safety by a private way.

The court finding the charges against me not sustained I was acquitted to the great satisfaction of my friends and vexation of my enemies; who were now once more set for me, but through the instrumentality of my new friend the Constable I was enabled to escape them, and make my way in safety to my wife's sister's house. where I found my wife—with whom I next day returned to my own house.

Draft 2

and quailed before them like criminals before a bar of justice.

The majority of the assembled multitude had now began to find that nothing could be sustained against me: even the Constable who arrested ⟨me,⟩ and treated me so badly—now came and apologized to me, and asked my forgiveness ⟨for⟩ of his behaviour towards me; and so far was he changed that he informed me that the mob were determined, that if the Court acquitted me; that they would have me, and rail ride me, and tar and feather me; and further, that he was willing to favour me, and lead me out in safety by another ⟨a private⟩ way.

The Court finding the charges against me, not sustained, I was accordingly acquitted,[197] to the great satisfaction of my friends, and vexation of my enemies, who were still determined upon molesting me, but through the instrumentality of my new friend, the Constable; I was enabled to escape them, and make my way in safety to my wifes sister's house,[198] where I found my wife awaiting with much anxiety the issue of these ⟨those⟩[199] ungodly proceedings: and with her in company next day arrived in safety at my own house.

Draft 3

~~addressed the court~~ like criminals at the bar of justice

The majority of the multitude now began to find that nothing could be sustained against me and even the constable who arrested me came and apologised ~~and asked~~ asking my forgiveness for the wrongs he had done me ~~and~~ He informed me that the Mob were determined if the court acquitted me to take justice into their own hands or in other words <u>tar</u> and <u>feather</u> and <u>ride</u> me on a <u>rail</u> but that he would lead me out in safety by ~~another~~ private way

~~The court~~ ⟨I was⟩ at length acquitted by the court to the great satisfaction of my friends and disappointment ⟨of my enemies⟩ ~~and~~ Through the instrumentality of my <u>new</u> friend the [p. 80] constable I escaped the hands of ~~an~~ ruthles[s] and cowardly mob and arrived safely ~~at my~~ home

In this transaction talent as well ~~both~~ ⟨as⟩ civil and moral power ⟨aided by physical for[c]e⟩ ~~to was~~ were brought in array against me ~~orded~~ to blast my reputation as a christian and a member of society—to convince community of ⟨the falsity and⟩ dangerous ~~tendency~~ tendencies of the doctrines I taught yet the results were such as to convince the <u>public</u>[200] that I sustained an unimpeachable moral character and the <u>honest</u> in <u>heart</u> that I was no fanatic that my doctrines were those of the Apostles and ancient Christians

NOTES

197. According to a report apparently originating with the justice of the peace who heard the case, JS "was discharged; he had not looked in the glass for two years to find money, &c.,—hence it was outlawed."[a] JS had participated in treasure seeking on behalf of Josiah Stowell in late 1825.[b] The New York statute relating to misdemeanors or "public offences" such as the charges against JS required that legal actions "be commenced within two years after the offence shall have been committed, and not after."[c] (a. "Mormonism," *Morning Star,* 16 Nov. 1832, 114.   b. JS History, vol. A-1, p. 234 herein [Draft 2].   c. Of the Time of Commencing Actions for Penalties and Forfeitures, *Revised Statutes of the State of New-York* [1827–1828], 2:297, part 3, chap. 4, title 2, art. 3, sec. 29.)

198. Probably the home of Benjamin and Elizabeth Hale Wasson, in Colesville Township, Broome County, New York. (1825 New York Census, Colesville, Broome Co., NY, [8], microfilm 806,800, U.S. and Canada Record Collection, FHL; 1830 U.S. Census, Broome Co., NY, 33.)

199. TEXT: Revision of "these" to "those" in unidentified handwriting, possibly that of James Mulholland.

200. TEXT: Double underlining in original.

Draft 1

After some few days however, Oliver Cowdery and myself again returned to Colesville for the purpose of confirming those whom we had [p. [21]] thus been forced to abandon for a time. We had scarcely however arrived at Mr Knights when the mob was seen collecting together to oppose us, and we considered it wisdom to leave for home, which we did without having waited even to refresh ourselves, by something to eat. ~~Four~~ enemies pursued us, and it was often times as much as we could do to elude them, however we managed to get home, after having traveled all night, except a short time which we were forced to rest ourselves under a large tree by the way side, sleeping and watching alternately. And thus were we persecuted on account of ⟨our⟩ religious faith—in a country the constitution of which guarantees to every man the indefeasable right to worship God according to the dictates of his own conscience. And by men too who were professors of religion, and who were not backward to maintain this right for themselves, though they thus wantonly could deny ⟨it to⟩ us. ~~the same privilege~~[201]

⟨for instance on[e] ⟨Cyrus⟩ McMaster, a presbyterian of high standing in his church, was one of the chief instigators of these persecutions, and told me personally ⟨named⟩ that he believed me culpable with out Judge or Jury. The celebrated Doct^r Buoyington⟨, also presbyterian⟩ was another instigater of the business. And a young man ⟨named Benton &⟩ of the same ⟨religious⟩ Faith swore out the first warrant against me,⟩

Draft 2

After a few days however, I again returned to Colesville, in company with Oliver Cowdery, for the purpose of confirming those whom we had thus been forced to abandon for a time. We had scarcely arrived at Mr Knight [Joseph Knight Sr.]'s when the mob was seen collecting together to oppose us, and we considered it wisdom to leave for home, which we did, without even waiting for any refreshment. Our enemies pursued us, and it was oftentimes as much as we could do to elude them; however we managed to get home, after having travelled all night, except a short time, during which we were forced to rest ourselve[s] under a large tree by the way side, sleeping and watching alternately. And thus were we persecuted on account of our religious faith—in a country, the constitution of which, guarantees to every man the indefeisible right, to worship God according to the dictates of his own conscience; and by men too, who were professors [p. 47] of religion, and who were not backward to maintain this privilege for themselves; though they thus wantonly could deny it to us.

For instance Cyrus McMaster a Presbyterian of high standing in his church was one of the chief instigators of these persecutions, and he at one time told me personally, that he considered me guilty without judge or jury.

The celebrated Doct^r Boyington [Nathan Boynton], also a presbyterian, was another instigator to those deeds of outrage: Whilst a young man named [Abram] Benton, of the same religious faith swore out the first warrant against me.[202] I could mention many others also, but for brevity's sake, will make these suffice for the present.[203]

Draft 3

After a few days I again returned to colesville in company with Olivers Cowdry for the purpose of confirming ~~of confirming~~ those whom we had been compelled to abandon for a time We had scarcely arrived at Mr Knights when the Mob commenced gathering together to oppose us and we thought it wisdom to leave the place which we did without even taking refreshment of any kind Our enemies pursued us and it was with much difficulty that we eluded them and arrived at home after travelling almost all night

How long shall men be persecuted on account of their religious faith in ⟨a⟩ country the constitution of which guarrantees to <u>every</u> man the right to worship God according to the dictates of his own conscience; and by men too who <u>profess</u> to be servants of the Most High—who are not backward to assert their own rights ~~and~~ yet with ~~what~~ avidity and eagerness deprive others of ~~theirs~~ ⟨the⟩ rights of conscience

For instance Cyrus McMaster a Presbyterian of high ~~stand~~ standing was one of the principal instigators of this persecution who told me he considered me guilty with out Judge or jury

The Celebrated Doc^t Boyington also a Presbyterian was another instigator [p. 81] of these deeds of violence. And a young man by the name of Benton of the same denomination impiously swore out the first warrant against me

201. TEXT: As he did elsewhere in the manuscript, James Mulholland left blank lines here, which he filled in later with the insertion that follows.

202. That is, the warrant that resulted in JS's trial at South Bainbridge. The fact that Benton wrote a letter nine months later to a Universalist periodical in Utica, New York, discussing legal proceedings against JS suggests that Benton may have been a Universalist rather than a Presbyterian. ("Mormonites," *Evangelical Magazine and Gospel Advocate,* 9 Apr. 1831, 120.)

203. William W. Phelps later inserted at this point what he labeled a "revelation to Joseph Smith Jun. given June 1830." The text he inserted corresponds with the first two and a half pages of JS's manuscript revision of the Old Testament. (See Old Testament Revision 1, pp. 1–3 [Moses 1].)

Draft 1

~~John Whitmer now came to live with~~
~~me and write for me.~~ [*blank lines*]
~~Revelation Page 111 &~~
~~Page 178 & Page 179~~[204]

Notwithstanding however all the rage of
our enemies, still we had much conselation,
and many things occurred to strengthen our
faith, and cheer our hearts amidst our trials, and persecutions. After we had returned home after our trial, the church at
Colesville, were, as might be expected, very
anxious concerning our again visiting
them, during which time, Sister Knight,
(wife to Newel Knight) had a dream which
enabled her to say that we would ~~soon~~ visit
them that day, which really came to pass,
for a few hours after she had told her dream
we arrived and thus was our faith much
strengthened, concerning the things of the
last days mentioned by the Prophet Joel. of
dreams & visions—

After our return to my ⟨own⟩ house as
above mentioned, we received the following Revelations,,, Rev page 111— page 179
page 178—[207]

Draft 2

Mean time, notwithstanding all the
rage of our enemies, still we had much
consolation, and many things occurred to
strengthen our faith, and cheer our hearts.

After our return from Colesville, the
church there, were, as might be expected,
very anxious concerning our again visiting
them, during which time, Sister [Sarah
(Sally) Coburn] Knight, (wife to Newel
Knight) had a dream, which enabled her to
say that we would visit them that day,
which really came to pass, for a few hours
afterwards we arrived, and thus was our
faith much strengthened, concerning
dreams and visions in the last days, foretold by the ancient Prophet Joel:[205] And although we, this time, were forced to seek
safety from our enemies by flight, yet did
we feel confidence that eventualy we
should come off victorious, if we only continued faithful to Him who had called us
forth from darkness, into the marvellous
light of the Everlasting Gospel of our Lord
Jesus Christ.

Shortly after our return home, we received the following commandments.

Revelation given to Joseph Smith Jr,
and Oliver Cowderry, Given at Harmony,
Pennsylvania, July, 1830.[208]

1 Behold thou wast called and chosen
to write the Book of Mormon, and to my
ministry; and I have lifted thee up, out of
thy afflictions, and have counselled thee,
that thou hast been delivered from all
thine enemies, and thou hast been delivered from the powers of Satan, and from
darkness! Nevertheless, thou art not excusable in thy transgressions; nevertheless, go thy way, and sin no more.

Draft 3

But during all this persecution and rage of our enemi[e]s we had much to console us and strengthen us in our faith The church at Colesville were very anxious that we should again visit them and sister Knight (wife of Newel Knight) had a dream which enabled her to say that we would visit them that day which actually came to pass for ⟨in⟩ a few hours afterwards we ~~actually~~ arrived. This circumstance served to confirm us in ~~the~~ ⟨our⟩ faith concerning dreams and visions in the last days as foretold by the prophets Joel And although we were compelled to fly from our enemies yet we felt confident that we should come off victorious ~~as we~~ for we were not fighting our own battles but were fighting those of the ~~Lord~~ <u>Great I Am</u>[206]

Shortly after ~~I retu~~ our return home we recieved the following Commandments July 1830

1 Behold. thou wast called and chosen to write the Book of Mormon and to my ministry and I have lifted thee up out of thine afflictions and have counselled thee that thou hast been delivered from all ~~of~~ thine enemies and thou hast been delivered from the ⟨powers⟩ ~~hands~~ of Satan and from darkness. Nevertheless thou art not excusable in thy transgressions: nevertheless go thy way and sin no more

NOTES

204. TEXT: James Mulholland inscribed an embellished circle around this reference, presumably to indicate the intent to supply text from the 1835 edition of the Doctrine and Covenants. These two sentences were originally inscribed before the paragraph inserted above them, serving as a placeholder as Mulholland left spaces in the manuscript to be filled in later.

205. See Joel 2:28–29.

206. TEXT: "Great I Am" has double underlining in original.

207. TEXT: James Mulholland inscribed this revelation reference and left a blank space to be filled in later. He subsequently inserted the text that follows (beginning on p. 424 herein), which flowed beyond the reserved space and into the space he left after the canceled sentence at the top of page 23 of Draft 1 (p. 424 herein). It is unclear exactly where the insertion ends and the original inscription recommences after the canceled passage.

208. Revelation, July 1830–A, in Doctrine and Covenants 9, 1835 ed. [D&C 24].

Draft 1

Draft 2

2 Magnify thine office; and after thou hast sowed thy fields, and secured them, go speedily unto the Church which is in Colesville, Fayette and Manchester, and they shall support thee; and I will bless them both spiritually and temporally; but if they receive thee not, I will send upon them a cursing instead of a blessing.

3 And thou shalt continue ⟨in⟩ calling upon God in my name, and writing the things which shall be given thee by the comforter, and expounding all scriptures unto the church, and it shall be given thee in the very moment, what thou shalt speak and write; and they shall hear it, or I will send unto them a cursing instead of a blessing:

4 For thou shalt devote all thy service in Zion. And in this thou shalt have strength. Be patient in afflictions, for thou shalt have many: but endure them, [p. 48] for lo, I am with you, even unto the end of thy days. And in temporal labours thou shalt not have strength, for this is not thy calling. Attend to thy calling and thou shalt have wherewith to magnify thine office, and to expound all scriptures. And continue in laying on of the hands, and confirming the churches.

5 And thy brother Oliver shall continue in bearing my name before the world; and also to the church. And he shall not suppose that he can say enough in my cause; and lo I am with him to the end. In me he shall have glory, and not of himself, whether in weakness or in strength, whether in bonds or free: And at all times and in all places, he shall open his mouth and declare my gospel as with the ~~sound~~ ⟨voice⟩ of a trump, both

Draft 3

2 Magnify thine office; and after thou hast sown the fields and secured them go quickly unto the church which is in Colesville, Fayette and manchester and they shall support the[e]; and I will bless them both spiritually and temporally. but if they recieve thee not I will send upon them a cursing [p. 82] instead of a blessing

3 And thou shalt continue ⟨in⟩ calling upon God in my name, and writing the things which shall be given thee by the comforter, and expounding all scriptures unto the church and it shall be given thee in the very moment what thou shalt say and write, and they shall hear it or I will ⟨send⟩ unto them ⟨a⟩ cursing instead of a blessing

4 For thou shalt devote all thy service in Zion and in this thou shalt have strength Be patient in afflictions for thou shalt have many: but endure them for lo I am with you even unto the end of ~~your~~ ⟨thy⟩ days And in temporal labors thou shalt not have strength for this is not thy calling Attend to thy calling and tho[u] shalt have wherewith to to magnify thine office, and to expound all scriptures And continue in laying on of the hands and confirmng the churches

5 And thy brother Oliver shall continue in bearing my name before the world and also to the church And he shall not suppose that he can say enough in my cause and lo I am with him to the end In me he shall have glory and not of himself whether in weakness or in strength whether in bonds or free And at all times in all places he shall open his mouth and declare my gospel as with the voeice of a trump both day and night,

Draft 1   **Draft 2**

day and night. and I will give unto him
strength, such as is not known among
men.

6 Require not miracles, except I shall
command you; except casting out devils,
healing the sick; and against poisonous
serpents; and against deadly poisons; and
these things ye shall not do, except it be
required of you, by them who desire it,
that the scriptures might be fulfilled, for
ye shall do according to that which is
written. And in whatsoever place ye shall
enter, and they receive you not, in my
name, ye shall leave a cursing instead of
a blessing, by casting off the dust of your
feet against them as a testimony, and
cleansing your feet by the way side.

7 And it shall come to pass, that whosoever shall lay their hands upon you by
violence, ye shall command to be smitten in my name, and behold I will smite
them according to your words, in mine
own due time. And whosoever shall go
to law with thee shall be cursed by the
law. And thou shalt take no purse, no
scrip, neither staves, neither two coats, for
the Church shall give unto thee in the
very hour, what thou needest for food,
and for raiment and for shoes, and for
money, and for scrip: For thou art called
to prune my vineyard with a mighty
pruning, yea, even for the last time. Yea,
and also, all those whom thou hast ordained. And they shall do even according to this pattern. Amen.

Revelation given at Harmony, Penn.
July 1830.[209]

1 Hearken unto the voice of the Lord
your God, while I speak unto you, Emma
Smith my daughter, for verily I say unto
you, all those who receive my gospel are
sons and daughters in my kingdom.

Draft 3

and I will give unto him strength such as is not known among men

6 Requi[r]e not miracles except I shall command you, except casting out devils. healing the sick and against poisonous serpents and against deadly poisons and these things ye shall not do except it be required of you by those who desire it that the scriptures might be fulfilled for ye shall do according to that which is ~~desired~~ written And into whatsoever place ye shall enter and they receive you not in my name, ye shall leave a cursing [p. 83] instead of a blessing by casting off the dust of your feet against them as a testimony and cleansing your feet by the way-side

7 And it shall come to pass that whosoeve[r] shall lay their hands upon you in violence ye shall command to be smitten in my name and behold I will smite them according to your words in mine own due time And whosoever shall go to law with thee shall be cursed by the law And thou shalt take no purse, no scrip neither stores neither two coats for the church shall give thee in the very hour what thou needest for food and for raiment and for shoes and for money and for scrip For thou art called to prune my vineyard with a mighty pruning yea even for the last time, Yea and also all those whom thou hast ordained And they shall do even according to this pattern Amen

Shortly after we recievd the following Revelation July 1830

1 Hearken unto the voice of the Lord your God while I speak unto you Emma Smith my daughter for verily I say unto you, all those who recieve my gospel are sons and daughters in my king⟨dom⟩

NOTES

209. Revelation, July 1830–C, in Doctrine and Covenants 48, 1835 ed. [D&C 25].

Draft 1   **Draft 2**

A revelation I give unto you concerning my will, and if thou art faithful and walk in the paths of virtue before me, I will preserve ~~your~~ ⟨thy⟩ life, and thou shalt receive an inheritance in Zion. Behold thy sins are forgiven thee, and thou art an elect lady, whom I have called. Murmur not because of the things which thou hast not seen, for they are withheld from thee, and from the world, which is wisdom in me in a time to come.

2 And the office of thy calling shall be for a comfort unto my servant Joseph Smith Jr. thy husband, in his afflictions with consoling words, in the spirit [p. 49] of meekness. And thou shalt go with him at the time of his going, and be unto him for a scribe, while there is no one to be a scribe for him, that I may send my servant Oliver Cowdery, whithersoever I will. And thou shalt be ordained under his hand to expound scriptures, and to exhort the Church, according as it shall be given thee by my Spirit: for he shall lay his hands upon thee, and thou shalt receive the Holy Ghost, and thy time shall be given to writing, and to learning much. And thou needst not fear, for thy husband shall support thee in the Church: for unto them is his calling, that all things might be revealed unto them, whatsoever I will, according to their faith.

3 And verily I say unto thee, that thou shalt lay aside the things of this world, and seek for the things of a better. And it shall be given thee, also, to make a selection of sacred Hymns, as it shall be given thee, which is pleasing unto me, to be had in my Church: for my soul delighteth in the song of the heart: yea, the song of the righteous is a prayer unto me. And it shall be answered with a blessing upon their heads.— Wherefore lift up

Draft 3

A revelation I I give unto you concerning my will, and if thou art faithful and
walk in the paths of virtue before me I
will preserve thy life and thou shalt recieve an inheritance in Zion Behold thy
sins are forgiven thee and thou art an
elect Lady whom I have called Murmur
not because of the things which thou
hast not seen for they are withheld from
thee and from the world which is wisdom in me in a time to come

2 And the office of thy ⟨calling⟩ shall
be for a comfort unto my servant Joseph
Smith Jr thy husband in his afflictions,
with consoling words in the [p. 84] spirit
of meekness And thou shalt go with him
at the time of his going and be unto him
for a scribe while there is none to be a
scribe for him that I may send my servant Oliver Cowdry whithersoeve[r] I
will And thou shalt be ordained under
his hand to expound scriptures and to
exhort the church according as it shall be
given thee by my spirit for he shall lay
his hands upon thee and thou shalt reciev
the Holy Ghost and thy time shall be
given to writing and learning much And
thou needst not fear: for thy husband
shall support thee in the church: for
unto them is his calling; that all things
might be revealed unto them, whatsoever I will according to their faith

3ᵈ And verily I say unto ~~you~~ thee that
thou shalt lay aside the things of this
world and seek for ~~a better~~ the things of
a better And it shall be given theee also
to make a selection of sacred Hymns as it
shall be given thee which is pleasing
unto me to be had in my church: for my
Soul delighteth in the song of the heart
yea the song of the rightious is a prayer
unto me; and it shall be answered with a
blessing upon their heads Wherefore lift

Draft 1

Draft 2

thy heart and rejoice, and cleave unto the covenants which thou hast made.

4 Continue in the spirit of meekness, and beware of pride. Let thy soul delight in thy husband, and the glory which shall come upon him. Keep my commandments continually, and a crown of righteousness thou shalt receive. And except thou do this, where I am you cannot come. And verily, verily I say unto you, that this is my voice unto all. Amen.

Revelation to Joseph Smith Jr. Oliver Cowdery and John Whitmer, given at Harmony, Penn, July 1830.[210]

1 Behold, I say unto you, that you shall let your time be devoted to the studying of the scriptures, and to preaching, and to confirming the Church at Colesville; and to performing your labors on the land, such as is required, untill after you shall go to the west, to hold the next conference,[211] and then it shall be made known what you shall do. And all things shall be done by common consent in the church, by much prayer and faith; for all things you shall receive by faith. Amen.

⟨Shortly afterwards, Oliver Cowdery returned to Mr Whitmer's, ~~house~~ ⟨and⟩ John Whitmer (who was now living with me) and my self began to arrange & copy the revelations and commandments which we had received from time⟩ [p. [22]] Septe^r ~~1st we met in general conference of the Church—at Mr Whitmers Fayette,~~ ⟨to time from our Heavenly Father, which engaged our attention for some time. Whilst thus ⟨and otherwise at intervals⟩ employed in the work appointed me by my great Creator I received a letter from Oliver Cowdery the contents of which gave me both sorrow and uneasiness. Not having that letter now in my possession I cannot of course give it

Shortly after we had received the above revelations, Oliver Cowdery returned to Mr Whitmers [Peter Whitmer Sr.'s], and I began to arrange and copy the revelations which we had received from time to time; in which I was assisted by John Whitmer, who now resided with me.

Whilst thus ⟨and otherwise at intervals⟩ employed in the work appointed me, by my Heavenly Father; I received a letter from Oliver Cowdery—the contents of which, gave me both sorrow and uneasiness. Not having that letter ⟨now⟩ in my possession, I cannot, of course give it here

Draft 3

up thy heart and rejoice and cleave unto the covenant which thou hast made

4 Continue in the spirit of meekness and beware of pride Let thy soul delight in thy husband and the glory which shall come upon him Keep my commandments continually and a crown of righteousness thou shalt recieve— And except thou do this where I am thou ~~cannot~~ canst—not come And verily verily I say unto you that this is my voice unto all Amen

During the same month the following revelation was given to Joseph Smith J^r Oliver Cowdry and John Whitmer

1 Behold I say unto you that you shall let your [p. 85] time be devoted to the studying of the scriptures and to preaching and to confirming the church at Colesville and to performng your labors on the land such as is required until after you shall go to the west to hold the next conference and then it shall be made known what you shall do And all things shall be done by common consent in the Church by much prayer and faith, Amen

~~After I~~ After we had recieved the above revelation, I commenced arranging and copying the revelations which had been given us in which I was assisted by John Whitmer who now resided with me

Whilst thus engaged I recieved a Letter from O Cowdry (who had returned to Mr Whitmers) which caused me much pain and ~~uneas~~ anxiety I can only give my readers an extract of the contents as the letter is now lost

NOTES

210. Revelation, July 1830–B, in Doctrine and Covenants 49, 1835 ed. [D&C 26].

211. Minutes of the 9 June 1830 church conference indicate that the next conference was to convene 26 September 1830 at Fayette. (Minute Book 2, 9 June 1830.)

Draft 1

here ⟨in⟩ full but merely an extract, of the most prominent part, which I can yet; and expect long to remember. It was ~~as follows.~~ to the effect that, he had discovered an error, in one of the commandments,,, see book of Covenants Section 2nd paragraph 7th "and truly manifest by their works that they have received of the Spirit of Christ unto the remission of their Sins"

the above quotation he said was erroneous, And ⟨added I⟩ command~~ed me~~ you in the name of God, To erase those words from that commandment, "that no priestcraft be amongst us".

I immediately wrote to him in reply, in which I asked him, by what authority he took upon him to command me to alter or erase, to add or diminish to or from a revelation or commandment from the Almighty God.

I shortly after paid him a visit when I found that he had persuaded Father Whitmer and most of the family that the above was an error— And it was with great difficulty, and much labour that I prevailed with any of them to reason calmly on the subject, however Christian Whitmer at length got convinced that it was reasonable and according to scripture and finally with his assistance I succeeded ⟨in⟩ bringing not only all the Whitmer family but also Oliver himself to acknowledge that they had been in error ⟨&⟩ that the above quotation was in accordance with the rest of the commandment.⟩^217 Early in the month of August Newel Knights and his wife paid us a visit at our place in Harmony. Neither his wife nor mine had been as yet confirmed, and it was proposed that we should ⟨have sacrament together &⟩ confirm them;

Draft 2

in full, but merely an extract of the most prominent parts, which I can yet, and expect long to remember.

He wrote to inform me, that he had discovered an error in one of the commandments, Book [p. 50] of "Doctrine and Covenants" Sect, 2nd Par. 7th "and truly manifest by their works that they have received of the Spirit of Christ unto the remission of their sins"^213

The above quotation he said was erroneous, and added; "I command you in the name of God to erase those words, that no priestcraft be amongst us."^214

I immediately wrote to him in reply, in which I asked him, by what authority he took upon him to command me to alter, or erase, to add or diminish to or from a revelation or commandment from Almighty God. In a few days afterwards I visited him and Mr Whitmer's family, when I found the family in general of his opinion concerning the words above quoted; and it was not without both labor and perseverance that I could prevail with any of them to reason calmly on the subject; however Christian Whitmer, at length got convinced that it was reasonable and according to scripture,^216 and finally, with his assistance I succeeded ~~of~~ ⟨in⟩ bringing not only the Whitmer family, but also Oliver Cowdery also to acknowledge that they had been in error, and that the sentence in dispute was in accordance of the rest of the commandment. And thus was this error rooted out, which having its rise in presumption and rash judgement, was the more particularly calculated (when ~~one~~ once fairly understood) to teach each and all of ~~the~~ us the necessity of humility, and

Draft 3

He wrote to inform me that he had discovered an error in ~~the~~ one of the Commandments—see Book of doctrine and Covenants Sec^t. 2^◊ Par^t 7^◊ (see also this History Page 56)[212] "and truly manifest by their works that they have recieved of the spirit of C~~c~~hrist unto the remission of their sins["]

~~This quotatition~~ This quotation he said was incorrect and added "I command you in the name of God to erase those words that no priest-craft be among us["]

I imediately wrote him in reply asking by what authority he commanded me to alter or erase to add to or diminish from <u>any</u> commandment or revelation from Almighty God

In a few days I visited him and found that Mr Whitmer and family had imbibed the same opinion and it was with great difficulty ~~and~~ that I could convin[c]e any of them that the doctrine contained in the sentance was in strict accordance with those of the scripture and was in fact a ~~command~~ <u>revelation</u> from <u>God</u>[215] At length Christian Whitmer became convinced [p. 86] that this was the case; and by his assistance succeeded in convincing the ~~others~~ remainder of the family. and Oliver Cowdry confessed his error We drew a lesson from this calculated ~~do us much good~~ to teach us the necessity of humility and prayer that he would teach us his ways and that we should not decide ~~in rashness~~ ⟨rashly⟩ or ⟨in⟩ haste

NOTES

212. See p. 343 herein.

213. The reference points to the 1835 edition of the Doctrine and Covenants; the wording in this passage is the same in the earlier copies of the "articles and covenants." (Revelation Book 1, p. 55, in *JSP*, MRB:81; Book of Commandments 24:30; "The Articles and Covenants of the Church of Christ," *The Evening and the Morning Star*, June 1832, [1]; "The Articles and Covenants of the Church of Christ," *The Evening and the Morning Star*, June 1833, [97] [D&C 20:37].)

214. Cowdery was present at the 9 June 1830 conference at Fayette at which the church's foundational "articles and covenants" were read by JS and were unanimously approved by the congregation. The document JS read included the passage to which Cowdery took exception in his letter. The account given here suggests that Cowdery did not raise his concern until later, apparently while examining an early copy of the document. Cowdery had recorded in about June 1829 a document titled "Articles of the Church of Christ," which he described in its introduction as a "commandment from God unto Oliver how he should build up his Church & the manner thereof." The requirement for baptismal candidates that Cowdery objected to in the 10 April 1830 document was not among the requirements listed in Cowdery's earlier "articles." (Minute Book 2, 9 June 1830; Articles and covenants, 10 Apr. 1830, in Revelation Book 1, pp. 52–58, in *JSP*, MRB:75–87 [D&C 20]; Oliver Cowdery, Articles of the Church of Christ, ca. June 1829, CHL.)

215. TEXT: Double underlining in original.

216. In the Book of Mormon account, baptismal candidates "were not baptized, save they brought forth fruit meet that they were worthy of it." (Book of Mormon, 1830 ed., 576 [Moroni 6:1].)

217. TEXT: The exact point at which this long insertion ends is unknown.

Draft 1

before he & his wife should leave us. ~~and that we~~

In order to prepare for these things I set out—to go to procure some wine for ~~our~~ the occasion. I had however gone but a short distance when I was met by a heavenly messenger, and had the following revelation. the first paragraph of which was written at this time, & the remainder in Sept[emb]er following Page 179— [p. [23]]

Draft 2

meekness before the Lord, that he might teach us of his ways; that we might walk in his paths, and live by every word which proceedeth forth from his mouth.

Early in the month of August, Newel Knight and his wife[218] paid us a visit, at my place at Harmony, Penn; and as neither his wife nor mine had been as yet confirmed, ~~and~~ it was proposed that we should confirm them, and partake together of the sacrament, before he and his wife should leave us.—

In order to prepare for this; I set out to go to procure some wine for the occasion, but had gone ~~but~~ ⟨only⟩ a short distance when I was met by a heavenly messenger, and received the following revelation; the first paragraph of which was written at this time, and the remainder in the September following.

Revelation given at Harmony Penn, August 1830.[219]

1 Listen to the voice of Jesus Christ, your Lord, your God and your redeemer, whose word is quick and powerful. For behold I say unto you, that it mattereth not what ye shall eat, or what you shall drink, when ye partake of the sacrament if it so be that ye do it with an eye single to my glory; remembering unto the Father my body which was laid down for you, and my blood which was shed for the remission of your sins: wherefore a commandment I give unto you, that you shall not purchase wine, neither strong drink of your enemies: wherefore you shall partake of none, except it is made new among you, yea, in this my Father's kingdom which shall be built up on the earth.

2 Behold this is wis[p. 51]dom in me: wherefore marvel not, for the hour cometh that I will drink of the fruit of the

Draft 3

NOTES

218. Polly Peck Knight.
219. Revelation, ca. Aug. 1830, in Doctrine and Covenants 50, 1835 ed. [D&C 27].

Early in August Newel Knight and Lady visited me in Harmony P,a. and as neither his wife ~~nor~~ nor mine had beed confirmed it was proposed that before our visit ~~be~~ ⟨come to⟩ ~~should be~~ closee we should attend to that ordinance as as well as that of administring the sacrament

Accordingly I started to ~~neighboring~~ neighbour⁵ ~~place~~ ⟨house⟩ to obtain wine but had gone but a short distance when I ~~met a~~ was met by a Heavenly Messenger who gave me the following Revelation

~~Revelation~~

1 Listen to the voice of Jesus Christ your Lord and your God and your Redeemer whose word is quick and powerful For behold I say unto you that it mattereth not what ye shall eat or what ye shall ~~eat~~ drink when ye partake of the sacrament if it so be ~~the~~ that ye do it with an eye single to my glory remembering unto the Father my body which was laid dow[n] for you and my blood which was shed for the remissio◊ of your sins wherefore a commandment I give unto you. that you shall not purchase wine neither strong drink of your enemies; wherefore you shall partake of none except it be made new among you, Yea in this my fathers kingdom which shall be built up ~~an~~ on the earth

2 Behold this is wisdom in me: wherefore marvil not for the hour cometh that I will drink of the fruit of the vine with

Draft 1   **Draft 2**

vine with you on the earth,[220] and with
Moroni, whom I have sent unto you, to
reveal the Book of Mormon, containing
the fulness of ~~the~~ my everlasting gospel;
to whom I have committed the keys of
the record of the stick of Ephraim;[221] and
also with Elias, to whom I have committed the keys of bringing to pass the restoration of all things, or the restorer of all
things spoken by the mouth of ⟨all⟩ the
holy prophets since the world began,
concerning the last days: and also John
the son of Zacharias, which Zacharias he
(Elias) visited and gave promise that he
should have a son, and his name should
be John, and he should be filled with the
spirit of Elias; which John I have sent
unto you my servants, Joseph Smith Jr,
and Oliver Cowdery, to ordain you unto
this first Priesthood which you have received, that you might be called and ordained even as Aaron:[222] And also Elijah,
unto whom I have committed the keys of
the power of turning the hearts of the fathers to the children, and the hearts of
the children to the fathers, that the
whole earth may not be smitten with a
curse:[223] and also, with Joseph, and Jacob,
and Isaac, and Abraham, your fathers; by
whom the promises remain: and also
with Michael, or Adam, the father of all,
the prince of all, the ancient of days:

3 And also with Peter, and James, and
John, whom I have sent unto you, by
whom I have ordained you and confirmed you to be apostles and especial
witnesses of my name, and bear the keys
of your ministry: and of the same things
which I revealed unto them: unto whom
I have committed the keys of my kingdom, and a dispensation of the gospel for
the last ~~days~~ times; and for the fulness of
times, in which I will gather together in

Draft 3

you on the earth and with Maroni whom I have sent unto you to reveal the Book of Mormon [p. 87] containing the fulness of my everlasting gospel to whom I have committed the keys of the record of the stick of Ephraim and also with Elias to whom I have committed the keys of bringing to pass the restoration of all things or the restorer of all things spoken by the mouth of all the holy Prophets since the world beegan concerning the last days: and also John the son of Zacharius which Zacharius he (Elias) visited and gave promise that he should have a son and his mane [name] should be John and he should be filled with the spirit of Elias: which John I have sent unto you my servants Joseph Smith Jr and Oliver Cowdrey to ordain you unto this first Priesthood which you have recieved that you might be called and ordained even as ~~aron~~ Aaron: and also Elijah unto whom I have committed the keys of the power of turning the hearts of the fathers to the children and the hearts of the children to the fathers that the whole earth may not be smitten with a curse and also with Joseph and Jacob and Isace and Abraham your fathers by whom the promises remain: and also with Michel or Adam the father of all the prince of all the ancient of days

3 3 And also with peter and James and John whom I have sent unto you and confirmed you to be apostles and especial witnesses of my name and bear the keys of your ministry and of the same things which I revealed unto ~~you~~ them: unto whom I have committed the keys of ⟨my⟩ ~~the~~ kingdom and a dispensation of the gospel for the last times and for the fulness of times in which I will gather together in ⟨one⟩ all things both which are

NOTES

220. The rest of this revelation is an expansion as first published in the 1835 edition of the Doctrine and Covenants. The earlier versions of the revelation instead have a much shorter conclusion: "and with all those whom my Father hath given me out of the world: Wherefore lift up your hearts and rejoice, and gird up your loins and be faithful until I come:— even so. Amen." (Revelation, ca. Aug. 1830, in Book of Commandments 28:6–7.)

221. That is, the Book of Mormon.

222. According to the account given earlier in this history, John the Baptist conferred "the priesthood of Aaron" upon JS and Oliver Cowdery on 15 May 1829. (JS History, vol. A-1, p. 292 herein [Draft 2].)

223. See Malachi 4:5–6.

Draft 1   **Draft 2**

one all things, both which are in Heaven
and which are on earth: and also with all
those whom my father hath given me out
of the world: wherefore lift up your
hearts and rejoice, and gird up your loins,
and take upon you my whole armor, that
you may be able to withstand the evil day,
having done all ye may be able to stand.

   Stand therefore, having your loins girt
about with truth; having on the breast
plate of righteousness; and your feet shod
with the preparation of the gospel of
peace which I have sent mine angels to
commit unto you, taking the shield of
faith wherewith ye shall be able to
quench the fiery darts of the wicked, and
take the helmet of salvation, and the
sword of my spirit, which I will pour out
upon you, and my word which I reveal
unto you, and be agreed as touching all
things whatsoever ye ask of me, and be
faithful untill I come, and ye shall be
caught up that where I am ye shall be also.
Amen.

agreeable to this revelation we prepared some wine of our own make, ~~and~~
⟨and⟩ held our meeting which consisted
only of five; viz: Newel Knight & wife myself & wife and John Whitmer. We partook together of the sacrament after which
we confirmed the two sisters into the
Church, and spent the ev[eni]ng in a glorious manner, The Spirit of the Lord was
poured out upon us and we praised God &
rejoiced exceedingly.

   About this time a ~~bitter~~ ⟨spirit⟩ of persecution began to ⟨be⟩ manifested towards us
in the neighborhood where I resided—[224]

   ⟨and was commenced & originated by
a man ~~who~~ of the Methodist persuasion,
who professed to be a minister of God. He
came to understand that my Father in law
was friendly and enquiring earnestly into

   In obedience to the above commandment we prepared some wine of our own
make, and held our meeting, consisting
only of five viz: Newel Knight and wife,
myself and my wife, and John Whitmer.
We partook together of the sacrament,
after which we confirmed these two sisters
into the church, and spent the evening in a
glorious manner. The Spirit of the Lord
was poured out [p. 52] upon us, we praised
the Lord God, and rejoiced exceedingly.

   About this time a spirit of persecution
began ⟨again⟩ to manifest itself against
us in the neighborhood where I now resided, which was commenced by a man of
the methodist persuasion, who professed to
be a minister of God, and whose name
was [*blank*]. This man came to understand,
that my father in law and his family had

Draft 3

in heaven and which are on earth and also with all those whom my father hath given me out of the world: wherefore lift up your hearts and rejoice and gird up your [p. 88] loins and take upon you my whole armour that you may be able to withstand the evil day having done all ye may be able to stand Stand therefore having your loins girt about with truth having on the breast plate of righteousness and your feet shod with the preperation of the gospel of peace which I have sent mine angels to commit unto you taking the shield of faith wherewith ye shall be able to quench the firey darts of the wicked and take the helmet of salvation and the sword of my spirit which I will pour out upon you and my word which I reveal unto you and be agreed as touching all things whatsoever ye ask of me and be faithful until I come and ye shall be caught up that where I am ye shall be also Amen

In obedience to the above ~~command~~ command we <u>made</u> wine from the native grape and after confirming the two sisters partook of the sacrament and spent the evening in praising God ~~and~~ and his spirit was poured out upon us in a most glorious maner and we rejoiced in god the rock of our salvation

About this time persecution again began to show itself and slander with ⟨an⟩ ~~its~~ iron tongue began its work of destruction; ~~intending not even permitting~~ in the neighborhood where I lived the principal instigator of which was a professing to be a <u>minister</u> of <u>God</u>[225] This man being informed that my father in law was friendly

224. TEXT: James Mulholland apparently inscribed the beginning of this paragraph and left a blank space, which he filled in later with the following insertion.

225. TEXT: Double underlining in original.

Draft 1

the work, and knowing that if he could ⟨get⟩ him and his family turned against me, my friends in that place would be few, accordingly he went to him and told him falsehoods of the most shameful nature which turned them entirely against me, insomuch that he would not so much as visit us or give us any more protection &c &c—⟩

Towards the latter end of August, I (in company with John & David Whitmer, and my brother Hyrum Smith) visited the Church at Colesville, N.Y. Well knowing the determined hostility of our enemies in that quarter and also knowing that it was our duty to visit the Church ⟨we⟩ had called upon our Heavenly Father in mighty prayer, that he would grant us an opportunity of meeting with ~~the Church~~ t[h]ere them, that he would blind the eyes of our enemies so that they would not know us, ~~on this occasion,~~ & that we might ⟨on⟩ this ~~time~~ ⟨occasion⟩ ~~escape~~ ⟨return⟩ unmolested.

Our prayers were not in vain, for ~~on~~ ⟨when⟩ ~~Saturday afternoon~~ ⟨within a little⟩ distance of Mʳ Knight's place, we encountered a large company working at the public road, among whom were many of our most bitter enemies they looked earnestly at us, but not knowing us, ~~thn left us our course clear a◊◊◊◊ arrived~~ ⟨we passed on without interruption.⟩ We that evening assembled the Church, and confirmed them, partook of the Sacrament, and held a happy meeting, having much reason to rejoice in the God of our Salvation and sing Hosannas to his holy name. Next morning we set out on our return home, and although our enemies had offered a reward of five dollars, to any one who would let them know of the arrival of Joe Smith, yet did we get

Draft 2

promised us protection, and were friendly; and enquiring into the work, and knowing that if he could get him turned against me, my friends in that place would be but few, he accordingly went to visit my father in law, and told him falsehoods concerning me, of the most shameful nature, which turned the Old gentleman and his family so much against us, that they would no longer promise us protection, nor believe our doctrines.[226]

Towards the latter end of August I (in company with John and David Whitmer, and my brother Hyrum Smith) visited the church at Colesville, N.Y. Well knowing the determined ~~hostilities~~ ⟨hostility⟩ of our enemies in that quarter, and also knowing that it was our duty to visit the church, we had called upon our Heavenly Father in mighty prayer, that he would grant us an opportunity of meeting with them; that he would blind the eyes of our enemies, so that they would not know us, and that we might on this occasion return unmolested.—

Our prayers were not in vain, for, when within a little distance of Mʳ Knights [Joseph Knight Sr.'s] place, we encountered a large company at work upon the public road, among ⟨whom⟩ were several of our most bitter enemies. They looked earnestly at us, but not knowing us, we passed on with out interruption.

We that evening assembled the church, and confirmed them, partook of the sacrament, and held a happy meeting, having much reason to rejoice in the God of our salvation, and sing Hosannas to his holy name.

Next morning we set out on our return home, and although our enemies had offered a reward of five dollars, to any one who would give them information of our

Draft 3

to the work and knowing that with his influence in my favour I was perfectly safe from all attempts ~~to~~ at least ⟨to⟩ injure my person: ~~He paid~~ paid my father in law a visit and with most shameful falsehoods in his mouth influenced the old gentleman against me so that he would no longer promise me protection [p. 89] or countenance my doctrines

Towards the last of August I determined (in company with John and David Whitmer and my Br Hiram) to visit the church at Colesville Knowing the hostility of some of the citizens of that place and having a great desire to see our brethren there we prayed ~~your~~ our heavenly Father to protect us and permit us to visit our friends and return unmolested

Our prayers ~~aviled~~ ⟨prevailed⟩ much with God for on our arrival in the neighborhood we passed a large company of men a number of whom were our most bitter enemies at work on the public Highway They looked earnestly at us but not knowing us permitted us to pass ~~on~~ unmolested

That evening we collected our friends to gather and confirmed some of them partook of the sacrament and had much cause to thank and praise the God of Our Salvation and sing Hossanna to his name

Next morning we returned in safety to our homes

NOTES

226. The informant to whom JS referred was likely Nathaniel Lewis, brother-in-law of Isaac Hale and uncle of Emma Smith. Lewis, a minister of the Methodist Episcopal Church, wrote in 1834 that JS was "not a man of truth and veracity" and that "his general character in this part of the country, is that of an impostor, hypocrite and liar." An accompanying statement by Lewis's son Levi asserted that JS and Martin Harris had said adultery was not a crime and that "Harris said he did not blame Smith for his (Smith's) attempt to seduce Eliza Winters," a friend of Emma Smith. Such allegations may have been passed along to Isaac Hale, leading him to withdraw his support of JS. (Howe, *Mormonism Unvailed,* 266–269.)

Draft 1

clear out of the Neighborhood without the least annoyance. and without our enemies having heard of our ~~arrival~~ ⟨visit⟩ at all, and arrived at home in safety.

Some few days afterwards however Newel Knight came to my place when we learnt from him, that very shortly after our departure the mob had heard of our having been there, when the[y] immediately collected together and had threatened the brethren and very much annoyed ⟨them⟩ during all that day, Meantime Brother Knight had came prepared ⟨with his waggon⟩ to move me and my wife, ~~out of this neighborhood~~ to Fayette N.Y. [p. [24]] Mʳ Whitmer having invited us to go and live with him, on account of the great persecution which had ⟨been⟩ got up against us, at Harmony Pa We arrived at Fayette, during the last week of august, amidst the congratulations of our brethren and friends.

To our great grief however we found that Satan had been, lying in wait to deceive, and seeking whom he might devour.

Brother Hyrum Page had got in his possession a certain stone ⟨by⟩ which he obtained to certain revelations concerning the upbuilding of Zion the order of the Church and so forth, but which were entirely at variance with the order of Gods House, as it is laid down ~~both in ancient and our modern~~ ⟨in the⟩ scriptures. ⟨and our own late revelations.⟩

As a conference meeting had been appointed for the 1ˢᵗ September I ~~did~~ ⟨thought it wisdom⟩ not ⟨to⟩ do much more than converse with the brethren on the subject untill the conference ~~was~~ ⟨should

Draft 2

arrival, yet did we get clear out of the neighborhood, without the least annoyance, and arrived at home in safety.—

Some few days afterwards however, Newel Knight came to my place, and from him we learnt that very shortly after our departure the mob had came to know of our having been there, when they immediately collected together, and had threatened the brethren and very much annoyed them during all that day.

Mean time Brother Knight had came, with his waggon, prepared to move my family, &c, &c, to Fayette, N Y. Mʳ Whitmer [Peter Whitmer Sr.] having heard of the persecutions which had been got up against us at Harmony, Penn, had invited ⟨us⟩ to go and live with him; and during the last week of August we arrived at Fayette, amidst the congratulations of our brethren and friends.

To our great grief however, we soon found that Satan had been lying in wait to deceive, and seeking whom he might devour.

Brother Hyrum [Hiram] [p. 53] Page had got in his possession, a certain stone, by which he had obtained to certain revelations, concerning the upbuilding of Zion, the order of the Church &c &c,²²⁷ all of which were entirely at variance with the order of Gods house, as laid down in the new Testament, as well as in our late revelations.

As a conference meeting had been appointed for the first day of September, I thought it wisdom not to do much more than to converse with the brethren on the subject, untill the conference should meet.²²⁸

Draft 3

NOTES
227. Newel Knight wrote that Page "had quite a roll of papers full of these revelations." (Knight, Autobiography, 146.)
228. The conference was appointed for 26 September and was in fact convened on that date. (Minute Book 2, 9 June and 26 Sept. 1830.)

A few days afterward I learned from Newel Knight who came to visit me that very shortly after ~~after~~ we left ~~the Mob collec~~ our enemies collected about his house demanding with much clamor if we were there threatning the brethren and causing them much uneasiness during all that day Mr Whitmer having heard of the persecutions which raged in Harmony invited us to remove to Fayette N,Y, Accordingly Bro Knight ~~took us to~~ removed my famly, he having his waggon with him Our friends at Fayettee evinced much pleasure and satisfaction ~~at~~ when we arrived among them

To our great grief ~~we soon learned that we must not expect to be exempt from persecution even in Fayette for~~ we found that Satan had been ~~laying~~ lying in wait to decieve and Seeking whom he might devour even among our frends ~~Bro~~ at Fayette [p. 90]

Bro Hyrum Page had got possession of a <u>Stone</u> by which he had obtained several revelation relativee to the building up of Zion the Order of the Church &c &c &c all of which were at varience with the order of Gods house as laid down in the New Testament as ~~well~~ well ~~well~~ as in our late revelations

~~As a conference had been appointed for the first day of September~~ I thought it wise to do nothing more than converse with the brethren on that subject until conference which was to meet on the first

Draft 1

be⟩ held. Finding however that many of the brethren (especialy the Whitmer family and Oliver Cowdery) were believing much in the things which were set forth by ~~the~~ ⟨this⟩ stone, a few of us got together and succeeded in obtaining the following revelations, which gave us much information on that & other subjects connected with our respective duties.

Rev page 181— and page 112

Draft 2

Finding however that many (especially the Whitmer family and Oliver Cowdery) were believing much in the things set forth by this stone, we thought best to enquire of the Lord concerning so important a matter, and before conference convened, we received the following,

Revelation to Oliver Cowdery, Given at Fayette, N,Y, September 1830.[229]

1 Behold I say unto thee, Oliver, that it shall be given unto thee, that thou shalt be heard by the church, in all things whatsoever thou shalt teach them by the comforter, concerning the revelations and commandments which I have given.

2 But behold, verily, verily I say unto thee, no one shall be appointed to receive commandments and revelations in this church, excepting my servant Joseph Smith Jr, for he receiveth them even as Moses; and thou shalt be obedient unto the things which I shall give unto him, even as Aaron, to declare faithfully the commandments and the revelations, with power and authority unto the church. And if thou art led at any time by the comforter to speak or teach, or at all times by the way of commandment unto the church, thou mayest do it. But thou shalt not write by way of commandment, but by wisdom: And thou shalt not command him who is at thy head, and at the head of the Church; for I have given him the keys of the mysteries and the revelations which are sealed, untill I shall appoint unto them another in his stead.

3 And now, behold I say unto you, that you shall go unto the Lamanites, and preach my gospel unto them; and inasmuch as they receive ~~their~~ ⟨thy⟩ teachings,

Draft 3

of Sept following Finding howevr that many (especially the Whitmer family and O Cowdrey) were believng ~~in~~ the things set forth by this Stone we thought it best to enquire of the Lord concerning ⟨it⟩ and obtained the following ~~Revelation~~ Revelation

NOTES

229. Revelation, Sept. 1830–B, in Doctrine and Covenants 51, 1835 ed. [D&C 28].

1 Behold I say unto ~~you~~ thee Oliver that it shall be given unto thee that thou shalt be heard by the church in all things whatsoeve[r] thou shalt teach them by the comforter concerning the revelations and commandme[n]ts which I have given

2 But behold verily verily I say unto thee no one shall be appointed to recieve commandments and revelations in this Church excepting my servant Joseph Smith J[r] for he recieveth them even as Moses and thou shalt be obedient unto the things which I shall give unto him even as Aaron to declare faithfully the commandments and revelations with power and authority unto the church And if thou art led at any time by the comforter to speak or teach ~~or~~ at all times by way of commandment unto the church thou mayest do it.

But thou shalt not write by way of commandment but by wisdom And thou shalt not command him [p. 91] who is thy head and at the head of the church for I have given him the keys of the mysteries, ⟨and⟩ the revelations which are sealed until I Shall appoint unto them another in his Stead

3 And now behold I say unto you that you shall go unto the Lamanites and preach my Gospel unto them and inasmuch as they reciev the teachings thou

Draft 1   **Draft 2**

thou shalt cause my church to be established among them, and thou shalt have
revelations but write them not by way of
commandment. And now behold I say
unto you, that it is not revealed, and no
man knoweth where the city shall be
built, but it shall be given hereafter.[230]
Behold I say unto you, that it shall be on
the borders by the Lamanites.

4 Thou shalt not leave this place until
after conference, and my servant Joseph
shall be appointed to preside over the
conference by the voice of it, and what
he saith to thee, thou shalt tell. And
again, thou shalt take thy brother Hiram
Page between him and thee alone, and
tell him that those things which he hath
written from that stone are not of me,
and that Satan deceiveth him: for behold
these things have not been appointed
unto him: neither shall any thing be appointed unto any of this church, contrary
to the church covenants, for all things
must [p. 54] be done in order and by
common consent in the church, by the
prayer of faith.

5 And thou shalt assist to settle all
these things, according to the covenants
of the church before thou shalt take thy
journey among the Lamanites. And it
shall be given thee from the time that
thou shalt go, untill the time that thou
shalt return, what thou shalt do. And
thou must open thy mouth at all times,
declaring my gospel with the sound of
rejoicing. Amen.

Revelation given in the presence of
six elders, in Fayette, N,Y.
September 1830.[231]

Listen to the voice of Jesus Christ,
your Redeemer, the Great I, AM, whose
arm of mercy hath atoned for your sins;
who will gather his people even as a hen

Draft 3

shalt cause my church to be establis[h]ed among them and thou shalt have revelations but write them not by way of commandme[n]t And now b[e]hold I say unto you that it is not revealed and no man knoweth where the city shall be built but it shall be given hereafter Behold I say unto you that it shall be on the borders of the Lamanites

4 Thou shalt not leave this place until after conference and my servint Joseph be appoint[e]d to preside over the conference by the voice of it and what he saith to thee thou shalt tell And again thou shalt take thy Bro Hyrum Page betwe[e]n him and thee alone and tell him that those things which he hath written from that stone are not of me and that Satan decieveth him for behold these things have not been appointed unto him; neither shall any thing be appointed unto any of this church contrary to the church covenants for ⟨all⟩ things must be done in order and by common consent in the church by the prayer of faith

5 And thou shalt assist to settle all ~~things~~ these things according to the covenants of the church before thou shalt take thy journey among the Lamanites And it shall be given thee from the time that thou shalt go until the time that thou shalt return what thou shalt do And thou open thy mouth at all tim[e]s declaring my gospel with the sound of rejoicing Amen [p. 92]

We recieved at the same time the following Revelation ⟨in the presence of six elders⟩

1 Listen to the voice. of Jesus Christ the Great I <u>am</u>[232] whose arm of mercy ~~doth~~ hath atoned for your sins: who will gather his people even as a hen gathereth

NOTES

230. In the Book of Mormon, Jesus prophesied that if "the Gentiles" would repent, he would "establish [his] church among them," and they would help "the rem[n]ant of Jacob; and also, as many of the house of Israel as shall come, that they may build a city, which shall be called the New Jerusalem." The mention of "the city" in the revelation copied here, without any introduction of the context, suggests that the revelation was responding to an ongoing conversation about the New Jerusalem. (Book of Mormon, 1830 ed., 500–501 [3 Nephi 21:14, 22–23].)

231. Revelation, Sept. 1830–A, in Doctrine and Covenants 10, 1835 ed. [D&C 29].

232. TEXT: Triple underlining in original.

Draft 1   **Draft 2**

gathereth her chickens under her wings,
even as many as will hearken to my voice,
and humble themselves before me, and
call upon me in mighty prayer. Behold,
verily, verily I say unto you, that at this
time your sins are forgiven you, therefore
you receive these things: but remember
to sin no more, lest perils shall come
upon you.

2 Verily I say unto you, that you are
chosen out of the world to declare my
gospel with the sound of rejoicing, as
with the voice of a trump: lift up your
hearts and be glad, for I am in your
midst, and am your advocate with the
father; and it is his good will to give you
the kingdom; and as it is written, Whatsoever ye shall ask in faith, being united
in prayer according to my command, ye
shall receive; and ye are called to bring to
pass the gathering of mine elect, for
mine elect hear my voice, and harden
not their hearts: wherefore the decree
hath gone forth from the Father, that
they shall be gathered in unto one place,
upon the face of this land, to prepare
their hearts, and be prepared in all
things, against the day when tribulation
and desolation are sent forth upon the
wicked: for the hour is nigh, and the day
soon at hand, when the earth is ripe: and
all the proud, and ~~all~~ ⟨they⟩ that do wickedly, shall be as stubble, and I will burn
them up, saith the lord of hosts, that
wickedness shall not be upon the earth:
for the hour is nigh, and that which was
spoken by ~~mine~~[234] mine apostles must be
fulfilled; for as they spoke so shall it
come to pass; for I will reveal myself from
heaven with power, and great glory, with
all the hosts thereof, and dwell in righteousness with men on earth a thousand
years, and the wicked shall not stand.

Draft 3

her chickens under her wings. even as many as will hearken unto my voice and humble themselves before me and call upon me ~~by~~ in mighty prayer Behold verily verily I say unto you that at this time your sins are forgiven you therefore ~~you~~ ⟨ye⟩ recieve these things: but remember to sin no more lest perils shall come upon you

2 Verily verily I say unto you that you are chosen out of this world to declar my gospel with the sound of rejoicing as with the voice of a trump. lift up your hearts and be glad for I am in your midst and am your advocate with the father and it is his good will to give you the kingdom; and as it is written "Whatsoeve[r] ye shall ask in faith being united in prayer according to my command ye shall recei[v]e["] and ye ar called to bring to pass the gathering of mine elect for mine elect hear my voice and harden not their hearts; wherefore the decree hath gone forth from the father that th[e]y shall be gathered in unto one place upon the face of this land to prepare their hearts and be prepared in all things against the day when tribulation and desolation are sent forth upon the wicked. for the hour is nigh and the day soon at hand when the earth is ripe. and all the proud ~~yea all~~ and they that do wickedly shall be as stubble and I will burn them up saith the Lord of Hosts that wickedness shall not be upon the earth; for the ~~Lord~~[233] ⟨hour⟩ is nigh and that which was spoken by mine apostles must be fulfilled. for as they spake so shall it come to pass for I will reveal myself from heave[n] with power and great glory with all the hosts thereof, and dwell in righteousness with men on earth a thousand years and the wicked shall not stand [p. 93]

NOTES

233. TEXT: "Lord" written over "hour" and then canceled.

234. TEXT: "mine" written over "my hol[y]" and then canceled.

Draft 1

Draft 2

3 And again, verily, verily I say unto you, and it hath gone forth in a firm decree, by the will of the Father, that mine apostles, the twelve which were with me in my ministry at Jerusalem, shall stand at my right hand at the day of my coming in a pillar of fire, being clothed with robes of righteousness, with crowns upon their heads, in glory even as I am, to judge the whole house of Israel, even as many as have loved me and kept my commandments, [p. 55] and none else; for a trump shall sound both long and loud, even as upon Mount Sinai, and all the earth shall quake, and they shall come forth: yea, even the dead which died in me, to receive a crown of righteousness, and to be clothed upon, even as I am, to be with me, that we may be one.

4 But behold, I say unto you, that before this great day shall come, the sun shall be darkened, and the moon shall be turned into blood, and the stars shall fall from heaven; and there shall be greater signs in heaven above, and in the earth beneath; and there shall be weeping and wailing among the hosts of men: and there shall be a great hailstorm sent forth to destroy the crops of the earth: and it shall come to pass, because of the wickedness of the world, that I will take vengeance upon the wicked, for they will not repent: for the cup of mine indignation is full; for behold my blood w̶i̶l̶l̶ ⟨shall⟩ not cleanse them, if they hear me not.

5 Wherefore I the Lord God will send forth flies upon the face of the earth, which shall take hold of the inhabitants thereof, and shall eat their flesh, and shall cause maggots to come in upon them, and their tongues shall be stayed, that they shall not utter against me, and their

Draft 3

3 And again verily verily I say unto
you and it hath gone forth in a firm decree by the will of the Father that mine
apostles the twelve that were with me
in my ministry at Jerusalem shall stand
at my right hand at the day of my coming in a pillar of fire. being clothed with
robes of righteousness with crowns upon
their heads in glory even as I am to judge
the whole house of Israel even as many as
have loved me and kept my commandments and none else for a trump shall
sound both long and loud even as upon
Mount Sinai and all the earth shall quake
and they shall come forth even the dead
which died in me, to recieve a crown of
righteousness, and to be clothed upon
even as I am to be with me that we may
be one

4 But behold I say unto you that before this great day shall come the sun
shall be darkened and the Moon shall be
turned into blood and the stars shall fall
from heaven; and there shall be greater
signs in the heavens above and in the
earth beneath, and there shall be weeping and wailing among the ~~children of~~
hosts of men; and there shall be a great
hail storm sent forth to destroy the crops
of the earth; and it shall come to pass because of the wickedness of the world, that
I will take veangeance upon the wicked
for they will not repent: for the cup of
mine indignation is full: for behold my
⟨blood⟩ shall not cleanse them if they
hear me not

5 Wherefore I the Lord will send flies
upon the ~~earth~~ face of the earth, which
shall take hold of the inhabitants thereof
and shall eat their flesh and shall cause
maggots to come in upon them. and
their tongues shall be stayed that they
shall ⟨not⟩ utter against me and their

Draft 1

Draft 2

flesh shall fall from off their bones, and their eyes from their sockets: and it shall come to pass, that the beasts of the forests, and the fowls of the air, shall devour them up: and that great and abominable church, which is the whore of all the earth, shall be cast down by devouring fire, according as it is spoken by the mouth of Ezekeil the prophet, which spoke of these things, which have not come to pass, but surely must, as I live, for abomination shall not reign.

6 And again, verily, verily I say unto you, that when the thousand years are ended, and men again begin to deny their God, then will I spare the earth but for a little season; and the end shall come, and the heaven and the earth shall be consumed, and pass away, and there shall be a new heaven and a new earth, for all old things shall pass away, and all things shall become new, even the heaven and the earth, and all the fulness thereof, both men and beasts: the fowls of the air, and the fishes of the sea, and not one hair, neither mote, shall be lost for it is the workmanship of mine hand.

7 But behold, verily I say unto you, before the earth shall pass away, Michael mine Archangel, shall sound his trump, and then shall all the dead awake, for their graves shall be opened, and they shall come forth; yea, even all; and the righteous shall be gathered on my right hand unto eternal life; and the wicked on my left hand will I be ashamed to own before the Father: wherefore I will say unto them, depart from me, ye cursed into everlasting fire, prepared for the devil and his angels.

Draft 3

flesh shall fall off their bones and their eyes from their sockets; and it shall come to pass that the beasts of the forests, and the fowls of the air shall devour them up; and that great and abominable church which is the whore of all the earth shall be cast down by [p. 94] devouring fire, according as it is spoken by the ~~prophet~~ mouth of Ezekiel the prophet, who spoke of these things which have not come to pass. but surely must as I live ~~saith~~ for abomanation shall not reign

6 And again verily verily I say unto you that when the thousand years are ended and men again begin to ~~destroy their~~ deny their God then will I spare the earth but for a little season; and the end shall come and the heaven and the earth shall be consumed and pass away ~~for all old things shall pass away and all things shall become new~~ and there shall be a new heaven and a new earth for all old things shall pass away and all things shall become new, even the heaven and the earth and all the fullness thereof; both men and beasts, the fowls of the air, and the fishes of the sea, and not one ~~mote~~ hair neither mote shall be lost for it is the workmanship of mine hand

7 But behold verily I say unto you before the earth shall pass away Michael mine archangel shall sound his trump and then shall all the dead awake for their graves shall be opened and they shall come forth; yea, [e]ven all: and the righteous shall be gathered on my right hand unto eternal life; and the wicked on my left hand will I be ashamed to own befo[r]e the father; wherefore I will say unto them depart from me ye cursed into everlasting fire prepared for the devil and hi[s] angels

Draft 1   **Draft 2**

8 And now behold I say unto you, never at any time, have I declared from mine own mouth, that they should return, for where I am they cannot come, for they have no power; but remember, that all my judgements are not given unto men: and as the words are ⟨have⟩ gone forth out of my mouth, even so shall they be [p. 56] fulfilled, that the first shall be last, and that the last shall be first in all things, whatsoever I have created by the word of my power, which is the power of my Spirit; for by the power of my spirit created I them: yea, all things both spiritual and temporal: firstly spiritual, secondly temporal, which is the beginning of my work: and again, firstly temporal, and secondly spiritual, which is the last of my work: Speaking unto you, that you may naturally understand, but unto myself my works have no end, neither beginning; but it is given unto you, that ye may understand, because ye have asked it of me, and are agreed.

9 Wherefore, verily I say unto you, that all things unto me are spiritual, and not at any time have I given unto you a law which was temporal, neither any man, nor the children of men: neither Adam your father, whom I created: behold I gave unto him that he should be an agent unto himself; and I gave unto him commandment, but no temporal commandment gave I unto him, for my commandments are spiritual; they are not natural, nor temporal, neither carnal nor sensual.

10 And it came to pass, that Adam being tempted of the devil, for behold the devil was before Adam, for he rebelled against me saying, give me thy power Give me thine honor, which is my

Draft 3

8 And now behold I say unto you never at any time have I declared from mine own mouth that they should return for where I am they can not come ~~fore~~ ⟨for⟩ they have no power: But remember that all my Judgements are not given unto men, and as the words ~~and as the~~ have gone forth out of my mouth. even so shall they be fulfilled that the ~~last shall be first~~ first shall be last ~~and the las~~ and that the last shall be first in all things whatsoevr I have created by the word of my power which is the power of my spirit, for by the power of my spirit. ~~I~~ created I them [p. 95] yea all things both spiritual and temporal, firstly spiritual secondly temporal which is the beginning of my work, And again firstly temporal and secondly spiritual, which is the last of my work, speaking unto you that you may naturally understand but unto myself my works hav no end neithe[r] beginn[i]ng, ~~butt~~ but it is givn unto you that ye may understand because ye have asked it of me and are agreed

9 Wherefo[r]e verily I say unto you that all things unto me are spiritual and not at any time have I given unto a law which was temporal, neither any man. nor the children of men, neither Adam your fathe[r] whom I created, Behold I gave unto him that he should be an agent unto himself. and I gave unto him a commandment, but no temporal commandment gave I unto him; ~~For~~ for my commandments are spiritual, they are not natural, nor temporal neither carnal nor sensual

10 And it came to pass that Adam being tempted of the devil for behold the devil was before Adam for he rebelled against me saying "Give me thine honor" which is my power, and also a

Draft 1   **Draft 2**

power: and also a third part of the hosts
of heaven turned he away from me because of their agency: and they were
thrust down, and thus came the devil and
his angels; and behold there is a place
prepared for them, from the beginning,
which place is hell: and it must needs be
that the devil should tempt the children
of men, or they could not be agents unto
themselves, for if they never should have
bitter, they could not know the sweet.

11 Wherefore, it came to pass, that
the devil tempted Adam, and he partook
the forbidden fruit, and transgressed the
commandment, wherein he became subject to the will of the devil, because he
yielded unto temptation. Wherefore I
the Lord God, caused that he should be
cast out ~~of~~ ⟨from⟩ the garden of Eden,
from my presence, because of his transgression: wherein he became spiritually
dead: which is the first death, even that
same death, which is the last death,
which is spiritual, which shall be pronounced upon the wicked when I shall
say, Depart ye cursed.

12 But behold I say unto you, that I the
Lord God gave unto Adam, and unto
his seed, that they should not die ~~unto~~ as
to the temporal death, untill I the Lord
God should send forth angels to declare
unto them repentance and redemption,
through faith on the name of mine only
begotten son: and thus I the the Lord
God appoint unto man, the days of his
probation; that by his natural death he
might be raised in immortality unto
eternal life, even as many as would believe, and they that believe not, unto
eternal damnation, for they cannot be
redeemed from their spiritual fall, because they repent not, for they love darkness rather than light, and their deeds

Draft 3

third part of the hosts of heaven turned
he away from me because of their agency;
and they were thrust down and thus
came the devil and his angels And behold there is a place prepared for them
from the beginning which place is Hell.
and it must needs be that the divil
should tempt the children of men or
they could not be agents unto themselves. for if they never should have bitter
they could not know the sweet

11 Wherefor it came came to pass that
the devil tempted Adam and he partook
the forbidden fruit and transgressed the
commandment wherein he became subject to the will of the devil, because he
yieelded unto temptation Wherefore I
the Lord God caused that he should be
cast out from the garden of Eden, from
my presence because of his transgressions whereine he became spiritually
dead which is the last death which is
spiritual. which [p. 96] shall be pronounced upon the wicked when I shall
say Depart ye cursed

12 But behold I say unto you that I the
Lord God gave unto Adam and ⟨unto⟩
his seed that they should not die as
to the temporal death. until I the Lord
God should send forth angels to declare
unto them repentance and redemption
through faith on the name of mine only
begotten son. And thus did I the Lord
God appoint unto man the days of his
probation. that by his natural death he
might ~~he might~~ be raised in immortality
unto eternal life; even as many as would
believ. And they that believe not. unto
eternal damnation. for they cannot be
redeemed ~~from~~ from their spiritual fall,
because they repent not. for they will
love darkness rather than light, and their

Draft 1

Draft 2

are evil, and they receive their wages of ~~him~~ whom they list to obey.

13. But behold I say unto you, that [p. 57] little children are redeemed from the foundation of the world, through mine Only begotten: Wherefore they cannot sin, for power is not given unto Satan to tempt little children, untill they begin to become accountable before me; for it is given unto them even as I will, according to mine own pleasure, that great things may be required at the hand of their fathers.

14 And again I say unto you, that whoso having knowledge, have I not commanded to repent, and he that hath no understanding, it remaineth in me to do according as it is written. And now I declare no more unto you at this time. Amen.

Conference at length assembled, the subject of the Stone &c was brought up, and after considerable discussion, reasoning &c and investigation Hyrum agreed to renounce the stone & its author, and the brethren unanimously agreed to renounce them also

We now partook of sacrament—confirmed and ordained many, and attended to a great variety of Church business— ~~during~~ ⟨on,⟩ that and the following day. During which time we had much of the power of God manifested, The Holy Ghost poured out upon ⟨us⟩ and obtained the following revelations—page 182 & page 183 [p. [25]] [*11 pages blank*]

[*end of Draft 1*]

At length, our conference assembled; the subject of the stone above mentioned, was discussed, and after considerable investigation, Brother Page, as well as the whole church who were present, renounced the said stone, and all things connected therewith, much to our mutual satisfaction and happiness.[235] We now partook of the sacrament, confirmed, and ordained many, and attended to a great variety of Church business on that and the following day;[236] during which time we had much of the power of God manifested amongst us; the Holy Ghost came upon us, and filled us with joy unspeakable; and peace, and faith, and hope, and charity abounded in our midst. Before we separated we obtained the following,

Revelation to David Whitmer,
Peter Whitmer Jr. and John Whitmer
given at Fayette, New York,
September, 1830.[237]

Draft 3

deeds are evil and they recieve their wages of whom they list to obey

13 But behold I say unto you. that little children are redeemed from the foundation of the world through mine only begotten; wherefo[r]e they cannot sin. for power is not given unto satan to tempt little children, until they begin to become accountable before me; for it is given unto them even as I will according to mine own pleasure. that great things may be required at the hands of their fathers

14 And again I say unto you that whoso having knowledge have I not commanded to ~~repent~~ repent; and he that hath no understanding it remaineth in me to do according as it is written And now I declare no more unto you at this time Amen

This was sufficient to influence those who had believed in the virtue of the stone to abandon it and all things connected with it and when conference convened we met together united in sentiment and partook of the Sacrament together in Love and fellowship At this Conference we ordained many to the ministry and confirmed several in their faith

Before we parted we recieved the following Revelation [p. 97]

~~1 Behold I say unto you David~~

~~To~~ David Peter, and John Whitmer

NOTES

235. According to a copy of the conference minutes, "Brother Joseph Smith jr. was appointed by the voice of the Conference to receive and write Revelations & Commandments for this Church." (Minute Book 2, 26 Sept. 1830.)

236. Minute Book 2 documents only one day of conference meetings; a subsequent entry in Draft 2 indicates that the conference "continued three days." (Minute Book 2, 26 Sept. 1830; JS History, vol. A–1, p. 458 herein [Draft 2].)

237. Revelations, Sept. 1830–C through E, in Doctrine and Covenants 52, 1835 ed. [D&C 30].

Draft 1   **Draft 2**

1 Behold I say unto you, David, that
you have feared man, and not relied on
me for strength, as you ought: but your
mind has been on the things of the earth
more than on the things of me, your
Maker, and the ministry whereunto you
have been called; and you have not given
heed unto my Spirit, and to those who
were set over you, but ~~you~~ have been persuaded by those whom I have not commanded:[238] wherefore you are left to enquire for yourself at my hand, and
ponder upon the things which you have
received. And your home shall be at your
father's house, untill I give unto you further commandments. And you shall attend to the ministry in the Church, and
before the world, and in the regions
round about. Amen.

2 Behold I say unto you, Peter, that
you shall take your journey with your
brother Oliver, for the time has come,
that it is expedient in me, that you shall
open your mouth to declare my gospel:
therefore, fear not but give heed unto the
words and advice of your brother, which
he shall give you.— And be you afflicted
in ⟨all⟩ his afflictions, ever lifting up
your heart unto me in prayer, and faith
for his and your deliverance: for I have
given unto him power, to build up my
church among the Lamanites: and none
have I appointed to be his counsellor,
over him, in the church, concerning
church matters, except it is his [p. 58]
brother Joseph Smith Jr. Wherefore give
heed unto these things, and be diligent
in keeping ~~these~~ my commandments,
and you shall be blessed unto eternal life.
Amen.

3 Behold I say unto you, my servant
John, that thou shalt commence from

Draft 3

1 Behold I say unto you David that you have feared man and not relied on me for strength as you ought; but your mind has been on the things of the earth more than on the the things of me your Maker, and the min[i]stry where unto you have been called, and you have not given heed ⟨unto⟩ ~~to~~ my spirit and to those who were set over you; but have been pursuaded by those whom I have not commanded: wherefore you are left to enquire for yourself at my hand and ponder upon the things which you have recieved

And your house shall be at your fathers house until I give unto you further commandments And you shall attend ⟨to⟩ the ministry in the church and before the world and in the regions around about Amen

2 Behold I say unto you Peter that you shall take your journey with you[r] brother Oliver for the time has come that it is expedient in me that you shall open your mouth to declare my gospel. Therefore fear not but give heed unto the words and advice of your brother. which he shall give you And be you afflicted in his afflictions ever lifting up your heart ⟨unto m⟩ ~~in prayer~~ unto me in prayer and faith for his and your deliverance. for I have given unto him power to build up my church among the Lamanites; and none have I appointed to be his counsellor over him in the church concerning Church matters except it be his brother Joseph Smith J^r Wherefo[r]e give heed unto these things and be diligent in keeping my commandments and you shall be b[l]essed unto eternal life Amen

3 Behold I say unto you my servant John that thou shalt commence from

NOTES

238. Likely a reference to members of the Whitmer's family espousing the revelations of Hiram Page. (See JS History, vol. A-1, p. 438 herein [Draft 2].)

Draft 1

Draft 2

this time forth to proclaim my gospel, as
with the voice of a trump. And your
labour shall be at your brother Philip
Burroughs', and in that region round
about yea, wherever you can be heard,
untill I command you to go from hence.
And your whole labor shall be in Zion,
with all your soul, from henceforth; yea,
you shall ever open your mouth in my
cause, not fearing what man can do, for
I[239] am with you. Amen.

    Revelation to Thomas B. Marsh,
    given at Fayette, September 1830.[240]

1 Thomas, my son, blessed are you because of your faith in my work. Behold
you have had many afflictions on account
of your family: nevertheless I will bless
you, and your family: yea, your little
ones, and the day cometh that they will
believe and know the truth, and be one
with you in my church.

2 Lift up your heart and rejoice for the
hour of your mission is come; and your
tongue shall be loosed; and you shall declare glad tidings of great joy unto this
generation. You shall declare the things
which have been revealed to my servant
Joseph Smith Jr. You shall begin to
preach from this time forth; yea, to reap
in the field which is white already to be
burned: therefore thrust in your sickle
with all your soul; and your sins are forgiven you; and you shall be laden with
sheaves upon your back, for the laborer is
worthy of his hire. Wherefore your family shall live.

3 Behold, verily I say unto you, go
from them only for a little time, and declare my word, and I will prepare a place
for them: yea, I will open the hearts of
the people and they will receive you.
And I will establish a church by your
hand; and you shall strengthen them and

Draft 3

this time fortt to proclaim my gospel as with the voice of a trump And your labour shall be at your brother Phillip Burrough's and in that region [p. 98] round about. yea wherever you can be heard until I command you to go from hence And your whole labour shall be in Zion, with all your soul from henceforth; yea, you shall ever open your mouth in my cause. not fearing what man can do, for I am with you Amen

At the same time and place we recievd the following for Thos B Marsh

1 Thomas my son. blessed are you because of your faith in my work. Behold you have had many afflictions on account of your family; nevertheless I will bless you. and your family. yea your little ones. and the day cometh ~~when~~ that they will believe and know the truth and be one with you in my church

2 Lift up your heart and rejoice for the hour of your mission is come and your tongue shall be loosed and you shall declare glad tidings of great joy unto this generation You shall declare the things which have been revealed to my servant Joseph Smith J$^\text{r}$ You shall begin to preach from this time forth yea to reap in the field which is white already to be burned. Therefore thrust in your sickle with all your soul, and your sins are forgiven you and you Shall be laden with sheaves upon your back for the laborer is worthy of his hire Wherefore your family shall live

3 Behold verily I say unto you go from them only a little time and declare my word and I will prepa[r]e a place for them, yea I will open the hearts of the peoplee and they will recieve you And I will establish a church by your hands and you shall strengthen them and prepare

NOTES

239. TEXT: "I" possibly a later insertion.
240. Revelation, Sept. 1830–F, in Doctrine and Covenants 53, 1835 ed. [D&C 31].

Draft 1   **Draft 2**

prepare them against the time when they
shall be gathered. Be patient in afflictions, revile not against those that revile.
Govern your house in meekness, and be
steadfast.

4 Behold I say unto you, that you shall
be a physician unto the church, but
not unto the world, for they will not receive you. Go your way whithersoever I
will, and it shall be given you by the
Comforter what you shall do, and
whither you shall go. Pray always, lest
you enter into temptation, and lose your
reward. Be faithful unto the end and, lo,
I am with you. These words are not of
man nor of men, but of me, even Jesus
Christ, your Redeemer, by the will of the
Father. Amen. [*3 lines blank*] [p. 59]

/²⁴²During this Conference which continued three days the utmost harmony prevailed and all things were settled satisfactory to all present, and a desire was manifest
by all the saints to go forward and labor
with all their power to spread the great and
glorious principles of truth which had been
revealed by our heavenly father.

A number were baptized during the conference and the work of the Lord spread and
prevailed.

At this time a great desire was manifest by several of the Elders respecting the
remnants of the house of Joseph—the
Lamanites residing in the west, knowing
that the purposes of God were great to that
people and hoping that the time had come
when the promises of the Almighty in regard to that people were about to be accomplished, and that they would receive
the gospel and enjoy its blessings. The desire being so great that it was agreed upon

Draft 3

them against the time when they shall be gathered Be patient in afflictions. revile not against those that revile Gove[r]n your house in meekness and be stedfast

4 Behold I say unto you that you Shall be a [p. 99] physician unto the church but not unto the world for they will not recieve you

And Go your way whither whithersoevr I will and it shall be given you by the comforter what you shall do and whithe[r] you shall go Pray always lest you enter into temptations and loose your reward Be faithful unto the end and lo I am with you These words are not of man nor of men but of me even Jesus Christ Your redeemer by the will of the Father Amen[241]

During this conference which continued three days the most perfect harmony prevailed and every thing was settled to the satisfaction of all parties concerned and all the Saints manifested a desire to go go forward and labour with all their powers to spread the great and glorious principles of truth which our heavenly father had revealed to us

Many who had not heretofoóre heretofore obeyed the Gospel now came forward and were babtised and recieved the Holy Ghost by the laying on of hands by the p

A great desire Many of the Elders became very anxious to know their duty relative to the Lamanites (Indians) of the west; knowing that the purposes of God were great towards them and hoping that the time had come when the promises of God should be fulfilled and they should recieve the gospel and recieve and enjoy the blessings of the gospel

This desire became so prevelant the [that] we concluded to enquire of the Lord

241. TEXT: The fair copy of Draft 3 ends at this point.
242. TEXT: James Mulholland handwriting ends; Robert B. Thompson begins.

Draft 1	Draft 2

Draft 2

we should enquire of the Lord respecting the propriety of sending som of the Elders among them, which we accordingly did and received the following revelation

Revelation to Parley P. Pratt and Ziba Peterson given Oct[r.] 1830[243]

1 And now concerning my servant Parley P. Pratt behold I say unto him that as I live I will ⟨that he shall⟩ declare my gospel and learn of me, and be meek and lowly of heart and that which I have appointed unto him is that he shall go with my servants Oliver Cowdery and Peter Whitmer Jr into the wilderness among the Lamanites; and Ziba Peterson also shall go with them, and I myself will go with them and be in their midst: and I am their advocate with the Father and nothing shall prevail. And they shall give heed to that which is written and pretend to no other revelations and they shall pray allways that I may unfold them to their understanding; and they shall give heed unto these words and trifle not and I will bless them. Amen.

Immediately on ~~the receipt~~ of receiving this revelation preparations were made for the journey of the brethren therin designated to the boarders of the Lamanites and a copy of the revelation was given them: [p. 60]

Having got ready for their journey they bade adieu to their Brethren and friends and commenced their journey, preaching by the way[245] and leaving a sealing testimony behind them lifting up their voice like a trump in the different villages through which they passed.

They continued their journey until they came to Kirtland Ohio,[246] where they tarried some time there being quite a number in that place who believed their testimony

Draft 3

respecting the propriety of embassadors to them; which we did and recieved the followin[g] Revelation to P. P. Pratt and Ziba Peterson given Oct. 1830 [p. 100]

1 And now behold my servant Parley P Pratt behold I say unto ~~you~~ him that as I live I will that he shall declare my gospel and learn of me and be meek and lowly in heart and that which I have appointed unto him is that he shall go with my servants Oliver Cowdry and Peter Whitmer J^r. into the wilderness among the Lamenites; and Ziba Peterson also shall go with them and I myself will go with them and be in their midst and I am their advocate with the Father and nothing shall prevail. And they shall give heed to that which is written and pretend to no other revelation and they shall pray always that I may unfold them to their understanding and they shall give heed unto these words and trifle not and I will bless them Amen

Immediately after recieving this revelation preperations were made for the departure of the brethren to the far west A copy of the revelations we had recieved were given them

They according bade adieu to their friends and in the[244] month of Oct ~~departed~~ commenced their jou[r]ney preaching by the way—lifting up their voice and proclaimng the everlasting gospel in the different towns and villages through which they passed whenever the[y] found an opportunity

On their arrival at Kirtland Geauga Co Ohio they called upon Mr Sidney Rigdon ~~an~~ a Preacher of the sect called Camp[b]ellites with whom P P Pratt ⟨had

NOTES

243. Revelation, Oct. 1830–A, in Doctrine and Covenants 54, 1835 ed. [D&C 32].

244. TEXT: Possibly "the◊".

245. Accounts by three of the participants, Oliver Cowdery, Parley P. Pratt, and Peter Whitmer Jr., mention preaching at only one location between Fayette, New York, and Mentor, Ohio—in the vicinity of Buffalo, New York, to the Cattaraugus band of the Seneca Indians. However, John Corrill's account of his own initial encounter with the missionaries shortly before they reached Mentor indicated that they shared their message more broadly. (Oliver Cowdery, Kirtland, OH, to "beloved brethren," 12 Nov. 1830, in Knight, Autobiography, 207–210; "History of Parley P. Pratt," 1, Historian's Office, Histories of the Twelve, ca. 1858–1880, CHL; Pratt, *Autobiography,* 49; Whitmer, Journal, Dec. 1831, [1]; Corrill, *Brief History,* [7], in *JSP,* H2:131.)

246. "Kirtland" was later corrected—probably in the handwriting of Willard Richards—to "Mentor." As JS's history subsequently indicated, Sidney Rigdon was the first person the missionaries contacted in Mentor. Parley P. Pratt, a recent convert to Mormonism, had joined a congregation of Reformed Baptists in 1829 in Ohio as a result of preaching by Rigdon, who had been his "friend and instructor." After proselytizing at Mentor, the missionaries soon continued on to Kirtland. (JS History, vol. A-1, 67, 72–74; Pratt, *Autobiography,* 31–32, 49.)

Draft 1   **Draft 2**

and came forward and obeyed the gospel
among the number was Elder Sidney S.
Rigdon and a large portion of the Church
over which he presided.

    As there has been a great rumor and
many false statements have been given to
the world respecting Elder Rigdons' connexion with the church of Jesus Christ,[247] it
[is] necessary that ⟨a⟩ correct account of the
same be given so, that the public mind may
be disabused on the subject. I shall therefore proceed to give a brief history of his
life drawn from Authentic sources, as also,
an account of his connexion with the
Church of Christ.[248]

Draft 3

some acquaintance⟩ It is hoped that the reader will notice that here commences Mr Rigdon's acquaintance with the Church of Jesus Christ of Latter Day Saints as well as that of the book of Mormon ~~The assertions of our one~~ notwithstanding our enemies assert that he was the ~~authour~~ author of that Book [p. 101] and the <u>inventer</u> of our system of Religion One or two facts will settle this point to the Satisfaction of every man

~~1ˢᵗ The Book of Mormon was published~~

1ˢᵗ The plates were ⟨obtained⟩ ~~discovered~~ in 1827 and in the year 1829 the translation was completed and in ~~the year~~ the beginning of 1830 they were published and yet Sidny Rigden resided in Ohio ~~and~~ a distance of ~~300 or 200~~ 400 Miles ~~And yet~~[249] ~~say the world O Sidney Rigdon is the progenitor of the Scheme~~ from the ⟨[*illegible*]⟩ place where I ~~resided~~ ⟨lived⟩ and up to the◊ time when the church was organized and the Book published had never seen one of the brethren much ~~more~~ less myself

And yet he was the ⟨projector⟩ ~~progenitor~~ of the Scheme!!!!![250] [*22 lines blank*] [p. [102]]

247. Following the publication of the Book of Mormon in March 1830, JS's critics began to suggest alternative explanations for its production. Most influential was Eber D. Howe's 1834 compilation of anti-Mormon material, *Mormonism Unvailed.* Howe presented a theory advanced by Doctor Philastus Hurlbut that sometime before Rigdon publicly staged his acceptance of Mormonism, he discovered a manuscript in a print shop in Pittsburgh, Pennsylvania, written by Solomon Spaulding. The manuscript, titled "Manuscript Found," was a historical romance that cast the first settlers of America as descendants of the lost tribes of Israel, discovered by a Roman ship blown off course. Spaulding died in 1816 and his manuscript was left with a printer who never published it. Hurlbut argued that after Rigdon discovered the work, he went on to work secretly with JS to create the Book of Mormon based on the story. Solomon Spaulding's original manuscript was discovered in 1884; a transcript may be found in Kent P. Jackson, ed., *Manuscript Found: The Complete Original "Spaulding Manuscript"* (Provo, UT: Religious Studies Center, Brigham Young University, 1996). (See also Howe, *Mormonism Unvailed,* chap. 19; and Jackson, *Manuscript Found,* ix–xi, xiv–xvi.)

248. In the original manuscript volume, the handwriting of Robert B. Thompson continues for thirteen more pages, giving a brief biography of Sidney Rigdon. The remainder of the volume is in the handwriting of William W. Phelps and Willard Richards, carrying the narrative up through 30 August 1834. A transcript of the entire volume is available at the Joseph Smith Papers website, josephsmithpapers.org.

249. TEXT: "yes" changed to "yet" and then canceled with the rest of the passage.

250. TEXT: Exclamation points upside down in original; possibly semicolons.

which they prepared to do with all po-sible dilligence. This was no sooner made known to the Governor, than he *ordered* out the militia, (report says THIRTY THOUSAND) about *twel e thousand* of which, were on the mar:h and issued his Edict, Maximim like, to have the saints EXTERMINATED, or EXPELLED from the State *forth-with.* Accordingly, many were mur-dered, or rather *martyred*!—about 60 thrust into prison—several hundred families driven from their homes, in the short space of *ten days,* in the midst of a very remarkable snow storm in the month of November—their pro-perty plundered—and the whole church, comprising about *twel e thou-san so ls,* expelled from the State!!

Thus you see, gentle reader, a mi-n te history of all those transactions mentioned above, will be a subject of no small moment; when we consider that they have all been performed in the midst of this *boaste* land of Liber-ty; whose whole fabric, rests upon this one pivot, *liberty of conscience.*

Deprive her citizens of this heav-enly boon, which is so freely granted to all, by the Author of our existance, and all her hopes of future prosp rity are blasted forever; she can stand no longer, as a free Republican Govern-ment, but must fall to rise no more.

With these brief remarks we shall sub it the Times and Seasons to an enlightened public, feeling assured that it will be hailed as a welcome guest, by every lover of freedom, and receive that encouragement which its merits may demand.

E. ROBINSON.
D. C. SMITH.

Extract,

FROM THE PRIVATE JOURNAL OF

JOSEPH SMITH JR.

On the fourteenth day of March, in the year of our Lord one thousand eight hundred and thirty eight, I with my family, arrived in Far West, Cald-well county Missouri, after a journey of more than one thousand mil s, in the winter season, and being about eight weeks on our Journey; during which we suffered great affliction, and met with considerable persecution on the road. However, the prospect of meeting my friends in the west, and anticipating the pleasure of dwelling in peace, and enjoying the blessings thereof, buoyed me up under the diffi-culties and trials which I had then to endure. However, I had not been there long before I was given to un-derstand that plots were laid, by wick-ed and designing men, for my destruc-tion, who sought every opportunity to take my life; and that a company on the Grindstone forks of Grand river, in the county of Daviess, had offered the sum of one thousand dollars for my scalp: persons of whom I had no knowledge whatever, and who, I sup-pose, were entire strangers to me; and in order to accomplish their wicked design. I was frequently waylaid &c.; consequently, my life was continually in jeopardy.

I could hardly have given credit to such statements, had they not been corroborated by testimony, the most strong and convincing; as shortly af-ter my arrival at Far West, while wa-tering my horse in Shoal Creek, I dis-tinctly heard three or four guns snap, which were undoubtedly intended for my destruction; however, I was mer-cifully preserved from those who sought to destroy me, by their lurking in the woods and hiding places, for this purpose

My enemies were not confined alone, to the ignorant and obscure, but men in office, and holding situations under the Governor of the State, proclaimed themselves my enemies, and gave en-couragement to others to destroy me; amongst whom, was Judge King, of the fifth Judicial circuit, who has fre-quently been heard to say, that I ought to be beheaded on account of my religion Expressions such as these, from individuals holding such impor-tant offices as Judge King's, could not fail to produce, and encourage perse-cution against me, and the people with whom I was connected. And in con-sequence of the pre udice which existed in the mind of this Judge, which he did not endeavor to keep secret, but made it as public as he could, the peo-ple took every advantage they possibly could, in abusing me, and threatening my life; regardless of the laws, whica

"Extract, from the Private Journal of Joseph Smith Jr." Once they had settled in Hancock County, Illinois, the Latter-day Saints began to publish a monthly paper, *Times and Seasons.* "Extract, from the Private Journal of Joseph Smith Jr." appeared in the first issue. The article is Joseph Smith's account of his 1838–1839 Missouri experiences. The first two-thirds of the article is based closely on Joseph Smith's "Bill of Damages against the State of Missouri," written in June 1839. *Times and Seasons,* July 1839, 1:2 (transcribed on pp. 468–470 herein). (Church History Library, Salt Lake City. Photograph by Welden C. Andersen.)

"EXTRACT, FROM THE PRIVATE JOURNAL OF JOSEPH SMITH JR.," JULY 1839

Source Note

JS, "Extract, from the Private Journal of Joseph Smith Jr.," in Times and Seasons *(Commerce, IL), July 1839, vol. 1, no. 1, pp. 2–9; edited by Ebenezer Robinson and Don Carlos Smith; includes typeset signature. The copy used for transcription is currently part of a bound volume held at CHL.*

The eight-page article is the second item in the first number of the *Times and Seasons.* This issue comprises eight leaves, making sixteen pages that measure 8⅝ × 5¼ inches (22 × 13 cm). The text on each page is set in two columns. It is unknown how long this copy of this issue of the *Times and Seasons* has been in church custody.

Historical Introduction

The historical account contained in "Extract, from the Private Journal of Joseph Smith Jr." was composed in the aftermath of the 1838 armed conflict between the Latter-day Saints and other Missourians, a struggle that culminated in the incarceration of JS and the expulsion of the Saints from the state. On 20 March 1839, from the jail in Liberty, Missouri, JS wrote to the Saints instructing them to document "all the facts and suffering and abuses put upon them by the people of this state and also of all the property and amount of damages which they have sustained."[1] A month later, on 16 April, JS escaped from the custody of Missouri lawmen, and on 22 April he was reunited with the Mormon exiles in Quincy, Illinois. Within days he arranged extensive land purchases for Mormon settlement at nearby Commerce, Illinois, and across the Mississippi River in Iowa Territory. JS himself was among the initial Latter-day Saints to relocate to Commerce in May 1839. On 4 June 1839, during a visit to Quincy, JS created a record of his own Missouri losses, titled "Bill of Damages against the state of Missouri."[2] Written in the handwriting of JS's recently appointed clerk, Robert B. Thompson, the bill of damages was created as a petition to the federal government for redress, and it became the basis of "Extract, from the Private Journal

---

1. JS et al., Liberty, MO, to the church members and Edward Partridge, Quincy, IL, 20 Mar. 1839, in Revelations Collection, CHL [D&C 123:1–2]. In a letter to the church written three months earlier, JS had reflected on some of the causes leading to the expulsion. (JS, Liberty, MO, to "the church," Caldwell Co., MO, 16 Dec. 1838, JS Collection, CHL.)

2. JS, "Bill of Damages against the State of Missouri[:] An Account of the Sufferings and Losses Sustained Therein," Quincy, IL, 4 June 1839, JS Collection, CHL; see also JS, Journal, 27 May–8 June 1839, in *JSP*, J1:340.

of Joseph Smith Jr.," published in July 1839. The reference to a "private journal" in the title notwithstanding, the article was not in fact based on a journal source; JS's bill of damages is the only known manuscript source. The manuscript is much more than a simple bill of damages, however, and the historical narrative it contains bridges the chronological gap between JS's last Missouri journal and his first Illinois journal.[3]

After an introduction stating that JS encountered enmity from the moment of his arrival in Missouri in March 1838, "Extract, from the Private Journal" covers most of the significant episodes in the Missouri conflict. The first specific historical event is the siege of the Mormon settlement at De Witt in Carroll County. The article then narrates the subsequent conflict around Adam-ondi-Ahman in Daviess County, the battle at Crooked River with militia from Ray County, and the siege at Far West in Caldwell County. Also recounted are JS's capture, imprisonment, and indictment, as well as the exodus of the Latter-day Saints to Illinois. The narrative draws to a close with JS's escape and his flight from Missouri. Where the bill of damages ends with a list of losses and sufferings for which remuneration is sought, the "Extract" concludes with an address to the American people at large, appealing to the principles of liberty and justice.

"Extract, from the Private Journal of Joseph Smith Jr." was published in the first issue of the church newspaper *Times and Seasons.* The prospectus published at the end of the issue declared that the newspaper would provide "a history of the unparalleled persecution, which we, as a people, received in Missouri"; the lead article in the issue, an "Address" from the editors, similarly announced that the newspaper's mission included publication of "a detailed history of the persecution and suffering" experienced in Missouri.[4] "Extract, from the Private Journal" directly follows, taking up half of the issue's sixteen pages. *Times and Seasons* editors Ebenezer Robinson and Don Carlos Smith printed only about two hundred copies of the July 1839 issue before a malaria epidemic left them debilitated.[5] Months later they published a reprint of the first issue, including JS's "Extract," under a November 1839 date.[6] JS's account of Missouri sufferings constituted part of a new genre of Mormon historical writing, and in the next issue, the *Times and Seasons* began publishing an eleven-part series on the Saints' Missouri persecutions.[7]

---

3. The last entry in JS's September–October 1838 journal is 5 October 1838. On that day, JS left Far West, Missouri, with a detachment of Mormon men to reinforce the besieged Saints in De Witt, Missouri; after an introductory overview, JS's "Bill of Damages" begins with the De Witt conflict. The bill ends with JS's escape from his captors on 16 April 1839 and his arrival in Quincy, Illinois, on 22 April 1839; the first two entries in JS's 1839 journal resume JS's journal keeping precisely at this point. (See *JSP,* J1:330, 336.)

4. "Prospectus of the Times and Seasons," *Times and Seasons,* July 1839, 1:16; Ebenezer Robinson and Don Carlos Smith, "Address," *Times and Seasons,* July 1839, 1:1.

5. "To the Patrons of the Times and Seasons," *Times and Seasons,* Nov. 1839, 1:15–16; Ebenezer Robinson, "Items of Personal History of the Editor," *The Return,* May 1890, 257–258.

6. It appears that there were three printings of the first issue of the *Times and Seasons:* the first in July; the second in November, from the same typesetting; and a third sometime thereafter, from a new setting of the text. The third printing, perhaps issued to satisfy increasing demand for the newspaper, retained the November 1839 date. Although minor spelling and punctuation changes appear in the later printings of the "Extract," no changes were made to the wording. (See Crawley, *Descriptive Bibliography,* 1:94–95.)

7. See "A History, of the Persecution," *Times and Seasons,* Dec. 1839–Oct. 1840, in *JSP,* H2:203–286.

First issue of *Times and Seasons*. About two hundred copies of the first issue of the *Times and Seasons* had been printed in July 1839 when editors Ebenezer Robinson and Don Carlos Smith became ill with "swamp fever." They began printing again in November 1839 by reissuing the first number. Several copies of this reissue, now bearing the November date, were printed with the typesetting saved from July. The editors subsequently reset the type for additional printings of the November issue, thus creating a third state for the first issue of *Times and Seasons*. This third state, which included slight changes to spelling and punctuation, can be identified by a printing error in the nameplate, as seen above: "TRUTH WILL PTEVAIL." All three printings of the inaugural issue included the historical article titled "Extract, from the Private Journal of Joseph Smith Jr." *Times and Seasons,* July 1839, 1:1; Nov. 1839, 1:1. (Church History Library, Salt Lake City. Photographs by Welden C. Andersen.)

JS's bill of damages was revised for publication as the "Extract" sometime between 4 June 1839, when the bill of damages was composed, and 12 July, when Wilford Woodruff recorded "looking over the proof sheet of the first number of the Times & seasons."[8] JS returned to Commerce from Quincy on 5 June and remained in the area until 12 July, except for a 15–26 June journey through western Illinois. Therefore, JS's narrative of Missouri persecutions was likely revised in Commerce between 5 and 14 June or between 27 June and 12 July.[9] The first issue of the *Times and Seasons* was probably published within a few days of 12 July, the day Wilford Woodruff helped check the proof sheet.

The first two-thirds of the "Extract" was based closely on "Bill of Damages," with only minor editorial changes. The changes softened some of the manuscript's more strident rhetoric, omitted particulars regarding JS's personal losses, and added details to emphasize the suffering of the Saints. Significant differences between the two documents are explained in footnotes herein. The final section of the article, which did not come from the bill of damages, may have been dictated or written by JS, perhaps with help from clerical assistants Robert B. Thompson, James Mulholland, and George Robinson. The published "Extract" was disseminated to Saints throughout the nation via the newspaper, and the document shaped their memory of the persecution in Missouri and their pattern for rehearsing it. JS clearly intended to reach not only the Latter-day Saints subscribing to the church newspaper but also the greater American public. As part of JS's effort to gain sympathy in the court of public opinion, this document became part of the broadening agenda of gaining redress for grievances suffered in Missouri.

———— ✢ ————

Extract,
FROM THE PRIVATE JOURNAL OF
JOSEPH SMITH JR.

On the fourteenth day of March, in the year of our Lord one thousand eight hundred and thirty eight, I with my family, arrived in Far West, Caldwell county Missouri, after a journey of more than one thousand miles, in the winter season, and being about eight weeks on our Journey; during which we suffered great affliction, and met with considerable persecution on the road.[10] However, the prospect of meeting my friends in the west, and anticipating the pleasure of dwelling in peace, and enjoying the blessings thereof, buoyed me

---

8. Woodruff, Journal, 12 July 1839.

9. JS's journal records that he was "dictating History" 10–14 June and 3–5 July 1839, which may have included the historical narrative in the "bill of damages" along with his ongoing work on a complete history of the church. (JS, Journal, 10–14 June and 3–5 July 1839, in *JSP*, J1:340, 345.)

10. JS's bill of damages notes that expenditures for the journey amounted to "about two hundred dollars." JS later recounted that tavern keepers in Paris, Illinois, had combined to deny the Latter-day Saints lodging, which JS and others secured for their families only after threatening the use of force. (JS, Journal, 29 Dec. 1842, in *JSP*, J2:196–197; see also JS, Journal, 29 Mar. 1838, in *JSP*, J1:245–246.)

Joseph Smith's "Bill of Damages." In March 1839, Joseph Smith instructed the Latter-day Saints to gather accounts of their losses and persecutions in Missouri. To follow his own instruction, Smith dictated a "Bill of Damages," created as a petition to the federal government for redress. The first two-thirds of the manuscript became the source for "Extract, from the Private Journal of Joseph Smith Jr.," published in the first issue of the *Times and Seasons;* the page shown above corresponds to the first four paragraphs of the "Extract" (transcribed on pp. 468–470 herein). Handwriting of Robert B. Thompson. JS, "Bill of Damages against the State of Missouri," Quincy, IL, 4 June 1839, p. 1, JS Collection, Church History Library, Salt Lake City. (Photograph by Welden C. Andersen.)

up under the difficulties and trials which I had then to endure.[11] However, I had not been there long before I was given to understand that plots were laid, by wicked and designing men, for my destruction, who sought every opportunity to take my life; and that a company on the Grindstone forks of Grand river, in the county of Daviess, had offered the sum of one thousand dollars for my scalp: persons of whom I had no knowledge whatever, and who, I suppose, were entire strangers to me; and in order to accomplish their wicked design, I was frequently waylaid &c.; consequently, my life was continually in jeopardy.

I could hardly have given credit to such statements, had they not been corroborated by testimony, the most strong and convincing; as shortly after my arrival at Far West, while watering my horse in Shoal Creek, I distinctly heard three or four guns snap, which were undoubtedly intended for my destruction; however, I was mercifully preserved from those who sought to destroy me, by their lurking in the woods and hiding places, for this purpose[12]

My enemies were not confined alone, to the ignorant and obscure, but men in office, and holding situations under the Governor of the State,[13] proclaimed themselves my enemies, and gave encouragement to others to destroy me; amongst whom, was Judge [Austin A.] King, of the fifth Judicial circuit,[14] who has frequently been heard to say, that I ought to be beheaded on account of my religion[.] Expressions such as these, from individuals holding such important offices as Judge King's, could not fail to produce, and encourage persecution against me, and the people with whom I was connected. And in consequence of the prejudice which existed in the mind of this Judge, which he did not endeavor to keep secret, but made it as public as he could, the people took every advantage they possibly could, in abusing me, and threatening my life;[15] regardless of the laws, which [p. 2] promise protection to every religious society, without distinction.[16]

During this state of things, I do not recollect that either myself, or the people with whom I was associated, had done any thing to deserve such treatment, but felt a desire to live at peace, and on friendly terms, with the citizens of that, and the adjoining counties, as well as with all men; and I can truly say,

---

11. The previous sentence does not appear in JS's bill of damages. On the conditions attending JS's departure from Ohio, see *JSP,* J1:228–229.

12. In the bill of damages, this sentence ends at "intended for my destruction."

13. Lilburn W. Boggs.

14. Missouri's fifth judicial circuit covered the western counties north of the Missouri River. (*History of Ray County, Mo.,* 260–261.)

15. JS's bill of damages notes here that he was subjected to "vexatious law suits."

16. Both Missouri's constitution and the Constitution of the United States included religious protection clauses. (Missouri Constitution of 1820, art. 13, secs. 4–5; U.S. Constitution, amend. 1.)

"for my love they were my enemies," and "sought to slay me without any cause,"[17] or the least shadow of a pretext.

My family was kept in a continual state of alarm, not knowing, when I went from home, that I should ever return again; or what would befall me from day to day.[18] But notwithstanding these manifestations of enmity, I hoped that the citizens would eventually cease from their abusive and murderous purposes, and would reflect with sorrow upon their conduct in endeavoring to destroy me, whose only crime was in worshiping the God of heaven, and keeping his commandments; and that they would soon desist from harrassing a people, who were as good citizens as the majority of this vast republic—who labored almost night and day, to cultivate the ground; and whose industry, during the time they were in tha[t][19] neighborhood, was proverbial.[20]

In the latter part of September, A. D. 1838, I took a journey, in company with some others,[21] to the lower part of the county of Caldwell, for the purpose of selecting a location for a Town. While on my journey, I was met by one of our brethren from Dewitt, in Carroll county, who stated that our people, who had settled in that place, were, and had been for some time, surrounded by a mob, who had threatened their lives, and had shot at them several times;[22] and that he was on his way to Far West, to inform the brethren there, of the facts. I was surprised on receiving this intelligence, although there had, previous to this time, been some manifestations of mobs, but I had hoped that the good sense of the ma[j]ority of the people, and their respect for the constitution, would have put down any spirit of persecution, which might have been manifested in that neighborhood.[23]

––––––––––––––––––

17. See Psalm 109:3, 4.

18. The bill of damages does not include the remainder of this paragraph.

19. TEXT: In this and other instances where one or two characters are supplied in the transcript, the characters were not set or did not get inked in the original; text is supplied based on the reprint of this article in *Times and Seasons,* Nov. 1839, 1:2–9.

20. Tensions between the Latter-day Saints and other Missourians stretched back over several years. (See LeSueur, *1838 Mormon War in Missouri,* chap. 2; Baugh, "Call to Arms," chap. 2; and Anderson, "Clarifications of Boggs's Order," 30–36.)

21. The bill of damages does not specify that JS journeyed with others.

22. The remainder of this paragraph is not found in JS's bill of damages.

23. Church leaders purchased 134 of De Witt's 304 lots in June 1838, and by October there were seventy to eighty Mormon families living there. As early as July, however, the Saints in De Witt were confronted with ultimatums to leave Carroll County. When the Missouri militia disbanded anti-Mormon vigilantes gathered in Daviess County, many regrouped in Carroll County, where they laid siege to the Saints in De Witt. (Murdock, Journal, 23 June 1838; see also LeSueur, *1838 Mormon War in Missouri,* 101–107; and Baugh, "Call to Arms," chap. 6.)

Immediately on receiving this intelligence, I made preparations to go to that place, and endeavor, if possible, to allay the feelings of the citizens,[24] and save the lives of my brethren who were thus exposed to their wrath.[25] I arrived at Dewitt, about the first of October,[26] and found that the accounts of the situation of that place, were correct; for it was with much difficulty, and by travelling unfrequented roads, that I was able to get there; all the principal roads being strongly guarded by the mob, who refused all ingress as well as egress.[27] I found my brethren, (who were only a handfull, in comparison to the mob, by which they were surrounded,) in this situation, and their provisions nearly exhausted, and no prospect of obtaining any more.[28]

We thought it necessary to send immediately to the Governor, to inform him of the circumstances; hoping, from the Executive, to receive the protection which we needed, and which was guaranteed to us, in common with other citizens. Several Gentlemen of standing and respectability, who lived in the immediate vicinity, (who were not in any wise connected with the church of Latter Day Saints,) who had witnessed the proceedings of our enemies; came forward and made affidavits to the treatment we had received, and concerning our perilous situation; and offered their services to go and present the case to the Governor themselves.[29] A messenger was accordingly despatched to his Excellency, who made known to him our situation. But instead of receiving any aid whatever, or even sympathy from his Excellency, we were told that "the quarrel was between the Mormons and the mob," and that "we might fight it

---

24. The remainder of this sentence was modified from the bill of damages, which continues as follows: "if not to make arrangements with those individuals of whom we had made purchases and to whom I was responsible and holden for part of the purchase money."

25. JS apparently returned to Far West to raise a relief force. Albert Rockwood recorded that word of the siege at De Witt arrived on 4 October. Soon thereafter, Seymour Brunson and JS led groups of men to De Witt. (Rockwood, Journal, 14 Oct. 1838; see also Reed Peck, Quincy, IL, to "Dear Friends," 18 Sept. 1839, p. 73, Henry E. Huntington Library, San Marino, CA.)

26. For "about the first of October" the bill of damages reads "on the [*blank*] day." As JS was still in Far West around ten o'clock on the morning of 5 October, he could not have arrived in De Witt, over fifty miles to the east, before 6 October. In 1845, Thomas Bullock wrote in JS's history that JS arrived in De Witt on 6 October. (JS, Journal, 5 Oct. 1838, in *JSP*, J1:330; JS History, vol. B-1, 833.)

27. This description of JS's journey to De Witt is not found in the bill of damages.

28. JS's bill of damages does not note the Mormon settlers' numerical disadvantage. Brigadier General Hiram Parks estimated two or three hundred militiamen under arms against the Latter-day Saints. He noted that the anti-Mormon forces hoped to number five hundred within a few days but surmised that even with those numbers the Mormons would probably win out if there were a battle. In fact, the number of Saints under arms was about one hundred thirty. Their commander, George M. Hinkle, may have inflated their numbers in representing them to outsiders. (Hiram Parks, "five miles from De Witt," MO, to David R. Atchison, [Boonville, MO], 7 Oct. 1838, Mormon War Papers, MSA; Baugh, "Call to Arms," 173; see also Samuel D. Lucas, Boonville, MO, to Lilburn W. Boggs, 4 Oct. 1838, Mormon War Papers.)

29. The previous sentence does not appear in JS's bill of damages.

out."[30] In the mean time, we had petitioned the Judges to protect us.[31] They sent out about one hundred of the militia, under the command of Brigadier General [Hiram] Parks; but almost immediately on their arrival, General Parks informed us that the greater part of his men under Capt. [Samuel] Bogart had mutinied, and that he should be obliged to draw them off from the place, for fear they would [j]oin the mob; consequently he could afford us no assistance.[32] [p. 3]

We had now, no hopes whatever, of successfully resisting the mob, who kept constantly increasing: our provisions were entirely exhausted and we being wearied out, by continually standing on guard, and watching the movements of our enemies; who, during the time I was there, fired at us a great many times.[33] Some of the brethren died, for want of the common necessaries of life, and perished from starvation; and for once in my life, I had the pain of beholding some of my fellow creatures fall victims to the spirit of persecution, which did then, and has since prevailed to such an extent in Upper Missouri— men too, who were virtuous, and against whom, no legal process could for one moment, be sustained; but who, in consequence of their love to God—attachment to his cause—and their determination to keep the *faith*, were thus brought to an untimely grave.[34]

Many houses, belonging to my brethren, were burned; their cattle d[r]iven away, and a great quantity of their property destroyed by the mob. Seeing no prospect of relief, the Governor having turned a deaf ear to our entreaties, the militia having mutinied, and the greater part of them ready to join the mob; the brethren came to the conclusion to leave that place, and seek a shelter elsewhere; they consequently took their departure, with about seventy waggons,

---

30. Longtime Missouri citizen A. L. Caldwell had departed De Witt about 2 or 3 October (prior to JS's arrival), appealed to Governor Lilburn W. Boggs, and returned with this report on 9 or 10 October. (John Murdock, Affidavit, Adams Co., IL, 10 Jan. 1840, photocopy, Material Relating to Mormon Expulsion from Missouri, 1839–1843, CHL; JS History, vol. B-1, 834–835.)

31. JS's bill of damages specifies that the Saints petitioned circuit judge Austin A. King. They may also have petitioned the Carroll County judges: William Crockett, Thomas Arnold, and John Standley. (*History of Carroll County, Missouri,* 387.)

32. Attempting to defuse the confrontation at De Witt, Major General David R. Atchison ordered Brigadier General Hiram Parks to disperse both Mormon and anti-Mormon vigilantes who had come to De Witt from other counties and to suggest that local Mormons sell out to local anti-Mormons. Atchison also wrote to Governor Boggs suggesting he come personally to De Witt to restore peace there. In a report to Atchison, Parks neglected to mention Bogart's actions. Bogart later complained to Governor Boggs that Parks had not allowed Bogart and his men to intercept Mormon reinforcements arriving from Caldwell County. (David R. Atchison, Boonville, MO, to Lilburn W. Boggs, [St. Louis, MO], 9 Oct. 1838; Hiram Parks, "five miles from De Witt," MO, to David R. Atchison, [Boonville, MO], 7 Oct. 1838; Samuel Bogart, Elk Horn, MO, to Lilburn W. Boggs, 13 Oct. 1838, Mormon War Papers, MSA.)

33. The previous sentence does not appear in JS's bill of damages.

34. JS's bill of damages does not specifically note starvation as a cause of death among the De Witt Saints, nor does it include the sentiments expressed here following "the spirit of persecution."

with the remnant of the property they had been able to save from their match-
less foes, and proceeded to Caldwell.[35] During our journey, we were continually
harrassed and threatened by the mob, who shot at us several times; whilst several of our brethren died from the fatigue and privations which they had to
endure, and we had to inter them by the wayside, without a coffin, and under
circumstances the most distressing.[36]

On my arrival in Caldwell I was informed by General [Alexander]
Doniphan of Clay county, that a company of mobbers[37] eight hundred strong,
were marching towards a settlement of our people's in Daviess county.[38] He
ordered out one of the officers to raise a force and march immediately to what
he called Wight's town[39] and defend our people from the attacks of the mob,
until he should raise the militia in his, and the adjoining counties to put them
down.[40] A small company of militia who were on their rout to Daviess county,
and who had passed through Far West, he ordered back again, stating that
they were not to be depended upon, as many of them were disposed to join the
mob; and to use his own expression, were "damned rotten hearted."[41] According
to orders Lieut. Colonel [George M.] Hinkle marched with a number of our

---

35. The evacuation from De Witt began on 11 October 1838. (John Murdock, Affidavit, Adams Co., IL,
10 Jan. 1840, photocopy, Material Relating to Mormon Expulsion from Missouri, 1839–1843, CHL;
Baugh, "Call to Arms," 179–181.)

36. Other eyewitnesses reported deaths that occurred during the evacuation of De Witt. (See Judd,
Autobiography of Zadoc Knapp Judd, 9; Tarlton Lewis, Statement, 20 May 1879, p. 1, Historian's Office,
History of Persecutions, 1879–1880, CHL; and Arza Judd Jr., Petition, 6 Jan. 1840, photocopy, Material
Relating to Mormon Expulsion from Missouri, 1839–1843, CHL.)

37. JS's bill of damages does not call the company "mobbers."

38. JS was evidently already aware that anti-Mormon forces were on their way to Daviess County, as he
had called for an armed expedition to Daviess on 14 October, the day before Brigadier General Alexander
Doniphan arrived at Far West. Doniphan may have confirmed rumors of the vigilante detachment or
apprised JS of the size of the force. (See Corrill, *Brief History*, 36–37, in *JSP*, H2:176–177; and [Rigdon],
Appeal to the American People, 41.)

39. Lyman Wight spearheaded settlement of Adam-ondi-Ahman, the principal Latter-day Saint com-
munity in Daviess County.[a] Wight was also the leader of the Adam-ondi-Ahman contingent of the
Danite society, a private Mormon militia.[b] (a. JS, Journal, 18 May–1 June and 4–5 June 1838, in *JSP*,
J1:270–275; Berrett, *Sacred Places*, 4:399–402, 416, 438–444. b. JS, Journal, 7–9 Aug. 1838, in *JSP*, J1:299;
Swartzell, *Mormonism Exposed*, 17, 20–23, 32; "History of Lyman Wight," 5, Historian's Office, Histories
of the Twelve, ca. 1858–1880, CHL.)

40. While Brigadier General Alexander Doniphan had authority to issue orders for Caldwell and
Daviess counties, Sidney Rigdon recounted that Doniphan "advised" and "recommended" that Latter-
day Saints from Caldwell County help defend their fellow Saints in Daviess County. ([Rigdon], *Appeal to
the American People*, 42.)

41. JS's bill of damages notes that the company numbered sixty. This was apparently the company of
Missouri militia commanded by Colonel William Dunn of Clay County that Brigadier General Hiram
Parks had sent to Daviess County. Dunn's company encamped near Far West awaiting Brigadier General
Doniphan's arrival. Doniphan, however, ordered Dunn to dismiss his troops. (Hiram Parks, Richmond,
MO, to David R. Atchison, 21 Oct. 1838, Mormon War Papers, MSA.)

people to Daviess county to afford what assistance they could to their breth-ren.[42] Having some property in that county and having a house building there, I went up at the same time.[43] While I was there a number of houses belonging to our people were burned by the mob, who committed many other depreda-tions, such as driving off horses, sheep, cattle, hogs &c. A number, whose houses were burned down as well as those who lived in scattered and lonely situations, fled into the town for safety, and for shelter from the inclemency of the weather, as a considerable snow storm had taken place just about that time; women and children, some in the most delicate situations were thus obliged to leave their homes, and travel several miles in order to effect their escape. My feelings were such as I cannot describe when I saw them flock into the village, almost entirely destitu[t]e of clothes, and only escaping with their lives.[44] During this state of affairs General Parks arrived at Daviess county,[45] and was at the house of Colonel Lyman Wight, when the intelligence was brought, that the mob were burning houses; and also when women and children were fleeing for safety. Colonel Wight who held a commission in the 59th regiment under his (General Parks) command, asked what was to be done. He told him that he must immediately, call out his men and go and put them down.[46] Accordingly, a force was immediately raised for the purpose of quelling the mob, and in a short time were on their march with a determination to drive the mob, or die in the attempt;[47] as they could bear such treatment no longer.[48] The mob having learned the orders of general Parks, and likewise being aware

---

42. Approximately one hundred fifty to three hundred men from Caldwell County arrived in Daviess County on 16 October. (John Smith, Journal, 16 Oct. 1838; Corrill, *Brief History,* 37, in *JSP,* H2:177; Foote, Autobiography, 21 Oct. 1838.)

43. JS remained in Daviess County over the next few days to oversee Mormon operations there. (LeSueur, *1838 Mormon War in Missouri,* 112–128; Baugh, "Call to Arms," 185–210.)

44. Mormon victims of these vigilante depredations included Agnes Coolbrith Smith, wife of JS's brother Don Carlos. Her husband was away from home on a church mission. ([Rigdon], *Appeal to the American People,* 43; Hyrum Smith, Testimony, Nauvoo, IL, 1 July 1843, p. 6, Nauvoo, IL, Records, CHL.)

45. Brigadier General Hiram Parks arrived 18 October. (Hiram Parks, Richmond, MO, to David R. Atchison, 21 Oct. 1838, Mormon War Papers, MSA.)

46. Wight had been commissioned as the colonel of the Caldwell County regiment of the state militia when he resided there, prior to moving to Daviess County. William Peniston, an antagonist to the Mormons, held the office of colonel in Daviess County.[a] Wight directed Mormon forces at Adam-ondi-Ahman as leader of the church's private militia there.[b] (a. "History of Lyman Wight," 5, Historian's Office, Histories of the Twelve, ca. 1858–1880, CHL; see also William Peniston, Daviess Co., MO, to Lilburn W. Boggs, 21 Oct. 1838, Mormon War Papers, MSA. b. JS, Journal, 7–9 Aug. 1838, in *JSP,* J1:299; Sampson Avard, Testimony, Richmond, MO, Nov. 1838, in State of Missouri, "Evidence"; Swartzell, *Mormonism Exposed,* 17, 20–23, 32; Baugh, "Call to Arms," 385.)

47. JS's bill of damages does not include "or die in the attempt."

48. According to Parks, the Latter-day Saints began their attack before he arrived. (Hiram Parks, Richmond, MO, to David R. Atchison, 21 Oct. 1838, Mormon War Papers, MSA.)

of the determination of the oppressed, they broke up their encampments and fled. The mob seeing that they could not succeed by force, now [p. 4] resorted to str[a]tagem; and after removing their property out of their houses, which were nothing but log cabins, they actually set fire to their own houses, and then reported to the authorities of the state that the Mormons were burning and destroying all before them.[49]

On the retreat of the mob from Daviess, I returned to Caldwell, hoping to have some respite from our enemies, at least for a short time; but upon my arrival there, I was informed that a mob had commenced hostilities on the borders of that county, adjoining to Ray co. and that they had taken some of our brethren prisoners, burned some houses, and had committed depredations on the peaceable inhabitants.[50] A company under the command of Capt. [David W.] Patten, was ordered out by Lieutenant Col. Hinckle to go against them, and stop their depredations, and drive them out of the county.[51] Upon

-----

49. Several Mormons later stated that non-Mormons burned their own homes and then blamed the Mormons in order to provoke state action against them. Other accounts added that non-Mormons burned their own homes after selling their property to the Mormons. In many instances, however, the Mormons did burn non-Mormon homes, as well as some stores. Soon not only the vigilantes but most of the non-Mormon population of Daviess fled the county. ([Rigdon], *Appeal to the American People,* 44; Hyrum Smith, Testimony, Nauvoo, IL, 1 July 1843, p. 7, Nauvoo, IL, Records, CHL; Pulsipher, "Zerah Pu[l]siphers History," 8; LeSueur, *1838 Mormon War in Missouri,* 117–124; Baugh, "Call to Arms," chap. 7.)

50. Responding to rumors of Mormon intentions to raid Ray County, Captain Samuel Bogart of the Ray County militia mobilized a company, including militiamen and volunteers, to patrol the border area between Ray County and Caldwell County and to guard against potential attacks. He then wrote to David R. Atchison, a major general in the state militia, for authorization. Atchison not only granted Bogart's request for permission to "range the line between Caldwell & Ray County" but also charged him "to enquire into the state of things in Daviess County." On 24 October, Bogart's rangers began harassing Saints living on both sides of the Ray-Caldwell border and took three prisoners: Addison Green, Nathan Pinkham Jr., and William Seely. Green, and possibly Pinkham, belonged to a group of Mormon scouts reconnoitering the border. Sidney Rigdon later testified that a messenger reported Bogart's men burned one house. (Samuel Bogart, Elk Horn, MO, to David R. Atchison, 23 Oct. 1838, Mormon War Papers, MSA; Samuel Bogart, Testimony, Richmond, MO, Nov. 1838, in State of Missouri, "Evidence"; Rockwood, Journal, 25 Oct. 1838; Sidney Rigdon, Testimony, Nauvoo, IL, 1 July 1843, p. [12], photocopy, Nauvoo, IL, Records, CHL; see also Baugh, "Call to Arms," 219–225.)

51. JS's bill of damages also notes that "about day light next morning," Hinkle "came up with them." Parley P. Pratt, a participant in the expedition, recounted that "Captain Killian (to whom Col. Hincle had committed the command of the troops in Far West, when he himself was not present) sent out a detachment. . . . This company, consisting of about sixty men, was sent to see what the matter was on the lines; and who was committing depredations, and if necessary, to protect or move in the families and property; and if possible, effect the release of the prisoners."[a] Although the company's commission may have included all the elements listed by JS and Pratt, other accounts focus on the mission of rescuing the men taken prisoner.[b] In an effort to free the Mormon prisoners held by Bogart, the company crossed over the Caldwell County line early on the morning of 25 October and attacked Bogart at his camp on Crooked River in the noncounty area attached to Ray County.[c] (a. Pratt, *History of the Late Persecution,* 33. b. See, for example, Charles C. Rich, Statement, ca. Feb. 1845, Historian's Office,

the approach of our people, the mob fired upon them, and after discharging their pieces, fled with great precipitation, with the loss of one killed and several wounded.[52] In the engagement Capt. Patten, (a man beloved by all who had the pleasure of his acquaintance,) was wounded and died shortly after.[53] Two others were likewise killed and several wounded.[54] Great excitement now prevailed, and mobs were heard of in every direction who seemed determined on our destruction. They burned the houses in the country and took off all the cattle they could find.[55] They destroyed cornfields, took many prisoners, and threatened death to all the Mormons. On the 28th of Oct. a large company of armed soldiery were seen approaching Far West,[56] They came up near to the town and then drew back about a mile and encamped for the night.[57] We were informed that they were Militia, ordered out by the Govornor for the purpose of stopping our proceedings; it having been represented to his excellency, by wicked and designing men from Daviess, that we were the aggressors, and had committed outrages in Daviess &c.[58] They had not yet got the Governors orders of *extermination*, which I believe did not arrive until the next day.[59] On

---

JS History Documents, ca. 1839–1856, CHL; and Greene, *Facts Relative to the Expulsion,* 21. *c.* Berrett, *Sacred Places,* 4:267–268.)

52. Moses Rowland was killed in the encounter, and at least six others of the Ray County militia were wounded. (Wyatt Cravens, Testimony, Richmond, MO, Nov. 1838, in State of Missouri, "Evidence.")

53. In his bill of damages, JS states that before Patten died he "sent for me to pray for him, which request I complied with."

54. Besides Patten, Gideon Carter was killed in battle*a* and Patrick (or Patterson) Obanion was fatally wounded.*b* Seven other Mormons were wounded.*c* (*a.* Rockwood, Journal, 28 Oct. 1838; [Rigdon], *Appeal to the American People,* 45. *b.* Young, "Lorenzo Dow Young's Narrative," 51; John P. Greene, Affidavit, Quincy, IL, 17 Mar. 1840, Mormon Redress Petitions, 1839–1845, CHL; John L. Lockhart, Testimony, Richmond, MO, Nov. 1838, in State of Missouri, "Evidence." *c.* Baugh, "Call to Arms," 238–240.)

55. JS's bill of damages notes that "amongst the cattle driven off were Two cows of mine."

56. Eighteen hundred militiamen under the command of Samuel D. Lucas arrived at Goose Creek, one mile south of Far West, on 30 October. (Samuel D. Lucas, "near Far West," MO, to Lilburn W. Boggs, 2 Nov. 1838, Mormon War Papers, MSA.)

57. The following three sentences do not appear in the bill of damages, which resumes with "The next day I was waited upon by Colonel Hinckle." The soldiers encamped on Goose Creek. (Berrett, *Sacred Places,* 4:300–301.)

58. The "designing men from Daviess" were later identified as William Morgan, Samuel Bogart (actually from Ray County), William Peniston, Samuel Venable, Jonathan J. Dryden, James Stone, and Thomas J. Martin. (JS History, vol. B-1, 837; see also William Morgan, Affidavit, 21 Oct. 1838; William Peniston, Daviess Co., MO, to Lilburn W. Boggs, 21 Oct. 1838; Samuel Venable, Affidavit, 22 Oct. 1838; Jonathan J. Dryden, Affidavit, 22 Oct. 1838; James Stone, Affidavit, 22 Oct. 1838; and Thomas J. Martin, Affidavit, 22 Oct. 1838, Mormon War Papers, MSA.)

59. Acting as commander in chief of the Missouri state militia, Governor Lilburn W. Boggs issued orders on 27 October 1838 that "the Mormons must be treated as enemies and must be exterminated or driven from the state if necessary for the public peace." Reed Peck, who parleyed with the militia on behalf of the Saints, wrote that the order did not arrive until "an hour or so before Sun Set." However, Major General Lucas reported to Governor Boggs that he had received a copy of the order on the previous

the following morning, a flag was sent, which was met by several of our people, and it was hoped that matters would be satisfactorily arranged after the officers had heard a true statement of all the circumstances.[60] Towards evening, I was waited upon by Colonel Hinckle, who stated that the officers of the Militia desired to have an interview with me, and some others, hoping that the difficulties might be settled without having occasion to carry into effect the exterminating orders, which they had received from the Governor.[61] I immediately complied with the request, and in company with elders [Sidney] Rigdon and [Parley P.] Pratt, Colonel Wight, and Geo. W. Robinson, went into the camp of the militia. But judge of my surprise, when instead of being treated with that respect which is due from one citizen to another, we were taken, as prisoners of war, and were treated with the utmost contempt.[62] The officers would not converse with us, and the soldiers, almost to a man, insulted us as much as they felt disposed, breathing out threats against me and my companions.[63] I cannot begin to tell the scene which I there witnessed. The loud cries and yells of more than one thousand voices, which rent the air and could be heard for miles; and the horrid and blasphemous threats and curses which were poured upon us in

---

day, 30 October, at the Log Creek crossing on the road to Far West, and that he postponed meeting with Hinkle and the Mormon party on 31 October until two o'clock in the afternoon because he was preoccupied with "receiving & encamping of fresh troops, who were hourly coming in." (Lilburn W. Boggs, Jefferson City, MO, to John B. Clark, Fayette, MO, 27 Oct. 1838, Mormon War Papers, MSA; Reed Peck, Quincy, IL, to "Dear Friends," 18 Sept. 1838, p. 109, Henry E. Huntington Library, San Marino, CA; Samuel D. Lucas, "near Far West," MO, to Lilburn W. Boggs, 2 Nov. 1838, Mormon War Papers, MSA.)

60. Reed Peck wrote that Brigadier General Alexander Doniphan named him along with John Cleminson, John Corrill, and William W. Phelps to meet with Doniphan and other members of the militia delegation and that JS added Seymour Brunson and George M. Hinkle to the number. Corrill wrote that the delegation consisted of only himself, Peck, and Hinkle. According to Corrill, JS instructed him to "beg like a dog for peace." (Reed Peck, Quincy, IL, to "Dear Friends," 18 Sept. 1839, pp. 108–109, Henry E. Huntington Library, San Marino, CA; Corrill, *Brief History*, 40–41, in *JSP*, H2:183.)

61. The Mormon emissaries reported back to JS the conditions under which General Samuel D. Lucas would forgo extermination. As summarized by Corrill, they were to surrender certain church leaders, surrender their arms, give up their property as reparations for damages, and leave the state. Church leaders surrendered as prisoners would be allowed to decide whether to abide by those terms and remain prisoners or return to Far West to fight. General Lucas's report to Governor Boggs specified that the Mormon prisoners were to be held as hostages to guarantee compliance with the conditions of surrender.[a] Corrill recounted that JS "said he had rather go to States-prison for twenty years, or had rather die himself than have the people exterminated."[b] Colonel George M. Hinkle later maintained that he left to JS the decision whether to surrender and that JS sent word the following morning to agree to the terms.[c] (a. Corrill, *Brief History*, 41–42, in *JSP*, H2:185–187; S. Lucas to L. Boggs, 2 Nov. 1838. b. Corrill, *Brief History*, 41, in *JSP*, H2:183. c. George M. Hinkle, Buffalo, Iowa Territory, to William W. Phelps, Nauvoo, IL, 14 Aug. 1844, *The Ensign*, Aug. 1844, 30–32.)

62. JS was taken prisoner on Wednesday, 31 October 1838. (S. Lucas to L. Boggs, 2 Nov. 1838.)

63. The previous sentence is not in JS's bill of damages.

torrents, were enough to appal the stoutest heart. In the evening we had to lie down on the cold ground surrounded by a strong guard, who were only kept back by the power of God from depriving us of life.[64] We petitioned the officers to know why we were thus treated, but they utterly refused to give us any answer, or to converse with us. The next day they held a court martial, and sentenced us to be shot, on Friday morning, on the puplic square, as an ensample to the Mormons. However notwithstanding their sentence, and determination, they were not permitted to carry their murderous sentence into execution.[65]

Having an opportunity of speaking to General [Moses] Wilson,[66] I inquired of him the cause why I was thus treated, I told him I was not sensible of having done any thing worthy of such treatment; that I[67] had always been a supporter of the constitution and of Democracy. His answer was "I know it, and that is the reason why I want to kill you, or have you killled." The militia then went into the town and without any restraint whatever, plunderd the [p. 5] houses, and abused the innocent and unoffending inhabitants. They went to my house and drove my family out of doors.[68] They carried away most of my property and left many destitute.—[69] We were taken to the town, into the public square; and before our departure from Far West, we, after much entreaties, were suffered to see our families, being attended all the while with a strong guard; I found my wife and children in tears, who expected we were shot by those who had sworn to take our lives, and that they should see me no more.[70]

---

64. The phrase "who were only kept back by the power of God from depriving us of life" is not found in JS's bill of damages.

65. A plan to execute JS was prevented by the intervention of Brigadier General Alexander Doniphan, who was also one of JS's attorneys. (Burnett, *Recollections and Opinions*, 63; see also Maynard, "Alexander William Doniphan, Man of Justice," 462–472; and Launius, "Alexander William Doniphan and the 1838 Mormon War," 67, 90–93.)

66. Major General Lucas committed JS and the other prisoners to the charge of Brigadier General Wilson. (S. Lucas to L. Boggs, 2 Nov. 1838.)

67. The bill of damages here identifies JS as "a Democrat."

68. According to the bill of damages, this was done "under sanction of general Clark." Major General John B. Clark, to whom Governor Boggs had assigned overall command of the expedition against the Mormons, did not arrive at Far West until 4 November, after General Moses Wilson had left for Independence with JS and other Mormon prisoners as directed by Major General Lucas. (John B. Clark, Richmond, MO, to Lilburn W. Boggs, 10 Nov. 1838; Samuel D. Lucas, Independence, MO, to Lilburn W. Boggs, 5 Nov. 1838, Mormon War Papers, MSA.)

69. JS's bill of damages lists stolen horses, harnesses, cattle, hogs, books, and store goods. Mormon exiles from Missouri later reported tremendous losses in plundered property. (See redress petitions in Material Relating to Mormon Expulsion from Missouri, 1839–1843, CHL, and in Mormon Redress Petitions, 1839–1845, CHL.)

70. JS's mother, Lucy Mack Smith, later recalled that when JS was taken prisoner she and Joseph Smith Sr. heard several gunshots and concluded that JS had been murdered. (Lucy Mack Smith, History, 1844–1845, bk. 16, [2].)

When I entered my house, they clung to my garments, their eyes streaming with tears, while mingled emotions of joy and sorrow were manifest in their countenances. I requested to have a private interview with them a few minutes, but this privilege was denied me, I was then obliged to take my departure, but who can realize my feelings which I experienced at that time; to be torn from my companion, and leaving her surrounded with monsters in the shape of men, and my children too, not knowing how their wants would be supplied; to be taken far from them in order that my enemies might destroy me when they thought proper to do so. My partner wept, my children clung to me and were only thrust from me by the swords of the guard who guarded me. I felt overwhelmed while I witnessed the scene, and could only reccomend them to the care of that God, whose kindness had followed me to the present time; and who alone could protect them, and deliver me from the hands of my enemies and restore me to my family[71]

I was then taken back to the camp and then I with the rest of my brethren, viz: Sidney Rigdon, Hyram [Hyrum] Smith, Parley P. Pratt, Lyman Wight, Amasa Lyman, and George W. Robinson, were removed to Independence, Jackson county. They did not make known what their intention or designs were in taking us there; but knowing that some of our most bitter enemies resided in that county, we came to the conclusion that their design was to shoot us, which from the testimony of others. I do think was a correct conclusion.[72] While there, we were under the care of Generals [Samuel D.] Lucas and Wilson, we had to find our own board, and had to sleep on the floor with nothing but a mantle for our covering, and a stick of wood for our pillow.[73] After remaining there a few days we were ordered by General [John B.] Clark to return; we were accordingly taken back as far as Richmond, and there we

---

71. The description of JS bidding farewell to his family was expanded from the bill of damages. The three sentences that follow are also an expansion of the bill's text, which reads only, "We were then removed to Jackson County."

72. On 2 November Clark sent orders to Lucas to hold the seven prisoners until Clark arrived at Far West. Lucas apparently did not receive those orders before departing with the prisoners for Independence. Clark then sent orders on 3 November for Lucas to take the prisoners to Richmond. Lucas explained to Governor Boggs that he refused to comply with Clark's 3 November order because Clark, being junior to Lucas in appointment as a major general in the Missouri militia, was not entitled to issue such a command to Lucas. By returning from the field of operations to his division headquarters in Independence and bringing the prisoners with him, Lucas maintained jurisdictional control over the situation. He reported to Boggs that he "march[ed] them to my head Quarters at Independence to await your further Orders." (John B. Clark, Jefferson City, MO, to Lilburn W. Boggs, 29 Nov. 1838; Samuel D. Lucas, Independence, MO, to Lilburn W. Boggs, 5 Nov. 1838, Mormon War Papers, MSA; see also JS, Independence, MO, to Emma Smith, Far West, MO, 4 Nov. 1838, JS, Materials, CCLA.)

73. Parley P. Pratt recalled that the prisoners were initially kept in a vacant house and then moved to a hotel. (Pratt, *History of the Late Persecution*, 46–47.)

were thrust into prison and our feet bound with fetters.[74] While in Richmond, we were under the charge of colonel [Sterling] Price from Chariton county, who suffered all manner of abuse to be heaped upon us.[75] During this time my afflictions were great, and our situation was truly painful. After remaining there a few days we were taken before the court of inquiry,[76] but were not prepared with witnesses, in consequence of the eruelty [cruelty] of the mob, who threatend destruction to all who had any thing to say in our favor: but notwithstanding their threats there were a few who did not think their lives dear so that they might testify to the truth, and in our behalf, knowing we were unlawfully confined; but the court who was prejudiced against us, would not suffer them to be examined according to law, but suffered the State's Attorney[77] to abuse them as he thought proper.[78] We were then removed to Liberty jail in Clay county, and there kept in close confinement in that place for more than four months.[79] while there, we petitioned Judge [Joel] Turnham for a writ of habeas corpus, but on account of the prejudice of the jailor all communication

---

74. According to JS's bill of damages, "While we were in Jackson, General Clark with his troops arrived in Caldwell and sent an order for our return—holding out the inducement that we were to be reinstated to our former priviledges: but instead of being taken to Caldwell we were taken to Richmond." Before arriving at Far West, Clark twice sent orders to Lucas to incarcerate the prisoners in the jail at Richmond. There is no indication in Clark's correspondence that he ordered them returned to Far West. The prisoners were kept in Independence 4–8 November 1838. They were moved from Independence to Richmond 8–9 November. (John B. Clark, Jefferson City, MO, to Lilburn W. Boggs, 29 Nov. 1838, Mormon War Papers, MSA; [Rigdon], *Appeal to the American People*, 62–65.)

75. Lieutenant Colonel Price served in Brigadier General Robert Wilson's second brigade in Major General John B. Clark's first division of the state militia. (See John B. Clark, Richmond, MO, to Lilburn W. Boggs, 10 Nov. 1838; and Robert Wilson, Adam-ondi-Ahman, MO, to John B. Clark, 12 Nov. 1838, Mormon War Papers, MSA.)

76. Austin A. King, judge of Missouri's fifth judicial circuit, presided over a preliminary court of inquiry for sixty-four Latter-day Saint defendants at Richmond on 12–29 November 1838. (Madsen, "Joseph Smith and the Missouri Court of Inquiry," 97–98; see also State of Missouri, "Evidence.")

77. Thomas C. Burch. ([Rigdon], *Appeal to the American People*, 29, 66; JS History, vol. C-1, 858.)

78. Sidney Rigdon claimed that some of the witnesses for JS and his codefendants were intimidated and fled the county before the hearing began, while those who did attend the hearing "were sworn at bayonet point." Rigdon's account of the hearing also claimed that Judge Austin A. King never allowed the defense attorneys to cross-examine the witnesses for the prosecution. King charged JS with "overt acts of Treason in Daviess county" and charged several other Latter-day Saints with treason, murder, larceny, and other crimes. ([Rigdon], *Appeal to the American People*, 66–67; *Document Containing the Correspondence*, 150; see also Madsen, "Joseph Smith and the Missouri Court of Inquiry," 98–101.)

79. JS was transported from Richmond, Daviess County, to Liberty, Clay County, on 30 November and 1 December, along with Sidney Rigdon, Hyrum Smith, Lyman Wight, Alexander McRae, and Caleb Baldwin. Some Mormon prisoners were transferred to other facilities. (Mittimus, 29 Nov. 1838, State of Missouri v. JS et al. for Treason [Daviess Co. Cir. Ct. 1839], copy, JS Collection, CHL; Hyrum Smith, Diary, [9]; see also Jessee, "Prison Experience," 24–25.)

was cut off;[80] at length however, we succeeded iin getting a petition conveyed
to him, but for fourteen days we received no answer. We likewise petitioned
the other Judges but with no success. After the expiration of fourteen days
Judge Turnham ordered us to appear before him, we went and took a number
of witnesses, which caused us considerable expense and trouble; but he altogether refused to hear any of our witnesses. The lawyers which we had
employed refused to act; being afraid of the people.[81] This being the case, we of
course could not succeed, and were consequently [re]manded back to our
prison house.—[82] We were sometimes visited by our friends whose kindness
and attention, [I] shall ever remember with feelings of [li]vely gratitude, but
frequently we were not sufiered to have that privilege. Our vituals were of the
coarsest [p. 6] kind, and served up in a manner which was disgusting. We continued in this situation, bearing up under the injuries and cruelties we suffered
as well as we could, until we were removed to Daviess county, where we were
taken in order to be tried for the crimes with which we had been charged.[83]
The grand jury (who were mostly intoxicated,) indibted [indicted] us for treason, etc. etc.—[84]

---

80. The Clay County jailer was Sheriff Samuel Hadley. (State of Missouri, Mittimus, 29 Nov. 1838,
State of Missouri v. JS et al. for Treason [Daviess Co. Cir. Ct. 1839], copy, JS Collection, CHL.)

81. JS's bill of damages also states, "We likewise petitioned to Judge King and to the Judges of the
supreme Court but they utterly refused."

82. Alexander Doniphan and Peter Burnett represented the prisoners at the 25 January 1839 habeas
corpus hearing in Clay County. No record of the proceedings has been found. Burnett later recounted
that Doniphan made a spirited defense of the prisoners at this time. Judge Turnham released Rigdon,
finding insufficient proof of his culpability in the record of the November 1838 court of inquiry over
which Judge Austin A. King presided. (Fearing for his safety, Rigdon remained in the prison until
5 February.) JS and the other prisoners were returned to jail pending a hearing before a Daviess County
grand jury, scheduled for April 1839. (Jessee, "Prison Experience," 29; Burnett, *Recollections and
Opinions,* 53–55; Sidney Rigdon, Testimony, Nauvoo, IL, 1 July 1843, pp. [23]–[24], Nauvoo, IL, Records,
CHL.)

83. JS and his fellow prisoners were moved 6–8 April 1839. (Hyrum Smith, Diary, [12], [21]–[22]; Baugh,
"We Took Our Change of Venue," 61–62.)

84. The hearing before the grand jury was held 9–11 April at Gallatin, Daviess County, Missouri. JS was
indicted for treason, riot, arson, larceny, and receiving stolen goods. (See the indictments issued during
the April 1839 term of the Daviess County, Missouri, Circuit Court in the following cases: State of
Missouri v. JS et al. for Treason, photocopy, Max H Parkin, Collected Missouri Court Documents, CHL;
State of Missouri v. JS et al. for Riot; State of Missouri v. Caleb Baldwin et al. for Arson; State of
Missouri v. Jacob Gates et al. for Arson, Historical Department, Nineteenth-Century Legal Documents
Collection, CHL; State of Missouri v. James Worthington et al. for Larceny, Daviess Co., MO,
Courthouse, Gallatin, MO; and State of Missouri v. JS for Receiving Stolen Goods, photocopy, Max H
Parkin, Collected Missouri Court Documents, CHL; see also Baugh, "We Took Our Change of Venue,"
63–65.)

While there, we got a change of venue to Boon[e] county,[85] and were conducted on our way to that place by a strong guard.[86] The second evening after our departure the guard got intoxicated[.] we thought it a favorable opportunity to make our escape; knowing that the only object of our enemies was our destruction;[87] and likewise knowing that a number of our brethren had been massacred by them on Shoal creek, amongst whom were two children;[88] and that they sought every opportunity to abuse others who were left in that state; and that they were never brought to an account for their barbarious proceedings, but were wincked at, and encouraged, by those in authority. We thought that it was necessary for us, inasmuch as we loved our lives, and did not wish to die by the hand of murderers and assasins; and inasmuch, as we loved our families and friends, to deliver ourselves from our enemies, and from that land of tyrany and oppression, and again take our stand amongst a people in whose bosoms dwell those feelings of republicanism and liberty which gave rise to our nation:— Feelings which the inhabitants of the state of Missouri were strangers to. Accordingly we took the advantage of the situation of our guard and took our departure,[89] and that night we travelled a cons[i]derable distance. We

85. Defense counsel initially sought a change of venue based on a newly enacted statute that allowed such a request to be supported by affidavits from the requesting parties. Judge Thomas Burch denied this request. A second motion to change venue was then made based on another Missouri statute that precluded an interested party from serving as a judge in the case. Because Judge Burch served as prosecuting attorney at the 12–19 November court of inquiry at Richmond, this statute specifically required disqualification. Burch granted this motion and the case was transferred to Boone County. (An Act to Amend an Act concerning Criminal Proceedings [13 Feb. 1839], *Laws of the State of Missouri* [1838–1839], 98; Daviess Co., MO, Circuit Court Record, Apr. 1839, vol. A, 66–70, Daviess Co., Courthouse, Gallatin, MO; Snow, Journal, 1838–1841, 47–49.)

86. William Morgan, sheriff of Daviess County, summoned William Bowman, Wilson McKinney, John Brassfield, and John Pogue as his guard to escort the prisoners. (William Morgan, Certificate, 1 July 1839; "Preamble," William Morgan, Papers, CHL.)

87. The next several lines are additions not found in JS's bill of damages, which resumes at "Accordingly we took the advantage."

88. On 30 October, Livingston County colonel Thomas Jennings led two to three hundred men in an attack on the small Latter-day Saint settlement of Hawn's Mill. The attackers shot at men, women, and children. Seventeen were killed, including Charles Merrick (age nine) and Sardius Smith (age ten). At least fourteen were wounded. (See Baugh, "Call to Arms," chap. 9; and "A History, of the Persecution," *Times and Seasons,* Aug. 1840, 1:145–150, in *JSP,* H2:259–271.)

89. JS and his fellow prisoners escaped 16 April 1839 while at Yellow Creek in Chariton County. The prisoners departed Gallatin on 12 April, four days earlier, but did not leave the confines of Daviess County—the county in which they had been charged—until 15 April. Hyrum Smith later testified that Daviess County sheriff William Morgan informed the prisoners that Judge Burch had privately instructed him not to escort the prisoners as far as Boone County. One of the guards sold two horses to the prisoners for their escape, and he later collected payment in Nauvoo. (JS, Journal, 16 Apr. 1839, in *JSP,* J1:336; Lyman Wight, Testimony, Nauvoo, IL, 1 July 1843, p. 32, Nauvoo, IL, Records, CHL; Baugh, "We Took Our Change of Venue," 65–71; Hyrum Smith, Testimony, Nauvoo, IL, 1 July 1843, pp. 25–26, Nauvoo, IL, Records, CHL; JS to John Brassfield, Promissory note, 16 Apr. 1839, JS Collection, CHL.)

continued on our journey both by night and by day, and after suffering much
fatigue and hunger, I arrived in Quincy Illinois, amidst the congratulations of
my friends and the embraces of my family.[90]

I have now resided in this neighborhood for several weeks as it is known to
thousands of the citizens of Illinois, as well as of the State of Missouri, but the
authorities of Mo., knowing that they had no justice in their crusade against
me, and the people with whom I was associated, have not yet to my knowledge, taken the first step towards having me arrested.[91]

Amongst those who have been the chief instruments, and leading characters, in the unparallelled persecutions against the church of Latter Day Saints;
the following stand conspicuous, viz: Generals Clark, Wilson, and Lucas,
Colonel Price, and Cornelius Guilliam [Gilliam].[92] Captain Bogart also, whose
zeal in the cause of oppression and injustlce, was unequalled, and whose delight
has been to rob, murder, and spread devastation amongst the Saints. He stole a
valuable horse, saddle and bridle from me; which cost two hundred dollars,
and then sold the same to General Wilson. On understanding this I applied to
General Wilson for the horse, who assured me, upon the honor of a gentleman,
and an officer, that I should have the horse returned to me; but this promise
has not been fulfilled.

All the threats, murders, and robberies which these officers have been
guilty of, are entirely looked over by the Executive of the state; who, to hide his
own iniquity, must of course shield and protect those whom he employed, to
carry into effect his murderous purposes.

I was in their hands as a prisoner about six months, but notwtihstanding
their determination to destroy me, with the rest of my brethren who were with
me; and although at three different times (as I was informed) we were sentenced
to be shot, without the least shadow of law, (as we were not military men,) and
had the time, and place apointed for that purpose;[93] yet, through the mercy of

---

90. JS arrived at Quincy, Illinois, 22 April. (JS, Journal, 16 and 22–23 Apr. 1839, in *JSP*, J1:336.)

91. The remainder of the text is not based on JS's bill of damages, which here terminates with a paragraph listing JS's claims against Missouri for losses sustained in Jackson, Daviess, and Caldwell counties
for "Lands: Houses Horses: Harness Cattle Hogs & Books & store Goods Expences while in Bonds:
of moneys paid out expences of moving out of the State & damages sustained by False imprisonment
threatnings: intimidation Exposure &c &c &c &c &c." JS calculated the total value lost at $100,000.

92. Gilliam led one of the vigilante groups that harassed and plundered the Saints. (LeSueur, *1838
Mormon War in Missouri*, 128–129, 192; Baugh, "Call to Arms," 300–302.)

93. As noted previously, Alexander Doniphan intervened to prevent JS's execution shortly after he was
taken prisoner. JS's brother Hyrum Smith later testified that Jedediah M. Grant, a Latter-day Saint, over-
heard a conversation between General Clark and militiamen at Richmond that indicated Clark's intention to have JS and fellow prisoners executed on 12 November. According to Smith, Clark abandoned that
plan after learning that military law made no provision for a court-martial for civilians. (Hyrum Smith,
Testimony, Nauvoo, IL, 1 July 1843, p. 17, Nauvoo, IL, Records, CHL.)

God, in answer to the prayers of the saints, I have been preserved, and delivered out of their hands, and can again enjoy the society of my friends and brethren, whom I love; and to whom I feel united in bonds that are stronger than death: and in a state where I believe the laws are respected, and whose citizens, are humane and charitable.

During the time I was in the hands of my enemies; I must say, that although I felt great anxiety, respecting my family and friends, who were so inhumanly treated and abused; and who had to mourn the loss of their husbands and children, who had been slain; and after having been robbed of [p. 7] nearly all that they possessed be driven from their homes, and forced to wander as strangers in a strange country,[94] in order, that they might save themselves and their little ones, from the destructions they were threatened with in Missouri: yet, as far as I was concerned, I felt perfectly calm, and resigned to the will of my heavenly Father. I knew my innocency, as well as that of the saints; and that we had done nothing to deserve such treatment from the hands of our oppressors: consequently, I could look to that God, who has the hearts of all men in his hands, and who had saved me frequently from the gates of death, for deliverance: and notwithstanding that every avenue of escape seemed to be entirely closed, and death stared me in the face, and that my destruction was determined upon, as far as man was concerned; yet, from my first entrance into the camp, I felt an assurance, that I with my brethren and our families should be delivered. Yes, that still small voice, which has so often whispered consolation to my soul, in the depth of sorrow and distress, bade me be of good cheer,[95] and promised deliverance, which gave me great comfort: and although the heathen raged, and the people imagined vain things,[96] yet the Lord of hosts, the God of Jacob, was my refuge;[97] and when I cried unto him in the day of trouble, he delivered me; for which I call upon my soul, and and all that is within me, to bless and praise his holy name:[98] For although I was "troubled on every side, yet not distressed; perplexed, but not in despair; persecuted, but not forsaken; cast down, but not destroyed."[99]

The conduct of the saints under their accumulated wrongs and sufferings, has been praise-worthy; their courage, in defending their brethren from the ravages of mobs; their attachment to the cause of truth, under circumstances the most trying and distressing, which humanity can possibly endure; their

---

94. See Exodus 2:22.
95. See 1 Kings 19:12; Acts 23:11; and Book of Mormon, 1837 ed., 49 [1 Nephi 17:45].
96. See Psalm 2:1; and Acts 4:25.
97. See Psalm 46:7, 11.
98. See Psalms 50:15, 103:1.
99. See 2 Corinthians 4:8–9.

love to each other; their readiness to afford assistance to me, and my brethren who were confined in a dungeon; their sacrifices in leaving the state of Missouri, and assisting the poor widows and orphans, and securing them houses in a more hospitable land; all conspire to raise them in the estimation of all good and virtuous men; and has secured them the favor and approbation of Jehovah; and a name, as imperishable as eternity. And their virtuous deeds, and heroic actions, while in defence of truth and their brethren: will be fresh and bloom- ing; when the names of their oppressors shall either be entirely forgotten, or only remembered, for their barbarity and cruelty. Their attention and affec- tion to me, while in prison, will ever be remembered by me; and when I have seen them thrust away, and abused by the jailor and guard, when they came to do any kind offices, and to cheer our minds while we were in the gloomy prison house, gave me feellings, which I cannot describe, while those who wished to insult and abuse us, by their threats and blasphemous language, were applauded and had every encouragement given them.

However, thank God, we have been deliverd; and although, some of our beloved brethren, have had to seal their testimony with their blood; and have died martyrs to the cause of truth; yet,

> Short, though bitter was their pain;
> Everlasting is their joy.[100]

Let us not sorrow as "those without hope," the time is fast approaching, when we shall see them again; and rejoice together, without being affraid of wicked men: Yes, those who have slept in Christ, shall he bring with him,[101] when he shall come to be glorified in his saints, and admired by all those who believe: but to take vengeance upon his enemies, and all those who obey not the gos- pel. At that time, the hearts of the widow and fatherless shall be comforted; and every tear shall be wiped from off their faces.

The trials they have had to pass through, shall work together for their good,[102] and prepare them for the society of those, who have come up out of great tribulation; and have washed their robes, and made them white in the blood of the Lamb.[103] Marvel not then, if you are persecuted, but remember the words of the Savior, "The servant is not above his Lord, if they have persecuted

---

100. Quoted inexactly from Hannah More (1745–1833), "The True Heroes: or, The Noble Army of Martyrs." The original lines are "Short, tho' bitter were their woes / Everlasting is their joy." (*Works of Hannah More*, 1:187.)

101. See 1 Thessalonians 4:13–14.

102. See Romans 8:28; see also JS et al., Liberty, MO, to the church members and Edward Partridge, Quincy, IL, 20 Mar. 1839, in Revelations Collection, CHL [D&C 122:7].

103. See Revelation 7:14.

me, they will persecute you also;"[104] and that all the afflictions through which the saints have to pass, are in fulfillment of the words of [p. 8] the prophets, which have spoken since the world began. We shall therefore do well to discern the signs of the times, as we pass along, that the day of the Lord may not "overtake us as a thief in the night."[105] Afflictions, persecutions, imprisonments and deaths, we must expect according to the scriptures, which tell us, that the blood of those whose souls were under the altar, could not be avenged on them that dwell on the earth, until their brethren should be slain, as they were.[106]

If these transactions had taken place among barbarians, under the authority of a despot; or in a nation, where a certain religion is established according to law, and all others proscribed; then there might have been some shadow of defence offered. But can we realize, that in a land which is the cradle of Liberty and equal rights; and where the voice of the conquerors, who had vanquished our foes, had scarcely died away upon our ears, where we frequently mingled with those who had stood amidst the "battle and the breeze;"[107] and whose arms have been nerved in the defence of their country and liberty: whose institutions are the theme of philosophers and poets, and held up to the admiration of the whole civilized world. In the midst of all these scenes, with which we were surrounded, a persecution, the most unwarrantable, was commenced; and a tragedy, the most dreadful, was enacted, by a large portion of the inhabitants, of one of those free and independent States, which comprise this vast republic; and a deadly blow was struck at the institutions, for which our Fathers had fought many a hard battle, and for which, many a Patriot had shed his blood; and suddenly, was heard, amidst the voice of joy and gratitude for our national liberty, the voice of mourning, lamentation and woe. Yes, in this land, a mob, regardless of those laws, for which so much blood had been spilled, dead to every feeling of virtue and patriotism, which animate the bosom of freemen; fell upon a people whose religious faith was different from their own; and not only destroyed their homes, drove them away, and carried off their property, but murderd many a free born son of America. A tragedy, which has no parrallel in modern, and hardly in ancient times; even the face of the Red man would be ready to turn pale at the recital of it.

It would have been some consolation, if the authorities of the State had been innocent in this affair, but they are involved in the guilt thereof; and the blood of innocence, even of *children*, cry for vengeance upon them. I ask the

---

104. See John 15:20.

105. See Revelation, 25 Nov. 1834, in Doctrine and Covenants 99:2, 1835 ed. [D&C 106:4]; compare 2 Peter 3:10.

106. See Revelation 6:9–11.

107. Phrase taken from Thomas Campbell (1777–1844), "Ye Mariners of England: A Naval Ode."

citizens of this vast republic, whether such a state of things is to be suffered to pass unnoticed, and the hearts of widows, orphans and patriots, to be broken, and their wrongs left without redress? No! I invoke the genius of our constitution, I appeal to the patriotism of Americans, to stop this unlawful and unholy proceedure; and pray that God may defend this nation from the dreadful effects of such outrages. Is there not virtue in the body politic? Will not the people rise up in their majesty, and with that promptitude and zeal, which is so characteristic of them, discountenance such proceedings, by bringing the offenders to that purnishment which they so richly deserve; and save the nation from that disgrace and ultimate ruin, which otherwise must inevitably fall upon it?

JOSEPH SMITH JR.

"CHURCH HISTORY,"
1 MARCH 1842

Source Note

JS, "Church History," in Times and Seasons *(Nauvoo, IL), 1 Mar. 1842, vol. 3, no. 9 (whole no. 45), pp. 706–710; edited by JS; includes typeset signature. The copy used for transcription is currently part of a bound volume held at CHL; includes later underlining.*

The five-page article is the second item in this number of the *Times and Seasons*. The issue comprises eight leaves, making sixteen pages that measure 9 × 5¾ inches (23 × 15 cm). The text on each page is set in two columns. The copy used for transcription has apparently been in continuous church custody since its purchase in the early twentieth century.[1]

Historical Introduction

In 1842, Boston lawyer George Barstow asked his friend John Wentworth, owner and editor of the weekly *Chicago Democrat*, to write to JS requesting a summary of the doctrines and history of the Latter-day Saints. Barstow was working on a history of New Hampshire, and he sought information about the Mormons for possible inclusion in the book. Barstow ultimately made 1819 the closing date of his study, and because the Mormons did not organize as a church until 1830, they did not have a place in his volume. JS's essay was published instead as "Church History" in the church's newspaper *Times and Seasons*.[2]

Opportunities for favorable treatment of the church in non-Mormon publications were rare, and some previous attempts had not been entirely successful. On 4 January 1833, JS wrote a letter to N. C. Saxton, editor of the New York newspaper *American Revivalist, and Rochester Observer.* JS told Saxton that the letter had been written "by the commandment of God" and asked the editor to publish the entire letter, but Saxton published only excerpts. JS wrote again on 12 February 1833 asking that the whole of his previous letter be

---

1. A previous owner's bookplate and stamp are found on the inside front cover, as is the selling price of the volume, marked in graphite now erased. A blank flyleaf has the same previous owner's stamp.

2. George Barstow, *The History of New Hampshire from Its Discovery, in 1614, to the Passage of the Toleration Act, in 1819* (Concord, NH: I. S. Boyd, 1842). Barstow's initial interest in Mormonism may have been prompted by recent Latter-day Saint missionary activity and church growth in New Hampshire and Massachusetts. (See Eli P. Maginn, Salem, MA, to JS, Nauvoo, IL, 22 Mar. 1842, *Times and Seasons*, 2 May 1842, 3:778–779; see also Williams, "Missionary Movements of the LDS Church in New England," 128–133, 147–156.)

706

vah, and I know the end from the beginning, therefore, my hand shall be over thee, and I will make of thee a great nation, and I will bless thee above measure, and make thy name great among all nations, and thou shalt be a blessing unto thy seed after thee, that in their hands they shall bear this ministry and priesthood unto all nations; and I will bless them through thy name; for as many as receive this gospel shall be called after thy name; and shall be accounted thy seed, and shall rise up and bless thee, as unto their father, and I will bless them that bless thee, and curse them that curse thee, and in thee, (that is, in thy Priesthood) and in thy seed, (that is thy Priesthood,) for I give unto thee a promise that this right shall continue in thee, and in thy seed after thee (that is to say, the literal seed, or the seed of the body,) shall all the families of the earth be blessed, even with the blessings of the gospel, which are the blessings of salvation, even of life eternal.

12. Now, after the Lord had withdrawn from speaking to me, and withdrawn his face from me, I said in mine heart, thy servent has sought thee earnestly, now I have found thee. Thou didst send thine angel to deliver me from the Gods of Elkenah, and I will do well to hearken unto thy voice, therefore let thy servant rise up and depart in peace. So I, Abram, departed as the Lord had said unto me, and Lot with me, and I, Abram, was sixty and two years old when I departed out of Haran. And I took Sarai, whom I took to wife when I was in Ur, in Chaldea, and Lot, my brother's son, and all our substance that we had gathered, and the souls that we had won in Haran, and came forth in the way to the land of Canaan, and dwelt in tents, as we came on our way: therefore, eternity was our covering, and our rock, and our salvation, as we journeyed from Haran by the way of Jershon, to come to the land of Canaan.

13. Now I, Abram, built an altar in the land of Jershon, and made an offering unto the Lord, and prayed that the famine might be turned away from my father's house, that they might not perish; and then we passed from Jershon through the land, unto the place of Sechem. It was situated in the plains of Moreh, and we had already came into the borders of the land of the Canaanites, and I offered sacrifice there in the plains of Moreh, and called on the Lord devoutly because we had already come into the land of this idolatrous nation.

CHURCH HISTORY.

At the request of Mr. John Wentworth, Editor, and Proprietor of the "Chicago Democrat," I have written the following sketch of the rise, progress, persecution, and faith of the Latter-Day Saints, of which I have the honor, under God, of being the founder. Mr. Wentworth says, that he wishes to furnish Mr. Bastow, a friend of his, who is writing the history of New Hampshire, with this document. As Mr. Bastow has taken the proper steps to obtain correct information all that I shall ask at his hands, is, that he publish the account entire, ungarnished, and without misrepresentation.

I was born in the town of Sharon Windsor co., Vermont, on the 23d of December, A. D. 1805. When ten years old my parents removed to Palmyra New York, where we resided about four years, and from thence we removed to the town of Manchester.

My father was a farmer and taught me the art of husbandry. When about fourteen years of age I began to reflect upon the importance of being prepared for a future state, and upon enquiring the plan of salvation I found that there was a great clash in religious sentiment; if I went to one society they referred me to one plan, and another to another; each one pointing to his own particular creed as the summum bonum of perfection: considering that all could not be right, and that God could not be the author of so much confusion I determined to investigate the subject more fully, believing that if God had a church it would not be split up into factions, and that if he taught one society to worship one way, and administer in one set of ordinances, he would not teach another principles which were diametrically opposed. Believing the word of God I had confidence in the declaration of James; "If any man lack wisdom let him ask of God who giveth to all men liberally and upbraideth not and it shall be given him," I retired to a secret place in a grove and began to call upon the Lord, while fervently engaged in supplication my mind was taken away from the objects with which I was surrounded, and I was enwrapped in a

Joseph Smith's "Church History" essay. In 1842, Joseph Smith received a letter from John Wentworth, asking him for information on the history and doctrines of the church. Wentworth's request was on behalf of his friend George Barstow, who was writing a history of New Hampshire. Although Barstow ultimately did not make use of the information, Joseph Smith's response, often referred to as the "Wentworth letter," was published in the church's newspaper. *Times and Seasons,* 1 Mar. 1842, 3:706 (transcribed on pp. 492–494 herein). (Church History Library, Salt Lake City. Photograph by Welden C. Andersen.)

"laid before the public," but Saxton did not publish it.[3] In 1836, in a volume titled *The Religious Creeds and Statistics of Every Christian Denomination in the United States and British Provinces,* editor John Hayward included a summary of the Book of Mormon and short excerpts from the Doctrine and Covenants as well as a statement of beliefs furnished by church member Joseph Young, but these materials were bracketed by negative statements from Isaac Hale (the father of JS's wife Emma Smith) and from the skeptical Hayward.[4] In 1839, the editor of the *St. Louis Gazette* asked church apostle John Taylor for an article about the church but then declined to print it; Taylor published the history himself as *A Short Account of the Murders, Roberies, Burnings, Thefts, and Other Outrages Committed by the Mob and Militia of the State of Missouri, upon the Latter Day Saints.*[5]

JS responded to Wentworth's request with a "sketch of the rise, progress, persecution, and faith of the Latter-Day Saints." In this history, which later came to be known among Latter-day Saints as the "Wentworth letter," JS recounted his first vision of Deity and the production of the Book of Mormon. He also included a thirteen-point summary of Latter-day Saint beliefs, known today as the Articles of Faith.[6] As he had done when he wrote Saxton nine years earlier, JS asked that Barstow "publish the account entire, ungarnished, and without misrepresentation."[7]

The essay appeared under the title "Church History" in the 1 March 1842 issue of the Nauvoo, Illinois, *Times and Seasons.*[8] No manuscript copy has been located, and it is not known how much of the history was originally written or dictated by JS. "Church History" echoes some wording from Orson Pratt's *A[n] Interesting Account of Several Remarkable Visions, and of the Late Discovery of Ancient American Records.*[9] Pratt's summary of church beliefs, upon which JS drew for the list of thirteen church beliefs in "Church History," was

---

3. "Mormonism," *American Revivalist, and Rochester [NY] Observer,* 2 Feb. 1833, [2]; JS, Kirtland, OH, to N. C. Saxton, Rochester, NY, 4 Jan. 1833, in JS Letterbook 1, pp. 14–18; JS, Kirtland, OH, to N. C. Saxton, Rochester, NY, 12 Feb. 1833, in JS Letterbook 1, p. 28.

4. Hayward, *Religious Creeds and Statistics,* 130–142. In 1842 Hayward published *The Book of Religions; Comprising the Views, Creeds, Sentiments, or Opinions, of All the Principal Religious Sects in the World, Particularly of All Christian Denominations in Europe and America; to Which Are Added Church and Missionary Statistics, together with Biographical Sketches* (Boston: John Hayward, 1842). After referring to the material on "Mormonites" in his 1836 volume, Hayward excerpted passages from "Church History." (Hayward, *Book of Religions,* 260–266.)

5. John Taylor, *A Short Account of the Murders, Roberies, Burnings, Thefts, and Other Outrages Committed by the Mob and Militia of the State of Missouri, upon the Latter Day Saints. The Persecutions They Have Endured for Their Religion, and Their Banishment from That State by the Authorities Thereof* ([Springfield, IL]: [By the author], [1839]).

6. In 1851, Franklin D. Richards published the Articles of Faith as part of a pamphlet titled *The Pearl of Great Price: Being a Choice Selection from the Revelations, Translations, and Narrations of Joseph Smith, First Prophet, Seer, and Revelator to the Church of Jesus Christ of Latter-day Saints.* The entire Pearl of Great Price, including the Articles of Faith, was canonized as scripture in 1880. (See Crawley, *Descriptive Bibliography,* 2:234–238; see also Whittaker, "Articles of Faith," 63–78.)

7. JS, "Church History," p. 492 herein.

8. The issue was published no earlier than 2 March, when JS read the proof sheets. (JS, Journal, 2 Mar. 1842, in *JSP,* J2:39–40.)

9. This document is transcribed in the appendix to the present volume. Light gray shading is employed in the appendix to indicate language or content later echoed in "Church History."

in turn based on a theological summary written by Parley P. Pratt.[10] Other individuals may have been involved in compiling the essay, including Willard Richards, who wrote extensively as JS's scribe during this period. Because William W. Phelps revised and expanded the text of "Church History" a year later in answer to a request from editor Israel Daniel Rupp, it is possible that Phelps helped compose the original essay.[11] However, Phelps's active role as scribe and composer for JS apparently did not commence until late 1842.

Whatever his debt to Phelps, Pratt, or others, JS took responsibility for "Church History" when it was published in the *Times and Seasons.* His name appears as author, and a note below his name further confirms his approval: "This paper commences my editorial career, I alone stand responsible for it, and shall do for all papers having my signature henceforward."[12] When the history was updated and sent to Rupp for publication, JS again accepted responsibility for the text.

———— ❧ ————

CHURCH HISTORY.

At the request of Mr. John Wentworth, Editor, and Proprietor of the "Chicago Democrat," I have written the following sketch of the rise, progress, persecution, and faith of the Latter-Day Saints, of which I have the honor, under God, of being the founder. Mr. Wentworth says, that he wishes to furnish Mr. Bastow [George Barstow], a friend of his, who is writing the history of New Hampshire, with this document. As Mr. Bastow has taken the proper steps to obtain correct information all that I shall ask at his hands, is, that he publish the account entire, ungarnished, and without misrepresentation.

I was born in the town of Sharon Windsor co., Vermont, on the 23d of December, A. D. 1805. When ten years old my parents removed to Palmyra New York,[13] where we resided about four years, and from thence we removed to the town of Manchester.[14]

My father was a farmer and taught me the art of husbandry.[15] When about fourteen years of age I began to reflect upon the importance of being prepared for a future state, and upon enquiring the plan of salvation I found that there

---

10. See Pratt and Higbee, *An Address . . . to the Citizens of Washington;* compare Pratt, *Late Persecution of the Church,* iii–xiii.

11. See pp. 503–506 herein.

12. "To Subscribers," *Times and Seasons,* 1 Mar. 1842, 3:710; see also Woodruff, Journal, 3 Feb. 1842.

13. Joseph Smith Sr. left Vermont in late summer or early fall 1816, when JS was ten years old. The rest of the Smith family joined him in Palmyra in early 1817, shortly after JS turned eleven. (Palmyra, NY, Record of Highway Taxes, 1817, Copies of Old Village Records, 1793–1867, microfilm 812,869, U.S. and Canada Record Collection, FHL; Lucy Mack Smith, History, 1844–1845, bk. 3, [3]–[6]; JS History, vol. A-1, 131nA.)

14. On the Smiths' move from Palmyra village, see 205n40 herein.

15. Some of the following language used to describe JS's early visions quotes Orson Pratt's *Interesting Account.* (See appendix herein.)

John Wentworth. 1847. As a favor to a friend, John Wentworth, a newspaper editor and lawyer, asked Joseph Smith for a summary of Latter-day Saint history and doctrine. The summary, often referred to as the "Wentworth letter," was published in 1842 in the church newspaper *Times and Seasons*. This photograph was taken during Wentworth's tenure in the United States House of Representatives. (Courtesy Chicago History Museum.)

was a great clash in religious sentiment; if I went to one society they referred me to one plan, and another to another; each one pointing to his own particular creed as the summum bonum of perfection: considering that all could not be right, and that God could not be the author of so much confusion I determined to investigate the subject more fully, believing that if God had a church it would not be split up into factions, and that if he taught one society to worship one way, and administer in one set of ordinances, he would not teach another principles which were diametrically opposed. Believing the word of God I had confidence in the declaration of James; "If any man lack wisdom let him ask of God who giveth to all men liberally and upbraideth not and it shall be given him,"[16] I retired to a secret place in a grove and began to call upon the Lord, while fervently engaged in supplication my mind was taken away from the objects with which I was surrounded, and I was enwrapped in a [p. 706] heavenly vision and saw two glorious personages who exactly resembled each other in features, and likeness, surrounded with a brilliant light which eclipsed the sun at noon-day.[17] They told me that all religious denominations were believing in incorrect doctrines, and that none of them was acknowledged of God as his church and kingdom. And I was expressly commanded to "go not after them,"[18] at the same time receiving a promise that the fulness of the gospel should at some future time be made known unto me.

On the evening of the 21st of September, A. D. 1823, while I was praying unto God, and endeavoring to exercise faith in the precious promises of scripture on a sudden a light like that of day, only of a far purer and more glorious appearance, and brightness burst into the room, indeed the first sight was as though the house was filled with consuming fire; the appearance produced a shock that affected the whole body; in a moment a personage stood before me surrounded with a glory yet greater than that with which I was already surrounded.[19] This messenger proclaimed himself to be an angel of God sent to bring the joyful tidings, that the covenant which God made with ancient Israel was at hand to be fulfilled, that the preparatory work for the second coming of the Messiah was speedily to commence; that the time was at hand

---

16. James 1:5.

17. JS identified these two personages as God the Father and Jesus Christ. (JS History Drafts, 1838–ca. 1841, p. 214 herein; see also JS History, ca. summer 1832, pp. 11–13 herein; JS, Journal, 9–11 Nov. 1835, in *JSP*, J1:87–88 [see also later version, pp. 115–116 herein]; and JS, "Latter Day Saints," p. 508 herein.)

18. See Luke 17:23.

19. JS also recounted this experience in JS History, ca. summer 1832, pp. 13–14 herein; JS, Journal, 9–11 Nov. 1835, in *JSP*, J1:88–89 (see also later version, pp. 116–117 herein); JS History Drafts, 1838–ca. 1841, pp. 220–233 herein; and JS, "Latter Day Saints," pp. 508–509 herein. He previously identified the messenger as Moroni. ([JS], Editorial, *Elders' Journal*, July 1838, 42–44.)

for the gospel, in all its fulness to be preached in power, unto all nations that a people might be prepared for the millennial reign.

I was informed that I was chosen to be an instrument in the hands of God to bring about some of his purposes in this glorious dispensation.

I was also informed concerning the aboriginal inhabitants of this country, and shown who they were, and from whence they came; a brief sketch of their origin, progress, civilization, laws, governments, of their righteousness and iniquity, and the blessings of God being finally withdrawn from them as a people was made known unto me: I was also told where there was deposited some plates on which were engraven an abridgement of the records of the ancient prophets that had existed on this continent. The angel appeared to me three times the same night and unfolded the same things. After having received many visits from the angels of God unfolding the majesty, and glory of the events that should transpire in the last days, on the morning of the 22d of September A. D. 1827, the angel of the Lord delivered the records into my hands.[20]

These records were engraven on plates which had the appearance of gold, each plate was six inches wide and eight inches long and not quite so thick as common tin. They were filled with engravings, in Egyptian characters and bound together in a volume, as the leaves of a book with three rings running through the whole. The volume was something near six inches in thickness, a part of which was sealed. The characters on the unsealed part were small, and beautifully engraved. The whole book exhibited many marks of antiquity in its construction and much skill in the art of engraving. With the records was found a curious instrument which the ancients called "Urim and Thummim," which consisted of two transparent stones set in the rim of a bow fastened to a breastplate.

Through the medium of the Urim and Thummim I translated the record by the gift, and power of God.

In this important and interesting book the history of ancient America is unfolded, from its first settlement by a colony that came from the tower of Babel, at the confusion of languages to the beginning of the fifth century of the Christian era. We are informed by these records that America in ancient times has been inhabited by two distinct races of people. The first were called Jaredites and came directly from the tower of Babel. The second race came directly from the city of Jerusalem, about six hundred years before Christ. They were principally Israelites, of the descendants of Joseph. The Jaredites

20. Much of the following account of the gold plates quotes Orson Pratt's *Interesting Account.* (See appendix herein.)

were destroyed about the time that the Israelites came from Jerusalem, who succeeded them in the inheritance of the country. The principal nation of the second race fell in battle towards the close of the fourth century. The remnant are the Indians that now inhabit this country. This book also tells us that our Saviour made his appearance upon this continent after his resurrection, that he planted the gospel here in all its fulness, and richness, and power, and blessing; that they had apostles, prophets, pastors, teachers and evangelists; the same order, the same priesthood, the [p. 707] same ordinances, gifts, powers, and blessing, as was enjoyed on the eastern continent, that the people were cut off in consequence of their transgressions, that the last of their prophets who existed among them was commanded to write an abridgement of their prophesies, history &c., and to hide it up in the earth, and that it should come forth and be united with the bible for the accomplishment of the purposes of God in the last days. For a more particular account I would refer to the Book of Mormon, which can be purchased at Nauvoo, or from any of our travelling elders.

As soon as the news of this discovery was made known, false reports, misrepresentation and slander flew as on the wings of the wind in every direction, the house was frequently beset by mobs, and evil designing persons, several times I was shot at, and very narrowly escaped, and every device was made use of to get the plates away from me, but the power and blessing of God attended me, and several began to believe my testimony.

On the 6th of April, 1830, the "Church of Jesus Christ of Latter-Day Saints," was first organized in the town of Manchester, Ontario co., state of New York.²¹ Some few were called and ordained by the spirit of revelation, and

---

21. JS organized the church in 1830 as the "Church of Christ"; an 1838 revelation established the full name of the church as used here.ᵃ The earliest sources place the meeting at Fayette, New York, and later JS documents support this designation.ᵇ Some later documents, including the present history, locate the meeting at Manchester. The discrepancy may originate with William W. Phelps, who was not involved with the church at the time of its organization and therefore appears to have misidentified the location. While preparing the Book of Commandments for publication based on Revelation Book 1, the editors (who included Phelps) added "given in Manchester, NY" to a 6 April 1830 revelation in chapter 22.ᶜ Records linked to Phelps or Orson Pratt (who was also not present at the church's organizational meeting and who later spoke of Fayette as the correct location) state that the 6 April meeting took place in Manchester.ᵈ Later printings of the Doctrine and Covenants and Pratt's *Interesting Account* either omit references to Manchester as the site or revise the meeting place to Fayette.ᵉ (*a.* Articles and covenants, 10 Apr. 1830, in Doctrine and Covenants 2:1, 1835 ed. [D&C 20:1]; Revelation, 26 Apr. 1838, in JS, Journal, 26 Apr. 1838, in *JSP,* J1:258 [D&C 115:3–4]. *b.* Revelation, 6 Apr. 1830, in Revelation Book 1, p. 28, in *JSP,* MRB:27 [D&C 21]; JS History, vol. A-1, pp. 364–366 herein [Draft 2]. *c.* See Book of Commandments 22 [D&C 21]; compare Revelation Book 1, pp. 28–29, in *JSP,* MRB:27–29. *d.* "Prospects of the Church," *The Evening and the Morning Star,* Mar. 1833, [4]; Pratt, *Interesting Account,* p. 540 herein; Orson Pratt, in *Journal of Discourses,* 7 Oct. 1869, 13:193. *e.* Doctrine and Covenants 45–46, 1835 ed. [D&C 21, 23]; Pratt, *Remarkable Visions,* 12.)

prophesy, and began to preach as the spirit gave them utterance, and though weak, yet were they strengthened by the power of God, and many were brought to repentance, were immersed in the water, and were filled with the Holy Ghost by the laying on of hands. They saw visions and prophesied, devils were cast out and the sick healed by the laying on of hands. From that time the work rolled forth with astonishing rapidity, and churches were soon formed in the states of New York, Pennsylvania, Ohio, Indiana, Illinois and Missouri; in the last named state a considerable settlement was formed in Jackson co.; numbers joined the church and we were increasing rapidly; we made large purchases of land, our farms teemed with plenty, and peace and happiness was enjoyed in our domestic circle and throughout our neighborhood; but as we could not associate with our neighbors who were many of them of the basest of men and had fled from the face of civilized society, to the frontier country to escape the hand of justice, in their midnight revels, their sabbath breaking, horseracing, and gambling, they commenced at first ridicule, then to persecute, and finally an organized mob assembled and burned our houses, tarred, and feathered, and whipped many of our brethren and finally drove them from their habitations; who houseless, and homeless, contrary to law, justice and humanity, had to wander on the bleak prairies till the children left the tracks of their blood on the prairie, this took place in the month of November, and they had no other covering but the canopy of heaven, in this inclement season of the year; this proceeding was winked at by the government and although we had warrantee deeds for our land, and had violated no law we could obtain no redress.

There were many sick, who were thus inhumanly driven from their houses, and had to endure all this abuse and to seek homes where they could be found. The result was, that a great many of them being deprived of the comforts of life, and the necessary attendances, died; many children were left orphans; wives, widows; and husbands widowers.— Our farms were taken possession of by the mob, many thousands of cattle, sheep, horses, and hogs, were taken and our household goods, store goods, and printing press, and type were broken, taken, or otherwise destroyed.

Many of our brethren removed to Clay where they continued until 1836, three years; there was no violence offered but there were threatnings of violence. But in the summer of 1836, these threatnings began to assume a more serious form; from threats, public meetings were called, resolutions were passed, vengeance and destruction were threatened, and affairs again assumed a fearful attitude, Jackson county was a sufficient precedent, and as the authorities in that county did not interfere, they boasted that they would not in this, which on application to the authorities we found to be too true, and after much violence, privation and loss of property we were again driven from our homes.[22]

We next settled in Caldwell, and Davies[s] counties, where we made large and extensive settlements, thinking to free ourselves from the power of oppression, by settling in new counties, with very few inhabitants in them; but here we were not allowed to live in peace, but in 1838 we were again attacked by mobs [p. 708] an exterminating order was issued by Gov. [Lilburn W.] Boggs,[23] and under the sanction of law an organized banditti ranged through the country, robbed us of our cattle, sheep, horses, hogs &c., many of our people were murdered in cold blood,[24] the chastity of our women was violated, and we were forced to sign away our property at the point of the sword, and after enduring every indignity that could be heaped upon us by an inhuman, ungodly band of maurauders, from twelve to fifteen thousand souls men, women, and children were driven from their own fire sides, and from lands that they had warrantee deeds of, houseless, friendless, and homeless (in the depth of winter,) to wander as exiles on the earth or to seek an asylum in a more genial clime, and among a less barbarous people.[25]

Many sickened and died, in consequence of the cold, and hardships they had to endure; many wives were left widows, and children orphans, and destitute. It would take more time than is allotted me here to describe the injustice, the wrongs, the murders, the bloodshed, the theft, misery and woe that has been caused by the barbarous, inhuman, and lawless, proceedings of the state of Missouri.

In the situation before alluded to we arrived in the state of Illinois in 1839, where we found a hospitable people and a friendly home; a people who were willing to be governed by the principles of law and humanity. We have commenced to build a city called "Nauvoo" in Hancock co., we number from six

---

22. Although some of the original settlers of Clay County were determined to see the Latter-day Saints leave the county, the conditions surrounding the Saints' departure were markedly less violent than was the earlier episode in Jackson County. (See Parkin, "History of the Latter-day Saints in Clay County," chap. 8.)

23. Boggs charged the state militia with restoring peace to northwest Missouri. If necessary, the governor ordered, the Mormons were to be "exterminated or driven from the state." (Lilburn W. Boggs, Jefferson City, MO, to John B. Clark, Fayette, MO, 27 Oct. 1838, Mormon War Papers, MSA.)

24. About twenty Mormons were killed during the "Mormon War" in Missouri. (LeSueur, *1838 Mormon War in Missouri*, 162–168; Baugh, "Call to Arms," 238–240, 253–298.)

25. Although the number of Mormons driven from Missouri is unknown, the estimate of "twelve to fifteen thousand" appears to be too high. Others estimated that about eight thousand Mormons were driven from Missouri. (Eliza R. Snow, Caldwell Co., MO, to Isaac Streator, Streetsborough, OH, 22 Feb. 1839, photocopy, CHL; see also Hartley, "Almost Too Intolerable a Burthen," 7n2.)

to eight thousand here[26] besides vast numbers in the county around and in almost every county of the state. We have a city charter granted us and a charter for a legion the troops of which now number 1500. We have also a charter for a university, for an agricultural and manufacturing society, have our own laws and administrators, and possess all the privileges that other free and enlightened citizens enjoy.[27]

Persecution has not stopped the progress of truth, but has only added fuel to the flame, it has spread with increasing rapidity, proud of the cause which they have espoused and conscious of their innocence and of the truth of their system amidst calumny and reproach have the elders of this church gone forth, and planted the gospel in almost every state in the Union; it has penetrated our cities, it has spread over our villages, and has caused thousands of our intelligent, noble, and patriotic citizens to obey its divine mandates, and be governed by its sacred truths. It has also spread into England, Ireland, Scotland and Wales: in the year of 1839 where a few of our missionaries were sent over five thousand joined the standard of truth,[28] there are numbers now joining in every land.

Our missionaries are going forth to different nations, and in Germany, Palestine, New Holland, the East Indies, and other places, the standard of truth has been erected:[29] no unhallowed hand can stop the work from progressing,

---

26. This may be an overstatement of the Nauvoo population. Although some estimates ran even higher (an article in the 1 October 1842 issue of the *Times and Seasons* described "a population of 14 or 15,000"), a circa February 1842 church census listed 3,413 Latter-day Saints in Nauvoo. ("Nauvoo," *Times and Seasons,* 1 Oct. 1842, 3:936–937; Platt, *Nauvoo,* vii; Leonard, *Nauvoo,* 179.)

27. The Nauvoo charter was passed by the Illinois legislature and signed by the governor in December 1840. It included a provision for a city university. The agricultural and manufacturing association was incorporated in February 1841. (*Journal of the Senate . . . of Illinois,* 9 Dec. 1840, 61; *Journal of the House of Representatives . . . of Illinois,* 12 Dec. 1840, 110; An Act to Incorporate the City of Nauvoo [16 Dec. 1840], *Laws of the State of Illinois* [1840–1841], 52–57; An Act to Incorporate the Nauvoo Agricultural and Manufacturing Association, in the County of Hancock [27 Feb. 1841], *Laws of the State of Illinois* [1840–1841], 139–141.)

28. A revelation dated 8 July 1838 commanded the Quorum of the Twelve to depart on a mission to Europe. Most of the quorum, along with several other missionaries, left Commerce, Illinois, in 1839, arriving in England in April 1840. They proselytized throughout the British Isles until April 1841, adding approximately five thousand people to the church. (Revelation, 8 July 1838–A, in JS, Journal, 8 July 1838, in *JSP,* J1:285 [D&C 118]; Allen et al., *Men with a Mission,* 54–302.)

29. Although this description of global missionary work reflected assignments and endeavors that had begun by this time, the effort was still in its infancy. After being appointed to fulfill a mission to the Jews, Orson Hyde traveled to Jerusalem, where on 24 October 1841 he dedicated the land in preparation for the gathering of "Judah's scattered remnants."[a] In July 1840, English convert William James Barratt emigrated to New Holland (now Australia) after being ordained an elder by George A. Smith.[b] The *Times and Seasons* noted that "Elder William Donaldson, member of the army" was "bound for the East Indies."[c] Simeon Carter was assigned to Germany, but the call was suspended.[d] (a. Orson Hyde, "Interesting News from Alexandria and Jerusalem," *LDS Millennial Star,* Jan. 1842, 2:132–136; see also Hyde, *Voice from*

persecutions may rage, mobs may combine, armies may assemble, calumny may defame, but the truth of God will go forth boldly, nobly, and independent till it has penetrated every continent, visited every clime, swept every country, and sounded in every ear, till the purposes of God shall be accomplished and the great Jehovah shall say the work is done.

We believe in God the Eternal Father, and in his son Jesus Christ, and in the Holy Ghost.

We believe that men will be punished for their own sins and not for Adam's transgression.

We believe that through the atonement of Christ all mankind may be saved by obedience to the laws and ordinances of the Gospel.

We believe that these ordinances are 1st, Faith in the Lord Jesus Christ; 2d, Repentance; 3d, Baptism by immersion for the remission of sins; 4th, Laying on of hands for the gift of the Holy Ghost.

We believe that a man must be called of God by "prophesy, and by laying on of hands"[30] by those who are in authority to preach the gospel and administer in the ordinances thereof.

We believe in the same organization that existed in the primitive church, viz: apostles, prophets, pastors, teachers, evangelists &c.[31]

We believe in the gift of tongues, prophesy, revelation, visions, healing, interpretation of tongues &c.

We believe the bible to be the word of God as far as it is translated correctly; we also believe the Book of Mormon to be the word of God.

We believe all that God has revealed, all that he does now reveal, and we be[p. 709]lieve that he will yet reveal many great and important things pertaining to the kingdom of God.

We believe in the literal gathering of Israel and in the restoration of the Ten Tribes. That Zion will be built upon this continent. That Christ will reign personally upon the earth, and that the earth will be renewed and receive its paradasaic glory.

We claim the privilege of worshipping Almighty God according to the dictates of our conscience, and allow all men the same privilege let them worship how, where, or what they may.

We believe in being subject to kings, presidents, rulers, and magistrates, in obeying, honoring and sustaining the law.

Jerusalem, 6–35. *b.* Devitry-Smith, "William James Barratt," 53–66. *c.* "News from the Elders," *Times and Seasons,* 1 Dec. 1840, 2:229. *d.* JS History, vol. C-1, 1224.)

30. See 1 Timothy 4:14.
31. See Ephesians 4:11.

We believe in being honest, true, chaste, benevolent, virtuous, and in doing good to *all men;* indeed we may say that we follow the admonition of Paul "we believe all things we hope all things,"[32] we have endured many things and hope to be able to endure all things. If there is any thing virtuous, lovely, or of good report or praise worthy we seek after these things.[33] Respectfully &c.,

JOSEPH SMITH.

---

32. See 1 Corinthians 13:7.
33. See Philippians 4:8.

I. D. Rupp's *Original History of the Religious Denominations.* Sometime in May or June 1844, Joseph Smith received a copy of *He Pasa Ekklesia* [The whole church]: *An Original History of the Religious Denominations at Present Existing in the United States,* to which he had contributed an essay titled "Latter Day Saints." On 5 June 1844, he wrote to editor Israel Daniel Rupp, expressing thanks for "so valueable a treasure" and praising "the design, the propriety, the wisdom of letting every sect tell its own story" (see p. 504 herein). As was common in books of the time, the title on the spine differs from the longer title on the title page itself. (Copy in private possession. Photograph by Welden C. Andersen.)

"LATTER DAY SAINTS," 1844

Source Note

JS, "Latter Day Saints," pp. 404–410 in Israel Daniel Rupp (ed.), He Pasa Ekklesia *[The whole church].* An Original History of the Religious Denominations at Present Existing in the United States. Containing Authentic Accounts of Their Rise, Progress, Statistics and Doctrines. Written Expressly for the Work by Eminent Theological Professors, Ministers, and Lay-Members, of the Respective Denominations. Projected, Compiled and Arranged by I. Daniel Rupp, of Lancaster, Pa. Author of "Der Maertyrer Geschichte," Etc. Etc.; *Philadelphia: James Y. Humphreys; Harrisburg, PA: Clyde and Williams; printed by C. Sherman; 1844; i–viii, 9–734 pp. The copy used for transcription is held at CHL; includes redactions and archival marking.*

The history is the twenty-second of forty-three chapters in the volume. It comprises seven pages that measure 9⅛ × 5⅝ inches (23 × 14 cm) within a book measuring 9½ × 6½ × 2 inches (24 × 17 × 5 cm). The copy used for transcription has apparently been in continuous church custody since its purchase in 1905.[1]

Historical Introduction

In July 1843, JS received a letter from Clyde, Williams & Co. of Harrisburg, Pennsylvania, announcing the planned publication of a volume of articles "written expressly for the Work, by distinguished Divines" from various religious denominations in the United States. The letter invited JS or "some other competent person" representing the Latter-day Saints to submit an "impartial account of the Rise and Progress, Faith and Practice" of the church.[2] On behalf of JS, William W. Phelps prepared a letter in reply, promising that an article would be "matured and forwarded in season to meet your anticipations."[3]

---

1. This copy was purchased 21 June 1905 from a Salt Lake City bookstore for the Church Historian's Office. The lower right corner of the inside front cover bears a sticker of the bookstore, "Shepard Book Company", and the upper left corner bears a sticker of the "Historian's Office Library". Several "Historian's Office" stamps are found throughout the book, including on the first page of the essay on the Latter-day Saints. A notation on the recto of the blank leaf preceding the title page indicates the day of purchase and a library number, "3493", written in ink and later erased. "3493" corresponds to an entry made sometime after 1930 in an early Church Historian's Office catalog book. ("Library Record," book no. 3493.)

2. Clyde, Williams & Co., Harrisburg, PA, to JS, Nauvoo, IL, ca. 15 July 1843, JS Collection, CHL.

3. JS per William W. Phelps, Nauvoo, IL, to Clyde, Williams & Co., Harrisburg, PA, 1 Aug. 1843, JS Collection, CHL. Volumes describing various religious denominations were not uncommon in this

The resulting essay, published as "Latter Day Saints," was a revised version of "Church History," an overview of Latter-day Saint history and doctrine recently written in response to a similar request and published in the church newspaper.[4] Taken as a whole, the revisions highlight JS's emphasis on revelation, with a new opening paragraph explaining the revelatory foundations of the church and JS's prophetic calling. The revised essay, composed in September 1843, also expanded on the achievements of the hardworking Latter-day Saints, noting the progress of Nauvoo, Illinois, during the eighteen months since the publication of "Church History." Whereas the earlier version noted simply, "We have commenced to build a city called 'Nauvoo'" and alluded only briefly to the city charter, the Nauvoo Legion, and the Saints' missionary outreach, "Latter Day Saints" elaborated on these now-implemented plans.[5] The Nauvoo Legion was growing in numbers, and the University of Nauvoo was to be a place "where all the arts and sciences will grow." The newly begun temple received a descriptive paragraph of its own. While "Church History" emphasized the departure of missionaries to many parts of the world, the updated version announced that "thousands have already gathered with their kindred saints, to this the cornerstone of Zion."

"Latter Day Saints" was written on behalf of JS and appeared under his name. JS approved of and may have collaborated on the content, but apparently it was William W. Phelps who wrote the additions to "Church History." Phelps's handwriting appears in a three-page document containing drafts of passages that correspond to the changes to "Church History," including both the initial paragraph of the revised text and the new section that precedes the concluding list of beliefs. The verso of the document's second page reads, "Additions to an article in the Times & Seasons. Sent to Clyde Williams and Co. Publishe[r]s—Harrisburgh—September—1843."[6] In early April 1844, JS's essay was published in the volume *He Pasa Ekklesia* [The whole church], edited by German-American author and translator Israel Daniel Rupp.[7] The text presented herein is a transcription of the published version, with notes indicating textual variations from Phelps's draft and from "Church History."

On 5 June 1844, JS wrote to Rupp acknowledging receipt of a copy of *He Pasa Ekklesia*: "I feel very thankful for so valueable a treasure. The design, the propriety, the wisdom of letting every sect tell its own story; and the elegant manner in which the work appears,

---

time period. In addition to John Hayward's 1836 *Religious Creeds and Statistics,* Robert Baird published *A View of Religion in America* in Glasgow in 1842, with a revised edition, titled *Religion in America,* printed in the United States two years later and reprinted many times thereafter. Other examples are P. Douglass Gorrie, *The Churches and Sects of the United States* (New York: Lewis Colby, 1850), and Joseph Belcher, *The Religious Denominations in the United States* (Philadelphia: J. E. Potter, 1854). Rupp's volume is distinctive in that it is a collection of essays written by representatives of the respective denominations.

4. See JS, "Church History," pp. 489–501 herein. When JS composed "Church History," he quoted from Orson Pratt's *A[n] Interesting Account of Several Remarkable Visions,* reproduced in the appendix herein. Light gray shading in the appendix indicates language used in "Church History" and in "Latter Day Saints."

5. JS, "Church History," pp. 498–499 herein.

6. William W. Phelps, "Additions to an Article in the Times & Seasons," Sept. 1843, CHL.

7. The book was published in or shortly after April 1844, the date found in its preface. (Rupp, *He Pasa Ekklesia,* vi.)

HARRISBURG, July   , 1843.

Sir: We, the undersigned, have it in contemplation to publish a work, entitled

HE PAS'ECCLESIA,

OR

THE WHOLE CHURCH OF THE UNITED STATES:

Consisting of entirely Original Articles, written expressly for the Work, by distinguished Divines, belonging to the several Denominations in the United States; and comprising an accurate and impartial account of the Rise and Progress, Faith and Practice of each Denomination.

Such a Work, we believe to be a desideratum; and would, no doubt, be eminently useful to all classes of a reading community.

But, to get up a good and valuable work===such as we believe to be needed, and as we intend ours to be===we have taken the liberty, hereby, to address you; and respectfully to request that you furnish the requisite Article of the Church to which you belong, either from your own pen, or through some other competent person in your denomination.

We confidently hope that you will comply with our wishes, and have the desired Article furnished with as little delay as possible, as we desire to publish the Work the ensuing Fall.

For your kindness and trouble in this business, we will allow you, if requested, any reasonable remuneration.

Please to inform us, by return of mail, what you are disposed to do for us in this matter;

And you will much oblige, your's truly,

CLYDE, WILLIAMS & Co.

To Elder J. Smith

Navoo

Illinois

Request for essay on church. Clyde, Williams & Co., publishers in Harrisburg, Pennsylvania, wrote to Joseph Smith asking that he or "some other competent person" contribute an article on the "Rise and Progress, Faith and Practice" of the Latter-day Saints to a forthcoming collection of essays on various denominations. William W. Phelps responded on 1 August 1843, promising that the requested article was forthcoming. In 1844 Joseph Smith's essay, "Latter Day Saints," was published in *He Pasa Ekklesia* [The whole church]: *An Original History of the Religious Denominations at Present Existing in the United States.* Clyde, Williams & Co., Harrisburg, PA, to JS, Nauvoo, IL, ca. 15 July 1843, JS Collection, Church History Library, Salt Lake City. (Photograph by Welden C. Andersen.)

have filled my breast with encomiums upon it, wishing you <u>God's speed</u>." He continued, "I shall be pleased to furnish further information, at a proper time, and render you such service as the work, and vast extension of our church may demand for the benefit of truth, virtue, and holiness." He then assured Rupp that "your work will be suitably noticed in our paper, for your benefit."[8] On 26 June, the day before JS was killed, the promised endorsement appeared in the Mormon-owned community newspaper, the *Nauvoo Neighbor,* noting that "every sect is its own witness" and declaring, "Such a work is actually worth its weight in gold. The author has our blessing for his success."[9]

─────── ❧ ───────

LATTER DAY SAINTS.
BY JOSEPH SMITH.
NAUVOO, ILLINOIS.

THE Church of Jesus Christ of Latter Day Saints, was founded upon direct revelation, as the true church of God has ever been, according to the scriptures (Amos, iii. 7, and Acts i. 2.) And through the will and blessings of God, I have been an instrument in his hands, thus far, to move forward the cause of Zion. Therefore, in order to fulfil the solicitation of your letter of July last, I shall commence with my life.[10]

I was born in the town of Sharon, Windsor county, Vermont, on the 23d of December, A. D. 1805. When ten years old, my parents removed to Palmyra, New York,[11] where we resided about four years, and from thence we removed to the town of Manchester, a distance of six miles.[12]

My father was a farmer, and taught me the art of husbandry. When about fourteen years of age, I began to reflect upon the importance of being prepared for a future state; and upon inquiring the place[13] of salvation, I found that there was a great clash in religious sentiment; if I went to one society they referred me to one place, and another to another; each one pointing to his own particular creed as the "summum bonum" of perfection. Considering that all could not be right, and that God could not be the author of so much confusion,

─────────────────

8. JS, Nauvoo, IL, to Israel Daniel Rupp, Lancaster City, PA, 5 June 1844, copy, JS Collection, CHL.

9. "He Pasa Ekklesia," *Nauvoo Neighbor,* 26 June 1844, [2].

10. This first paragraph is based on William W. Phelps, "Additions to an Article in the Times & Seasons," Sept. 1843, CHL.

11. Joseph Smith Sr. left Vermont in late summer or early fall 1816, when JS was ten years old. The rest of the Smith family joined him in Palmyra in early 1817, shortly after JS turned eleven. (Palmyra, NY, Record of Highway Taxes, 1817, Copies of Old Village Records, 1793–1867, microfilm 812,869, U.S. and Canada Record Collection, FHL; Lucy Mack Smith, History, 1844–1845, bk. 3, [3]–[6]; JS History, vol. A-1, 131nA.)

12. The last five words do not appear in "Church History." On the Smiths' move from Palmyra village, see 205n40 herein.

13. For both instances of "place" in this sentence, "Church History" has "plan." (See p. 492 herein.)

LATTER DAY SAINTS.

BY JOSEPH SMITH,
NAUVOO, ILLINOIS.

THE Church of Jesus Christ of Latter Day Saints, was founded upon direct revelation, as the true church of God has ever been, according to the scriptures (Amos, iii. 7, and Acts i. 2.) And through the will and blessings of God, I have been an instrument in his hands, thus far, to move forward the cause of Zion. Therefore, in order to fulfil the solicitation of your letter of July last, I shall commence with my life.

I was born in the town of Sharon, Windsor county, Vermont, on the 23d of December, A. D. 1805. When ten years old, my parents removed to Palmyra, New York, where we resided about four years, and from thence we removed to the town of Manchester, a distance of six miles.

My father was a farmer, and taught me the art of husbandry. When about fourteen years of age, I began to reflect upon the importance of being prepared for a future state; and upon inquiring the place of salvation, I found that there was a great clash in religious sentiment; if I went to one society they referred me to one place, and another to another; each one pointing to his own particular creed as the "summum bonum" of perfection. Considering that all could not be right, and that God could not be the author of so much confusion, I determined to investigate the subject more fully, believing that if God had a church, it would not be split up into factions, and that if he taught one society to worship one way, and administer in one set of ordinances, he would not teach another principles which were diametrically opposed. Believing the word of God, I had confidence in the declaration of James, "If any man lack wisdom let him ask of God, who giveth to all men liberally and upbraideth not, and it shall be given him."

I retired to a secret place in a grove, and began to call upon the

---

First page of Joseph Smith's "Latter Day Saints" essay. Joseph Smith's essay "Latter Day Saints" was one of forty-three contributions included in I. D. Rupp's *An Original History of the Religious Denominations at Present Existing in the United States.* "Latter Day Saints" duplicates much of "Church History" (also known as the "Wentworth letter"), but one addition composed especially for "Latter Day Saints" is the opening paragraph, setting forth the role of revelation. The "Historian's Office" stamp at the top of the page is a later archival designation. Rupp, *He Pasa Ekklesia,* 404 (transcribed on pp. 506–508 herein). (Church History Library, Salt Lake City. Photograph by Welden C. Andersen.)

I determined to investigate the subject more fully, believing that if God had a church, it would not be split up into factions, and that if he taught one society to worship one way, and administer in one set of ordinances, he would not teach another principles which were diametrically opposed. Believing the word of God, I had confidence in the declaration of James, "If any man lack wisdom let him ask of God, who giveth to all men liberally and upbraideth not, and it shall be given him."[14]

I retired to a secret place in a grove, and began to call upon the [p. 404] Lord. While fervently engaged in supplication, my mind was taken away from the objects with which I was surrounded, and I was enrapt in a heavenly vision, and saw two glorious personages, who exactly resembled each other in features and likeness, surrounded with a brilliant light, which eclipsed the sun at noonday.[15] They told me that all the religious denominations were believing in incorrect doctrines, and that none of them was acknowledged of God as his church and kingdom. And I was expressly commanded to "go not after them,"[16] at the same time receiving a promise that the fulness of the gospel should at some future time be made known unto me.

On the evening of the 21st September, A. D. 1823, while I was praying unto God and endeavouring to exercise faith in the precious promises of scripture, on a sudden a light like that of day, only of a far purer and more glorious appearance and brightness, burst into the room; indeed the first sight was as though the house was filled with consuming fire. The appearance produced a shock that affected the whole body. In a moment a personage stood before me surrounded with a glory yet greater than that with which I was already surrounded.[17] This messenger proclaimed himself to be an angel of God, sent to bring the joyful tidings, that the covenant which God made with ancient Israel was at hand to be fulfilled; that the preparatory work for the second coming of the Messiah was speedily to commence; that the time was at hand for the gospel in all its fulness to be preached in power, unto all nations, that a people might be prepared for the millennial reign.

---

14. James 1:5.

15. JS identified these two personages as God the Father and Jesus Christ. (JS History Drafts, 1838–ca. 1841, p. 214 herein; see also JS History, ca. summer 1832, pp. 11–13 herein; JS, Journal, 9–11 Nov. 1835, in *JSP*, J1:87–88 [see also later version, p. 115–116 herein]; and JS, "Church History," p. 494 herein.)

16. See Luke 17:23.

17. JS also recounted this experience in JS History, ca. summer 1832, pp. 13–14 herein; JS, Journal, 9–11 Nov. 1835, in *JSP*, J1:88–89 (see also later version, pp. 116–117 herein); JS History Drafts, 1838–ca. 1841, pp. 220–233 herein; and JS, "Church History," pp. 494–495 herein. He previously identified the messenger as Moroni. ([JS], Editorial, *Elders' Journal*, July 1838, 42–44.)

I was informed that I was chosen to be an instrument in the hands of God to bring about some of his purposes in this glorious dispensation.

I was informed also concerning the aboriginal inhabitants of this country, and shown who they were, and from whence they came;— a brief sketch of their origin, progress, civilization, laws, governments, of their righteousness and iniquity, and the blessings of God being finally withdrawn from them as a people, was made known unto me. I was also told where there was deposited some plates, on which was engraven an abridgment of the records of the ancient prophets that had existed on this continent. The angel appeared to me three times the same night and unfolded the same things. After having received many visits from the angels of God, unfolding the majesty and glory of the events that should transpire in the last days, on the morning of the 22d of September, A. D. 1827, the angel of the Lord delivered the records into my hands.

These records were engraven on plates which had the appearance of gold; each plate was six inches wide and eight inches long, and [p. 405] not quite so thick as common tin. They were filled with engravings in Egyptian characters, and bound together in a volume, as the leaves of a book, with three rings running through the whole. The volume was something near six inches in thickness, a part of which was sealed. The characters on the unsealed part were small and beautifully engraved. The whole book exhibited many marks of antiquity in its construction, and much skill in the art of engraving. With the records was found a curious instrument which the ancients called "Urim and Thummim," which consisted of two transparent stones set in the rim on[18] a bow fastened to a breastplate.

Through the medium of the Urim and Thummim I translated the record, by the gift and power of God.

In this important and interesting book the history of ancient America is unfolded, from its first settlement by a colony that came from the tower of Babel, at the confusion of languages, to the beginning of the fifth century of the Christian era.

We are informed by these records, that America, in ancient times, has been inhabited by two distinct races of people. The first were called Jaredites, and came directly from the tower of Babel. The second race came directly from the city of Jerusalem, about six hundred years before Christ. They were principally Israelites, of the descendants of Joseph. The Jaredites were destroyed, about the time that the Israelites came from Jerusalem, who succeeded them in the inheritance of the country. The principal nation of the second race fell in battle

---

18. "Church History" has "of." (See p. 495 herein.)

towards the close of the fourth century. The remnant are the Indians who now inhabit this country. This book also tells us that our Saviour made his appearance upon this continent after his resurrection; that he planted the gospel here in all its fulness, and richness, and power, and blessing; that they had apostles, prophets, pastors, teachers, and evangelists; the same order, the same priesthood, the same ordinances, gifts, powers, and blessing, as was enjoyed on the eastern continent; that the people were cut off in consequence of their transgressions; that the last of their prophets who existed among them was commanded to write an abridgment of their prophecies, history, &c., and to hide it up in the earth, and that it should come forth and be united with the Bible, for the accomplishment of the purposes of God, in the last days. For a more particular account, I would refer to the Book of Mormon, which can be purchased at Nauvoo, or from any of our travelling elders.

As soon as the news of this discovery was made known, false reports, misrepresentation and slander flew, as on the wings of the wind, in every direction; my house was frequently beset by mobs, [p. 406] and evil designing persons; several times I was shot at, and very narrowly escaped, and every device was made use of to get the plates away from me; but the power and blessing of God attended me, and several began to believe my testimony.

On the 6th April, 1830, the "Church of Jesus Christ of Latter Day Saints," was first organized, in the town of Manchester, Ontario Co., State of New York.[19] Some few were called and ordained by the Spirit of revelation and prophecy, and began to preach as the Spirit gave them utterance, and though weak, yet were they strengthened by the power of God; and many were brought to repentance, were immersed in the water, and were filled with the Holy Ghost by the laying on of hands. They saw visions and prophesied, devils were cast out, and the sick healed by the laying on of hands. From that time the work rolled forth with astonishing rapidity, and churches were soon formed in the States of New York, Pennsylvania, Ohio, Indiana, Illinois, and Missouri; in the last named state a considerable settlement was formed in Jackson county; numbers joined the church, and we were increasing rapidly; we made large purchases of land, our farms teemed with plenty, and peace and happiness were enjoyed in our domestic circle and throughout our neighbourhood; but as we could not associate with our neighbours,—who were, many of them, of the basest of men, and had fled from the face of civilized society to the frontier country, to escape the hand of justice—in their midnight revels, their sabbath-breaking, horse-racing, and gambling, they commenced at first to ridicule, then to persecute, and finally an organized mob assembled and

---

19. On the name of the church and the location of its organizational meeting, see 496n21 herein.

I. D. Rupp. Israel Daniel Rupp was the editor of *He Pasa Ekklesia* [The whole church]: *An Original History of the Religious Denominations at Present Existing in the United States.* This collection of essays, published in 1844, included Joseph Smith's "Latter Day Saints." (Courtesy Historical Society of Pennsylvania, Philadelphia.)

burned our houses, tarred and feathered and whipped many of our brethren, and finally drove them from their habitations; these, houseless and homeless, contrary to law, justice, and humanity, had to wander on the bleak prairies till the children left the tracks of their blood on the prairie. This took place in the month of November, and they had no other covering but the canopy of heaven, in that inclement season of the year. This proceeding was winked at by the government; and although we had warrantee deeds for our land, and had violated no law, we could obtain no redress. There were many sick who were thus inhumanly driven from their houses, and had to endure all this abuse, and to seek homes where they could be found. The result was, that a great many of them being deprived of the comforts of life, and the necessary attendance, died; many children were left orphans; wives, widows; and husbands, widowers. Our farms were taken possession of by the mob, many thousands of cattle, sheep, horses, and hogs were taken, and our household goods, store goods, and printing press and types were broken, taken, or otherwise destroyed. [p. 407]

Many of our brethren removed to Clay county, where they continued until 1836 (three years); there was no violence offered, but there were threatenings of violence. But in the summer of 1836 these threatenings began to assume a more serious aspect; from threats, public meetings were called, resolutions were passed, vengeance and destruction were threatened, and affairs again assumed a fearful attitude; Jackson county was a sufficient precedent, and as the authorities in that county did not interfere, they boasted that they would not in this; which on application to the authorities we found to be too true; and, after much violence, privation, and loss of property, we were again driven from our homes.[20]

We next settled in Caldwell and Daviess counties, where we made large and extensive settlements thinking to free ourselves from the power of oppression by settling in new counties, with a very few inhabitants in them; but here we were not allowed to live in peace; and in 1838 were again attacked by mobs; an exterminating order was issued by Governor [Lilburn W.] Boggs, and under the sanction of law, an organized banditti ravaged[21] the country, robbing us of

---

20. Although some of the original settlers of Clay County were determined to see the Latter-day Saints leave the county, the conditions surrounding the Saints' departure were markedly less violent than was the earlier episode in Jackson County. (See Parkin, "History of the Latter-day Saints in Clay County," chap. 8.)

21. "Church History" has "ranged through." Boggs charged the state militia with restoring peace to northwest Missouri. If necessary, the governor ordered, the Mormons were to be "exterminated or driven from the state." (Lilburn W. Boggs, Jefferson City, MO, to John B. Clark, Fayette, MO, 27 Oct. 1838, Mormon War Papers, MSA.)

our cattle, sheep, horses, hogs, &c.; many of our people were murdered in cold blood,[22] the chastity of our women was violated, and we were forced to sign away our property at the point of the sword; and after enduring every indignity that could be heaped upon us by an inhuman, ungodly band of marauders,— from twelve to fifteen thousand souls, men, women, and children, were driven from their own firesides, and from lands for which they had warrantee deeds, to wander houseless, friendless, and homeless, (in the depth of winter,) as exiles on the earth, or to seek an asylum in a more genial clime, and among a less barbarous people.[23]

Many sickened and died in consequence of the cold and hardships they had to endure, many wives were left widows, and children orphans and destitute.

It would take more time than I am able to devote to your service, at present, to describe the injustice, the wrongs, the murders, the bloodshed, thefts, misery and wo that have been committed upon our people by the barbarous, inhuman, and lawless proceedings of the State of Missouri. And I would refer you, and the readers of your history who may be desirous of further information on this topic, to the evidence taken on my recent trial before the Municipal Court of Nauvoo, on Saturday, July 1st, 1843, on a writ of habeas corpus, which is published in pamphlet form by Messrs. [John] Taylor & [Wilford] Woodruff, of this city.[24]

[25]After being thus inhumanly expelled by the government and people from Missouri, we found an asylum and friends in the State of [p. 408] Illinois.

---

22. About twenty Mormons were killed during the "Mormon War" in Missouri. (LeSueur, *1838 Mormon War in Missouri,* 162–168; Baugh, "Call to Arms," 238–240, 253–298.)

23. Although the number of Mormons driven from Missouri is unknown, the estimate of "twelve to fifteen thousand" appears to be too high. Others estimated that about eight thousand Mormons were driven from Missouri. (Eliza R. Snow, Caldwell Co., MO, to Isaac Streator, Streetsborough, OH, 22 Feb. 1839, photocopy, CHL; see also Hartley, "Almost Too Intolerable a Burthen," 7n2.)

24. This sentence does not appear in "Church History," and no manuscript source is known. The publication referred to is JS, *Evidence Taken on the Trial of Mr. Smith, before the Municipal Court of Nauvoo, on Saturday, July 1, 1843. Respecting the Late Persecution of the Latter Day Saints, in the State of Missouri, North America* (Nauvoo, IL: Taylor and Woodruff, [1843]). The thirty-eight-page pamphlet was reprinted from transcripts of the affidavits that appeared in both the *Nauvoo Neighbor* (5, 12, 19, and 26 July 1843) and the *Times and Seasons* (1 and 15 July and 1 August 1843); the signed affidavits may also be found in Nauvoo, IL, Records, CHL.

25. From this point, the text is based on William W. Phelps's manuscript providing additions to "Church History." The manuscript, which begins "From this awful, bloody, and inhuman expulsion by the government, and people, from Missouri," provides the basis for the text up until the commencement of the thirteen points of doctrine beginning "We believe in God." The only exception is the paragraph beginning "The temple of God," which does not appear in Phelps's manuscript. (William W. Phelps, "Additions to an Article in the Times & Seasons," Sept. 1843, CHL.)

Here, in the fall of 1839, we commenced a city called Nauvoo,[26] in Hancock county, which, in December, 1840, received an act of incorporation from the Legislature of Illinois, and is endowed with as liberal powers as any city in the United States.[27] Nauvoo, in every respect, connected with increase and prosperity, has exceeded the most sanguine expectations of thousands. It now contains near 1500 houses, and more than 15,000 inhabitants. The charter contains, amongst its important powers, privileges, or immunities, a grant for the "University of Nauvoo," with the same liberal powers of the city, where all the arts and sciences will grow with the growth, and strengthen the strength of this beloved city of the "saints of the last days."[28] Another very commendatory provision of the charter is, that that portion of the citizens subject to military duty are organized into a body of independent military men, styled the "Nauvoo Legion," whose highest officer holds the rank, and is commissioned lieutenant-general.[29] This legion, like other independent bodies of troops in this republican government, is at the disposal of the Governor of this State, and President of the United States. There is also an act of incorporation for an agricultural and manufacturing association, as well as the Nauvoo House Association.[30]

The temple of God, now in the course of erection, being already raised one story, and which is 120 feet by 80 feet, of stone, with polished pilasters, of an entire new order of architecture, will be a splendid house for the worship of

26. The Saints began settling in Commerce, Illinois, in spring 1839, and by that fall, they began referring to the area as Nauvoo. (See Leonard, *Nauvoo,* chap. 3; and "Nauvoo Journals, December 1841–April 1843," in *JSP,* J2:xv.)

27. The Nauvoo charter was passed by the Illinois legislature and signed by the governor in December 1840. (*Journal of the Senate . . . of Illinois,* 9 Dec. 1840, 61; *Journal of the House of Representatives . . . of Illinois,* 12 Dec. 1840, 110; An Act to Incorporate the City of Nauvoo [16 Dec. 1840], *Laws of the State of Illinois* [1840–1841], 52–57.)

28. The Nauvoo charter granted the city's university trustees "full power to pass, ordain, establish, and execute all such laws and ordinances as they may consider necessary for the welfare and prosperity of said university, its officers and students: Provided, That the said laws and ordinances shall not be repugnant to the Constitution of the United States or of this State." (An Act to Incorporate the City of Nauvoo [16 Dec. 1840], *Laws of the State of Illinois* [1840–1841], pp. 56–57, sec. 24; see also Bennett and Cope, "Chartering the City of Nauvoo," 23–25.)

29. See section 25 of the Nauvoo charter. (An Act to Incorporate the City of Nauvoo [16 Dec. 1840], *Laws of the State of Illinois* [1840–1841], p. 57, sec. 25.)

30. The Illinois legislature passed an act on 23 February 1841 to incorporate the Nauvoo House Association, authorizing the association to "erect and furnish a public house of entertainment" or boarding house to accommodate visitors to Nauvoo. Four days later, 27 February 1841, the legislature passed the act to incorporate the Nauvoo Agricultural and Manufacturing Association. (An Act to Incorporate the Nauvoo House Association [23 Feb. 1841], *Laws of the State of Illinois* [1840–1841], 131–132; An Act to Incorporate the Nauvoo Agricultural and Manufacturing Association, in the County of Hancock [27 Feb. 1841], *Laws of the State of Illinois* [1840–1841], 139–141.)

God, as well as an unique wonder for the world, it being built by the direct revelation of Jesus Christ for the salvation of the living and the dead.[31]

Since the organization of this church its progress has been rapid, and its gain in numbers regular. Besides these United States, where nearly every place of notoriety has heard the glad tidings of the gospel of the Son of God, England, Ireland, and Scotland, have shared largely in the fulness of the everlasting gospel,[32] and thousands have already gathered with their kindred saints, to this the cornerstone of Zion. Missionaries of this church have gone to the East Indies, to Australia, Germany, Constantinople, Egypt, Palestine, the Islands of the Pacific, and are now preparing to open the door in the extensive dominions of Russia.[33]

There are no correct data by which the exact number of members composing this now extensive, and still extending, Church of Jesus Christ of Latter Day Saints can be known. Should it be supposed at 150,000, it might still be short of the truth.[34]

Believing the Bible to say what it means and mean what it says; and guided by revelation according to the ancient order of the fathers [p. 409] to whom came what little light we enjoy; and circumscribed only by the eternal limits of truth: this church must continue the even tenor of her way, and "spread undivided, and operate unspent."[35]

We believe in God the Eternal Father, and in his son Jesus Christ, and in the Holy Ghost.

We believe that men will be punished for their own sins and not for Adam's transgression.

---

31. Revelation, 19 Jan. 1841, in Doctrine and Covenants 103:10–12, 1844 ed. [D&C 124:26–39], gave instructions for the building of the temple at Nauvoo and described its purpose as a holy place in which to perform rites for church members and by proxy for deceased persons.

32. The text omits Wales, which is included in "Church History." About 250 people had joined the church in Wales by 1844. (JS, "Church History," p. 499 herein; Dennis, "The Welsh and the Gospel," 237–241.)

33. In addition to the assignments mentioned in "Church History," JS here adds Constantinople, Egypt, the Pacific islands, and Russia as missionary destinations. Orson Hyde visited Constantinople and Egypt during his mission to the Jews.[a] Missionaries had by this time also been assigned to the Sandwich Islands, though they actually went to the Society Islands, in French Polynesia.[b] In spring 1843, Hyde and George J. Adams were appointed to open missionary work in Russia, though they did not fulfill the assignment.[c] (a. Hyde, *Voice from Jerusalem,* 22–23. b. JS, Journal, 23 May 1843, JS Collection, CHL; see also Pratt, Journals, 20 Sept. 1843–28 Apr. 1847; and Britsch, *Unto the Isles of the Sea,* chap. 1. c. "Recommendatory," *Times and Seasons,* 1 June 1843, 4:218.)

34. Historian Dean L. May gave a conservative estimate of approximately thirty thousand Latter-day Saints by 1846; other sources indicate as many as thirty-five to forty thousand. In any case, the figure given is too high. (May, "Demographic Portrait of the Mormons," 123.)

35. See Alexander Pope (1688–1744), *Essay on Man,* epistle 1, line 274.

We believe that through the atonement of Christ all men may be saved by obedience to the laws and ordinances of the gospel.

We believe that these ordinances are: 1st, Faith in the Lord Jesus Christ; 2d, Repentance; 3d, Baptism by immersion for the remission of sins; 4th, Laying on of hands for the gift of the Holy Ghost.

We believe that a man must be called of God by "prophecy, and by laying on of hands,"[36] by those who are in authority to preach the gospel and administer in the ordinances thereof.

We believe in the same organization that existed in the primitive church, viz. apostles, prophets, pastors, teachers, evangelists, &c.[37]

We believe in the gift of tongues, prophecy, revelation, visions, healing, interpretation of tongues, &c.

We believe the Bible to be the word of God as far as it is translated correctly; we also believe the Book of Mormon to be the word of God.

We believe all that God has revealed, all that he does now reveal, and we believe that he will yet reveal many great and important things pertaining to the kingdom of God.

We believe in the literal gathering of Israel, and in the restoration of the Ten Tribes. That Zion will be built upon this continent. That Christ will reign personally upon the earth, and that the earth will be renewed and receive its paradisal glory.

We claim the privilege of worshipping Almighty God according to the dictates of our conscience, and allow all men the same privilege, let them worship how, where, or what they may.

We believe in being subject to kings, presidents, rulers, and magistrates; in obeying, honouring, and sustaining the law.

We believe in being honest, true, chaste, benevolent, virtuous, and in doing good to all men; indeed we may say that we follow the admonition of Paul; "we believe all things: we hope all things:"[38] we have endured many things, and hope to be able to endure all things. If there is any thing virtuous, lovely, or of good report, or praiseworthy, we seek thereafter.[39] [p. 410]

---

36. See 1 Timothy 4:14.
37. See Ephesians 4:11.
38. See 1 Corinthians 13:7.
39. See Philippians 4:8.

APPENDIX: ORSON PRATT, *A[N] INTERESTING ACCOUNT OF SEVERAL REMARKABLE VISIONS*, 1840

Source Note

Orson Pratt, A Interesting Account of Several Remarkable Visions, and of the Late Discovery of Ancient American Records; *1–31 pp.; Edinburgh, Scotland: Ballantyne and Hughes, 1840. The copy used for transcription is held at CHL.*

Historical Introduction

Orson Pratt was twenty-three years old when he was appointed to the newly organized Quorum of the Twelve Apostles in 1835, and along with others of the Twelve, he served as a proselytizing missionary to the British Isles from 1840 to 1841. While traveling to his mission, he stopped for a number of weeks in the eastern United States and spent time in the company of JS, who was in the East petitioning the federal government for redress for the Latter-day Saints' Missouri losses. Pratt attended speeches that JS delivered during his stay in the area and accompanied him on a journey from Philadelphia, Pennsylvania, to Monmouth, New Jersey, in December 1839.[1] He likely heard JS recount his early visions, a subject JS publicly addressed while in the eastern states.[2] As a member of one of the Latter-day Saints' governing bodies, Pratt had earlier opportunities to hear JS speak of his early visionary experiences, but JS's lectures on the East Coast may have left those visions fresh in Pratt's mind as he journeyed across the Atlantic. The next year he published the pamphlet *A[n] Interesting Account of Several Remarkable Visions, and of the Late Discovery of Ancient American Records,* which focused on JS's personal history and included the earliest printed account of his first vision of Deity.[3] Pratt published the pamphlet in Edinburgh, Scotland, in late September 1840, and he informed fellow apostle George A. Smith, "I shall be at conference [in Manchester, England] on the 6th of Oct. if the Lord will. I shall bring about 2000 pamphlets with me which are now in the press."[4]

---

1. Orson Pratt, New York City, NY, to Sarah Bates Pratt, Nauvoo, IL, 6 Jan. 1840, *Times and Seasons,* Feb. 1840, 1:61.

2. See Benjamin Winchester, Philadelphia, PA, to "Dear Brother in the Lord," 10 Feb. 1840, *Times and Seasons,* May 1840, 1:104; and Pratt, *Autobiography, 330.*

3. Similarity of phrasing, especially in describing JS's rudimentary education, suggests that Pratt may have had access to JS's unpublished circa summer 1832 history. (See p. 11 herein.)

4. Orson Pratt, Edinburgh, Scotland, to George A. Smith, London, England, 24 Sept. 1840, George Albert Smith, Papers, CHL.

A

INTERESTING ACCOUNT

OF

SEVERAL REMARKABLE VISIONS,

AND OF

THE LATE DISCOVERY

OF

ANCIENT AMERICAN RECORDS.

BY O. PRATT,

MINISTER OF THE GOSPEL.

" For there is nothing covered, that shall not be revealed ; and hid, that shall not be known."—MATT. X. 26.

EDINBURGH :
PRINTED BY BALLANTYNE AND HUGHES,
MDCCCXL.

Orson Pratt's *Interesting Account.* In Edinburgh, Scotland, in 1840, Orson Pratt published the missionary pamphlet *A[n] Interesting Account of Several Remarkable Visions, and of the Late Discovery of Ancient American Records.* The pamphlet included the first published account of Joseph Smith's first vision of Deity. Two years later, the description of the vision in Joseph Smith's "Church History" drew upon Pratt's wording for many of the details. *Interesting Account* was reprinted many times and was translated into Danish, Dutch, and Swedish. Pratt, *Interesting Account,* [1]. (Church History Library, Salt Lake City. Photograph by Welden C. Andersen.)

Pratt began his thirty-one-page pamphlet by describing JS's first vision of Deity and the later visit JS received from "the angel of the Lord." In relating how JS obtained the gold plates of the Book of Mormon, Pratt quoted extensively from the historical letters by Oliver Cowdery printed in the *Latter Day Saints' Messenger and Advocate* in Kirtland, Ohio, in 1834–1835.[5] He summarized the contents of the Book of Mormon, reprinted the statements of two groups of witnesses who saw the gold plates, and concluded with a fifteen-point "sketch of the faith and doctrine of this Church."

In his description of the Book of Mormon, Orson Pratt superimposed his understanding of Book of Mormon geography onto the Western Hemisphere by placing the Nephites in South America and the Jaredites in North America. Pratt's association of Book of Mormon peoples with the history of all of North and South America matched common understanding of early Latter-day Saints. Shortly thereafter, when John Lloyd Stephens's *Incidents of Travel in Central America, Chiapas, and Yucatan* became available in Nauvoo in about 1842, JS greeted it enthusiastically and church members used it to map Book of Mormon sites in a Central American setting.[6]

Pratt's *Interesting Account of Several Remarkable Visions* proved to be one of the more influential Mormon tracts to come out of this period. The first American edition was printed in New York in 1841, and reprints appeared in Europe, Australia, and the United States.[7] Pratt's work was a principal source for Orson Hyde's German-language pamphlet *Ein Ruf aus der Wüste* [A cry out of the wilderness], the earliest church publication in a language other than English, and for the first French-language pamphlet, John Taylor's *Aux amis de la vérité religieuse* [To friends of religious truth].[8] Pratt's pamphlet was later translated into Danish, Swedish, and Dutch.[9]

Interesting Account is not a JS document, because JS did not write it, assign it, or supervise its creation. However, two JS documents in this volume, "Church History" (pages 489–501 herein) and "Latter Day Saints" (a later version of "Church History," pages 503–516

5. Cowdery's letters were copied into JS History, 1834–1836, pp. 40–89 herein.

6. John L. Stephens, *Incidents of Travel in Central America, Chiapas, and Yucatan,* 2 vols. (New York: Harper and Brothers, 1841); see also "Facts Are Stubborn Things," *Times and Seasons,* 15 Sept. 1842, 3:921–922; "Zarahemla," *Times and Seasons,* 1 Oct. 1842, 3:927–928; JS, Nauvoo, IL, to John Bernhisel, New York City, NY, 16 Nov. 1841, JS Collection, CHL; and Givens, *By the Hand of Mormon,* chaps. 4–5.

7. Orson Pratt, *An Interesting Account of Several Remarkable Visions, and of the Late Discovery of Ancient American Records,* 1st American ed. (New York: Joseph W. Harrison, 1841); Orson Pratt, *Remarkable Visions* (Liverpool: R. James, [1848]); Orson Pratt, *An Interesting Account of Several Remarkable Visions, and of the Late Discovery of Ancient American Records* (Sydney: Albert Mason, 1851); Orson Pratt, *An Interesting Account of Several Remarkable Visions, and of the Late Discovery of Ancient American Records,* 2nd American ed. (New York: Joseph W. Harrison, 1841); see also Crawley, *Descriptive Bibliography,* 1:160–161; 2:63–64, 262–265.

8. Orson Hyde, *Ein Ruf aus der Wüste, eine Stimme aus dem Schoose der Erde* (Frankfurt: Im Selbstverlage des Verfassers [by the author], 1842); John Taylor, *Aux amis de la vérité religieuse. Récit abrégé du commencement, des progrès, de l'établissement, des persécutions, de la foi et de la doctrine de l'Église de Jésus-Christ des Saints des Derniers Jours* (Paris: Marc Ducloux et Compagnie, 1850); see also Crawley, *Descriptive Bibliography,* 1:205–208; 2:166–167.

9. Orson Pratt, *Mærkværdige syner* (Copenhagen: F. E. Bording, 1851); Orson Pratt, *Märkwärdiga syner* (Copenhagen: F. E. Bording, 1860); Orson Pratt, *Merkwaardige verschijningen* (Amsterdam?, [ca. 1865]); see also Crawley, *Descriptive Bibliography,* 2:240.

herein), quote extensively from Pratt's pamphlet. These documents made use of Pratt's language to describe JS's early visionary experiences and built on Pratt's summary of the church's "faith and doctrine" for the thirteen-point statement of church beliefs that came to be known as the Articles of Faith. (The summary of beliefs in *Interesting Account* was in turn based on an earlier statement composed by Orson Pratt's brother, Parley P. Pratt.[10]) *Interesting Account* is therefore included as an appendix to this volume to allow convenient comparison with JS's histories. Gray highlighting in the text indicates passages that later provided wording or content for "Church History" and for "Latter Day Saints." Passages highlighted in Pratt's concluding statement of beliefs show parallels to JS's own list of beliefs in "Church History."

——— ☙ ———

A[11]

INTERESTING ACCOUNT
OF
SEVERAL REMARKABLE VISIONS,
AND OF
THE LATE DISCOVERY
OF
ANCIENT AMERICAN RECORDS.
BY O. PRATT,
MINISTER OF THE GOSPEL.

"For there is nothing covered, that shall not be revealed; and hid, that shall not be known."—MATT. x. 26.

EDINBURGH:
PRINTED BY BALLANTYNE AND HUGHES,
MDCCCXL. [p. [1]]

[*1 page blank*]

FACTS
IN RELATION TO THE LATE DISCOVERY OF
ANCIENT AMERICAN RECORDS.

MR JOSEPH SMITH, jun., who made the following important discovery, was born in the town of Sharon, Windsor county, Vermont, on the 23d of

---

10. See Pratt and Higbee, *An Address . . . to the Citizens of Washington;* compare Pratt, *Late Persecution of the Church,* iii–xiii.

11. Later copies from this printing omit this *A.* Pratt originally intended the title to begin "An Interesting Account," but the printer typeset the title as it appears here. When this error was discovered in the middle of the print run, the *A* was removed. (See Orson Pratt, Edinburgh, Scotland, to George A. Smith, London, England, 24 Sept. 1840, George Albert Smith, Papers, CHL; and Crawley, *Descriptive Bibliography,* 1:129.)

Orson Pratt. Pratt was the author of *A[n] Interesting Account of Several Remarkable Visions, and of the Late Discovery of Ancient American Records,* a missionary pamphlet published in 1840 in Edinburgh, Scotland. *Interesting Account* served as a source for Joseph Smith's essays "Church History" and "Latter Day Saints," especially for their account of his early visionary experiences and the thirteen-point statement of beliefs that came to be known as the Articles of Faith. (Church History Library, Salt Lake City.)

December, A.D. 1805. When ten years old, his parents, with their family, moved to Palmyra, New York; in the vicinity of which he resided for about eleven years, the latter part in the town of Manchester. Cultivating the earth for a livelihood was his occupation, in which he employed the most of his time. His advantages, for acquiring literary knowledge, were exceedingly small; hence, his education was limited to a slight acquaintance with two or three of the common branches of learning. He could read without much difficulty, and write a very imperfect hand; and had a very limited understanding of the ground rules of arithmetic. These were his highest and only attainments; while the rest of those branches, so universally taught in the common schools throughout the United States, were entirely unknown to him. When somewhere about fourteen or fifteen years old, he began seriously to reflect upon the necessity of being prepared for a future state of existence: but how, or in what way, to prepare himself, was a question, as yet, undetermined in his own mind: he perceived that it was a question of infinite importance, and that the salvation of his soul depended upon a correct understanding of the same. He saw, that if he understood not the [p. [3]] way, it would be impossible to walk in it, except by chance; and the thought of resting his hopes of eternal life upon chance, or uncertainties, was more than he could endure. If he went to the religious denominations to seek information, each one pointed to its particular tenets, saying—"This is the way, walk ye in it;"[12] while, at the same time, the doctrines of each were, in many respects, in direct opposition to one another. It, also, occurred to his mind, that God was not the author of but one doctrine, and therefore could not acknowledge but one denomination as his church; and that such denomination must be a people, who believe, and teach, that one doctrine, (whatever it may be,) and build upon the same. He then reflected upon the immense number of doctrines, now, in the world, which had given rise to many hundreds of different denominations. The great question to be decided in his mind, was—if any one of these denominations be the Church of Christ, which one is it? Until he could become satisfied, in relation to this question, he could not rest contented. To trust to the decisions of fallible man, and build his hopes upon the same, without any certainty, and knowledge, of his own, would not satisfy the anxious desires that pervaded his breast. To decide, without any positive and definite evidence, on which he could rely, upon a subject involving the future welfare of his soul, was revolting to his feelings. The only alternative, that seemed to be left him, was to read the Scriptures, and endeavour to follow their directions. He, accordingly, commenced perusing the sacred pages of the Bible, with sincerity, believing the

---

12. See Isaiah 30:21.

things that he read. His mind soon caught hold of the following passage:—"If any of you lack wisdom, let him ask of God, that giveth to all *men* liberally, and upbraideth not; and it shall be given him."—James i. 5. From this promise he learned, that it was the privilege of all men to ask God for wisdom, with the sure and certain expectation of receiving, liberally; without being upbraided for so doing. This was cheering information to him: tidings that gave him great joy. It was like a light shining forth in a dark place, to guide him to the path in which he should walk. He, now, saw that if he inquired of God, there was, not only, a possibility, but a probability; yea, more, a certainty, that he should [p. 4] obtain a knowledge, which, of all the doctrines, was the doctrine of Christ; and, which, of all the churches, was the church of Christ. He, therefore, retired to a secret place, in a grove, but a short distance from his father's house, and knelt down, and began to call upon the Lord. At first, he was severely tempted by the powers of darkness, which endeavoured to overcome him; but he continued to seek for deliverance, until darkness gave way from his mind; and he was enabled to pray, in fervency of the spirit, and in faith. And, while thus pouring out his soul, anxiously desiring an answer from God, he, at length, saw a very bright and glorious light in the heavens above; which, at first, seemed to be at a considerable distance. He continued praying, while the light appeared to be gradually descending towards him; and, as it drew nearer, it increased in brightness, and magnitude, so that, by the time that it reached the tops of the trees, the whole wilderness, for some distance around, was illuminated in a most glorious and brilliant manner. He expected to have seen the leaves and boughs of the trees consumed, as soon as the light came in contact with them; but, perceiving that it did not produce that effect, he was encouraged with the hopes of being able to endure its presence. It continued descending, slowly, until it rested upon the earth, and he was enveloped in the midst of it. When it first came upon him, it produced a peculiar sensation throughout his whole system; and, immediately, his mind was caught away, from the natural objects with which he was surrounded; and he was enwrapped in a heavenly vision, and saw two glorious personages, who exactly resembled each other in their features or likeness. He was informed, that his sins were forgiven. He was also informed upon the subjects, which had for some time previously agitated his mind, viz.—that all the religious denominations were believing in incorrect doctrines; and, consequently, that none of them was acknowledged of God, as his church and kingdom. And he was expressly commanded, to go not after them; and he received a promise that the true doctrine—the fulness of the gospel, should, at some future time, be made known to him; after which, the vision withdrew, leaving his mind in a state of calmness and peace, indescribable.[13] Some time after having received this glorious [p. 5] manifestation, being young, he was again entangled in the vanities of the world, of which he afterwards sincerely and truly repented.

And it pleased God, on the evening of the 21st of September, A.D. 1823, to again hear his prayers. For he had retired to rest, as usual, only that his mind was drawn out, in fervent prayer, and his soul was filled with the most earnest desire, "to commune with some kind messenger, who could communicate to him the desired information of his acceptance with God,"[14] and also unfold the principles of the doctrine of Christ, according to the promise which he had received in the former vision. While he thus continued to pour out his desires before the Father of all good; endeavouring to exercise faith in his precious promises; "on a sudden, a light like that of day, only of a purer and far more glorious appearance and brightness, burst into the room. Indeed, the first sight was as though the house was filled with consuming fire. This sudden appearance of a light so bright, as must naturally be expected, occasioned a shock or sensation visible to the extremities of the body. It was, however, followed with a calmness and serenity of mind, and an overwhelming rapture of joy, that surpassed understanding, and, in a moment, a personage stood before him."

Notwithstanding the brightness of the light which previously illuminated the room, "yet there seemed to be an additional glory surrounding or accompanying this personage, which shone with an increased degree of brilliancy, of which he was in the midst; and though his countenance was as lightning, yet, it was of a pleasing, innocent, and glorious appearance; so much so, that every fear was banished from the heart, and nothing but calmness pervaded the soul."

"The stature of this personage was a little above the common size of men in this age; his garment was perfectly white, and had the appearance of being without seam."

This glorious being declared himself to be an Angel of God,[15] sent forth, by commandment, to communicate to him that his sins were forgiven, and that

---

13. For JS's accounts of this vision of Deity, see JS History, ca. summer 1832, pp. 11–13 herein; JS, Journal, 9–11 Nov. 1835, in *JSP,* J1:87–88 (see also later version, pp. 115–116 herein); JS History Drafts, 1838–ca. 1841, pp. 210–215 herein; JS, "Church History," p. 494 herein; and JS, "Latter Day Saints," p. 508 herein.

14. Pratt's quotation marks in this and the two following paragraphs indicate quotations or close paraphrases from Oliver Cowdery, "Letter IV," *LDS Messenger and Advocate,* Feb. 1835, 1:78–79 (see also later version, pp. 57–58 herein).

15. JS identified this angel as Moroni, the last prophet to write in the Book of Mormon. ([JS], Editorial, *Elders' Journal,* July 1838, 42–44; see also 223n56 herein. For JS's other accounts of this experience, see JS History, ca. summer 1832, pp. 13–14 herein; JS, Journal, 9–11 Nov. 1835, in *JSP,* J1:88–89 [see also later version, pp. 116–117 herein]; JS History Drafts, 1838–ca. 1841, pp. 220–233 herein; JS, "Church History," pp. 494–495 herein; and JS, "Latter Day Saints," pp. 508–509 herein.)

his prayers were heard; and also, to bring the joyful tidings, that the covenant which God made with ancient Israel, concerning their [p. 6] posterity, was at hand to be fulfilled; that the great preparatory work for the second coming of the Messiah, was speedily to commence; that the time was at hand for the gospel, in its fulness, to be preached in power unto all nations; that a people might be prepared with faith and righteousness, for the Millennial reign of universal peace and joy.

He was informed, that he was called and chosen to be an instrument in the hands of God, to bring about some of his marvellous purposes in this glorious dispensation. It was also made manifest to him, that the "American Indians" were a remnant of Israel; that when they first emigrated to America, they were an enlightened people, possessing a knowledge of the true God, enjoying his favour, and peculiar blessings from his hand; that the prophets, and inspired writers among them, were required to keep a sacred history of the most important events transpiring among them: which history was handed down for many generations, till at length they fell into great wickedness: the most part of them were destroyed, and the records, (by commandment of God, to one of the last prophets among them,) were safely deposited, to preserve them from the hands of the wicked, who sought to destroy them. He was informed, that these records contained many sacred revelations pertaining to the gospel of the kingdom, as well as prophecies relating to the great events of the last days; and that to fulfil his promises to the ancients, who wrote the records, and to accomplish his purposes, in the restitution of their children, &c., they were to come forth to the knowledge of the people. If faithful, he was to be the instrument, who should be thus highly favoured in bringing these sacred things to light: at the same time, being expressly informed, that it must be done with an eye single to the glory of God, that no one could be entrusted with those sacred writings, who should endeavour to aggrandize himself, by converting sacred things to unrighteous and speculative purposes. After giving him many instructions concerning things past and to come, which would be foreign to our purpose to mention here, he disappeared, and the light and glory of God withdrew, leaving his mind in perfect peace, while a calmness and serenity indescribable pervaded the soul. But, before morning, the vision was [p. 7] twice renewed, instructing him further, and still further, concerning the great work of God, about to be performed on the earth. In the morning, he went out to his labour as usual; but soon the vision was renewed—the Angel again appeared; and having been informed by the previous visions of the night, concerning the place where those records were deposited, he was instructed to go immediately and view them.

Accordingly, he repaired to the place, a brief description of which shall be given, in the words of a gentleman, by the name of Oliver Cowdery, who has visited the spot.[16]

"As you pass on the mail-road, from Palmyra, Wayne county, to Canandaigua, Ontario county, New York, before arriving at the little village of Manchester, say from three to four, or about four miles from Palmyra, you pass a large hill on the east side of the road. Why I say large, is because it is as large, perhaps, as any in that country.

"The north end rises quite suddenly until it assumes a level with the more southerly extremity; and I think, I may say, an elevation higher than at the south, a short distance, say half or three-fourths of a mile. As you pass towards Canandaigua, it lessens gradually, until the surface assumes its common level, or is broken by other smaller hills or ridges, water-courses and ravines. I think I am justified in saying, that this is the highest hill for some distance round, and I am certain, that its appearance, as it rises so suddenly from a plain on the north, must attract the notice of the traveller as he passes by."—"The north end," which has been described as rising suddenly from the plain, forms "a promontory without timber, but covered with grass. As you pass to the south, you soon come to scattering timber, the surface having been cleared by art or wind; and a short distance further left, you are surrounded with the common forest of the country. It is necessary to observe, that even the part cleared, was only occupied for pasturage; its steep ascent, and narrow summit not admitting the plough of the husbandman, with any degree of ease or profit. It was at the second mentioned place, where the record was found to be deposited, on the west side of the hill, not far from the top down its side; and when myself visited the place in the year 1830, there were several trees standing—enough to cause a shade in [p. 8] summer, but not so much as to prevent the surface being covered with grass—which was also the case when the record was first found.

"How far below the surface these records were" anciently "placed, I am unable to say; but from the fact, that they had been some fourteen hundred years buried, and that, too, on the side of a hill so steep, one is ready to conclude, that they were some feet below, as the earth would naturally wear, more or less, in that length of time. But they, being placed toward the top of the hill, the ground would not remove as much as at two-thirds, perhaps. Another circumstance would prevent a wearing of the earth: in all probability, as soon as

---

16. Pratt quotes from and paraphrases Oliver Cowdery, "Letter VII," *LDS Messenger and Advocate,* July 1835, 1:158; and Oliver Cowdery, "Letter VIII," *LDS Messenger and Advocate,* Oct. 1835, 2:195–199 (see also later version, pp. 76 and 79–85 herein).

timber had time to grow, the hill was covered," "and the roots of the same would hold the surface. However, on this point, I shall leave every man to draw his own conclusion, and form his own speculation." But, suffice to say, "a hole of a sufficient depth was dug. At the bottom of this was laid a stone of suitable size, the upper surface being smooth. At each edge, was placed a large quantity of cement, and into this cement, at the four edges of this stone, were placed erect four others; *their* bottom edges resting *in* the cement, at the outer edges of the first stone. The four last named, when placed erect, formed a box: the corners, or where the edges of the four came in contact, were also cemented so firmly, that the moisture from without was prevented from entering. It is to be observed, also, that the inner surfaces of the four erect or side stones, were smooth. This box was sufficiently large to admit a breastplate, such as was used by the ancients, to defend the chest, &c., from the arrows and weapons of their enemy. From the bottom of the box, or from the breastplate, arose three small pillars, composed of the same description of cement used on the edges; and upon these three pillars were placed the records."—"This box, containing the records, was covered with another stone, the bottom surface being flat, and the upper crowning." When it was first visited by Mr Smith, on the morning of the 22d of September 1823, "a part of the crowning stone was visible above the surface, while the edges were concealed by the soil and grass." From which circumstance, it may be seen, "that however deep this box might have been placed at first, the time had been [p. 9] sufficient to wear the earth, so that it was easily discovered, when once directed, and yet, not enough to make a per-ceivable difference to the passer-by."—"After arriving at the repository, a little exertion in removing the soil from the edges of the top of the box, and a light pry, brought to his natural vision its contents." While viewing and contemplat-ing this sacred treasure with wonder and astonishment, behold! the Angel of the Lord, who had previously visited him, again stood in his presence, and his soul was again enlightened as it was the evening before, and he was filled with the Holy Spirit, and the heavens were opened, and the glory of the Lord shone round about and rested upon him. While he thus stood gazing and admiring, the Angel said, "Look!" And as he thus spake, he beheld the Prince of Darkness, surrounded by his innumerable train of associates. All this passed before him, and the heavenly messenger said, "All this is shown, the good and the evil, the holy and impure, the glory of God, and the power of darkness, that you may know hereafter the two powers, and never be influenced or over-come by that wicked one. Behold, whatsoever enticeth and leadeth to good and to do good, is of God, and whatsoever doth not, is of that wicked one. It is he that filleth the hearts of men with evil, to walk in darkness and blaspheme God; and you may learn from henceforth, that his ways are to destruction, but the way of holiness is peace and rest. You cannot at this time obtain this record, for the commandment of God is strict, and if ever these sacred things are obtained, they must be by prayer and faithfulness in obeying the Lord. They are not deposited here for the sake of accumulating gain and wealth for the glory of this world; they were sealed by the prayer of faith, and because of the knowledge which they contain, they are of no worth among the children of men, only for their knowledge. On them is contained the fulness of the gospel of Jesus Christ, as it was given to his people on this land; and when it shall be brought forth by the power of God, it shall be carried to the Gentiles, of whom many will receive it, and after will the seed of Israel be brought into the fold of their Redeemer by obeying it also. Those who kept the commandments of the Lord on this land, desired this at his hand, and through the prayer of faith obtained the promise, that [p. 10] if their descendants should transgress and fall away, that a record should be kept, and in the last days come to their children. These things are sacred, and must be kept so, for the promise of the Lord concerning them must be fulfilled. No man can obtain them if his heart is impure, because they contain that which is sacred." . . .[17] "By them will the Lord work a great and marvellous work; the wisdom of the wise shall become as nought, and the understanding of the prudent shall be hid, and because the power of God shall be displayed, those who profess to know the truth, but walk in deceit, shall tremble with anger; but with signs and with wonders, with gifts and with healings, with the manifestations of the power of God, and with the Holy Ghost, shall the hearts of the faithful be comforted. You have now beheld the power of God manifested, and the power of Satan; you see that there is nothing desirable in the works of darkness; that they cannot bring happiness; that those who are overcome therewith are miserable; while, on the other hand, the righteous are blessed with a place in the kingdom of God, where joy unspeakable surrounds them. There they rest beyond the power of the enemy of truth, where no evil can disturb them. The glory of God crowns them, and they continually feast upon his goodness, and enjoy his smiles. Behold, notwithstanding you have seen this great display of power, by which you may ever be able to detect the evil one, yet I give unto you another sign, and when it comes to pass then know that the Lord is God, and that he will fulfil his purposes, and that the knowledge which this record contains will go to every nation, and kindred, and tongue, and people under the whole heaven. This is the sign: when these things begin to be known, that is, when it is known that the Lord has shown you these things, the workers of iniquity will seek your

---

17. TEXT: Ellipses in original. Pratt here omits a fifty-five-word section of Cowdery's letter. (Oliver Cowdery, "Letter VIII," *LDS Messenger and Advocate,* Oct. 1835, 2:198 [see also later version, p. 84 herein].)

overthrow. They will circulate falsehoods to destroy your reputation; and also will seek to take your life; but remember this, if you are faithful, and shall hereafter continue to keep the commandments of the Lord, you shall be preserved to bring these things forth; for in due time he will give you a commandment to come and take them. When they are interpreted, the Lord will give the holy priesthood to some, and they shall begin to proclaim this gospel and baptize by water, and after that, they shall have power to give the Holy Ghost by the laying on of their [p. 11] hands. Then will persecution rage more and more; for the iniquities of men shall be revealed, and those who are not built upon the Rock will seek to overthrow the church; but it will increase the more opposed, and spread farther and farther, increasing in knowledge till they shall be sanctified, and receive an inheritance where the glory of God will rest upon them; and when this takes place, and all things are prepared, the ten tribes of Israel will be revealed in the north country, whither they have been for a long season; and when this is fulfilled will be brought to pass that saying of the prophet,—'And the Redeemer shall come to Zion, and unto them that turn from transgression in Jacob, saith the Lord.'[18] But, notwithstanding the workers of iniquity shall seek your destruction, the arm of the Lord will be extended, and you will be borne off conqueror if you keep all his commandments. Your name shall be known among the nations, for the work which the Lord will perform by your hands shall cause the righteous to rejoice and the wicked to rage; with the one it shall be had in honour, and with the other in reproach; yet, with these it shall be a terror, because of the great and marvellous work which shall follow the coming forth of this fulness of the gospel. Now, go thy way, remembering what the Lord has done for thee, and be diligent in keeping his commandments, and he will deliver thee from temptations and all the arts and devices of the wicked one. Forget not to pray, that thy mind may become strong, that when he shall manifest unto thee, thou mayest have power to escape the evil, and obtain these precious things."

We here remark, that the above quotation is an extract from a letter written by Elder Oliver Cowdery, which was published in one of the numbers of the "Latter Day Saints' Messenger and Advocate."[19]

Although many more instructions were given by the mouth of the angel to Mr Smith, which we do not write in this book, yet the most important items are contained in the foregoing relation. During the period of the four following years, he frequently received instruction from the mouth of the heavenly

---

18. See Isaiah 59:20.
19. See 526n16 herein.

messenger. And on the morning of the 22d of September, A. D. 1827, the angel
of the Lord delivered the records into his hands.

These records were engraved on plates, which had the [p. 12] appearance of
gold. Each plate was not far from seven by eight inches in width and length,
being not quite as thick as common tin. They were filled on both sides with
engravings, in Egyptian characters, and bound together in a volume, as the
leaves of a book, and fastened at one edge with three rings running through
the whole. This volume was something near six inches in thickness, a part of
which was sealed. The characters or letters upon the unsealed part were small,
and beautifully engraved. The whole book exhibited many marks of antiquity
in its construction, as well as much skill in the art of engraving. With the
records was found "a curious instrument, called by the ancients the Urim and
Thummim, which consisted of two transparent stones, clear as crystal, set in
the two rims of a bow. This was in use, in ancient times, by persons called
seers. It was an instrument, by the use of which, they received revelation of
things distant, or of things past or future."[20]

In the mean time, the inhabitants of that vicinity, having been informed
that Mr Smith had seen heavenly visions, and that he had discovered sacred
records, began to ridicule and mock at those things. And after having obtained
those sacred things, while proceeding home through the wilderness and fields,
he was waylaid by two ruffians, who had secreted themselves for the purpose of
robbing him of the records. One of them struck him with a club before he
perceived them; but being a strong man, and large in stature, with great exertion he cleared himself from them, and ran towards home, being closely pursued until he came near his father's house, when his pursuers, for fear of being
detected, turned and fled the other way.

Soon the news of his discoveries spread abroad throughout all those parts.
False reports, misrepresentations, and base slanders, flew as if upon the wings
of the wind in every direction. The house was frequently beset by mobs and
evil designing persons. Several times he was shot at, and very narrowly escaped.
Every device was used to get the plates away from him. And being continually
in danger of his life, from a gang of abandoned wretches, he at length concluded to leave the place, and go to Pennsylvania; and, accordingly, packed up
his goods, putting the plates into a barrel of beans, and proceeded upon his
jour[p. 13]ney. He had not gone far, before he was overtaken by an officer with
a search-warrant, who flattered himself with the idea, that he should surely

20. In this paragraph, Pratt quotes from and paraphrases Parley P. Pratt, "Discovery of an Ancient
Record in America," *LDS Millennial Star,* June 1840, 1:30. Other similarities between the two works
indicate that Orson Pratt relied on his brother Parley's article for his summary of the Book of Mormon.

obtain the plates; after searching very diligently, he was sadly disappointed at not finding them. Mr Smith then drove on; but before he got to his journey's end, he was again overtaken by an officer on the same business, and after ransacking the waggon very carefully, he went his way, as much chagrined as the first, at not being able to discover the object of his research. Without any further molestation, he pursued his journey until he came into the northern part of Pennsylvania, near the Susquehannah river, in which part his father-in-law resided.[21]

Having provided himself with a home, he commenced translating the record, by the gift and power of God, through the means of the Urim and Thummim; and being a poor writer, he was under the necessity of employing a scribe, to write the translation as it came from his mouth.

In the mean time, a few of the original characters were accurately transcribed and translated by Mr Smith, which, with the translation, were taken by a gentleman by the name of Martin Harris, to the city of New York, where they were presented to a learned gentleman by the name of [Charles] Anthon, who professed to be extensively acquainted with many languages, both ancient and modern. He examined them; but was unable to decipher them correctly; but he presumed, that if the original records could be brought, he could assist in translating them.

But to return. Mr Smith continued the work of translation, as his pecuniary circumstances would permit, until he finished the unsealed part of the records. The part translated is entitled the "Book of Mormon," which contains nearly as much reading as the Old Testament.

In this important and most interesting book, we can read the history of ancient America, from its early settlement by a colony who came from the tower of Babel, at the confusion of languages, to the beginning of the fifth century of the Christian era. By these Records we are informed, that America, in ancient times, has been inhabited by two distinct races of people. The first, or more ancient race, came directly from the great tower, being called Jaredites. The second race came directly from the city of Jerusalem, about six hundred years before Christ, being Israelites, [p. 14] principally the descendants of Joseph. The first nation, or Jaredites, were destroyed about the time that the Israelites came from Jerusalem, who succeeded them in the inheritance of the country. The principal nation of the second race, fell in battle towards the close of the fourth century. The remaining remnant, having dwindled into an uncivilized

---

21. In December 1827, JS and Emma Smith relocated to Harmony, Susquehanna County, Pennsylvania, where Isaac and Elizabeth Hale resided. (JS History, ca. summer 1832, p. 15 herein.)

state, still continue to inhabit the land, although divided into a "multitude of nations," and are called by Europeans the "American Indians."

We learn from this very ancient history, that at the confusion of languages, when the Lord scattered the people upon all the face of the earth, the Jaredites, being a righteous people, obtained favour in the sight of the Lord, and were not confounded. And because of their righteousness, the Lord miraculously led them from the tower to the great ocean, where they were commanded to build vessels, in which they were marvellously brought across the great deep to the shores of North America.[22]

And the Lord God promised to give them America, which was a very choice land in his sight, for an inheritance. And He swore unto them in his wrath, that whoso should possess this land of promise, from that time henceforth and forever, should serve him, the true and only God, or they should be swept off when the fulness of his wrath should come upon them, and they were fully ripened in iniquity. Moreover, he promised to make them a great and powerful nation, so that there should be no greater nation upon all the face of the earth.

Accordingly, in process of time, they became a very numerous and powerful people, occupying principally North America; building large cities in all quarters of the land; being a civilized and enlightened nation. Agriculture and machinery were carried on to a great extent. Commercial and manufacturing business flourished on every hand; yet, in consequence of wickedness, they were often visited with terrible judgments. Many prophets were raised up among them from generation to generation, who testified against the wickedness of the people, and prophesied of judgments and calamities which awaited them, if they did not repent, &c. Sometimes they were visited by pestilence and plagues, and sometimes by famine and war, until at length (having occupied the land some fifteen or [p. 15] sixteen hundred years) their wickedness became so great, that the Lord threatened, by the mouth of his prophets, to utterly destroy them from the face of the land. But they gave no heed to these warnings; therefore the word of the Lord was fulfilled; and they were entirely destroyed; leaving their houses, their cities, and their land desolate; and their sacred records also, which were kept on gold plates, were left by one of their last prophets whose name was Ether, in such a situation, that they were discovered by the remnant of Joseph, who soon afterwards were brought from Jerusalem to inherit the land.[23]

---

22. The narrative of the Jaredite migration is found in Book of Mormon, 1837 ed., 569–575, 578–579 [Ether 1:33–3:28, 6:2–12].

23. See Book of Mormon, 1837 ed., 602–604, 183, 159–160 [Ether 15; Mosiah 8:7–11; Omni 1:20–22].

This remnant of Joseph were also led in a miraculous manner from Jerusalem, in the first year of the reign of Zedekiah, king of Judah. They were first led to the eastern borders of the Red Sea; then they journeyed for some time along the borders thereof, nearly in a south-east direction; after which, they altered their course nearly eastward, until they came to the great waters, where, by the commandment of God, they built a vessel, in which they were safely brought across the great Pacific ocean, and landed upon the western coast of South America.[24]

In the eleventh year of the reign of Zedekiah, at the time the Jews were carried away captive into Babylon, another remnant were brought out of Jerusalem; some of whom were descendants of Judah. They landed in North America; soon after which they emigrated into the northern parts of South America, at which place they were discovered by the remnant of Joseph, something like four hundred years after.[25]

From these ancient records, we learn, that this remnant of Joseph, soon after they landed, separated themselves into two distinct nations. This division was caused by a certain portion of them being greatly persecuted, because of their righteousness, by the remainder. The persecuted nation emigrated towards the northern parts of South America, leaving the wicked nation in possession of the middle and southern parts of the same. The former were called Nephites, being led by a prophet whose name was Nephi. The latter were called Lamanites, being led by a very wicked man whose name was Laman. The Nephites had in their possession a copy of the Holy Scriptures, viz. the five books of Moses, and the prophecies of the holy [p. 16] prophets, down to Jeremiah, in whose days they left Jerusalem. These Scriptures were engraved on plates of brass, in the Egyptian language.[26] They themselves also made plates, soon after their landing, on which they began to engrave their own history, prophecies, visions, and revelations. All these sacred records were kept by holy and righteous men, who were inspired by the Holy Ghost; and were carefully preserved and handed down from generation to generation.

And the Lord gave unto them the whole continent, for a land of promise, and he promised, that they, and their children after them, should inherit it, on condition of their obedience to his commandments; but if they were disobedient, they should be cut off from his presence. And the Nephites began to prosper in the land, according to their righteousness, and they multiplied and

---

24. See Book of Mormon, 1837 ed., 42–43, 45–46, 51–53 [1 Nephi 16:12–14; 17:1–8; 18], for the account of these events.

25. See Book of Mormon, 1837 ed., 159 [Omni 1:13–17].

26. See Book of Mormon, 1837 ed., 163–164, 567 [Mosiah 1:3–4; Mormon 9:32].

spread forth to the east, and west, and north; building large villages, and cities, and synagogues, and temples, together with forts, and towers, and fortifications, to defend themselves against their enemies. And they cultivated the earth, and raised various kinds of grain in abundance. They also raised numerous flocks of domestic animals, and became a very wealthy people; having in abundance gold, silver, copper, tin, iron, &c. Arts and sciences flourished to a great extent. Various kinds of machinery were in use. Cloths, of various kinds, were manufactured. Swords, cimeters, axes, and various implements of war were made, together with head-shields, arm-shields, and breastplates, to defend themselves in battle with their enemies. And in the days of their righteousness, they were a civilized, enlightened, and happy people.

But, on the other hand, the Lamanites, because of the hardness of their hearts, brought down many judgments upon their own heads; nevertheless, they were not destroyed as a nation; but the Lord God sent forth a curse upon them, and they became a dark, loathsome, and filthy people. Before their rebellion, they were white and exceedingly fair, like the Nephites; but the Lord God cursed them in their complexions, and they were changed to a dark colour; and they became a wild, savage, and ferocious people; being great enemies to the Nephites, whom they sought, by every means, to destroy, and many times came [p. 17] against them, with their numerous hosts to battle, but were repulsed by the Nephites, and driven back to their own possessions, not, however, generally speaking, without great loss on both sides; for tens of thousands were very frequently slain, after which they were piled together in great heaps upon the face of the ground, and covered with a shallow covering of earth, which will satisfactorily account for those ancient mounds, filled with human bones, so numerous at the present day, both in North and South America.

The second colony, which left Jerusalem eleven years after the remnant of Joseph left that city, landed in North America, and emigrated from thence, to the northern parts of South America; and about four hundred years after, they were discovered by the Nephites, as we stated in the foregoing.

They were called the people of Zarahemla. They had been perplexed with many wars among themselves; and having brought no records with them, their language had become corrupted, and they denied the being of God; and at the time they were discovered by the Nephites they were very numerous, and only in a partial state of civilization; but the Nephites united with them, and taught them the Holy Scriptures, and they were restored to civilization, and became one nation with them.[27] And in process of time, the Nephites began to build ships near the Isthmus of Darien, and launch them forth into the western

---

27. See Book of Mormon, 1837 ed., 159 [Omni 1:13–19].

ocean, in which great numbers sailed a great distance to the northward, and began to colonize North America.[28] Other colonies emigrated by land, and in a few centuries the whole continent became peopled. North America, at that time, was almost entirely destitute of timber, it having been cut off by the more ancient race, who came from the great tower, at the confusion of languages; but the Nephites became very skilful in building houses of cement; also, much timber was carried by the way of shipping from South to North America. They also planted groves and began to raise timber, that in time their wants might be supplied. Large cities were built in various parts of the continent, both among the Lamanites and Nephites. The law of Moses was observed by the latter. Numerous prophets were raised up from time to time throughout their generations. [p. 18] Many records, both historical and prophetical, which were of great size, were kept among them; some on plates of gold and other metals, and some on other materials. The sacred records, also, of the more ancient race who had been destroyed, were found by them. These were engraved on plates of gold. They translated them into their own language by the gift and power of God, through the means of the Urim and Thummim. They contained an historical account from the creation down to the Tower of Babel, and from that time down until they were destroyed, comprising a period of about thirty-four hundred, or thirty-five hundred years. They also contained many prophecies, great and marvellous, reaching forward to the final end and consummation of all things, and the creation of the new heaven and new earth.

The prophets also among the Nephites prophesied of great things. They opened the secrets of futurity, and saw the coming of Messiah in the flesh, and prophesied of the blessings to come upon their descendants in the latter times, and made known the history of unborn generations, and unfolded the grand events of ages to come, and viewed the power, and glory, and majesty of Messiah's second advent, and beheld the establishment of the kingdom of peace, and gazed upon the glories of the day of righteousness, and saw creation redeemed from the curse, and all the righteous filled with songs of everlasting joy.

The Nephites knew of the birth and crucifixion of Christ, by certain celestial and terrestrial phenomena, which, at those times, were shown forth in fulfilment of the predictions of many of their prophets. Notwithstanding the many blessings with which they had been blessed, they had fallen into great wickedness, and had cast out the saints and the prophets, and stoned and killed them. Therefore, at the time of the crucifixion of Christ, they were visited in

---

28. See Book of Mormon, 1837 ed., 429 [Alma 63:5–9]. Pratt here associates the "narrow neck" mentioned in the Book of Mormon with the Isthmus of Darien or Panama.

great judgment. Thick darkness covered the whole continent. The earth was terribly convulsed. The rocks were rent into broken fragments, and afterwards found in seams and cracks upon all the face of the land. Mountains were sunk into valleys, and valleys raised into mountains. The highways and level roads were broken up and spoiled. Many cities were laid in ruins. Others were buried up in the depths of the earth, and mountains occupied their place. [p. 19] While others were sunk, and waters came up in their stead, and others still were burned by fire from heaven.[29]

Thus, the predictions of their prophets were fulfilled upon their heads. Thus, the more wicked part, both of the Nephites and Lamanites, were destroyed. Thus, the Almighty executed vengeance and fury upon them, that the blood of the saints and prophets might no longer cry from the ground against them.

Those who survived these terrible judgments, were favoured with the personal ministry of Christ. For after He arose from the dead, and finished his ministry at Jerusalem, and ascended to heaven, he descended in the presence of the Nephites, who were assembled round about their temple in the northern parts of South America. He exhibited to them his wounded hands, and side, and feet; and commanded the law of Moses to be abolished; and introduced and established the Gospel in its stead; and chose twelve disciples from among them to administer the same; and instituted the sacrament; and prayed for and blessed their little children; and healed their sick, and blind, and lame, and deaf, and those who were afflicted in any way, and raised a man from the dead, and showed forth his power in their midst; and expounded the Scriptures, which had been given from the beginning down to that time; and made known unto them all things which should take place down until He should come in his glory, and from that time down to the end, when all people, nations, and languages should stand before God to be judged, and the heaven and the earth should pass away, and there should be a new heaven and new earth. These teachings of Jesus were engraved upon plates, some of which are contained in the book of Mormon; but the more part are not revealed in that book, but are hereafter to be made manifest to the saints.[30]

After Jesus had finished ministering unto them, he ascended into heaven; and the twelve disciples, whom he had chosen, went forth upon all the face of the land, preaching the gospel; baptizing those who repented for the remission of sins, after which they laid their hands upon them, that they might

---

29. See Book of Mormon, 1837 ed., 496–498 [3 Nephi 8].

30. See Book of Mormon, 1837 ed., 502–540 [3 Nephi 11–28], for the account of the visitation and ministry of Christ to the people of the Book of Mormon.

receive the Holy Spirit. Mighty miracles were wrought by them, and also by many of the church. The Nephites and Lamanites were all converted unto the Lord, both in South and North America: and they dwelt [p. 20] in righteousness above three hundred years; but towards the close of the fourth century of the Christian era, they had so far apostatized from God, that he suffered great judgments to fall upon them. The Lamanites, at that time, dwelt in South America, and the Nephites in North America.

A great and terrible war commenced between them, which lasted for many years, and resulted in the complete overthrow and destruction of the Nephites. This war commenced at the Isthmus of Darien, and was very destructive to both nations for many years. At length, the Nephites were driven before their enemies, a great distance to the north, and north-east; and having gathered their whole nation together, both men, women, and children, they encamped on, and round about the hill Cumorah, where the records were found, which is in the State of New York, about two hundred miles west of the city of Albany. Here they were met by the numerous hosts of the Lamanites, and were slain, and hewn down, and slaughtered, both male and female—the aged, middle aged, and children. Hundreds of thousands were slain on both sides; and the nation of the Nephites were destroyed, excepting a few who had deserted over to the Lamanites, and a few who escaped into the south country, and a few who fell wounded, and were left by the Lamanites on the field of battle for dead, among whom were Mormon and his son Moroni, who were righteous men.[31]

Mormon had made an abridgement, from the records of his forefathers, upon plates, which abridgement he entitled the "Book of Mormon;" and, (being commanded of God,) he hid up in the hill Cumorah, all the sacred records of his forefathers which were in his possession, except the abridgement called the "Book of Mormon," which he gave to his son Moroni to finish. Moroni survived his nation a few years, and continued the writings, in which he informs us, that the Lamanites hunted those few Nephites who escaped the great and tremendous battle of Cumorah, until they were all destroyed, excepting those who were mingled with the Lamanites, and that he was left alone, and kept himself hid, for they sought to destroy every Nephite who would not deny the Christ. He furthermore states, that the Lamanites were at war one with another, and that the [p. 21] whole face of the land was one continual scene of murdering, robbing, and plundering.[32] He continued the history until the four hundred and twentieth year of the Christian era, when, (by the commandment

---

31. See Book of Mormon, 1837 ed., 558–559 [Mormon 6].
32. See Book of Mormon, 1837 ed., 561–562, 605 [Mormon 8:1–14; Moroni 1:1–3].

of God,) he hid up the records in the hill Cumorah, where they remained concealed, until by the ministry of an angel they were discovered to Mr Smith, who, by the gift and power of God, translated them into the English language, by the means of the Urim and Thummim, as stated in the foregoing.

After the book was translated, the Lord raised up witnesses to bear testimony to the nations of its truth, who, at the close of the volume, send forth their testimony, which reads as follows:—

TESTIMONY OF THREE WITNESSES.

"Be it known unto all nations, kindreds, tongues, and people, unto whom this work shall come, that we, through the grace of God the Father, and our Lord Jesus Christ, have seen the plates which contain this record, which is a record of the people of Nephi, and also of the Lamanites, their brethren, and also of the people of Jared, who came from the tower of which hath been spoken; and we also know that they have been translated by the gift and power of God, for his voice hath declared it unto us; wherefore we know of a surety, that the work is true. And we also testify that we have seen the engravings which are upon the plates; and they have been shown unto us by the power of God, and not of man. And we declare, with words of soberness, that an angel of God came down from heaven, and he brought and laid before our eyes, that we beheld and saw the plates, and the engravings thereon; and we know that it is by the grace of God the Father, and our Lord Jesus Christ, that we beheld and bear record that these things are true; and it is marvellous in our eyes, nevertheless, the voice of the Lord commanded us that we should bear record of it; wherefore, to be obedient unto the commandments of God, we bear testimony of these things. And we know that if we are faithful in Christ, we shall rid our garments of the blood of all men, and be found spotless before the judgment seat of Christ, and shall dwell with him eternally in the heavens. And the honour be to the Father, and to the Son, and to the Holy Ghost, which is one God. Amen.

OLIVER COWDERY,
DAVID WHITMER,
MARTIN HARRIS." [p. 22]

AND ALSO THE TESTIMONY OF EIGHT WITNESSES.

"Be it known unto all nations, kindreds, tongues, and people, unto whom this work shall come, that Joseph Smith, Jr. the translator of this work, has shown unto us the plates of which hath been spoken, which have the appearance of gold; and as many of the leaves as the said Smith has translated, we did handle with our hands: and we also saw the engravings thereon, all of which has the appearance of ancient work, and of curious workmanship. And this we bear record with words of soberness, that the said Smith has shown unto us, for we have seen and hefted, and know of a surety, that the said Smith has got the plates of which we have spoken. And we give our names unto the world, to witness unto the world that which we have seen; and we lie not, God bearing witness of it.

> CHRISTIAN WHITMER,
> JACOB WHITMER,
> PETER WHITMER, Jr.
> JOHN WHITMER,
> HIRAM PAGE,
> JOSEPH SMITH, Sen.
> HYRUM SMITH,
> SAMUEL H. SMITH."[33]

Also, in the year 1829, Mr Smith and Mr Cowdery, having learned the correct mode of baptism, from the teachings of the Saviour to the ancient Nephites, as recorded in the "Book of Mormon," had a desire to be baptized; but knowing that no one had authority to administer that sacred ordinance in any denomination, they were at a loss to know how the authority was to be restored, and while calling upon the Lord with a desire to be informed on the subject, a holy angel appeared and stood before them, and laid his hands upon their heads, and ordained them, and commanded them to baptize each other, which they accordingly did.[34]

In the year 1830, a large edition of the "Book of Mormon" first appeared in print. And as some began to peruse its sacred pages, the spirit of the Lord bore record to them that it was true; and they were obedient to its requirements, by coming forth, humbly repenting before the Lord, and being immersed in water, for the remission of sins, after which, by the commandment of God, hands were laid upon them in the name of the Lord, for the gift of the Holy Spirit.

---

33. The statements of the three and eight witnesses found here match the versions in the second edition of the Book of Mormon. ("Testimony of Three Witnesses" and "Testimony of Eight Witnesses," in Book of Mormon, 1837 ed., [620]–[621].)

34. According to JS, the angel identified himself as John the Baptist. (JS History, vol. A-1, p. 294 herein [Draft 2].)

And on the sixth of April, in the year of our Lord one thousand eight hundred and thirty, the "Church of Jesus Christ of Latter Day Saints" was organized, in the town [p. 23] of Manchester, Ontario County, State of New York, North America.[35] Some few were called and ordained by the spirit of revelation and prophecy, and began to preach and bear testimony, as the spirit gave them utterance; and although they were the weak things of the earth, yet they were strengthened by the Holy Ghost, and gave forth their testimony in great power, by which means many were brought to repentance, and came forward with broken hearts and contrite spirits, and were immersed in water confessing their sins, and were filled with the Holy Ghost by the laying on of hands; and saw visions and prophesied. Devils were cast out, and the sick were healed by the prayer of faith, and laying on of hands. Thus was the word confirmed unto the faithful by signs following. Thus the Lord raised up witnesses, to bear testimony of his name, and lay the foundation of his kingdom in the last days. And thus the hearts of the saints were comforted, and filled with great joy. In the foregoing, we have related the most important facts concerning the visions and the ministry of the angel to Mr Smith; the discovery of the records; their translation into the English language, and the witnesses raised up to bear testimony of the same.

We have also stated when, and by whom they were written; that they contain the history of nearly one-half of the globe, from the earliest ages after the flood, until the beginning of the fifth century of the Christian era; that this history is interspersed with many important prophecies, which unfold the great events of the last days, and that in it also is recorded the gospel in its fulness and plainness, as it was revealed by the personal ministry of Christ to the ancient Nephites. We have also given an account of the restoration of the authority in these days, to administer in the ordinances of the gospel; and of the time of the organization of the church; and of the blessings poured out upon [t]he same while yet in its infancy.

We now proceed to give a sketch of the faith and doctrine of this Church.[36]

First, We believe in God the Eternal Father, and in his Son Jesus Christ, and in the Holy Ghost, who bears record of them, the same throughout all ages and for ever.

We believe that all mankind, by the transgression of their first parents, and not by their own sins, were brought un[p. 24]der the curse and penalty of that

---

35. On the name of the church and the location of its organizational meeting, see 496n21 herein.

36. Compare this list of beliefs with the list in JS's "Church History" that became known as the Articles of Faith, pp. 500–501 herein. Orson Pratt expanded on a list of church beliefs already published by Parley P. Pratt. (See Pratt and Higbee, *An Address . . . to the Citizens of Washington;* compare Pratt, *Late Persecution of the Church,* iii–xiii.)

transgression, which consigned them to an eternal banishment from the presence of God, and their bodies to an endless sleep in the dust, never more to rise, and their spirits to endless misery under the power of Satan; and that, in this awful condition, they were utterly lost and fallen, and had no power of their own to extricate themselves therefrom.

We believe, that through the sufferings, death, and atonement of Jesus Christ, all mankind, without one exception, are to be completely, and fully redeemed, both body and spirit, from the endless banishment and curse, to which they were consigned, by Adam's transgression; and that this universal salvation and redemption of the whole human family from the endless penalty of the original sin, is effected, without any conditions whatsoever on their part; that is, that they are not required to believe, or repent, or be baptized, or do any thing else, in order to be redeemed from that penalty; for whether they believe or disbelieve, whether they repent or remain impenitent, whether they are baptized or unbaptized, whether they keep the commandments or break them, whether they are righteous or unrighteous, it will make no difference in relation to their redemption, both soul and body, from the penalty of Adam's transgression. The most righteous man that ever lived on the earth, and the most wicked wretch of the whole human family, were both placed under the same curse, without any transgression or agency of their own, and they both, alike, will be redeemed from that curse, without any agency or conditions on their part. Paul says, Rom. v. 18, "Therefore, as by the offence of one, judgment came upon ALL *men* to condemnation; even so, by the righteousness of one, the free gift came upon ALL *men* unto the justification of life." This is the reason, why ALL *men* are redeemed from the grave. This is the reason, that the spirits of ALL *men* are restored to their bodies. This is the reason that ALL *men* are redeemed from their first banishment, and restored into the presence of God, and this is the reason that the Saviour said, John xii. 32, "If I be lifted up from the earth I will draw ALL *men* unto me." After this full, complete, and universal redemption, restoration, and salvation of the whole of Adam's race, through the atonement of Jesus Christ, without faith, re[p. 25]pentance, baptism, or any other works, then, all and every one of them, will enjoy eternal life and happiness, never more to be banished from the presence of God, IF *they themselves have committed no sin:* for the penalty of the original sin can have no more power over them at all, for Jesus hath destroyed its power, and broken the bands of the first death, and obtained the victory over the grave, and delivered all its captives, and restored them from their first banishment into the presence of his Father; hence eternal life will then be theirs, IF *they themselves are not found transgressors of some law.*

We believe that all mankind, in their infant state, are incapable of knowing good and evil, and of obeying or disobeying a law, and that, therefore, there is no law given to them, and that where there is no law, there is no transgression; hence they are innocent, and if they should all die in their infant state, they would enjoy eternal life, not being transgressors themselves, neither accountable for Adam's sin.

We believe that all mankind, in consequence of the fall, after they grow up from their infant state, and come to the years of understanding, know good and evil, and are capable of obeying or disobeying a law, and that a law is given against doing evil, and that the penalty affixed is a second banishment from the presence of God, both body and spirit, *after* they have been redeemed from the FIRST *banishment* and restored into his presence.

We believe, that the penalty of this second law can have no effect upon persons who have not had the privilege, in this life, of becoming acquainted therewith; for although the light that is in them, teaches them good and evil, yet that light does not teach them the law against doing evil, nor the penalty thereof. And although they have done things worthy of many stripes, yet the law cannot be brought to bear against them, and its penalty be inflicted, because they can plead ignorance thereof. Therefore they will be judged, not by the revealed law which they have been ignorant of, but by the law of their conscience, the penalty thereof being a few stripes.

We believe that all who have done evil, having a knowledge of the law, or afterwards, in this life, coming to the knowledge thereof, are under its penalty, which is not [p. 26] inflicted in this world, but in the world to come. Therefore such, in this world, are prisoners, shut up under the sentence of the law, awaiting, with awful fear, for the time of judgment, when the penalty shall be inflicted, consigning them to a *second banishment* from the presence of their Redeemer, who had redeemed them from the penalty of the FIRST law. But, enquires the sinner, is there no way for my escape? Is my case hopeless? Can I not devise some way by which I can extricate myself from the penalty of this SECOND *law*, and escape this SECOND *banishment?* The answer is, if thou canst hide thyself from the all-searching eye of an Omnipresent God, that he shall not find thee, or if thou canst prevail with him to deny justice its claim, or if thou canst clothe thyself with power, and contend with the Almighty, and prevent him from executing the sentence of the law, then thou canst escape. If thou canst cause repentance, or baptism in water, or any of thine own works, to *atone* for the least of thy transgressions, then thou canst deliver thyself from the awful penalty that awaits thee. But, be assured, O sinner, that thou canst not devise any way of thine own to escape, nor do any thing that will *atone* for thy sins. Therefore, thy case is hopeless, unless God hath devised some way for thy deliverance; but do not let despair seize upon thee: for though thou art under the sentence of a broken law, and hast no power to atone for thy sins, and redeem thyself therefrom, yet there is hope in thy case; for he, who gave the law, has devised a way for thy deliverance. That same Jesus, who hath atoned for the original sin, and will redeem all mankind from the penalty thereof, hath also atoned for thy sins, and offereth salvation and deliverance to thee, on certain conditions to be complied with on thy part.

We believe that the first condition to be complied with on the part of sinners is, to *believe* in God, and in the sufferings and death of his Son Jesus Christ, to atone for the sins of the whole world, and in his resurrection and ascension on high, to appear in the presence of his Father, to make intercessions for the children of men, and in the Holy Ghost, which is given to all who obey the gospel.

That the second condition is, to *repent*, that is, all who believe, according to the first condition, are required to [p. 27] come humbly before God, and confess their sins with a broken heart and contrite spirit, and to turn away from them, and cease from all their evil deeds, and make restitution to all they have in any way injured, as far as it is in their power.

That the third condition is, to be *baptized* by immersion in water, in the name of the Father, Son, and Holy Ghost, *for remission of sins;* and that this ordinance is to be administered by one who is called and authorized of Jesus Christ to baptize, otherwise it is illegal, and of no advantage, and not accepted by him; and that it is to be administered only to those persons, who believe and repent, according to the two preceding conditions.

And that the fourth condition is, to receive the *laying on of hands*, in the name of Jesus Christ, for the gift of the Holy Ghost; and that this ordinance is to be administered by the apostles or elders, whom the Lord Jesus hath called and authorized to lay on hands, otherwise it is of no advantage, being illegal in the sight of God; and that it is to be administered only to those persons, who believe, repent, and are baptized into this church, according to the three preceding conditions. These are the first conditions of the gospel. All who comply with them receive forgiveness of sins, and are made partakers of the Holy Ghost. Through these conditions, they become the adopted sons and daughters of God. Through this process, they are born again, first of water, and then of the spirit, and become children of the kingdom—heirs of God—saints of the most High—the church of the first-born—the elect people, and heirs to a celestial inheritance, eternal in the presence of God. After complying with these principles, their names are enrolled in the book of the names of the righteous.

They are then required to be humble, to be meek and lowly in heart, to watch and pray, to deal justly; and inasmuch as they have the riches of this world, to feed the hungry and clothe the naked, according to the dictates of wisdom and prudence; to comfort the afflicted, to bind up the broken-hearted, and to do all the good that is in their power: and besides all these things, they are required to meet together as often as circumstances will admit, and partake of bread and wine, in remembrance of the broken [p. 28] body, and shed blood of the Lord Jesus; and, in short, to continue faithful to the end, in all the duties enjoined upon them by the word and spirit of Christ.

"It is the duty and privilege of the saints thus organized upon the everlasting gospel, to believe in and enjoy all the gifts, powers, and blessings which flow from the Holy Spirit. Such, for instance, as the gifts of revelation, prophecy, visions, the ministry of angels, healing the sick by the laying on of hands in the name of Jesus, the working of miracles, and, in short, all the gifts as mentioned in Scripture, or as enjoyed by the ancient saints."[37] We believe that inspired apostles and prophets, together with all the officers as mentioned in the New Testament, are necessary to be in the Church in these days.

We believe that there has been a general and awful apostacy from the religion of the New Testament, so that all the known world have been left for centuries without the Church of Christ among them; without a priesthood authorized of God to administer ordinances; that every one of the churches has perverted the gospel; some in one way, and some in another. For instance, almost every church has done away *immersion for remission of sins.* Those few who have practised *it for remission of sins*, have done away the ordinance of the *"laying on of hands"* upon baptized believers for the gift of the Holy Ghost. Again, the few who have practised this last ordinance, have perverted the first, or have done away the ancient gifts, and powers, and blessings, which flow from the Holy Spirit, or have said to inspired apostles and prophets, we have no need of you in the body in these days. Those few, again, who have believed in, and contended for the miraculous gifts and powers of the Holy Spirit, have perverted the ordinances, or done them away. Thus all the churches preach false doctrines, and pervert the gospel, and instead of having authority from God to administer its ordinances, they are under the curse of God for perverting it. Paul says, Gal. i. 8, "Though we, or an angel from heaven, preach any other gospel unto you than that which we have preached unto you, let him be accursed."

We believe that there are a few, sincere, honest, and humble persons, who are striving to do according to the best of their understanding; but, in many

37. Pratt, *Late Persecution of the Church,* v.

respects, they [p. 29] err in doctrine, because of false teachers and the precepts of men, and that they will receive the fulness of the gospel with gladness, as soon as they hear it.

The gospel in the "Book of Mormon," is the same as that in the New Testament, and is revealed in great plainness, so that no one that reads it can misunderstand its principles. It has been revealed by the angel, to be preached as a witness to all nations, first to the Gentiles, and then to the Jews, then cometh the downfall of Babylon. Thus fulfilling the vision of John, which he beheld on the Isle of Patmos, Rev. xiv. 6, 7, 8, "And I saw," says John, "another angel fly in the midst of heaven, having the everlasting gospel to preach unto them that dwell on the earth, and to every nation, and kindred, and tongue, and people, saying, with a loud voice, Fear God, and give glory to him, for the hour of his judgment is come: and worship him that made heaven, and earth, and the sea, and the fountains of waters. And there followed another angel, saying, Babylon is fallen, is fallen, that great city, because she made all nations drink of the wine of the wrath of her fornication."

Many revelations and prophecies have been given to this church since its rise, which have been printed and sent forth to the world. These also contain the gospel in great plainness, and instructions of infinite importance to the saints. They also unfold the great events that await this generation; the terrible judgments to be poured forth upon the wicked, and the blessings and glories to be given to the righteous. We believe that God will continue to give revelations by visions, by the ministry of angels, and by the inspiration of the Holy Ghost, until the saints are guided unto all truth, that is, until they come in possession of all the truth there is in existence, and are made perfect in knowledge. So long, therefore, as they are ignorant of any thing past, present, or to come, so long, we believe, they will enjoy the gift of revelation. And when in their immortal and perfect state—when they enjoy "the measure of the stature of the fulness of Christ"[38]—when they are made perfect in one, and become like their Saviour, then they will be in possession of all knowledge, wisdom, and intelligence: then all things will be theirs, whether [pr]incipalities[39] or powers, thrones or dominions; and, i[n][40] [p. 30] short, then they will be filled with all the fulness of God. And what more can they learn? What more can they know? What more can they enjoy? Then they will no longer need revelation.

We believe that wherever the people enjoy the religion of the New Testament, there they enjoy visions, revelations, the ministry of angels, &c.

---

38. See Ephesians 4:13.
39. TEXT: Original has "incipalities", preceded by a one-character space.
40. TEXT: Original has "i", followed by a one-character space.

And that wherever these blessings cease to be enjoyed, there they also cease to enjoy the religion of the New Testament.

We believe that God has raised up this church, in order to prepare a people for his second coming in the clouds of heaven, in power, and great glory; and that then the saints who are asleep in their graves will be raised, and reign with him on earth a thousand years.

And we now bear testimony to all, both small and great, that the Lord of Hosts hath sent us with a message of glad tidings—the everlasting gospel, to cry repentance to the nations, and prepare the way of his second coming. Therefore *repent*, O ye nations, both Gentiles and Jews, and cease from all your *evil deeds*, and come forth with broken hearts and contrite spirits, and be *baptized* in water, in the name of the Father, Son, and Holy Ghost, *for remission of sins*, and ye shall receive the gift of the Holy Spirit, by the *laying on of the hands* of the Apostles or Elders of this church; and signs shall follow them that believe, and if they continue faithful to the end, they shall be saved. But woe unto them, who hearken not to the message which God has now sent, for the day of vengeance and burning is at hand, and they shall not escape. Therefore, REMEMBER, O reader, and *perish not!*

EDINBURGH: PRINTED BY BALLANTYNE AND HUGHES, PAUL'S WORK. [p. 31]

REFERENCE
MATERIAL

Chronology for the Years 1805–1844

This brief chronology includes significant events from JS's life and from the early history of the Latter-day Saint movement. It emphasizes events related to the creating and publishing of histories written by JS or initiated by official church assignment during JS's lifetime. Although this chronology spans most of JS's life, it is not a comprehensive list of major events; periods covered in more detail in the volume receive more extensive treatment here. Readers wishing to conduct further research into events in JS's life may consult the documented chronology found on the Joseph Smith Papers website, josephsmithpapers.org.

1805

December	23	JS born in Sharon, Vermont.

ca. 1812

JS contracted typhoid fever; complications required surgery on leg, West Lebanon, New Hampshire.

1816–1817

Winter	Smith family moved to Palmyra, New York.

1819

ca. January	Smith family moved to farm two miles south of Palmyra village.

1820

Spring	JS's first vision of Deity, near Smith home on south border of Palmyra Township.

1823

September	21–22	JS's first visions of angel Moroni, in which JS learned of ancient record inscribed on gold plates buried nearby, Palmyra and Manchester townships, New York.
November	19	Death of JS's brother Alvin Smith, Palmyra Township.

1824

September	22	JS made first annual trip to nearby hill to receive instruction from angel Moroni, Manchester Township.

1825

| September | 22 | JS made second annual trip to nearby hill to receive instruction from angel Moroni, Manchester Township. |
| November | 1 | JS, Joseph Smith Sr., Josiah Stowell, Isaac Hale, and five others apparently signed agreement concerning search for silver mine. |

1826

March	20	JS tried and acquitted on charges of being disorderly person and imposter, South Bainbridge, New York.
September	22	JS made third annual trip to nearby hill to receive instruction from angel Moroni, Manchester Township.
November		JS began working for Joseph Knight Sr., Colesville Township, New York.

1827

January	18	JS married Emma Hale, South Bainbridge.
September	22	JS obtained Book of Mormon plates, Manchester Township.
December		JS and Emma Smith moved from Manchester Township to Harmony Township, Pennsylvania.

1828

February		Martin Harris took transcript of characters copied from gold plates to show scholars in New York City and Albany, New York.
April–June		JS translated portion of Book of Mormon with Martin Harris acting as scribe, Harmony Township.
June	15	Unnamed son born to JS and Emma Smith; did not survive birth, Harmony Township.
July	early	JS traveled to parents' home in Manchester Township and learned Martin Harris lost manuscript pages of Book of Mormon.
		Plates temporarily taken from JS; first recorded revelation chastised JS but affirmed his status as translator, Harmony Township.
ca. October		Oliver Cowdery began teaching school in Manchester district and became acquainted with Smith family.
		Oliver Cowdery met David Whitmer, and both began investigating rumors of JS's acquisition of gold plates, Palmyra.

1829

| ca. Winter–Spring | | Revelation to Oliver Cowdery convinced him of JS's divine calling, Manchester Township. |
| February | | Joseph Smith Sr. visited JS and Emma Smith, Harmony Township. |

March		Revelation calling for three witnesses to see and testify of plates, Harmony Township.
ca. April		Revelation instructing JS not to retranslate Book of Mormon pages for which initial translation was lost, Harmony Township.
April	5	Oliver Cowdery arrived in Harmony Township to assist JS with Book of Mormon translation.
	7	JS recommenced Book of Mormon translation, with Oliver Cowdery assisting as scribe, Harmony Township.
May		Joseph Knight Sr. traveled from Colesville Township to Harmony Township, bringing JS needed supplies.
	15	JS and Oliver Cowdery received authority from John the Baptist and baptized each other, Harmony Township; sometime thereafter, received higher authority.
	15 or 25	Oliver Cowdery baptized Samuel Smith, Harmony Township.
June	ca. 1	David Whitmer arrived in Harmony, met JS for first time, and helped JS and Oliver Cowdery move to Whitmer farm in Fayette Township.
	early	Book of Mormon translation resumed at Whitmer home and continued throughout the month, Fayette Township.
		JS began visiting printers in Palmyra and Rochester, New York, to arrange for printing of Book of Mormon; eventually reached agreement with E. B. Grandin in Palmyra.
	11	Initial copyright requirement for Book of Mormon met by court filing of title page, Utica, New York.
	late	Three witnesses—Oliver Cowdery, David Whitmer, and Martin Harris—saw plates from which Book of Mormon was translated, Fayette Township; eight witnesses—Christian Whitmer, Jacob Whitmer, Peter Whitmer Jr., John Whitmer, Hiram Page, Joseph Smith Sr., Hyrum Smith, and Samuel Smith—saw and handled plates near Smith home, Palmyra Township.
	26	Book of Mormon title page published in *Wayne Sentinel,* Palmyra.
ca. June		"The word of the Lord" commanded JS and Oliver Cowdery to ordain each other elders and perform other ordinances when previously baptized "brethren" could be assembled to approve their ordination, Fayette Township.
July	ca. 1	Translation of Book of Mormon completed, Fayette Township.
August	25	Martin Harris pledged farm to assure payment to E. B. Grandin for printing five thousand copies of Book of Mormon, Palmyra.
	ca. 25–31	Hyrum Smith delivered first pages of Book of Mormon manuscript for typesetting, Palmyra.
October	4	JS moved back to Harmony Township.
December	late	Printing for Book of Mormon completed and binding process begun, Palmyra.

1830

March	26	*Wayne Sentinel* announced Book of Mormon available for purchase, Palmyra.
April	6	Church of Christ organized; revelation directing Saints to keep record and acknowledge JS as revelator, apostle, and elder, Fayette Township.
Summer		JS and John Whitmer began arranging and copying recorded revelations, Harmony Township.
		JS dictated "visions of Moses" to Oliver Cowdery, Fayette Township or Harmony Township.
		JS began inspired revision of Bible with Oliver Cowdery and John Whitmer as scribes, Fayette Township or Harmony Township.
June		Church branch established in Colesville Township.
	9	Church conference held; church approved "articles and covenants" outlining church organization and government; Oliver Cowdery appointed to keep church record and conference minutes, Fayette Township.
	ca. 28–July 1	JS arrested, tried, and acquitted on charges of being disorderly person, first at South Bainbridge, then Colesville.
July		Revelation instructing Emma Smith on preparation of hymnbook and other duties, Harmony Township.
August		With brother Hyrum Smith and John and David Whitmer, JS traveled to Colesville Township and encountered hostility.
September	early	JS and family relocated to Fayette Township because of opposition in Harmony Township.
October	28	Oliver Cowdery, Ziba Peterson, Parley P. Pratt, and Peter Whitmer Jr. arrived in Geauga County, Ohio, from New York en route to mission to unorganized territory west of Missouri. Remained for several weeks to preach and baptized more than one hundred individuals, including Sidney Rigdon and Frederick G. Williams, before moving on, accompanied by Williams.
December	early	Sidney Rigdon and Edward Partridge arrived in New York from Geauga County.
	7	Revelation calling Sidney Rigdon to act as scribe for JS's work on Bible revision, near Fayette Township.
	30	Revelation in Canandaigua, New York, commanding Saints to gather to Ohio.

1831

January	2	Third church conference held; revelation on gathering to Ohio and caring for poor, Fayette Township.
	14	Oliver Cowdery and companions preached to Delaware and Shawnee nations west of Missouri. Lacking government permission, they were

soon ordered to leave and instead began preaching in Jackson County, Missouri.

	late	JS, Emma Smith, Sidney Rigdon, Edward Partridge, Ezra Thayer, Joseph Knight Sr., Polly Knight, and Elizabeth Knight departed New York for move to Kirtland, Ohio.
February	4	JS arrived in Kirtland.
March	ca. 8	Revelation instructing John Whitmer "to Keep the Church Record & History continually," Kirtland.
April	9	John Whitmer appointed by council of elders to keep church record and history, Kirtland.
	30	Unnamed twins, a boy and girl, born to JS and Emma Smith; both died within hours of birth, Kirtland.
May	9	JS and Emma Smith adopted infant twins Joseph and Julia Murdock, Kirtland.
June	3–6	Conference of elders held, Kirtland.
	12	John Whitmer commenced writing history, Kirtland.
	19	JS, Sidney Gilbert, Edward Partridge, William W. Phelps, Sidney Rigdon, and others departed Kirtland on journey to Independence to designate location of Zion.
July	14	JS and party arrived in Independence.
	20	Revelation identifying Independence as "centre place" for Zion.
August	1	Revelation concerning Latter-day Saints in new gathering place, Jackson County.
	2	JS and company symbolically laid foundation for land of Zion; Sidney Rigdon dedicated land for gathering, Kaw Township, Jackson County.
	3	JS and company dedicated city of Zion and site for temple, Independence.
	9	JS, Oliver Cowdery, Sidney Gilbert, William W. Phelps, Sidney Rigdon, and others departed Independence on return journey to Kirtland.
	27	JS arrived in Kirtland by stage.
September	12	JS and family moved to John Johnson farm, Hiram Township, Ohio.
October	25–26	JS presided over meetings at which fifteen elders were ordained high priests, Orange, Ohio.
November	1	Church conference held at Hiram Township; passed resolution to publish ten thousand copies (later reduced to three thousand copies) of Book of Commandments.
	11	Revelation at Hiram Township directing John Whitmer to continue writing history and to carry revelation manuscript book to Missouri with Oliver Cowdery.
	20	Oliver Cowdery and John Whitmer departed Ohio for Missouri.

1832

January	5	Oliver Cowdery and John Whitmer arrived in Independence.
	25	JS appointed president of the high priesthood, Amherst Township, Ohio.
February	16	JS and Sidney Rigdon's vision of degrees of heavenly glory, Hiram Township.
March	8	Sidney Rigdon and Jesse Gause selected as counselors to JS in presidency of the high priesthood, Hiram Township.
	24	JS and Sidney Rigdon tarred and feathered, Hiram Township.
	29	Death of Joseph Murdock Smith, adopted son of JS and Emma Smith, Hiram Township.
April	1	JS departed Hiram Township on journey to Independence to meet with Latter-day Saints and conduct church business.
June		JS returned to Ohio from journey to Independence.
July	20	Frederick G. Williams appointed JS's scribe, Kirtland.
September	12	JS and family moved back from Hiram to Kirtland and lived above Newel K. Whitney's store.
Fall		JS departed Kirtland on journey with Newel K. Whitney to New York City and other cities in eastern United States to buy merchandise and proselytize.
November	6	Joseph Smith III born to JS and Emma Smith, Kirtland.
		JS returned to Kirtland from journey to eastern United States.
	27	JS wrote to William W. Phelps concerning record-keeping duties of church clerk, Kirtland.
December	27–28	Revelation mandating establishment of "house of God," or temple, in Kirtland and instruction and purification for those called to ministry, Kirtland. Additional revelation on same subject, 3 January 1833.

1833

January	4	JS wrote to N. C. Saxton, editor of *American Revivalist, and Rochester [NY] Observer,* asking him to publish letter expounding Mormon doctrine, Kirtland.
	11	JS wrote to William W. Phelps, editor of Missouri church periodical *The Evening and the Morning Star,* instructing him to publish information about rise and progress of church, Kirtland.
	by 22	Frederick G. Williams selected as counselor to JS in presidency of the high priesthood, Kirtland.
	23	JS conducted first session of School of the Prophets, Kirtland.
April		William W. Phelps published "Rise and Progress of the Church of Christ" in *The Evening and the Morning Star,* Independence.
June	1	Revelation chastising Saints for failure to build God's house as earlier mandated, Kirtland.

	6	Latter-day Saints began construction on temple, Kirtland.
	25	From Kirtland, JS sent plat for city of Zion with temple plan to Missouri Saints.
July	2	JS concluded work on Bible revision, Kirtland.
	20	Vigilantes, demanding removal of Latter-day Saints from Jackson County, destroyed printing office and tarred and feathered Edward Partridge and Charles Allen, Independence; a few dozen copies of unfinished Book of Commandments survived.
	23	JS participated in laying cornerstones of Kirtland temple.
		Under duress, Latter-day Saints in Jackson County agreed to demands of vigilantes to leave county.
August	9	Oliver Cowdery arrived in Kirtland with news of Jackson County citizens' demands for expulsion of Saints.
September	late	Mormons in Jackson County petitioned Missouri governor Daniel Dunklin with grievances; he advised settling matter through courts.
October	early	JS instructed Latter-day Saints in Jackson County that only those who had signed agreement and those who feared for personal safety should leave.
	5	JS departed Kirtland on proselytizing mission to Mount Pleasant, Upper Canada.
	31	Forty or fifty vigilantes attacked Saints at Whitmer settlement, Kaw Township.
November	1	Vigilantes attacked Gilbert and Whitney Store as well as homes of many Latter-day Saints, Independence.
	2	Vigilantes attacked Blue River settlement, Kaw Township, but retreated when Saints returned gunfire.
	4	One Mormon and two antagonists killed during confrontation, Whitmer settlement.
		Several church leaders imprisoned in Jackson County but released the following day after promising that all Mormons would depart from county.
		JS returned to Kirtland from journey to Mount Pleasant.
	5	County militia called out and assembled against Mormons, Independence.
	by 8	Latter-day Saints were fleeing Jackson County, migrating primarily to Clay County, Missouri.
	13	JS observed early-morning meteor shower, Kirtland; display seen as sign of imminent return of Jesus Christ by Mormon refugees in Missouri.
	25	JS notified by Orson Hyde and John Gould that Latter-day Saints had been expelled from Jackson County earlier in month, Kirtland.

1834

February	17	JS organized first high council, Kirtland.
	22	JS notified of condition of exiled Latter-day Saints in Clay County by Parley P. Pratt and Lyman Wight, Kirtland.
	24	Revelation in Kirtland commanding organization of expedition (later known as "Camp of Israel" or "Zion's Camp") to relieve Saints driven from Jackson County and to help them return to their homes.
	26	JS departed Kirtland on journey to Pennsylvania and New York to raise funds and recruit volunteers for Camp of Israel.
March	28	JS returned to Kirtland from journey to New York and Pennsylvania.
April	20–21	JS attended church conference in Norton, Ohio, to raise funds and recruit volunteers for Camp of Israel.
May	3	Name of church changed from "Church of Christ" to "Church of the Latter Day Saints," Kirtland.
	5	JS departed Kirtland on journey to Missouri at head of Camp of Israel.
June	ca. 15	JS received word that Missouri governor Daniel Dunklin would not assist in reclaiming Jackson County land.
	19	Camp of Israel arrived in Clay County; vigilantes assembled to attack Camp of Israel but abandoned venture because of severe rainstorm, Fishing River Township, Clay County.
	22	Revelation in Washington, Clay County, effectively disbanded Camp of Israel, stating redemption of Zion must wait until elders were "endowed with power from on high" in Kirtland temple.
	late	Camp of Israel, including JS, afflicted with cholera, Clay County; more than a dozen camp members and Clay County Saints died.
July	3, 7	JS organized high council for church in Missouri, ordained David Whitmer president of church in Missouri and potential successor, and ordained William W. Phelps and John Whitmer assistant presidents, Liberty Township, Clay County.
August	ca. 1	JS returned to Kirtland from expedition to Missouri.
	16	In Kirtland, JS urged Missouri high council to sign petition to Missouri governor Daniel Dunklin to request federal protection for Saints on their Jackson County properties; declared 11 September 1836 as "the appointed time for the redemption of Zion."
September	5	JS traveled with Oliver Cowdery to attend church conference in New Portage, Ohio.
	7	Oliver Cowdery wrote first of eight historical letters published in *LDS Messenger and Advocate,* Kirtland.
October	16	JS departed Kirtland on journey to Pontiac, Michigan, to meet with Latter-day Saints and proselytize.
	late	JS returned to Kirtland.

December	5	JS ordained Oliver Cowdery an assistant president of the high priesthood, Kirtland.
	6	JS ordained brother Hyrum Smith and father, Joseph Smith Sr., assistant presidents of the high priesthood, Kirtland.
	9	JS received patriarchal blessing from Joseph Smith Sr., Kirtland.

1835

January	14	Copyright for Doctrine and Covenants secured, Ohio.
February	14	Three Witnesses to the Book of Mormon selected Quorum of the Twelve Apostles, Kirtland.
	17	JS and counselors wrote preface to Doctrine and Covenants, Kirtland.
	28	JS organized Quorum of the Seventy, Kirtland.
May	4	Twelve Apostles departed Kirtland on journey to northeastern states and Upper Canada to supervise outlying branches of church.
July		With help of others, JS purchased Egyptian mummies and papyri associated with later Book of Abraham translation, Kirtland.
August ca. 10–23		JS traveled from Kirtland to Michigan to visit Latter-day Saints.
	17	Church conference approved publication of Doctrine and Covenants, Kirtland.
September	14	Oliver Cowdery appointed church recorder, Kirtland.
	24	JS and high council resolved that exiled Mormons should petition Missouri governor Daniel Dunklin for resettlement on Jackson County lands, Kirtland.
Fall		JS worked periodically on Book of Abraham translation, Kirtland.
October	7–11	JS attended father, Joseph Smith Sr., during serious illness, Kirtland.
	29	Warren Parrish hired as JS's scribe, Kirtland.
November	9–11	JS hosted Robert Matthews, whom he ultimately denounced, Kirtland.
	12	JS instructed apostles about ordinance of washing of feet and forthcoming endowment, Kirtland.
	19	JS visited Kirtland temple and observed interior finishing work.
	24	JS solemnized his first recorded wedding, marrying Newel Knight and Lydia Goldthwaite Bailey, Kirtland.
December	16	William Smith became enraged during debating school argument and attacked JS, Kirtland.
ca. 17–29		JS's parents moved into his home, Kirtland.

1836

January	1	JS reconciled with William Smith, Kirtland.
	4	JS organized school for study of Hebrew language, Kirtland.

	13	JS presided over meeting of church leaders in which Kirtland bishop's council and high councils of Kirtland and Missouri were fully organized, Kirtland.
	21	JS administered and received first ritual washings and anointings with priesthood leaders; saw vision of celestial kingdom, Kirtland.
	26	First day of formal instruction of Hebrew School, Kirtland.
March	27	JS dedicated temple, Kirtland.
	29	JS administered and received ritual washing of feet with priesthood leaders in temple, Kirtland.
	30	Solemn assembly held in temple, Kirtland.
	31	JS repeated temple dedication ceremonies for those who could not be seated on 27 March, Kirtland.
ca. April		Warren Cowdery began work as JS's clerk; assignments included inscription in JS's history, Kirtland.
April	3	JS and Oliver Cowdery's visions of Jesus Christ, Moses, Elias, and Elijah in temple, Kirtland.
June	20	Frederick Granger Williams Smith born to JS and Emma Smith, Kirtland.
	29	Clay County citizen committee demanded that Mormons stop immigrating to county and that those without substantial farms leave after fall harvest.
July	25	JS and associates departed Kirtland on journey to conduct business in New York City and to search for rumored cache of money in house in Salem, Massachusetts.
August	8	Church funds used to purchase plot for future site of Far West, Missouri.
September		JS returned to Kirtland from journey to New York and Massachusetts.
December	29	Missouri governor Lilburn W. Boggs signed bill creating Caldwell County for Mormon settlement, Jefferson City, Missouri.

1837

January	9	Kirtland Safety Society Anti-Banking Company, although denied state banking charter, opened doors to public, Kirtland.
February		JS traveled to Monroe, Michigan, in connection with recent investment in Bank of Monroe.
	19	JS spoke in temple denouncing dissenters, Kirtland.
April	5	Missouri high council confronted John Whitmer and William W. Phelps concerning business conduct, Far West, Caldwell County.
	6	JS held solemn assembly in temple on anniversary of church's organization, Kirtland.
	13	JS charged with hiring men to kill Grandison Newell, Painesville, Ohio.

May	28	JS defended himself in worship service against accusations of dissenters, Kirtland.
June	8	JS completed withdrawal from Kirtland Safety Society, apparently recognizing likelihood of failure, having made arrangements for resolution of outstanding debts, Kirtland.
	9	JS discharged in Grandison Newell case, Chardon, Ohio.
	11	JS instructed and set apart as missionaries to England apostles Heber C. Kimball and Orson Hyde and priest Joseph Fielding, Kirtland; two days later, with Willard Richards, they departed to fulfill mission.
	12	JS suffered onset of severe illness, Kirtland.
July	ca. 19	Heber C. Kimball and six other missionaries arrived in Liverpool, England.
	28	JS departed Kirtland on journey to Toronto, Upper Canada, to visit Latter-day Saints.
	late	Church newspaper acknowledged failure of Kirtland Safety Society, Kirtland.
August	27	JS returned to Kirtland from journey to Toronto.
September	3	JS presided over conference at which apostles Luke Johnson, Lyman Johnson, and John F. Boynton were disfellowshipped; on 10 September all three confessed errors and were received back into church fellowship, Kirtland.
	17	JS appointed 109 missionaries; George W. Robinson appointed general church clerk and recorder, Kirtland.
	27	JS departed Kirtland on journey to northwest Missouri to put Missouri church in order and identify places for Latter-day Saints to settle.
November	7	JS held church conference, Far West, at which Frederick G. Williams was removed from presidency and Hyrum Smith appointed in his place.
December	ca. 10	JS returned to Kirtland from journey to Missouri; faced dissenters forming rival church, Kirtland.
	late	High council excommunicated twenty-eight dissenters, including Martin Harris, Warren Parrish, and apostles Luke Johnson and John F. Boynton, Kirtland.

1838

January	12	JS and Sidney Rigdon fled Kirtland for Far West.
March	10	Church council excommunicated John Whitmer and William W. Phelps, Far West.
	14	JS arrived at Far West.
April	6	John Corrill and Elias Higbee appointed historians; George W. Robinson retained as general church recorder and appointed clerk for

First Presidency; Ebenezer Robinson appointed church clerk, Far West.

9 Letter from JS and Sidney Rigdon demanded surrender of John Whitmer's "notes" on church history in order to revise and publish them, Far West.

12 Church council excommunicated Oliver Cowdery, Far West.

13 Church council excommunicated David Whitmer and Lyman Johnson, Far West.

26 Revelation clarifying name of church as "the Church of Jesus Christ of Latter Day Saints" and commanding Saints to build house of the Lord, Far West.

27 With Sidney Rigdon and George W. Robinson, JS commenced writing detailed history of church, Far West.

May 18 JS departed Far West on journey to Daviess County, Missouri, to select sites for new Mormon settlements.

19 JS planned Mormon settlement at Spring Hill (soon renamed Adam-ondi-Ahman), Daviess County.

June Led by Sampson Avard, Jared Carter, and George W. Robinson, group later known as "Danites" began meeting to discuss and act on problem of dissenters in church, Far West.

1 JS returned to Far West from journey to Daviess County.

2 Alexander Hale Smith born to JS and Emma Smith, Far West.

17 Sidney Rigdon delivered "Salt Sermon," criticizing dissenters, Far West; two days later, Oliver Cowdery, Lyman Johnson, and David and John Whitmer fled Far West.

28 JS organized stake at Adam-ondi-Ahman with John Smith as president.

July 4 JS presided over Independence Day celebration, which included ceremonial laying of temple cornerstones and public address by Sidney Rigdon declaring Latter-day Saints' intent to defend themselves from persecution, Far West.

6 About five hundred Saints constituting "Kirtland Camp" departed Kirtland, migrating to Missouri.

30–31 JS attended circuit court; received visit from Judge Austin A. King, Far West.

August 6 Fighting broke out at Gallatin, Daviess County, during attempt to prevent Mormons from voting in election; injuries and rumor of deaths resulted.

8 With large company of armed men, JS called upon Daviess County justice of the peace Adam Black, demanding he uphold the law, Grand River Township, Daviess County.

10 Writs for arrest of JS and Lyman Wight issued by Austin A. King, Richmond, Ray County, Missouri.

	11	JS departed Far West on journey to "forks of Grand River," non-county territory northwest of Daviess County, to warn company of Canadian Latter-day Saints who settled outside of Adam-ondi-Ahman area contrary to his directions.
	13	JS returned to Far West.
September	4	JS hired David R. Atchison and Alexander Doniphan as legal counsel, Far West.
	7	JS appeared for preliminary hearing with Lyman Wight before Austin A. King on charges arising from confrontation with Adam Black; gave bonds for later court appearance, Honey Creek Township, Daviess County.
October	1	Vigilantes began armed siege of Mormon settlement in De Witt, Carroll County, Missouri; Mormons sought help from Missouri governor Lilburn W. Boggs and other civil authorities.
	2	Members of Kirtland Camp arrived in Far West.
	5–13	JS led rescue company to defend besieged Mormons at De Witt; assisted with evacuation and migration to Far West.
	ca. 9	Messenger informed Latter-day Saints at De Witt that Missouri governor Lilburn W. Boggs declined to intervene on their behalf.
	ca. 13	JS arrived in Far West after evacuation from De Witt.
	14	Clay County militia company under Colonel William Dunn encamped near Far West; Dunn informed JS that armed force of vigilantes was en route from Carroll to Daviess County; JS requested that company of Mormon soldiers prepare to leave for Daviess County.
	15	Brigadier General Alexander Doniphan arrived in Far West and advised Latter-day Saints to prepare to defend themselves; JS and Mormon cavalry departed Far West for Adam-ondi-Ahman.
	16	Fearing anti-Mormon mutiny, Alexander Doniphan ordered his troops back to Clay County; JS arrived with Mormon reinforcements at Adam-ondi-Ahman.
	17	Heavy snow prevented movement by Mormon and Missouri militias.
	18–21	Mormon forces plundered and burned residences and businesses of perceived opponents and communities supportive of anti-Mormon vigilantes, Daviess County.
	18	General Hiram Parks arrived in Daviess County.
	22–23	JS returned to Far West from Adam-ondi-Ahman.
	24	Thomas B. Marsh and Orson Hyde signed affidavits criticizing actions of Saints, Richmond.
	25	Mormon militia attacked volunteers from Ray County who had captured two Mormon spies; two Latter-day Saints, their guide, and one Ray County militiaman killed at Crooked River, near borderline of Caldwell and Ray counties.

27   Governor Lilburn W. Boggs issued order authorizing extermination or expulsion of Mormons from state, Jefferson City.

30   General Samuel D. Lucas and nearly two thousand troops approached Far West.

Vigilantes attacked outlying community of Latter-day Saints, killing seventeen and wounding fourteen, Hawn's Mill settlement, Grand River Township, Caldwell County.

31   JS and four others surrendered to Samuel D. Lucas; taken prisoner by state militia, Far West.

November   1   Mormon prisoners sentenced to death by military court; Alexander Doniphan objected, thus preventing execution, Goose Creek camp, Rockford Township, Caldwell County.

9   JS and others confined at Richmond, pending outcome of court of inquiry.

12–29   JS and others appeared at court of inquiry before Austin A. King, Richmond.

29   Mormon prisoners bound over for trial in Daviess, Caldwell, and Ray counties for treason and other charges, Richmond.

December   1   JS, Hyrum Smith, Sidney Rigdon, Lyman Wight, Caleb Baldwin, and Alexander McRae incarcerated, Liberty, Clay County.

1839

January   25   Hearing of JS and others before Judge Joel Turnham, Liberty.

29   Sidney Rigdon released but remained in jail as safety precaution until 5 February, Liberty.

February   Beginning of large-scale evacuation of Saints from Missouri to Illinois.

6   JS and others made unsuccessful attempt to escape jail, Liberty.

11   John Corrill registered copyright for *A Brief History of the Church of Christ of Latter Day Saints,* St. Louis, Missouri.

March   4   JS and others made second unsuccessful attempt to escape jail, Liberty.

17   John Corrill excommunicated in absentia, Quincy, Illinois.

20   JS commenced writing epistle from jail to exiled Latter-day Saints, completing it by 22 March, Liberty; letter instructed Edward Partridge and Saints to record depredations and losses suffered in Missouri.

April   6–8   JS transferred from Liberty to Gallatin to attend grand jury hearing on crimes allegedly committed in Daviess County.

11   In Gallatin, JS indicted by grand jury for treason and other charges but granted change of venue.

12   JS departed Gallatin on journey to Columbia, Boone County, Missouri, to stand trial.

16   JS and companions allowed to escape while en route to Columbia for trial, Chariton County, Missouri.

	22	JS reunited with wife and children, who were residing in home of John and Sarah Cleveland, Quincy.
	ca. 25	JS began investigating land for Mormon settlement, Illinois and Iowa.
	30	Church agents made initial purchases of land for Mormon settlement in Commerce, Illinois, area.
May	6	Almon Babbitt, Erastus Snow, and Robert B. Thompson appointed to compile accounts of Missouri injustices, Quincy.
	9–10	JS and family moved from Quincy to log home in Commerce area.
	27	Death of Edward Partridge, Commerce area.
June	4	JS dictated "Bill of Damages against the State of Missouri," Quincy.
	11	JS resumed recording history with scribe James Mulholland, Commerce area.
July		First issue of church newspaper *Times and Seasons* published at Commerce; included "Extract, from the Private Journal of Joseph Smith Jr."
		JS and others administered faith healings to Saints in areas of Commerce, Illinois, and Montrose, Iowa.
August	8	John Taylor and Wilford Woodruff departed Commerce for British Isles, initiating overseas proselytizing mission of Quorum of the Twelve Apostles.
October	5–7	JS presided over general church conference at Commerce and organized stakes in Commerce area and Iowa.
	ca. 29	JS departed Illinois for Washington DC to seek redress for Mormon property losses in Missouri.
November		First number of *Times and Seasons* reissued at Commerce.
	3	Death of James Mulholland, JS's scribe, Commerce area.
	28	JS arrived in Washington DC.
December		From this month until October 1840, *Times and Seasons* published twelve installments of "A History, of the Persecution, of the Church of Jesus Christ, of Latter Day Saints in Missouri," including three installments by Edward Partridge, Commerce/Nauvoo, Illinois.
	5	JS and Elias Higbee sent letter from Washington DC to Hyrum Smith, reporting visit with U.S. president Martin Van Buren.

1840

March	early	JS returned to Commerce from Washington DC.
April	6	Orson Hyde and John Page appointed to meet with Jewish leaders in London, Amsterdam, Constantinople, Jerusalem, and elsewhere.
	mid	Howard Coray began work as JS's clerk, Commerce/Nauvoo.
	21	United States postmaster general officially changed name of Commerce post office to Nauvoo.
June	13	Don Carlos Smith born to JS and Emma Smith, Nauvoo.

August	15	JS introduced doctrine of proxy baptism for deceased persons, Nauvoo.
September	1	Missouri governor Lilburn W. Boggs initiated extradition proceedings against JS and others, Independence.
	14	Death of Joseph Smith Sr., Nauvoo.
	late	Orson Pratt published *A[n] Interesting Account of Several Remarkable Visions,* with first printed account of JS's first vision of Deity, Edinburgh, Scotland.
October	3	Robert B. Thompson appointed general church clerk, Nauvoo.
	19	From Nauvoo, JS and Hyrum Smith wrote letter of reproof to Latter-day Saints in Kirtland.
December		JS dictated letter from Nauvoo to apostles on missions in Great Britain, agreeing to their request to return in spring.
	16	State of Illinois granted official charter to city of Nauvoo.

1841

January	19	Revelation regarding church callings and construction of temple and Nauvoo House, Nauvoo.
February	1	Charter for city of Nauvoo (approved by Illinois legislature and governor in December 1840) took effect, and first general elections held, Nauvoo.
June	5	JS arrested at Bear Creek, Illinois, based on requisition that former Missouri governor Lilburn W. Boggs issued to Illinois governor Thomas Carlin to extradite JS as fugitive from justice; obtained writ of habeas corpus at Quincy, Illinois.
	7	JS departed Quincy for hearing in Monmouth, Illinois.
	10	Judge Stephen A. Douglas ruled arrest warrant invalid and discharged JS, Monmouth.
July	4	Brigham Young, John Taylor, and Heber C. Kimball, first apostles to return from Great Britain, reported on missions to congregation of five thousand, Nauvoo.
August	15	Death of Don Carlos Smith, son of JS and Emma Smith, Nauvoo.
	16	"Special conference of the Church" in Nauvoo approved JS's proposal that Quorum of the Twelve Apostles be elevated "to stand in their place next to the First Presidency."
	27	Death of Robert B. Thompson, JS's clerk, Nauvoo.
October	2	James Sloan appointed to replace Robert B. Thompson as general church clerk, Nauvoo.
	24	Orson Hyde dedicated Palestine for return of "Judah's scattered remnants."
November	21	First proxy baptisms for deceased persons in Nauvoo temple performed in temple font.

December	13	JS appointed Willard Richards recorder for Nauvoo temple and scribe for private office of JS, Nauvoo.

1842

February	6	Unnamed son born to JS and Emma Smith; did not survive birth, Nauvoo.
March	1	JS's account of church history and summary of foundational beliefs—previously sent to Chicago newspaper editor John Wentworth—published in *Times and Seasons,* Nauvoo.
	17	JS organized Female Relief Society of Nauvoo and appointed Emma Smith president, Nauvoo.
May	4	JS presented sacred ceremonies and instructions known as "endowment" to Hyrum Smith, Brigham Young, and others in upper room of JS's red brick store, Nauvoo.
June	16	William W. Phelps assigned to continue work on JS's history, Nauvoo.
August	8	JS arrested on charge of being accessory in shooting of Lilburn W. Boggs, Nauvoo. Nauvoo Municipal Court issued writ of habeas corpus; JS remained in Nauvoo while officers took writ and arrest warrant to Quincy seeking Governor Thomas Carlin's advice.
	by 10	JS went into hiding; in and out of hiding for about four months, Nauvoo and surrounding area.
September	20	Governor Thomas Carlin issued proclamation for JS's arrest.
	26	Death of John Corrill, Adams County, Illinois.
December	1	JS appointed Willard Richards to work on history with William W. Phelps, Nauvoo.

1843

January	4, 5	JS appeared in federal court for habeas corpus hearing; Judge Nathaniel Pope ruled that Lilburn W. Boggs's affidavit, upon which Missouri writ of extradition was based, was defective and that JS should be discharged from arrest, Springfield, Illinois.
	6	Illinois governor Thomas Ford signed order discharging JS from arrest and declaring previous proclamation and arrest warrants for JS void, Springfield.
	20	JS instructed William W. Phelps and Willard Richards regarding history, Nauvoo.
May	11	At Nauvoo, church clerk James Sloan called on mission to Ireland.
	28	JS and Emma Smith married for eternity in JS's red brick store, Nauvoo.
June	8	Death of Elias Higbee, Nauvoo.
	10	Letter sent from Missouri informing Thomas Ford that JS had been indicted for treason by grand jury in Daviess County.

	17	Thomas Ford issued arrest warrant in connection with treason charge, Springfield.
	23	JS arrested by Missouri sheriff and Illinois constable on charge of treason against Missouri, near Dixon, Illinois.
July		JS received request from publisher Clyde, Williams & Co. for article on church to be published in collection of religious essays, Nauvoo.
	1	JS discharged by Nauvoo Municipal Court on writ of habeas corpus, Nauvoo.
	12	Revelation on plural wives and eternal marriage recorded, Nauvoo.
	30	At Nauvoo, Willard Richards appointed general church recorder, replacing James Sloan.
September	7	Historical article sent to Clyde, Williams & Co. under JS's name for publication in I. Daniel Rupp's *He Pasa Ekklesia* [The whole church], Nauvoo.

1844

ca. April	JS's essay "Latter Day Saints" published in *He Pasa Ekklesia*.

Maps

The following maps show nearly every town and city mentioned in this volume of *The Joseph Smith Papers,* along with other features and boundaries, as they existed during the period indicated on each map.

To locate a particular place on these maps, consult the map index at the end of the maps section, on page 576 herein. The map index provides grid coordinates and full jurisdictional identification for each place.

568

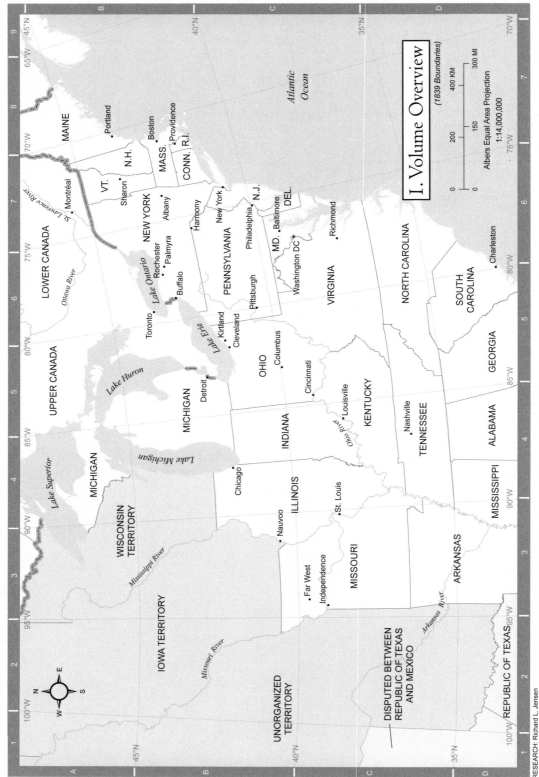

I. Volume Overview
(1839 Boundaries)

Albers Equal Area Projection
1:14,000,000

300 MI

400 KM

RESEARCH: Richard L. Jensen
CARTOGRAPHY: Brent Beck, Kent Simons, Benjamin Clift, Tyler Jones, BYU Geography

569

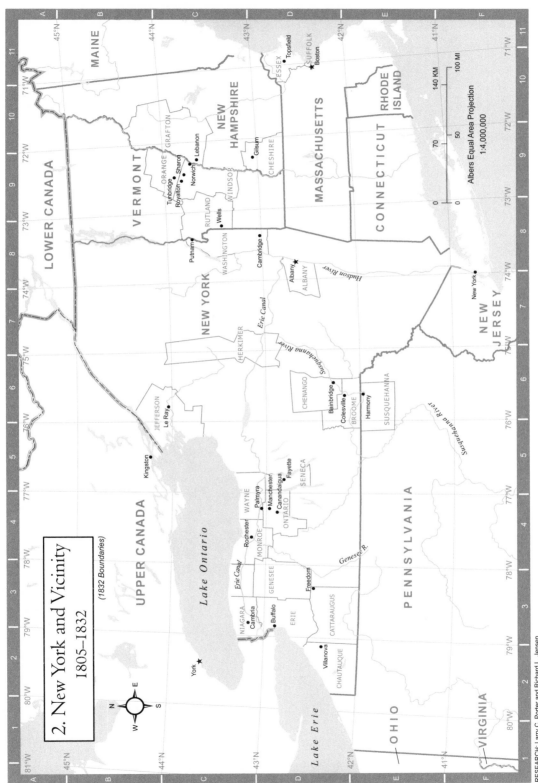

2. New York and Vicinity
1805–1832
(1832 Boundaries)

RESEARCH: Larry C. Porter and Richard L. Jensen
CARTOGRAPHY: Isaac Montague, Benjamin Clift, Tyler Jones, BYU Geography

570

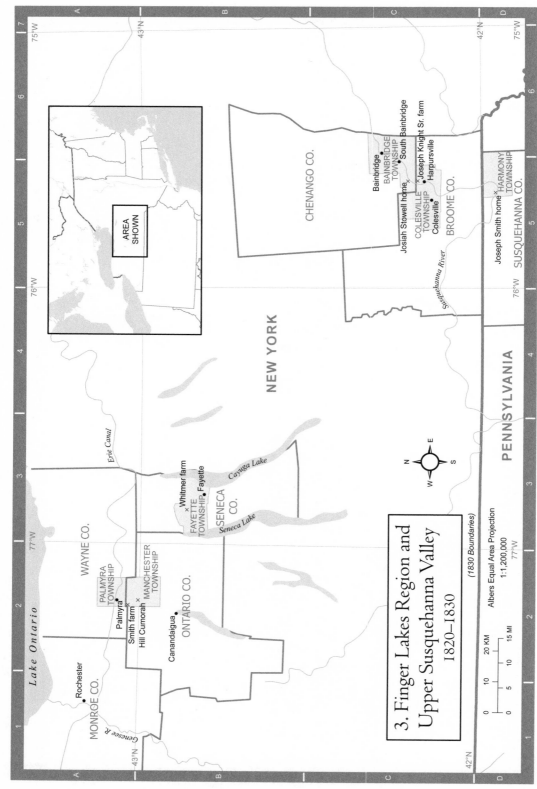

3. Finger Lakes Region and Upper Susquehanna Valley

1820–1830

(1830 Boundaries)

Albers Equal Area Projection

1:1,200,000

0   10   20 KM
0 5 10 15 MI

NEW YORK

PENNSYLVANIA

CHENANGO CO.

BROOME CO.

SUSQUEHANNA CO.

MONROE CO.

WAYNE CO.

ONTARIO CO.

SENECA CO.

Lake Ontario

Genesee R.

Erie Canal

Cayuga Lake

Seneca Lake

Susquehanna River

Rochester

Palmyra

PALMYRA TOWNSHIP

MANCHESTER TOWNSHIP

Smith farm

Hill Cumorah

Canandaigua

Whitmer farm

Fayette

FAYETTE TOWNSHIP

Bainbridge

BAINBRIDGE TOWNSHIP

South Bainbridge

Josiah Stowell home

Joseph Knight Sr. farm

Harpursville

COLESVILLE TOWNSHIP

Colesville

Joseph Smith home

HARMONY TOWNSHIP

AREA SHOWN

N
E
S
W

75°W
76°W
77°W

43°N
42°N

RESEARCH: Richard L. Jensen
CARTOGRAPHY: Tyler Jones, BYU Geography

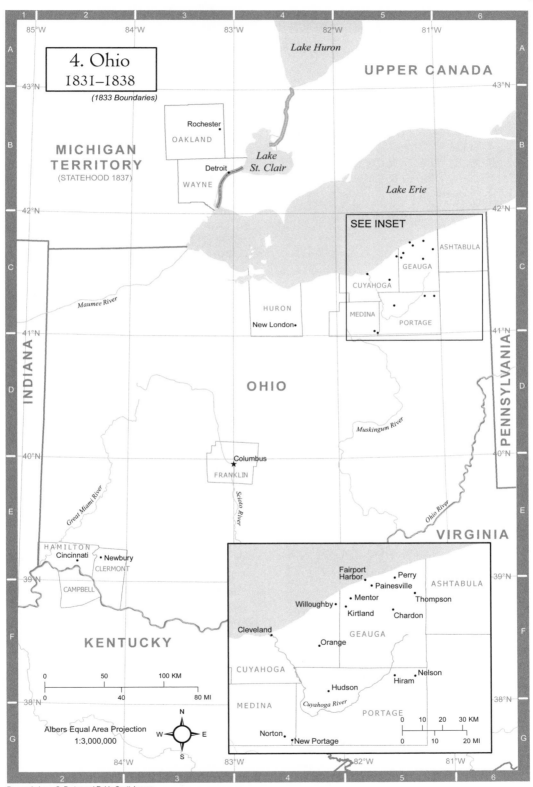

4. Ohio
1831–1838
(1833 Boundaries)

Lake Huron

UPPER CANADA

MICHIGAN TERRITORY
(STATEHOOD 1837)

OAKLAND

Rochester

Lake St. Clair

Detroit

WAYNE

Lake Erie

SEE INSET

ASHTABULA

GEAUGA

CUYAHOGA

MEDINA

PORTAGE

Maumee River

HURON

New London

OHIO

INDIANA

Muskingum River

PENNSYLVANIA

Columbus

FRANKLIN

Scioto River

Great Miami River

Ohio River

VIRGINIA

HAMILTON

Cincinnati

Newbury

CLERMONT

CAMPBELL

KENTUCKY

0 50 100 KM
0 40 80 MI

Albers Equal Area Projection
1:3,000,000

N
W E
S

Inset:

Fairport Harbor

Perry

Painesville

ASHTABULA

Willoughby

Mentor

Thompson

Kirtland

Chardon

Cleveland

GEAUGA

Orange

CUYAHOGA

Nelson

Hiram

Hudson

MEDINA

Cuyahoga River

PORTAGE

0 10 20 30 KM
0 10 20 MI

Norton

New Portage

Research: Larry C. Porter and Robin Scott Jensen
Cartography: Isaac Montague, Brent Beck, Kent Simons, Benjamin Clift, Tyler Jones, BYU Geography

Portion of Kirtland Township, Ohio
31 December 1835

Selected Structures

A. Loud-Lyman gristmill
B. Loud-Lyman sawmill
C. Milldam
D. Newel K. and Elizabeth Ann Whitney house
E. N. K. Whitney & Co. red store
F. N. K. Whitney & Co. white store
G. Tannery
H. Bark mill
I. Tannery vats
J. John Johnson inn
K. Distillery
L. Sawmill
M. Ashery
N. Schoolhouse on the flats
O. Joseph Smith Jr. and Emma Smith house
P. Joseph Smith Sr. and Lucy Mack Smith house
Q. Methodist Episcopal church
R. John Johnson Sr. and Elsa Johnson house
S. Schoolhouse/printing office
T. House of the Lord (temple)
U. Sidney and Phoebe Rigdon house

Selected Properties and Owners

1. N. K. Whitney & Co.
2. N. K. Whitney & Co.
3. N. K. Whitney & Co.
4. Austin Loud and Azariah Lyman
5. Austin Loud and Azariah Lyman
6. Austin Loud
7. Frederick G. Williams
8. Frederick G. Williams
9. Elijah Smith
10. Ira Bond
11. Azariah Lyman
12. Newel K. Whitney
13. Martha Raymond
14. Newel K. Whitney
15. Sidney Rigdon
16. Samuel Smith
17. Elijah Smith
18. N. K. Whitney & Co.
19. N. K. Whitney & Co.
20. Jacob Bump
21. Newel K. Whitney
22. Ira Bond
23. Leonard Rich
24. Joseph Smith Jr.
25. Newel K. Whitney
26. Newel K. Whitney
27. Oliver Cowdery
28. Newel K. Whitney
29. Oliver Cowdery
30. Joseph Smith Jr.
31. Sidney Rigdon
32. Joseph Smith Jr.
33. Edmund Bosley
34. Joseph Smith Jr.
35. Jacob Bump

Index of Selected Owners

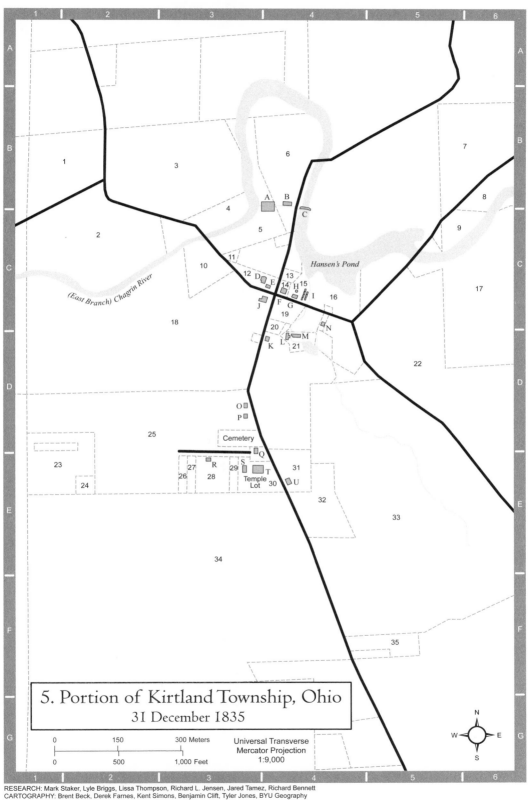

5. Portion of Kirtland Township, Ohio
31 December 1835

0   150   300 Meters
0   500   1,000 Feet

Universal Transverse
Mercator Projection
1:9,000

N
W · E
S

RESEARCH: Mark Staker, Lyle Briggs, Lissa Thompson, Richard L. Jensen, Jared Tamez, Richard Bennett
CARTOGRAPHY: Brent Beck, Derek Farnes, Kent Simons, Benjamin Clift, Tyler Jones, BYU Geography

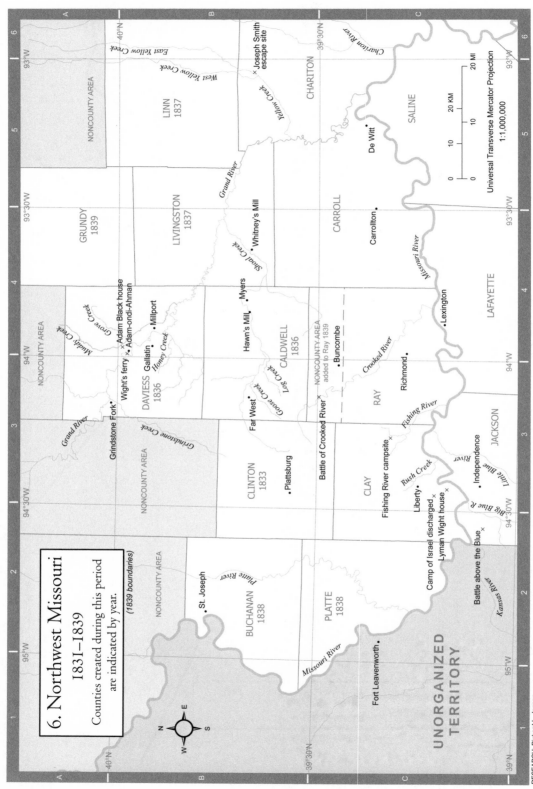

6. Northwest Missouri
1831–1839
Counties created during this period
are indicated by year.
(1839 boundaries)

NONCOUNTY AREA

LINN
1837

West Yellow Creek
East Yellow Creek

× Joseph Smith
escape site

CHARITON

Chariton River

GRUNDY
1839

LIVINGSTON
1837

Grand River

Yellow Creek

SALINE

De Witt •

CARROLL

Carrollton •

Whitney's Mill •
Shoal Creek

Grove Creek
Muddy Creek

Wight's ferry × Adam Black house
× Adam-ondi-Ahman
Gallatin • Millport
Honey Creek

DAVIESS
1836

Myers •
Hawn's Mill •

CALDWELL
1836

Lost Creek

NONCOUNTY AREA
added to Ray 1839

Buncombe •

Missouri River

Lexington •

LAFAYETTE

Grand River
Grindstone Fork •

Grindstone Creek

Far West •
Goose Creek

× Battle of Crooked River

Crooked River

Richmond •

RAY

Fishing River

NONCOUNTY AREA

CLINTON
1833

Plattsburg •

Fishing River campsite ×
Liberty •
Camp of Israel discharged ×
Lyman Wight house ×

CLAY

Rush Creek

Independence •

JACKSON

Little Blue River

St. Joseph •

Platte River

BUCHANAN
1838

PLATTE
1838

NONCOUNTY AREA

Battle above the Blue ×
Big Blue R.

Kansas River

Missouri River

Fort Leavenworth •

UNORGANIZED
TERRITORY

20 MI
20 KM
Universal Transverse Mercator Projection
1:1,000,000

N
W E
S

RESEARCH: Richard L. Jensen
CARTOGRAPHY: Brent Beck and Tyler Jones, BYU Geography

575

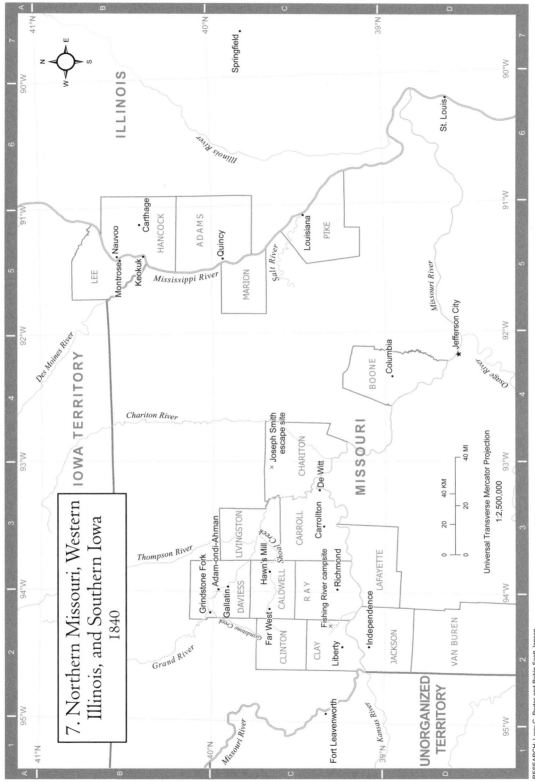

7. Northern Missouri, Western Illinois, and Southern Iowa
1840

RESEARCH: Larry C. Porter and Robin Scott Jensen
CARTOGRAPHY: Isaac Montague, Brent Beck, Kent Simons, Benjamin Clift, Tyler Jones, BYU Geography

Map Index

This is an index to the maps that appear on pages 568–575 herein. Entries are listed alphabetically, with map number and grid coordinates. Jurisdictional information is given for each entry, and spellings of the time period have been used. This map index includes only those places relevant to the volume. For example, even though Georgia appears on map 1, it is not indexed.

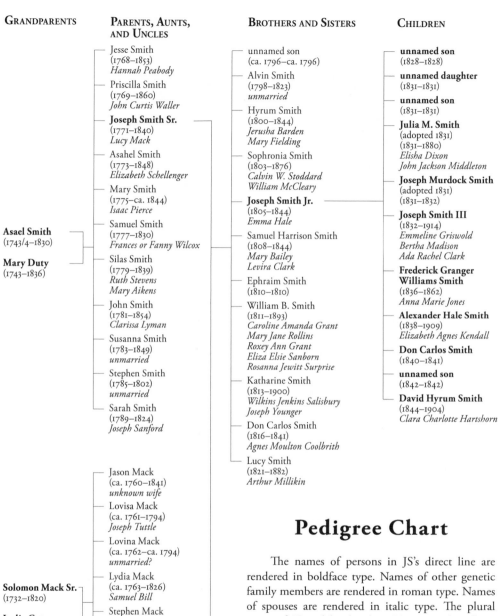

GRANDPARENTS	PARENTS, AUNTS, AND UNCLES	BROTHERS AND SISTERS	CHILDREN
	Jesse Smith (1768–1853) *Hannah Peabody*	unnamed son (ca. 1796–ca. 1796)	**unnamed son** (1828–1828)
	Priscilla Smith (1769–1860) *John Curtis Waller*	Alvin Smith (1798–1823) *unmarried*	**unnamed daughter** (1831–1831)
	Joseph Smith Sr. (1771–1840) *Lucy Mack*	Hyrum Smith (1800–1844) *Jerusha Barden* *Mary Fielding*	**unnamed son** (1831–1831)
	Asahel Smith (1773–1848) *Elizabeth Schellenger*	Sophronia Smith (1803–1876) *Calvin W. Stoddard* *William McCleary*	**Julia M. Smith** (adopted 1831) (1831–1880) *Elisha Dixon* *John Jackson Middleton*
	Mary Smith (1775–ca. 1844) *Isaac Pierce*	**Joseph Smith Jr.** (1805–1844) *Emma Hale*	**Joseph Murdock Smith** (adopted 1831) (1831–1832)
Asael Smith (1743/4–1830)	Samuel Smith (1777–1830) *Frances or Fanny Wilcox*	Samuel Harrison Smith (1808–1844) *Mary Bailey* *Levira Clark*	**Joseph Smith III** (1832–1914) *Emmeline Griswold* *Bertha Madison* *Ada Rachel Clark*
Mary Duty (1743–1836)	Silas Smith (1779–1839) *Ruth Stevens* *Mary Aikens*	Ephraim Smith (1810–1810)	**Frederick Granger Williams Smith** (1836–1862) *Anna Marie Jones*
	John Smith (1781–1854) *Clarissa Lyman*	William B. Smith (1811–1893) *Caroline Amanda Grant* *Mary Jane Rollins* *Roxey Ann Grant* *Eliza Elsie Sanborn* *Rosanna Jewitt Surprise*	**Alexander Hale Smith** (1838–1909) *Elizabeth Agnes Kendall*
	Susanna Smith (1783–1849) *unmarried*	Katharine Smith (1813–1900) *Wilkins Jenkins Salisbury* *Joseph Younger*	**Don Carlos Smith** (1840–1841)
	Stephen Smith (1785–1802) *unmarried*	Don Carlos Smith (1816–1841) *Agnes Moulton Coolbrith*	**unnamed son** (1842–1842)
	Sarah Smith (1789–1824) *Joseph Sanford*	Lucy Smith (1821–1882) *Arthur Millikin*	**David Hyrum Smith** (1844–1904) *Clara Charlotte Hartshorn*
	Jason Mack (ca. 1760–1841) *unknown wife*		
	Lovisa Mack (ca. 1761–1794) *Joseph Tuttle*		
	Lovina Mack (ca. 1762–ca. 1794) *unmarried?*		
	Lydia Mack (ca. 1763–1826) *Samuel Bill*		
Solomon Mack Sr. (1732–1820)	Stephen Mack (1766–1826) *Temperance Bond*		
Lydia Gates (1732–ca. 1818)	Daniel Gates Mack (ca. 1770–by 1841) *Sally Ball*		
	Solomon Mack Jr. (1773–1851) *Esther Hayward* *Hulda Hayward Whipple* *Betsy Way Alexander*		
	Lucy Mack (1775–1856) *Joseph Smith Sr.*		

Pedigree Chart

The names of persons in JS's direct line are rendered in boldface type. Names of other genetic family members are rendered in roman type. Names of spouses are rendered in italic type. The plural wives of JS and his brothers Hyrum and William Smith are not listed here. A list of JS's plural wives will appear in a forthcoming volume. Further information about many of the people listed here can be found in the Biographical Directory. Readers wishing to conduct further research may consult the documented pedigree chart posted on the Joseph Smith Papers website, josephsmithpapers.org.

Biographical Directory

This register contains brief biographical sketches for most of the persons mentioned in this volume. These persons include church leaders, members of JS's family, people JS encountered on his travels, his acquaintances, and other figures from the earliest decades of the Latter-day Saint movement. The directory also includes information about the scribes of documents in this volume. Plural wives of JS, his brothers Hyrum and William Smith, and others are not listed here. A list of JS's plural wives will appear in a forthcoming volume.

The biographical entries identify persons by complete name (correctly spelled), birth and death dates, and additional information, such as parentage and birth place, migrations and places of residence, dates of marriage and names of spouses, occupation and denominational affiliation, religious and civic positions, and place of death. Occupations listed in an entry may not be comprehensive. Key figures with major significance to JS's activities receive the fullest biographical sketches. Others receive much briefer descriptions, often with less data than is available. Because unverified and sometimes incorrect data has been recirculated for decades, professional genealogists on the staff of the Joseph Smith Papers Project have utilized original sources whenever possible.

Entries for women are generally listed under their final married names, with appropriate cross-references under maiden names or earlier married names. Partial names in the text are not included in this directory when research could not determine the full name. In some cases, a footnote in the text provides possible identifications. The index found in *Histories, Volume 2* can often lead the reader to helpful information.

Locations that are noted include city or town, county, and state, when identified, for the first mention of a locale in each sketch. The counties and states of a handful of well-known cities have been omitted. "LDS church" refers to the church established by JS in 1830 and later known as the Church of Jesus Christ of Latter-day Saints. "RLDS church" refers to the church known originally as the New Organization and subsequently as the Reorganized Church of Jesus Christ of Latter Day Saints (1860–2001) and the Community of Christ (2001 to the present).

Even the fullest entries in this directory provide, of necessity, only a bare skeleton of a person's life. Readers wishing to conduct further research may consult the documented biographical directory posted on the Joseph Smith Papers website, josephsmithpapers.org.

Angell, Truman Osborn (5 June 1810–16 Oct. 1887), carpenter, joiner, architect, farmer. Born at North Providence, Providence Co., Rhode Island. Son of James W. Angell and Phebe Morton. Joined Freewill Baptist Church, ca. 1829. Married Polly Johnson of Genesee Co., New York, 7 Oct. 1832. Baptized into LDS church, Jan. 1833, and ordained an elder five weeks later. Served mission with Joseph Holbrook to New York and Massachusetts, spring 1833. Moved to Lima, Livingston Co., New York, July 1833. Moved to Kirtland, Geauga Co., Ohio, fall 1835. Labored on Kirtland temple. Appointed member of Second

Quorum of the Seventy, 1836. Moved to Missouri, spring 1838; to Quincy, Adams Co., Illinois, winter 1838–1839; and to Nauvoo, Hancock Co., Illinois, 1841. Directed joiner work of Nauvoo temple under architect William Weeks. Migrated with family to Salt Lake Valley, 1848. Served as architect for LDS church, ca. 1848–1861. Began work on Salt Lake temple, 1853. Served mission to Europe to study architecture and preach, 1856. Again appointed church architect, 1867. Served as president of Fourteenth Quorum of the Seventy in Salt Lake City. Ordained a high priest and a patriarch, Feb. 1884. Died at Salt Lake City.

Anthon, Charles (17 Nov. 1797–29 July 1867), college professor, lawyer. Born in New York City. Son of George Christian Anthon and Genevieve Judot. Attended Columbia College, 1811–1815, in New York City. Studied law; admitted to bar, 1819. Adjunct professor of Greek and Latin at Columbia College, 1820–1830. Rector of grammar school, 1830–1864. Full professor at Columbia College, 1830–1867. Produced numerous classical textbooks for college students. Died in New York City.

Austin, Emily M. Coburn (Jan. 1813–after 1900), milliner, teacher, nurse. Born in Tioga Co., Pennsylvania. Daughter of Amariah Coburn and Rose Linda Lyon. Moved to Unadilla River area of Otsego Co., New York, 1818; to Greene, Chenango Co., New York, by 1820; to Guilford, Chenango Co.; and to Sanford, Broome Co., New York, ca. 1827. Joined Presbyterian church, 1829, in Sanford. Baptized into LDS church, June 1830, and joined Latter-day Saints at Colesville, Broome Co. Moved to Kirtland, Geauga Co., Ohio, Mar. 1831. Moved to Kaw Township, Jackson Co., Missouri, July 1831. Married first Clark Slade, 1833, in Jackson Co. Moved to Clay Co., Missouri, 1834; to Far West, Missouri, 1836; and to Pittsfield, Pike Co., Illinois, 1839. Husband died, 1842. Moved to Nauvoo, Hancock Co., Illinois, winter 1842–1843. Moved to Wayne, Ashtabula Co., Ohio, 1843. Returned briefly to Nauvoo, ca. June 1846. Moved to Espyville, Crawford Co., Pennsylvania, 1847. Joined Methodist church, 1847, in Espyville. Moved to Meadville, Crawford Co., by 1850. Moved to Madison, Dane Co., Wisconsin, 1851. Married second James Brannon Finch, 19 May 1852, in Madison. Moved to Bellevue, Jackson Co., Iowa, 1853. Returned to Nauvoo, by June 1860. Married third James H. Ward in Nauvoo. Moved to Fort Madison, Lee Co., Iowa, by 1871. Married fourth Philander Austin, 4 Jan. 1877, in Madison, Dane Co., Wisconsin. Resided in Sun Prairie, Dane Co., June 1880. Published *Mormonism; or, Life among the Mormons,* her reminiscences of living among Latter-day Saints, 1882. Resided in Quincy, Adams Co., Illinois, June 1900.

Averitt, Julia Ann Stringham (28 Feb. 1818–30 Apr. 1886). Born in Broome Co., New York. Daughter of William Stringham and Esther Knight. Baptized into LDS church, 28 June 1830, in Colesville, Broome Co. Moved with Colesville branch to Thompson, Geauga Co., Ohio, May 1831, and to Kaw Township, Jackson Co., Missouri, July 1831. Moved to Clay Co., Missouri, Dec. 1833; to Caldwell Co., Missouri, 1836; and to Springfield, Sangamon Co., Illinois, by 1840. Married first Person G. Boman, 24 Mar. 1842, in Springfield. Married second Thomas Averitt, 11 Nov. 1849, in Morgan Co., Illinois. Died in Springfield.

Babbitt, Almon Whiting (9 Oct. 1812–Sept. 1856), postmaster, editor, attorney. Born at Cheshire, Berkshire Co., Massachusetts. Son of Ira Babbitt and Nancy Crosier. Baptized into LDS church, ca. 1830. Located in Amherst, Lorain Co., Ohio, July 1831. Served mission to New York, fall 1831. Served mission to Pomfret, Chautauque Co., New

York, fall 1833. Married Julia Ann Johnson, 23 Nov. 1833, in Kirtland, Geauga Co., Ohio. Participated in Camp of Israel expedition to Missouri, 1834. Appointed member of First Quorum of the Seventy, Feb. 1835. Served mission to Upper Canada, 1837–1838. Led company of Canadian Latter-day Saints to Missouri, 1838. Appointed to gather reports and publications circulated against LDS church, 4 May 1839, at Quincy, Adams Co., Illinois. Appointed president of Kirtland stake, 3 Oct. 1840, at Nauvoo, Hancock Co., Illinois. Disfellowshipped, 1841. Moved to Ramus (later Webster), Hancock Co. Attended church conference, restored to fellowship, and appointed presiding elder of Ramus, 1843. Appointed commander of Ramus militia. Elected to Illinois legislature, representing Hancock Co., 1844. Member of Council of Fifty. Appointed one of five trustees responsible for financial and temporal affairs in Nauvoo, 1846. Appointed postmaster of Nauvoo, 1846. Participated in battle at Nauvoo and signed surrender treaty, Sept. 1846. Migrated to Salt Lake Valley, 1849. Elected delegate to U.S. Congress for provisional state of Deseret, 5 July 1849. Disfellowshipped, 1849, 1851. Appointed secretary of Utah Territory, 1852. Excommunicated, May 1854. Killed at Ash Hollow, Garden Co., Nebraska Territory.

Badlam, Alexander, Sr. (28 Nov. 1808–30 Nov./1 Dec. 1894), coachmaker, realtor, inventor, author. Born at Dorchester, Suffolk Co., Massachusetts. Son of Ezra Badlam and Mary Lovis. Married Mary Ann Brannan, ca. 1833, near Saco, York Co., Maine. Participated in Camp of Israel expedition to Missouri, 1834. Appointed member of First Quorum of the Seventy, 28 Feb. 1835. Ordained an elder and a seventy, 1 Mar. 1835. Lived at Daviess Co. and Caldwell Co., Missouri. Member of Missouri high council, Aug. 1835. Fled Missouri to Illinois, 1839. Resided in Nauvoo, Hancock Co., Illinois, 1842. Presided over Boston branch of church, ca. 1847–1848. Sailed for California from Boston, 1849. Lived at Sacramento, Sacramento Co., California. Returned to Massachusetts and migrated with his family to Utah Territory, 1850. Left LDS church, ca. 1855. Moved to Sacramento, by 1860. Moved to Hot Springs Township (area of present-day Calistoga and St. Helena), Napa Co., California, by 1870. Moved to San Francisco, by 1880. Died at San Francisco.

Bailey, Lydia Goldthwaite. See McClellan, Lydia Goldthwaite.

Baker, Elizabeth (Betsey). See Carrico, Elizabeth (Betsey) Baker.

Barden, Jerusha. See Smith, Jerusha T. Barden.

Barstow, George (19 June 1812–9 Sept. 1883), college professor, lawyer, historian. Born in Haverhill, Grafton Co., New Hampshire. Son of William Barstow and Abigail Townsend. Attended Dartmouth College, 1835, in Hanover, Grafton Co. Moved to Yarmouth Port, Barnstable Co., Massachusetts, 1835–1836. Moved to Boston, 1836, and studied law. Wrote *The History of New Hampshire, from Its Discovery, in 1614, to the Passage of the Toleration Act, in 1819,* published in 1842. Married Emily E. Shipley (Shepley), 11 June 1844, in York Co., Maine. Moved to Hillsborough, Hillsborough Co., New Hampshire, 1844; to Manchester, Hillsborough Co., 1845; to New York City, ca. 1850; and to San Francisco, 1858. Served as professor of medical jurisprudence at University of the Pacific, beginning ca. 1858. Member of California House of Representatives, 1861–1862, 1878. Died in San Francisco.

Beman (Beaman), Alvah (22 May 1775–15 Nov. 1837), farmer. Born at New Marlboro, Berkshire Co., Massachusetts. Son of Reuben Beman and Mariam. Married Sarah (Sally) Burt, 18 Aug. 1796. Moved to Livonia, Ontario Co., New York, 1799. Moved to Avon,

Livingston Co., New York, 1831. Among first to be acquainted with JS and his work at Palmyra, Wayne Co., New York. Assisted JS in concealing Book of Mormon plates from Palmyra mob and in fashioning box to contain plates. Baptized into LDS church. Moved to Kirtland, Geauga Co., Ohio, after Oct. 1835. Appointed to preside over elders quorum in Kirtland, 15 Jan. 1836. Died at Kirtland.

Benton, Abram Willard (16 July 1805–9 Mar. 1867), physician, merchant. Born in New York. Studied medicine with physician Nathan Boynton, before 1830, in Bettsburg, Chenango Co., New York. Member of Presbyterian church. Moved to South Bainbridge (later Afton), Chenango Co., by Oct. 1830. Became member of Chenango County Medical Society, 13 Oct. 1830. Married Hannah Johnston, ca. 1830. Wrote letter attacking JS to editors of *Evangelical Magazine and Gospel Advocate,* published Apr. 1831. Moved to Sterling, Whiteside Co., Illinois, 1837. Moved to Fulton, Whiteside Co., by 1854. Served as Fulton town supervisor, 1854–1855, and town trustee, 1855. Died at Fulton.

Bisbee, Harriet Jolly (Apr. 1816–May 1865). Born in New York, likely at Fayette, Seneca Co. Daughter of William Jolly and Elizabeth Stones. Baptized into LDS church by David Whitmer, June 1830, in Seneca Lake, Seneca Co. Moved to Parkman, Geauga Co., Ohio, 1831. Married Arza Bisbee, 3 Nov. 1833, at Geauga Co. Moved to Richmond, Ray Co., Missouri, 1840. Likely died at Richmond.

Bishop, Francis Gladden (19 June 1809–30 Nov. 1864), watchmaker, minister. Born at Livonia, Ontario Co., New York. Son of Isaac Gates Bishop and Mary Hyde. Served as minister in Freewill Baptist Church, by 1831. Baptized into LDS church and ordained an elder, 2 July 1832, in Olean Point (later Olean), Cattaraugus Co., New York. Engaged in extensive missionary work from North Carolina to Upper Canada, 1833–1840. Moved to Kirtland, Geauga Co., Ohio, by 1836. Ordained a seventy, Feb. 1836, in Kirtland. Appointed secretary of church conference held in Rochester, Columbiana Co., Ohio, 28 Oct. 1837. Moved to Nauvoo, Hancock Co., Illinois, by 1842. Excommunicated, 11 Mar. 1842, in Nauvoo. Organized schismatic movement called "Kingdom of God," 1842. Lived at Kirtland, 1850. Participated in eight religious movements, 1847–ca. 1860. Moved to Council Bluffs, Pottawattamie Co., Iowa, by Mar. 1853. Moved to Cincinnati, by Apr. 1855. Appointed Indian agent for Utah Territory, spring 1858; maintained a residence in Little Sioux, Harrison Co., Iowa, until 1860. Resided in Denver and Golden City, Jefferson Co., Colorado, early 1860s. Moved to Salt Lake City, after Mar. 1864. Died in Salt Lake City.

Bissell (Bissel), Benjamin (1805–13 Oct. 1878), lawyer, senator, judge. Born at Hartwick, Otsego Co., New York. Son of Benjamin Bissell and Elizabeth Heath. Moved to Painesville, Geauga Co., Ohio, Jan. 1829. Married Sarah Bright, 10 Apr. 1829, at Painesville. Partner with Salmon B. Axtell in law firm Bissell & Axtell, Aug. 1837–1842, in Painesville. Defended JS in several lawsuits during Kirtland, Geauga Co., period. Ohio state senator, 1839–1840. Moved to Red Oak, Montgomery Co., Iowa, ca. 1873. Died in Red Oak. Buried in Painesville.

Bogart, Samuel (2 Apr. 1797–11 Mar. 1861), preacher, military officer, farmer. Born in Carter Co., Tennessee. Son of Cornelius Bogart and Elizabeth Moffett. Served in War of 1812. Married Rachel Hammer, 19 May 1818, in Washington Co., Tennessee. Moved to Illinois and became Methodist minister. Served as commissioner in Schuyler Co., Illinois. Served as major in Black Hawk War, 1832. Located at Ray Co., Missouri, mid-1830s.

Captain of company of mounted volunteers from Ray Co. during Mormon War, 1838; contended with Mormon militia at Battle of Crooked River, near Ray Co., 25 Oct. 1838. Appointed to arrest Mormons who participated in Battle of Crooked River and to summon witnesses for court hearing at Richmond, Ray Co. Elected judge, Nov. 1839, at Caldwell Co., Missouri. Shot and killed opponent's nephew, Beatty Hines, during election-day argument; fled to escape prosecution. Settled in Washington Co., Republic of Texas, 1839. Moved to what became Collin Co., Republic of Texas, 1845. Elected to Texas legislature, 1847, 1849, 1851, and 1859. Likely died near McKinney, Collin Co.

Boggs, Lilburn W. (14 Dec. 1796–14 Mar. 1860), bookkeeper, bank cashier, merchant, Indian agent and trader, lawyer, doctor, postmaster, politician. Born at Lexington, Fayette Co., Kentucky. Son of John M. Boggs and Martha Oliver. Served in War of 1812. Moved to St. Louis, ca. 1816, and engaged in business. Married first Julia Ann Bent, July 1817, at St. Louis. Moved to Franklin, Howard Co., Missouri, 1817; to Fort Osage, Howard Co., ca. 1818; to St. Louis, 1820; and back to Fort Osage, spring 1821. Married second Panthea Grant Boone, July 1823. Moved to Harmony Mission (Indian mission for Great Osage Nation; later near Papinville, Bates Co.), Missouri, by 1824. Located at Independence, Jackson Co., Missouri, 1826; elected to state senate on Democratic ticket, 1826, 1828. Elected lieutenant governor, 1832. Became governor upon resignation of predecessor, Daniel Dunklin, 1836, and served through 1840. Moved to Jefferson City, Cole Co., Missouri, 1836. Authorized 1838 expulsion of Mormons from Missouri under what was termed his "extermination order." Returned to Independence, before 1842. Severely wounded by assassin, 6 May 1842; accused JS of complicity with Orrin Porter Rockwell in perpetrating the crime. Returned to Jefferson City, 1842. Served in state senate, 1842–1846. Moved to Cass Co., Missouri, by 1843; returned to Independence, by 1845. Migrated to Sonoma, Mexico (later in Sonoma Co., California), 1846. In 1852, moved to Napa Valley, Napa Co., California, where he died.

Bond, Ira (19 Jan. 1798–30 Nov. 1887), farmer. Born at Caldwell, Essex Co., New Jersey. Son of Abner Bond and Mary Elisabeth Gould. Moved to Mendon, Monroe Co., New York, before 1830. Married Charlotte Wilcox in Honeoya Falls, Monroe Co. Baptized into LDS church by Joseph Young, 1833, at Mendon. Moved to Kirtland, Geauga Co., Ohio, 1834. Labored on Kirtland temple. Appointed to preside over Kirtland deacons quorum, 15 Jan. 1836. Member of Kirtland Safety Society, 1837. Affiliated with RLDS church. Died in Kirtland.

Boynton, John Farnham (20 Sept. 1811–20 Oct. 1890), merchant, lecturer, scientist, inventor. Born at East Bradford (later Groveland), Essex Co., Massachusetts. Son of Eliphalet Boynton and Susanna Nichols. Baptized into LDS church by JS, Sept. 1832, at Kirtland, Geauga Co., Ohio. Ordained an elder by Sidney Rigdon, 1832. Served missions to Pennsylvania, 1832, with Zebedee Coltrin; to Maine, 1833–1834; and to Painesville, Geauga Co., Ohio, Nov. 1834, with William E. McLellin. Ordained member of Quorum of the Twelve, Feb. 1835, in Kirtland. Served mission to eastern states and Canada with Quorum of the Twelve. Married first to Susannah (Susan) Lowell by JS, 20 Jan. 1836, at Kirtland. Dissented over handling of temporal matters associated with Kirtland Safety Society; disfellowshipped from Quorum of the Twelve, 3 Sept. 1837. Reinstated to church and membership in Quorum of the Twelve, 10 Sept. 1837. Excommunicated, 1837. Visited

JS in Nauvoo, Hancock Co., Illinois, Sept. 1842. Settled at Syracuse, Onondaga Co., New York, ca. 1851. Wife died, 7 Aug. 1859. Assisted in running boundary line between U.S. and Mexico. Married second Caroline Foster Harriman, 20 Jan. 1883. Died at Syracuse.

Boynton, Nathan (30 June 1788–ca. 1860), lumber dealer, miller, postmaster, physician, merchant. Born in Wendell, Hampshire Co., Massachusetts. Son of Caleb Boynton and Sarah Flagg. Moved to Worcester, Otsego Co., New York, 1795. Moved to Madrid, St. Lawrence Co., New York, 1806. Studied medicine at Fairfield Medical College in Fairfield, Herkimer Co., New York. Moved to Guilford, Chenango Co., New York, 1814. Married Sepha Stowell, ca. 1818, in Bainbridge, Chenango Co. Served as surgeon's mate in 133rd Regiment for Chenango Co., 1818. Member of Presbyterian church. Resided at Bainbridge, by Aug. 1820. Elected trustee of South Bainbridge Presbyterian Society, 7 Feb. 1825. Moved to Southport, Tioga Co., New York, 1833. Served as Southport town clerk. Moved to Elmira, Chemung Co., New York, 1839. Lived with his son in Southport, 1860.

Brannan, Samuel (2 Mar. 1819–5 May 1889), printer, editor, publisher, miner, businessman, land developer. Born at Saco, York Co., Maine. Son of Thomas Brannan and Sarah Emery. Moved to Kirtland, Geauga Co., Ohio, 1833. Baptized into LDS church, 1833, in Kirtland. Printer's apprentice for three years; reportedly resided with family of JS. Ordained an elder, 1838, in Kirtland. Married first Harriet Hatch, 1841, in Ohio. Married second Ann Eliza Corwin, ca. 1842, in New York. A founder of *The Prophet,* 1844, in New York City. Appointed presiding elder in New York City, 25 Oct. 1844. Led group of 238 Latter-day Saints from New York to Yerba Buena, Mexico (later San Francisco), via Hawaii by ship, 1846. Moved to Sacramento, Mexico (later Sacramento Co., California), fall 1847, and opened store later named Brannan & Co. Returned to San Francisco, 1849. Excommunicated, 1 Sept. 1851, in San Francisco. Elected senator of California, 1853. Divorced wife, 1870. Moved to Guaymas, Sonora, Mexico. Married third Carmelita de Llaguno, ca. 1871. Moved to Escondido, San Diego Co., California, before 1889. Died at Escondido.

Brown, Eliza. See Perry, Eliza Brown.

Brunson, Seymour (1 Dec. 1798–10 Aug. 1840), farmer. Born at Plattsburg, Clinton Co., New York. Son of Reuben Brunson and Sally Clark. Served in War of 1812. Married Harriet Gould of Hector, Tompkins Co., New York, ca. 1823. Baptized into LDS church by Solomon Hancock, Jan. 1831, at Strongsville, Cuyahoga Co., Ohio. Ordained an elder by John Whitmer, Jan. 1831. Ordained a high priest, 1 Dec. 1831. Served mission to Ohio, Kentucky, and Virginia, 1832. Moved to Caldwell Co., Missouri. Located at Quincy, Adams Co., Illinois, 1839. Located at Commerce (later Nauvoo), Hancock Co., Illinois, 1839. Appointed to Commerce high council, Oct. 1839. Died at Nauvoo.

Bump, Jacob (1791–by 10 Oct. 1865), brickmason, plasterer, carpenter, mechanic, farmer, craftsman. Born at Butternuts, Otsego Co., New York. Son of Asa Bump and Lydia Dandley. Married Abigail Pettingill, ca. 1811. Moved to Meadville, Crawford Co., Pennsylvania, by 1826. Baptized into LDS church, by 1833. Moved to Kirtland, Geauga Co., Ohio, by 1833. Participated in Camp of Israel expedition to Missouri, 1834. Labored on Kirtland temple, 1835. Joined dissenters in Kirtland to depose JS. Used influence with dissenters to prevent mob violence against Mormons leaving Kirtland, 1838. Appointed bishop in Kirtland stake of James J. Strang's Church of Jesus Christ of Latter Day Saints,

7 Aug. 1846. Broke with Strang and reconstituted Church of Christ with William E. McLellin, Jan. 1847. Lived at Kirtland, 1860.

Burch, Thomas C. (ca. 1807–ca. Sept. 1839), attorney, judge. Likely born in Tennessee. Married first Ann Ross, 20 Jan. 1824, at Howard Co., Missouri. Began law practice, 1831, at Richmond, Ray Co., Missouri. Married second Celenary (Selinary) Jacobs, 23 Jan. 1834, at Ray Co. Circuit attorney for Ray Co., 1838. Appointed judge of Eleventh Judicial Circuit, 1838. On 15 Apr. 1839, JS and other prisoners with him secured change of venue to Boone Co., Missouri, because of Burch's new judicial appointment. His office posed conflict of interest, as he had been prosecuting attorney for state at hearing in Richmond, Nov. 1838. Died at Keytesville, Chariton Co., Missouri.

Burdick, Thomas (17 Nov. 1795–6 Nov. 1877), farmer, teacher, judge, postmaster, clerk, civil servant. Born at Canajoharie, Montgomery Co., New York. Son of Gideon Burdick and Catherine Robertson. Married Anna Higley, 1828, at Jamestown, Chautauque Co., New York. Baptized into LDS church and moved to Kirtland, Geauga Co., Ohio, by Oct. 1834. Ordained an elder, by Jan. 1836. Appointed church clerk to record membership licenses, 24 Feb. 1836. Appointed elders quorum treasurer, 9 Nov. 1836. Appointed member of Kirtland high council, 7 Nov. 1837. Appointed bishop of Kirtland, 22 May 1841. Moved to Burlington, Des Moines Co., Iowa Territory, 1845. Moved to what became Council Bluffs, Pottawattamie Co., Iowa Territory, 1846. Located at San Bernardino, San Bernardino Co., California, 1853. Settled at San Gabriel Township, Los Angeles Co., California, winter 1853–1854. Died at Los Angeles Co.

Burroughs, Philip (1794–25 July 1865), farmer. Born in New Jersey. Son of Jonathan Burroughs and Mercy Edington. Served in War of 1812. Married Anna Parker, 12 Mar. 1815, in Fayette, Seneca Co., New York. Moved to Junius, Seneca Co., by 1819. Moved to Seneca Falls, Seneca Co., by 1830. LDS church meeting held in his home, Sept. 1830, near Fayette. Wife baptized into LDS church, but no record of his membership. Moved to Portage, Allegany Co., New York, by 1840. Died in Portage.

Cahoon, Reynolds (30 Apr. 1790–29 Apr. 1861), farmer, tanner, builder. Born at Cambridge, Washington Co., New York. Son of William Cahoon Jr. and Mehitable Hodges. Married Thirza Stiles, 11 Dec. 1810. Moved to northeastern Ohio, 1811. Located at Harpersfield, Ashtabula Co., Ohio. Served in War of 1812. Moved near Kirtland, Geauga Co., Ohio, 1825. Baptized into LDS church by Parley P. Pratt, 12 Oct. 1830. Ordained an elder by Sidney Rigdon and a high priest by JS, 4 June 1831. Appointed counselor to Bishop Newel K. Whitney at Kirtland, 10 Feb. 1832. Appointed to serve mission with David W. Patten to Warsaw, Wyoming Co., New York, 23 Mar. 1833. Member of committee to oversee building of Kirtland temple. Member of Kirtland stake presidency. Moved to Missouri, June 1838. Appointed counselor to stake president at Adam-ondi-Ahman, Daviess Co., Missouri, 28 June 1838. Located in Iowa Territory following exodus from Missouri. Appointed counselor in Iowa stake, Lee Co., Iowa Territory, 1839. Appointed guard in Nauvoo Legion, Mar. 1841. Served on building committee for Nauvoo temple. Member of Nauvoo Masonic Lodge. Member of Council of Fifty, 11 Mar. 1844. Resided at Winter Quarters, unorganized U.S. territory (later in Omaha, Douglas Co., Nebraska), 1846. Migrated to Salt Lake Valley, 1848. Died in Salt Lake City.

Cahoon, William Farrington (**7 Nov. 1813–6 Apr. 1893**), shoemaker, carpenter, joiner. Born at Harpersfield, Ashtabula Co., Ohio. Son of Reynolds Cahoon and Thirza Stiles. Baptized into LDS church by Parley P. Pratt, 16 Oct. 1830, at Kirtland, Geauga Co., Ohio. Ordained a priest by Oliver Cowdery, 25 Oct. 1831, at Orange, Cuyahoga Co., Ohio. Served mission to Ohio, Pennsylvania, and New York, 1832–1833. Ordained an elder, 1833. Participated in Camp of Israel expedition to Missouri, 1834. Ordained a seventy, 28 Feb. 1835. Married to Nancy Miranda Gibbs by JS, 17 Jan. 1836, at Kirtland. Member of Kirtland Safety Society, 1837. Moved to Far West, Caldwell Co., Missouri, spring 1838. Moved to Adam-ondi-Ahman, Daviess Co., Missouri, fall 1838. Located at Montrose, Lee Co., Iowa Territory, fall 1839. Moved to Nauvoo, Hancock Co., Illinois, spring 1842. Migrated to Salt Lake Valley, 1849. Served in presiding council of Second Quorum of the Seventy. Died at Salt Lake City.

Capron, Henry (**14 Mar. 1815–18 Jan. 1865**), farmer, town officer. Born in New York. Son of Joseph Capron and Sabra Avery. Moved to Perrinton, Ontario Co., New York, by 1820. Lived next to JS's family at Manchester, Ontario Co. Visited JS, 30 Nov. 1835, in Kirtland, Geauga Co., Ohio. Moved to Auburn, Geauga Co., ca. 1835. Married Laura Brown, 10 Oct. 1838, at Geauga Co. In Auburn, served as constable, 1840–1841; assessor, 1845; trustee, 1848; and justice, 1860, 1863. Died in Auburn.

Carrico, Elizabeth (Betsey) Baker (**4 Dec. 1811–2 May 1883**). Born at Bethlehem, Grafton Co., New Hampshire. Married to Thomas Carrico Jr. by JS, 14 Jan. 1836, at Kirtland, Geauga Co., Ohio. Baptized into LDS church at Kirtland. Moved to Missouri with husband. Lived at Nauvoo, Hancock Co., Illinois, 1840s. Later affiliated with RLDS church. Moved to Jefferson, Harrison Co., Iowa, by June 1870. Died near Logan, Harrison Co.

Carrico, Thomas, Jr. (**20 Sept. 1801–22 Feb. 1882**), shoemaker. Born at Beverly, Essex Co., Massachusetts. Son of Thomas Carrico and Deborah Wallis. Baptized into Unitarian church, 27 Sept. 1801, at Beverly. Married first Mary E. Raymond, 30 Aug. 1827, at Beverly. Wife died, 1833. Baptized into LDS church by John F. Boynton, 24 Mar. 1834, at New Rowley (later Georgetown), Essex Co. Moved to Kirtland, Geauga Co., Ohio, Aug. 1835. Married second to Elizabeth (Betsey) Baker by JS, 14 Jan. 1836, at Kirtland. Ordained a teacher, 1 Feb. 1836, at Kirtland. Lived in Missouri and then settled at Nauvoo, Hancock Co., Illinois, Apr. 1842. Appointed counselor to Bishop Jonathan H. Hale at Nauvoo. Ordained a high priest, Sept. 1842, at Nauvoo. Later joined RLDS church. Moved to Galena, Jo Daviess Co., Illinois, by 1850; to Boyer, Harrison Co., Iowa, by 1860; and to Jefferson, Harrison Co., by 1870. Died near Logan, Harrison Co.

Carter, Gideon Hayden (Haden) (**1798–25 Oct. 1838**). Born at Killingworth, Middlesex Co., Connecticut. Son of Gideon Carter and Johanna Sims. Moved to Benson, Rutland Co., Vermont, after Apr. 1807. Married first Hilah (Hilda) Burwell, 1822. Moved to Amherst, Lorain Co., Ohio, 1831. Baptized into LDS church by JS and ordained a priest by Oliver Cowdery, 25 Oct. 1831, at Orange, Cuyahoga Co., Ohio. In Amherst, ordained an elder and appointed to serve mission to Ohio, 25 Jan. 1832. Moved to Kirtland, Geauga Co., Ohio, by Sept. 1832. Left to serve mission to Pennsylvania, Apr. 1832. Married second Charlotte Woods, 31 Dec. 1833. Served on Kirtland high council, 1837. Member of Kirtland Safety Society, 1837. Migrated to Far West, Caldwell Co., Missouri, 1838. Killed in Battle of Crooked River, near Ray Co., Missouri.

Carter, Jared (14 June 1801–6 July 1849). Born at Killingworth, Middlesex Co., Connecticut. Son of Gideon Carter and Johanna Sims. Moved to Benson, Rutland Co., Vermont, by 1810. Married Lydia Ames, 20 Sept. 1823, at Benson. Moved to Chenango, Broome Co., New York, by Jan. 1831. Baptized into LDS church by Hyrum Smith, 20 Feb. 1831, in Colesville, Broome Co. Moved with Colesville branch to Thompson, Geauga Co., Ohio, May 1831. Ordained a priest, June 1831. Ordained an elder, Sept. 1831. Appointed to serve missions to eastern U.S., 22 Sept. 1831 and Mar. 1832. Left to serve mission to Michigan, Dec. 1832. Appointed to serve mission to eastern U.S., Mar. 1833. Ordained a high priest, by May 1833. Appointed to obtain funds for Elders School, 4 May 1833. Member of Kirtland temple building committee, 1833. Appointed to first Kirtland high council, 17 Feb. 1834. Appointed to serve mission to Upper Canada, 20 Feb. 1834. Labored on Kirtland temple. Shareholder of Kirtland Safety Society, Jan. 1837. Appointed president of Kirtland high council, 9 Sept. 1837. Removed family to Far West, Caldwell Co., Missouri, 1837. Appointed member of Far West high council, 3 Mar. 1838. Prominent in Missouri Danite activities, 1838. Moved from Far West to Commerce (later Nauvoo), Hancock Co., Illinois, 1839. Member of Nauvoo Masonic Lodge. Affiliated with James J. Strang's Church of Jesus Christ of Latter Day Saints, 1846. Excommunicated from Strangite movement, 8 Nov. 1846. Returned to LDS church. By June 1849, moved to DeKalb Co., Illinois, where he died.

Carter, Simeon (7 June 1794–3 Feb. 1869), farmer. Born at Killingworth, Middlesex Co., Connecticut. Son of Gideon Carter and Johanna Sims. Moved to Benson, Rutland Co., Vermont, by 1810. Married Lydia Kenyon, 2 Dec. 1818, at Benson. Moved to Amherst, Lorain Co., Ohio, by 1830. Baptized into LDS church and ordained an elder and a high priest, 1831. Appointed to serve mission to Missouri with Solomon Hancock, June 1831. President of branch at Big Blue River, Kaw Township, Jackson Co., Missouri, 1833. Member of high council in Clay Co., Missouri, 1834, and of high council in Far West, Caldwell Co., Missouri, 1837. Exiled from Missouri, 1838. Located at Lee Co., Iowa Territory, 1840. Served mission to England, 1846–1849. Arrived at Salt Lake Valley, 1849. Moved to Brigham City, Box Elder Co., Utah Territory, by 1860. Died at Brigham City.

Clark, John Bullock (17 Apr. 1802–29 Oct. 1885), lawyer, politician. Born at Madison Co., Kentucky. Moved to Howard Co., Missouri, 1818. Practiced law in Fayette, Howard Co., beginning 1824. Clerk of Howard Co. courts, 1824–1834. Appointed brigadier general in Missouri militia, 1830. Appointed major general in Missouri militia. Appointed to command Missouri militia operations against Mormon forces, 27 Oct. 1838; arrived in Far West, Caldwell Co., Missouri, 4 Nov. 1838, after Saints had surrendered. Insisted Saints leave Missouri; transported Mormon prisoners to Richmond, Ray Co., Missouri, where they underwent a preliminary hearing. Member of Missouri House of Representatives, 1850–1851. Member of U.S. House of Representatives, 1857–1861. Died at Fayette.

Clark, Josiah (ca. 1794–Aug. 1869), farmer. Born in New Jersey. Married Parthenia. Lived at Columbia, Hamilton Co., Ohio, 1830. Moved to Campbell Co., Kentucky, by May 1833. Subscriber to *LDS Messenger and Advocate,* 1836. Represented Cincinnati branch of church at conference held at Springdale, Hamilton Co., 4 Sept. 1841. Died at Dayton Precinct, Campbell Co.

Cobb, Mary (Polly) Harris. See Parker, Mary (Polly) Harris.

Coburn, Emily M. See Austin, Emily M. Coburn.

Coburn, Sarah (Sally). See Knight, Sarah (Sally) Coburn.

Coray, Howard (6 May 1817–16 Jan. 1908), bookkeeper, clerk, teacher, farmer. Born in Dansville, Steuben Co., New York. Son of Silas Coray and Mary Stephens. Moved to Providence, Luzerne Co., Pennsylvania, ca. 1827; to Williams, Northampton Co., Pennsylvania, by 1830; and to Pike Co., Illinois, by 1840. Baptized into LDS church, 24/25 Mar. 1840, near Perry, Pike Co. Moved to Nauvoo, Hancock Co., Illinois, ca. Apr. 1840. Served as clerk for JS and helped compile church history. Ordained an elder by JS, 3 Sept. 1840. Married Martha Jane Knowlton, 6 Feb. 1841, in Hancock Co. Served mission to Pennsylvania, Nov. 1842–1843. Ordained a high priest, 4 June 1843, at Nauvoo. With wife, helped Lucy Mack Smith write history of JS, 1844–1845. Arrived in Salt Lake City, spring 1850. Moved to E. T. City (later Lake Point), Tooele Co., Utah Territory, ca. 1854; to Provo, Utah Co., Utah Territory, 1857; to Juab Co., Utah Territory, 1871; and back to Provo, fall 1880. Served mission to Smyth Co., Virginia, June 1882–Apr. 1883. Lived in Salt Lake City, by 1900. Died in Salt Lake City.

Corrill, John (17 Sept. 1794–26 Sept. 1842), surveyor, politician, author. Born at Worcester Co., Massachusetts. Married Margaret Lyndiff, ca. 1830. Lived at Harpersfield, Ashtabula Co., Ohio, 1830. Baptized into LDS church, 10 Jan. 1831, at Kirtland, Geauga Co., Ohio. Ordained an elder, Jan. 1831, at Kirtland. Served mission to New London, Huron Co., Ohio, 1831. Ordained a high priest by Lyman Wight, 4 June 1831, at Kirtland. Appointed second counselor to Bishop Edward Partridge. Moved to Jackson Co., Missouri. Branch president in Independence, Jackson Co., 1831–1833. Appointed one of ten high priests to watch over the ten Missouri branches, 11 Sept. 1833. In Nov. 1833, expelled from Jackson Co. and located at Clay Co., Missouri, where he continued as counselor to Bishop Partridge. Returned to Kirtland and labored on temple, 1834–1836. Returned to Missouri and became a founder of Far West (later in Caldwell Co.), Missouri, after Mar. 1836. Appointed "Keeper of the Lord's store House," at Far West, 22 May 1837. Released as counselor to Bishop Partridge, Aug. 1837. Elected state representative from Caldwell Co., 1838. Appointed church historian, 1838. Testified for state at JS's hearing in Richmond, Ray Co., Missouri, Nov. 1838. Moved to Illinois, 1839. Excommunicated, 17 Mar. 1839, at Quincy, Adams Co., Illinois. Published *A Brief History of the Church of Christ of Latter Day Saints, (Commonly Called Mormons),* 1839. Died in Adams Co.

Covey, Almira Mack (28 Apr. 1805–10 Mar. 1886). Born at Tunbridge, Orange Co., Vermont. Daughter of Stephen Mack and Temperance Bond. Moved to Detroit, 1822. Moved to Pontiac, Oakland Co., Michigan Territory, 1823. Baptized into LDS church by David Whitmer and confirmed by JS, May 1830, at Palmyra, Wayne Co., New York. Married first William Scobey, 7 Aug. 1831. Husband died, by 1835. Moved to Clay Co., Missouri, 1835. Married second Benjamin Covey, Oct. 1836, at Kirtland, Geauga Co., Ohio. Moved to Far West, Caldwell Co., Missouri, by Aug. 1837; part of forced exodus from Missouri, 1839. Settled in Commerce (later Nauvoo), Hancock Co., Illinois. Moved to Winter Quarters, unorganized U.S. territory (later in Omaha, Douglas Co., Nebraska), 1846. Migrated to Salt Lake Valley; arrived 21 Sept. 1848. Served colonizing mission with husband to Carson City, Ormsby Co., Utah Territory (later in Nevada), 1856. Returned to Salt Lake City, 1857. Died at Salt Lake City.

Cowdery, Elizabeth Ann Whitmer (22 Jan. 1815–7 Jan. 1892). Born in Fayette, Seneca Co., New York. Daughter of Peter Whitmer and Mary Musselman. Baptized into LDS church by Oliver Cowdery, 18 Apr. 1830, in Seneca Co. Moved to Jackson Co., Missouri, by 1832. Married Oliver Cowdery, 18 Dec. 1832, in Kaw Township, Jackson Co. Moved to Kirtland, Geauga Co., Ohio, by Sept. 1833; to Far West, Caldwell Co., Missouri, 1837; to Richmond, Ray Co., Missouri, summer 1838; back to Kirtland, fall 1838; to Tiffin, Seneca Co., Ohio, 1840; to Elkhorn, Walworth Co., Wisconsin Territory, 1847; and to Richmond, by 1849. Husband died, Mar. 1850. Joined RLDS church, after 1860. Moved to Southwest City, McDonald Co., Missouri, after 1870; to El Paso Co., Colorado, by June 1880; and back to Southwest City. Died at Southwest City.

Cowdery, Oliver (3 Oct. 1806–3 Mar. 1850), clerk, teacher, justice of the peace, lawyer, newspaper editor. Born at Wells, Rutland Co., Vermont. Son of William Cowdery and Rebecca Fuller. Raised Congregationalist. Moved to western New York and clerked at a store, ca. 1825–1828. Taught term as local schoolmaster at Manchester, Ontario Co., New York, 1828–1829. Assisted JS as principal scribe in translation of Book of Mormon, 1829. With JS, baptized and received priesthood authority, 1829. Moved to Fayette, Seneca Co., New York, and was one of the Three Witnesses of the Book of Mormon, June 1829. Helped oversee printing of Book of Mormon by E. B. Grandin, 1829–1830. Among six original members of LDS church, 6 Apr. 1830. Served as church recorder, 1830, 1835–1837. Led missionaries through Ohio and to Missouri, 1830–1831. With John Whitmer, left Ohio to take revelations to Missouri for publication, Nov. 1831. Assisted William W. Phelps in conducting church's printing operations at Jackson Co., Missouri, 1832–1833. Married Elizabeth Ann Whitmer, 18 Dec. 1832, in Kaw Township, Jackson Co. Edited *The Evening and the Morning Star,* 1833. Moved to Kirtland, Geauga Co., Ohio, by Sept. 1833. Member of United Firm, Literary Firm, and Kirtland high council. Appointed assistant president of church, 5 Dec. 1834. Edited Kirtland continuation of *The Evening and the Morning Star,* 1833, and edited reprint under modified title *Evening and Morning Star,* 1835–1836. Edited *LDS Messenger and Advocate,* 1834–1835, 1836–1837, and *Northern Times,* 1835. Elected justice of the peace in Kirtland, 1837. Moved to Far West, Caldwell Co., Missouri, 1837. Moved to Richmond, Ray Co., Missouri, summer 1838. Excommunicated, 1838. Returned to Kirtland, 1838, and briefly practiced law. Moved to Tiffin, Seneca Co., Ohio, where he continued law practice and held political offices, 1840–1847. Attended Methodist Protestant Church at Tiffin. Moved to Elkhorn, Walworth Co., Wisconsin Territory, 1847. Ran unsuccessfully for Wisconsin State Assembly, 1848. Coeditor of *Walworth County Democrat,* 1848. Requested and received readmission to LDS church, 1848, at Kanesville (later Council Bluffs), Pottawattamie Co., Iowa. Died at Richmond, Ray Co., Missouri.

Cowdery, Warren A. (17 Oct. 1788–23 Feb. 1851), physician, druggist, farmer, editor. Born at Wells, Rutland Co., Vermont. Son of William Cowdery and Rebecca Fuller. Married Patience Simonds, 22 Sept. 1814, in Pawlet, Rutland Co. Moved to Freedom, Cattaraugus Co., New York, 1816. Became first town postmaster of Freedom, 1824. Baptized into LDS church, fall 1831. Appointed presiding elder of church at Freedom, 25 Nov. 1834. Moved to Kirtland, Geauga Co., Ohio, Feb. 1836. Involved in managing bookbindery and printing office in Kirtland. Assisted in writing dedicatory prayer delivered by JS in Kirtland temple, 1836. Editor of *LDS Messenger and Advocate* and clerk to JS, 1836–1837. Served on

Kirtland high council, 1837. Became disaffected with church leadership, 1838. Served as justice of the peace, 1838–1840. Served as election judge in Kirtland, 1841–1842. In 1850, farmed at Kirtland. Died at Kirtland.

Cowdery, William, Jr. (5 Sept. 1765–26 Feb. 1847), farmer, physician. Born at East Haddam, Middlesex Co., Connecticut. Son of William Cowdery and Hannah Emmons. Raised Congregationalist. Married first Rebecca Fuller. Moved to Wells, Rutland Co., Vermont, ca. 1787. Appointed surveyor of highways, 1792 and 1803, at Wells. Moved to Middletown, Rutland Co., 1809. Wife died, 1809. Married second Keziah Pearce Austin, 18 Mar. 1810, at Middletown Springs, Rutland Co. Moved to Williamson, Ontario Co., New York, 1810; back to Middletown, ca. 1813; and to Poultney, Rutland Co., by 1820. Baptized into LDS church and moved to Kirtland, Geauga Co., Ohio. Served as president of Kirtland priests quorum. Died at Kirtland.

Culver, Aaron (ca. 1772–1831). Son of Nathan Culver and Eunice. Married Esther Peck. Resided at Wardsboro, Windham Co., Vermont, 1800; at Guilford, Windham Co., 1810; and at Colesville, Broome Co., New York, 1830. Baptized into LDS church by Oliver Cowdery, 28 June 1830, at Colesville. Sold hundred-acre farm and moved with Colesville branch to Thompson, Geauga Co., Ohio, May 1831, and to Kaw Township, Jackson Co., Missouri, July 1831. Participated in symbolic log-laying ceremony, 2 Aug. 1831, in Kaw Township. Likely died in Kaw Township.

Culver, Esther Peck (10 July 1766–11 Oct. 1836). Born at Attleboro, Bristol Co., Massachusetts. Daughter of Joseph Peck and Elizabeth Read. Married Aaron Culver. Resided at Wardsboro, Windham Co., Vermont, 1800; at Guilford, Windham Co., 1810; and at Colesville, Broome Co., New York, 1830. Baptized into LDS church by Oliver Cowdery, 28 June 1830, at Colesville. Sold hundred-acre farm and moved with Colesville branch to Thompson, Geauga Co., Ohio, May 1831, and to Kaw Township, Jackson Co., Missouri, July 1831. Husband died, 1831. Later resided with nephew Newel Knight's family. Died at home of Newel Knight, Turnham's Landing (later in Avondale), Clay Co., Missouri.

Cushman, Nathan (16 Dec. 1782–12 Aug. 1874), innkeeper. Born at Bennington, Bennington Co., Vermont. Son of Charles Cushman and Desiah Branch. Married Polly Weeks, 9 Dec. 1802, at Bennington. Lived at Rutland, Rutland Co., Vermont, 1820. Lived at Willoughby, Cuyahoga Co., Ohio, 1835–1860. Wife died, 1865. Lived at East Cleveland, Cuyahoga Co., Ohio, 19 Sept. 1866. Died at Cleveland.

Davidson, James (ca. 1779–9 June 1847), farmer. Likely born in Guilford, Cumberland Co., New York (later in Windham Co., Vermont). Son of James Davidson and Lydia Wetherbee. Moved to Jericho, Tioga Co. (later Bainbridge, Chenango Co.), New York, as early as 1797. Married Betsey. Died in Bainbridge.

Doniphan, Alexander William (9 July 1808–8 Aug. 1887), lawyer, military general, insurance/bank executive. Born near Maysville, Mason Co., Kentucky. Son of Joseph Doniphan and Ann Smith. Father died, 1813; sent to live with older brother George, 1815, in Augusta, Bracken Co., Kentucky. Attended Augusta College, 1822–1826. Studied law in office of jurist Martin Marshall in Augusta. Passed Kentucky and Ohio bar examinations, 1829. Located at St. Louis, Mar. 1830. Moved to Lexington, Lafayette Co., Missouri, and opened law office there, 1830. Moved to Liberty, Clay Co., Missouri, 1833. Employed as legal counsel by Latter-day Saints during their expulsion from Jackson Co., Missouri, 1833. Elected to Missouri General Assembly representing Clay Co., 1836, 1840, and 1854. Married Elizabeth Jane Thornton, 21 Dec. 1837. Appointed brigadier general in state militia. Prevented intended execution of JS and other church leaders at Far West, Caldwell Co., Missouri, Nov. 1838. Again defended JS and others in courts, 1838–1839. Served in Mexican War, 1846–1847. Returned to Liberty. Moved to St. Louis, 1863. Moved to Richmond, Ray Co., Missouri, ca. 1869. Died at Richmond.

Dort, David (6 Jan. 1793–10 Mar. 1841), farmer, miller. Born at Gilsum, Cheshire Co., New Hampshire. Son of John Dort and Elishaba Briggs. Married first JS's cousin Mary (Polly) Mack, 2 June 1813, at Gilsum. After Mary's death, married her sister Fanny Mack. Moved to Pontiac, Oakland Co., Michigan Territory. Baptized into LDS church, 1831. Participated in Camp of Israel expedition to Missouri, 1834. Member of high council in Kirtland, Geauga Co., Ohio, 1837. In 1838, moved to Far West, Caldwell Co., Missouri, where he served on high council. Located at Commerce (later Nauvoo), Hancock Co., Illinois, following exodus from Missouri, 1839, and became member of high council there. Died at Nauvoo.

Dunklin, Daniel (14 Jan. 1790–25 July 1844), farmer, tavern owner, businessman, investor, lawyer, politician. Born near Greenville, Greenville District, South Carolina. Son of Joseph Dunklin Jr. and Sarah Margaret Sullivan. Moved to what became Caldwell Co., Kentucky, 1806; to St. Genevieve, St. Genevieve District, Louisiana Territory (later in St. Genevieve Co., Missouri Territory), Dec. 1810; and to Potosi, St. Genevieve District (later in Washington Co., Missouri Territory), Feb. 1811. Served in War of 1812 in Missouri territorial militia. Married Emily W. Haley, 1815. Sheriff of Washington Co., Missouri Territory, 1815–1819. Elected member of Missouri constitutional convention, 1820. Served in Missouri House of Representatives, 1822–1823. Elected lieutenant governor of Missouri, 1828, and governor, 1832. Resigned as governor, 1836, to accept appointment as surveyor general of Missouri and Illinois. Moved to Herculaneum, Jefferson Co., Missouri, 1840. Appointed commissioner of Missouri to adjust the Missouri-Arkansas boundary, 1843. Died near Herculaneum.

Eaton, Frazier (23 Jan. 1780–after 1855), surveyor. Born at Goffstown, Hillsborough Co., New Hampshire. Son of Enoch Eaton and Esther Williams. Married Lucinda Metcalf, by 1800. Moved to Cavendish, Windsor Co., Vermont, by Aug. 1800. Moved to Bridgewater, Luzerne Co., Pennsylvania, by Aug. 1810. Lived at Rushford, Allegany Co., New York, by 1820. Moved to Portage, Allegany Co., by June 1830; returned to Rushford, by Nov. 1833. Baptized into LDS church, by May 1835. Donated substantial sum for building Kirtland temple. Lived in Hancock Co., Illinois, 1840; returned to Rushford, by June 1850. Buried at Rushford.

Elliott, David (18 Nov. 1799–2 Dec. 1855), blacksmith. Born at Charleston, Montgomery Co., New York. Son of Peter Elliott and Phebe Holley. Married first Almira Holliday of Solon, Cortland Co., New York, ca. 1821. Married second Margery Quick. Lived at Ithaca, Tompkins Co., New York, 1830. Baptized into LDS church, 2 Jan. 1831. Married third Mary Cahoon, 21 May 1831, at Kirtland, Geauga Co., Ohio. Participated in Camp of Israel expedition to Missouri, 1834. Appointed member of First Quorum of the Seventy, 1835. Married fourth Miranda Pratt, 11 Mar. 1838, in Cuyahoga Co., Ohio. Moved to Missouri with Kirtland Camp, 1838. Following exodus from Missouri, settled at Springfield, Sangamon Co., Illinois. Married fifth Margaret Straway, 12 Mar. 1848, in Henry Co., Iowa. Lived at Mount Pleasant, Henry Co., 1850. Migrated to Salt Lake Valley, 1852. Died in Salt Lake City.

Emmett, James (22 Feb. 1803–28 Dec. 1852), farmer, policeman, explorer, miner. Born at Boone Co., Kentucky. Son of Silas Emmett and Elizabeth Trowbridge. Married Phebe Jane Simpson, 13 Apr. 1823. Baptized into LDS church, 1831, in Boone Co. Moved to Jackson Co., Missouri, by Apr. 1832. Ordained an elder, by Sept. 1834. Served mission to Illinois, Indiana, Kentucky, Ohio, and Missouri, 1835. Moved to Far West, Caldwell Co., Missouri, by 1837. Member of Far West high council, 1838. Moved to Adams Co., Illinois, 1839. Moved to Lee Co., Iowa Territory, by Apr. 1841. Appointed to Iowa stake high council, Lee Co., 24 Apr. 1841. Moved to Nauvoo, Hancock Co., Illinois, by Dec. 1843. Appointed to Nauvoo police force, 29 Dec. 1843. Bodyguard to JS. Appointed by JS to explore western U.S. and select new location for Latter-day Saints, 21 Feb. 1844. Led advance party of Latter-day Saint settlers from vicinity of Nauvoo to vicinity of present-day Vermillion, Clay Co., South Dakota, 1845–1846. Moved to Waubonsie, Fremont Co., Iowa, by Apr. 1847. Migrated west, 1849. Resided at Tuolumne Co., California, by June 1850. Moved to San Bernardino, Los Angeles Co., California, where he died.

Follett, King (24/26 July 1788–9 Mar. 1844). Born at Winchester, Cheshire Co., New Hampshire. Son of John Follett and Hannah Oak (Oake) Alexander. Married Louisa Tanner, by 1815. Baptized into LDS church, spring 1831. Member of Whitmer branch at Jackson Co., Missouri, by 1833. Moved to Clay Co., Missouri, 1833. Moved to what became Caldwell Co., Missouri, 1835. Ordained an elder, 28 Jan. 1836, at Kirtland, Geauga Co., Ohio. During difficulties in Missouri in 1839, imprisoned at Richmond, Ray Co., Missouri, and Columbia, Boone Co., Missouri. Moved to Illinois, 1839. Died at Nauvoo, Hancock Co., Illinois.

Fordham, Elijah (12 Apr. 1798–9 Sept. 1879), carpenter. Born at New York City. Son of George Fordham and Mary Baker. Married first Jane Ann Fisher, 23 Nov. 1822. Married second Bethiah Fisher, 12 Apr. 1830. Lived at Pontiac, Oakland Co., Michigan Territory, 1831–1833. Baptized into LDS church, by May 1834. Participated in Camp of Israel expedition to Missouri, 1834. Ordained an elder, 2 Jan. 1836, in Kirtland, Geauga Co., Ohio. Ordained a seventy, by Apr. 1836. Ordained a high priest, by 22 Jan. 1837. Returned to New York City, by June 1837. Married third Anna Bibbins Chaffee, 3 Oct. 1838, in Ashford, Windham Co., Connecticut. Moved to Montrose, Lee Co., Iowa Territory, by 22 July 1839. Appointed to Iowa stake high council, 5 Oct. 1839, in Lee Co. Member of Nauvoo Legion. Migrated to Utah Territory, 1850. Died at Wellsville, Cache Co., Utah Territory.

Gee, Salmon (16 Oct. 1792–13 Sept. 1845), farmer. Born at Lyme, New London Co., Connecticut. Son of Zopher Gee and Esther Beckwith. Moved to Lebanon, Warren Co., Ohio, by 1814. Married Sarah (Sally) Watson Crane, 15 Nov. 1814, at Ashtabula Co., Ohio. Baptized into LDS church by Zebedee Coltrin, July 1832, at Geauga Co., Ohio. Ordained an elder by Sidney Rigdon, 4 Feb. 1833. Moved to Kirtland, Geauga Co., Apr. 1834. Member of Second Quorum of the Seventy, 1836. Appointed a president of the Seventy, 6 Apr. 1837. Member of Kirtland high council under Almon W. Babbitt, 1841–1844. Moved to Ambrosia, Lee Co., Iowa Territory, 1844. Died at Ambrosia.

Gilliam, Cornelius (13 Apr. 1798–24 Mar. 1848), politician, military officer. Born near Mount Pisgah, Buncombe Co., North Carolina. Son of Epaphroditus Gilliam and Sarah Ann Israel. Moved to Missouri, before 1820. Married Mary Crawford, 1820/1821, in Ray Co. (later in Clay Co.), Missouri. Sheriff of Clay Co., 1830–1834. Served in Black Hawk War, 1832. Served as captain in Seminole War, 1837. Participated in Mormon War, 1838. Served as state senator, 1838–1844. Led group of emigrants from Missouri to Oregon Country (later in Oregon Territory), May–Dec. 1844. Ordained a Baptist minister, 1845, in Yamhill District (later in Polk Co.), Oregon Country. Appointed superintendent of postal matters for Oregon Country, 1847. Commanded Oregon troops in campaign against Cayuse Indians, 1847–1848. Died near Umatilla River, Clackamas Co., Oregon Country.

Gould, Dean C. (ca. 1810/1820–after 1841). Participated in Camp of Israel expedition to Missouri, 1834. During expedition, baptized into LDS church by Lyman Wight, 15 June 1834, in Chariton River, Missouri. Member of elders quorum in Kirtland, Geauga Co., Ohio, 1836. Lived at Kirtland, 1840. Applied for marriage license with Louisa Wilcox, 22 Apr. 1841, in Geauga Co.

Gould, John (21 Dec. 1784–25 June 1855), pastor, farmer. Born in New Hampshire. Married first Oliva Swanson of Massachusetts. Resided at Portsmouth, Rockingham Co., New Hampshire, 1808. Lived in Vermont. Moved to northern Pennsylvania, 1817. Served as minister in Freewill Baptist Church, 1817–1832, in New York and Pennsylvania. Lived at Spafford, Onondaga Co., New York, 1830. Baptized into LDS church by Reynolds Cahoon, 16 Dec. 1832, in Chautauque Co., New York. Ordained an elder by David W. Patten, 17 Dec. 1832, in Chautauque Co. Moved to Kirtland, Geauga Co., Ohio, ca. 1833. Traveled from Kirtland with Orson Hyde to inform church leaders in Missouri of JS's instructions to obtain redress through legal channels for impending eviction from Jackson Co., Missouri, Aug. 1833. Assisted JS in recruiting volunteers for Camp of Israel expedition to Missouri, 1834. Attended church conference at Freedom, Cattaraugus Co., New York, 24–25 Jan. 1835. Member of Second Quorum of the Seventy, by Apr. 1836. Served as a president of the Seventy, 6 Apr.–3 Sept. 1837. In 1846, located in Knoxville, Knox Co., Illinois, where he affiliated with James J. Strang's Church of Jesus Christ of Latter Day Saints. Married second Delia Metcalf, 9 July 1848, at Knox Co. Died at Truro Township, Knox Co.

Grandin, Egbert Bratt (30 Mar. 1806–16 Apr. 1845), printer, butcher, shipper, tanner. Born in Freehold, Monmouth Co., New Jersey. Son of William Grandin and Amy Lewis. Moved to Williamson, Ontario Co., New York, by 1810; to Pultneyville, Ontario Co., after 1820; and to Palmyra, Wayne Co., New York, by 1828. Married Harriet Rogers, 23 Dec. 1828, in Palmyra. Printed first edition of Book of Mormon, 1829–1830, in Palmyra. Served as village corporation trustee, 1831; clerk of village board of election inspectors, 1834; constable and collector, 1835; and town assessor, 1839–1841, 1843. Buried in Palmyra City Cemetery, Palmyra.

Greene, John Portineus (3 Sept. 1793–10 Sept. 1844), farmer, shoemaker, printer, publisher. Born at Herkimer, Herkimer Co., New York. Son of John Coddington Greene and Anna Chapman. Married first Brigham Young's sister Rhoda Young, 11 Feb. 1813. Moved to Aurelius, Cayuga Co., New York, 1814; to Brownsville, Ontario Co., New York, 1819; to Watertown, Jefferson Co., New York, 1821; and to Mentz, Cayuga Co., 1826.

Member of Methodist Episcopal Church; later, member of Methodist Reformed Church. A founder of Methodist Protestant Church, 1828. Moved to Conesus, Livingston Co., New York, 1829. Moved to Mendon, Monroe Co., New York, by 1832. Baptized into LDS church by Eleazer Miller, Apr. 1832, at Mendon; ordained an elder by Eleazer Miller shortly after. Organized branch of church at Warsaw, Genesee Co., New York, 1832. Moved to Kirtland, Geauga Co., Ohio, Oct. 1832. Appointed to preside over branch in Parkman, Geauga Co., spring 1833. Returned to Kirtland, fall 1833. Ordained a high priest and left to serve mission to eastern U.S., 16 Sept. 1833. Left to serve mission to western New York and Canada, 25 Feb. 1834. Served mission to eastern U.S., 1835. Author of booklet on Mormon expulsion from Missouri, 1839. Served mission to Ohio to raise funds for Kirtland temple, Mar. 1836. Left to serve mission to New York, 13 July 1836. Member of Kirtland high council. Left to serve mission to Canada, 16 Nov. 1837. Moved to Far West, Caldwell Co., Missouri, 1838. Member of Caldwell Co. militia. Participated in Battle of Crooked River, near Ray Co., Missouri, 25 Oct. 1838. Moved to Quincy, Adams Co., Illinois, Nov. 1838. Served mission to Ohio, Pennsylvania, and New York, 1839. Moved to Nauvoo, Hancock Co., Illinois, spring 1840. Member of Nauvoo City Council, 1841–1843. Married second Mary Eliza Nelson, 6 Dec. 1841, in Nauvoo. Member of Nauvoo Masonic Lodge. Author of booklet on Mormon expulsion from Missouri, 1839. Served mission to Ohio and New York, Aug. 1842. Elected Nauvoo city marshal, Dec. 1843. Assessor and collector of Nauvoo Fourth Ward. Carried out orders of JS and city council to suppress *Nauvoo Expositor* press, 10 June 1844. Died at Nauvoo.

Grover, Thomas (22 July 1807–20 Feb. 1886), farmer, boat operator. Born at Whitehall, Washington Co., New York. Son of Thomas Grover and Polly Spaulding. Married first Caroline Whiting of Whitehall, 1828. Became a Methodist preacher, by 1834. Moved to Freedom, Cattaraugus Co., New York, by 1834. Baptized into LDS church by Warren A. Cowdery, Sept. 1834, at Freedom. Moved to Kirtland, Geauga Co., Ohio, spring 1835. Appointed to Kirtland high council, 1836. Removed his family to Far West, Caldwell Co., Missouri, where he served on high council, 1837. Member of committee at Far West to supervise removal of Latter-day Saints from Missouri, Jan. 1839. Moved to Adams Co., Illinois, by 7 May 1839. Located at Commerce (later Nauvoo), Hancock Co., Illinois, 1839. Appointed to Commerce high council, 1839. Member of Nauvoo Legion, 1841. Married second Caroline Nickerson Hubbard, 20 Feb. 1841, in Nauvoo. Served three short missions during early 1840s. Moved to Winter Quarters, unorganized U.S. territory (later in Omaha, Douglas Co., Nebraska), winter 1846–1847. Migrated to Salt Lake Valley, Oct. 1847; settled at Deuel Creek (later in Centerville), Davis Co., Utah Territory. Collected tithing in California, winter 1848–1849. Moved to Farmington, Davis Co., 1849. Moved to Kanesville (later Council Bluffs), Pottawattamie Co., Iowa, 1850; returned to Farmington, 1853. Member of Davis Co. high council. Served in Utah territorial legislature. Probate judge in Davis Co. Served mission to eastern U.S., 1874–1875. Died at Farmington.

Hale, Emma. See Smith, Emma Hale.

Hale, Isaac (21 Mar. 1763–11 Jan. 1839), farmer, hunter, innkeeper. Born in Waterbury, New Haven Co., Connecticut. Son of Reuben Hale and Diantha Ward. Member of Methodist church. Moved to Wells, Albany Co., New York (later in Rutland Co., Vermont), ca. 1771, to live with maternal grandfather, Arah Ward. Served in

Revolutionary War, beginning 1780. Married Elizabeth Lewis, 20 Sept. 1790, in Wells. Moved to Harmony (later Oakland), Luzerne Co., Pennsylvania, before 1792. Likely died at Harmony.

Hall, Levi (ca. 1802–16 May 1867), farmer. Born in Canada. Son of Roxanna. Married Ruth. Moved to Windsor, Broome Co., New York, ca. 1827. Baptized into LDS church by Oliver Cowdery, 28 June 1830, at Colesville, Broome Co. Apparently remained in Windsor when Colesville branch migrated to Ohio in 1831. Died at Windsor.

Hancock, Solomon (15 Aug. 1793/1794–2 Dec. 1847). Born at Springfield, Hampden Co., Massachusetts. Son of Thomas Hancock and Amy Ward. Moved to Wolcott, Seneca Co., New York, by 1810. Joined Methodist church, 1814. Married first Alta Adams, 12 Mar. 1815. Moved to Columbia, Hamilton Co., Ohio, by 1823. Moved to Chagrin (later Willoughby), Cuyahoga Co., Ohio, by 1830. Baptized into LDS church, 16 Nov. 1830, in Ohio. Ordained an elder, by June 1831. Ordained a high priest by Lyman Wight, 4 June 1831, at Geauga Co., Ohio. Appointed to serve mission with Simeon Carter to Missouri, June 1831. Lived in Jackson Co., Missouri, by 1833. Appointed to Clay Co., Missouri, high council, 1834. Served mission to eastern states, fall 1834. Wife died, 1836. Married second Phebe Adams, 28 June 1836. Moved to Caldwell Co., Missouri, by Dec. 1836. Appointed member of Far West, Caldwell Co., high council, 7 Nov. 1837. Exiled from Missouri, spring 1839; located at Adams Co., Illinois. Moved to Lima, Adams Co., 1841. Appointed member of Lima high council, 1843. Moved to Yelrome (Morley's Settlement, later in Tioga), Hancock Co., Illinois, ca. 1844, and presided over Yelrome branch of church. Died near what became Council Bluffs, Pottawattamie Co., Iowa.

Harris, Emer (29 May 1781–28 Nov. 1869), carpenter, scribe, sawmill operator, blacksmith. Born at Easton, Albany Co., New York. Son of Nathan Harris and Rhoda Lapham. Moved with parents to area of Swift's Landing (later in Palmyra), Ontario Co., New York, 1793. Married first Roxana Peas, 22 July 1802. Moved to Luzerne Co., Pennsylvania, ca. 1805. Divorced wife, 1818. Married second Deborah Lott, 16 Jan. 1819. Wife died, 1825. Married third Parna Chapell, 29 Mar. 1826. Baptized into LDS church by Hyrum Smith and Newel Knight, 10 Feb. 1831, while living near Windham, Luzerne Co. Ordained an elder, by June 1831. Moved to Brownhelm, Lorain Co., Ohio, summer 1831. Ordained a high priest, 25 Oct. 1831, in Orange, Cuyahoga Co., Ohio. Appointed scribe for JS, 27 Oct. 1831. Served mission to Pennsylvania and Ohio, 1832. Moved to Florence, Huron Co., Ohio, Dec. 1833. Labored on temple in Kirtland, Geauga Co., Ohio, 1835. Moved near Kirtland, spring 1836. Migrated to Missouri, Oct. 1838. Expelled from Missouri; relocated at Quincy, Adams Co., Illinois, 1838. Settled at Commerce (later Nauvoo), Hancock Co., Illinois, 1839. Labored on Nauvoo temple. Member of Nauvoo Legion. Moved to Pottawattamie Co., Iowa Territory, fall 1846. Migrated to Utah Territory, 1852, and settled in Ogden, Weber Co. Moved to Provo, Utah Co., Utah Territory, by Oct. 1853. Ordained a patriarch, 8 Oct. 1853. Appointed to preside over high priests in Provo, 2 Sept. 1855. Moved to southern Utah Territory, 1862. Returned to northern Utah Territory, 1867. Died at Logan, Cache Co., Utah Territory.

Harris, Lucy Harris (1 May 1792–summer 1836). Born at Swift's Landing (later in Palmyra), Ontario Co., New York. Daughter of Rufus Harris and Lucy Hill. Affiliated with Religious Society of Friends (Quakers). Married her first cousin Martin Harris, 27 Mar. 1808, in Palmyra. Partially deaf, by 1827. One of five to whom JS gave Martin

Harris permission to show 116 pages of Book of Mormon transcription, 1828. Separated from husband, after June 1830. Died in Palmyra.

Harris, Martin (18 May 1783–10 July 1875), farmer. Born at Easton, Albany Co., New York. Son of Nathan Harris and Rhoda Lapham. Moved with parents to area of Swift's Landing (later in Palmyra), Ontario Co., New York, 1793. Married first his first cousin Lucy Harris at Palmyra, 1808. Served in War of 1812 in New York militia. Became landowner of some 320 acres at Palmyra. Reportedly investigated Quakers, Universalists, Restorationists, Baptists, Methodists, and Presbyterians. Took transcript of Book of Mormon characters to Charles Anthon and Samuel Latham Mitchill at New York City, Feb. 1828. Assisted JS as scribe during translation of first 116 manuscript pages of Book of Mormon, ca. 12 Apr.–14 June 1828. One of the Three Witnesses of the Book of Mormon, June 1829. Baptized into LDS church by Oliver Cowdery, 6 Apr. 1830. Ordained a priest, by 9 June 1830. Paid printing costs for publication of Book of Mormon through sale of 151 acres. Led members of Manchester, Ontario Co., branch from Palmyra to Kirtland, Geauga Co., Ohio, May 1831. Ordained a high priest by Lyman Wight, 4 June 1831, at Kirtland. Participated in Camp of Israel expedition to Missouri, 1834. Member of Kirtland high council, 1834. Married second Caroline Young, 1837. Excommunicated, Dec. 1837. Rebaptized into LDS church, 1842, at Kirtland. Member of high council of James J. Strang's Church of Jesus Christ of Latter Day Saints at Kirtland, 7 Aug. 1846. Joined with William E. McLellin's religious movement, 1847. Initiated a new movement with William Smith and Chilton Daniels at Kirtland, likely 1855. Migrated to Salt Lake Valley, 1870. Rebaptized into LDS church, 1870. Died at Clarkston, Cache Co., Utah Territory.

Harris, Mary (Polly). See Parker, Mary (Polly) Harris.

Harris, Nathan (23 Mar. 1758–17 Nov. 1835), farmer. Born at Smithfield, Providence Co., Rhode Island. Son of Preserved Harris and Martha Mowry. Married Rhoda Lapham, before 1781. Lived at Cambridge, Charlotte Co., New York, 1781. Resided in Easton, Albany Co., New York, 1783. Moved to area of Swift's Landing (later in Palmyra), Ontario Co., New York, 1793. Lived at Northampton, Ontario Co., 1800. Lived at Palmyra, 1810–1830. One of five to whom JS gave Martin Harris permission to show 116 pages of Book of Mormon transcription, 1828. Died at Mentor, Geauga Co., Ohio.

Harris, Preserved (ca. 1785–18 Apr. 1867). Born at Easton, Albany Co., New York. Son of Nathan Harris and Rhoda Lapham. Moved with parents to area of Swift's Landing (later in Palmyra), Ontario Co., New York, 1793. Married Nancy Warren. One of five to whom JS gave Martin Harris permission to show 116 pages of Book of Mormon transcription, 1828. Baptized into LDS church, ca. 1831. Located at Mentor, Lake Co., Ohio, 1840. Member of high council of James J. Strang's Church of Jesus Christ of Latter Day Saints at Kirtland, Lake Co., by Aug. 1846. Died at Mentor.

Harris, Rhoda Lapham (27 Apr. 1759–11 Oct. 1849). Born in Providence, Providence Co., Rhode Island. Daughter of Solomon Lapham and Sylvia. Married Nathan Harris, before 1781. Lived at Cambridge, Charlotte Co., New York, 1781. Resided in Easton, Albany Co., New York, 1783. Moved to area of Swift's Landing (later in Palmyra), Ontario Co., New York, 1793. Lived at Northampton, Ontario Co., 1800. Lived at Palmyra, 1810–1830. One of five to whom JS gave Martin Harris permission to show 116 pages of Book of

Mormon transcription, 1828. Husband died, 1835. Lived at Mentor, Lake Co., Ohio, with son Preserved Harris, 1840. Died at Mentor.

Higbee, Elias (23 Oct. 1795–8 June 1843), clerk, judge, surveyor. Born at Galloway, Gloucester Co., New Jersey. Son of Isaac Higbee and Sophia Somers. Moved to Clermont Co., Ohio, 1803. Married Sarah Elizabeth Ward, 10 Sept. 1818, in Tate Township, Clermont Co. Lived at Tate Township, 1820. Located at Fulton, Hamilton Co., Ohio, 1830. Baptized into LDS church, summer 1832, at Jackson Co., Missouri. Ordained an elder by Isaac Higbee, 20 Feb. 1833, at Cincinnati. Migrated to Jackson Co., Apr. 1833. Driven from Jackson Co. into Clay Co., Missouri, Nov. 1833. Ordained a high priest by Orson Pratt, 7 Aug. 1834, in Clay Co. Served mission to Missouri, Illinois, Indiana, and Ohio, 1835. Labored on Kirtland temple. Returned to Clay Co. Member of Clay Co. high council, 1836. Moved to what became Caldwell Co., Missouri, spring 1836. Presiding judge of Caldwell Co. Appointed to high council in Far West, Caldwell Co., 1837. With John Corrill, appointed church historian, 6 Apr. 1838, at Far West. Prominent in Missouri Danite activities, 1838.Participated in Battle of Crooked River, near Ray Co., Missouri, 25 Oct. 1838. Fled Missouri; located at Quincy, Adams Co., Illinois, 1839. Member of committee that investigated lands offered for sale by Isaac Galland, 1839. Settled at Commerce (later Nauvoo), Hancock Co., Illinois, 1839. Traveled to Washington DC with JS to seek redress for Missouri grievances, Oct. 1839–Mar. 1840. Appointed member of Nauvoo temple committee, 6 Oct. 1840. Appointed guard in Nauvoo Legion, Mar. 1841. Member of Nauvoo Masonic Lodge. Died at Nauvoo.

Hill, Isaac (28 Sept. 1806–25 June 1879), blacksmith, brick maker. Born near Brighton, Beaver Co., Pennsylvania. Son of John Hill and Nancy Warrick. Moved to East Liverpool, Columbiana Co., Ohio, by Dec. 1826. Married first Mary Bell, 7 June 1827, at East Liverpool. Joined Methodist church, 2 Aug. 1828. Baptized into LDS church by Joseph Wood, Aug. 1833, at Liverpool, Columbiana Co. Moved to Kirtland, Geauga Co., Ohio, 1834. Wife died, 1835. Married second Eliza Wright, 7 July 1836, at Geauga Co. Moved to Missouri, 1836; to Iowa Territory, 1839; and to Nauvoo, Hancock Co., Illinois, 1840. Ordained a priest, 9 Mar. 1842. Served mission to Pennsylvania, 1842–1843. Ordained a high priest by Isaac Higbee, 8 Dec. 1844, at Nauvoo. Moved to Utah Territory, by 1850. Bishop of Salt Lake City Second Ward, 1854–1864. Served mission to Province of Canada, 1857–1858. Moved near Bear Lake, 1864. Lived at St. Charles, Rich Co., Utah Territory (later in Bear Lake Co., Idaho), 1870. Died at Fish Haven, Bear Lake Co. Buried at St. Charles.

Hinkle, George M. (13 Nov. 1801–Nov. 1861), merchant, physician, publisher, minister, farmer. Born in Jefferson Co., Kentucky. Son of Michael Hinkle and Nancy Higgins. Married first Sarah Ann Starkey. Baptized into LDS church, 1832. Moved to Far West (later in Caldwell Co.), Missouri, 1836. Served on high councils at Clay Co., Missouri, and Caldwell Co., 1836–1838. Commissioned colonel in Missouri state militia. During Missouri conflict in 1838, directed defense of De Witt, Carroll Co., Missouri, and commanded Mormon militia defending Far West. While assisting in negotiation of truce between state militia and Latter-day Saints at Far West, surrendered church leaders to General Samuel D. Lucas. Excommunicated, 17 Mar. 1839, at Quincy, Adams Co., Illinois. Moved to Duncan Prairie, Mercer Co., Illinois, 1839. Organized religious society named The Church of Jesus Christ, the Bride, the Lamb's Wife, 24 June 1840, at Moscow, Muscatine Co., Iowa

Territory. Affiliated briefly with Sidney Rigdon and Church of Christ, 1845. Moved to Iowa Territory, by Dec. 1845. Wife died, 1 Dec. 1845. Returned to Mercer Co., by June 1850. Married second Mary Loman Hartman. Moved to Decatur Co., Iowa, by 1852. Moved to Adair Co., Iowa. Served in Civil War, 1861. Died at Decatur, Decatur Co.

Hitchcock, Jesse (10 Aug. 1801–ca. 1846). Born in Ashe Co., North Carolina. Son of Isaac Hitchcock and Elizabeth Wheeler. Married Mary Polly Hopper, 4 July 1821, at Lafayette Co., Missouri. Baptized into LDS church. Ordained an elder by Oliver Cowdery, 20 July 1831. Located with Colesville, Broome Co., New York, branch in Jackson Co., Missouri, 1831–1833. Ordained a high priest, 26 Sept. 1833, in Jackson Co. Fled Jackson Co., Nov. 1833. Member of Missouri high council, 1836–1837. In 1843, served mission in Illinois to "disabuse the public mind" over arrest of JS. Member of the Seventy at Nauvoo, Hancock Co., Illinois. Died at Mount Pisgah, Clarke Co., Iowa Territory, en route to Salt Lake Valley.

Hollister, John (12 Oct. 1792–1839), farmer. Born at Marbletown, Ulster Co., New York. Son of Isaac Hollister and Elizabeth Newcomb. Married Lavina (Vina) Clearwater, ca. 1817. Lived at Tompkins Co., New York, ca. 1820–ca. 1835. Moved to Portage Co., Ohio, ca. 1835. Member of Closed Communion Baptist Church. Met with JS, Dec. 1835, at Portage Co. Died in Illinois.

Holmes, Erastus (12 Oct. 1800–26 Aug. 1863), clerk, trader, merchant. Born at Salisbury, Litchfield Co., Connecticut. Son of George Holmes and Betsy Ball. Moved to Newbury (probably later Mulberry), Miami Township, Clermont Co., Ohio, 1821. Married Mary Ann Leming, after Jan. 1823, in Clermont Co. Member of Methodist church. Visited JS at Kirtland, Geauga Co., Ohio, to inquire about LDS church, 14–17 Nov. 1835. Served as postmaster at Mulberry, 1839–1846. Moved to Cincinnati, by June 1850; returned to Miami Township, by June 1860. Died at Milford, Clermont Co.

Holmes, Milton (16 Jan. 1811–30 Apr. 1881), shoemaker, farmer. Born at Rowley, Essex Co., Massachusetts. Son of Nathaniel Holmes and Sarah Harriman. Lived at Napoli, Cattaraugus Co., New York, 1830. Baptized into LDS church, by 1834. Moved to Kirtland, Geauga Co., Ohio, 1834. Assigned proselytizing mission to Upper Canada with Lyman E. Johnson, 20 Feb. 1834. Participated in Camp of Israel expedition to Missouri, 1834. Served mission to Tennessee and Illinois, 1835. Ordained a seventy, 3 Jan. 1837. Served mission to Upper Canada and eastern U.S., 1837. Member of Wilford Woodruff company traveling from Fox Islands, Maine, to Kirtland, 6 Oct. 1838. Moved from Kirtland to Illinois, 1839. Served mission to England, 1844. Appointed president of church conference, 15 Sept. 1845, held at Manchester, Lancashire, England. Returned to U.S. and settled in Georgetown, Essex Co., Massachusetts. Married Aphia S. Woodman, 25 Jan. 1846, in Wilton, Franklin Co., Maine. Excommunicated, 1847. Lived near Boston, 1847, when affiliated with James J. Strang's Church of Jesus Christ of Latter Day Saints. Moved to Wilton, by June 1850. Died at Wilton.

Howe, Harriet (ca. 1796–1856). Born at Clifton Park, Saratoga Co., New York. Daughter of Samuel William Howe and Mabel Dudley. Sister of Eber D. Howe. Resided near Queenstown, Lincoln Co., Niagara District (later in Queenston, Regional Municipality of Niagara, Ontario), Upper Canada, 1811. Moved to Lewiston, Niagara Co., New York, 1812; to Batavia, Genesee Co., New York, Dec. 1813; and to Cleveland, 1817.

Member of First Presbyterian Church of Cleveland at its organization, 19 Sept. 1820. Moved to Painesville, Geauga Co., Ohio, ca. 1820. Joined Reformed Baptist (later Disciples of Christ or Campbellite) movement. Baptized into LDS church, ca. 1831. Member of Kirtland Safety Society. Disaffected from church. Died at Akron, Summit Co., Ohio.

Hulett, Anne Schott (1801–19 Nov. 1866). Born in Pennsylvania. Daughter of Frederick Schott and Anna Rathfon. Moved to Washington (later Fayette), Cayuga Co., New York, 1802. Married first Christian Whitmer, 22 Feb. 1825, at Seneca Co., New York. Baptized into LDS church, 11 Apr. 1830, in Fayette. Moved to Kirtland, Geauga Co., Ohio, 1831; to Jackson Co., Missouri, 1832; and to Clay Co., Missouri, 1833. Husband died, 27 Nov. 1835. Married second Sylvester Hulett, ca. 1836, in Clay Co. Moved to Far West, Caldwell Co., Missouri, by 25 Mar. 1838; to Nauvoo, Hancock Co., Illinois, by 1842; and back to Fayette, by 1850. Died at Fayette.

Hunt, Susanna (Susan) Bailey Smith (27 Oct. 1835–14 Dec. 1905), schoolteacher. Born at Kirtland, Geauga Co., Ohio. Daughter of Samuel H. Smith and Mary Bailey. Moved to Far West, Caldwell Co., Missouri, Mar. 1838. Moved to Quincy, Adams Co., Illinois, Apr. 1839; to Macomb, McDonough Co., Illinois, summer 1839; to Nauvoo, Hancock Co., Illinois, Nov. 1841; and to Plymouth, Hancock Co., fall 1842. Orphaned, 1844; lived with mother's sister in Wisconsin. Married Alonzo A. Hunt, ca. 1858. Resided at Osage, Mitchell Co., Iowa, June 1860; in Moody Co., Dakota Territory, June 1880; and at Enterprise, Moody Co., South Dakota, June 1900. Died at Dell Rapids, Minnehaha Co., South Dakota.

Hyde, Orson (8 Jan. 1805–28 Nov. 1878), laborer, clerk, storekeeper, teacher, editor, businessman, lawyer, judge. Born at Oxford, New Haven Co., Connecticut. Son of Nathan Hyde and Sally Thorpe. Moved to Derby, New Haven Co., 1812. Moved to Kirtland, Geauga Co., Ohio, 1818. Joined Methodist church, ca. 1827. Later affiliated with Reformed Baptists (later Disciples of Christ or Campbellites). Baptized into LDS church by Sidney Rigdon and ordained an elder by JS and Sidney Rigdon, 30 Oct. 1831, at Kirtland. Ordained a high priest by JS and appointed to serve mission to Ohio, Nov. 1831, in Orange, Cuyahoga Co., Ohio. Baptized many during proselytizing mission with Samuel H. Smith to eastern states, 1832. Appointed clerk to church presidency, 1833. Appointed to serve mission to Jackson Co., Missouri, summer 1833. Served mission to Pennsylvania and New York, winter and spring 1834. Member of Kirtland high council, 1834. Participated in Camp of Israel expedition to Missouri, 1834. Married to Marinda Nancy Johnson by Sidney Rigdon, 4 Sept. 1834, at Kirtland. Ordained member of Quorum of the Twelve by Oliver Cowdery, David Whitmer, and Martin Harris, 15 Feb. 1835, in Kirtland. Served mission to western New York and Upper Canada, 1836. Served mission to England with Heber C. Kimball, 1837–1838. Moved to Far West, Caldwell Co., Missouri, summer 1838. Sided with dissenters against JS, 1838. Lived in Missouri, winter 1838–1839. Removed from Quorum of the Twelve, 4 May 1839. Restored to Quorum of the Twelve, 27 June 1839, at Commerce (later Nauvoo), Hancock Co., Illinois. Served mission to Palestine to dedicate land for gathering of Israel, 1840–1842. Member of Nauvoo Masonic Lodge, 1842. Member of Nauvoo City Council, 1843–1845. Participated in plural marriage during JS's lifetime. Departed Nauvoo during exodus to the West, mid-May 1846. Served mission to Great Britain, 1846–1847. Presided over Latter-day Saints in Iowa before migrating to Utah Territory. Appointed president of Quorum of the Twelve, 1847. Published *Frontier Guardian* at Kanesville (later

Council Bluffs), Pottawattamie Co., Iowa, 1849–1852. Migrated to Utah Territory, 1852. Appointed associate judge of U.S. Supreme Court for Utah Territory, 1852. Elected to Utah territorial legislature, 27 Nov. 1852, 1858. Presided over church in Carson Co., Utah Territory (later in Nevada Territory), 1855–1856. Served colonizing mission to Sanpete Co., Utah Territory, by 1860; presided as ecclesiastical authority there, 1860–1877. Died at Spring City, Sanpete Co.

Jackman, Levi (28 July 1797–23 July 1876), carpenter, wainwright. Born at Vershire, Orange Co., Vermont. Son of Moses French Jackman and Elizabeth Carr. Moved to Batavia, Genesee Co., New York, 1810. Married first Angeline Myers Brady, 13 Nov. 1817, at Alexander, Genesee Co. Moved to Portage Co., Ohio, 1830. Baptized into LDS church by Harvey G. Whitlock, 7 May 1831, in Portage Co.; ordained an elder by Oliver Cowdery a few days later. Ordained a high priest, Nov. 1831. Left for Jackson Co., Missouri, 2 May 1832. Moved to Clay Co., Missouri, Nov. 1833. Appointed member of Clay Co. high council, summer 1834. Moved to Kirtland, Geauga Co., Ohio, July 1835. Labored on Kirtland temple, 1835–1836. Returned to Clay Co., 1836. Moved to Far West, Missouri, June 1836. Elected justice of the peace, 1836. Appointed to Far West high council, Nov. 1837. Obtained land at Commerce (later Nauvoo), Hancock Co., Illinois, 1839. Labored on Nauvoo temple. Served mission, 1844. Married second Sally Plumb, 1846. Moved to Winter Quarters, unorganized U.S. territory (later in Omaha, Douglas Co., Nebraska), winter 1846–1847. Migrated with Brigham Young pioneer company to Salt Lake Valley, 1847. Appointed member of first high council in Salt Lake Valley. Ordained a patriarch. Moved to Salem, Utah Co., Utah Territory, Mar. 1864. Died at Salem.

Jackson, Truman (ca. 1802–after 1880), farmer. Born in Vermont. Lived in Verona, Oneida Co., New York, 1830. Baptized into LDS church. Appointed member of elders quorum in Kirtland, Geauga Co., Ohio, 27 Feb. 1836. Ordained a seventy, 3 Jan. 1837, in Kirtland. Married to Ann Brown by Oliver Cowdery, 10 Sept. 1837, at Kirtland. Returned to Verona, by June 1840. Lived in Nauvoo, Hancock Co., Illinois, by 1842. Moved to Gold Township, Bureau Co., Illinois, by 1858. Lived at Greenville, Bureau Co., 1880.

James, Samuel (1814–Apr. 1876). Born in Washington Co., Pennsylvania. Baptized into LDS church. Ordained a high priest and appointed to Kirtland high council, 13 Jan. 1836. Married Marian Evans, 6 Jan. 1841, at Montrose, Lee Co., Iowa Territory. Appointed to serve mission in England, 11 May 1843. Followed Sidney Rigdon after death of JS. Lived at Jefferson Co., Ohio, 1850–1870. Died at Steubenville, Jefferson Co.

Johnson, John (14 Apr. 1779–30 July 1843), farmer, innkeeper. Born at Chesterfield, Cheshire Co., New Hampshire. Son of Israel Johnson and Abigail Higgins. Married Alice (Elsa) Jacobs, 22 June 1800. Moved to Pomfret, Windsor Co., Vermont, ca. 1803. Settled at Hiram, Portage Co., Ohio, 1818. Associated with Methodist church. Baptized into LDS church, ca. 1831. JS lived at Johnson home, 1831–1832. Moved to Kirtland, Geauga Co., Ohio, 1833. Ordained an elder by JS, 17 Feb. 1833, in Kirtland. Ordained a high priest, 4 June 1833, in Kirtland. Provided funds to church for purchase of Peter French properties. Member of Kirtland high council, 1834–1837. Disaffected from church, 1837–1838. Died at Kirtland.

Johnson, Luke (3 Nov. 1807–8 Dec. 1861), farmer, teacher, doctor. Born at Pomfret, Windsor Co., Vermont. Son of John Johnson and Alice (Elsa) Jacobs. Lived at Hiram,

Portage Co., Ohio, when baptized into LDS church by JS, 10 May 1831. Ordained a priest by Christian Whitmer shortly after baptism. Ordained an elder, by Oct. 1831. Ordained a high priest, 25 Oct. 1831. Served missions to Ohio, Pennsylvania, Virginia, and Kentucky, 1831–1833. Married first Susan Harminda Poteet, 1 Nov. 1833, in Cabell Co., Virginia (later in West Virginia). Appointed to high council, 17 Feb. 1834, at Kirtland, Geauga Co., Ohio. Participated in Camp of Israel expedition to Missouri, 1834. Member of Quorum of the Twelve, 1835–1837. Served mission to eastern states, 1835, and to New York and Upper Canada, 1836. Constable in Kirtland. Disfellowshipped, 3 Sept. 1837. Reinstated to church and membership in Quorum of the Twelve, 10 Sept. 1837. Excommunicated, 1838. Taught school in Virginia and also studied medicine, which he practiced at Kirtland. Rebaptized into LDS church by Orson Hyde, 8 Mar. 1846, at Nauvoo, Hancock Co, Illinois. Wife died, 1846. Married second America Morgan Clark, Mar. 1847. Member of Brigham Young pioneer company to Salt Lake Valley, 1847. Moved to St. John, Tooele Co., Utah Territory, 1858. Bishop at St. John. Died at Salt Lake City.

Johnson, Lyman Eugene (24 Oct. 1811–20 Dec. 1859), merchant, lawyer, hotelier. Born at Pomfret, Windsor Co., Vermont. Son of John Johnson and Alice (Elsa) Jacobs. Moved to Hiram, Portage Co., Ohio, Mar. 1818. Baptized into LDS church by Sidney Rigdon, Feb. 1831. Ordained an elder by JS, 1831. Ordained a high priest by JS, 25 Oct. 1831, at Orange, Cuyahoga Co., Ohio. Served missions with Orson Pratt to eastern states and New England, 1832–1833, and to Upper Canada, 1834. Participated in Camp of Israel expedition to Missouri, 1834. Married Sarah Lang (Long), 4 Sept. 1834, in Geauga Co., Ohio. Member of Quorum of the Twelve, 1835–1838. Charter member of Kirtland Safety Society, 1837. Disfellowshipped, 3 Sept. 1837; restored to fellowship, 10 Sept. 1837. Migrated to Far West, Caldwell Co., Missouri. Excommunicated, 13 Apr. 1838. Member of Nauvoo Masonic Lodge, 1842. Lived in Iowa Territory, 1842. Remained friendly to church. Practiced law at Davenport, Scott Co., Iowa Territory, and at Keokuk, Lee Co., Iowa Territory. Died near Prairie du Chien, Crawford Co., Wisconsin.

Johnson, Orson (15 June 1803–21 Mar. 1883), shoemaker, innkeeper, farmer. Born at Chesterfield, Cheshire Co., New Hampshire. Son of Thomas Johnson and Elizabeth (Betsey) Smith. Married first Nancy Mason, 24 Oct. 1827, at Bath, Grafton Co., New Hampshire. Baptized into LDS church by Orson Pratt and Lyman E. Johnson, 1832, in Bath. Attended church conference for elders near Big Blue River, Jackson Co., Missouri, 27 Sept. 1832. Participated in Camp of Israel expedition to Missouri, 1834. Moved to Kirtland, Geauga Co., Ohio. Member of Kirtland high council, 28 Aug. 1834. Excommunicated, by 3 Sept. 1837. Moved to Copperas, Peoria Co., Illinois, by June 1840. Married second Caroline M. C. Hassler, 22 May 1855, in Boston. Moved to Trivoli, Peoria Co., by June 1860; to Altona, Knox Co., Illinois, by June 1870; and to San Bernardino Co., California, after 1870. Died at San Bernardino Co.

Jolly, Elizabeth Stones (1788–22 Oct. 1843). Married William Jolly, before 1809, likely in New York. Resided at Fayette, Seneca Co., New York, by 1810. Baptized into LDS church by Oliver Cowdery, 18 Apr. 1830, in Seneca Lake, Seneca Co. Moved to Parkman, Geauga Co., Ohio, 1831. Died at Parkman.

Jolly, Harriet. See Bisbee, Harriet Jolly.

Jolly, John (2 Mar. 1812–11 Feb. 1885), farmer. Born in New York, likely at Fayette, Seneca Co. Son of William Jolly and Elizabeth Stones. Baptized into LDS church by David Whitmer, June 1830, in Seneca Lake, Seneca Co. Moved to Parkman, Geauga Co., Ohio, 1831. Married Hamuthiel Rowler, 21 June 1849, at Warren, Trumbull Co., Ohio. Died at Parkman.

Jolly, Julia Ann. See Whitmer, Julia Ann Jolly.

Jolly, Vincent (1809–18 Dec. 1866), farmer. Born in New York, likely at Fayette, Seneca Co. Son of William Jolly and Elizabeth Stones. Baptized into LDS church by Oliver Cowdery, 18 Apr. 1830, in Seneca Lake, Seneca Co. Moved to Geauga Co., Ohio, 1831, and settled in Parkman. Married Betsy Curtis, 24 Apr. 1834, in Geauga Co. Buried in Parkman's Overlook Cemetery, Parkman.

Jolly, William (1777–3 Apr. 1863), farmer. Born in New York. Son of John Jolly. Resided at Fayette, Seneca Co., New York, as early as 1804. Married Elizabeth Stones, before 1809, likely in New York. Baptized into LDS church by Oliver Cowdery, 18 Apr. 1830, in Seneca Lake, Seneca Co. Moved to Parkman, Geauga Co., Ohio, 1831. Died at Parkman.

Kimball, Heber Chase (14 June 1801–22 June 1868), blacksmith, potter. Born at Sheldon, Franklin Co., Vermont. Son of Solomon Farnham Kimball and Anna Spaulding. Married Vilate Murray, 22 Nov. 1822, at Mendon, Monroe Co., New York. Member of Baptist church at Mendon, 1831. Baptized into LDS church by Alpheus Gifford, 15 Apr. 1832, at Mendon. Ordained an elder by Joseph Young, 1832. Moved to Kirtland, Geauga Co., Ohio, 1833. Participated in Camp of Israel expedition to Missouri, 1834. Ordained member of Quorum of the Twelve, 1835. Served mission to the East with Quorum of the Twelve, 1835. Presided over first Latter-day Saint missionaries to British Isles, 1837–1838. Moved from Kirtland to Far West, Caldwell Co., Missouri, 1838. Worked closely with Brigham Young and others in supervising removal of Latter-day Saints from Missouri, 1838–1839. Present at Far West temple site, 26 Apr. 1839, when members of Quorum of the Twelve formally began their missionary assignment to British Isles. In removing from Missouri, initially located at Quincy, Adams Co., Illinois, and then at Commerce (later Nauvoo), Hancock Co., Illinois, May 1839. Served mission with Quorum of the Twelve to British Isles, 1839–1841. Member of Nauvoo City Council, 1841–1845. Member of Nauvoo Masonic Lodge. Participated in plural marriage during JS's lifetime. Served mission to eastern states, 1843. Labored on Nauvoo temple. Joined exodus from Illinois into Iowa Territory, Feb. 1846. Member of Brigham Young pioneer company to Salt Lake Valley; arrived July 1847. Sustained as first counselor to Brigham Young in First Presidency at what became Council Bluffs, Pottawattamie Co., Iowa, 27 Dec. 1847. Elected lieutenant governor in provisional state of Deseret. Served in Utah territorial legislature. Died at Salt Lake City.

King, Austin Augustus (21 Sept. 1802–22 Apr. 1870), attorney, judge, politician, farmer. Born at Sullivan Co., Tennessee. Son of Walter King and Nancy Sevier. Married first Nancy Harris Roberts, 13 May 1828, at Jackson, Madison Co., Tennessee. In 1830, moved to Missouri, where he practiced law at Columbia, Boone Co. Served as colonel in Black Hawk War, 1832. Elected to state legislature as Jacksonian Democrat from Boone Co., 1834, 1836. In 1837, removed to Richmond, Ray Co., Missouri, where he received appointment as circuit judge in northwestern Missouri by Governor Lilburn W. Boggs. Between 1837 and 1848, served as judge of Missouri's Fifth Judicial Circuit, consisting of counties of Clinton, Ray, Caldwell, Clay, Daviess, Carroll, and Livingston. In Nov. 1838, presided at preliminary hearing of JS and other Mormons at Richmond; committed them to jail pending trials to be held Mar. 1839. Governor of Missouri, 1848–1852. Married second Martha Anthony Woodson, 10 Aug. 1858, in Kingston, Caldwell Co. Represented Missouri in U.S. Congress, 1863–1865. Died at St. Louis.

Kingsbury, Horace (ca. 1798–12 Mar. 1853), jeweler, silversmith. Born in New Hampshire. Married first Dianthe Stiles, 20 July 1826. Moved to Painesville, Geauga Co., Ohio, 1827. Elected Painesville trustee, 1847, and mayor, 1848. Married second Marana Norton Seymour, 18 Feb. 1848. Died at Painesville.

Kingsbury, Joseph Corrodon (2 May 1812–15 Oct. 1898), mining superintendent, store clerk, teacher, farmer, ferry operator, tithing storehouse supervisor, Temple Square guide. Born at Enfield, Hartford Co., Connecticut. Son of Solomon Kingsbury and Bathsheba Amanda Pease. Moved from Enfield to Painesville, Geauga Co., Ohio, ca. Sept. 1812. Baptized into LDS church by Burr Riggs, 15 Jan. 1832. Ordained an elder, 23 July 1833, at Kirtland, Geauga Co. Served mission to eastern states, 1835. Ordained a high priest and appointed to Kirtland high council, 13 Jan. 1836. Married to Caroline Whitney by JS, 3 Feb. 1836, at Kirtland. Moved to Far West, Caldwell Co., Missouri, May–Sept. 1838. Joined exodus from Missouri, Jan. 1839, and finally located at Montrose, Lee Co., Iowa Territory. Appointed to Zarahemla high council, 24 Apr. 1841, at Montrose. Clerk in JS's red brick store in Nauvoo, Hancock Co., Illinois, 1841–1842. Wife died, Oct. 1842. Served mission to eastern states, 1843–1844. Entered Salt Lake Valley, Sept. 1847. Appointed bishop of Salt Lake City Second Ward, July 1851. Supervisor of tithing storehouse, 1865–1889. Ordained a patriarch, 25 Jan. 1883. Died at Salt Lake City.

Knight, Joseph, Jr. (21 June 1808–3 Nov. 1866), miller, carder, millwright. Born at Halifax, Windham Co., Vermont. Son of Joseph Knight Sr. and Polly Peck. Moved to Jericho (later Bainbridge), Chenango Co., New York, ca. 1809. Moved to Windsor (later in Colesville), Broome Co., New York, 1811. Became acquainted with JS when Knight's father hired JS, 1826. Baptized into LDS church by Oliver Cowdery, 28 June 1830, at Colesville. Moved with Colesville branch to Thompson, Geauga Co., Ohio, May 1831, and to Kaw Township, Jackson Co., Missouri, July 1831. Married Betsey Covert, 22 Mar. 1832, at Kirtland, Geauga Co. Moved to Clay Co., Missouri, 1833; to Far West, Caldwell Co., Missouri, 1837; to Lima, Adams Co., Illinois, 1839; to Nauvoo, Hancock Co., Illinois, 1840; and to La Harpe, Hancock Co. Ordained a priest at La Harpe. Moved back to Nauvoo, 1844. Captain in emigrant company traveling through Iowa Territory, 1846. Moved to what became Council Bluffs, Pottawattamie Co., Iowa Territory, 1846. Migrated to Salt Lake City, 1850. Died at Salt Lake City.

Knight, Joseph, Sr. (3 Nov. 1772–2 Feb. 1847), farmer, miller. Born at Oakham, Worcester Co., Massachusetts. Son of Benjamin Knight and Sarah Crouch. Lived at Marlboro, Windham Co., Vermont, by 1780. Married first Polly Peck, 1795, at Windham Co. Moved to Jericho (later Bainbridge), Chenango Co., New York, ca. 1809. Moved to Windsor (later in Colesville), Broome Co., New York, 1811. Universalist. Hired JS, 1826. Present at Smith family farm when JS retrieved gold plates, 1827, at Manchester, Ontario Co., New York. Baptized into LDS church by Oliver Cowdery, 28 June 1830, at Colesville. Moved with Colesville branch to Thompson, Geauga Co., Ohio, May 1831, and to Kaw

Township, Jackson Co., Missouri, July 1831. Married second Phebe Crosby Peck, by Oct. 1833, in Missouri. Lived at Liberty, Clay Co., Missouri, by 1834. Moved to Nauvoo, Hancock Co., Illinois, by 1840. Ordained a high priest, ca. Sept. 1844, at Nauvoo. Member of Nauvoo Masonic Lodge. Died at Mount Pisgah, Clarke Co., Iowa.

Knight, Lydia Goldthwaite. See McClellan, Lydia Goldthwaite.

Knight, Newel (13 Sept. 1800–11 Jan. 1847), miller, merchant. Born at Marlborough, Windham Co., Vermont. Son of Joseph Knight Sr. and Polly Peck. Moved to Jericho (later Bainbridge), Chenango Co., New York, ca. 1809. Moved to Windsor (later in Colesville), Broome Co., New York, 1811. Married first Sarah (Sally) Coburn, 7 June 1825. Became acquainted with JS when Knight's father hired JS, 1826. Baptized into LDS church by David Whitmer, last week of May 1830, in Seneca Co., New York. Ordained a priest, 26 Sept. 1830. President of Colesville branch of church; led branch from Broome Co. to Thompson, Geauga Co., Ohio, May 1831. Ordained an elder, before June 1831. Moved again with Colesville branch to Kaw Township, Jackson Co., Missouri, July 1831. Ordained a high priest, by July 1832. Expelled from Jackson Co. and moved to Clay Co., Missouri, 1833. Appointed member of Clay Co. high council, July 1834. Wife died, Sept. 1834. Lived at Kirtland, Geauga Co., Ohio, spring 1835–spring 1836. Married second to Lydia Goldthwaite Bailey by JS, 24 Nov. 1835, at Kirtland. Lived at Clay Co., 1836. Member of high council at Far West, Caldwell Co., Missouri, 1837–1838. Left Missouri during exodus and moved to Commerce (later Nauvoo), Hancock Co., Illinois, 1839. Member of Commerce/Nauvoo high council, 1839–1845. Left Nauvoo, 1846. Died in present-day northern Nebraska.

Knight, Polly. See Stringham, Polly Knight.

Knight, Polly Peck (6 Apr. 1774–6 Aug. 1831). Born in Guilford, Cumberland Co., New York (later in Windham Co., Vermont). Daughter of Joseph Peck and Elizabeth Read. Married Joseph Knight Sr., 1795, in Windham Co. Moved to Jericho (later Bainbridge), Chenango Co., New York, ca. 1809. Moved to Windsor (later in Colesville), Broome Co., New York, 1811. Universalist. Baptized into LDS church by Oliver Cowdery, 28 June 1830, at Colesville. Moved with Colesville branch to Thompson, Geauga Co., Ohio, May 1831, and to Kaw Township, Jackson Co., Missouri, July 1831. Died in Kaw Township.

Knight, Sarah (Sally) Coburn (1804–15 Sept. 1834). Born in Oxford (later in Guilford), Chenango Co., New York. Daughter of Amariah Coburn and Rose Linda Lyon. Resided in Oxford, Chenango Co., by 1810. Moved to Greene, Chenango Co., by 1820. Moved to Colesville, Broome Co., New York, by 1825. Married Newel Knight, 7 June 1825. Baptized into LDS church, 28 June 1830, in Colesville. Moved with Colesville branch to Thompson, Geauga Co., Ohio, May 1831, and to Kaw Township, Jackson Co., Missouri, July 1831. Moved to Turnham's Landing (later in Avondale), Clay Co., Missouri, fall 1833. Died at Turnham's Landing.

Knight, Vinson (14 Mar. 1804–31 July 1842), farmer, druggist, school warden. Born at Norwich, Hampshire Co., Massachusetts. Son of Rudolphus Knight and Rispah (Rizpah) Lee. Married Martha McBride, 14 Mar. 1826. Moved to Perrysburg, Cattaraugus Co., New York, by Mar. 1834. Owned farm at Perrysburg when baptized into LDS church, spring 1834. Moved to Kirtland, Geauga Co., Ohio, by Dec. 1835. Ordained an elder, 2 Jan. 1836. Ordained a high priest and appointed counselor to Bishop Newel K. Whitney, 13 Jan. 1836, at Kirtland. Appointed township clerk, 1837. Member of Kirtland Safety Society,

Jan. 1837. Served mission, 1837. Moved to Far West, Caldwell Co., Missouri, by Nov. 1837. Appointed to Far West high council, 6 Nov. 1837. Located at Adam-ondi-Ahman, Daviess Co., Missouri, summer 1838. Appointed acting bishop at Adam-ondi-Ahman, 28 June 1838. Exiled from Missouri; located at Quincy, Adams Co., Illinois, 1839. Church land agent; with others purchased approximately 19,000 acres of Half-Breed Tract in Lee Co., Iowa Territory, from Isaac Galland, and about 190 acres in Hancock Co., Illinois, from Galland and Hugh White, 1839. Appointed bishop in Commerce (later Nauvoo), Hancock Co., 4 May 1839. Appointed bishop of Lower Ward at Commerce, 5 Oct. 1839. Instructed in JS revelation to buy stock for building Nauvoo House, 19 Jan. 1841. Appointed presiding bishop of church, 19 Jan. 1841. Member of Nauvoo City Council, 1841–1842. Served as warden of Nauvoo common schools and member of Nauvoo University building committee, 1841–1842. Appointed guard in Nauvoo Legion, Mar. 1841. Member of Nauvoo Masonic Lodge. Died at Nauvoo.

Lane, George (13 Apr. 1784–6 May 1859), teacher, merchant, minister. Born near Kingston, Ulster Co., New York. Son of Nathan Lane and Dorcas Muscroft. Joined Methodist church, ca. 1803, in New York. Circuit preacher, beginning 1804. Ordained a deacon in Methodist church, 1807. Ordained an elder in Methodist church, 1809. Married first Sarah Harvey, 31 May 1810, at Plymouth, Luzerne Co., Pennsylvania. Appointed presiding elder in Methodist church of Ontario District (area near Palmyra, Wayne Co., New York), 1824. Lived in Berwick, Columbia Co., Pennsylvania, 1825–1834. Married second Lydia Bunting, 24 Jan. 1837. Resided in New York City, 1837. Published *Northern Christian Advocate* for several years. Moved to Mount Holly, Burlington Co., New Jersey, 1852. Died in Wilkes-Barre, Luzerne Co., Pennsylvania.

Lewis, Job L. (10 Sept. 1776–after 1836). Born at Exeter, Washington Co., Rhode Island. Son of Joseph Lewis and Mary Stanton. Married Margaret Lowers, New York, ca. 1807. Lived at Westfield, Chautauque Co., New York, 1830. Baptized into LDS church. Excommunicated, 1836.

Lewis, Lloyd L. (18 July 1807–24 Dec. 1902), farmer, millwright, county officer. Born at Onondaga Co., New York. Son of Job L. Lewis and Margaret Lowers. Moved to Westfield, Chautauque Co., New York, by 1830. Baptized into LDS church, by 1835, at Westfield. Married Elizabeth Donnelly, 23 Sept. 1848, at Knoxville, Knox Co., Illinois. Moved to Black River, Crawford Co., Wisconsin, by 1850. Moved to Isabelle, Pierce Co., Wisconsin, by 1860. Served as register of deeds and county clerk in Pierce Co., 1865–1867. Moved to Hartland, Pierce Co., by 1870; to Ellsworth, Pierce Co., by 1880; and to Superior, Douglas Co., Wisconsin, by 1900. Died at Minong, Washburn Co., Wisconsin.

Lewis, Lorenzo L. (ca. 1809–ca. May 1897), millwright. Born in New York. Son of Job L. Lewis and Margaret Lowers. Baptized into LDS church, probably at Westfield, Chautauque Co., New York. Ordained an elder, 13 May 1835, in Kirtland, Geauga Co., Ohio. Appointed to serve mission to Pennsylvania, 24 May 1835. Excommunicated, 28 Sept. 1835. Married Mandana Isabel Gould in Illinois. Moved to Black River, Crawford Co., Wisconsin, by June 1850. Elected superintendent of schools in La Crosse, La Crosse Co., Wisconsin, Apr. 1851. Elected La Crosse assessor, 1857, 1858. Moved to El Paso, Pierce Co., Wisconsin, by June 1860. Moved to Salem, Marion Co., Oregon, before 1897. Died at Salem.

Lucas, Samuel D. (19 July 1799–23 Feb. 1868), store owner, recorder of deeds. Born at Washington Co., Kentucky. Son of Samuel Lucas Sr. Married Theresa Bartlett Allen, 10 Nov. 1823, in Harrison Co., Kentucky. Member of Presbyterian church. Lived at Independence, Jackson Co., Missouri, by 1827. Jackson Co. court justice, 1831. Secretary of citizens committee that met in Independence to negotiate departure of Latter-day Saints from Jackson Co., July 1833. Major general in Missouri militia; in absence of designated commander, John B. Clark, led militia forces and confronted Mormon forces near Far West, Caldwell Co., Missouri, Oct. 1838. Disbanded Mormon forces, took JS and other Mormon leaders prisoner, and escorted them to Independence before Clark arrived. County clerk, 1842, and clerk of circuit court, 1848, in Jackson Co. Died in Independence.

Lyman, Amasa Mason (30 Mar. 1813–4 Feb. 1877), boatman, gunsmith, farmer. Born at Lyman, Grafton Co., New Hampshire. Son of Boswell Lyman and Martha Mason. Baptized into LDS church by Lyman E. Johnson, 27 Apr. 1832. Moved to Hiram, Portage Co., Ohio, May–June 1832. Ordained an elder by JS and Frederick G. Williams, 23 Aug. 1832, at Hiram. Left to serve mission to southern Ohio and Virginia, 24 Aug. 1832. Left to serve mission to New York and New Hampshire, 21 Mar. 1833. Ordained a high priest by Lyman E. Johnson and Orson Pratt, 11 Dec. 1833, in Elk Creek, Otsego Co., New York. Participated in Camp of Israel expedition to Missouri, 1834. Ordained a seventy by JS, Oliver Cowdery, and Sidney Rigdon, ca. Mar. 1835. Married Maria Louisa Tanner, 10 June 1835, at Kirtland, Geauga Co., Ohio. Served mission to New York, spring 1836. Charter member of Kirtland Safety Society, 1837. Moved to Far West, Caldwell Co., Missouri, 1837; to McDonough Co., Illinois, winter 1839–1840; to Lee Co., Iowa Territory, spring 1840; and to Nauvoo, Hancock Co., Illinois, spring 1841. Served mission to northern Illinois and Wisconsin Territory, 1841. Appointed to serve mission to raise funds for construction of Nauvoo temple and Nauvoo House, Oct. 1841. Served mission to Tennessee, spring 1842. Member of Nauvoo Masonic Lodge. Member of Nauvoo City Council, 1842–1843. Ordained member of Quorum of the Twelve, 20 Aug. 1842, at Nauvoo. Elected a regent of University of Nauvoo, 20 Aug. 1842. Served mission to southern Illinois, 1842. Served colonizing mission to Shokokon, Henderson Co., Illinois, Feb.–June 1843; returned to Nauvoo, summer 1843. Counselor in First Presidency, 1843–1844. Moved to Winter Quarters, unorganized U.S. territory (later in Omaha, Douglas Co., Nebraska), 1846. Captain of wagon companies to Salt Lake Valley, 1847, 1848. Appointed to establish settlement at San Bernardino, Los Angeles Co., California, 1851. Migrated to Salt Lake Valley, 1858. President of European mission, 1860–1862. Moved to Fillmore, Millard Co., Utah Territory, 1862. Deprived of apostleship, 6 Oct. 1867, and excommunicated, 12 May 1870. President of Godbeite Church of Zion, 1870. Died at Fillmore.

Lyon, Windsor Palmer (8 Feb. 1809–Jan. 1849), physician, druggist, merchant. Born at Orwell, Addison Co., Vermont. Son of Aaron Child Lyon and Roxana Palmer. Baptized into LDS church, 1832, in New York. Lived at Willoughby, Cuyahoga Co., Ohio, 1835–1836, where he owned a store. Owned land in Far West, Missouri, 1836. Married Sylvia Porter Sessions, Mar. 1838, at Far West. Moved to Hancock Co., Illinois, by Feb. 1841. Lived in Nauvoo Fourth Ward, 1842, at Nauvoo, Hancock Co. Appointed aide-de-camp to major general in Nauvoo Legion, June 1842. Opened drug and variety store at Nauvoo. Ordained a high priest, by 3 Feb. 1846. Moved to Johnson Co., Iowa Territory, by Nov. 1846. Resided at Iowa City, Johnson Co., 1848. Died at Iowa City.

Mack, Almira. See Covey, Almira Mack.

Mack, Solomon, Sr. (15 Sept. 1732–23 Aug. 1820), farmer, manufacturer, merchant, shipmaster, real estate investor, freighter. Born in Lyme, New London Co., Connecticut. Son of Ebenezer Mack and Hannah. Served in French and Indian War, 1755–1759. Married Lydia Gates, 4 Jan. 1759, in Lyme. Moved to Marlow, New Hampshire, 1761. Moved to Gilsum, Cheshire Co., New Hampshire, by 1773. Served in American Revolution, 1776. Buried in Bond Cemetery, Gilsum.

Marsh, Thomas Baldwin (1 Nov. 1800–Jan. 1866), farmer, hotel worker, waiter, horse groom, grocer, type foundry worker, teacher. Born at Acton, Middlesex Co., Massachusetts. Son of James Marsh and Molly Law. Married Elizabeth Godkin, 1 Nov. 1820, at New York City. Joined Methodist church at Boston. Migrated to Palmyra, Wayne Co., New York, by Sept. 1830. Baptized into LDS church by David Whitmer, 3 Sept. 1830, at Cayuga Lake, Seneca Co., New York. Ordained an elder by Oliver Cowdery, Sept. 1830. Moved to Kirtland, Geauga Co., Ohio, with Manchester, Ontario Co., New York, branch of church, May 1831. Ordained a high priest by Lyman Wight, 4 June 1831, at Kirtland. Served mission to Missouri, June–Aug. 1831. Moved to Jackson Co., Missouri, 10 Nov. 1832. Appointed president of Big Blue River, Jackson Co., branch. Expelled from Jackson Co., 1833. Member of Clay Co., Missouri, high council, 1834. Ordained member of Quorum of the Twelve, 26 Apr. 1835, at Kirtland. Sustained as president of Quorum of the Twelve, 2 May 1835. Served mission with the Twelve to eastern states and Upper Canada, 1835. President pro tempore of church in Far West, Caldwell Co., Missouri, 5 Feb. 1838. Withdrew from church at Far West, 22 Oct. 1838. Excommunicated in absentia, 17 Mar. 1839, at Quincy, Adams Co., Illinois. Sought readmittance, Jan. 1857. Rebaptized into LDS church at Florence, Douglas Co., Nebraska, 16 July 1857. Migrated to Utah Territory, 1857. Settled at Spanish Fork, Utah Co., Utah Territory. Moved to Ogden, Weber Co., Utah Territory, latter part of 1862. Died at Ogden.

Matthews, Robert (1788–ca. 1841), carpenter, joiner, merchant, minister. Born at Cambridge, Washington Co., New York. Raised in Anti-Burgher Secession Church. Married Margaret Wright, 1813, at New York City. Adopted beliefs of Methodism and then Judaism. Moved to Albany, ca. 1825. Claimed to be God the Father reincarnated in body of Matthias, the ancient apostle. Prophesied destruction of Albany, 1830. Left Albany and his family to embark on apostolic preaching tour through eastern and southern U.S. Upon returning to New York, recruited local religious figures Elijah Pierson and Benjamin Folger. Committed to hospital for the insane at Bellevue, New York City, for a time. Little is known of Matthews after his 1835 visit with JS at Kirtland, Geauga Co., Ohio. Reported to have died in Iowa Territory.

McBride, Reuben (16 June 1803–26 Feb. 1891), farmer. Born at Chester, Washington Co., New York. Son of Daniel McBride and Abigail Mead. Married Mary Ann Anderson, 16 June 1833. Baptized into LDS church, 4 Mar. 1834, at Villanova, Chautauque Co., New York. Participated in Camp of Israel expedition to Missouri, 1834. Appointed member of Second Quorum of the Seventy, Feb. 1835. Lived at Kirtland, Geauga Co., Ohio, ca. 1836–1848. Assigned to oversee church interests there after departure of main body of Latter-day

Saints in 1838. Appointed counselor in Kirtland bishopric, 22 May 1841. Migrated to Salt Lake Valley, 1850. Returned to Kirtland, 1851. Settled at Fillmore, Millard Co., Utah Territory, by 1853. Appointed to serve mission to Europe, 1857. Served mission to England, 1867. Member of Millard stake high council, 1877–1884. Died at Fillmore.

McCleary, Sophronia Smith (16 May 1803–22 July 1876). Born at Tunbridge, Orange Co., Vermont. Daughter of Joseph Smith Sr. and Lucy Mack. Moved to Royalton, Windsor Co., Vermont, 1804; to Sharon, Windsor Co., by Aug. 1804; to Tunbridge, by Mar. 1808; to Royalton, by Mar. 1810; and to Lebanon, Grafton Co., New Hampshire, 1811. Migrated with family from Norwich, Windsor Co., Vermont, to Palmyra, Ontario Co., New York, 1816–Jan. 1817. Joined Presbyterian church, ca. 1820. Moved to Manchester, Ontario Co., 1825. Married first Calvin W. Stoddard, 30 Dec. 1827, at Palmyra, Wayne Co., New York. Lived at Macedon, Wayne Co., 1830. Lived at Kirtland, Geauga Co., Ohio, by 1832. Husband died, 1836. Married second William McCleary, 11 Feb. 1838, at Kirtland. Left Ohio for Far West, Caldwell Co., Missouri, May 1838. Fled to Illinois, Feb. 1839. Lived at Macedonia (later Webster), Hancock Co., Illinois, 1843. Lived at Tennessee, McDonough Co., Illinois, 1860. Received into RLDS church, 8 Apr. 1873, based on original baptism. Died at Fountain Green, Hancock Co.

McClellan, Lydia Goldthwaite (9 June 1812–3 Apr. 1884), boardinghouse operator, weaver, teacher. Born at Sutton, Worcester Co., Massachusetts. Daughter of Jesse G. Goldthwaite and Sally Burt. Married first Calvin Bailey, fall 1828, but deserted by him, 1832. Moved to home of Eleazer Freeman Nickerson at Mount Pleasant, Brantford Township, Wentworth Co. (later in Brant Co.), Gore District (later in Ontario), Upper Canada, Feb. 1833. Baptized into LDS church by JS, 27 Oct. 1833, at Mount Pleasant. Moved to New York, 1834. Moved to Kirtland, Geauga Co., Ohio, May 1835. Assisted Jerusha Smith, wife of Hyrum Smith, in operating boarding home in Kirtland, Oct. 1835. Married second to Newel Knight by JS, 24 Nov. 1835, at Kirtland. Moved to Missouri, 1836, and Illinois, 1839. Joined Female Relief Society, 1842, in Nauvoo. Left Nauvoo with Mormon exodus, 1846. Traveled with Newel Knight and others to Camp Ponca on Niobrara River in present-day Knox Co., Nebraska, 1846. Husband died, 1847. Migrated to Salt Lake Valley, 1850. Married third John Dalton, 1852; divorced, ca. 1857. Moved to Provo, Utah Co., Utah Territory, by Sept. 1860. Moved to Payson, Utah Co., by 1864. Married fourth James McClellan, 1864, in Payson. Served colonizing mission with husband to Santa Clara, Washington Co., Utah Territory, by 1870. Appointed to serve in temple at St. George, Washington Co. Husband died, 1880. Moved to St. George, 1880. Died at St. George.

McLellin, William E. (18 Jan. 1806–13/14 Mar. 1883), schoolteacher, physician, publisher. Born at Smith Co., Tennessee. Son of Charles McLellin. Married first Cynthia Ann, 30 July 1829. Baptized into LDS church by Hyrum Smith, 20 Aug. 1831, in Jackson Co., Missouri. Ordained an elder by Hyrum Smith and Edward Partridge, 24 Aug. 1831. Served two short-term missions. Wife died, by 1832. Married second Emeline Miller, 26 Apr. 1832, at Portage Co., Ohio. Left Ohio for Independence, Jackson Co., Missouri, 2 May 1832. Served mission to Missouri and Illinois with Parley P. Pratt, Jan.–June 1833. Fled with fellow Latter-day Saints from Jackson Co. into Clay Co., Missouri, Nov. 1833. Proselytized in Indiana on way to Kirtland, Geauga Co., Ohio, 1834. Appointed instructor in Kirtland School, 19 Nov. 1834. Appointed and ordained member of Quorum of the Twelve, 15 Feb.

1835. Disfellowshipped over difficulties arising during eastern mission with Quorum of the Twelve; reinstated, 26 Sept. 1835. Wrote letter of withdrawal from church, Aug. 1836. Again sustained to Quorum of the Twelve, 3 Sept. 1837, at Kirtland. In Far West, Caldwell Co., Missouri, commissioned captain in First Company, Fifty-Ninth Regiment, Second Brigade, Third Division of Missouri state militia, 22 Nov. 1837. Associated with factions organized under leadership of George M. Hinkle, William Law, Sidney Rigdon, James J. Strang, David Whitmer, and Granville Hedrick. Broke with all organized religion, 1869. Died at Independence.

McMaster, Cyrus (ca. 1801–2 Jan. 1879), dairyman, farmer. Likely born at Sidney, Delaware Co., New York. Son of David McMaster and Abigail Smith. Married Electa Bridgeman. Member of Presbyterian church. Moved to Bainbridge, Chenango Co., New York, by 1830. Resided in Afton, Chenango Co., by 1860. Likely died at Afton.

McWethy (McWithey), Eliza Ann. See Webb, Eliza Ann McWethy (McWithey).

McWithy, Isaac (1778–4 May 1851), farmer. Born in New York. Married Hannah Taylor of Vermont. Moved to Covington, Genesee Co., New York, by 1820. Lived at Bennington, Genesee Co., with family of five, 1830. Ordained an elder, 15 Feb. 1833. Lived at Kirtland, Geauga Co., Ohio, 1835. Appointed to Zion high council, 13 Jan. 1836, in Kirtland. Died at Kirtland.

Middleton, Julia M. Smith (30 Apr. 1831–12 Sept. 1880). Born in Warrensville, Cuyahoga Co., Ohio. Daughter of John Murdock and Julia Clapp. After death of mother, adopted by JS and Emma Smith at age of nine days. Lived in Hiram, Portage Co., Ohio, 1831. Moved to Kirtland, Geauga Co., Ohio, 1832; to Far West, Caldwell Co., Missouri, 1838; near Quincy, Adams Co., Illinois, 1839; and to Commerce (later Nauvoo), Hancock Co., Illinois, later that year. Member of Nauvoo Fourth Ward, 1842. Married first Elisha Dixon, by 1850. Moved to Galveston, Galveston Co., Texas, ca. 1851. Moved back to Nauvoo, 1853, following husband's death. Married second John Jackson Middleton, 19 Nov. 1856, in Hancock Co. Converted to Catholicism. Lived in Sonora Township, Hancock Co., by 1860. Likely died in Sonora Township.

Millet, Artemus (11 Sept. 1790–19 Nov. 1874), farmer, lumberman, merchant, builder, stonemason. Born at Westmoreland, Cheshire Co., New Hampshire. Son of Ebenezer Millet and Catherine Dryden. Moved to Stockbridge, Windsor Co., Vermont, fall 1800; to Shelburn, Chittenden Co., Vermont, 1809; and to Louisville, St. Lawrence Co., New York, 1810. Returned to Stockbridge, 1811. Married first Ruth Grannis of Milton, Chittenden Co., 17 May 1815. Moved near Plattsburg, Clinton Co., New York, 1815. Moved to Volney, Oswego Co., New York, fall 1816. Member of Methodist church. Moved to Long Island, Queens Co., New York, 1822. Moved to Ernestown (later in Lennox and Addington Co., Ontario), Upper Canada, 1823. Married second Susanna Peters, 15 Jan. 1832, in Ernestown. Baptized into LDS church by Brigham Young and confirmed by Joseph Young, Jan. 1833, at Loughborough, Frontenac Co., Midland District (later in Ontario), Upper Canada. In Oct. 1833, moved to Kirtland, Geauga Co., Ohio, where he supervised construction of temple. Ordained an elder and served mission to Highland Co., Ohio, 1836. Member of Kirtland Safety Society, 1837. Moved back to Upper Canada, ca. 1837; returned to Ohio, 1841. Returned to body of church in Nauvoo, Hancock Co., Illinois, Apr. 1843. Married third Catherine Almira Pritchard Oaks, 20 Apr. 1843. Ordained a high priest by

Noah Packard, 8 Oct. 1844, in Nauvoo. Left Nauvoo, summer 1846. Married fourth Triphenia Booth, Oct. 1847, in Iowa. Married fifth Nancy Lemaster, 11 Mar. 1849, in Kanesville (later Council Bluffs), Pottawattamie Co., Iowa. Moved to northern Missouri, 1849. Migrated to Utah Territory, Oct. 1850. Arrived at Manti, Sanpete Co., Utah Territory, to serve colonizing mission, 18 Nov. 1850. Appointed president of Manti high council, 30 Apr. 1851. Served colonizing missions to various locations in present-day southern Utah and Nevada. Died at Scipio, Millard Co., Utah Territory.

Milliken, Nathaniel (25 Dec. 1793–Aug. 1874), farmer, post office clerk. Born at Buxton, York Co., Maine. Son of Nathaniel Milliken and Mary Lord. Married first Mary Fairfield Hayes, 22 Apr. 1819. Baptized into LDS church, 1 Oct. 1833, at Buxton. Moved to Kirtland, Geauga Co., Ohio, ca. 1834. Appointed member of Second Quorum of the Seventy, Apr. 1836. Excommunicated, by 7 Jan. 1838. Wife died, 1853. Married second Mary Beckwith, 26 Jan. 1862. Died at Kirtland.

Millikin, Lucy Smith (18 July 1821–9 Dec. 1882). Born at Palmyra, Ontario Co., New York. Daughter of Joseph Smith Sr. and Lucy Mack. Moved to Manchester, Ontario Co., 1825. Baptized into LDS church, possibly 1830. Migrated from Seneca Falls, Seneca Co., New York, to Kirtland, Geauga Co., Ohio, May 1831. Moved to Far West, Caldwell Co., Missouri, summer 1838. Migrated to Quincy, Adams Co., Illinois, Feb. 1839. Located at Commerce (later Nauvoo), Hancock Co., Illinois, May 1839. Married to Arthur Millikin by JS, 4 June 1840, at Nauvoo. Joined Female Relief Society, 24 Mar. 1842, in Nauvoo. Moved to Maine, 1843; returned to Nauvoo, 1844. Cared for Lucy Mack Smith for several years. Settled at Colchester, McDonough Co., Illinois, early 1850s. Received into RLDS church, 8 Apr. 1873, based on original baptism. Died near Colchester.

Mitchill, Samuel Latham (20 Aug. 1764–7 Sept. 1831), lawyer, surveyor, author, editor, poet, physician, college professor. Born in North Hempstead, Queens Co., New York. Son of Robert Mitchill and Mary Latham. Raised in Quaker faith. Studied medicine at University of Edinburgh, 1786, in Edinburgh, Midlothian, Scotland. Appointed a commissioner to purchase western New York lands from Iroquois Indians, 1788. Professor of chemistry, botany, and natural history at Columbia College, 1792–1801, in New York City. A founder of State Society for the Promotion of Agriculture, 1793. Elected to New York legislature, 1790, 1797. Married Catherine Akerly Cock, 23 June 1799. Served in U.S. Congress, 1801–1813. Served in U.S. Navy during War of 1812. Appointed surgeon general of New York state militia, 1818. Founder and president of Lyceum of Natural History of New York. A founder of New York Literary and Philosophical Society, Institution for the Deaf and Dumb, and Rutgers Medical College. Professor at New York's College of Physicians and Surgeons. Died in New York City.

Morey, George (30 Nov. 1803–15 Dec. 1875), farmer. Born at Pittstown, Rensselaer Co., New York. Son of William Morey and Anda Martin. Moved to Collinsville, Butler Co., Ohio, 1814. Married Sylvia Butterfield, 29 Oct. 1825, at Butler Co. Moved to Vermillion Co., Illinois, 1831. Baptized into LDS church, 1833. Located in Clay Co., Missouri, 1834; in Kirtland, Geauga Co., Ohio, 1835–1836; and in Far West, Caldwell Co., Missouri, by Aug. 1837. Member of Far West high council, 1837–1838. Participated in Battle of Crooked River, near Ray Co., Missouri, 25 Oct. 1838. Returned to Vermillion Co., by June 1840. Moved to Nauvoo, Hancock Co., Illinois, by 1841. Ordained a high priest, 1841. Constable in Nauvoo,

1841. Member of Nauvoo Legion. Supported Sidney Rigdon as successor to JS. Moved to Brown Co., Illinois, late 1844; to DeKalb Co., Illinois, 1849; and to Whiteside Co., Illinois, 1851. Settled at Hamilton Township, Decatur Co., Iowa, 1852. Presided over Little River branch of RLDS church, in Pleasanton, Decatur Co., 1859. Died near Pleasanton.

Morley, Isaac (11 Mar. 1786–24 June 1865), farmer, cooper, merchant, postmaster. Born at Montague, Hampshire Co., Massachusetts. Son of Thomas Morley and Editha (Edith) Marsh. Family affiliated with Presbyterian church. Moved to Kirtland, Geauga Co., Ohio, before 1812. Married Lucy Gunn, June 1812, at Montague; immediately returned to Kirtland. Served in War of 1812 as private and captain in Ohio militia. Elected trustee of Kirtland, 1818. Baptized into Reformed Baptist (later Disciples of Christ or Campbellite) faith by Sidney Rigdon, 1828. Baptized into LDS church by Parley P. Pratt, 15 Nov. 1830. Latter-day Saints migrating from New York settled on his farm at Kirtland, 1831. Ordained a high priest by Lyman Wight, 4 June 1831. Counselor to Bishop Edward Partridge at Kirtland, 1831, and in Missouri, 1831–1838. Lived at Independence, Jackson Co., Missouri, 1831. Appointed to set in order branches of church in Missouri, 3 Dec. 1832. Appointed bishop, 25 June 1833. Driven from Jackson Co. into Clay Co., Missouri, Nov. 1833. Member of Missouri high council, by 19 Dec. 1833. Left to serve mission to eastern states with Edward Partridge, 17 Feb. 1835. Returned to Missouri and moved family to what became Far West, Caldwell Co., Missouri, Apr. 1836. Ordained a patriarch by JS, Sidney Rigdon, and Hyrum Smith, 7 Nov. 1837. Moved to Hancock Co., Illinois, 1839; founded Yelrome (Morley's Settlement, later in Tioga), where he served as bishop and was appointed president of stake at Lima, Adams Co., Illinois, 22 Oct. 1840. Member of Masonic lodge in Nauvoo, Hancock Co. Moved to Winter Quarters, unorganized U.S. territory (later in Omaha, Douglas Co., Nebraska), 1846. Migrated to Salt Lake Valley, 1848. Elected senator of provisional state of Deseret, 12 Mar. 1849. Led initial settlement of Latter-day Saints at Sanpete Valley, unorganized U.S. territory (later in Sanpete Co., Utah Territory), 28 Oct. 1849, and presided at Manti, Sanpete Co., 1849–1853. Member of Utah territorial legislature, 1851–1857. Died at North Bend (later Fairview), Sanpete Co.

Mulholland, James (1804–3 Nov. 1839). Born in Ireland. Baptized into LDS church. Married Sarah Scott, 8 Feb. 1838, at Far West, Caldwell Co., Missouri. Engaged in clerical work for JS, 1838, at Far West. Ordained a seventy, 28 Dec. 1838. After expulsion from Missouri, lived at Quincy, Adams Co., Illinois, spring 1839. Relocated at Commerce (later Nauvoo), Hancock Co., Illinois, May 1839. Scribe for two of JS's journals, fall 1838 and 1839. Scribe in dictation of JS's personal history, beginning 11 June 1839. Appointed clerk for land contracts and subtreasurer of church at Commerce, 20 Oct. 1839. Died at Commerce.

Murdock, John (15 July 1792–23 Dec. 1871), farmer. Born at Kortright, Delaware Co., New York. Son of John Murdock Sr. and Eleanor Riggs. Joined Lutheran Dutch Church, ca. 1817, then Presbyterian Seceder Church shortly after. Moved to Orange, Cuyahoga Co., Ohio, ca. 1819. Baptized into Baptist church at Orange. Married first Julia Clapp of Mentor, Geauga Co., Ohio, 14 Dec. 1823. Joined Reformed Baptist (later Disciples of Christ or Campbellite) faith, ca. 1827. Baptized into LDS church by Parley P. Pratt, 5 Nov. 1830, at Kirtland, Geauga Co. Ordained an elder by Oliver Cowdery, 7 Nov. 1830, at Mayfield, Cuyahoga Co. Organized branches of church at Orange and Warrensville, Cuyahoga Co., 1831. Wife died following birth of twins, 30 Apr. 1831, at Warrensville. JS and Emma Smith adopted the twins, Joseph and Julia. Ordained a high priest by JS, 4 June 1831, at Kirtland. Left to serve mission to Missouri with Hyrum Smith, June 1831. Left to serve mission to eastern states with Zebedee Coltrin, Apr. 1833. Participated in Camp of Israel expedition to Missouri, 1834. Member of Clay Co., Missouri, high council, 1834. President of high council in Far West, Missouri, ca. 1835. Served mission to Vermont and New York, 1835–1836. Married second Amoranda Turner, 4 Feb. 1836; wife died, 1837. Married third Electra Allen, 3 May 1838. With George M. Hinkle, purchased large number of lots for Mormon settlement in De Witt, Carroll Co., Missouri, 23 June 1838. Forced out of De Witt by vigilantes, 11 Oct. 1838; returned to Far West, 14 Oct. 1838. Left Far West for Quincy, Adams Co., Illinois, 4 Feb. 1839. Lived near Lima, Adams Co., 1839–1841. Moved to Nauvoo, Hancock Co., Illinois, spring 1841. Bishop of Nauvoo Fifth Ward, 1842–1844. Served mission to Indiana, Nov. 1844–Mar. 1845. Wife died, 1845. Married fourth Sarah Zufelt, 13 Mar. 1846, in Fulton Co., Illinois. Arrived in Salt Lake Valley, 24 Sept. 1847. Member of Salt Lake high council, ca. 1847–1849, and appointed bishop of Salt Lake City Fourteenth Ward, 1849. Served in Utah territorial legislature, 1849–1851. Served mission to Australia, 1851–1853. Moved to Lehi, Utah Co., Utah Territory, ca. 1854. Served as patriarch, Apr. 1854–Mar. 1867. Moved to Beaver, Beaver Co., Utah Territory, fall 1867. Died at Beaver.

Murdock, Joseph S. See Smith, Joseph Murdock.

Murdock, Julia. See Middleton, Julia M. Smith.

Olney, Oliver H. (11 Aug. 1796–ca. 1845), wool manufacturer, farmer. Born at Eastford, Windham Co., Connecticut. Son of Ezekiel Olney and Lydia Brown. Married first Alice (Elsa) Johnson, daughter of John Johnson and Alice (Elsa) Jacobs, 14 Sept. 1820, at Hiram, Portage Co., Ohio. President of Kirtland teachers quorum, 1836. Ordained a seventy by Hazen Aldrich, 20 Dec. 1836, at Kirtland, Geauga Co., Ohio. Driven out of De Witt, Carroll Co., Missouri, into Caldwell Co., Missouri, 1838. Wife died, 1841. Excommunicated, 1842, at Nauvoo, Hancock Co., Illinois. Printed anti-Mormon tract titled *The Absurdities of Mormonism Portrayed,* spring 1843. Married second Phebe Wheeler, 19 Oct. 1843, at Nauvoo. In St. Louis, published exposé on polygamy titled *Spiritual Wifery at Nauvoo Exposed,* 1845.

Ousley, Electa Rockwell (May 1816–12 Nov. 1900), farmer. Likely born in Belchertown, Hampshire Co., Massachusetts. Daughter of Orin Rockwell and Sarah Witt. Moved to Farmington, Ontario Co., New York, by Aug. 1820. Baptized into LDS church by David Whitmer, ca. 9 June 1830, in Seneca Lake, Seneca Co., New York. Moved to Ohio, 1831. Moved to Jackson Co., Missouri, 1831. Married Samuel Marshall Ousley, 11 Jan. 1837, in Clay Co., Missouri. Moved to what became Andrew Co., Missouri, 1839. Moved to Nodaway, Buchanan Co., Missouri, by 1840. Migrated to California, winter 1852–1853; settled in Deer Creek, El Dorado Co., California, July 1853. Moved to Gilroy, Santa Clara Co., California, 1854. Husband died, 1855. Buried in Gilroy.

Packard, Noah (7 May 1796–17 Feb. 1860), farmer, surveyor, miner. Born at Plainfield, Hampshire Co., Massachusetts. Son of Noah Packard and Molly Hamblin. Moved to Parkman, Geauga Co., Ohio, 1817. Married Sophia Bundy, 29 June 1820, at Parkman. Baptized into LDS church by Parley P. Pratt, June 1832, in Parkman. Ordained a priest by JS, 3 Dec. 1832, at Kirtland, Geauga Co. Appointed to serve mission to Parkman,

5 Dec. 1832. Left to serve mission to eastern U.S., 22 Apr. 1833. Ordained an elder by John Gould, 6 May 1833, at Westfield, Chautauque Co., New York. Appointed president of Parkman branch, 1833. Moved to Kirtland, 1835. Ordained a high priest, 13 Jan. 1836. Member of Kirtland high council, 1836. Member of Kirtland Safety Society, 1837. Left Ohio for Missouri, late fall 1838, but instead spent winter at Wellsville, Columbiana Co., Ohio. Located at Quincy, Adams Co., Illinois, 1839. Moved to Commerce (later Nauvoo), Hancock Co., Illinois, 18 May 1839. Served as counselor in Nauvoo high priests quorum presidency under Don Carlos Smith and then George Miller, 1840–1846. Served missions to various U.S. states, 1841–1843, 1845. Agent for church to collect funds in Michigan for Nauvoo temple, 1845. Moved to Hazelgreen, Orren Co., Wisconsin, spring 1846. Migrated to Utah Territory, 18 Sept. 1850. In 1851, settled at Springville, Utah Co., Utah Territory, where he was appointed first counselor in branch presidency. Alderman in Springville city government. Died at Springville.

Page, Catherine Whitmer (ca. 1807–after 1880), farmer. Likely born in Harrisburg, Dauphin Co., Pennsylvania. Daughter of Peter Whitmer Sr. and Mary Musselman. Moved to Fayette, Seneca Co., New York, by 1810. Married Hiram Page, 10 Nov. 1825, likely in Fayette. Baptized into LDS church, 11 Apr. 1830, in Seneca Lake, Seneca Co. Moved to Kirtland, Geauga Co., Ohio, 1831; near Independence, Jackson Co., Missouri, 1832; to Clay Co., Missouri, 1833; to Far West, Missouri, 1836; and near present-day Excelsior Springs, Ray Co., Missouri, 1838. Husband died, 1852. Moved to Grape Grove, Ray Co., by 1860. Moved to Richmond, Ray Co., by 1880.

Page, Hiram (1800–12 Aug. 1852), physician, farmer. Born in Vermont. Married Catherine Whitmer, 10 Nov. 1825, likely in Fayette, Seneca Co., New York. One of the Eight Witnesses of the Book of Mormon, June 1829. Baptized into LDS church by Oliver Cowdery, 11 Apr. 1830, at Seneca Lake, Seneca Co. Ordained a teacher, by 9 June 1830, in New York. Claimed to receive revelations for church, 1830; later denounced them in response to JS revelation. Moved to Kirtland, Geauga Co., Ohio, 1831; near Independence, Jackson Co., Missouri, 1832; and to Clay Co., Missouri, 1833. Helped found Far West, Missouri, 1836. Left church and moved to Ray Co., Missouri, 1838. Briefly joined William E. McLellin's Church of Christ, 1848. Died near present-day Excelsior Springs, Ray Co.

Palmer, Ambrose (15 Sept. 1784–before Sept. 1838), farmer, tavern keeper, surveyor, glass worker, manufacturer, justice of the peace. Born at Winchester, Litchfield Co., Connecticut. Moved to Trumbull Co., Ohio, by 1807. Married Lettis (Lettice) Hawkins of Castleton, Rutland Co., Vermont, ca. 1810. Served in War of 1812 as captain of an Ohio company. Masonic lodge meetings held at his tavern in Vernon Township, Trumbull Co., 1814–1817. Moved to Norton, Medina Co., Ohio, 1818. Elected justice of the peace in Norton, Apr. 1818. Moved to New Portage, Medina Co., after 1820; returned to Norton, by June 1830; returned to New Portage, by 1833. Baptized into LDS church, Apr. 1833, in New Portage. Presiding elder at New Portage, 1835. Moved to Far West, Caldwell Co., Missouri, by Sept. 1836. Resident of Far West, June 1838. Died at Far West.

Parker, Mary (Polly) Harris (ca. 1794–ca. 19 Dec. 1871). Born in Rhode Island. Daughter of Rufus Harris and Lucy Hill. Married first Freeman Cobb, 1812, at Palmyra, Ontario Co., New York. Resided at Williamson, Ontario Co., 1820. One of five to whom JS gave Martin Harris permission to show 116 pages of Book of Mormon transcription, 1828.

Married second William Parker, 1828. Resided at Hartland, Niagara Co., New York, 1830; at Lewiston, Niagara Co., 1840; and at Newfane, Niagara Co., 1850. Died at Newfane.

Parks, Hiram Gartrell (ca. 1807–after 1880), farmer, military officer, sheriff, real estate agent, hatter. Born in Tennessee. Married first Nancy McGhee, 22 Apr. 1828, in Knox Co., Tennessee. Resided in Knoxville, Knox Co., 1830. Moved to Richmond, Ray Co., Missouri, by 1835. Ray Co. treasurer, 1835–1836. Member of board of trustees, 1835, at Richmond. Brigadier general in Missouri militia. Served in Mormon War, 1838. Moved to California, 1849. Married second Louise, ca. 1854, in California. Married third Sarah Miller, 7 June 1858, at Analy (later in Sebastopol), Sonoma Co., California. Moved to Bodega, Sonoma Co., by 1860. Married fourth Louisa McDonald, 23 June 1865. Served intermittently as sheriff and deputy sheriff, 1865–1880, at Santa Rosa, Sonoma Co. Patient at Sonoma County Hospital, 1880.

Parrish, Martha H. Raymond (1 Dec. 1804–1/14 July 1875). Born in Massachusetts. Married to Warren F. Parrish by JS, 3 Dec. 1835, at Kirtland, Geauga Co., Ohio. Lived at Chardon, Geauga Co., 1840; at Mendon, Monroe Co., New York, 1850; at Rockford, Winnebago Co., Illinois, 1860; and at Emporia, Lyon Co., Kansas, 1870. Died at Emporia.

Parrish, Warren Farr (10 Jan. 1803–3 Jan. 1877), clergyman, gardener. Born in New York. Son of John Parrish and Ruth Farr. Married first Elizabeth (Betsey) Patten of Westmoreland Co., New Hampshire, 1826. Lived at Alexandria, Jefferson Co., New York, 1830. Purchased land at Chaumont, Lyme Township, Jefferson Co., 1831. Baptized by Brigham Young, 20 May 1833, at Theresa, Jefferson Co. Participated in Camp of Israel expedition to Missouri, 1834. Wife died of cholera at Rush Creek, Clay Co., Missouri, while accompanying Warren on expedition, 27 June 1834. Served mission to Missouri, Kentucky, and Tennessee with David W. Patten, 1834–1835. Appointed member of First Quorum of the Seventy, 1835. Served mission to Kentucky and Tennessee with Wilford Woodruff, Mar.–July 1835. Started clerical work and began serving as scribe for JS, 29 Oct. 1835. Married second to Martha H. Raymond by JS, 3 Dec. 1835, at Kirtland, Geauga Co., Ohio. Appointed secretary and treasurer of Kirtland Safety Society, 2 Jan. 1837. Found guilty of speculation, costing bank estimated $25,000. Led movement of reformers opposed to JS. Excommunicated, ca. Dec. 1837. Lived at Chardon, Geauga Co., 1840. Baptist clergyman in Fox River area of Wisconsin/Illinois, 1844. Clergyman at Mendon, Monroe Co., New York, 1850. Lived at Rockford, Winnebago Co., Illinois, 1860. Lived at Emporia, Lyon Co., Kansas, 1870. Died at Emporia.

Partridge, Edward (27 Aug. 1793–27 May 1840), hatter. Born at Pittsfield, Berkshire Co., Massachusetts. Son of William Partridge and Jemima Bidwell. Moved to Painesville, Geauga Co., Ohio. Married Lydia Clisbee, 22 Aug. 1819, at Painesville. Initially a Universal Restorationist but adhered to Reformed Baptist (later Disciples of Christ or Campbellite) faith when first contacted by Mormon missionaries in Nov. 1830. With Sidney Rigdon, visited JS at Fayette, Seneca Co., New York. Baptized into LDS church by JS, 11 Dec. 1830, in nearby Seneca River. Ordained an elder by Sidney Rigdon, Dec. 1830. Named first bishop in church, Feb. 1831, at Kirtland, Geauga Co. Ordained a high priest by Lyman Wight, 4 June 1831, at Kirtland. Accompanied JS to Missouri and called to oversee settlement of Latter-day Saints in Missouri, summer 1831. Involved in administering stewardships of land under law of consecration. Tarred and feathered during mob violence in

Jackson Co., Missouri, July 1833. Fled with family to Clay Co., Missouri, Nov. 1833. Served as bishop in Clay Co. Served mission to Illinois, Iowa, Ohio, and Indiana, Jan.–May 1835. Served mission to New York and New England, June–Oct. 1835. In fall 1836, forced to move from Clay Co. to what soon became Caldwell Co., Missouri, where he continued to serve as bishop. Jailed at Richmond, Ray Co., Missouri, fall 1838. Exiled from state, 1839. Appointed bishop of Upper Ward at Commerce (later Nauvoo), Hancock Co., Illinois, 1839. Died at Nauvoo.

Patten, David Wyman (14 Nov. 1799–25 Oct. 1838), farmer. Born in Vermont. Son of Benoni Patten and Edith Cole. Moved to Theresa, Oneida Co., New York, as a young child. Moved to Dundee, Monroe Co., Michigan Territory, as a youth. Married Phoebe Ann Babcock, 1828, in Dundee. Affiliated with Methodists. Baptized into LDS church by his brother John Patten, 15 June 1832, at Fairplay, Greene Co., Indiana. Ordained an elder by Elisha H. Groves, 17 June 1832. Served mission to Michigan Territory, 1832. Ordained a high priest by Hyrum Smith, 2 Sept. 1832. Served mission to eastern states, 1832–1833. Moved family from Michigan Territory to Florence, Erie Co., Ohio, 1833. With William Pratt, carried dispatches from JS to church leaders in Clay Co., Missouri, Dec. 1833. Served mission to southern U.S. with Warren F. Parrish, 1834–1835. Ordained member of Quorum of the Twelve, 15 Feb. 1835, at Kirtland, Geauga Co., Ohio. Served mission to Tennessee, spring 1835. With the Twelve, served mission to eastern states, summer 1835. Moved from Kirtland to Far West, Missouri, 1836. Member of presidency pro tempore of church in Far West, 1838. Captain of local militia in Caldwell Co., Missouri. Mortally wounded during Battle of Crooked River, near Ray Co., Missouri, 25 Oct. 1838. Died near Far West.

Peck, Hezekiah (19 Jan. 1782–25 Aug. 1850), millwright. Born at Guilford, Cumberland Co., New York (later in Windham Co., Vermont). Son of Joseph Peck and Elizabeth Read. Moved to Jericho (later Bainbridge), Chenango Co., New York, by 1812. Married Martha Long, by 1812. Baptized into LDS church by Oliver Cowdery, 28 June 1830, at Joseph Knight Sr. farm, Colesville, Broome Co., New York. Moved with Colesville branch to Thompson, Geauga Co., Ohio, May 1831, and to Kaw Township, Jackson Co., Missouri, July 1831. Approved for high priest ordination, 25 June 1833. Relocated at Clay Co., Missouri, by Nov. 1835. Located in Far West, Caldwell Co., Missouri, by 1837; at Adams Co., Illinois, by Mar. 1840; and at Hancock Co., Illinois, by June 1842. Bishop of Nauvoo Tenth Ward, 1844. Lived at Jackson Township, Andrew Co., Missouri, June 1850. Died in Andrew Co.

Peck, Polly. See Knight, Polly Peck.

Peixotto, Daniel Levy Maduro (18 July 1800–13 May 1843), physician, author, linguist. Born at Amsterdam, Holland. Son of Moses Peixotto and Judith Lopez Salzedo. Moved to Curaçao, West Indies, before 1807. Moved to New York City, 18 July 1807. Married Rachel M. Seixas, 19 Mar. 1823. Graduated from Columbia College, 1825. Returned to West Indies; returned to New York City, 1827. Pioneer in field of preventive medicine. Became a Mason, 1828. Physician at New York City Dispensary. President of New York County Medical Society, 1830–1832. Editor of *New-York Medical and Physical Journal,* first quarterly medical journal printed in English. Revised George Gregory's medical textbook, *Elements of the Theory and Practice of Physic,* 1830. Served on committees that promoted regulating medical practice by city and state governments, beginning 1831. Moved to Ohio, ca. 1835. Appointed professor of "Theory and Practice of Medicine and Obstetrics" at newly established Willoughby Medical College of Lake Erie in Willoughby, Cuyahoga Co., Ohio—the only institution for regular medical training in northeastern Ohio. By 1841, returned to New York City, where he resumed his practice. Died at New York City.

Perry, Eliza Brown (5 Oct. 1808–18 Sept. 1885). Born at Sherburne, Chenango Co., New York. Daughter of George Brown and Sally Burniss. Received patriarchal blessing, 12 Mar. 1835, at Kirtland, Geauga Co., Ohio. Married William C. Perry, 25 Oct. 1835, at Kirtland. Lived among Latter-day Saints in Missouri and Illinois. Moved to Quincy, Adams Co., Illinois, by June 1840; to Nodaway Co., Missouri, by June 1850; to Washington, De Kalb Co., Missouri, by June 1870; and to Stewartsville, De Kalb Co., by June 1880. Died at Stewartsville.

Perry, William Chadwick (26 Jan. 1812–9 May 1893), farmer, carpenter. Born at Madison, Madison Co., New York. Son of Asahel Perry and Polly Chadwick. Lived at Middlebury, Genesee Co., New York, 1815–1830. Baptized into LDS church, 1835. Ordained an elder, 7 Mar. 1835, in Kirtland, Geauga Co., Ohio. Married Eliza Brown, 25 Oct. 1835, at Kirtland. Member of Second Quorum of the Seventy, by 31 Dec. 1836. Migrated to Missouri with Kirtland Camp, 1838. Located at Quincy, Adams Co., Illinois, by May 1839. Member of high council at Nauvoo, Hancock Co., Illinois, by 1 June 1844. Moved to Missouri, by 1849; to Nodaway Co., Missouri, by June 1850; and to Washington, De Kalb Co., Missouri, by June 1870. Moved to Stewartsville, De Kalb Co., by June 1880. Died at Stewartsville.

Peterson, Ziba (ca. 1810–1849), teacher, farmer, law officer. Born in New York. Lived in Macedon, Wayne Co., New York, ca. 1830. Baptized into LDS church. Ordained an elder, by 9 June 1830. Served mission to Ohio and Missouri, 1830–1831. Missionary appointment and elder's license revoked, 1 Aug. 1831, at Jackson Co., Missouri. Married Rebecca Hopper, 11 Aug. 1831, at Clay Township, Lafayette Co., Missouri. Reordained an elder by Lyman Wight, 2 Oct. 1832, in Missouri. Excommunicated, by 25 June 1833, in Missouri. Resided in Lafayette Co., 1840. In 1848, moved to Dry Diggins (later Hangtown), California, where he served as sheriff, 1848–1849. Died at Hangtown (later Placerville, El Dorado Co.).

Phelps, William Wines (17 Feb. 1792–7 Mar. 1872), writer, teacher, printer, newspaper editor, publisher, postmaster, lawyer. Born at Hanover, Morris Co., New Jersey. Son of Enon Phelps and Mehitabel Goldsmith. Moved to Homer, Cortland Co., New York, 1800. Married Sally Waterman, 28 Apr. 1815, in Smyrna, Chenango Co., New York. Editor of *Western Courier.* Moved to Wooster, Wayne Co., Ohio, by 3 July 1819. Returned to Homer, by Nov. 1821. Moved to Trumansburg, Tompkins Co., New York, 1823. Edited Anti-Masonic newspaper *Lake Light.* Moved to Canandaigua, Ontario Co., New York, Apr. 1828, and there published Anti-Masonic newspaper *Ontario Phoenix.* Obtained copy of Book of Mormon, 1830. Met JS, 24 Dec. 1830. Migrated to Kirtland, Geauga Co., Ohio, 1831. Baptized into LDS church, 16 June 1831, at Kirtland. Ordained an elder by JS, June 1831, at Kirtland. Appointed church printer, 20 July 1831. Ordained a high priest, 1831. Moved to Jackson Co., Missouri, late 1831. Became editor of *The Evening and the Morning Star* and *Upper Missouri Advertiser,* published 1832–1833 at Independence, Jackson Co. Published partially completed Book of Commandments, but most copies destroyed by mob action when printing office was razed, 20 July 1833. Exiled from Jackson Co. to Clay Co.,

Missouri, Nov. 1833. Appointed counselor/assistant president to David Whitmer, president of church in Missouri, 3 July 1834. Returned to Kirtland and served as JS's scribe. Helped compile Doctrine and Covenants and first Latter-day Saint hymnal, 1835, at Kirtland. Prolific writer of hymns. Appointed to draft regulations for Kirtland temple, 13 Jan. 1836. Returned from Kirtland to Clay Co., where he resumed duties with Missouri presidency, 1836. Appointed postmaster, 27 May 1837, at Far West, Caldwell Co., Missouri. Excommunicated, 17 Mar. 1838. Moved to Dayton, Montgomery Co., Ohio, before Mar. 1840. Reconciled with church, July 1840; rebaptized into LDS church, 1841. Returned to Kirtland, by May 1841. Appointed to serve mission to eastern U.S., 23 May 1841. Appointed recorder of church licenses, 2 Oct. 1841, in Kirtland. Moved to Nauvoo, Hancock Co., Illinois, by Dec. 1841. Acted as clerk to JS and assisted John Taylor in editing *Times and Seasons* and *Nauvoo Neighbor.* Assisted Willard Richards in writing JS's history, by Jan. 1843. Elected fire warden, 11 Feb. 1843. Elected to Nauvoo City Council, early 1844. Member of Council of Fifty, by 11 Mar. 1844. Migrated to Salt Lake Valley, 1848. Served as counselor to Parley P. Pratt on exploration mission to southern Utah Territory, Nov. 1849. Admitted to Utah territorial bar, 1851. Member of Utah territorial legislative assembly, 1851–1857. Died at Salt Lake City.

Pratt, Orson (19 Sept. 1811–3 Oct. 1881), farmer, writer, teacher, merchant, surveyor, editor, publisher. Born at Hartford, Washington Co., New York. Son of Jared Pratt and Charity Dickinson. Moved to New Lebanon, Columbia Co., New York, 1814; to Canaan, Columbia Co., fall 1823; to Hurl Gate, Queens Co., New York, spring 1825; and to New York City, spring 1826. Returned to Hurl Gate, fall 1826, and to Canaan, spring 1827. Moved to Lorain Co., Ohio, fall 1827; to Chagrin (later Willoughby), Cuyahoga Co., Ohio, spring 1828; and to Connecticut, fall 1828. Returned to Hurl Gate, winter 1828–1829, and to Canaan, spring 1829. Baptized into LDS church by Parley P. Pratt, 19 Sept. 1830, at Canaan. Ordained an elder by JS, 1 Dec. 1830, in Fayette, Seneca Co., New York, and appointed to serve mission to Colesville, Broome Co., New York. With Samuel H. Smith, traveled from New York to Kirtland, Geauga Co., Ohio; arrived, 27 Feb. 1831. Served mission to Missouri, summer 1831. Moved to Hiram, Portage Co., Ohio, Dec. 1831. Ordained a high priest by Sidney Rigdon, 2 Feb. 1832, in Hiram. Served mission with Lyman E. Johnson to the East from Kirtland, Feb. 1832. Participated in Camp of Israel expedition to Missouri, 1834. Ordained member of Quorum of the Twelve by David Whitmer and Oliver Cowdery, 26 Apr. 1835, at Kirtland. Married Sarah Marinda Bates, 4 July 1836, at Henderson, Jefferson Co., New York. Served mission to Upper Canada, 1836. Served mission to Great Britain with other members of Quorum of the Twelve, 1839–1841. Member of city council, 1841–1845, in Nauvoo, Hancock Co., Illinois. Member of Nauvoo Masonic Lodge. Excommunicated, 20 Aug. 1842, at Nauvoo. Rebaptized into LDS church, 20 Jan. 1843, and ordained to his former office in Quorum of the Twelve. Moved to what became Council Bluffs, Pottawattamie Co., Iowa Territory, 1846. Entered Salt Lake Valley with Mormon pioneers, 1847. Presided over church in Great Britain, 1848–1849, 1856–1857. Member of Utah territorial legislature. Appointed church historian, 1874. Died at Salt Lake City.

Pratt, Parley Parker (12 Apr. 1807–13 May 1857), farmer, editor, publisher, teacher, school administrator, legislator, explorer, author. Born at Burlington, Otsego Co., New York. Son of Jared Pratt and Charity Dickinson. Traveled west with brother to acquire land, 1823. Affiliated with Baptist church at age eighteen. Lived in Ohio, 1826–1827. Married first Thankful Halsey, 9 Sept. 1827, at Canaan, Columbia Co., New York. Converted to Reformed Baptist (later Disciples of Christ or Campbellite) faith by Sidney Rigdon, 1829. Baptized into LDS church and ordained an elder by Oliver Cowdery, 1 Sept. 1830, at Seneca Lake, Seneca Co., New York. Served mission to unorganized Indian Territory and Missouri with Oliver Cowdery and others, 1830–1831. En route, stopped at Kirtland, Geauga Co., Ohio, and vicinity; missionaries baptized some 130 individuals. Returned to Kirtland, 3 Apr. 1831. Ordained a high priest by Lyman Wight, 4 June 1831. Served mission to western U.S., 7 June 1831–May 1832. Moved to Jackson Co., Missouri, summer 1832. Appointed president of Elders School in Independence, Jackson Co. Left to serve mission to eastern U.S., Mar. 1834. Participated in Camp of Israel expedition to Missouri, 1834. Moved to Kirtland, Oct. 1834. Ordained member of Quorum of the Twelve, 21 Feb. 1835. Served mission to eastern U.S., spring–28 Aug. 1835. Served mission to Canada, Apr.–June 1836. Shareholder of Kirtland Safety Society, 1837. Wife died, 25 Mar. 1837. Married second Mary Ann Frost Stearns, 14 May 1837, at Kirtland. Left to serve mission to New York City, July 1837. Moved to Far West, Caldwell Co., Missouri, Apr. 1838. First lieutenant in Missouri state militia, 1838. Participated in Battle of Crooked River, near Ray Co., Missouri, 25 Oct. 1838. Jailed at Richmond, Ray Co., and Columbia, Boone Co., Missouri, 1838–1839. Reunited with family, 11 July 1839, in Illinois. Served mission to England, 1839–1842. Edited first number of *LDS Millennial Star,* published in Manchester, England, 27 May 1840. President of British mission, 1841–1842. Arrived at Nauvoo, Hancock Co., Illinois, 7 Feb. 1843. Member of Nauvoo Masonic Lodge. Participated in plural marriage during JS's lifetime. Directed affairs of church in New York City, 1844–1845. Moved to Mount Pisgah, Clarke Co., Iowa Territory, 14 Feb. 1846. Left to serve mission to England, 31 July 1846. Arrived at Winter Quarters, unorganized U.S. territory (later in Omaha, Douglas Co., Nebraska), 8 Apr. 1847. Arrived in Salt Lake Valley, 28 Sept. 1847. Led exploration party into southern Utah Territory, Nov. 1849–Feb. 1850. Served mission to Chile, 16 Mar. 1851– 18 Oct. 1852. Served mission to eastern U.S., beginning Sept. 1856. Murdered at Van Buren, Crawford Co., Arkansas.

Price, Sterling (ca. Sept. 1809–29 Sept. 1867), farmer, merchant, military officer. Born near Farmville, Prince Edward Co., Virginia. Son of Pugh Williamson Price and Elizabeth Marshall Williamson. Moved to Missouri, 1831. Married Martha Head, 14 May 1833, in Randolph Co., Missouri. Member of Missouri House of Representatives, 1836– 1838, 1840–1844. Served in Missouri militia, 1838–1839, and participated in Mormon War. Moved to Chariton Co., Missouri, by June 1840. Elected to U.S. Congress, 1844; resigned to serve in Mexican War, 12 Aug. 1846. Became military governor of what became New Mexico, 1847. Served as Missouri governor, 1852–1856. Commissioned major general in Confederate army in Civil War, 1862. Moved to Mexico. Moved to St. Louis, 11 Feb. 1867. Died in St. Louis.

Raymond, Martha H. See Parrish, Martha H. Raymond

Redfield, David Harvey (31 Aug. 1807–27 Dec. 1878), teamster, farmer, merchant, coroner. Born at Herkimer, Herkimer Co., New York. Son of Samuel Russell Redfield and Sarah Gould. Baptized into LDS church, by 1831. Ordained a priest by Sidney Rigdon, 11 Nov. 1831, at Hiram, Portage Co., Ohio. Lived in Missouri at time Mormons were expelled from Jackson Co., Missouri, 1833. Moved to Kirtland, Geauga Co., Ohio, by 1837.

Married Frances (Fanny) Atherton (McAtherton), 26 Oct. 1837, at Kirtland. Migrated from
Ohio to Missouri with Kirtland Camp, 1838. Moved to Quincy, Adams Co., Illinois,
ca. 1839. Moved to Commerce (later Nauvoo), Hancock Co., Illinois, ca. 1839. Ordained
a high priest, by 1845. Migrated to Salt Lake Valley, 1849. In winter 1851, settled at Nicolaus,
Sutter Co., California. Died near Nicolaus.

Reed, John Savage (ca. 1785–1878), farmer, lawyer. Born in Massachusetts. Son of
Amos Reed and Hannah Slade. Married first Submit Joiner. Moved to Bainbridge,
Chenango Co., New York, ca. 1823. Defended JS in trials in Chenango Co. and Broome
Co., New York. Visited Nauvoo, Hancock Co., Illinois, May 1844, as delegate from
Chemung Co., New York, to elect JS as U.S. president. Moved to Mexico, Oswego Co.,
New York, by 1855. Married second Mercy Foster, by 1855. Buried in Three Mile Creek
Cemetery, Clayton, Jefferson Co., New York.

Rich, Leonard (1800–1868), farmer. Born in New York. Married first Keziah. Lived
at Warsaw, Genesee Co., New York, 1830. Participated in Camp of Israel expedition to
Missouri, 1834. Served as a president of First Quorum of the Seventy, 1835–1837. Moved to
Kirtland, Geauga Co., Ohio, by 1840. Sustained in Sidney Rigdon's Church of Christ as
president of Quorum of the Seventy, 15 Mar. 1845, at Pittsburgh. With William E. McLellin
and Jacob Bump, organized the Church of Christ at Kirtland, Jan. 1847. Wife died, 1853.
Married second Marina Bassett, 7 Mar. 1858, in Kirtland. Died at Kirtland.

Richards, Willard (24 June 1804–11 Mar. 1854), teacher, lecturer, doctor, clerk,
printer, editor, postmaster. Born at Hopkinton, Middlesex Co., Massachusetts. Son of
Joseph Richards and Rhoda Howe. Moved to Richmond, Berkshire Co., Massachusetts,
1813. Moved to Chatham, Columbia Co., New York, by Nov. 1820; returned to Richmond,
by Nov. 1821. Moved to Nassau, Rensselaer Co., New York, by 6 Apr. 1823. Traveled
through New England, giving lectures on scientific subjects for several years, beginning
1827. Practiced medicine at Thomsonian infirmary, beginning 1834, in Boston. Moved to
Holliston, Middlesex Co., 1835. Moved to Kirtland, Geauga Co., Ohio, by Dec. 1836.
Baptized into LDS church by Brigham Young, 31 Dec. 1836, in Kirtland. Appointed to
serve mission to eastern U.S., 13 Mar. 1837. Served mission to England, 1837–1841. Married
Jennetta Richards, 24 Sept. 1838, in Walker Ford, Chaigley, Lancashire, England.
Ordained member of Quorum of the Twelve, 14 Apr. 1840, at Preston, Lancashire. Moved
to Nauvoo, Hancock Co., Illinois. Moved to Warsaw, Hancock Co., 31 Aug. 1841;
returned to Nauvoo, 1841. Member of Nauvoo City Council, 1841–1843. Appointed recorder
for Nauvoo temple and JS's scribe, 13 Dec. 1841. Member of Nauvoo Masonic Lodge.
Appointed JS's private secretary, Dec. 1842; church historian, ca. Dec. 1842; church
recorder, 30 July 1843; Nauvoo city recorder, Aug. 1843; and clerk of municipal court.
Participated in plural marriage during JS's lifetime. Before death of JS, completed personal
history of JS up to Aug. 1838. With JS in jail in Carthage, Hancock Co., when JS and
Hyrum Smith were murdered. Moved to Winter Quarters, unorganized U.S. territory (later
in Omaha, Douglas Co., Nebraska), 1846. Migrated to Salt Lake Valley and returned to
Winter Quarters, 1847. Appointed second counselor to Brigham Young in church presi-
dency, 27 Dec. 1847, at what became Council Bluffs, Pottawattamie Co., Iowa. Returned to
Salt Lake Valley. Appointed secretary and president of legislative council for provisional

state of Deseret. Secretary of Utah Territory, postmaster of Salt Lake City, and editor of *Deseret News.* Died at Salt Lake City.

Rigdon, Sidney (19 Feb. 1793–14 July 1876), tanner, farmer, minister. Born at St. Clair, Allegheny Co., Pennsylvania. Son of William Rigdon and Nancy Gallaher. Joined United Baptists, 1817. Preached at Warren, Trumbull Co., Ohio, and vicinity, 1819–1821. Married Phebe Brook, 12 June 1820, at Warren. Minister of First Baptist Church of Pittsburgh, 1821–1824. Later joined Reformed Baptist (later Disciples of Christ or Campbellite) movement and became influential preacher. Moved to Bainbridge, Geauga Co., Ohio, 1826. Moved to Mentor, Geauga Co., 1827. Introduced to Mormonism by his former proselyte to Reformed Baptist faith, Parley P. Pratt, who was en route with Oliver Cowdery and others on mission to unorganized Indian Territory. Baptized into LDS church by Oliver Cowdery, Nov. 1830. Scribe for JS, 1830. Ordained a high priest by Lyman Wight, 4 June 1831, in Kirtland, Geauga Co. Moved to Hiram, Portage Co., Ohio, 1831. Counselor/assistant president in church presidency, 1832–1844. Accompanied JS to Upper Canada on proselytizing mission and helped keep JS's diary during trip, 1833. Arrived at Far West, Caldwell Co., Missouri, from Kirtland, 4 Apr. 1838. With JS in jail at Liberty, Clay Co., Missouri, Nov. 1838–Feb. 1839. After release, found refuge at Quincy, Adams Co., Illinois. Accompanied JS to Washington DC to seek redress for Missouri grievances, 1839–1840. Member of city council in Nauvoo, Hancock Co., Illinois, 1841. Appointed postmaster of Nauvoo, 24 Feb. 1841. Member of Nauvoo Masonic Lodge. Claimed right to lead church after death of JS; excommunicated, 1844. Moved to Pittsburgh to lead schismatic Church of Jesus Christ of Latter Day Saints, 1844; name of church changed to Church of Christ, 1845. Located near Greencastle, Antrim Township, Franklin Co., Pennsylvania, May 1846. Removed to Friendship, Allegany Co., New York, where he died.

Robinson, Angelina (Angeline) Eliza Works (22 Aug. 1814–8 Apr. 1880), schoolteacher. Born at Aurelius, Cayuga Co., New York. Daughter of Asa Works and Abigail Marks. Sister of Brigham Young's first wife, Miriam Works Young. Baptized into LDS church, 1835, at Kirtland, Geauga Co., Ohio. Married Ebenezer Robinson, 13 Dec. 1835, at Kirtland. Moved to Far West, Caldwell Co., Missouri, 1837. Lived at Commerce (later Nauvoo), Hancock Co., Illinois, 1839. Joined with Sidney Rigdon at Pittsburgh following death of JS, 1844. Lived at Greencastle, Franklin Co., Pennsylvania, 1846–1855. Moved to Decatur Co., Iowa, 1855. Affiliated with RLDS church, ca. 1863. Died near Pleasanton, Decatur Co.

Robinson, Ebenezer (25 May 1816–11 Mar. 1891), printer, editor, publisher. Born at Floyd (near Rome), Oneida Co., New York. Son of Nathan Robinson and Mary Brown. Moved to Utica, Oneida Co., ca. 1831, and learned printing trade at *Utica Observer.* Moved to Ravenna, Portage Co., Ohio, Aug. 1833, and worked as compositor on the *Ohio Star.* Moved to Kirtland, Geauga Co., Ohio, May 1835, and worked in printing office. Baptized into LDS church by JS, 16 Oct. 1835. Married first Angelina (Angeline) Eliza Works, 13 Dec. 1835, at Kirtland. Ordained an elder, 29 Apr. 1836, and a seventy, 20 Dec. 1836. Served mission to Richland Co., Ohio, June–July 1836, and shortly after served mission to New York. Moved to Far West, Caldwell Co., Missouri, spring 1837. Assisted with publication of *Elders' Journal,* summer 1838. Recorder and clerk of Missouri high council and church clerk, 1838. Member of Far West high council, Dec. 1838. Justice of the peace, 1839. When driven from Missouri, moved to Quincy, Adams Co., Illinois, and worked on *Quincy Whig,* 1839. Became publisher, coeditor, and editor of *Times and Seasons,* 1839–1842, at Commerce (later Nauvoo), Hancock Co., Illinois. Member of Nauvoo Masonic Lodge. Justice of the peace in Hancock Co., by 1842. Served mission to New York, 1843. Moved to Pittsburgh, June 1844. Affiliated with Sidney Rigdon and served as his counselor. In May 1846, moved to Greencastle, Franklin Co., Pennsylvania, where he edited Rigdonite *Messenger and Advocate of the Church of Christ.* Moved to Decatur Co., Iowa, Apr. 1855. Baptized into RLDS church by William W. Blair, 29 Apr. 1863, at Pleasanton, Decatur Co. Wife died, 1880. Married second Martha A. Cunningham, 5 Feb. 1885. Affiliated with David Whitmer's Church of Christ, 1888. Edited Whitmerite periodical *The Return,* 1889–1891. Died at Davis City, Decatur Co.

Robinson, George W. (14 May 1814–10 Feb. 1878), clerk, postmaster, merchant, clothier, miller, banker. Born at Pawlet, Rutland Co., Vermont. Baptized into LDS church and moved to Kirtland, Geauga Co., Ohio, by 1836. Clerk and recorder for Kirtland high council, beginning Jan. 1836. Married Athalia Rigdon, oldest daughter of Sidney Rigdon, fall 1836, in Salem, Essex Co., Massachusetts. In Sept. 1837, appointed general church recorder to replace Oliver Cowdery. Moved to Far West, Caldwell Co., Missouri, 28 Mar. 1838. Sustained as general church recorder and clerk to First Presidency at Far West, Apr. 1838. Imprisoned with JS and other church leaders in Missouri, Nov. 1838. Ordained a seventy, before May 1839. Moved to Quincy, Adams Co., Illinois, winter 1839. Moved to Commerce (later Nauvoo), Hancock Co., Illinois, before 1840. Appointed first postmaster in Nauvoo, Apr. 1840. Member of Nauvoo Masonic Lodge. Left LDS church, by July 1842. Moved to Cuba, Allegany Co., New York, by 1846. Affiliated with Sidney Rigdon's Church of Christ as an apostle. Moved to Friendship, Allegany Co., 1847. Charter member of Masonic lodge in that community. Founder and president of First National Bank, 1 Feb. 1864. Died at Friendship.

Rockwell, Caroline. See Smith, Caroline Rockwell.

Rockwell, Electa. See Ousley, Electa Rockwell.

Rockwell, Orrin Porter (28 June 1813–9 June 1878), ferry operator, herdsman, farmer. Born in Belchertown, Hampshire Co., Massachusetts. Son of Orin Rockwell and Sarah Witt. Moved to Farmington (later in Manchester), Ontario Co., New York, 1817. Neighbor to JS. Baptized into LDS church, 1830, in Ontario Co. Moved to Ohio and then to Big Blue settlement, Kaw Township, Jackson Co., Missouri, 1831. Married first Luana Beebe, 2 Feb. 1832, in Jackson Co. Moved to Clay Co., Missouri. Moved to Far West, Caldwell Co., Missouri, by 1838. Ordained a deacon, 6 July 1838, in Far West. Traveled to Washington DC with JS to seek redress for Missouri grievances, Oct. 1839–Mar. 1840. Moved to Hancock Co., Illinois, by 1840. Member of Nauvoo Masonic Lodge. Imprisoned in Missouri, Mar. 1843, on suspicion of attempting to kill former Missouri governor Lilburn W. Boggs. Grand jury declined to indict him on that charge; released Dec. 1843 after serving five-minute sentence for jailbreak. Ordained a high priest, before 5 Jan. 1846. Migrated with Brigham Young pioneer company to Salt Lake Valley, 1847. Married second Mary Ann Neff; wife died, 28 Sept. 1866. Married third Christine Olsen. Died in Salt Lake City.

Rolfe, Samuel Jones (26 Aug. 1794–July 1867), carpenter. Born at Concord, Merrimack Co., New Hampshire. Son of Benjamin Rolfe and Mary (Molly) Swett. Moved to Maine, 1810. Married Elizabeth Hathaway, 4 Mar. 1818. Lived at Rumford, Oxford Co., Maine, when baptized into LDS church, 1835. Moved to Kirtland, Geauga Co., Ohio, 1835. Lived in Caldwell Co., Missouri, 1837. Following expulsion from Missouri, located at Clayton, Adams Co., Illinois. Moved to Nauvoo, Hancock Co., Illinois, by 1841. President of Nauvoo priests quorum, 1841. Ordained a high priest, 12 Nov. 1845, in Nauvoo. Bishop at Winter Quarters, unorganized U.S. territory (later in Omaha, Douglas Co., Nebraska), 1846–1847. Arrived in Salt Lake Valley, Sept. 1847. Settled at San Bernardino, Los Angeles Co., California, 1851. Elected county treasurer. Served as counselor in stake presidency in Los Angeles Co. Returned to Utah Territory, before 1867. Died at Lehi, Utah Co., Utah Territory.

Roundy, Shadrach (1 Jan. 1789–4 July 1872), merchant. Born at Rockingham, Windham Co., Vermont. Son of Uriah Roundy and Lucretia Needham. Married Betsy Quimby, 22 June 1814, at Rockingham. Lived at Spafford, Onondaga Co., New York. Member of Freewill Baptist Church in Spafford. There are two versions of story of his baptism into LDS church: first, that he sought out JS at Fayette, Seneca Co., New York, and was baptized by JS following their first interview, winter 1830–1831 (reportedly 23 Jan. 1831); second, that William E. McLellin baptized him, as reported in McLellin's journal entry for 30 Jan. 1832. Ordained an elder by Orson Hyde and Samuel H. Smith, 16 May 1832. Lived at Elk Creek, Erie Co., Pennsylvania, 1833. Moved to Willoughby, Cuyahoga Co., Ohio, by 1834. Member of the Seventy, 1836. Migrated to Far West, Caldwell Co., Missouri. Located at Warsaw, Hancock Co., Illinois, 1839. Moved to Nauvoo, Hancock Co., 1840. Commissioned aide-de-camp in Nauvoo Legion, Apr. 1841. Member of a bishopric in Nauvoo, 1841. Member of Nauvoo Masonic Lodge. Joined Nauvoo police force, 1843. Ordained a high priest, by 25 Dec. 1845. Bishop of Winter Quarters Fifth Ward at Winter Quarters, unorganized U.S. territory (later in Omaha, Douglas Co., Nebraska). Member of Brigham Young pioneer company, arriving in Salt Lake Valley July 1847. Bishop of Salt Lake Sixteenth Ward, 1849–1856. Died at Salt Lake City.

Rudd, John, Jr. (16 June 1779–after 1835), distiller. Born at Bennington, Bennington Co., Vermont. Son of John Rudd and Chloe Hills. Moved to Richfield, Otsego Co., New York, by Aug. 1800. Married first Avis Whitaker, 1 Feb. 1801. A pioneer settler of Springfield, Erie Co., Pennsylvania, 1802. Married second Rosanna Jackson of Bennington, ca. 1804. Purchased land in Salem Township (later Conneaut Township), Ashtabula Co., Ohio, 14 Feb. 1809. Moved to Salem Township, by 1812. Served in War of 1812. Served as Salem Township clerk, 1814. Returned to Springfield, by Aug. 1820. Baptized into LDS church by Samuel H. Smith, ca. 22 Feb. 1832, at Springfield. JS stayed at Rudd home while traveling to and from the East, 1833. Gave small sum of money to assist JS in meeting his obligations, Dec. 1835.

Rupp, Israel Daniel (10 July 1803–31 May 1878), bookseller, editor, historian, insurance agent, teacher, translator. Born in East Pennsboro (later in Hampden), Cumberland Co., Pennsylvania. Son of George Rupp and Christina Boeshor. Member of Reformed faith. Moved to Allen, Cumberland Co., by 1810. Married Caroline Aristide, 19 July 1827, at Carlisle, Cumberland Co. Moved to Harrisburg, Dauphin Co., Pennsylvania, 1827. Electioneered for John Quincy Adams, 1828, in Pennsylvania. Moved to Montgomery,

Hamilton Co., Ohio, by 1830; to Silver Spring Township, Cumberland Co., by 1833; to Lancaster, Lancaster Co., Pennsylvania, ca. 1842; to Jonestown, Lebanon Co., Pennsylvania, by 1860; and to Philadelphia, 1860. Died in Philadelphia.

Salisbury, Katharine Smith. See Younger, Katharine Smith.

Salisbury, Wilkins Jenkins (6 Jan. 1809–28 Oct. 1853), lawyer, blacksmith. Born at Rushville, Yates Co., New York. Son of Gideon Salisbury and Elizabeth Shields. Baptized into LDS church in New York. Moved to Kirtland, Geauga Co., Ohio, by 1831. Married JS's sister Katharine Smith, 8 June 1831, at Kirtland. Settled at Chardon, Geauga Co. Participated in Camp of Israel expedition to Missouri, 1834. Appointed member of First Quorum of the Seventy, 1835. Left Ohio for Far West, Caldwell Co., Missouri, May 1838. Exiled from Missouri; located at Bardolph, McDonough Co., Illinois, Feb. 1839. Moved to Plymouth, Hancock Co., Illinois, by 1842; to Alexandria, Clark Co., Missouri, spring 1846; to Warsaw, Hancock Co., late 1846; and to Webster, Hancock Co., fall 1847. Died at Plymouth.

Scobey, Almira Mack. See Covey, Almira Mack.

Seixas, Joshua (4 June 1802–1874), Hebraist, textbook writer, teacher. Probably born at New York City. Son of Gershom Mendez Seixas and Hannah Manuel. Married Henrietta Raphael of Richmond, Henrico Co., Virginia. Taught Hebrew at New York and Charlestown, Massachusetts. His work *Manual Hebrew Grammar for the Use of Beginners* was published at Andover, Essex Co., Massachusetts, 1833. Taught at Oberlin College, Ohio, 1835. Among his students was Lorenzo Snow, whose sister Eliza was a Latter-day Saint and lived in JS household at Kirtland, Geauga Co., Ohio. (JS possibly first heard of Seixas from the Snows or from Daniel Peixotto, whose wife, Rachel, was Seixas's cousin.) Taught private course in Hebrew for six weeks at Western Reserve College at Hudson, Portage Co., Ohio, Dec. 1835–23 Jan. 1836 and probably summer 1836. On 26 Jan. 1836, arrived at Kirtland, where he taught Hebrew, 26 Jan.–29 Mar. 1836. Returned to New York, by 1838.

Seymour, William (ca. 1780–28 Dec. 1848), lawyer, justice of the peace, judge, politician. Born in Connecticut. Moved to Windsor, Tioga Co., New York, ca. 1793. Moved to Binghamton, Tioga Co., ca. 1802. Admitted to bar, 1806. Moved back to Windsor, ca. 1807. Served as justice of the peace, 1812–1828, at Windsor. Corporator of Windsor Bridge Company, 23 Apr. 1823. Moved to Binghamton, 1833. Judge of Broome Co. Court of Common Pleas, 1833–1835, 1837–1847. Member of U.S. House of Representatives, 4 Mar. 1835–3 Mar. 1837. Died in Binghamton.

Sherman, Lyman Royal (22 May 1804–ca. 15 Feb. 1839). Born at Monkton, Addison Co., Vermont. Son of Elkanah Sherman and Asenath Hurlbut. Married Delcena Didamia Johnson, 16 Jan. 1829, at Pomfret, Chautauque Co., New York. Baptized into LDS church, Jan. 1832. Located at Kirtland, Geauga Co., Ohio, 1833. Participated in Camp of Israel expedition to Missouri, 1834. Appointed a president of First Quorum of the Seventy, 28 Feb. 1835. Issued elder's certificate, 30 Mar. 1836, at Kirtland. Ordained a high priest and appointed to Kirtland high council, 2 Oct. 1837. Moved to Far West, Caldwell Co., Missouri, by Oct. 1838. Appointed temporary member of Far West high council, 13 Dec. 1838. Appointed member of Quorum of the Twelve, 16 Jan. 1839, but died at Far West before notified and ordained.

Smith, Alvin (11 Feb. 1798–19 Nov. 1823), farmer, carpenter. Born at Tunbridge, Orange Co., Vermont. Son of Joseph Smith Sr. and Lucy Mack. Moved to Randolph, Orange Co., 1802; returned to Tunbridge, 1803. Moved to Royalton, Windsor Co., Vermont, 1804, and to Sharon, Windsor Co., by Aug. 1804; returned to Tunbridge, by Mar. 1808. Returned to Royalton, by Mar. 1810. Moved to Lebanon, Grafton Co., New Hampshire, 1811; to Norwich, Windsor Co., 1813; and to Palmyra, Ontario Co., New York, 1816–Jan. 1817. Played prominent role in family economy, working to pay for 99.5-acre farm at Farmington (later Manchester), Ontario Co., jointly articled for with his father, 1820. Supervised construction of Smiths' frame home in Manchester. Supporter of JS's claims of heavenly manifestations. Experienced severe stomach cramps, perhaps caused by appendicitis, 15 Nov. 1823; situation was apparently complicated by overdose of calomel. Died at Palmyra.

Smith, Caroline Rockwell (ca. 1812–20 Feb. 1887). Born in Massachusetts. Daughter of Orin Rockwell and Sarah Witt. Moved to Farmington, Ontario Co., New York, by Aug. 1820. Baptized into LDS church by David Whitmer, ca. 9 June 1830, in Seneca Lake, Seneca Co., New York. Moved to Ohio, 1831. Moved to Jackson Co., Missouri, 1831. Married Horton Smith, 7 Jan. 1834, in Geauga Co. Moved to Hambden, Geauga Co., by 1840. Died in Hambden.

Smith, David Hyrum (17 Nov. 1844–29 Aug. 1904). Born at Nauvoo, Hancock Co., Illinois. Son of JS and Emma Hale. Ordained an elder in RLDS church, 8 Oct. 1863. Married Clara Charlotte Hartshorn, 10 May 1870, at Sandwich, De Kalb Co., Illinois. Second counselor to his brother Joseph Smith III in RLDS church presidency, 1873–1885. Patient at Illinois State Hospital for the Insane, 1877–1904, at Elgin, Kane Co., Illinois. Died at Elgin.

Smith, Don Carlos (25 Mar. 1816–7 Aug. 1841), farmer, printer, editor. Born at Norwich, Windsor Co., Vermont. Son of Joseph Smith Sr. and Lucy Mack. Moved to Palmyra, Ontario Co., New York, 1816–Jan. 1817. Moved to Manchester, Ontario Co., 1825. Baptized into LDS church by David Whitmer, ca. 9 June 1830, at Seneca Lake, Seneca Co., New York. Accompanied his father on mission to Asael Smith family in St. Lawrence Co., New York, Aug. 1830. Migrated from Seneca Falls, Seneca Co., to Kirtland, Geauga Co., Ohio, with Lucy Mack Smith company of Fayette, Seneca Co., branch of Latter-day Saints, May 1831. Employed by Kirtland printing shop under Oliver Cowdery, fall 1833. Married Agnes Moulton Coolbrith, 30 July 1835, at Kirtland. Ordained a high priest and appointed president of Kirtland high priests quorum, 15 Jan. 1836. Served mission to Pennsylvania and New York, 1836. Continued working in Kirtland printing shop, including involvement with *Elders' Journal.* Moved to New Portage, Medina Co., Ohio, Dec. 1837. Served mission to Virginia, Pennsylvania, and Ohio, spring 1838. Left Ohio for Far West, Caldwell Co., Missouri, May 1838. Served mission to Kentucky and Tennessee, 1838. Expelled from Far West, Feb. 1839; moved to Quincy, Adams Co., Illinois. Lived at Macomb, McDonough Co., Illinois, and then moved to Commerce (later Nauvoo), Hancock Co., Illinois, 1839. President of high priests in Commerce, 1839. Editor and publisher of *Times and Seasons* with Ebenezer Robinson, 1839–1841, at Nauvoo. Elected member of Nauvoo City Council, 1 Feb. 1841. Appointed a regent of University of Nauvoo, 3 Feb. 1841. Elected brigadier general in Nauvoo Legion, 5 Feb. 1841. Died at Nauvoo.

Smith, Don Carlos (13 June 1840–15 Aug. 1841). Born in Nauvoo, Hancock Co., Illinois. Son of JS and Emma Hale. Died in Nauvoo.

Smith, Emma Hale (10 July 1804–30 Apr. 1879), clerk, scribe, editor, author, boardinghouse operator, clothier. Born at Harmony (later in Oakland), Susquehanna Co., Pennsylvania. Daughter of Isaac Hale and Elizabeth Lewis. Member of Methodist church at Harmony. Married first to JS by Zechariah Tarble, 18 Jan. 1827, at South Bainbridge (later Afton), Chenango Co., New York. Assisted JS as scribe during translation of Book of Mormon at Harmony, 1828, and joined him during completion of translation at Peter Whitmer Sr. farm, Fayette, Seneca Co., New York. Baptized into LDS church by Oliver Cowdery, 28 June 1830, at Colesville, Broome Co., New York. Migrated from New York to Kirtland, Geauga Co., Ohio, Jan.–Feb. 1831. Lived at John Johnson home at Hiram, Portage Co., Ohio, while JS worked on revision of Bible, 1831–1832. Edited *A Collection of Sacred Hymns, for the Church of the Latter Day Saints,* published 1835, at Kirtland. Fled Ohio for Far West, Caldwell Co., Missouri, Jan.–Mar. 1838. Exiled from Missouri, Feb. 1839; located near Quincy, Adams Co., Illinois. Moved to Commerce (later Nauvoo), Hancock Co., Illinois, 10 May 1839. Appointed president of Female Relief Society in Nauvoo, 17 Mar. 1842. Husband murdered, 27 June 1844. Fled to Fulton, Fulton Co., Illinois, Sept. 1846–Feb. 1847, then returned to Nauvoo. Married second Lewis Crum Bidamon, 23 Dec. 1847, at Nauvoo. Affiliated with RLDS church, 1860. Died at Nauvoo.

Smith, Ephraim (13 Mar. 1810–24 Mar. 1810). Born at Royalton, Windsor Co., Vermont. Son of Joseph Smith Sr. and Lucy Mack. Died at Royalton.

Smith, Frederick Granger Williams (20 June 1836–13 Apr. 1862), farmer, merchant. Born at Kirtland, Geauga Co., Ohio. Son of JS and Emma Hale. Married Anna Marie Jones, 13 Sept. 1857, in Hancock Co., Illinois. Died in Nauvoo, Hancock Co.

Smith, George Albert (26 June 1817–1 Sept. 1875). Born at Potsdam, St. Lawrence Co., New York. Son of John Smith and Clarissa Lyman. Baptized into LDS church by Joseph H. Wakefield, 10 Sept. 1832, at Potsdam. Moved to Kirtland, Geauga Co., Ohio, 1833. Labored on Kirtland temple. Participated in Camp of Israel expedition to Missouri, 1834. Appointed member of First Quorum of the Seventy, 1 Mar. 1835, at Kirtland. Served mission to eastern states with Lyman Smith, 1835. Served mission to Ohio, 1836. Arrived at Far West, Caldwell Co., Missouri, from Kirtland, 16 June 1838, and soon located at Adam-ondi-Ahman, Daviess Co., Missouri. Member of Adam-ondi-Ahman high council, 1838. In exodus from Missouri, located north of Quincy, Adams Co., Illinois. Ordained member of Quorum of the Twelve, 26 Apr. 1839, at Far West. Served mission to England, 1839–1841. Moved to Nauvoo, Hancock Co., Illinois, 1841. Married to Bathsheba W. Bigler by Don Carlos Smith, 25 July 1841, at Nauvoo. Moved to Zarahemla, Lee Co., Iowa Territory, 1841. Member of Nauvoo Masonic Lodge. Member of Nauvoo City Council, 1842–1843. Nauvoo city alderman, 1843–1844. Member of Brigham Young pioneer company that journeyed to Salt Lake Valley, 1847. Appointed church historian and recorder, 1854. Member of Utah territorial supreme court, 1855. First counselor to Brigham Young in church presidency, 1868. Died at Salt Lake City.

Smith, Hyrum (9 Feb. 1800–27 June 1844), farmer, cooper. Born at Tunbridge, Orange Co., Vermont. Son of Joseph Smith Sr. and Lucy Mack. Moved to Randolph, Orange Co., 1802; to Tunbridge, 1803; to Royalton, Windsor Co., Vermont, May 1804; to Sharon,

Windsor Co., by Aug. 1804; to Tunbridge, by Mar. 1808; to Royalton, by Mar. 1810; to Lebanon, Grafton Co., New Hampshire, 1811; to Norwich, Windsor Co., 1813; and to Palmyra, Ontario Co., New York, 1816–Jan. 1817. Member of Western Presbyterian Church of Palmyra, early 1820s. Lived at Palmyra, 1817–1825. Lived at Manchester, Ontario Co., 1825–1826. Married first Jerusha Barden, 2 Nov. 1826, at Manchester. Returned to Palmyra, 1826. Baptized by JS, June 1829, at Seneca Lake, Seneca Co., New York. One of the Eight Witnesses of the Book of Mormon, June 1829. Assisted in arrangements for publication of Book of Mormon, 1829–1830, at Palmyra. Among six original members of LDS church, 6 Apr. 1830. Presided over branch of church at Colesville, Broome Co., New York, 1830–1831. Migrated to Kirtland, Geauga Co., Ohio, 1831. Ordained a high priest by JS, 4 June 1831. Member of committee to supervise construction of Kirtland temple, 1833–1836. Participated in Camp of Israel expedition to Missouri, 1834. Appointed to Kirtland high council, 24 Sept. 1834. Sustained as assistant counselor in presidency of church, 3 Sept. 1837. Wife died, 13 Oct. 1837. Appointed counselor in First Presidency, 7 Nov. 1837. Married second Mary Fielding, 24 Dec. 1837, at Kirtland. Migrated to Far West, Caldwell Co., Missouri, Mar.–May 1838. Imprisoned at Liberty, Clay Co., Missouri, with his brother JS, 1838–1839. Allowed to escape during change of venue, 16 Apr. 1839, en route from trial in Gallatin, Daviess Co., Missouri, to Columbia, Boone Co., Missouri. Arrived at Quincy, Adams Co., Illinois, 22 Apr. 1839. Moved to Commerce (later Nauvoo), Hancock Co., Illinois, 1839. In JS revelation dated 19 Jan. 1841, instructed to buy stock for building Nauvoo House, appointed patriarch of church, released as counselor in First Presidency, and appointed a prophet, seer, and revelator in First Presidency. Elected to Nauvoo City Council, 1 Feb. 1841. Appointed chaplain in Nauvoo Legion, Mar. 1841. Member of Nauvoo Masonic Lodge. Vice mayor of Nauvoo, 1842–1843. Appointed to replace Elias Higbee as member of Nauvoo temple committee, 10 Oct. 1843. Participated in plural marriage during JS's lifetime. Murdered at Carthage, Hancock Co.

Smith, Jerusha T. Barden (15 Feb. 1805–13 Oct. 1837). Born in Norfolk, Litchfield Co., Connecticut. Daughter of Seth Barden and Sarah. Moved to Greene, Chenango Co., New York, by 1820. Married Hyrum Smith, 2 Nov. 1826, in Manchester, Ontario Co., New York. Moved to Palmyra, Wayne Co., New York, 1826. Baptized into LDS church by David Whitmer, ca. 9 June 1830, in Seneca Lake, Seneca Co., New York. Moved to Colesville, Broome Co., New York, 1830. Moved to Kirtland, Geauga Co., Ohio, 1831. Member of Kirtland Safety Society, 1837. Died in Kirtland.

Smith, John (16 July 1781–23 May 1854), farmer. Born at Derryfield (later Manchester), Rockingham Co., New Hampshire. Son of Asael Smith and Mary Duty. Member of Congregational Church. Appointed overseer of highways at Potsdam, St. Lawrence Co., New York, 1810. Married Clarissa Lyman, 11 Sept. 1815. Baptized into LDS church by Solomon Humphrey, 9 Jan. 1832. Confirmed and ordained an elder by Joseph Wakefield and Solomon Humphrey, 9 Jan. 1832. Moved to Kirtland, Geauga Co., Ohio, 1833. Ordained a high priest, June 1833. President of Kirtland high council. Served mission to eastern states with his brother Joseph Smith Sr., 1836. Appointed assistant counselor in First Presidency, 1837; member of Kirtland stake presidency, 1838. Left Kirtland for Far West, Caldwell Co., Missouri, 5 Apr. 1838. Appointed president of stake in Adam-ondi-Ahman, Daviess Co., Missouri, 28 June 1838. Expelled from Missouri; arrived in Illinois, 28 Feb.

1839. Moved to Commerce (later Nauvoo), Hancock Co., Illinois, June 1839. Appointed president of stake in Lee Co., Iowa Territory, 5 Oct. 1839. Member of Nauvoo Masonic Lodge. Appointed to preside at Macedonia (later Webster), Hancock Co., Illinois, 1843–1844. Ordained a patriarch, 10 Jan. 1844. Appointed Nauvoo stake president, 7 Oct. 1844. Joined westward exodus of Latter-day Saints into Iowa Territory, 9 Feb. 1846. Arrived in Salt Lake Valley, 23 Sept. 1847. Presided over Salt Lake stake, 1847–1848. Ordained patriarch of church, 1 Jan. 1849. Died at Salt Lake City.

Smith, Joseph, III (6 Nov. 1832–10 Dec. 1914), clerk, hotelier, farmer, justice of the peace, editor, minister. Born at Kirtland, Geauga Co., Ohio. Son of JS and Emma Hale. Moved to Far West, Caldwell Co., Missouri, 1838; to Quincy, Adams Co., Illinois, 1839; and to Commerce (later Nauvoo), Hancock Co., Illinois, 1839. Baptized into LDS church by JS, Nov. 1843, at Nauvoo. Appointed clerk of city council in Canton, Fulton Co., Illinois, Jan. 1855. Married first Emmeline Griswold, 22 Oct. 1856, at Nauvoo. Appointed president of RLDS church, 6 Apr. 1860, in Amboy, Lee Co., Illinois. Moved to Plano, Kendall Co., Illinois, 1865. Married second Bertha Madison, 12 Nov. 1869, at Sandwich, Kendall Co. Moved to Little Rock, Kendall Co., by June 1870. Returned to Plano, by June 1880. Moved to Lamoni, Decatur Co., Iowa, 1881. Founded Graceland College in Lamoni and served as chairman of board of trustees, 1893–1898. Married third Ada Rachel Clark, 12 Jan. 1898, at Amaranth, Dufferin Co., Ontario, Canada. Moved to Fayette, Decatur Co., by June 1900. Moved to Independence, Jackson Co., Missouri, 1906. Died at Independence.

Smith, Joseph, Sr. (12 July 1771–14 Sept. 1840), cooper, farmer, teacher, merchant. Born at Topsfield, Essex Co., Massachusetts. Son of Asael Smith and Mary Duty. Nominal member of Congregationalist church at Topsfield. Married to Lucy Mack by Seth Austin, 24 Jan. 1796, at Tunbridge, Orange Co., Vermont. Joined Universalist Society at Tunbridge, 1797. Entered mercantile business at Randolph, Orange Co., ca. 1802, and lost all in a ginseng root investment. Moved to Tunbridge, before May 1803; to Royalton, Windsor Co., Vermont, 1804; to Sharon, Windsor Co., by Aug. 1804; to Tunbridge, by Mar. 1808; to Royalton, by Mar. 1810; to Lebanon, Grafton Co., New Hampshire, 1811; to Norwich, Windsor Co., 1813; to Palmyra, Ontario Co., New York, 1816; and to Manchester, Ontario Co., 1825. One of the Eight Witnesses of the Book of Mormon, June 1829. Baptized into LDS church by Oliver Cowdery, 6 Apr. 1830. Served mission to family of his father in St. Lawrence Co., New York, Aug. 1830. Lived at The Kingdom, unincorporated settlement near Waterloo, Seneca Co., New York, Nov. 1830–1831. Moved to Kirtland, Geauga Co., Ohio, 1831. Ordained a high priest, 4 June 1831. Ordained patriarch of church and assistant president, 6 Dec. 1834. Member of Kirtland high council, 1834. Labored on Kirtland temple. Served mission to eastern states with his brother John Smith, 1836. Sustained as assistant counselor in First Presidency, 1837. Moved to Far West, Caldwell Co., Missouri, summer 1838. Fled to Quincy, Adams Co., Illinois, Feb. 1839. Located at Commerce (later Nauvoo), Hancock Co., Illinois, spring 1839. Died at Nauvoo.

Smith, Joseph Murdock (30 Apr. 1831–30 Mar. 1832). Born in Warrensville Township (later near University Heights), Cuyahoga Co., Ohio. Son of John Murdock and Julia Clapp. After death of mother, adopted by JS and Emma Smith at age of nine days. Lived in Hiram, Portage Co., Ohio, 1831. Died in Hiram from measles and possibly from exposure to cold air during attack on JS six days earlier.

Smith, Julia M. See Middleton, Julia M. Smith.

Smith, Katharine. See Younger, Katharine Smith.

Smith, Lucy. See Millikin, Lucy Smith.

Smith, Lucy Mack (8 July 1775–14 May 1856), oilcloth painter, nurse, fund-raiser, author. Born at Gilsum, Cheshire Co., New Hampshire. Daughter of Solomon Mack Sr. and Lydia Gates. Moved to Montague, Franklin Co., Massachusetts, 1779; to Tunbridge, Orange Co., Vermont, 1788; to Gilsum, 1792; and to Tunbridge, 1794. Married to Joseph Smith Sr. by Seth Austin, 24 Jan. 1796, at Tunbridge. Moved to Randolph, Orange Co., 1802; to Tunbridge, before May 1803; to Royalton, Windsor Co., Vermont, 1804; to Sharon, Windsor Co., by Aug. 1804; to Tunbridge, by Mar. 1808; to Royalton, by Mar. 1810; to Lebanon, Grafton Co., New Hampshire, 1811; to Norwich, Windsor Co., 1813; to Palmyra, Ontario Co., New York, 1816–Jan. 1817; and to Manchester, Ontario Co., 1825. Member of Western Presbyterian Church of Palmyra, early 1820s. Baptized into LDS church, 6 Apr. 1830, at Seneca Lake, Seneca Co., New York. Lived at The Kingdom, unincorporated settlement near Waterloo, Seneca Co., Nov. 1830–May 1831. Led company of approximately eighty Fayette, Seneca Co., branch members from Seneca Co. to Kirtland, Geauga Co., Ohio, May 1831. Migrated to Far West, Caldwell Co., Missouri, summer 1838. Fled to Quincy, Adams Co., Illinois, Feb. 1839. Located at Commerce (later Nauvoo), Hancock Co., Illinois, spring 1839. Husband died, 1840. Joined Female Relief Society, Mar. 1842, in Nauvoo, Hancock Co., Illinois. Lived with daughter Lucy Smith Millikin in Colchester, McDonough Co., Illinois, 1846–1853. Returned to Nauvoo, 1853. Died in Nauvoo. Her narrative history of Smith family, published as *Biographical Sketches of Joseph Smith,* 1853, has been an invaluable resource for study of JS and early church.

Smith, Lyman (ca. 1817–1837). Born at Potsdam, St. Lawrence Co., New York. Participated in Camp of Israel expedition to Missouri, 1834. Appointed member of First Quorum of the Seventy, 1835. Married Clarissa Lyman, 4 Nov. 1835, at Kirtland, Geauga Co., Ohio. Reportedly died in Illinois.

Smith, Mary Bailey (20 Dec. 1808–25 Jan. 1841). Born at Bedford, Hillsborough Co., New Hampshire. Daughter of Joshua Bailey and Hannah Boutwell. Baptized into LDS church by Samuel H. Smith, 26 June 1832, at Boston. Migrated from Boston to Kirtland, Geauga Co., Ohio, 1833. Married Samuel H. Smith, 13 Aug. 1834, at Kirtland. Moved to Missouri, 1838. Located at Commerce (later Nauvoo), Hancock Co., Illinois, 1839. Died at Nauvoo.

Smith, Samuel Harrison (13 Mar. 1808–30 July 1844), farmer, logger, scribe, builder, tavern operator. Born at Tunbridge, Orange Co., Vermont. Son of Joseph Smith Sr. and Lucy Mack. Moved to Royalton, Windsor Co., Vermont, by Mar. 1810; to Lebanon, Grafton Co., New Hampshire, 1811; to Norwich, Windsor Co., 1813; to Palmyra, Ontario Co., New York, 1816–Jan. 1817; and to Manchester, Ontario Co., 1825. Member of Western Presbyterian Church of Palmyra, 1820. Baptized by Oliver Cowdery, May 1829, at Harmony (later in Oakland), Susquehanna Co., Pennsylvania. One of the Eight Witnesses of the Book of Mormon, June 1829. Among six original members of LDS church, 6 Apr. 1830. Ordained an elder, 9 June 1830, at Fayette, Seneca Co., New York. Began mission to New York, 30 June 1830. Sent to serve mission to Kirtland, Geauga Co., Ohio, Dec. 1830. Migrated from New York to Kirtland; arrived, Feb. 1831. Ordained a high priest by Lyman

Wight, 4 June 1831. Served mission to Missouri with Reynolds Cahoon, 1831. Served mission to eastern states with Orson Hyde, 1832. Appointed member of first Kirtland high council, 17 Feb. 1834. Married first Mary Bailey, 13 Aug. 1834, at Kirtland. Committee member and general agent for Literary Firm in Kirtland, 1835. Member of Kirtland Safety Society, 1837. Appointed president of Kirtland high council, 2 Oct. 1837. Moved to Far West, Caldwell Co., Missouri, where he lived briefly before moving to Marrowbone, Daviess Co., Missouri, 1838. Participated in Battle of Crooked River, near Ray Co., Missouri, 25 Oct. 1838. Among first Latter-day Saints to seek refuge at Quincy, Adams Co., Illinois, 1838. Hired to farm for George Miller near Macomb, McDonough Co., Illinois, Mar. 1839. Moved to Nauvoo, Hancock Co., Illinois, 1841. Wife died, Jan. 1841. Appointed a bishop at Nauvoo, 1841. Nauvoo city alderman, 1841–1842. Appointed guard in Nauvoo Legion, Mar. 1841. Married second Levira Clark, 30 May 1841, in Scott Co., Illinois. Appointed a regent of University of Nauvoo. Moved to Plymouth, Hancock Co., Jan. 1842. Member of Nauvoo Masonic Lodge. Member of Nauvoo City Council, 1842–1843. Died at Nauvoo.

Smith, Sophronia. See McCleary, Sophronia Smith.

Smith, Susanna (Susan) Bailey. See Hunt, Susanna (Susan) Bailey Smith.

Smith, Sylvester (25 Mar. 1806–22 Feb. 1880), farmer, carpenter, lawyer, realtor. Born at Tyringham, Berkshire Co., Massachusetts. Son of Chileab Smith and Nancy Marshall. Moved to Amherst, Lorain Co., Ohio, ca. 1815. Married Elizabeth Frank, 27 Dec. 1827, likely in Chautauque Co., New York. Baptized into LDS church and ordained an elder, by June 1831. Ordained a high priest by Oliver Cowdery, 25 Oct. 1831. Served mission to New England with Gideon Carter, 1832. Moved to Kirtland, Geauga Co., Ohio, by 1834. Member of Kirtland high council, 1834. Participated in Camp of Israel expedition to Missouri, 1834. Tried by Kirtland high council for making false charges against JS, confessed, and retained his membership, 1834. Appointed a president of First Quorum of the Seventy, 1835. Temporary scribe to JS during illness of Warren F. Parrish, 1836. Left church, by 1838. Moved to Council Bluffs, Pottawattamie Co., Iowa, 1853. Served as Pottawattamie Co. school fund commissioner and justice of the peace. Died at Council Bluffs.

Smith, unnamed son (15 June 1828–15 June 1828). Born at Harmony (later in Oakland), Susquehanna Co., Pennsylvania. Son of JS and Emma Hale. Did not survive birth.

Smith, unnamed daughter (30 Apr. 1831–30 Apr. 1831). Born at Kirtland, Geauga Co., Ohio. Daughter of JS and Emma Hale. Did not survive birth.

Smith, unnamed son (30 Apr. 1831–30 Apr. 1831). Born at Kirtland, Geauga Co., Ohio. Son of JS and Emma Hale. Did not survive birth.

Smith, William B. (13 Mar. 1811–13 Nov. 1893), farmer, newspaper editor. Born at Royalton, Windsor Co., Vermont. Son of Joseph Smith Sr. and Lucy Mack. Moved from Norwich, Windsor Co., to Palmyra, Ontario Co., New York, 1816–Jan. 1817. Moved to Farmington (later Manchester), Ontario Co., 1818. Baptized into LDS church by David Whitmer, ca. 9 June 1830, at Seneca Lake, Seneca Co., New York. Lived at The Kingdom, unincorporated settlement in Seneca Falls, Seneca Co., by 1830. Ordained a teacher, 5 Oct. 1830. Moved to Kirtland, Geauga Co., Ohio, May 1831. Ordained an elder by Lyman Johnson, 19 Dec. 1832, at Kirtland. Served mission to Erie Co., Pennsylvania, Dec. 1832. Married first Caroline Amanda Grant, 14 Feb. 1833, at Kirtland. Ordained a high priest,

21 June 1833. Participated in Camp of Israel expedition to Missouri, 1834. Appointed member of Quorum of the Twelve, 14 Feb. 1835, at Kirtland. Moved to Far West, Caldwell Co., Missouri, spring 1838. Disfellowshipped, 4 May 1839. Restored to Quorum of the Twelve, 25 May 1839. Settled at Plymouth, Hancock Co., Illinois, ca. 1839, where he kept a tavern. Restored to fellowship. Member of Masonic lodge in Nauvoo, Hancock Co. Member of Nauvoo City Council, 1842–1843. Editor of Nauvoo newspaper *The Wasp*, 1842. Represented Hancock Co. in Illinois House of Representatives, 1842–1843. Wife died, May 1845. Ordained patriarch of church, 24 May 1845. Married second Mary Jane Rollins, 22 June 1845, at Nauvoo. Excommunicated, 12 Oct. 1845. Sustained James J. Strang as successor to JS, 1 Mar. 1846. Married third Roxey Ann Grant, 19 May 1847, in Knox Co., Illinois. Ordained patriarch and apostle of Strang's Church of Jesus Christ of Latter Day Saints, 11 June 1846, at Voree, Walworth Co., Wisconsin Territory. Excommunicated from Strangite movement, 8 Oct. 1847. Affiliated briefly with Lyman Wight, 1849–1850. Initiated a new movement with Martin Harris and Chilton Daniels at Kirtland, likely 1855. Married fourth Eliza Elsie Sanborn, 12 Nov. 1857, at Kirtland. Moved to Venango, Erie Co., Pennsylvania, by 1860, and to Elkader, Clayton Co., Iowa, shortly after. Enlisted in U.S. Army during Civil War and apparently adopted middle initial *B* at this time. Spent active duty time in Arkansas. Joined RLDS church, 1878. Wife died, Mar. 1889. Married fifth Rosanna Jewitt Surprise, 21 Dec. 1889, at Clinton, Clinton Co., Iowa. Moved to Osterdock, Clayton Co., 1890. Died at Osterdock.

Snow, Zerubbabel (29 Mar. 1809–27 Sept. 1888), clerk, teacher, merchant, lawyer. Born at St. Johnsbury, Caledonia Co., Vermont. Son of Levi Snow and Lucina Streeter. Baptized into LDS church by Orson Pratt and Lyman E. Johnson, 1832. Married first Susan Slater Lang, Oct. 1833. Migrated to Kirtland, Geauga Co., Ohio, 1834. Participated in Camp of Israel expedition to Missouri, 1834. Appointed member of First Quorum of the Seventy, 1835, at Kirtland. Appointed to serve mission to eastern states, Mar. 1835. Practiced law in Ohio, 1839–1850. Married second Mary Augusta Hawkins at Streetsboro, Portage Co., Ohio, 25 Aug. 1841. Appointed associate justice for Utah Territory, 1850; migrated to Utah Territory, 1851, and served as associate justice, 1851–1854. Ordained a high priest by William and Willard Snow, 20 Sept. 1851. Served mission to Australia, 1856–1858. Attorney general of Utah Territory, 1869–1874. Died at Salt Lake City.

Squires, Andrew Jackson (17 Sept. 1815–3 Sept. 1897), physician, politician. Born at Aurora, Portage Co., Ohio. Son of Ezekiel Squires and Clarissa Stuart (Stewart). Baptized into LDS church and ordained an elder. Left church and joined briefly with the Methodists. Returned to LDS church, 1835. Practiced medicine at Mantua, Portage Co., 1843–1864. Married Martha Wilmot, 17 Jan. 1850, at Portage Co. Served in Ohio state legislature, 1859–1861. Moved to Hiram Center, Portage Co., 1864, and continued to practice medicine. Died at Portage Co.

Stanley, Harvey (21 Dec. 1812–16 Feb. 1862), stonecutter, dairyman. Born in Vermont. Son of Benjamin Stanley and Ruth. Baptized into LDS church, by Apr. 1834. Participated in Camp of Israel expedition to Missouri, 1834. Labored on temple in Kirtland, Geauga Co., Ohio. Ordained a seventy by JS, Sidney Rigdon, and Oliver Cowdery, 28 Feb. 1835, in Kirtland. Served mission to New York. Married Lerona Cahoon, 17 Jan. 1836, at Kirtland.

Moved to Lee Co., Iowa Territory, by Nov. 1839. Lived at Keokuk, Lee Co., Iowa, 1850. Migrated to Petaluma, Marin Co., California, by June 1860. Died at Marin Co.

Stoddard, Calvin W. (7 Sept. 1801–19 Nov. 1836), farmer. Born at Palmyra, Ontario Co., New York. Son of Silas Stoddard and Bathsheba Sheffield. Lived at Ontario Co., 1810. Married Sophronia Smith, 30 Dec. 1827, at Palmyra. Resident of Macedon, Wayne Co., New York, June 1830. Solicited sales of Book of Mormon, 1830. Migrated to Kirtland, Geauga Co., Ohio, with Lucy Mack Smith company of Fayette, Seneca Co., New York, branch members, 1831. Ordained a priest in LDS church at Orange, Cuyahoga Co., Ohio, 25 Oct. 1831. Ordained an elder, 1832. Became estranged from church. Died at Macedon.

Stoddard, Sophronia Smith. See McCleary, Sophronia Smith.

Stowell, Josiah, Sr. (22 Mar. 1770–12 May 1844), farmer, sawmill owner. Born in Winchester, Cheshire Co., New Hampshire. Son of Israel Stowell and Mary Butler. Member of Presbyterian church. Moved to Jericho, Tioga Co. (later Bainbridge, Chenango Co.), New York, 1791. Married Miriam Bridgeman of Jericho, ca. 1791. Hired JS to dig for Spanish silver in Harmony (later in Oakland), Susquehanna Co., Pennsylvania, 1825. Witness for JS's defense at court proceedings in South Bainbridge (later Afton), Chenango Co., 1826, 1830. Present at Smith home in Manchester, Ontario Co., New York, when JS arrived with gold plates, 1827. Baptized into LDS church, ca. 1830, likely in Bainbridge. Moved to Smithboro, Tioga Co., New York, 1833. Moved to Elmira, Chemung Co., New York, by 1844. Died in Smithboro.

Stringham, Esther Knight (25 Apr. 1798–ca. 1831). Born in Marlborough, Windham Co., Vermont. Daughter of Joseph Knight Sr. and Polly Peck. Moved to Jericho (later Bainbridge), Chenango Co., New York, 1809. Moved to Windsor (later in Colesville), Broome Co., New York, 1811. Married William Stringham, ca. 1816. Member of Universalist church. Baptized into LDS church by Oliver Cowdery, 28 June 1830, in Colesville. Moved with Colesville branch to Thompson, Geauga Co., Ohio, May 1831, and to Kaw Township, Jackson Co., Missouri, July 1831. Died at Kaw Township.

Stringham, Julia Ann. See Averitt, Julia Ann Stringham.

Stringham, Polly Knight (7 Mar. 1811–28 Apr. 1844). Born in Jericho (later Bainbridge), Chenango Co., New York. Daughter of Joseph Knight Sr. and Polly Peck. Moved to Windsor (later in Colesville), Broome Co., New York, 1811. Baptized into LDS church by Oliver Cowdery, 28 June 1830, in Colesville. Moved with Colesville branch to Thompson, Geauga Co., Ohio, May 1831, and to Kaw Township, Jackson Co., Missouri, July 1831. Moved to Clay Co., Missouri, ca. 1833. Married William Stringham, ca. 1835, in Missouri. Likely moved to Far West, Caldwell Co., Missouri, ca. 1838. Moved to Commerce (later Nauvoo), Hancock Co., Illinois, 1839. Member of Female Relief Society in Nauvoo. Died in Nauvoo.

Stringham, William (10 Mar. 1788–3 Nov. 1865), farmer, tailor. Born in North Hempstead, Queens Co., New York. Son of James Stringham and Martha Willis. Married first Esther Knight, ca. 1816. Resident of Windsor (later in Colesville), Broome Co., New York, by Aug. 1820. Baptized into LDS church, 1830, in Colesville. Moved with Colesville branch to Thompson, Geauga Co., Ohio, May 1831, and to Kaw Township, Jackson Co., Missouri, July 1831. Moved to Clay Co., Missouri, ca. 1833. Married second Polly Knight, ca. 1835. Signed petition warning dissidents to leave Caldwell Co., Missouri, 1838, at Far

West, Caldwell Co. Moved to Commerce (later Nauvoo), Hancock Co., Illinois, 1839. Ordained a high priest, 1 Dec. 1844, in Nauvoo. Married third Eliza Lake, 22 Jan. 1846, in Nauvoo. Moved to Garden Grove (later in Decatur Co.), Iowa Territory, by 1847. Moved to Wapello Co., Iowa, by June 1850. Rebaptized, 1855, in Jacksonville, Morgan Co., Illinois. Moved to Salt Lake City, fall 1856. Moved to Manti, Sanpete Co., Utah Territory, 1857. Died at Manti.

Tanner, John (15 Aug. 1778–13 Apr. 1850), farmer, timberland owner. Born at Hopkinton, Washington Co., Rhode Island. Son of Joshua Tanner and Thankful Tefft. Moved to Greenwich, Washington Co., New York, ca. 1791. Married first Tabitha Bentley, 1800. Wife died, Apr. 1801. Married second Lydia Stewart, fall 1801. Moved to Northwest Bay (near Bolton), Warren Co., New York, 1818. Moved to Bolton, 1823. Wife died, 1825. Married third Elizabeth Beswick, 1825. Baptized into LDS church, 17 Sept. 1832, at Bolton's Landing, Warren Co. Ordained a priest by Orson Pratt, 2 Feb. 1833, at Bolton. Moved to Kirtland, Geauga Co., Ohio, Dec. 1834. Loaned and donated substantial monies to JS and church. Left Kirtland for Far West, Caldwell Co., Missouri, 1838. Severely beaten during conflict between Latter-day Saints and other Missourians, fall 1838. Moved to New Liberty, Pope Co., Illinois, Mar.–Apr. 1839. Located near Montrose, Lee Co., Iowa Territory, Mar. 1840. Materially assisted in building of temple in Nauvoo, Hancock Co., Illinois. Served mission to New York, 1844. Ordained a high priest, by Dec. 1845. Moved to what became Council Bluffs, Pottawattamie Co., Iowa Territory, spring 1846. Moved to Salt Lake Valley, 1848. Died at South Cottonwood, Salt Lake Valley.

Taylor, John (1 Nov. 1808–25 July 1887), preacher, editor, publisher, politician. Born at Milnthorpe, Westmoreland Co., England. Son of James Taylor and Agnes Taylor, members of Church of England. At age fifteen, joined Methodists and was local preacher. Migrated from England to York, York Township, York Co., Home District, Upper Canada, 1828–1829. Married Leonora Cannon, 28 Jan. 1833, at York. Baptized into LDS church by Parley P. Pratt, 9 May 1836, and ordained an elder shortly after. Appointed to preside over churches in Upper Canada. Ordained a high priest by JS and others, 21 Aug. 1837. Moved to Kirtland, Geauga Co., Ohio. Moved to Far West, Caldwell Co., Missouri, 1838. Ordained member of Quorum of the Twelve by Brigham Young and Heber C. Kimball, 19 Dec. 1838, at Far West. Served mission to England, 1839–1841. In Nauvoo, Hancock Co., Illinois, served as member of city council, judge advocate of Nauvoo Legion, and editor of *Times and Seasons* and *Nauvoo Neighbor*. Member of Nauvoo Masonic Lodge. Participated in plural marriage during JS's lifetime. With JS when JS and Hyrum Smith were murdered in jail at Carthage, Hancock Co., 27 June 1844. Served mission to England, 1846–1847. Arrived in Salt Lake Valley, 1847. Elected associate judge of provisional state of Deseret, 12 Mar. 1849. Served mission to France and Germany, 1849–1852; arranged for translation of Book of Mormon into French and published *L'Etoile du Deseret* (The star of Deseret). In Germany, supervised translation of Book of Mormon into German and published *Zions Panier* (Zion's banner). Appointed to preside over branches in eastern states, 1854. Editor of *The Mormon,* New York City, 1855–1857. Member of Utah territorial legislature, 1857–1876. Following death of Brigham Young, presided over church from 1877 to 1887. Ordained president of church, 10 Oct. 1880. Died at Kaysville, Davis Co., Utah Territory. Buried in Salt Lake City.

Taylor, Jonathan (6 June 1793–after 1846). Born at Burlington, Hartford Co., Connecticut. Son of Eliza Taylor. Married first Lydia Azula Taylor, 12 June 1828. Lived at Norton, Medina Co., Ohio, 1830. Visited by JS at his home at Norton, 1834. Baptized into LDS church. Sold Medina Co. land holdings, 1838. Listed in Nauvoo Third Ward, 1842. Married second Martha Pierce at Nauvoo, Hancock Co., Illinois, 22 Jan. 1846. Sold land at Nauvoo, 14 May 1846.

Thayer, Ezra (ca. 1792–6 Sept. 1862), farmer, gardener, builder. Born in New York. Married Elizabeth Frank. Lived at Bloomfield, Ontario Co., New York, 1820. Lived at Farmington, Ontario Co., 1830. Baptized into LDS church by Parley P. Pratt and confirmed by JS, fall 1830, at Ontario Co. or Palmyra, Wayne Co., New York. Ordained a high priest by Lyman Wight, 4 June 1831, at Kirtland, Geauga Co., Ohio. Commissioned to superintend land purchases in Kirtland, 1833. Participated in Camp of Israel expedition to Missouri, 1834. Church membership suspended, 2 May 1835, at Kirtland. Apparently reinstated. Appointed member of high council at Adam-ondi-Ahman, Daviess Co., Missouri, 28 June 1838. Lived at Brighton, Monroe Co., New York, 1840. Present at church conference at Comstock, Kalamazoo Co., Michigan, 1 June 1844. Lived at Chili, Monroe Co., 1850. Affiliated briefly with James J. Strang at Voree, Walworth Co., Wisconsin, but soon returned to New York. Rebaptized into LDS church, Sept. 1854, in New York. Lived at Jefferson, Cass Co., Michigan, 1860. Baptized into RLDS church, 11 Sept. 1860, at Galien, Berrien Co., Michigan. Died in Cass Co.

Thompson, Robert Blashel (1 Oct. 1811–27 Aug. 1841), clerk, editor. Born in Great Driffield, Yorkshire, England. Member of Methodist church. Immigrated to Upper Canada, 1834. Baptized into LDS church by Parley P. Pratt, May 1836, in Upper Canada. Ordained an elder by John Taylor, 22 July 1836, in Upper Canada. Resided at Churchville, Chinguacousy Township, York Co. (later in Ontario), Upper Canada, 24 Apr. 1837. Moved to Kirtland, Geauga Co., Ohio, May 1837. Married Mercy Rachel Fielding, 4 June 1837, in Kirtland. Began serving mission to Upper Canada, June 1837. Returned to Kirtland, Mar. 1838. Moved to Far West, Caldwell Co., Missouri, with Hyrum Smith's family, June 1838. Fought in Battle of Crooked River, near Ray Co., Missouri, 25 Oct. 1838. After Missouri expulsion, moved to Quincy, Adams Co., Illinois, 1839. Appointed to gather reports and publications circulated against LDS church, 4 May 1839, at Quincy. Ordained a seventy, 6 May 1839. Moved to Nauvoo, Hancock Co., Illinois, by 1840. Appointed to Nauvoo incorporation committee, 1840. Regent of University of Nauvoo, 1840. Appointed aide-de-camp to lieutenant general in Nauvoo Legion, Mar. 1841. Served as scribe to JS and church clerk, 1840–1841. Preached sermon at funeral for Joseph Smith Sr., 15 Sept. 1840. Elected Nauvoo city treasurer, 3 Feb. 1841. Associate editor of *Times and Seasons,* May–Aug. 1841. Died in Nauvoo, apparently from severe lung infection.

Tippets, John Harvey (5 Sept. 1810–14 Feb. 1890), mail carrier, farmer. Born at Wilton, Rockingham Co., New Hampshire. Son of John Tippets and Abigail Pearce. Lived at Lewis, Essex Co., New York, 1813–1834. Baptized into LDS church by Elijah Collins, July 1832. Married first Abigail (Abby) Jane Smith, Oct. 1834, at Bolton, Washington Co., New York. Lived at Kirtland, Geauga Co., Ohio, 1834–1835; in Missouri, 1835–1839; and at Quincy, Adams Co., Illinois, 1839–1840. Ordained a seventy by Joseph Young, 12 May 1839, in Quincy. Lived at Nauvoo, Hancock Co., Illinois, 1840–1846. Married second Caroline

Fidelia Calkins Pew, 25 Sept. 1840, at Nauvoo. Served mission to Illinois and Indiana, fall 1842. Member of Mormon Battalion in U.S. war with Mexico, 1846–1847. Helped lead Pueblo detachment of battalion and Mississippi Latter-day Saints to Salt Lake Valley, 1847. Served mission to England, 1856–1857. Moved to Farmington, Davis Co., Utah Territory, 1864. Ordained a patriarch, 1878. Died in Farmington.

Tippets, Joseph Harrison (4 June 1814–12 Oct. 1868), locksmith, cabinetmaker, farmer. Born at Lewis, Essex Co., New York. Son of Joseph Tippets and Abigail Lewis. Baptized into LDS church. Moved to Kirtland, Geauga Co., Ohio, 1834. Moved to Missouri, 1835. Married first Rosalia Elvira Perry, 1 Jan. 1837, in Clinton Co., Missouri. After Missouri expulsion, moved to Quincy, Adams Co., Illinois, and later to Nauvoo, Hancock Co., Illinois, 1840. Wife died, 1841. Married second Amanda Melvina Perry, 26 June 1842, at Nauvoo. Ordained an elder, by 1846. Lived in Pottawattamie Co., Iowa, 1848–1850. Traveled west to Utah Territory, 1852. Settled in Farmington, Davis Co., Utah Territory. Moved to Brigham City, Box Elder Co., Utah Territory, by 1858. Wife died, 1864. Married third Rose Wickham, 10 May 1865. Died at Brigham City.

Tippets, William Plummer (26 June 1812–29 Mar. 1877), farmer. Born at Groton, Grafton Co., New Hampshire. Son of John Tippets and Abigail Pearce. Baptized into LDS church, by 1834. Lived at Kirtland, Geauga Co., Ohio, 1834–1835. Participated in Camp of Israel expedition to Missouri, 1834. Married first Caroline, 30 July 1835, in Geauga Co. Moved to Missouri, 23 Sept. 1835. Married second Jeanette Stebbins (Styles). Married third Sophia Burnham Mead, 1 Jan. 1842. Migrated to Utah Territory, 1850. Moved to Three Mile Creek (later in Perry), Box Elder Co., Utah Territory, spring 1853. Died at Three Mile Creek.

Turnham, Joel (23 Sept. 1783–24 Aug. 1862), judge, farmer. Born in Virginia. Married Elizabeth Rice, ca. Feb. 1806, in Jefferson Co., Kentucky. Moved to Jessamine Co., Kentucky, by 1810. Served in War of 1812 in Kentucky militia. Moved to Clay Co., Missouri, by 1822. Clay Co. court judge, 1827–1830, 1838–1844, 1854–1856. Built tobacco warehouse at Liberty Landing (later Liberty), Clay Co., winter 1830–1831. Lived in Fishing River, Clay Co., 1850. Moved to Milam Co., Texas, by 1860. Died in Milam Co.

Weaver, Russell (27 July 1788–24 Apr. 1865), farmer, preacher, physician. Born at Shaftsbury, Bennington Co., Vermont. Son of Thomas Weaver and Lois Greene. Married Lydia Cowell, 1 June 1808, in Otsego Co., New York. Lived at Cambria, Niagara Co., New York, by 1809. Preacher for Christian or Unitarian church. Introduced to JS by Joseph Rose, 12 Jan. 1836, while visiting at Kirtland, Geauga Co., Ohio. Died at Cambria.

Webb, Catherine Noramore (17 Dec. 1809–11 July 1884), midwife, nurse. Born at Staco, New Baltimore Township, Greene Co., New York. Daughter of John Noramore and Lydia Hoag. Married first Eber Edward Wilcox, 14 Sept. 1826. Baptized into LDS church and moved to Kirtland, Geauga Co., Ohio. Husband died, 26 June 1834. Married second to John Webb by JS, 14 Jan. 1836, at Kirtland. Lived at Adams Co., Illinois; in Clark Co., Missouri; and in present-day Clay Co., Iowa, during 1840s. Arrived in Salt Lake Valley, Sept. 1850. Moved to Fillmore, Millard Co., Utah Territory, Oct. 1851. Moved to Escalante, Iron Co., Utah Territory, by June 1880. Moved to Coyote (later Antimony), Garfield Co., Utah Territory, after 1880. Died at Coyote.

Webb, Edwin Densmore (ca. 1813–after 1902), blacksmith, carpenter. Born at Hanover, Chautauque Co., New York. Son of James Webb and Hannah Griswold. Baptized into LDS church, likely 1834. Moved to Kirtland, Geauga Co., Ohio, before Dec. 1835. Married first Eliza Ann McWethy (McWithey), 13 Dec. 1835, at Kirtland. Member of the Seventy in Kirtland, 1836. Member of Kirtland Safety Society, 1837. Served mission to Illinois, 1839. Moved to Nauvoo, Hancock Co., Illinois, by 1842; to Racine, Racine Co., Wisconsin Territory, 1842; to Nauvoo, 1843; and to Marquette Co., Wisconsin, by June 1850. Migrated to Salt Lake Valley, 1853. Moved to Fillmore, Millard Co., Utah Territory, by June 1860. Married second Jane H., by Nov. 1868. Moved to Sacramento, Sacramento Co., California, by June 1870. Registered voter in Sacramento, 1882–1902.

Webb, Eliza Ann McWethy (McWithey) (1817–before 1860). Born in New York. Daughter of Isaac McWithy and Hannah Taylor. Married to Edwin Densmore Webb by JS, 13 Dec. 1835, at Kirtland, Geauga Co., Ohio. Moved to Rochester, Peoria Co., Illinois, by June 1840. Lived in Nauvoo, Hancock Co., Illinois, 1842. Lived at Marquette Co., Wisconsin, 1850. Migrated to Utah Territory, 1853. Died in Utah Territory.

Webb, John (2 May 1808–3 May 1894), wainwright, wheelwright, farmer. Born at Manheim, Herkimer Co., New York. Son of James Webb and Betsy Faville (Caville). Moved to Kirtland, Geauga Co., Ohio, by 1836. Married to Catherine Noramore Wilcox by JS, 14 Jan. 1836, at Kirtland. Baptized into LDS church by F. Weight, Apr. 1839. Lived in Adams Co., Illinois, early 1840s. Arrived in Salt Lake Valley, 1848. Ordained a seventy by Chancy Webb, Apr. 1848. Settled on Pioneer Creek (later in Holden), Millard Co., Utah Territory, 15 June 1855. Moved to Meadow, Millard Co., 1858; to Fillmore, Millard Co., by June 1860; to Petersburg (later near Kanosh), Millard Co., by June 1870; and to Escalante, Iron Co., Utah Territory, by June 1880. Died at Coyote (later Antimony), Garfield Co., Utah Territory.

Wentworth, John (5 Mar. 1815–16 Oct. 1888), teacher, newspaper editor and owner, lawyer, politician, historian. Born in Sandwich, Strafford Co., New Hampshire. Son of Paul Wentworth and Lydia Cogswell. Graduated from Dartmouth College, 1836. Moved to Chicago, 25 Oct. 1836. Became editor of *Chicago Democrat,* 1836; purchased newspaper, 1839. Appointed aide-de-camp to Illinois governor Thomas Carlin, 1839. Admitted to Illinois state bar, 1841. Served in U.S. House of Representatives, 1843–1851, 1853–1855, 1865–1867. Married Roxanna Marie Loomis, 13 Nov. 1844, in Troy, Rensselaer Co., New York. Mayor of Chicago, 1857–1858, 1860. Appointed police commissioner, 1863. Authored three-volume *The Wentworth Genealogy: English and American,* by 1878. Died in Chicago.

Whitlock, Harvey Gilman (1809–after 1880), physician. Born in Massachusetts. Married Minerva Abbott, 21 Nov. 1830. Baptized into LDS church, 1831. Ordained an elder, by June 1831. Ordained a high priest, 4 June 1831. In 1831, moved his household to Missouri, where he became member of Whitmer branch. Expelled from Jackson Co., Missouri, 1833. Conference of First Presidency recommended he be rebaptized and re-ordained, 30 Jan. 1836. Withdrew from church, 1838. Moved to Cedar Co., Iowa Territory, by 1840. Baptized into Sidney Rigdon's Church of Christ at West Buffalo, Scott Co., Iowa Territory, 1845. Migrated to Salt Lake Valley, by 1850. Rebaptized into LDS church, 1858. By 1860, moved to San Bernardino, San Bernardino Co., California, where he was baptized into RLDS church. President of Pacific Slope area of RLDS church, 1866. Excommunicated from RLDS church, 1868. Moved to Contra Costa Co., California, by 1870. Lived at Bishop Creek, Inyo Co., California, 1880. Likely died in California.

Whitmer, Anne Schott. See Hulett, Anne Schott.

Whitmer, Christian (18 Jan. 1798–27 Nov. 1835), shoemaker. Born in Pennsylvania. Son of Peter Whitmer Sr. and Mary Musselman. Married Anne Schott, 22 Feb. 1825, at Seneca Co., New York. Ensign in New York militia, 1825. Constable of Fayette, Seneca Co., 1828–1829. Member of German Reformed Church. One of several Book of Mormon scribes. One of the Eight Witnesses of the Book of Mormon, June 1829. Baptized into LDS church by Oliver Cowdery, 11 Apr. 1830, at Seneca Co. Ordained a teacher, by 9 June 1830. Ordained an elder, 1831. Moved to Kirtland, Geauga Co., Ohio, 1831. Moved to Jackson Co., Missouri, 1832. Served as president of elders in Jackson Co., 1832. Ordained a high priest by Simeon Carter, 21 Aug. 1833, at Jackson Co. Moved to Clay Co., Missouri, 1833. Served as high councilor of church in Missouri, 1834–1835. Died at Clay Co.

Whitmer, David (7 Jan. 1805–25 Jan. 1888), farmer, livery keeper. Born near Harrisburg, Dauphin Co., Pennsylvania. Son of Peter Whitmer Sr. and Mary Musselman. Moved to Ontario Co., New York, shortly after birth. Raised Presbyterian. Arranged for completion of translation of Book of Mormon in his father's home, Fayette, Seneca Co., New York, June 1829. Baptized by JS, June 1829, in Seneca Lake, Seneca Co. One of the Three Witnesses of the Book of Mormon, 1829. Among six original members of church and ordained an elder, 6 Apr. 1830. Married Julia Ann Jolly, 9 Jan. 1831, at Seneca Co. Migrated from Fayette to Kirtland, Geauga Co., Ohio, 1831. Ordained a high priest, 25 Oct. 1831, at Orange, Cuyahoga Co., Ohio. Served mission to Jackson Co., Missouri, with Harvey G. Whitlock, 1831. Driven from Jackson Co. by vigilantes, Nov. 1833; located in Clay Co., Missouri. Appointed president of church in Missouri and ordained as potential successor to JS, 7 July 1834. Left for Kirtland, Sept. 1834. Moved to Far West, Caldwell Co., Missouri, by 1837. Rejected as president in Missouri at meetings in Far West, 5–9 Feb. 1838. Excommunicated, 13 Apr. 1838, at Far West. In 1838, moved to Clay Co. and then to Richmond, Ray Co., Missouri, where he operated a livery stable. Ordained by William E. McLellin to preside over McLellinite Church of Christ, 1847, but later rejected that movement. Elected mayor of Richmond, 1867–1868. Later set forth his claims in *An Address to All Believers in Christ, by a Witness to the Divine Authenticity of the Book of Mormon,* 1887. Died at Richmond.

Whitmer, Elizabeth Ann. See Cowdery, Elizabeth Ann Whitmer.

Whitmer, Elizabeth Ann Schott (1803–4 Apr. 1876). Born in Cayuga Co., New York. Daughter of Frederick Schott and Anna Rathfon. Resided in Fayette, Seneca Co., New York, by 1820. Married Jacob Whitmer, 29 Sept. 1825. Baptized into LDS church, 11 Apr. 1830, in Seneca Lake, Seneca Co. Moved to Ohio, early 1831; to Jackson Co., Missouri, by 1833; to Clay Co., Missouri; to Far West, Missouri, by Nov. 1836; and near Richmond, Ray Co., Missouri, 1838.

Whitmer, Jacob (27 Jan. 1800–21 Apr. 1856), shoemaker, farmer. Born in Pennsylvania. Son of Peter Whitmer Sr. and Mary Musselman. Married Elizabeth Schott, 29 Sept. 1825, at Seneca Co., New York. One of the Eight Witnesses of the Book of Mormon, June 1829. Baptized into LDS church by Oliver Cowdery, 11 Apr. 1830, in Seneca Lake, Seneca Co. Moved to Ohio, 1831. Moved to Jackson Co., Missouri, by 1833; to Clay

Co., Missouri, 1833; and to what became Caldwell Co., Missouri, by Nov. 1836. Received elder's license, 7 Dec. 1837, in Far West, Caldwell Co. Disaffected from church, 1838. Moved near Richmond, Ray Co., Missouri, 1838. Died near Richmond.

Whitmer, John (27 Aug. 1802–11 July 1878), farmer, stock raiser, newspaper editor. Born in Pennsylvania. Son of Peter Whitmer Sr. and Mary Musselman. Member of German Reformed Church, Fayette, Seneca Co., New York. Evidently baptized by Oliver Cowdery, June 1829, in Seneca Lake, Seneca Co. Acted as scribe during translation of Book of Mormon at Whitmer home. One of the Eight Witnesses of the Book of Mormon, June 1829. Ordained an elder, by 9 June 1830. Copied revelations as scribe to JS, July 1830. Sent by JS to Kirtland, Geauga Co., Ohio, ca. Dec. 1830. Appointed church historian, ca. 8 Mar. 1831. Worked on a church history, 1831–ca. 1847. Ordained a high priest, 4 June 1831, at Kirtland. With Oliver Cowdery, left Ohio to take revelations to Missouri for publication, Nov. 1831. Married to Sarah Maria Jackson by William W. Phelps, 10 Feb. 1833, at Kaw Township, Jackson Co., Missouri. Expelled from Jackson Co. into Clay Co., Missouri, Nov. 1833. Appointed an assistant to his brother David Whitmer in Missouri church presidency, July 1834. Editor of *LDS Messenger and Advocate,* Kirtland, 1835–1836. Lived in Clay Co., 1836. Helped establish Latter-day Saints at Far West, Caldwell Co., Missouri. Excommunicated, 10 Mar. 1838, at Far West. Left Far West for Richmond, Ray Co., Missouri, June 1838. Returned to Far West after departure of Latter-day Saints. In Sept. 1847, met with his brother David Whitmer and William E. McLellin at Far West in an attempt to reconstitute Church of Christ under presidency of David Whitmer. Died at site of Far West.

Whitmer, Julia Ann Jolly (7 Feb. 1815–25 Feb. 1889). Born in New York, likely at Fayette, Seneca Co. Daughter of William Jolly and Elizabeth Stones. Baptized into LDS church by David Whitmer, June 1830, in Seneca Lake, Seneca Co. Married David Whitmer, 9 Jan. 1831, at Fayette. Moved to Kirtland, Geauga Co., Ohio, 1831; to Jackson Co., Missouri; and to Clay Co., Missouri, by 1833. Moved back to Kirtland, by 1835; to Far West, Caldwell Co., Missouri, 1837; and to Richmond, Ray Co., Missouri, 1838. Died at Richmond.

Whitmer, Mary Musselman (27 Aug. 1778–Jan. 1856). Born in Germany. Immigrated to Pennsylvania. Married Peter Whitmer Sr., before 1798. Lived in Lebanon Township, Dauphin Co., Pennsylvania, by 1800. Moved to Fayette, Seneca Co., New York, by 1809. Member of German Reformed Church. Baptized into LDS church by Oliver Cowdery, 11 Apr. 1830, in Fayette. Moved to area near Kirtland, Geauga Co., Ohio, 1831; settled in Hiram, Portage Co., Ohio. Moved to Jackson Co., Missouri, 1832; to Clay Co., Missouri, ca. late 1833; to Far West, Caldwell Co., Missouri, by 1838; and to Richmond, Ray Co., Missouri, 1838. Died at Richmond.

Whitmer, Peter, Jr. (27 Sept. 1809–22 Sept. 1836), tailor. Born at Fayette, Seneca Co., New York. Son of Peter Whitmer Sr. and Mary Musselman. Baptized by Oliver Cowdery, June 1829, in Seneca Lake, Seneca Co. One of the Eight Witnesses of the Book of Mormon, June 1829. Among six original members of LDS church, 6 Apr. 1830. Served mission to unorganized Indian Territory on western border of Missouri, 1830–1831. Ordained a high priest by Oliver Cowdery, 25 Oct. 1831, in Jackson Co., Missouri. Married to Vashti

Higley by Oliver Cowdery, 14 Oct. 1832, at Jackson Co. Moved to Clay Co., Missouri, 1833. Appointed to Clay Co. high council, Jan. 1836. Died near Liberty, Clay Co.

Whitmer, Peter, Sr. (14 Apr. 1773–12/13 Aug. 1854), farmer. Born in Pennsylvania. Son of Peter Whitmer. Member of Presbyterian church. Married Mary Musselman, before 1798, in Pennsylvania. Lived in Lebanon Township, Dauphin Co., Pennsylvania, by 1800. Moved to Fayette, Seneca Co., New York, by 1809. Member of German Reformed Church. Served as overseer of highways, 1826–1827, in Fayette. Boarded JS and family, June 1829, in Fayette. Organizational meeting for LDS church held at his home, 6 Apr. 1830. First public LDS church service held at his home, 11 Apr. 1830. Baptized into LDS church by Oliver Cowdery, 18 Apr. 1830, in Seneca Lake, Seneca Co., New York. Moved to area near Kirtland, Geauga Co., Ohio, 1831; settled in Hiram, Portage Co., Ohio. Moved to Jackson Co., Missouri, 1832; to Clay Co., Missouri, ca. late 1833; to Far West, Caldwell Co., Missouri, by 1838; and to Richmond, Ray Co., Missouri, 1838. Disaffected from church. Died in Richmond.

Whitney, Elizabeth Ann Smith (26 Dec. 1800–15 Feb. 1882). Born at Derby, New Haven Co., Connecticut. Daughter of Gibson Smith and Polly Bradley. Moved to Ohio, 1819. Married Newel K. Whitney, 20 Oct. 1822, at Kirtland, Geauga Co., Ohio. Shortly after, joined Reformed Baptist (later Disciples of Christ or Campbellite) movement. Baptized into LDS church by missionaries to unorganized Indian Territory, Nov. 1830. Left Kirtland for Far West, Caldwell Co., Missouri, fall 1838, but at St. Louis learned that Latter-day Saints were being driven from Missouri. Located at Carrollton, Greene Co., Illinois, winter 1838–1839. Moved to Quincy, Adams Co., Illinois, winter 1839–1840, and then to Commerce (later Nauvoo), Hancock Co., Illinois, spring 1840. Appointed counselor in presidency of Female Relief Society in Nauvoo, 17 Mar. 1842. Moved to Winter Quarters, unorganized U.S. territory (later in Omaha, Douglas Co., Nebraska), Feb. 1846. Migrated to Salt Lake Valley, arriving 24 Sept. 1848. Husband died, 1850. Second counselor to Eliza R. Snow in Relief Society presidency, 1880–1882. Died at Salt Lake City.

Whitney, Newel Kimball (3/5 Feb. 1795–23 Sept. 1850), trader, merchant. Born at Marlborough, Windham Co., Vermont. Son of Samuel Whitney and Susanna Kimball. Merchant at Plattsburg, Clinton Co., New York, 1814. Mercantile clerk for Algernon Sidney Gilbert at Painesville, Geauga Co., Ohio, ca. 1817. Opened store in Kirtland, Geauga Co., by 1822. Married Elizabeth Ann Smith, 20 Oct. 1822, in Geauga Co. Member of Reformed Baptist (later Disciples of Christ or Campbellite) faith. Entered partnership with Algernon Sidney Gilbert in N. K. Whitney & Co. store, by 1827. Baptized into LDS church by missionaries to unorganized Indian Territory, Nov. 1830. Appointed bishop at Kirtland, 1831. Traveled with JS to Missouri and then to New York City, Albany, and Boston, 1832. Member of United Firm, 1832, in Kirtland. En route to Missouri, fall 1838, when difficulties in that state were confirmed at St. Louis. Located his family temporarily at Carrollton, Greene Co., Illinois, and returned to Kirtland to conduct business. Moved family from Carrollton to Quincy, Adams Co., Illinois, and then to Commerce (later Nauvoo), Hancock Co., Illinois. Appointed bishop of Middle Ward at Commerce, Oct. 1839. Nauvoo city alderman, 1841–1843. Member of Nauvoo Masonic Lodge. Member of Council of Fifty, 1844. Ordained a high priest, by Dec. 1845. Joined exodus of Latter-day Saints into Iowa Territory and Winter Quarters, unorganized U.S. territory (later in Omaha, Douglas Co.,

Nebraska), 1846. Sustained as presiding bishop of church, 6 Apr. 1847. Migrated to Salt Lake Valley, Oct. 1848. Bishop of Salt Lake Eighteenth Ward and justice of the peace, 1849. Died at Salt Lake City.

Wight, Lyman (9 May 1796–31 Mar. 1858), farmer. Born at Fairfield, Herkimer Co., New York. Son of Levi Wight Jr. and Sarah Corbin. Served in War of 1812. Married Harriet Benton, 5 Jan. 1823, at Henrietta, Monroe Co., New York. Moved to Warrensville, Cuyahoga Co., Ohio, ca. 1826. Baptized into Reformed Baptist (later Disciples of Christ or Campbellite) faith by Sidney Rigdon, May 1829. Moved to Isaac Morley homestead at Kirtland, Geauga Co., Ohio, and joined with other Reformed Baptist families having all things in common, Feb. 1830. Lived at Mayfield, Cuyahoga Co., when baptized into LDS church in Chagrin River, 14 Nov. 1830, and confirmed by Oliver Cowdery at Kirtland, 18 Nov. 1830. Ordained an elder by Oliver Cowdery, 20 Nov. 1830. Ordained a high priest by JS, 4 June 1831. Ordained JS and Sidney Rigdon high priests, 4 June 1831. Served mission to Jackson Co., Missouri, via Detroit and Pontiac, Michigan Territory, June–Aug. 1831. Joined by family at Jackson Co., Sept. 1831; located at Prairie branch, Jackson Co. Moved to and presided over Big Blue settlement, Jackson Co. Driven from Jackson Co. into Clay Co., Missouri, Nov. 1833. Recruited volunteers for Camp of Israel expedition to Missouri, 1834. Member of Clay Co. high council, 1834. Moved to Caldwell Co., Missouri, 1837. Elected colonel at organization of Caldwell Co. militia, Aug. 1837. Moved to Adam-ondi-Ahman, Daviess Co., Missouri, 1838. Member of Adam-ondi-Ahman stake presidency, 1838. Prominent in Missouri Danite activities, 1838. Imprisoned with JS at Richmond, Ray Co.; Liberty, Clay Co.; and Gallatin, Daviess Co., Missouri, 1838–1839. Allowed to escape Missouri imprisonment during change of venue to Columbia, Boone Co., Missouri. Moved to Quincy, Adams Co., Illinois, summer 1839. Counselor in Zarahemla stake presidency, Lee Co., Iowa Territory, Oct. 1839. Member of Nauvoo House Association. Ordained member of Quorum of the Twelve, 8 Apr. 1841, at Nauvoo, Hancock Co., Illinois. Member of Nauvoo City Council, 1841–1843. Member of Nauvoo Masonic Lodge. Leader in procuring lumber for Nauvoo temple and Nauvoo House from pineries on Black River, Wisconsin Territory, 1843–1844. Served mission to eastern states to campaign for JS as candidate for U.S. president, 1844. Returned to Wisconsin Territory, 1844–1845. Led company of some 150 Latter-day Saints from Wisconsin Territory to Republic of Texas, arriving in Nov. 1845. Moved to Zodiac, Gillespie Co., Texas. Excommunicated, 3 Dec. 1848. Died at Dexter, Medina Co., Texas.

Wilcox, Catherine Noramore. See Webb, Catherine Noramore.

Williams, Frederick Granger (28 Oct. 1787–10 Oct. 1842), ship's pilot, teacher, physician, justice of the peace. Born at Suffield, Hartford Co., Connecticut. Son of William Wheeler Williams and Ruth Granger. Moved to Newburg, Cuyahoga Co., Ohio, 1799. Practiced Thomsonian botanical system of medicine as physician. Married Rebecca Swain, Dec. 1815. Lived at Warrensville, Cuyahoga Co., by 1816. Worshipped with Sidney Rigdon's Reformed Baptist (later Disciples of Christ or Campbellite) congregation. Moved to Chardon, Geauga Co., Ohio, by 1828. Moved to Kirtland, Geauga Co., 1830. Baptized into LDS church and ordained an elder, Oct./Nov. 1830, by missionaries under leadership of Oliver Cowdery who were en route to Missouri and unorganized Indian Territory. Accompanied Cowdery to Missouri frontier on mission. Appointed clerk and scribe to JS,

20 July 1832. Assistant president/counselor in presidency of church, 1833–1837. Consecrated by deed to JS roughly 142 prime acres in Kirtland, 1834. Participated in Camp of Israel expedition to Missouri, 1834. Editor of *Northern Times* and member of publications committee that printed Doctrine and Covenants and Emma Smith's *A Collection of Sacred Hymns, for the Church of the Latter Day Saints* under auspices of firm F. G. Williams & Co., 1835. Helped organize and was a trustee of School of the Prophets. Elected justice of the peace, Kirtland, 1837. Officer in Kirtland Safety Society, 1837. Removed from church presidency, 7 Nov. 1837. Moved to Far West, Caldwell Co., Missouri, late 1837. An 8 July 1838 JS revelation directed Williams be ordained an elder and preach abroad. Rebaptized into LDS church, by 5 Aug. 1838. Excommunicated, 17 Mar. 1839, at Quincy, Adams Co., Illinois. Restored to fellowship at Nauvoo, Hancock Co., Illinois, Apr. 1840. Died at Quincy.

Wilson, Moses Greer (1795–ca. 1868), farmer, merchant, land developer, postmaster. Born in Virginia. Moved to Greene Co., Tennessee, by Dec. 1818. Married first Margaret Guin, 23 Dec. 1829, in Greene Co. Moved to Pike Co., Illinois, by Apr. 1832. Served in Black Hawk War, 1832. Moved to Independence, Jackson Co., Missouri, by 1833. Operated store at Independence. Leader in movement to expel Saints from Jackson Co. Elected brigadier general in Missouri militia, Nov. 1833. Served as justice of Jackson Co. court, beginning 1834. Participated in Mormon War, 1838. A developer of Kansas City, Jackson Co., incorporated 14 Nov. 1838. Moved near McKinney, Collin Co., Texas, by 1846. Elected first district clerk, 13 July 1846, in Collin Co. Moved to Houston, after 17 Aug. 1847. Moved to Washington Co., Texas, by 1854. Married second Sophia Lewis, 1 Dec. 1857, in Washington Co. Served as postmaster in Vine Grove (near present-day Burton), Washington Co., ca. 1866.

Woodruff, Wilford (1 Mar. 1807–2 Sept. 1898), farmer, miller. Born at Farmington, Hartford Co., Connecticut. Son of Aphek Woodruff and Beulah Thompson. Moved to Richland, Oswego Co., New York, 1832. Baptized into LDS church by Zera Pulsipher, 31 Dec. 1833, near Richland. Ordained a teacher, 2 Jan. 1834, at Richland. Moved to Kirtland, Geauga Co., Ohio, Apr. 1834. Participated in Camp of Israel expedition to Missouri, 1834. Ordained a priest, 5 Nov. 1834. Served mission to Arkansas, Tennessee, and Kentucky, 1834–1836. Ordained an elder, 1835. Appointed member of the Seventy, 31 May 1836. Married to Phoebe Carter by Frederick G. Williams, 13 Apr. 1837, at Kirtland. Served missions to New England and Fox Islands off coast of Maine, 1837–1838. Ordained member of Quorum of the Twelve by Brigham Young, 26 Apr. 1839, at Far West, Caldwell Co., Missouri. Served mission to Great Britain, 1839–1841. Member of city council, 1841–1843, in Nauvoo, Hancock Co., Illinois. Member of Nauvoo Masonic Lodge. Served mission to eastern states to raise funds for building Nauvoo temple, 1843. Served mission to eastern states to campaign for JS as candidate for U.S. president, 1844. Presided over British mission, Aug. 1844–Apr. 1846. Member of Brigham Young pioneer company that journeyed to Salt Lake Valley, 1847. Served mission to eastern states, 1848–1850. Member of Utah territorial legislature. Appointed assistant church historian, 7 Apr. 1856. President of temple in St. George, Washington Co., Utah Territory, 1877. President of Quorum of the Twelve, 1880. Sustained as church historian and general church recorder, 1883. President of church, 7 Apr. 1889–2 Sept. 1898. Died at San Francisco.

Works, Angelina (Angeline) Eliza. See Robinson, Angelina (Angeline) Eliza Works.

Young, Brigham (1 June 1801–29 Aug. 1877), carpenter, painter, glazier, colonizer. Born at Whitingham, Windham Co., Vermont. Son of John Young and Abigail (Nabby) Howe. Brought up in Methodist household; later joined Methodist church. Moved to Sherburne, Chenango Co., New York, 1804. Married first Miriam Angeline Works of Aurelius, Cayuga Co., New York, 8 Oct. 1824. Lived at Mendon, Monroe Co., New York, when baptized into LDS church by Eleazer Miller, 9/15 Apr. 1832. Wife died, 8 Sept. 1832. Served missions to New York and Upper Canada, 1832–1833. Migrated to Kirtland, Geauga Co., Ohio, 1833. Labored on Kirtland temple. Married second Mary Ann Angell, 31 Mar. 1834, in Geauga Co. Participated in Camp of Israel expedition to Missouri, 1834. Ordained member of Quorum of the Twelve, 14 Feb. 1835. Served mission to New York and New England, 1835–1837. Fled Kirtland, 22 Dec. 1837. Joined JS en route to Far West, Caldwell Co., Missouri; arrived, 14 Mar. 1838. Member of presidency pro tempore of church in Far West, 1838. Directed Mormon evacuation from Missouri. Forced to leave Far West; reached Quincy, Adams Co., Illinois, Feb. 1839. Served mission to England, 1839–1841, departing from Commerce (later Nauvoo), Hancock Co., Illinois. Member of Nauvoo City Council, 1841–1845. Member of Nauvoo Masonic Lodge. Participated in plural marriage during JS's lifetime. Officiator in proxy baptisms for the dead in Nauvoo, 1843. Served mission to campaign for JS as candidate for U.S. president, 1844. With the Twelve, sustained to administer affairs of church after JS's death, 8 Aug. 1844, at Nauvoo. Directed Mormon migration from Nauvoo to Salt Lake Valley, 1846–1848. Appointed president of church, Dec. 1847. Governor of Utah Territory, 1850–1857. Superintendent of Indian affairs for Utah Territory, 1851–1857. Directed establishment of hundreds of communities in western U.S. Died at Salt Lake City.

Young, Joseph (7 Apr. 1797–16 July 1881), farmer, painter, glazier. Born at Hopkinton, Middlesex Co., Massachusetts. Son of John Young and Abigail (Nabby) Howe. Moved to Auburn, Cayuga Co., New York, before 1830. Joined Methodist church, before Apr. 1832. Baptized into LDS church by Daniel Bowen, 6 Apr. 1832, at Columbia, Bradford Co., Pennsylvania. Ordained an elder by Ezra Landon, Apr. 1832. Served mission to New York, spring 1832. Served mission to Upper Canada, summer 1832. Moved to Kirtland, Geauga Co., Ohio, fall 1832. Served mission to Upper Canada, winter 1832–1833. Married Jane Adeline Bicknell, 18 Feb. 1834, at Geneseo, Livingston Co., New York. Participated in Camp of Israel expedition to Missouri, 1834. Ordained a seventy, 28 Feb. 1835, in Kirtland. Appointed a president of First Quorum of the Seventy, 1 Mar. 1835. Served missions to eastern states, 1835, 1836. Member of Kirtland Safety Society, 1837. Moved from Kirtland to Missouri, July–Oct. 1838, and witnessed massacre at Hawn's Mill, Caldwell Co., Missouri. During exodus from Missouri, located temporarily at Quincy, Adams Co., Illinois. Moved to Nauvoo, Hancock Co., Illinois, 1840. Resided at Winter Quarters, unorganized U.S. territory (later in Omaha, Douglas Co., Nebraska), and at Carterville, Iowa, 1846–1850. Migrated to Utah Territory, Sept. 1850. Served in Utah territorial legislature. Served mission to British Isles, 1870. Died at Salt Lake City.

Young, Lorenzo Dow (19 Oct. 1807–21 Nov. 1895), farmer, plasterer, gardener, blacksmith, nurseryman. Born at Smyrna, Chenango Co., New York. Son of John Young and Abigail (Nabby) Howe. Married Persis Goodall, 6 June 1826, at Watertown, Jefferson Co., New York. Baptized into LDS church by John P. Greene, 1832. Moved to Kirtland,

Geauga Co., Ohio, by 1834. Moved to Missouri, Sept. 1837, and settled in Daviess Co., spring 1838. Moved to Far West, Caldwell Co., Missouri, Oct. 1838. Participated in Battle of Crooked River, near Ray Co., Missouri, 25 Oct. 1838. Moved to Scott Co., Illinois, 1839; to Macedonia, Hancock Co., Illinois, 1841; and to Nauvoo, Hancock Co., 1842. Participated in plural marriage during JS's lifetime. Served mission to Ohio, 1844. Member of Brigham Young pioneer company that journeyed to Salt Lake Valley, 1847. Bishop of Salt Lake City Eighteenth Ward, 1851–1878. Ordained a patriarch, 1877. Died at Salt Lake City.

Young, Phineas Howe (16 Feb. 1799–10 Oct. 1879), printer, saddler, farmer. Born at Hopkinton, Middlesex Co., Massachusetts. Son of John Young and Abigail (Nabby) Howe. Moved to Whitingham, Windham Co., Vermont, ca. 1801. Moved to New York. Married first Clarissa Hamilton, 28 Sept. 1818. Lived in Hector, Tompkins Co., New York, 1820. Baptized into Methodist church, fall 1824. Moved to Cheshire, Ontario Co., New York, ca. 1825. Moved to Mendon, Monroe Co., New York, spring 1828. Baptized into LDS church by Ezra Landon, 5 Apr. 1832, at Bradford Co., Pennsylvania. Began serving mission to Canada with Elial Strong, Eleazer Miller, and Enos Curtis, June 1832. Moved to Pittsburgh, 1832. Moved to Kirtland, Geauga Co., Ohio, ca. summer 1833. Served mission to New York with Oliver Granger, ca. 1834. Married second Lucy Pearce Cowdery, half sister of Oliver Cowdery, 28 Sept. 1834, at Kirtland. Served missions to Virginia, eastern states, and Michigan Territory, 1835. Purchased land at Caldwell Co., Missouri, 1837, and then moved to Clinton Co., Missouri. Forced to flee Missouri, fall 1838. Lived at Morgan Co., Illinois, for about one year. Moved to Winchester, Scott Co., Illinois. Moved to Nauvoo, Hancock Co., Illinois, 1840. Ordained a high priest by Brigham Young and George Miller, fall 1842. Moved to Cincinnati to preside over church in southern district of Ohio, late 1842. Served mission to eastern states, 1843–1844, preaching mainly in Ohio and New York. Member of Brigham Young pioneer company, 1847. Bishop of Salt Lake City Second Ward, 1864–1871. Died at Salt Lake City.

Younger, Katharine Smith (28 July 1813–2 Feb. 1900), seamstress, weaver. Born at Lebanon, Grafton Co., New Hampshire. Daughter of Joseph Smith Sr. and Lucy Mack. Moved to Norwich, Windsor Co., Vermont, fall 1813; to Palmyra, Ontario Co., New York, 1816–Jan. 1817; and to Manchester, Ontario Co., 1825. Reported hearing JS's recitals concerning heavenly visitations and reported lifting gold plates. Baptized into LDS church by David Whitmer, ca. 9 June 1830, at Seneca Lake, Seneca Co., New York. Migrated to Kirtland, Geauga Co., Ohio, from Seneca Co., May 1831. Married first to Wilkins Jenkins Salisbury by Sidney Rigdon, 8 June 1831, at Kirtland. After marriage, settled at Chardon, Geauga Co., 1831. Left Ohio for Far West, Caldwell Co., Missouri, May 1838. After expulsion from Missouri, located near present-day Bardolph, McDonough Co., Illinois, 1839. Moved to Plymouth, Hancock Co., Illinois, by 1842. Moved to Nauvoo, Hancock Co., by 1845. Lived at Webster, Hancock Co., fall 1847. Husband died, 28 Oct. 1853, in Plymouth. Married second Joseph Younger, 3 May 1857, in Hancock Co. Received into RLDS church, 1873, based on original baptism. Died at Fountain Green, Hancock Co.

Glossary

This glossary defines terms appearing in this volume that have particular meaning in Mormon usage, especially ordinances, offices, and organizations. Terms are defined as they were used in JS's time. Readers wishing to conduct further research may consult the fully documented glossary posted on the Joseph Smith Papers website, josephsmithpapers.org.

Aaronic Priesthood. The lower or lesser of two orders of priesthood in the church. Sometimes called the "Levitical Priesthood." It was named for Aaron, the brother of Moses, "because it was conferred upon Aaron and his seed" in antiquity (Instruction on priesthood, ca. Apr. 1835, in Doctrine and Covenants 3:8, 1835 ed. [D&C 107:13]). This authority held "the keys of the ministring of angels, and to administer in outward ordinances—the letter of the gospel—the baptism of repentance for the remission of sins" (Instruction on priesthood, ca. Apr. 1835, in Doctrine and Covenants 3:10, 1835 ed. [D&C 107:20]). JS said that the Aaronic Priesthood was conferred upon Oliver Cowdery and himself by John the Baptist on 15 May 1829.

Adam-ondi-Ahman. The term *Adam-ondi-Ahman* was introduced into Latter-day Saint vocabulary by a revelation that stated that God had "established the foundations of Adam-ondi-Ahman" (Revelation, 1 Mar. 1832, in Doctrine and Covenants 75:3, 1835 ed. [D&C 78:15–16]). A revelation of circa April 1835 explicitly applied the term to a place, "the valley of Adam-ondi-Ahman," where Adam gave his posterity his "last blessing" (Instruction on priesthood, ca. Apr. 1835, in Doctrine and Covenants 3:28, 1835 ed. [D&C 107:53]). JS's journal indicates that a site in Daviess County, Missouri, which was selected on 19 May 1838 for a settlement of the Saints, was "after wards named by the mouth of [the] Lord and was called Adam Ondi Awmen, because said he it is the place where Adam shall come to visit his people, or the Ancient of days shall sit as spoken of by Daniel the Prophet" (JS, Journal, 19 May 1838, in *JSP*, J1:271 [D&C 116]; compare Daniel 7:13–14).

Anoint. Following a biblical pattern, JS on 21 January 1836 instituted the ordinance of anointing with oil on the head or body as a sign of sanctification and consecration in preparation for the endowment of "power from on high" (Prayer, 27 Mar. 1836, in *Prayer, at the Dedication of the Lord's House,* 1 [D&C 109:35]). This anointing was combined with the ordinance of washing. In addition, the ordinance of blessing of the sick included anointing with oil. Latter-day Saints also used the term *anointed* in the metaphorical sense to mean chosen, elected, or otherwise designated by God to some position or responsibility.

Apostle. JS's revelations first used the term *apostle,* from the Greek for "envoy" or "messenger," to denote individuals with proselytizing responsibilities. JS and Oliver Cowdery were called "apostles and especial witnesses" of Jesus Christ (Revelation, ca. Aug. 1830, in Doctrine and Covenants 50:3, 1835 ed. [D&C 27:12]). An 1829 revelation indicated that twelve disciples would be "called to go into all the world to preach my gospel" (Revelation, June 1829-B, in Doctrine and Covenants 43:5, 1835 ed. [D&C 18:28]). After the organization of the Quorum of the Twelve Apostles in February 1835, use of the term *apostle* became increasingly restricted to those who held that specific priesthood office. These apostles had responsibility to act as "special witnesses of the name of Christ, in all the world" (Instruction on priesthood, ca. Apr. 1835, in Doctrine and Covenants 3:11, 1835 ed. [D&C 107:23]). Nevertheless, JS occasionally referred to the "seventy apostles," and a broader definition of *apostle* that included members of the Quorums of Seventy persisted for some time.

Assistant president. See "First Presidency" and "Presidency."

Baptism. Water baptism by immersion, an ordinance of salvation. New converts were to be received into the church by baptism after they "humble themselves before God and . . . witness before the church that they have truly repented of all their sins and are willing to take upon them the name of Jesus Christ" (Articles and covenants, 10 Apr. 1830, in Doctrine and Covenants 2:7, 1835 ed. [D&C 20:37]). An early revelation directed that converts who had previously been baptized into other denominations must be rebaptized. Baptism was not to be performed for infants, but for those who had "arriven to the years of accountability" (Revelation, June 1829–B, in Doctrine and Covenants 43:6, 1835 ed. [D&C 18:42]), an age defined in 1831 as eight years old.

Bishop. Priesthood office whose duties included caring for church members' material needs, acting as a "judge in Israel" in settling disputes, and sitting "in judgment upon transgressors" (Instruction on priesthood, ca. Apr. 1835, in Doctrine and Covenants 3:32, 1835 ed. [D&C 107:72]). JS appointed Edward Partridge in February 1831 as the first bishop; Partridge served first in Ohio and then, beginning later that year, in Missouri. JS appointed Newel K. Whitney as bishop for Ohio in December 1831. In early 1835, a revelation explained that the bishop was the highest office in the Aaronic, or lower, order of the priesthood and that bishoprics presided over the Aaronic Priesthood generally and over local priests in particular. Bishops were high priests.

Bishopric. Eventually used to describe the ecclesiastical body comprising the bishop and his counselors, the term was also used in the 1830s to describe priesthood positions generally, as in, for example, the idea that one could have his "bishoprick" taken from him (see Acts 1:20).

Bishop's council. Used to designate a bishop and his assistants or counselors as they carried out ecclesiastical or administrative responsibilities. The term also denoted the officers who served in a bishop's court.

Bishop's court. Official church proceedings convened to handle disputes or allegations of misconduct. The officers of the court were a bishop, his assistants or counselors, and additional high priests or elders assembled on an ad hoc basis. Until high councils were established in 1834, matters that could not be settled satisfactorily by the bishop's council were referred to a court, or council, of twelve high priests over which the president of the church presided. Thereafter, appeals of bishop's court decisions were directed to high councils or, if necessary, to the church's presidency. Allegations of misconduct against a president of the church were to be considered by a council consisting of a bishop and twelve high priests.

Blessing of the sick. JS's revelations instructed elders to lay their hands on those who were ill and offer a blessing of healing. Beginning in the mid-1830s, blessings usually included a preliminary anointing with oil. As in the New Testament, having faith was a necessary component of being healed.

Branch. See "Stake."

Camp of Israel. The name of the spring 1834 military expedition from Kirtland, Ohio, to Clay County, Missouri. It later came to be known as "Zion's Camp." This relief expedition, appointed by revelation and led by JS, consisted of about two hundred armed but largely untrained men who hoped to reinstate the exiled Latter-day Saints to their lands in Jackson County, Missouri. Despite the sacrifice of the marchers in journeying on foot more than eight hundred miles under difficult circumstances, the expedition did not fulfill its ostensible mission. A revelation directed that the Camp of Israel be disbanded and that its members "wait for a little season for the redemption of Zion" (Revelation, 22 June 1834, in Doctrine and Covenants 102:3, 1844 ed. [D&C 105:9]). Members of the original Quorum of the Twelve and the original Quorum of the Seventy were later selected primarily from those who made this trek to Missouri with JS.

Celestial kingdom. Highest kingdom of glory among the multiple heavens described in a vision dated 16 February 1832. According to this vision, inheritors of the highest kingdom "are they who received the testimony of Jesus, and believed on his name, and were baptized . . . and receive the Holy Spirit by the laying on of the hands . . . who overcome by faith." Those so qualified are "given all things," "are gods, even the sons of God," and "dwell in the presence of God and his Christ forever and ever" (Vision, 16 Feb. 1832, in Doctrine and Covenants 91:5, 1835 ed. [D&C 76:51–53, 55, 58, 62]). Additionally, a 21 January 1836 vision declared that all who had died without "knowledge of this gospel" could "be heirs of the celestial kingdom" if they would have received the gospel had they "been permitted to tarry" (Vision, 21 Jan. 1836, in JS, Journal, 21 Jan. 1836, in *JSP*, J1:168 [D&C 137:7]).

Chapel. See "House of the Lord."

Church of Jesus Christ of Latter Day Saints. The first name used to denote the church JS organized on 6 April 1830 was "the church of Christ" (Articles and covenants, 10 Apr. 1830, in Book of Commandments 24:1 [D&C 20:1]). At a 3 May 1834 conference, church leaders approved changing the name to "The Church of the Latter Day Saints" ("Communicated," *The Evening and the Morning Star,* May 1834, 160). A revelation dated 26 April 1838 incorporated both previous official names: "For thus shall my Church be called in the Last days even the Church of Jesus Christ of Latter Day Saints" (Revelation, 26 Apr. 1838, in JS, Journal, 26 Apr. 1838, in *JSP*, J1:258 [D&C 115:4]). Usage during JS's lifetime varied.

Communion. See "Sacrament."

Conference. Most church business was transacted at meetings called conferences, originally to be held quarterly or as otherwise needed. Conferences were convened by church leaders and were attended by lay members and representatives of various church branches. Many meetings referred to as conferences in early church records were priesthood meetings for reports or for instruction and deliberation regarding policies, appointments, ordinations, and church discipline. Conferences provided an opportunity for decisions to be ratified by the general membership of the church according to the law of "common consent." Since they were also important occasions for preaching, conferences often included a meeting to which the general public was invited. Beginning in May 1835, the Quorum of the Twelve conducted a series of meetings in New York and New England at which branches of the church under their jurisdiction were incorporated into geographic areas for church governance, each of which was called a conference. "General" conferences held in May and October 1839 began the establishment of a pattern of semiannual meetings at which business was transacted for the entire church.

Confirmation. After baptism, new converts were "confirmed" members of the church and given the gift of the Holy Ghost in an ordinance by the laying on of hands. JS stated that the first confirmations were given at the organization of the church on 6 April 1830. The term *confirmation* was also used more generally to describe any bestowal of spiritual blessings, such as priesthood ordination by the laying on of hands.

Consecration. An 1831 revelation outlined a church law of community-based economic arrangements to provide for the poor and contribute to the building up of the church. In obedience to this law, individual church members would donate, or consecrate, their property to the church and receive back a "stewardship" based on their circumstances, needs, and wants. Local bishops were to oversee the application of the law. Initially, the church sought to retain ultimate ownership rights for the church and provide usage rights for individual stewards, but JS eventually directed that each steward would own his or her property, whether or not he or she remained in the church. After the initial consecration of property, it was expected that each steward would contribute any yearly surplus to a bishop's storehouse, from which the needy could be supported. A revelation dated 8 July 1838 did away with the initial consecration of property but instructed Latter-day Saints to give "all their surplus property" to the bishop and then a "tenth of all their interest annually" thereafter (Revelation, 8 July 1838–C, in JS, Journal, 8 July 1838, in *JSP*, J1:288 [D&C 119:1, 4]). The system was thus significantly adjusted during JS's ministry, but the principles continued to guide church efforts to cooperatively share resources in building up communities and the church.

Danites. The common name for the "Daughter of Zion," a military society organized among the Mormons in Missouri in June 1838 to defend the church from both internal and external opposition. The official name was apparently derived from Micah 4:13: "Arise and thresh, O daughter of Zion: for I will make thine horn iron, and I will make thy hoofs brass: and thou shalt beat in pieces many people: and I will consecrate their gain unto the Lord, and their substance unto the Lord of the whole earth." The more common nickname was derived from the Israelite warrior tribe of Dan. JS later indicated that the nickname originated with him. The society began in connection with the effort to intimidate dissenters into leaving Far West, Missouri. It promoted political candidates favored by the First Presidency and facilitated the economic program of consecration. The Danites were organized into companies of tens and fifties led by captains, modeling the structure of the Israelite armies of the Old Testament. Parallel to state militia organization, the hierarchy also included generals, colonels, and other officers. According to its constitution, the society sought to protect the God-given rights of the Latter-day Saints and to resist oppression. Its constitution vested executive authority in JS and his counselors in the First Presidency. JS attended at least one of the society's meetings and reportedly expressed approval of its aims, but the precise nature of his involvement with and approval of the organization is unclear. The society's activity in the summer of 1838 is evident by their participation in the Independence Day commemoration at Far West on 4 July, in the election-day brawl in Daviess County on 6 August, and in the expedition that afterwards demanded a statement of neutrality from local justice of the peace Adam Black. As troubles with other Missourians mounted, the Danites were apparently absorbed into the larger Mormon militia that conducted Mormon military operations during September and October 1838. Following the surrender of Far West and the ensuing court hearing, JS wrote on 16 December that he had only recently learned that Sampson Avard, one of the Danite generals, had presented "false and pernicious" teachings as having come from the First Presidency. While there is no credible evidence that the Danite society outlived the Mormon War in Missouri, its brief existence contributed to widespread and lasting rumors of an enduring secret society of Mormon avengers.

Deacon. An office in the Aaronic Priesthood. Deacons were "to warn, expound, exhort, and teach, and invite all to come unto Christ" (Articles and covenants, 10 Apr. 1830, in Doctrine and Covenants 2:11, 1835 ed. [D&C 20:59]). The first known deacon ordinations occurred by 1831.

Dispensation. A period of God's work on earth, such as the "dispensation of the gospel of Abraham" (Vision, 3 Apr. 1836, in JS, Journal, 3 Apr. 1836, in *JSP,* J1:222 [D&C 110:12]). The biblical phrase "dispensation of the fulness of times" (Ephesians 1:10) appears often in the writing of early Latter-day Saints; they typically used it to describe the final dispensation, the "last times" "wated [awaited] with anxious expectation" when God would bring together the work of all dispensations and complete his earthly work (Revelation, ca. Aug. 1830, in Doctrine and Covenants 50:3, 1835 ed. [D&C 27:13]; JS et al., Liberty, MO, to the church members and Edward Partridge, Quincy, IL, 20 Mar. 1839, in Revelations Collection, CHL [D&C 121:27]). Revelations stated that JS had been given "the Keys of this dispensation" (Vision, 3 Apr. 1836, in JS, Journal, 3 Apr. 1836, in *JSP,* J1:222 [D&C 110:16]).

Elder. Before the designation of a specific priesthood office, elders were leading members in the movement that became the Church of Christ in April 1836. That usage of the term *elder* continued throughout the 1830s and beyond. The founding articles of the church outlined the duty of an elder as a specific priesthood office "to baptize, and to ordain other elders, priests, teachers, and deacons, and to administer bread and wine . . .; to teach, expound exhort, . . . and watch over the church; and to confirm the church . . . and to take the lead of all meetings" (Articles and covenants, 10 Apr. 1830, in Doctrine and Covenants 2:8, 1835 ed. [D&C 20:38–44]). JS and Oliver Cowdery were designated the "first" and "second" elders, respectively, at the church's organizational meeting in 1830, indicative not only of their being the first ordained elders but also of their serving as the infant church's presiding officers. After the term *Melchizedek Priesthood* was applied to the higher priesthood in late 1831, *elder* was one of the offices included therein. The term was also used to signify proselytizing missionaries generally.

Elders School. See "School of the Prophets."

Endowment. The terms *endow, endowed,* and *endowment*—as well as *endued* and *enduement*—were used to describe the bestowal of spiritual blessings upon the Latter-day Saints. In common usage, these terms meant essentially the same thing: to clothe, to put on, to furnish, or to supply with. In revelations in 1831, Latter-day Saints were promised an endowment "with power from on high" (Revelation, 2 Jan. 1831, in Doctrine and Covenants 12:7, 1835 ed. [D&C 38:32]), and by 1833 the promises were associated with the House of the

Lord, then under construction in Kirtland, Ohio. In one reference, the promises were made analogous to the New Testament instruction to the apostles that they should tarry at Jerusalem until they were "endued with power from on high" (Luke 24:49). Many Latter-day Saints considered the outpouring of spiritual power, including speaking in tongues, visions, and prophesying, that they experienced in Kirtland in March 1836 to be their endowment with power. Church members later referred to a specific temple ordinance introduced in 1842 in Nauvoo, Illinois, as an endowment.

Endue. See "Endowment."

Evangelist. See "Patriarch."

F. G. Williams & Co. After the destruction of the church printing office in Missouri in 1833, the United Firm formed F. G. Williams & Co. as a commercial entity in Kirtland, Ohio, with publishing as its primary purpose. Following the dissolution of the United Firm in 1834, F. G. Williams & Co. continued as a stewardship assigned to Oliver Cowdery and Frederick G. Williams. Its financial books show that the company contributed support to the whole church presidency. The business's church printing projects included publication of the first edition of the Doctrine and Covenants, the first hymnbook, and church and local newspapers. The partnership was dissolved 7 June 1836.

First elders. In 1830, JS was designated by revelation as the "first elder" in the specific sense of his authority as the church's presiding officer. During the period before the elaboration of church offices, he functioned in this role with Oliver Cowdery as "second elder," or second presiding officer. The term "first elders" in later records generally meant "leading elders," especially in reference to those who were to prepare for the endowment of power in the House of the Lord.

First Presidency. The presiding body of the church. From the day of the church's organization on 6 April 1830, JS and Oliver Cowdery led the church in their capacity as elders. An 11 November 1831 revelation directed that "the duty of the president of the office of the high priesthood is to preside over the whole church" (Revelation, 11 Nov. 1831–B, in Doctrine and Covenants 3:42, 1835 ed. [D&C 107:91]). JS was ordained to that office on 25 January 1832. A presidency of the church was first organized 8 March 1832 when JS ordained Jesse Gause and Sidney Rigdon as his counselors in the presidency of the high priesthood. Gause served only briefly, and by March 1833 Frederick G. Williams was appointed his successor. The term "first presidency of the church," used first in 1834 (Minutes, 17 Feb. 1834, in Doctrine and Covenants 5:11, 14, 1835 ed. [D&C 102:26, 33]), did not become standard until 1838. The presidency consisted of a president (JS) and two or more counselors or assistant presidents. After standing high councils were organized in 1834 and the quorums of the Twelve Apostles and the Seventy were organized in February 1835, revelation indicated that those bodies were each nominally equal in authority to the presidency of the church, but the Seventy were to officiate under the direction of the Twelve and the Twelve under the direction of the presidency. The presidency's jurisdiction included the entire church, and they were to "preside in counsel and set in order all the affairs of this church" (Revelation, 8 Mar. 1833, in Doctrine and Covenants 84:5, 1835 ed. [D&C 90:16]), whereas the jurisdiction of the Twelve and the Seventy was primarily outside Zion and its stakes, and the high councils were responsible for Zion and the stakes. For several months in 1835 and 1836 when Missouri church officers were visiting Kirtland,

Ohio, while preparing for the solemn assembly in the House of the Lord, the Missouri church presidency was incorporated into the general church presidency in what was sometimes called a council, or quorum, of presidents. After the Missouri presidency's departure from Kirtland, a 3 September 1837 conference sustained JS, Sidney Rigdon, and Frederick G. Williams as "the three first presidnts of the Church" and Oliver Cowdery, Joseph Smith Sr., Hyrum Smith, and John Smith as "assistant Councillors." The minutes of the meeting explained, "These last four are allso, together with the first three to be concidered the heads of the Church" (Minute Book 1, 3 Sept. 1837). By 7 November 1838 only the three members of the First Presidency were mentioned in official records as the presidency of the church.

Fulness of times. See "Dispensation."

Gathering. As directed by early revelations, Latter-day Saints "gathered" in communities. In December 1830, Latter-day Saints living in New York were commanded to "assemble together" with the church members in Ohio (Revelation, 30 Dec. 1830, in Doctrine and Covenants 58:2, 1835 ed. [D&C 37:3]). In July 1831, "Zion" in western Missouri was designated as a gathering place. Along with the practical benefits living among fellow believers afforded, the Latter-day Saints considered living in close proximity to be essential for the church in the "last days." A revelation dated September 1830, for instance, instructed elders "to bring to pass the gathering of [the] elect" who would "be gathered in unto one place, upon the face of this land" (Revelation, Sept. 1830–A, in Doctrine and Covenants 10:2, 1835 ed. [D&C 29:7–8]). Proselytizing efforts of missionaries gained converts who converged at these points of gathering. Those so concentrated together would "prepare their hearts, and be prepared in all things, against the day when tribulation and desolation are sent forth upon the wicked" (Revelation, Sept. 1830–A, in Doctrine and Covenants 10:2, 1835 ed. [D&C 29:8]). Even after repeated friction with neighbors caused some Latter-day Saints to question the wisdom of gathering together, the majority of the Saints continued in building up "gathered" communities. JS taught that ultimately Latter-day Saints gathered for the same reason Israel gathered anciently—to build a temple where God could reveal knowledge and ordinances. Latter-day Saints also anticipated a gathering, or restoration, of scattered Israel to Palestine.

Gentiles. For Latter-day Saints, this term generally meant "non–Latter-day Saint," although the meaning also extended to include "non-Jewish" and "non-Lamanite."

Hebrew School. Educational program instituted by JS in Kirtland, Ohio, in January 1836 for the study of the Hebrew language. Class was usually held in the westernmost room in the third, or attic, story of the House of the Lord in Kirtland. Under the tutelage of Joshua Seixas, a Hebraist and language scholar, at least eighty students gained a basic knowledge of Hebrew in sessions that met regularly until the end of March of that year. Seixas apparently conducted an additional term of the Hebrew School in Kirtland in the summer of 1836.

High council. Although JS utilized councils of elders and high priests earlier in church government, the first standing high council of the church was organized in Kirtland, Ohio, on 17 February 1834. The second high council was organized a few months later in Clay County, Missouri. These high councils ultimately consisted of twelve high priests and were organized "for the purpose of settling important difficulties, which might arise in the church, which could not be settled by the church, or the bishop's council, to the satisfaction of the parties" (Minutes, 17 Feb. 1834, in Doctrine and Covenants 5:1, 1835 ed. [D&C 102:2]). In addition to providing a judicial function, high councils played an important administrative role in the church. For congregations outside the jurisdiction of the standing high councils in Zion and her stakes, the Quorum of the Twelve constituted a traveling high council to regulate church affairs.

High priest. An office in the Melchizedek Priesthood, first instituted on 3 June 1831 with several ordinations to the high priesthood. Revelations set forth that high priests had "a right to officiate in their own standing, under the direction of the presidency, in administering spiritual things" (Instruction on priesthood, ca. Apr. 1835, in Doctrine and Covenants 3:5, 1835 ed. [D&C 107:10]) and that they could serve as bishops or bishops' counselors, officiate in all lesser offices, constitute high councils, and serve in the church's presidency. High priests were organized into a quorum by January 1836, at which time JS's brother Don Carlos Smith was sustained as president of the high priests, an office distinct from JS's role as "president of the high priesthood."

High priesthood. Variously used to denote the authority held by individuals ordained to the office of high priest, the high priests as a body, and the Melchizedek Priesthood. The president of the high priesthood was "to preside over the whole church" (Revelation, ca. Apr. 1835, in Doctrine and Covenants 3:42, 1835 ed. [D&C 107:91]).

House of the Lord. The sacred edifice in Kirtland, Ohio, since known as the Kirtland temple. Although the term *temple* in the early days of the church designated a category of buildings, the proper name applied to the structure in Kirtland was "House of the Lord." JS and the Latter-day Saints also referred to it as "the chapel" and, in rare instances, "the temple." Revelations relating to the construction of the House of the Lord in Kirtland made clear that it would serve as a place of religious instruction and a place of God's presence, where he would manifest himself to faithful Latter-day Saints and endow his servants "with power from on high" (Revelation, 1 June 1833, in Doctrine and Covenants 95:2, 1835 ed. [D&C 95:8]). The building became a focal point for the religious community, providing a place for church meetings, office space for church leaders, rooms for schools, and sacred space for ordinances and revelation. The term "House of the Lord" was intended to be used more widely than just in Kirtland. In June 1833, JS and the presidency directed that twenty-four temples were to be built in Independence, Missouri, eighteen of which would bear proper names beginning with "House of the Lord."

Jaredite. In the Book of Mormon, the Jaredites are a people whose progenitors sailed from Mesopotamia to the New World sometime between roughly 3100 and 1750 BC. Their history is found largely in the book of Ether within the Book of Mormon.

Keys. Early revelations equated "keys" with authority, which parallels biblical use of the term. Keys were often associated with the presiding officers of the church. Revelation described JS as having the "keys of the kingdom" of heaven on earth (Revelation, 15 Mar. 1832, in Doctrine and Covenants 79:1, 1835 ed. [D&C 81:2]). He stated that he received the several keys, which constituted the authority necessary to lead the church, from divine messengers. The imagery of a key was especially powerful with respect to the Quorum of the Twelve, upon whom were conferred the keys "to unlock the door of the kingdom" to the nations of the earth (Revelation, 23 July 1837, in JS, Journal, 23 July 1837, in *JSP*,

J1:307 [D&C 112:17]). JS's revelations also connected the idea of keys to essential knowledge or understanding.

Lamanite. In the Book of Mormon, the Lamanites are an Israelite people whose progenitors migrated from the vicinity of Jerusalem to the New World in about 600 BC. Early Saints used the term *Lamanites* to refer to American Indians, the presumed descendants of these early immigrants to the New World, and later to native peoples of the Americas.

Laying on of hands. A ritual bestowing of power, authority, or other blessings. One holding priesthood authority placed his hands upon another's head to confer the gift of the Holy Ghost, confer the priesthood, set apart to an office or calling, or offer a blessing for counsel, comfort, or healing. JS stated that John the Baptist appeared to Oliver Cowdery and JS in May 1829 to confer the Aaronic Priesthood upon them by the laying on of hands.

License. The founding articles of the church instructed each holder of the priesthood to obtain a certificate from the person who ordained him which "shall authorize him to perform the duties of his calling" (Articles and covenants, 10 Apr. 1830, in Doctrine and Covenants 2:15, 1835 ed. [D&C 20:64]). Licenses were routinely issued to those ordained to the priesthood to certify their standing and authority in the church and could be revoked as a measure of church discipline. Church licensing practices were standardized in March 1836.

Lord's Supper. See "Sacrament."

Melchizedek Priesthood. The greater or higher of two orders of priesthood in the church. Also known as "the holy priesthood, after the order of the Son of God," "the high priesthood," and "the high and holy priesthood." This priesthood held the "right of presidency," the responsibility "to administer in spiritual things," and the "keys of all the spiritual blessings of the church" (Instruction on priesthood, ca. Apr. 1835, in Doctrine and Covenants 3:1, 3, 9, 1835 ed. [D&C 107:3, 8, 18]). The name honors the Old Testament priest Melchizedek, to whom Abraham paid tithes, and was also used to respectfully avoid too frequent repetition of the name of Deity. Those holding offices in the Melchizedek Priesthood were to preside over the church and its stakes and branches as well as to officiate in ordinances. Those holding the Aaronic Priesthood could also perform some ordinances, but JS's revelations stipulated that only in the ordinances of the higher priesthood was "the power of godliness . . . manifest" (Revelation, 22 and 23 Sept. 1832, in Doctrine and Covenants 4:3, 1835 ed. [D&C 84:19–20]). Latter-day Saints believed that both the Aaronic and Melchizedek priesthoods were held anciently but that the higher priesthood was taken away from ancient Israel. Peter, James, John, and other members of Christ's early church were understood to have held the Melchizedek Priesthood, which was again taken from the earth after the time of Christ and was later restored to JS after a similar restoration of the Aaronic Priesthood.

Nephite. In the Book of Mormon, the Nephites are an Israelite people whose progenitors migrated from the vicinity of Jerusalem to the New World in about 600 BC. They are the primary group who kept the record known as the Book of Mormon.

New and everlasting covenant. This phrase and a shortened version, "everlasting covenant," appeared in JS's revelations as synonymous with the "fulness of [the] gospel"—the sum total of the church's message—or with individual elements of it (Revelation, 1 Nov. 1831–B, in Doctrine and Covenants 1:3–4, 1835 ed. [D&C 1:15, 22]; Revelation, 29 Oct. 1831, in Doctrine and Covenants 74:1, 1835 ed. [D&C 66:2]). Baptism by priesthood authority, for instance, was identified as a "new and an everlasting covenant" in an early revelation (Revelation, 16 Apr. 1830, in Doctrine and Covenants 47:1, 1835 ed. [D&C 22:1]). The phrase was later used with reference to marriage sealings by church priesthood authority.

New Jerusalem. See "Zion."

Official member. Common term for church members who were also officials; men who held priesthood offices.

Ordain, ordination. Priesthood offices were conferred on males, primarily adults, by the laying on of hands "by those who are in authority" (JS, "Church History," *Times and Seasons,* p. 500 herein [Articles of Faith 1:5]; 1 Timothy 4:14). This conferral was frequently referred to as an *ordination.* The term was also occasionally used in the generic sense, meaning to appoint, decree, or establish.

Ordinance. Any of a number of religious rituals that early Latter-day Saints believed God had instituted for the blessing of humanity. Ordinances were performed by priesthood authority, were generally authorized by presiding officers, and often involved the making or renewing of covenants with God. A September 1832 revelation stated that in the ordinances of the Melchizedek Priesthood "the power of godliness is manifest" (Revelation, 22 and 23 Sept. 1832, in Doctrine and Covenants 4:3, 1835 ed. [D&C 84:19–20]). Revelations singled out some ordinances, such as baptism and bestowal of the gift of the Holy Ghost, as necessary for eternal glory.

Patriarch. An office in the Melchizedek Priesthood with the authority and responsibility to give inspired blessings similar to those given by the Old Testament patriarchs. Joseph Smith Sr. was the first appointed patriarch to the church, ordained in December 1834. According to the Book of Patriarchal Blessings, he held "the keys of the patriarchal priesthood over the Kingdom of God on earth" (Patriarchal Blessings, 1:9). Additional patriarchs were called thereafter. Joseph Smith Sr. periodically held "patriarchal meetings" or "blessing meetings" to administer such blessings. JS sometimes referred to patriarchs as "evangelical ministers" or "evangelists." The blessings they gave were recorded and preserved as church records.

Patriarchal blessing. See "Patriarch."

Presidency. Priesthood quorums and various bodies of Latter-day Saints were overseen by presidencies. As early as November 1831, a revelation outlined the need for the organization of a formal church presidency, and by 1832, JS and two counselors constituted the general presidency over the church. In the years that followed, other individuals were called as counselors—or sometimes assistant presidents—in this presidency. A local presidency was formed in 1834, when David Whitmer, William W. Phelps, and John Whitmer were appointed to serve as the presidency of the church in Missouri under the direction of the general presidency of the church. In Kirtland, Ohio, in 1835–1836, in preparation for the solemn assembly in the House of the Lord, the Missouri group frequently joined the church presidency to function as a unit, designated variously as the "quorem of the presedincy" and the "council of the presidency" (JS, Journal, 28 Jan. 1836, in *JSP,* J1:174). During this period, this council consisted of some or all of nine individuals: JS, Oliver Cowdery, Sidney Rigdon, Frederick G. Williams, Hyrum Smith, Joseph Smith Sr., David Whitmer, William W. Phelps, and John Whitmer. That combination ended with the departure of the Missouri presidency from Kirtland. In the aftermath of the dissension and apostasy that disrupted the church in 1837 and 1838, the general presidency of the church consisted of one president with two counselors. Presidencies of individual church stakes generally followed this same pattern of one president with two counselors, as did presidencies of quorums of high priests, elders, priests, teachers, and deacons. Bishops and their counselors were designated in revelation as presidencies of the Aaronic Priesthood. A single president presided over the Quorum of the Twelve Apostles, and seven presidents led the original Quorum of the Seventy.

Priest. An office in the Aaronic Priesthood. The founding articles of the church outlined the duties of the priest as including the following: "to preach, teach, expound, exhort, and baptize, and administer the sacrament, and visit the house of each member, and . . . ordain other priests, teachers, and deacons" (Articles and covenants, 10 Apr. 1830, in Doctrine and Covenants 2:10, 1835 ed. [D&C 20:46–48]). Priests were to take charge of church meetings in the absence of elders.

Priestcraft. The misuse of religious authority for monetary gain, power, or other personal ambition.

Priesthood. Power and authority from God delegated to man to govern the church and perform ordinances. Priesthood officers held responsibility for administering the memorial sacrament of the Lord's Supper and other ordinances, overseeing pastoral duties, preaching, and proselytizing. JS oversaw the conferral of priesthood by the laying on of hands on ordinary male members of the church in good standing. No specialized training was required for ordination. Priesthood officers belonged to one of two general priesthood levels, which JS designated in 1835 as the Aaronic Priesthood and the higher Melchizedek Priesthood. Officers belonged to "quorums" organized by office. JS reported having received "keys," or governing authority in the priesthood, from biblical figures who appeared to himself and Oliver Cowdery.

Quorum. Refers especially to a group to which individuals ordained to the Aaronic or Melchizedek priesthoods belonged. Quorums were organized by office, such as an "elders quorum." The organization of quorums provided leadership and a manageable structure for varied priesthood responsibilities.

Redemption of Zion. See "Camp of Israel" and "Zion."

Sacrament. In Latter-day Saint usage, this term primarily applied to the sacrament of the Lord's Supper, or Communion, as opposed to other religious sacraments. The founding articles of the church directed "that the church meet together often to partake of bread and wine in remembrance of the Lord Jesus" (Articles and covenants, 10 Apr. 1830, in Doctrine and Dovenants 50:1, 1835 ed. [D&C 27:4]). A revelation later that year directed that "it mattereth not what ye shall eat, or what ye shall drink, when ye partake of the sacrament" if the Saints partook of it "with an eye single to my glory" and that whatever wine they used was to be "made new among you" (Revelation, ca. Aug. 1830, in Doctrine and Covenants 50:1, 1835 ed. [D&C 27:2, 4]).

School. See "Hebrew School" and "School of the Prophets."

School of the Prophets. In response to revelation, the Latter-day Saints established a "School of the Prophets" in Kirtland, Ohio, in January 1833 to prepare leading elders of the church for their ministry. Those who attended that winter and early spring were instructed in church doctrine and various secular topics. In accordance with the 1833 instructions, members were initiated into the school by the ordinance of the washing of feet and met each other with a formal, prescribed greeting at each school meeting. A similar school convened in Jackson County, Missouri, during summer 1833. In late 1834, ministerial training resumed under the name "Elders School" or "School of the Elders." Although it differed from the original School of the Prophets in that its attendance was expanded to include additional bearers of the priesthood beyond church leaders and did not include the footwashing ordinance or the formal greeting, JS and others sometimes referred to the Elders School as the "School of the Prophets." Additional sessions of the Elders School were held in winter 1835–1836.

Seal. To confirm, to solemnize, and to conclude. Early revelations adopted biblical usage of the term *seal;* for example, "seal up the testimony" referred to proselytizing and testifying of the gospel with finality with the approach of the end-time (Revelation, 27 and 28 Dec. 1832 and 3 Jan. 1833, in Doctrine and Covenants 7:23, 1835 ed. [D&C 88:84]). JS and other early Latter-day Saints also used forms of the word *seal* when describing confirmations of religious proceedings, prayers, blessings, anointings, or marriages. Such sealings were performed in many ways: by the laying of hands on the person's head, with uplifted hands, by prayer, by announcement, with hosannas or amens, or by combinations of these. *Sealing* was also used in connection with the notion of power sufficient to bind (or loose) on earth and be recognized in heaven, or to consign to God's punishment or to salvation. JS explained in October 1831 that high priests had authority to seal church members to salvation.

Seventy. An office in the Melchizedek Priesthood patterned after the seventy envoys called by Jesus in the New Testament. The first members of the Quorum of the Seventy were called in February 1835. Revelation stipulated that "the seventy are also called to preach the gospel, and to be especial witnesses unto the Gentiles and in all the world" and "to act in the name of the Lord, under the direction of the twelve . . . in building up the church and regulating all the affairs of the same, in all nations: first unto the Gentiles and then to the Jews" (Instruction on priesthood, ca. Apr. 1835, in Doctrine and Covenants 3:11, 13, 1835 ed. [D&C 107:25, 34]). JS occasionally referred to the Seventy as "seventy elders" or "seventy apostles." The Seventy were led by seven presidents, who could choose additional quorums of the Seventy "until seven times seventy, if the labor in the vineyard of necessity requires it" (Instruction on priesthood, ca. Apr. 1835, in Doctrine and Covenants 3:43, 1835 ed. [D&C 107:96]).

Solemn assembly. Generally, a special church meeting, such as the meeting of the School of the Prophets on 23 January 1833 and the dedication of the House of the Lord in Kirtland, Ohio, on 27 March 1836. In particular, it referred to the meeting held in the House of the Lord on 30 March 1836. A June 1833 revelation promised that selected church officials would be endowed "with power from on high" in connection with a solemn assembly in the planned building prior to going forth to preach (Revelation, 1 June 1833, in Doctrine and Covenants 95:2, 1835 ed. [D&C 95:8]). The solemn assembly was to be preceded by a period of preparation, which would include instructions, ordinances of washing and anointing, and renewals of commitment. Many people who were present during the dedication of the House of the Lord in Kirtland, the 30 March 1836 solemn assembly in that same structure, and related events reported having experienced manifestations of spiritual power, including speaking in tongues, seeing visions, and prophesying.

Stake. The ecclesiastical organization of Latter-day Saints in a particular locale. The terms *stake, branch,* and *church* were used in a roughly similar way, although the latter was also used to denote the church in its entirety or the Latter-day Saints generally in an area. Unlike smaller branches, which were headed by a teacher or a presiding elder, stakes were typically larger local organizations of church members ideally headed by a presidency, a high council, and a bishopric. Additionally, revelations dated January 1838 made clear that only the First Presidency could designate stakes and that such designation required prior recognition of the authority of the First Presidency by a vote of the members in that jurisdiction. Some revelations refer to stakes "to" or "of" Zion—places where substantial congregations of Latter-day Saints could be found outside the central place of gathering. This conceptualization drew on Old Testament imagery of the tent of Zion supported by cords fastened to stakes. During the years of gathering in Missouri, the term *stake* was not used in reference to the principal Mormon community in that state, which was "Zion" itself. However, several stakes were later planned for upper Missouri, and one in Adam-ondi-Ahman was operational before the forced exodus in 1838.

Teacher. An office in the Aaronic Priesthood. The founding articles of the church outlined the duties of a teacher as including the following: "to watch over the church, . . . see that there is no iniquity in the church, . . . see that the church meet together often, and also see that all the members do their duty . . . to take the lead of meetings in the absence of the elder or priest" (Articles and covenants, 10 Apr. 1830, in Doctrine and Covenants 2:11, 1835 ed. [D&C 20:53–56]).

Temple. See "House of the Lord."

Twelve Apostles. The Quorum of the Twelve Apostles was organized in February 1835. Its members were to be "special witnesses of the name of Christ, in all the world" and to act "under the direction of the presidency of the church" in preaching the gospel and in building up and regulating the church. Initially, the Twelve constituted a "travelling, presiding high council" (Instruction on priesthood, ca. Apr. 1835, in Doctrine and Covenants 3:11–12, 1835 ed. [D&C 107:23, 33]) and had governing authority only outside of Zion and organized stakes, where local high councils had jurisdiction. An exception was the service of apostles Thomas B. Marsh, David W. Patten, and Brigham Young as the acting presidency of the church in Missouri after the removal of the existing presidency. At the dedication of the House of the Lord in Kirtland, Ohio, JS, "the Presidency," and the Twelve were presented and upheld as "Prophets and Seers" (JS, Journal, 27 Mar. 1836, in *JSP*, J1:203–204). At a 16 August 1841 conference, the Twelve were additionally authorized to assist the First Presidency "in managing the affairs of the Kingdom" at church headquarters and in the stakes (General Church Minutes, 16 Aug. 1841).

Urim and Thummim. Named in the Old Testament as an instrument or device of divination used by designated individuals; term was applied by Latter-day Saints to the "two stones in silver bows" (JS History, vol. A-1, p. 222 herein [Draft 2]). JS used in translating the gold plates and to the "seer stones" he used for the same purpose.

Washing of feet. Ordinance symbolizing unity and cleanliness. Revelation directed that the "president, or presiding elder of the church" was to administer the ordinance "in the house of the Lord, in the school of the prophets" (Revelation, 27 and 28 Dec. 1832 and 3 Jan. 1833, in Doctrine and Covenants 7:44–46, 1835 ed. [D&C 88:136–141]), in accordance with the pattern set by Jesus at the Last Supper. It was initially performed in the School of the Prophets in 1833. As Latter-day Saints prepared for the endowment of power in the House of the Lord in Kirtland, Ohio, in 1836, JS established the sequence of washings, anointings, blessings, and sealings, which culminated with the washing of feet of priesthood officers during the solemn assembly on 30 March 1836.

Washings. Washings of bodies as an ordinance began on 21 January 1836, when JS had priesthood holders wash to prepare for the endowment "with power from on high" connected with the dedication of the House of the Lord in Kirtland, Ohio (Revelation, 1 June 1833, in Doctrine and Covenants 95:2, 1835 ed. [D&C 95:8]). Biblical in origin, ritual washing symbolized a cleansing of body and spirit to be worthy of God's presence. It was performed in preparation for the ordinance of anointing with oil.

Zion. In JS's earliest revelations, *Zion* was a synonym for God's work generally, but it soon came to mean the ideal society that JS sought to establish, mirroring Enoch's righteous, unified, poverty-free community also called Zion. It also came to mean the place where God's people were to establish a holy city. On 20 July 1831, JS designated Independence, Jackson County, Missouri, as the site for the city of Zion—and Missouri generally as the "land" of Zion. The term *Zion* was subsequently used for the Missouri church headquartered in Clay County and then Caldwell County. Ancillary communities of Latter-day Saints called "stakes," figuratively tethered to the tent of Zion, were to collectively sustain the center.

Zion's Camp. See "Camp of Israel."

Essay on Sources

The span of history covered in the documents in this volume breaks naturally into four periods. The early period begins in 1805 with JS's birth in Vermont and continues into 1831. Unfolding primarily in New York and Pennsylvania, it covers JS's early visions, the translation of the Book of Mormon, the organization of the church, and the labors of the missionaries who left New York in fall 1830 to proselytize west of Missouri. In early 1831, JS and many other Mormons living in New York migrated to Ohio to join a large group of converts there, commencing the second period of Latter-day Saint history. In this second period, the church built a temple in Kirtland, Ohio, and grew to a membership of about two thousand in that vicinity before most of the Saints migrated to Missouri in 1838. The third period, contemporaneous with the second, covers the church's activities in Missouri beginning in July 1831 with JS's declaration that the latter-day Zion was to be built there. The end of the Missouri period is marked by the April 1839 escape of JS and other church leaders from their incarceration in Missouri. The final period, which receives only light treatment in this volume, centers on the church's activities in western Illinois from 1839 to 1844.

While most sources cited in the annotation focus largely or exclusively on only one of the four periods, a few sources provide essential background for the entire volume. Probably most important of these are the texts of JS's revelations, which are heavily quoted, paraphrased, and alluded to in the histories. For convenience, the annotation primarily refers to the versions of revelations that were canonized in the early compilations known as the Book of Commandments (1833) and Doctrine and Covenants (1835), but most of the revelations also exist in earlier manuscript form and some were published in church newspapers before being canonized. For detailed background on early efforts to record, preserve, and publish the revelations, consult the first and second volumes of the Revelations and Translations series. To further study the individual revelations in historical context, consult the Documents series. The King James Version of the Bible and the Book of Mormon—which is classified in *The Joseph Smith Papers* as a translation rather than a revelation—are also useful for identifying many direct and indirect references that appear in most of the histories.

After these works, the source most routinely appearing in the annotation is the multivolume manuscript history of the church, often abbreviated herein as volumes A-1 through F-1 of "JS History." Compiled from 1838 to 1856, the history consists primarily of copies and adaptations drawn from JS's journals, letters, and other documents and as such is mostly a secondary source. Nonetheless, it contains a significant amount of original narrative material authored by JS, especially for the years 1805 through 1830. This volume of the Histories series includes three early drafts of this massive history, presenting the work in progress as it appeared in about 1841. The entire multivolume history will be published digitally at josephsmithpapers.org. Several early histories written by scribes and others under assignment from JS will be published in volume 2 of the Histories series. Researchers may consult that volume for more information about many of the events recounted in the histories found here in volume 1.

Articles, editorials, correspondence, and other materials published in Latter-day Saint newspapers also help contextualize most of the documents transcribed in this volume. The church's first newspaper, *The Evening and the Morning Star,* was edited by William W. Phelps in Independence, Missouri, from June 1832 to July 1833. Printing resumed in Kirtland, Ohio, in December 1833 under the editorship of Oliver Cowdery, who produced another ten issues. Beginning in January 1835, the entire run of twenty-four issues was reprinted with modifications under a shortened title, *Evening and Morning Star.* In October 1834, the *Latter Day Saints' Messenger and Advocate* replaced *The Evening and the Morning Star* as the principal church periodical. Edited by Oliver Cowdery and others, it was published monthly in Kirtland until September 1837. The *Messenger and Advocate* gave way to the *Elders' Journal of the Church of Latter Day Saints,* later renamed *Elders' Journal of the Church of Jesus Christ of Latter Day Saints.* Only four issues of the *Elders' Journal* were ever published, two in Kirtland in fall 1837 and two in Far West, Missouri, in summer 1838. Following the *Elders' Journal,* the primary church organ was the *Times and Seasons,* published in Commerce (later Nauvoo), Illinois, from November 1839 to February 1846.

Other sources appearing in the annotation tend to relate more specifically to one of the four periods described previously. The New York and Pennsylvania period is treated most heavily in JS's circa summer 1832 history, in the 1838–circa 1841 history, and in the Orson Pratt pamphlet found in the appendix, but also figures prominently in most of the other narratives. For this period, the retrospective account of JS's mother supplies helpful context. Lucy Mack Smith dictated her history in the winter of 1844–1845 to scribe Martha Jane Knowlton Coray, who with her husband, Howard, produced a revised and somewhat expanded manuscript in 1845. The history was published in 1853 in Liverpool by Orson Pratt under the title *Biographical Sketches of Joseph Smith, the Prophet, and His Progenitors for Many Generations.* Oliver Cowdery's series of eight historical letters, published in the *Latter Day Saints' Messenger and Advocate* from October 1834 to October 1835 and copied into JS's 1834–1836 history (pages 39–89 herein), also provide an account of key events of the New York and Pennsylvania period and can be compared with various passages of the histories in the present volume. One of the best secondary sources for this early period is the updated version of Larry C. Porter's doctoral dissertation, published as *A Study of the Origins of the Church of Jesus Christ of Latter-day Saints in the States of New York and Pennsylvania, 1816–1831,* Dissertations in Latter-day Saint History (Provo, UT: Joseph Fielding Smith Institute for Latter-day Saint History; BYU Studies, 2000).

The Ohio period of church history is treated most heavily herein in JS's 1834–1836 history. JS's second journal, created from 1835 to 1836, was the source for the final section of this history. A portion of the records in Minute Book 2, copied from minutes taken in 1831, and Minute Book 1, created from 1832 to 1837, supply helpful information regarding meetings mentioned in the histories.

The Missouri period is the sole focus of "Extract, from the Private Journal of Joseph Smith Jr." JS's "Church History" and "Latter Day Saints" articles also track Latter-day Saint activities in Missouri from the initial settlement in Jackson County in summer 1831 through the forced exodus from the state in the winter of 1838–1839. Important contextual material for the middle and late Missouri period is found in the lengthy retrospective account written by Reed Peck, a disaffected Mormon, in fall 1839. JS's principal Missouri journal, created March through September 1838 and also including copies of documents from as early as September 1837, supplies valuable information for the late Missouri period from the perspective of JS and his scribe, George W. Robinson. Many affidavits, letters, and other documents created during or shortly after the fall 1838 "Mormon War" in Missouri also illuminate the historical accounts of this conflict. Many such documents were gathered by order of the Missouri legislature in the wake of the conflict and now constitute the Mormon War Papers collection, housed in the Missouri State Archives. Some of the materials within this collection were published in 1841 in *Document Containing the Correspondence, Orders, &c., in Relation to the Disturbances with the Mormons; and the Evidence Given before the Hon. Austin A. King, Judge of the Fifth Judicial Circuit of the State of Missouri, at the Court-House in Richmond, in a Criminal Court of Inquiry, Begun November 12, 1838, on the Trial of Joseph Smith, Jr., and Others, for High Treason and Other Crimes against the State* (Fayette, MO: Boon's Lick Democrat). The National Archives of the United States and the Church History Library, Salt Lake City, hold hundreds of affidavits and other statements contributed by individual Latter-day Saints in 1839 and 1840 that detail losses and abuses they suffered in Missouri in the 1830s. Most of these and other related documents were published in Clark V. Johnson, ed., *Mormon Redress Petitions: Documents of the 1833–1838 Missouri Conflict,* Religious Studies Center Monograph Series 16 (Provo, UT: Religious Studies Center, Brigham Young University, 1992). Testimony before the municipal court of Nauvoo on 1 July 1843 in connection with the case *State of Missouri v. JS for Treason* provides additional information about experiences in Missouri. Various dissertations and monographs also help in navigating the Missouri period. Among those relied on here are Stephen C. LeSueur, *The 1838 Mormon War in Missouri* (Columbia: University of Missouri Press, 1987), and Alexander L. Baugh, "A Call to Arms: The 1838 Mormon Defense of Northern Missouri" (PhD diss., Brigham Young University, 1996).

Of the documents featured in this volume, only JS's brief "Church History" and "Latter Day Saints" articles supply detail for the Illinois period, and therefore annotation pertaining to this period is slim. The Illinois act incorporating the city of Nauvoo, signed into law 16 December 1840 and formally titled "An Act to Incorporate the City of Nauvoo," provides essential background for any historical treatment of Nauvoo's court system, city council, militia, or fledgling university.

Works Cited

This list of sources serves as a comprehensive guide to all sources cited in this volume (documentation supporting the reference material in the back of this volume may be found on the Joseph Smith Papers website, josephsmithpapers.org). Annotation has been documented with original sources where possible and practical. In entries for manuscript sources, dates identify when the manuscript was created, which is not necessarily the time period the manuscript covers. Newspaper entries are listed under the newspaper titles used during the time period covered by this volume. Newspaper entries also provide beginning and ending years for the publication. Since newspapers often changed names or editors over time, such dates typically approximate the years the paper was active under a particular editor; when it is impractical to provide beginning and ending publication dates by an editor's tenure, dates may be determined by major events in the paper's history, such as a merger with another sizable newspaper.

Some sources cited in this volume are referred to on first and subsequent occurrences by a conventional shortened citation. For convenience, some documents are referred to by editorial titles rather than by their original titles or by the titles given in the catalogs of their current repositories, in which case the list of works cited provides the editorial title followed by full bibliographic information.

Transcripts and images of a growing number of Joseph Smith's papers are available on the Joseph Smith Papers website.

Scriptural References

The annotation within volumes of *The Joseph Smith Papers* includes numerous references to works accepted as scripture by The Church of Jesus Christ of Latter-day Saints. The principal citations of Mormon scripture appearing in annotation are to JS-era published or manuscript versions. However, for reader convenience, these citations also include a bracketed reference to the current and widely available Latter-day Saint scriptural canon. All versions of scripture cited in this volume, early or modern, are identified in the list of works cited.

The church's current scriptural canon consists of the King James (or Authorized) Version of the Bible (KJV), plus three other volumes: the Book of Mormon, the Doctrine and Covenants, and the Pearl of Great Price. The following paragraphs provide more detailed information about uniquely Mormon scriptures and how they are cited in this volume.

Book of Mormon. The first edition of the Book of Mormon was printed for JS in 1830. He oversaw the publication of subsequent editions in 1837 and 1840. The Book of Mormon, like the Bible, consists of a number of shorter books. However, the present volume cites early editions of the Book of Mormon by page numbers because these editions were not divided into numbered verses. The bracketed references to the modern (1981) Latter-day Saint edition of this work identify the book name with modern chapter and verse.

Doctrine and Covenants. JS authorized publication of early revelations beginning in 1832 in *The Evening and the Morning Star,* the church's first newspaper, and initiated the publication of a compilation of revelations, which first appeared in 1833 under the title Book of Commandments. Revised and expanded versions of this compilation were published in 1835 and 1844 under the title Doctrine and Covenants. Since JS's time, The Church of Jesus Christ of Latter-day Saints has continued to issue revised and expanded versions of the Doctrine and Covenants, as has the Community of Christ (formerly the Reorganized Church of Jesus Christ of Latter Day Saints). The bracketed references to the modern (1981) Latter-day Saint edition of the Doctrine and Covenants, which cite by section number and verse, use the abbreviation D&C in the place of Doctrine and Covenants. A table titled Corresponding Section Numbers in Editions of the Doctrine and Covenants, which appears after the list of works cited, aligns the corresponding section numbers of the three JS-era compilations and the current editions of the Doctrine and Covenants published by The Church of Jesus Christ of Latter-day Saints and by the Community of Christ. For more information about the format of Doctrine and Covenants citations, see the Editorial Method.

Joseph Smith Bible revision. Beginning in June 1830, JS systematically reviewed the text of the KJV and made revisions and additions to it. JS largely completed the work in 1833, but only a few excerpts were published in his lifetime. The Reorganized Church of Jesus Christ of Latter Day Saints published the entire work in 1867 under the title Holy Scriptures and included excerpts from the writings of Moses in two sections of its Doctrine and Covenants. The Church of Jesus Christ of Latter-day Saints, which today officially refers to JS's Bible revisions as the Joseph Smith Translation, has never published the entire work, but two excerpts are canonized in the Pearl of Great Price and many other excerpts are included in the footnotes and appendix of the modern (1979) Latter-day Saint edition of the KJV. In the *Papers,* references to JS's Bible revision are cited to the original manuscripts, with a bracketed reference given where possible to the relevant book, chapter, and verse of the Joseph Smith Translation.

Pearl of Great Price. The Pearl of Great Price, a collection of miscellaneous writings that primarily originated with JS, was first published in 1851 and was canonized by The Church of Jesus Christ of Latter-day Saints in 1880. The modern (1981) edition of this work consists of the following: selections from the Book of Moses, an extract from JS's Bible revision manuscripts; the Book of Abraham, writings translated from papyri JS and others acquired in 1835 and first published in the *Times and Seasons* in 1842; Joseph Smith—Matthew, another extract from JS's Bible revision manuscripts; Joseph Smith—History, a selection from the history that JS began working on in 1838 (see pages 204–244, 276, and 292–296 herein for the manuscript source of this publication); and the Articles of Faith, a statement of beliefs included in a JS letter to Chicago newspaper editor John Wentworth and published in the *Times and Seasons* in 1842 (see pages 500–501 herein). Except in the case of Joseph Smith—History, citations in this volume to early versions of each of these works also include a bracketed reference to the corresponding chapter and verse in the modern Latter-day Saint canon. The Pearl of Great Price is not part of the canon of the Community of Christ.

Court Abbreviations

Citations to legal cases in this volume usually reference the name of the case, the deciding court, and the year of the court's decision. Jurisdictions and court names used in legal citations are contemporary to the year of the cited case and do not necessarily correspond to modern courts or jurisdictions. The following abbreviations are used within this volume:

Daviess Co. Cir. Ct.	Daviess County, Missouri, Circuit Court
J.P. Ct.	Justice of the Peace Court
Mo. 5th Cir. Ct.	Fifth Judicial Circuit Court of Missouri

Abbreviations for Frequently Cited Repositories

BYU	L. Tom Perry Special Collections, Harold B. Lee Library, Brigham Young University, Provo, Utah
CCLA	Community of Christ Library-Archives, Independence, Missouri
CHL	Church History Library, The Church of Jesus Christ of Latter-day Saints, Salt Lake City
FHL	Family History Library, The Church of Jesus Christ of Latter-day Saints, Salt Lake City
MSA	Missouri State Archives, Jefferson City

———— ❧ ————

Abraham (Book of). See *Pearl of Great Price* (1981).

Adams, Dale W. "Grandison Newell's Obsession." *Journal of Mormon History* 30 (Spring 2004): 159–188.

Allen, James B., Ronald K. Esplin, and David J. Whittaker. *Men with a Mission, 1837–1841: The Quorum of the Twelve Apostles in the British Isles.* Salt Lake City: Deseret Book, 1992.

An American Dictionary of the English Language; Exhibiting the Origin, Orthography, Pronunciation, and Definitions of Words. Edited by Noah Webster. New York: Harper and Brothers, 1845.

American Home Missionary Society Papers, 1816–1894. Series 1, *Incoming Correspondence, 1816–1893.* Microfilm ed. Glen Rock, NJ: Microfilming Corporation of America, 1975. The original manuscripts are held by the Amistad Research Center, Tulane University, New Orleans.

American Revivalist and Rochester Observer. Rochester, NY. 1827–1833.

Ames, Ira. Autobiography and Journal, 1858. CHL.

Anderson, Richard Lloyd. "Circumstantial Confirmation of the First Vision through Reminiscences." *BYU Studies* 9 (Spring 1969): 373–404.

———. "Clarifications of Boggs's 'Order' and Joseph Smith's Constitutionalism." In *Regional Studies in Latter-day Saint Church History: Missouri,* edited by Arnold K. Garr and Clark V. Johnson, 27–83. Provo, UT: Department of Church History and Doctrine, Brigham Young University, 1994.

————. "Who Were the Six Who Organized the Church on 6 April 1830?" *Ensign,* June 1980, 44–45.

Arrington, Leonard J. "James Gordon Bennett's 1831 Report on 'The Mormonites.'" *BYU Studies* 10 (Spring 1970): 353–364.

The Articles of Faith of the Church of Jesus Christ of Latter-day Saints. See *Pearl of Great Price* (1981).

Austin, Emily M. *Mormonism; or, Life among the Mormons: Being an Autobiographical Sketch; Including an Experience of Fourteen Years of Mormon Life.* Madison, WI: M. J. Cantwell, 1882.

Backman, Milton V., Jr. *The Heavens Resound: A History of the Latter-day Saints in Ohio, 1830–1838.* Salt Lake City: Deseret Book, 1983.

————. Ohio Research Papers, ca. 1975. CHL.

Backman, Milton V., Jr., and James B. Allen. "Membership of Certain of Joseph Smith's Family in the Western Presbyterian Church of Palmyra." *BYU Studies* 10 (Summer 1970): 482–490.

Baugh, Alexander L. "A Call to Arms: The 1838 Mormon Defense of Northern Missouri." PhD diss., Brigham Young University, 1996. Also available as *A Call to Arms: The 1838 Mormon Defense of Northern Missouri,* Dissertations in Latter-day Saint History (Provo, UT: Joseph Fielding Smith Institute for Latter-day Saint History; BYU Studies, 2000).

————. "'We Took Our Change of Venue to the State of Illinois': The Gallatin Hearing and the Escape of Joseph Smith and the Mormon Prisoners from Missouri, April 1839." *Mormon Historical Studies* 2, no. 1 (2001): 59–82.

Bennett, Richard E. "'Read This I Pray Thee': Martin Harris and the Three Wise Men of the East." *Journal of Mormon History* 36 (Winter 2010): 178–216.

Bennett, Richard E., and Rachel Cope. "'A City on a Hill'—Chartering the City of Nauvoo." *John Whitmer Historical Association Journal* (2002): 17–42.

Berrett, LaMar C., ed. *Sacred Places: A Comprehensive Guide to Early LDS Historical Sites.* 6 vols. Salt Lake City: Deseret Book, 1999–2007.

The Book of Abraham. See *Pearl of Great Price* (1981).

A Book of Commandments, for the Government of the Church of Christ, Organized according to Law, on the 6th of April, 1830. Zion [Independence], MO: W. W. Phelps, 1833. Also available in Robin Scott Jensen, Richard E. Turley Jr., and Riley M. Lorimer, eds., *Revelations and Translations, Volume 2: Published Revelations.* Vol. 2 of the Revelations and Translations series of *The Joseph Smith Papers,* edited by Dean C. Jessee, Ronald K. Esplin, and Richard Lyman Bushman (Salt Lake City: Church Historian's Press, 2011).

Book of Doctrine and Covenants: Carefully Selected from the Revelations of God, and Given in the Order of Their Dates. Independence, MO: Herald Publishing House, 2004.

Book of Mormon, Printer's Manuscript, 1829–1830. CCLA.

The Book of Mormon: An Account Written by the Hand of Mormon, upon Plates Taken from the Plates of Nephi. Palmyra, NY: E. B. Grandin, 1830.

The Book of Mormon: An Account Written by the Hand of Mormon, upon Plates Taken from the Plates of Nephi. 2nd ed. Kirtland, OH: P. P. Pratt and J. Goodson, 1837.

The Book of Mormon: Another Testament of Jesus Christ. Salt Lake City: The Church of Jesus Christ of Latter-day Saints, 1981.

The Book of Moses (selections from). See *Peal of Great Price* (1981).

Bouvier, John. *A Law Dictionary, Adapted to the Constitution and Laws of the United States of America, and of the Several States of the American Union; with References to the Civil and Other Systems of Foreign Law.* 2nd ed. 2 vols. Philadelphia: T. and J. W. Johnson, 1843.

Bradshaw, M. Scott. "Joseph Smith's Performance of Marriages in Ohio." *BYU Studies* 39, no. 4 (2000): 23–69.

Britsch, R. Lanier. *Unto the Islands of the Sea: A History of the Latter-day Saints in the Pacific.* Salt Lake City: Deseret Book, 1986.

Burgess, G. A., and J. T. Ward. *Free Baptist Cyclopedia. Historical and Biographical. The Rise of the Freewill Baptist Connection and of Those General and Open Communion Baptists Which, Merging Together, Form One People. . . .* Chicago: Free Baptist Cyclopedia, 1889.

Burnett, Peter H. *Recollections and Opinions of an Old Pioneer.* New York: D. Appleton, 1880.

Bushman, Richard Lyman. *Joseph Smith: Rough Stone Rolling.* With the assistance of Jed Woodworth. New York: Knopf, 2005.

Cahoon, Reynolds. Diaries, June 1831–Aug. 1832. CHL.

Cahoon, William F. Autobiography, 1878. CHL.

Campbell, Alexander. *Delusions. An Analysis of the Book of Mormon; with an Examination of Its Internal and External Evidences, and a Refutation of Its Pretences to Divine Authority.* Boston: Benjamin H. Greene, 1832.

Cannon, Donald Q. "Licensing in the Early Church." *BYU Studies* 22 (Winter 1982): 96–105.

"Caractors," [ca. 1829–1830]. CCLA.

Cheesman, Paul R. "An Analysis of the Accounts Relating Joseph Smith's Early Visions." Master's thesis, Brigham Young University, 1965.

Clark, John A. *Gleanings by the Way.* Philadelphia: W. J. and J. K. Simon, 1842.

Cole, David J., Eve Browning, and Fred E. H. Schroeder. *Encyclopedia of Modern Everyday Inventions.* Westport, CT: Greenwood Press, 2003.

A Collection of Sacred Hymns, for the Church of the Latter Day Saints. Edited by Emma Smith. Kirtland, OH: F. G. Williams, 1835.

Cook, Lyndon W. *Joseph Smith and the Law of Consecration.* Provo, UT: Grandin Book, 1985.

Copyright for Book of Mormon, 11 June 1829. Retained copy. CHL.

Coray, Howard. Reminiscences, after 1883. Microfilm. CHL.

Corrill, John. *A Brief History of the Church of Christ of Latter Day Saints, (Commonly Called Mormons;) Including an Account of Their Doctrine and Discipline; with the Reasons of the Author for Leaving the Church.* St. Louis: By the author, 1839.

Cosslett, Tess, ed. *Science and Religion in the Nineteenth Century.* New York: Cambridge University Press, 1984.

Cowdery, Oliver. Articles of the Church of Christ, ca. June 1829. CHL.

————. Diary, Jan.–Mar. 1836. CHL. Also available as Leonard J. Arrington, "Oliver Cowdery's Kirtland, Ohio, 'Sketch Book,'" *BYU Studies* 12 (Summer 1972): 410–426.

————. Letterbook, 1833–1838. Henry E. Huntington Library, San Marino, CA.

Crawley, Peter. *A Descriptive Bibliography of the Mormon Church.* 2 vols. Provo, UT: Religious Studies Center, Brigham Young University, 1997, 2005.

Cumming, John, and Audrey Cumming. *The Pilgrimage of Temperance Mack.* Mount Pleasant, MI: By the authors, 1967.

D&C. See *Doctrine and Covenants of the Church of Jesus Christ of Latter-day Saints* (1981).

Daviess County, Missouri. Circuit Court Record, vol. A, July 1837–Oct. 1843. Daviess County Courthouse, Gallatin, MO.

Dennis, Ronald D. "The Welsh and the Gospel." In *Truth Will Prevail: The Rise of the Church of Jesus Christ of Latter-day Saints in the British Isles, 1837–1987,* edited by V. Ben Bloxham, James R. Moss, and Larry C. Porter, 236–267. Cambridge: The Church of Jesus Christ of Latter-day Saints, 1987.

Deseret News. Salt Lake City. 1850–.

Devitry-Smith, John. "William James Barratt: The First Mormon 'Down Under.'" *BYU Studies* 28 (Summer 1988): 53–66.

Dibble, Philo. "Philo Dibble's Narrative." In *Early Scenes in Church History,* Faith-Promoting Series 8, pp. 74–96. Salt Lake City: Juvenile Instructor Office, 1882.

Dictionary of the History of Ideas: Studies of Selected Pivotal Ideas. Edited by Philip P. Weiner. 4 vols. New York: Charles Scribner's Sons, 1973.

Doctrine and Covenants, 2004 Community of Christ edition. See *Book of Doctrine and Covenants.*

Doctrine and Covenants of the Church of the Latter Day Saints: Carefully Selected from the Revelations of God. Compiled by Joseph Smith, Oliver Cowdery, Sidney Rigdon, and Frederick G. Williams. Kirtland, OH: F. G. Williams, 1835. Also available in Robin Scott Jensen, Richard E. Turley Jr., and Riley M. Lorimer, eds., *Revelations and Translations, Volume 2: Published Revelations.* Vol. 2 of the Revelations and Translations series of *The Joseph Smith Papers,* edited by Dean C. Jessee, Ronald K. Esplin, and Richard Lyman Bushman (Salt Lake City: Church Historian's Press, 2011).

The Doctrine and Covenants of the Church of Jesus Christ of Latter Day Saints; Carefully Selected from the Revelations of God. Compiled by Joseph Smith. 2nd ed. Nauvoo, IL: John Taylor, 1844. Selections also available in Robin Scott Jensen, Richard E. Turley Jr., and Riley M. Lorimer, eds., *Revelations and Translations, Volume 2: Published Revelations.* Vol. 2 of the Revelations and Translations series of *The Joseph Smith Papers,* edited by Dean C. Jessee, Ronald K. Esplin, and Richard Lyman Bushman (Salt Lake City: Church Historian's Press, 2011).

The Doctrine and Covenants of the Church of Jesus Christ of Latter-day Saints: Containing Revelations Given to Joseph Smith, the Prophet, with Some Additions by His Successors in the Presidency of the Church. Salt Lake City: The Church of Jesus Christ of Latter-day Saints, 1981.

Document Containing the Correspondence, Orders, &c., in Relation to the Disturbances with the Mormons; and the Evidence Given before the Hon. Austin A. King, Judge of the Fifth Judicial Circuit of the State of Missouri, at the Court-House in Richmond, in a Criminal

Court of Inquiry, Begun November 12, 1838, on the Trial of Joseph Smith, Jr., and Others, for High Treason and Other Crimes against the State. Fayette, MO: Boon's Lick Democrat, 1841.

Edelman, Jonathan. "A Brief History of Tape." *Ambidextrous* 5 (Fall 2006): 45–46.

Elders' Journal of the Church of Latter Day Saints. Kirtland, OH, Oct.–Nov. 1837; Far West, MO, July–Aug. 1838.

Elder's license for John Whitmer, 9 June 1830. Western Americana Collection. Beinecke Rare Book and Manuscript Library, Yale University, New Haven, CT.

The Ensign. Independence, MO. 1844–1845.

Esplin, Ronald K. "The Emergence of Brigham Young and the Twelve to Mormon Leadership, 1830–1841." PhD diss., Brigham Young University, 1981. Also available as *The Emergence of Brigham Young and the Twelve to Mormon Leadership, 1830–1841,* Dissertations in Latter-day Saint History (Provo, UT: Joseph Fielding Smith Institute for Latter-day Saint History; BYU Studies, 2006).

Evangelical Magazine and Gospel Advocate. Utica, NY. 1830–1850.

The Evening and the Morning Star. Independence, MO, June 1832–July 1833; Kirtland, OH, Dec. 1833–Sept. 1834.

Evidence Taken on the Trial of Mr. Smith, before the Municipal Court of Nauvoo, on Saturday, July 1, 1843. Respecting the Late Persecution of the Latter Day Saints, in the State of Missouri, North America. Nauvoo, IL: Taylor and Woodruff, [1843].

Faulring, Scott H. "An Annotated Catalog of the Joseph Smith Collection (Ms 155): In the Archives Division of the Historical Department of The Church of Jesus Christ of Latter-day Saints, Salt Lake City, Utah." Unpublished manuscript.

Faulring, Scott H., Kent P. Jackson, and Robert J. Matthews, eds. *Joseph Smith's New Translation of the Bible: Original Manuscripts.* Provo, UT: Religious Studies Center, Brigham Young University, 2004.

Foote, Warren. Autobiography, not before 1903. CHL.

General Church Minutes, 1839–1877. CHL.

Gee, John. "Eyewitness, Hearsay, and Physical Evidence of the Joseph Smith Papyri." In *The Disciple as Witness: Essays on Latter-day Saint History and Doctrine in Honor of Richard Lloyd Anderson,* edited by Stephen D. Ricks, Donald W. Parry, and Andrew H. Hedges, 175–217. Provo, UT: Foundation for Ancient Research and Mormon Studies, 2000.

Geneva Gazette. Geneva, NY. 1809–1833.

Gilbert, John H. Memorandum, 8 Sept. 1892. Photocopy. CHL.

Givens, Terryl L. *By the Hand of Mormon: The American Scripture That Launched a New World Religion.* Oxford: Oxford University Press, 2002.

Goldman, Shalom. "Joshua/James Seixas (1802–1874): Jewish Apostasy and Christian Hebraism in Early Nineteenth-Century America." *Jewish History* 7 (Spring 1993): 65–88.

Gravell, Thomas L., George Miller, and Elizabeth Walsh. *American Watermarks: 1690–1835.* 2nd ed. New Castle, DE: Oak Knoll Press, 2002.

Greene, John P. *Facts Relative to the Expulsion of the Mormons or Latter Day Saints, from the State of Missouri, under the "Exterminating Order."* Cincinnati: R. P. Brooks, 1839.

Gregory, George. *Elements of the Theory and Practice of Physic, Designed for the Use of Students.* New York: M. Sherman, 1830.

Hartley, William G. "'Almost Too Intolerable a Burthen': The Winter Exodus from Missouri, 1838–39." *Journal of Mormon History* 18 (Fall 1992): 6–40.

Hatch, Ebenezer. Bill of services, 4 July 1830. Chenango County Historical Society, Norwich, NY.

Hayward, John. *The Book of Religions; Comprising the Views, Creeds, Sentiments, or Opinions, of All the Principal Religious Sects in the World, Particularly of All Christian Denominations in Europe and America; to Which Are Added Church and Missionary Statistics, together with Biographical Sketches.* Boston: John Hayward, 1842.

———. *The Religious Creeds and Statistics of Every Christian Denomination in the United States and British Provinces. With Some Account of the Religious Sentiments of the Jews, American Indians, Deist, Mahometans, &c.* Boston: By the author, 1836.

Hill, Marvin S. "Joseph Smith and the 1826 Trial: New Evidence and New Difficulties." *BYU Studies* 12 (Winter 1972): 223–233.

Historian's Office. Catalogs and Inventories, 1846–1904. CHL.

———. Histories of the Twelve, ca. 1858–1880. CHL.

———. History of Persecutions, 1879–1880. CHL.

———. Joseph Smith History Documents, ca. 1839–1856. CHL.

Historical Department. Journal History of the Church, 1896–. CHL.

———. Microfilm Reports, 1949–1975. CHL.

———. Nineteenth-Century Legal Documents Collection, ca. 1825–1890. CHL.

History of Carroll County, Missouri, Carefully Written and Compiled from the Most Authentic Official and Private Sources. . . . St. Louis: Missouri Historical Company, 1881.

"History [of] Charles Coulson Rich," after 1833. In Historian's Office, Biographies of Quorum of Twelve, ca. 1883. CHL.

History of Erie County, Pennsylvania. Containing a History of the County; Its Townships, Towns, Villages, Schools, Churches, Industries, Etc. . . . Chicago: Warner, Beers and Co., 1884.

History of Geauga and Lake Counties, Ohio, with Illustrations and Biographical Sketches of Its Pioneers and Most Prominent Men. Philadelphia: Williams Brothers, 1878.

History of Ray County, Mo., Carefully Written and Compiled from the Most Authentic Official and Private Sources. . . . St. Louis: Missouri Historical Co., 1881.

The Holy Bible, Containing the Old and New Testaments Translated Out of the Original Tongues: And with the Former Translations Diligently Compared and Revised, by His Majesty's Special Command. Authorized King James Version with Explanatory Notes and Cross References to the Standard Works of the Church of Jesus Christ of Latter-day Saints. Salt Lake City: The Church of Jesus Christ of Latter-day Saints, 1979.

Hotchkin, James H. *A History of the Purchase and Settlement of Western New York, and of the Rise, Progress, and Present State of the Presbyterian Church in That Section.* New York: M. W. Dodd, 1848.

Howe, Eber D. *Mormonism Unvailed: or, A Faithful Account of That Singular Imposition and Delusion, from Its Rise to the Present Time. With Sketches of the Characters of Its Propagators, and a Full Detail of the Manner in Which the Famous Golden Bible Was*

Brought before the World. To Which Are Added, Inquiries into the Probability That the Historical Part of the Said Bible Was Written by One Solomon Spalding, More Than Twenty Years Ago, and by Him Intended to Have Been Published as a Romance. Painesville, OH: By the author, 1834.

Hughes, Richard T., and C. Leonard Allen. *Illusions of Innocence: Protestant Primitivism in America, 1630–1875.* Chicago: University of Chicago Press, 1988.

Hyde, Orson. *A Voice from Jerusalem, or a Sketch of the Travels and Ministry of Elder Orson Hyde, Missionary of the Church of Jesus Christ of Latter Day Saints, to Germany, Constantinople, and Jerusalem. . . .* Liverpool: P. P. Pratt, 1842.

Indictment, Apr. 1839. State of Missouri v. James Worthington et al. for Larceny (Daviess Co. Cir. Ct. 1840). Daviess Co., MO, Courthouse, Gallatin, MO.

"Inventory of President Joseph Fielding Smith's Safe," 23 May 1970. First Presidency, General Administration Files, 1921–1972. CHL.

Jackson, Kent P., ed. *Manuscript Found: The Complete Original "Spaulding Manuscript."* Provo, UT: Religious Studies Center, Brigham Young University, 1996.

Jensen, Robin Scott. "Ignored and Unknown Clues of Early Mormon Record Keeping." In *Preserving the History of the Latter-day Saints,* edited by Richard E. Turley Jr. and Steven C. Harper, 135–164. Provo, UT: Religious Studies Center, Brigham Young University, 2010.

Jessee, Dean C. "The Early Accounts of Joseph Smith's First Vision." *BYU Studies* 9 (Spring 1969): 275–294.

———. "The Original Book of Mormon Manuscript." *BYU Studies* 10 (Spring 1970): 259–278.

———, ed. *Personal Writings of Joseph Smith.* Rev. ed. Salt Lake City: Deseret Book; Provo, UT: Brigham Young University Press, 2002.

———. "Priceless Words and Fallible Memories: Joseph Smith as Seen in the Effort to Preserve His Discourses." *BYU Studies* 31 (Spring 1991): 19–40.

———. "The Reliability of Joseph Smith's History," *Journal of Mormon History* 3 (1976): 23–46.

———. "'Walls, Grates and Screeking Iron Doors': The Prison Experiences of Mormon Leaders in Missouri, 1838–1839." In *New Views of Mormon History: A Collection of Essays in Honor of Leonard J. Arrington,* edited by Davis Bitton and Maureen Ursenbach Beecher, 19–42. Salt Lake City: University of Utah Press, 1987.

———. "The Writing of Joseph Smith's History." *BYU Studies* 11 (Summer 1971): 439–473.

Jeter, Jeremiah B. *Baptist Principles Reset.* Richmond, VA: Religious Herald Co., 1901.

The Jewish Encyclopedia: A Descriptive Record of the History, Religion, Literature, and Customs of the Jewish People from the Earliest Times to the Present Day. Edited by Isidore Singer. 12 vols. New York and London: Funk and Wagnalls, 1901–1906.

Johnson, Jeffery O. *Register of the Joseph Smith Collection in the Church Archives, the Church of Jesus Christ of Latter-day Saints.* Salt Lake City: Historical Department of the Church of Jesus Christ of Latter-day Saints, 1973.

Johnson, Paul E., and Sean Wilentz. *The Kingdom of Matthias.* New York: Oxford University Press, 1994.

Joseph Smith Translation. See *Holy Bible.*

Journal of the House of Representatives of the Twelfth General Assembly of the State of Illinois, Convened by Proclamation of the Governor, Being Their First Session, Begun and Held in the City of Springfield, November 23, 1840. Springfield, IL: Wm. Walters, 1840.

Journal of the Senate of the Twelfth General Assembly of the State of Illinois, Convened by Proclamation of the Governor, Being Their First Session, Begun and Held in the City of Springfield, November 23, 1840. Springfield, IL: Wm. Walters, 1840.

JS. In addition to the entries that immediately follow, see entries under "Smith, Joseph."

JS Family Bible / Joseph Smith Family Bible, ca. 1831–1866. Private possession. A copy of JS's genealogical information as found in this Bible is available in Joseph Smith Sr. Family Reunions Files, 1972–2003, CHL.

JS History / Smith, Joseph, et al. History, 1838–1856. Vols. A-1–F-1 (originals), A-2–E-2 (fair copies). CHL. The history for the period after 5 Aug. 1838 was composed after the death of Joseph Smith.

JS Letterbook 1 / Smith, Joseph. "Letter Book A," 1832–1835. Joseph Smith Collection. CHL.

JS Letterbook 2 / Smith, Joseph. "Copies of Letters, &c. &c.," 1839–1843. Joseph Smith Collection. CHL.

JSP, H2 / Davidson, Karen Lynn, Richard L. Jensen, and David J. Whittaker, eds. *Histories, Volume 2: Assigned Historical Writings, 1831–1847.* Vol. 2 of the Histories series of *The Joseph Smith Papers,* edited by Dean C. Jessee, Ronald K. Esplin, and Richard Lyman Bushman. Salt Lake City: Church Historian's Press, 2012.

JSP, J1 / Jessee, Dean C., Mark Ashurst-McGee, and Richard L. Jensen, eds. *Journals, Volume 1: 1832–1839.* Vol. 1 of the Journals series of *The Joseph Smith Papers,* edited by Dean C. Jessee, Ronald K. Esplin, and Richard Lyman Bushman. Salt Lake City: Church Historian's Press, 2008.

JSP, J2 / Hedges, Andrew H., Alex D. Smith, and Richard Lloyd Anderson, eds. *Journals, Volume 2: December 1841–April 1843.* Vol. 2 of the Journals series of *The Joseph Smith Papers,* edited by Dean C. Jessee, Ronald K. Esplin, and Richard Lyman Bushman. Salt Lake City: Church Historian's Press, 2011.

JSP, MRB / Jensen, Robin Scott, Robert J. Woodford, and Steven C. Harper, eds. *Manuscript Revelation Books.* Facsimile edition. First volume of the Revelations and Translations series of *The Joseph Smith Papers,* edited by Dean C. Jessee, Ronald K. Esplin, and Richard Lyman Bushman. Salt Lake City: Church Historian's Press, 2009.

Judd, Zadoc Knapp. *Autobiography of Zadoc Knapp Judd (1827–1909).* [Provo, UT]: Brigham Young University Library, 1954. Copy at CHL.

Kansas City Daily Journal. Kansas City, MO. 1878–1896.

Kirtland Camp. Journal, Mar.–Oct. 1838. CHL.

Kirtland Egyptian Papers, ca. 1835–1836. CHL.

Kirtland Elders' Certificates / Kirtland Elders Quorum. "Record of Certificates of Membership and Ordinations of the First Members and Elders of the Church of Jesus Christ of Latter Day Saints Dating from March 21st 1836 to June 18th 1838 Kirtland Geauga Co. Ohio," 1836–1838. CHL.

Kirtland Elders Quorum. "A Record of the First Quorurum of Elders Belonging to the Church of Christ: In Kirtland Geauga Co. Ohio," 1836–1838, 1840–1841. CCLA.

Knight, Joseph. Reminiscences, after 1835. CHL.

Knight, Newel. Autobiography and Journal, ca. 1846. CHL.

Latimer, E. *The Three Brothers: Sketches of the Lives of Rev. Aurora Seager, Rev. Micah Seager, Rev. Schuyler Seager, D. D.* New York: Phillips and Hunt, 1880.

Latter Day Saints' Messenger and Advocate. Kirtland, OH. Oct. 1834–Sept. 1837.

Latter-day Saints' Millennial Star. Liverpool. 1840–1970.

Launius, Roger D. "Alexander William Doniphan and the 1838 Mormon War in Missouri." *John Whitmer Historical Association Journal* 18 (1998): 63–110.

Laws of the State of Illinois, Passed by the Twelfth General Assembly, at Their Session, Began and Held at Springfield, on the Seventh of December, One Thousand Eight Hundred and Forty. Springfield, IL: Wm. Walters, 1841.

Laws of the State of Missouri, Passed at the First Session of the Tenth General Assembly, Begun and Held at the City of Jefferson, on Monday, the Nineteenth Day of November, in the Year of Our Lord, One Thousand Eight Hundred and Thirty-Eight. Jefferson City, MO: Calvin Gunn, 1838.

Laws of the State of New-York, Passed at the Forty-Sixth Session of the Legislature. Begun at the City of Albany the First Day of January, and Continued Till April 24, 1823. . . . Albany: Leake and Croswell, 1823.

Laws of the State of New-York, Revised and Passed at the Thirty-Sixth Session of the Legislature, with Marginal Notes and References. . . . 2 vols. Albany, NY: H. C. Southwick, 1813.

Leonard, Glen M. *Nauvoo: A Place of Peace, a People of Promise.* Salt Lake City: Deseret Book; Provo, UT: Brigham Young University Press, 2002.

Leopard, Buel, and Floyd C. Shoemaker, comps. *The Messages and Proclamations of the Governors of the State of Missouri.* Vol. 1. Columbia, MO: State Historical Society of Missouri, 1922.

LeSueur, Stephen C. *The 1838 Mormon War in Missouri.* Columbia: University of Missouri Press, 1987.

"Library Record for the Listing or Cataloguing of Books." In Historian's Office, Library Accession Records, ca. 1890–ca. 1930. CHL.

Madsen, Gordon A. "Joseph Smith and the Missouri Court of Inquiry: Austin A. King's Quest for Hostages." *BYU Studies* 43, no. 4 (2004): 93–136.

———. "Joseph Smith's 1826 Trial: The Legal Setting," *BYU Studies* 30 (Spring 1990): 91–108.

Manchester, NY, Public School Records, 1828–1915. Microfilm 900, no. 62. BYU.

Marquardt, H. Michael. *The Rise of Mormonism: 1816–1844.* Longwood, FL: Xulon Press, 2005.

Material Relating to Mormon Expulsion from Missouri, 1839–1843. Photocopy. CHL.

May, Dean L. "A Demographic Portrait of the Mormons, 1830–1980." In *After 150 Years: The Latter-day Saints in Sesquicentennial Perspective,* edited by Thomas G. Alexander and Jessie L. Embry, 38–69. [Provo, UT]: Charles Redd Center for Western Studies, 1983.

Maynard, Gregory P. "Alexander William Doniphan: Man of Justice." *BYU Studies* 13 (Summer 1973): 462–472.

McCabe, James M. "Early Ledgers and Account Books: A Source for Local Vermont History." *Vermont History* 37 (Winter 1969): 5–12.

Messinger, George, Jr. Letter, South Bainbridge, NY, to S. Presson Landers, Prompton, PA, 1 Aug. 1837. Andover-Harvard Theological Library, Harvard Divinity School, Harvard University, Cambridge, MA.

Millennial Harbinger. Bethany, VA. 1830–1870.

Miller, Reuben. Journals, 1848–1849. CHL.

Minute Book 1 / "Conference A," 1832–1837. CHL.

Minute Book 2 / "The Conference Minutes and Record Book of Christ's Church of Latter Day Saints," 1838–ca. 1839, 1842, 1844. CHL.

Missouri, State of. "Evidence." Hearing Record, Richmond, MO, 12–29 Nov. 1838, State of Missouri v. Joseph Smith et al. for Treason and Other Crimes (Mo. 5th Cir. Ct. 1838). Eugene Morrow Violette Collection, 1806–1921, Western Historical Manuscript Collection. University of Missouri and State Historical Society of Missouri, Ellis Library, University of Missouri, Columbia.

Morgan, Sara, comp. *Cemetery Records, Palmyra, Wayne, New York.* Salt Lake City: Genealogical Society, 1945. Copy at FHL.

Morgan, William. Papers, 1838–1839. CHL.

Mormon Redress Petitions, 1839–1845. CHL.

Mormon War Papers, 1838–1841. MSA.

Morning Courier and New-York Enquirer. New York City. 1829–1861.

Morning Star. Limerick, ME, 1826–1833; Dover, NH, 1833–1874; Boston, 1875–1878; Dover, NH, 1879–1885; Boston, 1885–1904.

Morris, Larry E. "The Conversion of Oliver Cowdery." In *Journal of Book of Mormon Studies* 16, no. 1 (2007): 4–17.

Moses (selections from the Book of). See *Pearl of Great Price* (1981).

Mulholland, James. Journal, Apr.–Oct. 1839. In Joseph Smith, Journal, Sept.–Oct. 1838. Joseph Smith Collection. CHL.

Murdock, John. Autobiography, ca. 1859–1867. CHL.

———. Journal, ca. 1830–1859. CHL.

Nauvoo, IL. Records, 1841–1845. CHL.

Nauvoo Neighbor. Nauvoo, IL. 1843–1845.

Neibaur, Alexander. Journal, 1841–1862. CHL.

New Testament Revision 2, part 2 / New Testament Revision Manuscript 2, part 2, 1831–1832. CCLA. Also available in Scott H. Faulring, Kent P. Jackson, and Robert J. Matthews, eds., *Joseph Smith's New Translation of the Bible: Original Manuscripts* (Provo, UT: Religious Studies Center, Brigham Young University, 2004).

Old Testament Revision 1 / "A Revelation Given to Joseph the Revelator June 1830," 1830–1831. CCLA. Also available in Scott H. Faulring, Kent P. Jackson, and Robert J. Matthews, eds., *Joseph Smith's New Translation of the Bible: Original Manuscripts* (Provo, UT: Religious Studies Center, Brigham Young University, 2004), 75–152.

"The Original Prophet. By a Visitor to Salt Lake City." *Fraser's Magazine* 7, no. 28 (Feb. 1873): 225–235.

The Oxford English Dictionary. Edited by James A. H. Murray, Henry Bradley, W. A. Craigie, and C. T. Onions. 12 vols. 1933. Reprint. Oxford: Oxford University Press, 1970.

Painesville Telegraph. Painesville, OH. 1831–1838.

Palmyra, NY, Attendance record, first school district. Macedon Historical Society, Macedon, NY.

Parkin, Max H. Collected Missouri Court Documents, 1838–1840. Photocopy. CHL.

———. "A History of the Latter-day Saints in Clay County, Missouri, from 1833 to 1837." PhD diss., Brigham Young University, 1976.

Partridge, Edward. Journal, Jan. 1835–July 1836. CHL.

Patriarchal Blessings, 1833–. CHL.

The Pearl of Great Price: Being a Choice Selection from the Revelations, Translations, and Narrations of Joseph Smith, First Prophet, Seer, and Revelator to the Church of Jesus Christ of Latter-day Saints. Liverpool: F. D. Richards, 1851.

The Pearl of Great Price: A Selection from the Revelations, Translations, and Narrations of Joseph Smith, First Prophet, Seer, and Revelator to the Church of Jesus Christ of Latter-day Saints. Salt Lake City: The Church of Jesus Christ of Latter-day Saints, 1981.

Peck, George. *Early Methodism within the Bounds of the Old Genesee Conference from 1788 to 1828; or, The First Forty Years of Wesleyan Evangelism in Northern Pennsylvania, Central and Western New York, and Canada. . . .* New York: Carlton and Porter, 1860.

Peck, Reed. Letter, Quincy, IL, to "Dear Friends," 18 Sept. 1839. Henry E. Huntington Library, San Marino, CA.

Perrin, William Henry, ed. *History of Summit County, with an Outline Sketch of Ohio.* Chicago: Baskin and Bettey, 1881.

Petition of the Latter-Day Saints, Commonly Known as Mormons, Stating That They Have Purchased Lands of the General Government, Lying in the State of Missouri, from Which They Have Been Driven with Force by the Constituted Authorities of the State, and Prevented from Occupying the Same; and Have Suffered Other Wrongs, for Which They Pray Congress to Provide a Remedy. H.R. 22, 26th Cong., 2nd Sess. (1840).

Petty, Charles B. *The Albert Petty Family: A Genealogical and Historical Story of a Sturdy Pioneer Family of the West. Based on Records of the Past and Knowledge of the Present.* Salt Lake City: Deseret News, [1953].

Phelps, William W. "Additions to an Article in the Times & Seasons," Sept. 1843. CHL.

Pittsburgh Weekly Gazette. Pittsburgh. 1841–1859.

Pilkington, William. Autobiography and statements, 1934–1939. CHL.

Plat of City of Zion, 1833. CHL.

Plat of Kirtland, OH, ca. 1833. CHL.

Plat of Kirtland, OH, ca. 1837. CHL.

Platt, Lyman De. *Nauvoo: Early Mormon Records Series, 1839–1846.* Vol. 1. Highland, UT, 1980.

Porter, Larry C. "The Colesville Branch and the Coming Forth of the Book of Mormon." *BYU Studies* 10, no. 3 (Spring 1970): 365–385.

———. "Reverend George Lane—Good 'Gifts,' Much 'Grace,' and Marked 'Usefulness.'" *BYU Studies* 9 (Spring 1969): 321–340.

———. "A Study of the Origins of the Church of Jesus Christ of Latter-day Saints in the States of New York and Pennsylvania, 1816–1831." PhD diss., Brigham Young University, 1971.

———. *A Study of the Origins of the Church of Jesus Christ of Latter-day Saints in the States of New York and Pennsylvania, 1816–1831.* Dissertations in Latter-day Saint History. Provo, UT: Joseph Fielding Smith Institute for Latter-day Saint History; BYU Studies, 2000.

Pratt, Addison. Autobiography and journals, 1843–1852. CHL.

Pratt, Orson. *Remarkable Visions.* Liverpool: R. James, 1848.

Pratt, Parley P. *The Autobiography of Parley Parker Pratt, One of the Twelve Apostles of the Church of Jesus Christ of Latter-Day Saints, Embracing His Life, Ministry and Travels, with Extracts, in Prose and Verse, from His Miscellaneous Writings.* Edited by Parley P. Pratt Jr. New York: Russell Brothers, 1874.

———. *History of the Late Persecution Inflicted by the State of Missouri upon the Mormons, in Which Ten Thousand American Citizens Were Robbed, Plundered, and Driven from the State, and Many Others Imprisoned, Martyred, &c. for Their Religion, and All This by Military Force, by Order of the Executive. By P. P. Pratt, Minister of the Gospel. Written during Eight Months Imprisonment in That State.* Detroit: Dawson and Bates, 1839.

———. *Late Persecution of the Church of Jesus Christ, of Latter Day Saints. Ten Thousand American Citizens Robbed, Plundered, and Banished; Others Imprisoned, and Others Martyred for Their Religion. With a Sketch of Their Rise, Progress and Doctrine. By P. P. Pratt, Minister of the Gospel, Written in Prison.* New York: J. W. Harrison, 1840.

Pratt, Parley P., and Elias Higbee. *An Address by Judge Higbee and Parley P. Pratt, Ministers of the Gospel, of the Church of Jesus Christ of "Latter-day Saints," to the Citizens of Washington, and to the Public in General.* N.p., 1840.

Prayer, at the Dedication of the Lord's House in Kirtland, Ohio, March 27, 1836—By Joseph Smith, Jr. President of the Church of the Latter Day Saints. Kirtland, OH: 1836.

Pulsipher, Zerah. "Zerah Pu[l]siphers History." In Zerah Pulsipher, Record Book, ca. 1858–1878. CHL.

Quinn, D. Michael, ed. "The First Months of Mormonism: A Contemporary View by Rev. Diedrich Willers." *New York History* 54 (July 1973): 317–333.

Quorum of the Twelve Apostles, Record / Quorum of the Twelve Apostles. "A Record of the Transactions of the Twelve Apostles of the Church of the Latter Day Saints from the Time of Their Call to the Apostleship Which Was on the 14th Day of Feby. AD 1835," Feb.–Aug. 1835. In Patriarchal Blessings, 1833–, vol. 2. CHL.

Record of Seventies / First Council of the Seventy. "Book of Records," 1837–1843. Bk. A. In First Council of the Seventy, Records, 1837–1885. CHL.

"Records of the Session of the Presbyterian Church in Palmyra," 1828–1848. Microfilm 900, no. 59. BYU.

The Return. Davis City, IA, 1889–1891; Richmond, MO, 1892–1893; Davis City, 1895–1896; Denver, 1898; Independence, MO, 1899–1900.

Revelation Book 1 / "A Book of Commandments and Revelations of the Lord Given to Joseph the Seer and Others by the Inspiration of God and Gift and Power of the Holy Ghost Which Beareth Re[c]ord of the Father and Son and Holy Ghost Which Is One God Infinite and Eternal World without End Amen," 1831–1835. CHL.

Revelations Collection, 1831–ca. 1844, 1847, 1861, ca. 1876. CHL.

The Revised Statutes of the State of New-York, Passed during the Years One Thousand Eight Hundred and Twenty-Seven, and One Thousand Eight Hundred and Twenty-Eight: To Which Are Added, Certain Former Acts Which Have Not Been Revised. 3 vols. Albany: Packard and Van Benthuysen, 1829.

Richards, Franklin D. "Bibliography of Utah," 1884. Hubert H. Bancroft, Utah and the Mormons Collection, before 1889. Microfilm. CHL.

Richards, Willard. Journals, 1836–1853. Willard Richards, Papers, 1821–1854. CHL.

[Rigdon, Sidney]. *An Appeal to the American People: Being an Account of the Persecutions of the Church of Latter Day Saints; and of the Barbarities Inflicted on Them by the Inhabitants of the State of Missouri.* Cincinnati: Glezen and Shepard, 1840.

Robison, Elwin C. *The First Mormon Temple: Design, Construction, and Historic Context of the Kirtland Temple.* Provo, UT: Brigham Young University Press, 1997.

Rockwood, Albert Perry. Journal Entries, Oct. 1838–Jan. 1839. CHL.

Rupp, Israel Daniel, ed. *He Pasa Ekklesia* [The whole church]. *An Original History of the Religious Denominations at Present Existing in the United States, Containing Authentic Accounts of Their Rise, Progress, Statistics and Doctrines. Written Expressly for the Work by Eminent Theological Professors, Ministers, and Lay-Members, of the Respective Denominations.* Philadelphia: James Y. Humphreys; Harrisburg, PA: Clyde and Williams, 1844.

Saints' Herald. Independence, MO. 1860–.

Salt Lake Daily Tribune. Salt Lake City. 1871–.

Scott, Stephen. *Why Do They Dress That Way?* Intercourse, PA: Good Books, 1986.

Seixas, Joshua. *Manual Hebrew Grammar for the Use of Beginners.* 2nd ed., enl. and impr. Andover, MA: Gould and Newman, 1834.

Skousen, Royal, ed. *The Original Manuscript of the Book of Mormon: Typographical Facsimile of the Extant Text.* Provo, UT: Foundation for Ancient Research and Mormon Studies, Brigham Young University, 2001.

———, ed. *The Printer's Manuscript of the Book of Mormon: Typographical Facsimile of the Entire Text in Two Parts. Part 1, Copyright, 1830 Preface, 1 Nephi 1:0–Alma 17:26.* Provo, UT: Foundation for Ancient Research and Mormon Studies, Brigham Young University, 2001.

Smith, Emma. Letter, Nauvoo, IL, to Joseph Smith, Washington DC, 6 Dec. 1839. In Charles Aldrich Autograph Collection. State Historical Society of Iowa, Des Moines.

Smith, George Albert. Papers, 1834–1877. CHL.

Smith, Hyrum. Diary and Account Book, Nov. 1831–Feb. 1835. Hyrum Smith, Papers, ca. 1832–1844. BYU.

———. Diary, Mar.–Apr. 1839, Oct. 1840. CHL.

Smith, Hyrum, and Joseph Smith. Letter, Nauvoo, IL, to Oliver Granger, 30 Aug. 1841. Henry E. Huntington Library, San Marino, CA.

Smith, James H. *History of Chenango and Madison Counties, New York, with Illustrations and Biographical Sketches of Some of Its Prominent Men and Pioneers.* Syracuse, NY: D. Mason, 1880.

Smith, John. Journal, 1833–1841. John Smith, Papers, 1833–1854. CHL.

Smith, Joseph. In addition to the entries that immediately follow, see entries under "JS."

Smith, Joseph. Collection, 1827–1846. CHL.

———. Materials, 1832–1844, 1883. CCLA.

Smith, Joseph, et al. Memorial to U.S. Senate and House of Representatives, 27 Jan. 1840. In Record Group 46, Records of the U.S. Senate, Committee on the Judiciary, Records, 1816–1982. National Archives, Washington DC.

Smith, Joseph Fielding. Papers, 1893–1973. CHL.

Smith, Lucy Mack. *Biographical Sketches of Joseph Smith the Prophet, and His Progenitors for Many Generations*. Liverpool: S. W. Richards, 1853.

———. History, 1844–1845. 18 books. CHL. Also available in Lavina Fielding Anderson, ed., *Lucy's Book: A Critical Edition of Lucy Mack Smith's Family Memoir* (Salt Lake City: Signature Books, 2001).

———. History, 1845. CHL.

Snow, Eliza R. Letter, Caldwell Co., MO, to Isaac Streator, Streetsborough, OH, 22 Feb. 1839. Photocopy. CHL.

Snow, Erastus. Journals, 1835–1851, 1856–1857. CHL.

Snow, LeRoi C. "Who Was Professor Joshua Seixas?" *Improvement Era*, Feb. 1936, 67–71.

Staker, Mark L. *Hearken, O Ye People: The Historical Setting of Joseph Smith's Ohio Revelations*. Salt Lake City: Greg Kofford Books, 2009.

State of Missouri. See Missouri, State of.

Stevenson, Edward. Journal, 1852–1892. CHL.

Stott, David Keith. "Legal Insights into the Organization of the Church in 1830." *BYU Studies* 49, no. 2 (2010): 121–148.

Swartzell, William. *Mormonism Exposed, Being a Journal of a Residence in Missouri from the 28th of May to the 20th of August, 1838, together with an Appendix, Containing the Revelation concerning the Golden Bible, with Numerous Extracts from the 'Book of Covenants,' &c., &c.* Pekin, OH: By the author, 1840.

Taylor, John. Collection, 1829–1894. CHL.

Teacher's license for Christian Whitmer, 9 June 1830. Western Americana Collection. Beinecke Rare Book and Manuscript Library, Yale University, New Haven, CT.

Theodore Schroeder Papers: Corres., Writings and Printed Ephemera Relating to Mormonism. Microfilm. New York: New York Public Library Photographic Service, 1986. Copy at CHL.

Tiffany's Monthly. New York City. 1856–1859.

Times and Seasons. Commerce/Nauvoo, IL. Nov. 1839–Feb. 1846.

Trial Bill, 1 June 1830. People of Chenango County, New York v. Joseph Smith (J.P. Ct. 1830). Chenango County Courthouse, Norwich, NY.

Tucker, Pomeroy. *Origin, Rise, and Progress of Mormonism. Biography of Its Founders and History of Its Church. Personal Remembrances and Historical Collections Hitherto Unwritten*. New York: D. Appleton, 1867.

Tuckett, Madge Harris, and Belle Harris Wilson. *The Martin Harris Story, with Biographies of Emer Harris and Dennison Lott Harris*. Provo, UT: Vintage Books, 1983.

Turley, Richard E., Jr., ed. *Selected Collections from the Archives of the Church of Jesus Christ of Latter-day Saints*. 2 vols. 74 DVDs. Provo, UT: Brigham Young University Press, 2002.

Tyler, R. H. *American Ecclesiastical Law: The Law of Religious Societies, Church Government and Creeds, Disturbing Religious Meetings, and the Law of Burial Grounds in the United States. With Practical Forms.* Albany, NY: William Gould, 1866.

U.S. Bureau of the Census. Population Schedules. Microfilm. FHL.

U.S. and Canada Record Collection. FHL.

Vogel, Dan, ed. *Early Mormon Documents.* 5 vols. Salt Lake City: Signature Books, 1996–2003.

The Wasp. Nauvoo, IL. Apr. 1842–Apr. 1843.

Wayne Sentinel. Palmyra, NY. 1823–1852, 1860–1861.

Whiting, Linda Shelley. *David W. Patten: Apostle and Martyr.* Springville, UT: Cedar Fort, 2003.

Whiting, William. "Paper-Making in New England." In *The New England States: Their Constitutional, Judicial, Educational, Commercial, Professional and Industrial History,* edited by William T. Davis, vol. 1, pp. 303–333. Boston: D. H. Hurd, 1897.

Whitmer, David. *An Address to All Believers in Christ.* Richmond, MO: By the author, 1887.

Whitmer, History / Whitmer, John. "The Book of John, Whitmer Kept by Comma[n]d," ca. 1838–ca. 1847. CCLA.

Whitmer, Peter, Jr. Journal, Dec. 1831. CHL.

Whitney, Orson F. "The Aaronic Priesthood." *Contributor,* Jan. 1885, 123–132.

Whittaker, David J. "The 'Articles of Faith' in Early Mormon Literature and Thought." In *New Views of Mormon History: A Collection of Essays in Honor of Leonard J. Arrington,* edited by Davis Bitton and Maureen Ursenbach Beecher, 63–92. Salt Lake City: University of Utah Press, 1987.

———. "The Book of Daniel in Early Mormon Thought." In *By Study and Also by Faith: Essays in Honor of Hugh W. Nibley on the Occasion of His Eightieth Birthday, 27 March 1990,* edited by John M. Lundquist and Stephen D. Ricks, vol. 1, pp. 155–201. Salt Lake City: Deseret Book; Provo, UT: Foundation for Ancient Research and Mormon Studies, 1990.

Williams, Frederick G. "Frederick Granger Williams of the First Presidency of the Church." *BYU Studies* 12 (Spring 1972): 243–261.

Williams, Frederick G. Papers, 1834–1842. CHL.

Williams, Richard Shelton. "The Missionary Movements of the LDS Church in New England, 1830–1850." Master's thesis, Brigham Young University, 1969.

Wirthlin, LeRoy S. "Nathan Smith (1762–1828) Surgical Consultant to Joseph Smith." *BYU Studies* 17 (Spring 1977): 319–337.

Woman's Exponent. Salt Lake City. 1872–1914.

Woodruff, Wilford. Journals, 1833–1898. Wilford Woodruff, Journals and Papers, 1828–1898. CHL. Also available as *Wilford Woodruff's Journals, 1833–1898,* edited by Scott G. Kenney, 9 vols. (Midvale, UT: Signature Books, 1983–1985).

The Works of Hannah More. 4 vols. Dublin: D. Graisberry, 1803.

Young, Lorenzo Dow. "Lorenzo Dow Young's Narrative." In *Fragments of Experience,* Faith-Promoting Series 6, pp. 22–54. Salt Lake City: Juvenile Instructor Office, 1882.

Corresponding Section Numbers
in Editions of the Doctrine and Covenants

The Book of Commandments, of which a number of partial copies were printed in 1833, was superseded by the Doctrine and Covenants. Because the numbering of comparable material in the Book of Commandments and different editions of the Doctrine and Covenants varies extensively, the following table is provided to help readers refer from the version of a canonized item cited in this volume to other published versions of that same item. This table includes revelations announced by JS—plus letters, records of visions, articles, minutes, and other items, some of which were authored by other individuals—that were published in the Book of Commandments or Doctrine and Covenants in or before 1844, the year of JS's death. The table also includes material originating with JS that was first published in the Doctrine and Covenants after 1844. Such later-canonized material includes, for example, extracts of JS's 20 March 1839 letter written from the jail in Liberty, Missouri. These extracts, first canonized in 1876, are currently found in sections 121 through 123 of the Latter-day Saint edition of the Doctrine and Covenants.

The 1835 and 1844 editions of the Doctrine and Covenants included a series of lectures on the subject of faith, which constituted part 1 of the volume. Only part 2, the compilation of revelations and other items, is represented in the table. Further, the table does not include materials originating with JS that were not canonized in his lifetime and that have never been canonized by The Church of Jesus Christ of Latter-day Saints or by the Community of Christ. As only one of many examples, JS's journal entry for 3 November 1835 contains a JS revelation concerning the Twelve. This revelation has never been canonized and therefore does not appear in the table. More information about documents not listed on the table below will be provided in other volumes of *The Joseph Smith Papers* and on the Joseph Smith Papers website, josephsmithpapers.org.

Some material was significantly revised after its initial publication in the canon. For instance, the revelation in chapter 28 of the Book of Commandments included twice as much material when it was republished in the Doctrine and Covenants in 1835. As another example, chapter 65 of the Book of Commandments stops abruptly before the end of the revelation because publication of the volume was disrupted; the revelation was not published in its entirety until 1835. These and other substantial changes of greater or lesser significance are not accounted for in the table, but they will be identified in the appropriate volumes of the Documents series.

The far left column of the table gives the standard date of each item, based on careful study of original sources. The "standard date" is the date a revelation was originally dictated or recorded. If that date is ambiguous or unknown, the standard date is the best approximation of the date, based on existing evidence. The standard date provides a way to identify each item and situate it chronologically with other documents, but it cannot be assumed that every date corresponds to the day an item was first dictated or recorded. In some cases, an item was recorded without a date notation. It is also possible that a few items were first dictated on a date other than the date surviving manuscripts bear. The dates found in this table were assigned based on all available evidence, including later attempts by JS and his contemporaries to recover date, place, and circumstances.

Where surviving sources provide conflicting information about dating, editorial judgment has been exercised to select the most likely date (occasionally only an approximate month), based on the most reliable sources. In cases in which two or more items bear the same date, they have been listed in the order in which they most likely originated, and a letter of the alphabet has been appended, providing each item a unique editorial title (for example, May 1829–A or May 1829–B). Information on dating issues will accompany publication of these items in the Documents series.

The remaining five columns in the table provide the number of the chapter (in the case of the Book of Commandments) or section (in the case of editions of the Doctrine and Covenants) in which the item was published in one or more of five different canonical editions, the first three of which were initiated by JS. Full bibliographic information about these five editions is given in the list of works cited. See also the Scriptural References section in the introduction to Works Cited for more information about the origins of the Doctrine and Covenants and other Mormon scriptures.

Key to column titles

1833: Book of Commandments
1835: Doctrine and Covenants, 1835 edition, part 2
1844: Doctrine and Covenants, 1844 edition, part 2[1]
1981: Doctrine and Covenants, 1981 edition, The Church of Jesus Christ of
      Latter-day Saints[2]
2004: Doctrine and Covenants, 2004 edition, Community of Christ[3]

	JS-Era Canon				
Date	1833	1835	1844	1981	2004
21 Sept. 1823				2[4]	
July 1828	2	30	30	3	2
Feb. 1829	3	31	31	4	4
Mar. 1829	4	32	32	5	5

1. The 1844 edition of the Doctrine and Covenants included one item written after the death of JS (section 111). That item is not included in this table.

2. The 1981 Latter-day Saint edition of the Doctrine and Covenants includes some items written after the death of JS. Those items are not included in this table. Any item for which information appears only in the "1981" column and in the "Date" column is a later-canonized JS item, as discussed in the first paragraph of the preceding introduction.

3. The 2004 Community of Christ edition of the Doctrine and Covenants includes two extracts from JS's Bible revision (sections 22 and 36) and items written after the death of JS. Neither the extracts nor the later items are included in this table.

4. This section, an extract from the history JS initiated in 1838, is here dated by the date of the event described in the section rather than the date of the document's creation.

Date	JS-Era Canon			1981	2004
	1833	1835	1844		
Apr. 1829–A	5	8	8	6	6
ca. Apr. 1829	9	36	36	10	3
Apr. 1829–B	7	34	34	8	8
Apr. 1829–C	6	33	33	7	7
Apr. 1829–D	8	35	35	9	9
15 May 1829				13[5]	
May 1829–A	10	37	37	11	10
May 1829–B	11	38	38	12	11
June 1829–A	12	39	39	14	12
June 1829–B	15	43	43	18	16
June 1829–C	13	40	40	15	13
June 1829–D	14	41	41	16	14
June 1829–E		42	42	17	15
Mar. 1830	16	44	44	19	18
6 Apr. 1830	22	46	46	21	19
Apr. 1830–A	17	45:1	45:1	23:1–2	21:1
Apr. 1830–B	18	45:2	45:2	23:3	21:2
Apr. 1830–C	19	45:3	45:3	23:4	21:3
Apr. 1830–D	20	45:4	45:4	23:5	21:4
Apr. 1830–E	21	45:5	45:5	23:6–7	21:5
10 Apr. 1830	24	2	2	20	17
16 Apr. 1830	23	47	47	22	20
July 1830–A	25	9	9	24	23
July 1830–B	27	49	49	26	25
July 1830–C	26	48	48	25	24
ca. Aug. 1830	28	50	50	27	26
Sept. 1830–A	29	10	10	29	28
Sept. 1830–B	30	51	51	28	27
Sept. 1830–C	31	52:1	52:1	30:1–4	29:1
Sept. 1830–D	32	52:2	52:2	30:5–8	29:2
Sept. 1830–E	33	52:3	52:3	30:9–11	29:3
Sept. 1830–F	34	53	53	31	30
Oct. 1830–A		54	54	32	31
Oct. 1830–B	35	55	55	33	32

---

5. This section, an extract from the history JS initiated in 1838, is here dated by the date of the event described in the section rather than the date of the document's creation.

| Date | JS-Era Canon | | | | |
	1833	1835	1844	1981	2004
4 Nov. 1830	36	56	56	34	33
ca. Dec. 1830		73	74	74	74
7 Dec. 1830	37	11	11	35	34
9 Dec. 1830	38	57	57	36	35
30 Dec. 1830	39	58	58	37	37
2 Jan. 1831	40	12	12	38	38
5 Jan. 1831	41	59	59	39	39
6 Jan. 1831	42	60	60	40	40
4 Feb. 1831	43	61	61	41	41
9 Feb. 1831[6]	44	13:1–19	13:1–19	42:1–73	42:1–19
Feb. 1831–A	45	14	14	43	43
Feb. 1831–B	46	62	62	44	44
23 Feb. 1831	47	13:21–23, 20	13:21–23, 20	42:78–93, 74–77	42:21–23, 20
ca. 7 Mar. 1831	48	15	15	45	45
ca. 8 Mar. 1831–A	49	16	16	46	46
ca. 8 Mar. 1831–B	50	63	63	47	47
10 Mar. 1831	51	64	64	48	48
7 May 1831	52	65	65	49	49
9 May 1831	53	17	17	50	50
20 May 1831		23	23	51	51
6 June 1831	54	66	66	52	52
8 June 1831	55	66[7]	67	53	53
10 June 1831	56	67	68	54	54
14 June 1831	57	68	69	55	55
15 June 1831	58	69	70	56	56
20 July 1831		27	27	57	57
1 Aug. 1831	59	18	18	58	58
7 Aug. 1831	60	19	19	59	59
8 Aug. 1831	61	70	71	60	60
12 Aug. 1831	62	71	72	61	61
13 Aug. 1831	63	72	73	62	62
30 Aug. 1831	64	20	20	63	63

---

6. See also the following entry for 23 Feb. 1831.

7. The second of two sections numbered 66. Numbering remains one off for subsequent sections within the 1835 edition.

| | JS-Era Canon | | | | |
Date	1833	1835	1844	1981	2004
11 Sept. 1831	65	21	21	64	64
29 Oct. 1831		74	75	66	66
30 Oct. 1831		24	24	65	65
1 Nov. 1831–A		22	22	68	68
1 Nov. 1831–B	1	1	1	1	1
2 Nov. 1831		25	25	67	67
3 Nov. 1831		100	108	133	108
11 Nov. 1831–A		28	28	69	69
11 Nov. 1831–B[8]		3 (partial[9])	3 (partial[10])	107 (partial[11])	104 (partial[12])
12 Nov. 1831		26	26	70	70
1 Dec. 1831		90	91	71	71
4 Dec. 1831		89	90	72	72
10 Jan. 1832		29	29	73	73
25 Jan. 1832		87	88	75	75
16 Feb. 1832		91	92	76	76
ca. Mar. 1832				77	
1 Mar. 1832		75	76	78	77
7 Mar. 1832		77	78	80	79
12 Mar. 1832		76	77	79	78
15 Mar. 1832		79	80	81	80
26 Apr. 1832		86	87	82	81
30 Apr. 1832		88	89	83	82
29 Aug. 1832		78	79	99	96
22 and 23 Sept. 1832		4	4	84	83
27 Nov. 1832				85	
6 Dec. 1832		6	6	86	84
25 Dec. 1832				87	
27 and 28 Dec. 1832 and 3 Jan. 1833		7	7	88	85
27 Feb. 1833		80	81	89	86
8 Mar. 1833		84	85	90	87
9 Mar. 1833		92	93	91	88

8. See also the following entry for ca. Apr. 1835.

9. Verses 31–33, 35–42, 44.

10. Verses 31–33, 35–42, 44.

11. Verses 59–69, 71–72, 74–75, 78–87, 91–92, 99–100.

12. Verses 31–33, 35–42, 44.

	JS-Era Canon				
Date	1833	1835	1844	1981	2004
15 Mar. 1833		93	94	92	89
6 May 1833		82	83	93	90
1 June 1833		95	96	95	92
4 June 1833		96	97	96	93
2 Aug. 1833–A		81	82	97	94
2 Aug. 1833–B		83	84	94	91
6 Aug. 1833		85	86	98	95
12 Oct. 1833		94	95	100	97
16 and 17 Dec. 1833		97	98	101	98
17 Feb. 1834		5	5	102	99
24 Feb. 1834			101	103	100
23 Apr. 1834		98	99	104	101
22 June 1834			102	105	102
25 Nov. 1834		99	100	106	103
ca. Apr. 1835[13]		3	3	107	104
ca. Aug. 1835 ("Marriage")		101	109		111
ca. Aug. 1835 ("Of Governments and Laws in General")		102	110	134	112
26 Dec. 1835				108	
21 Jan. 1836				137	
27 Mar. 1836				109	
3 Apr. 1836				110	
6 Aug. 1836				111	
23 July 1837			104	112	105
Mar. 1838				113	
11 Apr. 1838				114	
26 Apr. 1838				115	
19 May 1838				116	
8 July 1838–A				118	
8 July 1838–C[14]			107	119	106
8 July 1838–D				120	
8 July 1838–E				117	

---

13. See also the preceding entry for 11 Nov. 1831–B.

14. This table skips from 8 July 1838–A to 8 July 1838–C because the revelation not shown here, 8 July 1838–B, has never been canonized.

	JS-Era Canon				
Date	**1833**	**1835**	**1844**	**1981**	**2004**
20 Mar. 1839				121–123	
19 Jan. 1841			[103]	124	107[15]
Mar. 1841				125	
9 July 1841				126	
1 Sept. 1842			105	127	109[16]
7 Sept. 1842			106	128	110[17]
9 Feb. 1843				129	
2 Apr. 1843				130	
16–17 May 1843				131	
12 July 1843				132	

15. The 2004 Community of Christ edition provides the following note regarding this section: "Placed in the Appendix by action of the 1970 World Conference: the Appendix was subsequently removed by the 1990 World Conference."

16. The 2004 Community of Christ edition provides the following note regarding this section: "Placed in the Appendix by action of the 1970 World Conference: the Appendix was subsequently removed by the 1990 World Conference."

17. The 2004 Community of Christ edition provides the following note regarding this section: "Placed in the Appendix by action of the 1970 World Conference: the Appendix was subsequently removed by the 1990 World Conference."

Acknowledgments

In an undertaking as large and complex as the Joseph Smith Papers Project, hundreds of people, in many areas of expertise, are called upon to contribute. The editors of the two letterpress volumes of the Histories series are grateful to many colleagues and friends who have given of their time and knowledge to move these volumes forward. In addition, the Histories volumes build on some important already-existing scholarly works, particularly volume 1 of *The Papers of Joseph Smith,* edited by Dean C. Jessee and published in 1989.

The resources of various archives and repositories have been essential to the Histories volumes. We thank the management and staff of the Church History Library, Salt Lake City, where the Joseph Smith Papers Project is housed; the Family History Library, Salt Lake City; and the L. Tom Perry Special Collections, Harold B. Lee Library, Brigham Young University, Provo, Utah. We express deep appreciation to the staff of the Community of Christ Library-Archives, Independence, Missouri, and to the historians and site directors of the Community of Christ; the suggestions of Ronald E. Romig were particularly helpful, as was the assistance of Mark Scherer, Barbara J. Bernauer, and Lachlan MacKay. We are also indebted to the Andover-Harvard Theological Library, Harvard Divinity School, Harvard University, Cambridge, Massachusetts; the Beinecke Rare Book and Manuscript Library, Yale University, New Haven, Connecticut; the Chenango County Courthouse, Norwich, New York; the Daviess County, Missouri, Courthouse, Gallatin; the Henry E. Huntington Library, San Marino, California; the J. Willard Marriott Library, University of Utah, Salt Lake City; the Missouri History Museum, St. Louis; and the Missouri State Archives, Jefferson City.

The Joseph Smith Papers Project relies on the skills and dedication of employees and volunteers in the Church History Department of The Church of Jesus Christ of Latter-day Saints, on faculty, researchers, and editors at Brigham Young University, and on independent scholars and editors. Those who have assisted us include Linda Hunter Adams, Gayle Y. Anderson, Grant A. Anderson, Angela Ashurst-McGee, Alexander L. Baugh, Richard S. Bennett, Donald Bradley, Eleanor Brainard, Alex D. Braunberger, Anya Bybee, Lee Ann Clanton, Joseph F. Darowski, James Wesley Davidson, Gerrit J. Dirkmaat, Patrick C. Dunshee, Jay R. Eastley, Naoma W. Eastley, Glen Ellsworth, Donald L. Enders, Mark Esplin, Barbara Faulring, Scott Faulring, Amanda Kae Fronk, Matthew C. Godfrey, Jared Hamon, William G. Hartley, Andrew H. Hedges, Peter V. Hilton, Whitney Hinckley, Tyler Humble, Jacqueline Jacobsen, Elizabeth L. Jensen, Emily W. Jensen, Jeffery O. Johnson, David H. Kitterman, Melissa Rehon Kotter, Michael O. Landon, Jamie Layton, Riley M. Lorimer, Mary C. Lynn, Allison Mathews, Chris McAfee, Kaitlin Merkley, Pauline K. Musig, Michael Nelson, Veneese Nelson, Sharon E. Nielsen, Amanda Owens, Benson Parkinson, Sarah Gibby Peris, Elizabeth Pinborough, Ronald Read, Leslie Sherman, William W. Slaughter, Alex D. Smith, Mark L. Staker, Elizabeth Stubbs, Norman E. Waite, Nick Walker, April Williamson, Julia K. Woodbury, Robert J. Woodford, and Ellen N. Yates.

We express our thanks to Glenn N. Rowe, Church History Department, The Church of Jesus Christ of Latter-day Saints, for his tireless assistance with the documents; to Gordon A. Madsen, Joseph Smith Papers, for assistance in understanding legal issues referred to in these documents; and to Larry E. Morris, Joseph Smith Papers, for drafting the chronology. Welden C. Andersen of the Audiovisual Department, The Church of Jesus Christ of Latter-day Saints, shot the textual photographs in this volume and helped prepare them for the press. We also thank Anna Staley and Viola Knecht for administrative assistance.

As the project made the transition to an XML-based platform, expert assistance was provided by Clark D. Christensen, Darren Shipley, Lisa Liddle, David Hale, and Dennis Sagers of the Information and Communication Services Department; Gary K. Jestice, Church History Department, The Church of Jesus Christ of Latter-day Saints; and Stephen Perkins, Paul Hayslett, Helen Langone, Allan Orsnes, and their colleagues at IDM USA.

Over the years these volumes have been in production, many student researchers at Brigham Young University, under the guidance of Kay Darowski of the Joseph Smith Papers, have provided valuable research support. They include Kendall Buchanan, Jared P. Collette, Justin Collings, Lia Suttner Collings, Christopher K. Crockett, Eric Dowdle, James A. Goldberg, David W. Grua, Angella L. Hamilton, Christopher C. Jones, Cort Kirksey, Mary-Celeste Lewis, Jason N. Olson, Benjamin E. Park, Daren E. Ray, Sandra Mason Roller, Timothy D. Speirs, Virginia E. Stratford, M. Nathaniel Tanner, Kathryn Jensen Wall, and Stephen Whitaker.

The maps in this volume were prepared in consultation with Max H Parkin of the Joseph Smith Papers and developed under the direction of Brandon Plewe of the Department of Geography, Brigham Young University, with assistance from Brent Beck, Lyle Briggs, Benjamin Clift, Derek Farnes, Vania Hernandez, Tyler Jones, Isaac Montague, Kent Simons, Jared Tamez, and Lissa Thompson.

We thank the management and staff at Deseret Book Company, Salt Lake City, for their assistance with the design, printing, and distribution of this volume. Especially appreciated are the contributions of Sheri L. Dew, Cory H. Maxwell, Anne Sheffield, Richard Erickson, Suzanne Brady, Gail Halladay, Derk Koldewyn, Rebecca B. Chambers, and Vicki Parry.

In addition to generous support from the Church History Library and Brigham Young University, our institutional sponsors, we acknowledge the ongoing encouragement and financial support of the Larry H. Miller and Gail Miller Family Foundation. The Millers are true friends of Mormon historical scholarship.

The first two volumes of the Histories series will be indexed cumulatively in the second volume of the series. A printable, searchable index will also available at the Joseph Smith Papers website.